NEGOTIATION

NEGOTIATION

Fourth Edition

Roy J. Lewicki
The Ohio State University

Bruce Barry
Vanderbilt University—Nashville

David M. Saunders
University of Calgary

John W. Minton
Havatar Associates, Inc.

Boston   Burr Ridge, IL   Dubuque, IA   Madison, WI   New York
San Francisco   St. Louis   Bangkok   Bogotá   Caracas   Kuala Lumpur
Lisbon   London   Madrid   Mexico City   Milan   Montreal   New Delhi
Santiago   Seoul   Singapore   Sydney   Taipei   Toronto

Irwin

McGraw-Hill Higher Education
A Division of The McGraw-Hill Companies

NEGOTIATION
Published by McGraw-Hill/Irwin, a business unit of The McGraw-Hill Companies, Inc., 1221 Avenue of the Americas, New York, NY, 10020. copyright © 2003, 1999, 1994, 1985 by The McGraw-Hill Companies, Inc. All rights reserved. No part of this publication may be reproduced or distributed in any form or by any means, or stored in a database or retrieval system, without the prior written consent of The McGraw-Hill Companies, Inc., including, but not limited to, in any network or other electronic storage or transmission, or broadcast for distance learning. Some ancillaries, including electronic and print components, may not be available to customers outside the United States.

This book is printed on acid-free paper.

domestic   1 2 3 4 5 6 7 8 9 0 DOC/DOC 0 9 8 7 6 5 4 3 2
international 1 2 3 4 5 6 7 8 9 0 DOC/DOC 0 9 8 7 6 5 4 3 2

ISBN 0-07-243255-1

Publisher: *John E. Biernat*
Senior editor: *John Weimeister*
Editorial coordinator: *Trina Hauger*
Senior marketing manger: *Ellen Cleary*
Producer, Media technology: *Mark Molsky*
Senior project manager: *Christine A. Vaughan*
Production supervisor: *Gina Hangos*
Coordinator freelance design: *Mary L. Christianson*
Supplement producer: *Joyce J. Chappetto*
Senior digital content specialist: *Brian Nacik*
Freelance cover designer: *Sarah Studnicki*
Typeface: *10/12 Times Roman*
Compositor: *Electronic Publishing Services, Inc., TN*
Printer: *R. R. Donnelley*

Library of Congress Cataloging-in-Publication Data

Negotiation / Roy J. Lewicki ... [et al.].— 4th ed.
   p. cm.
  Rev. ed. to: Negotiation / Roy J. Lewicki. 3rd ed. c1999.
  Companion vol. to: Negotiation : reading, exercises, and cases.
  Includes bibliographical references and indexes.
  ISBN 0-07-243255-1 (alk. paper) — ISBN 0-07-112315-6 (international : alk. paper)
  1. Negotiation in business. I. Lewicki, Roy J. II. Lewicki, Roy J. Negotiation.
HD58.6 .N437 2003
658.4'052—dc21

INTERNATIONAL EDITION ISBN 0-07-112315-6
Copyright © 2003. Exclusive rights by The McGraw-Hill Companies, Inc. for manufacture and export. This book cannot be re-exported from the country to which it is sold by McGraw-Hill. The International Edition is not available in North America.

www.mhhe.com

We dedicate this book to all negotiation, mediation, and dispute resolution professionals who try to make the world a more peaceful and prosperous place.

About the Authors

Roy J. Lewicki is the Dean's Distinguished Teaching Professor and Professor of Management and Human Resources at the Max. M. Fisher College of Business, The Ohio State University. He has authored or edited 24 books, as well as numerous research articles. Professor Lewicki has served as the President of the International Association of Conflict Management, and received the first David Bradford Outstanding Educator award from the Organizational Behavior Teaching Society for his contributions to the field of teaching in negotiation and dispute resolution.

Bruce Barry is Associate Professor of Management and Sociology at Vanderbilt University, and also Director of the Ph.D. program at Vanderbilt's Owen Graduate School of Management. His research on negotiation, influence, power, and justice has appeared in numerous scholarly journals and volumes. Professor Barry served a term as President of the International Association for Conflict Management (2002–2003), a professional society of researchers, teachers, and practitioners specializing in the fields of conflict, dispute resolution, and negotiation.

David M. Saunders is Dean of the Haskayne School of Management at the University of Calgary. He has coauthored several articles on negotiation, conflict resolution, employee voice, and organizational justice. Prior to accepting his current appointment, he was Director of the McGill MBA Japan program in Tokyo, and he has traveled extensively throughout Asia, Europe, and South America.

John W. Minton is the President and CEO of Havatar Associates, Inc., a management consultation, development, coaching, and recruiting firm specializing in meeting the needs of small and medium-sized organizations. He has taught in the business schools of Appalachian State and Duke Universities, and at Pfeiffer University where he was the Jefferson-Pilot Professor of Management. He is currently an Adjunct Professor at Gardner-Webb University, and has served as a volunteer mediator and arbitrator.

Preface

Welcome to the fourth edition of *Negotiation.* We are delighted to present this new and updated revision to you.

First, we welcome to the author team Prof. Bruce Barry of Vanderbilt University. Bruce has impressive professional credentials as a researcher in the fields of negotiation and conflict management, and as an experienced teacher of negotiation at the Owen Graduate School of Management.

For those of you who are familiar with the third edition, you will note little change in the fundamental chapter organization of the book. For those of you who are not familiar with previous editions, a brief overview is appropriate. The text is organized into 13 chapters. The first four chapters introduce the reader to negotiation fundamentals. Chapter 1 introduces the field of negotiation and conflict management, describes the basic elements of interdependence with other people, and briefly explores the challenges of managing that interdependence. The second chapter describes the fundamental prework that negotiators must do to get ready for a negotiation: framing the dispute (deciding what the negotiation is all about), defining negotiation objectives, and planning the steps one will pursue to achieve those objectives. Chapters 3 and 4 then present the two core approaches to negotiation: the basic dynamics of competitive (win-lose) bargaining (Chapter 3) and the basic dynamics of integrative (win-win) negotiation (Chapter 4).

The next three chapters present fundamental psychological subprocesses of negotiation: perception, cognition, communication, persuasion and leverage, and ethical judgment. In Chapter 5, we review the basic processes of perception, cognition, and communication in negotiation; we specifically examine communication dynamics, and a number of common cognitive and judgment biases made by negotiators. In Chapter 6, we look at the ways negotiators can use to pressure the other side, using the tools of power and persuasion to get the other to change his or her perspective or give in to their arguments. Finally, in Chapter 7, we examine the ethical standards and criteria that surround negotiation and create unique challenges for negotiators in deciding how fully and completely they are going to disclose their bargaining positions.

The next four chapters examine the social contexts in which these negotiations occur, and which also therefore influence how they evolve. In Chapter 8, we specifically examine the ways that the negotiation process changes when the parties have an established relationship with each other, and how the type of relationship affects the negotiation process. We also examine how negotiations change when negotiators are representing the interests of other parties, rather than simply negotiating for themselves.

In Chapter 9, we look at the group context for negotiation; we show how many group decision-making and problem-solving discussions can be viewed as negotiations, and how negotiators must often build alliances and partnerships in order to achieve a larger consensus in a group or organization. In Chapter 10, we delve into the extensive work that has been done to understand individual differences in personality and gender, and how these differences might predict different approaches to the negotiation process and conflict resolution. Finally, in Chapter 11, we attempt to clarify how national cultures shape the diverse ways that parties approach negotiations.

The last two chapters emphasize the strategies that can be used by the parties to resolve breakdowns in the negotiation process. Chapter 12 explores the techniques that negotiators can use on their own to get negotiations back on track. Chapter 13 describes the ways that third parties (arbitrators, mediators, and facilitators) become involved to help the parties find a resolution.

For those instructors who are familiar with previous editions, the most visible changes will be in the updated content of the book, as follows:

1. The content of the book has been revised and updated. Every chapter was reviewed by the authors, based on extensive feedback from faculty who have used the book in previous editions. Many of the chapters have been reorganized to present the material more effectively.

2. In our continued effort to enhance the book's readability, we have also updated and revised all of the "boxes" and cartoons that offer real-life perspectives on negotiation dynamics.

3. Several of the chapters have been extensively revised and updated. In Chapter 2, we reorganized the content, and expanded the sections on framing dynamics and on the planning process. In Chapter 5, we reorganized the content, expanded the section on cognitive biases, and improved the discussion of communication processes. In Chapter 8, we elaborated and clarified the nature of negotiating in relationships, as much new research has emerged in this area. In Chapter 12, we added a section on the nature of intractable disputes and reorganized much of the content in this chapter.

4. The structure of this book parallels that of a completely revised readings and class-room activities book, *Negotiation: Readings, Exercises and Cases* by Lewicki, Saunders, Minton, and Barry (4th ed.), also published by McGraw-Hill/Irwin. This text and reader can be used together, or separately. A shorter version of this text, *Essentials of Negotiation,* 3rd ed. (2003), by Lewicki, Barry, Saunders, and Minton, can also be used in conjunction with the readings book. We encourage instructors to contact their local McGraw-Hill/Irwin representative for an examination copy (or call 800-634-3963, or visit the website at www.mhhe.com).

5. **Instructional resources, including a test bank and PowerPoint slides, are available to accompany this volume. Instructors should contact their McGraw-Hill/Irwin representative.**

Once again, this book could not have been completed without the assistance of numerous people. We especially thank

- Many of our colleagues in the negotiation and dispute resolution field, whose research efforts have made the growth of this field possible, and who have given us helpful feedback about earlier editions to improve the content of this edition.

- The excellent editorial assistance of Steve Stenner, specifically for his help on copyediting, permissions, and bibliography.

- The outstanding skills of Eric Pincus, for refining the test bank and PowerPoint slides.

- The staff of McGraw-Hill/Irwin, especially our current editor, John Weimeister, and our previous editors, John Biernat, Kurt Strand, and Karen Johnson; Trina Hauger and Tracy Jensen, editorial assistants who can solve almost any problem; and Christine Vaughan, tireless project manager who turns our confusing instructions and tedious prose into eminently readable and usable volumes!

- Our families, who continue to provide us with the time, inspiration, and opportunities for continued learning about effective negotiation, and the personal support required to sustain this project.

Roy J. Lewicki
Bruce Barry
David M. Saunders
John W. Minton

Contents in Brief

Contents

CHAPTER 1

The Nature of Negotiation

JOE AND SUE CARTER

The day started early, as usual. Over breakfast, Sue Carter raised the question of where she and her husband, Joe, would go for their summer vacation. She wanted to sign up for a tour of the Far East being sponsored by her college's alumni association. However, two weeks on a guided tour with a lot of other people was not what Joe had in mind. He needed to get away from people, crowds, and schedules, and he wanted to charter a sailboat and cruise the New England coast. In addition, they were still not sure whether the children would go with them. The two kids really wanted to go to camp, and Joe and Sue couldn't afford both summer camp and a vacation for the four of them. The Carters had not argued (yet), but it was clear that they had a real problem here. Some of their friends handled problems like this by taking separate vacations. With both of them working full-time, though, one thing Joe and Sue did agree on was that they would take their vacation together.

As Joe drove to work, he thought about the vacation problem. What bothered Joe most was that there seemed to be no good way to manage the conflict productively. With some conflicts, they could compromise; but given what each wanted this time, compromise didn't seem possible. At other times they would flip a coin; that might work for choosing a restaurant, but it seemed unwise in this case because of how much money was involved and how important vacation time was to them. In addition, flipping a coin might be more likely to make one of them feel like a loser and the other feel guilty than to help both feel really satisfied.

Walking through the parking lot, Joe met his company's purchasing manager, Ed Laine. Joe was the head of the engineering design group for MicroWatt, a manufacturer of small electric motors. Ed reminded Joe that they had to settle a problem created by the engineers in Joe's department: The engineers were contacting vendors directly rather than going through MicroWatt's purchasing department. Joe knew that purchasing wanted all contacts with a vendor to go through them; but he also knew that his engineers badly needed technical information for design purposes, and waiting for the information to come through purchasing slowed things considerably. Ed Laine was aware of Joe's views about this problem, and Joe thought the two of them could probably find some way to resolve this if they really sat down to work on it. Joe and Ed were also both aware that upper management expected middle managers to settle differences among themselves; if this problem "went upstairs" to senior management, it would make both of them look bad.

Shortly after reaching his desk, Joe received a telephone call from an automobile salesman with whom he had been talking about a new car. The salesman asked how Sue felt about the car and whether she wanted to drive it. Joe wasn't quite sure that Sue would go along with his choice; Joe had picked out a luxury import, and he expected Sue to say it is too expensive. Joe was pleased with the latest offer the salesman had made, but thought he might still get a few more concessions out of him, so he introduced Sue's concerns to put more pressure on the salesman to lower the price.

As soon as Joe hung up the phone, it rang again. It was Sue, calling to vent her frustration to Joe over some of the procedures at the local bank where she worked as a senior loan officer. Sue was frustrated working for an old "family-run" bank that was not very automated, was heavily bureaucratic, and was slow to respond to customer needs. The competition would approve certain types of loans within three hours that took Sue a week to get approved. While the bank staff was oriented to the public and polite to customers, they were losing clients to large state and multinational banks that had entered the city and were providing more efficient services. It seemed that every week Sue was losing more and more of her clients to the larger banks. Whenever she tried to discuss this with senior management, she was met with resistance and a lecture on traditional values.

Most of Joe's afternoon was taken up by the annual budget meeting. Joe hated these meetings. The people from the finance department came in and arbitrarily cut everyone's figures by 30 percent, and then all the managers had to argue endlessly to try to get some of their new-project money reinstated. Joe had learned to work with a lot of people, some of whom he did not like very much, but these people from finance were the most arrogant and arbitrary number crunchers imaginable. He could not understand why the top brass did not see how much harm these people were doing to the engineering group's research and development efforts. Joe considered himself a reasonable guy, but the way these people acted made him feel like he didn't want to give them an inch. He was prepared to draw the line and fight it out for as long as it took.

In the evening, Sue and Joe attended a meeting of their town's Conservation Commission, which, among other things, was charged with protecting the town's streams, wetlands, and nature preserves. Sue is a member of the Conservation Commission, and Sue and Joe both strongly believe in sound environmental protection and management. This evening's case involved a request by a real estate development firm to drain a swampy area and move a small creek to build a new regional shopping mall. All projections showed that the new shopping mall would attract jobs and revenue to the area and considerably fatten the town's treasury. The new mall was badly needed to replace several others that had closed, putting a sizable number of people out of work and reducing the town's tax revenues. But the plan might also do irreparable damage to the wetlands and the wildlife in that area. The initial plan proposed by the development firm had serious problems, and the commission had asked Sue to see if an acceptable solution could be developed. Eventually a site plan had been worked out that would have considerably more benefits than drawbacks. But now Sue was having difficulties with some members of the commission who were ardent conservationists and argued against *any* change in the wetlands on that lot. In addition, word about the application had leaked out, and even some members of the town council had decided to join the conservationists in the fight.

Joe and Sue discussed their respective days as they drove home from the council meeting. Each thought that life is kind of strange, because sometimes things go very smoothly and other times things seem much too complicated. As they went to sleep later, they each thought about how they might have approached certain situations differently during the day and were thankful that they had a relationship where they could discuss things openly with each other.

INTRODUCTION

People negotiate all the time. Friends negotiate to decide where to have dinner. Children negotiate to decide which television program to watch. Businesses negotiate to purchase materials and to sell their products. Lawyers negotiate to settle legal claims before they go to court. The police negotiate with terrorists to free hostages. Nations negotiate to open their borders for free trade. Negotiation is not a process reserved only for the skilled diplomat, top salesperson, or ardent advocate for organized labor; it is something that *everyone* does, almost daily. Although the stakes are not usually as dramatic as peace accords or large corporate mergers, everyone, like Joe and Sue Carter, negotiates; sometimes people negotiate for major things like a new job, other times for relatively minor things, such as who will wash the dishes. The structure and processes of negotiation are fundamentally the same at the personal level as they are at the diplomatic and corporate levels.

Negotiations occur for one of two reasons: (1) to create something new that neither party could do on his or her own, or (2) to resolve a problem or dispute between the parties. A large number of perspectives can be used to understand different aspects of negotiations, including theory and research from economics, psychology, political science, communication, labor relations, law, sociology, and anthropology. The same negotiation outcome may also be explained simultaneously from several different perspectives (e.g., Hochberg and Kressel, 1996; Oliver, Balakrishnan, and Barry, 1994; Olekalns, Smith, and Walsh, 1996; Weiss, 1997). Because people can negotiate about so many different things, understanding the fundamental processes of negotiation is essential for anyone who works with other people. We will draw from several different research traditions throughout the book, but our focus will always be on promoting a deeper understanding of the negotiation process.

Sometimes people fail to negotiate because they do not recognize that they are in a bargaining situation. By choosing options other than negotiation, they may fail to identify a good opportunity and not achieve their goals, or they may not manage their problems as smoothly as they might like to. People may also recognize the need for bargaining but do poorly because they misunderstand the process and do not have good negotiating skills (Weingart, Hyder, and Prietula, 1996). After reading this book, people should be well prepared to recognize negotiation situations; understand what the process of bargaining involves; know how to analyze, plan, and implement successful negotiations; and, perhaps most important, be able to obtain better negotiation outcomes than before.

We will use the words *bargaining* and *negotiation* interchangeably throughout the book. In most conversations the words mean the same thing, but sometimes they are used as if they mean different things. For example, bargaining is like the competitive haggling over price that happens during a yard sale or flea market, whereas negotiation is a more formal process that occurs when parties are trying to find a mutually acceptable solution to a complex conflict. In Chapters 3 and 4, when we describe the differences between two very different forms of negotiation, we will call one *bargaining* and the other *negotiation* to make the comparisons between the two clearer.

To illustrate further what this book is about, and the breadth and scope of negotiation in our professional and personal lives, we will return to the hypothetical, but not unrealistic, Joe and Sue Carter story that opened this chapter.

CHARACTERISTICS OF A NEGOTIATION SITUATION

The Joe and Sue Carter story highlights the variety of situations that can be handled by negotiation. Any of us might encounter one or more of these situations over the course of a few days or weeks. We identify them as *negotiation situations* because they have fundamentally the same characteristics as peace negotiations between countries at war, business negotiations between two corporations, or a standoff between police and hostage takers. There are several characteristics common to all negotiation situations (see Lewicki, 1992; Rubin and Brown, 1975):

1. There are two or more parties—that is, two or more individuals, groups, or organizations. Although people can "negotiate" with themselves—as when someone debates whether to spend the afternoon studying, playing tennis, or going to the football game—we will discuss negotiation as an *interpersonal, intragroup,* or *intergroup* process. In the Carter story, Joe negotiates with his wife, the purchasing manager, and the auto salesman, and Sue negotiates with her husband, senior management at the bank, and the Conservation Commission, among others.

2. There is a conflict of interest between two or more parties—that is, what one wants is not necessarily what the other one wants—and the parties must search for a way to resolve the conflict. Joe and Sue negotiate over vacations, budgets, automobiles, and company procedures.

3. The parties negotiate because they think they can use some form of influence to get a better deal that way than by simply taking what the other side will voluntarily give them or let them have. Negotiation is largely a voluntary process. It is a strategy pursued by choice; seldom are we required to negotiate (see Box 1.1 for examples of when we should *not* negotiate).

4. The parties, at least for the moment, prefer to search for agreement rather than to fight openly, have one side capitulate, permanently break off contact, or take their dispute to a higher authority to resolve it. Negotiation occurs when there is no system—no fixed or established set of rules or procedures—for resolving the conflict, or when the parties prefer to work outside of the system to invent their own solution. If we keep a rented movie too long, the store will charge us a fee, but we might be able to negotiate that fee if we have a good excuse as to why the tape is being returned late. Similarly, attorneys negotiate or plea-bargain for their clients who would rather be assured of a negotiated settlement than take their chances with a judge and jury in the courtroom. In the Carter story, Joe pursues negotiation rather than letting his wife decide on the vacation, accepting a fixed

---

BOX 1.1
When You Shouldn't Negotiate

There are times when you should avoid negotiating. In these situations, stand your ground and you'll come out ahead.

When you'd lose the farm
If you're in a situation where you could lose everything, choose other options rather than negotiate.

When you're sold out
When you're running at capacity, don't deal. Raise your prices instead.

When the demands are unethical
Don't negotiate if your counterpart asks for something that you cannot support because it's illegal, unethical, or morally inappropriate. When your character or your reputation is compromised, you lose in the long run.

When you don't care
If you have no stake in the outcome, don't negotiate. You have everything to lose and nothing to gain.

When you don't have time
When you're pressed for time, you may choose not to negotiate. If the time pressure works against you, you'll make mistakes, and you may fail to consider the implications of your concessions. When under the gun, you'll settle for less than you could otherwise get.

When they act in bad faith
Stop the negotiation when your counterpart shows signs of acting in bad faith. If you can't trust their negotiating, you can't trust their agreement. In this case, negotiation is of little or no value. Stick to your guns and cover your position, or discredit them.

When waiting would improve your position
Perhaps you'll have a new technology available soon. Maybe your financial situation will improve. Another opportunity may present itself. If the odds are good that you'll gain ground with a delay, wait.

When you're not prepared
If you don't prepare, you'll think of all your best questions, responses, and concessions on the way home. Gathering your reconnaissance and rehearsing the negotiation will pay off handsomely. If you're not ready, just say "no."

SOURCE: J. C. Levinson, M. S. A. Smith, and O. R. Wilson, *Guerrilla Negotiating: Unconventional Weapons and Tactics to Get What You Want* (New York: John Wiley, 1999), pp. 22–23. This material is used by permission of John Wiley & Sons, Inc.

---

price for the car, or accepting the budget cut without question. Sue uses negotiation to try to change the bank's procedures rather than accepting the status quo, and she works to influence the outcome of the shopping mall plan rather than letting others decide how to resolve the problem or watching it go to court.

5. When we negotiate, we expect give and take. We expect that both sides will modify or give in somewhat on their opening statements, requests, or demands.

BOX 1.2
The Dangerous Role of Ego in Negotiation

Experienced negotiators understand that the process of reaching an agreement can often be emotional and traumatic. However, savvy negotiators also know that allowing emotion to color their perceptions of a negotiated outcome can be devastating.

Take, for example, discussions surrounding corporate mergers. Theoretically, mergers, unlike corporate takeovers, create companies that are run by management teams from both organizations. However, if some members of top management teams refuse to share power or give up control, the result can be a missed merger opportunity that would have provided benefits to both companies and to their shareholders.

In contrast, top leaders' willingness to talk candidly about individual roles and responsibilities as part of the merger negotiation can pave the way for successful future operations. When Lockheed and Martin Marietta merged in 1994, the two chief executives talked candidly about their expectations and were subsequently able to finalize their arrangement in a three-minute phone call. Lockheed chairman Daniel Tellep was 62 years old and did not want to give up immediate control so soon before retirement. Martin Marietta's chief executive, at 58 years old, did not feel the same time pressures. The two agreed that Tellep would serve first as both chairman and CEO of Lockheed Martin, the new company, but would phase Marietta's CEO, Norman Augustine, into both jobs over a two-year period. They agreed that Tellep would retire at 64 and formally turn full control over to Augustine at that time. Because both men were willing to discuss their emotional needs candidly, the merger produced the world's largest aerospace and defense company with relatively little commotion.

SOURCE: Steven Lipin, "In Many Merger Deals, Ego and Pride Play Big Roles in the Way Talks Go," *The Wall Street Journal,* August 22, 1996, pp. C1, C6.

Although the parties may at first argue strenuously for what they want, each pushing the other side for concessions, usually both sides will modify their positions and each will move toward the other. As we will discuss, however, truly creative negotiations may not require compromise; instead the parties may invent a solution that meets the objectives of all sides.

6. Successful negotiation involves the management of *intangibles* as well as the resolving of *tangibles* (e.g., the price or the terms of agreement). Intangible factors are the underlying psychological motivations that may directly or indirectly influence the parties during a negotiation. Some examples of intangibles are (*a*) the need to "look good" to the people you represent, (*b*) the desire to book more business than any other salesperson in your office, and (*c*) the fear of setting precedent in the negotiations. Intangibles can also include core beliefs and values. Intangible factors can have an enormous influence on negotiation processes and outcomes, and need to be managed proactively during negotiations. For example, Joe may not want to make Ed Laine angry about the purchasing problem because he needs Ed's support in the upcoming budget negotiations, but Joe also doesn't want to lose face to his engineers, who expect him to back them up. (See Box 1.2 about the dangerous role of ego.)

INTERDEPENDENCE

In negotiation, both parties need each other. A buyer cannot buy unless someone else sells, and vice versa. This situation of mutual dependency is called *interdependence*. Interdependent relations are complex and have their own special challenge. They are more complex than situations in which one party is independent of the other or in which one is simply dependent on the other. Independent parties can, if they choose, have a relatively detached, indifferent, uninvolved outlook. One who is dependent on another must accept and accommodate that other party's demands and idiosyncrasies. For example, if an employee is totally dependent on an employer for a job, the employee will have to either do the job as instructed or quit. Interdependent parties, however, have an opportunity to influence each other, and many options are open to both. Managing and dealing with those options can be difficult, however, because of the complexity of the interdependent relationship.

Interdependent relationships are characterized by interlocking goals—the parties need each other in order to accomplish their goals. For instance, in a business project management team, no single person could complete a complex project alone within the time limit imposed by the organization. For the group to accomplish its goals, each person needs to rely on the other project team members. In that sense, the goals of the project team members are interdependent. Note that having interdependent goals does not mean that everyone wants or needs exactly the same thing. Different project team members may need different things, but they must work together. This mix of personal and group goals is typical of interdependent situations. Another example of interdependence is two people playing a competitive game of squash. On the one hand, both players want to win the game, so their goals are in conflict (only one person can win). On the other hand, both want to play the game, so their goals converge (one cannot play squash alone). This mix of convergent and conflicting goals characterizes many interdependent relationships (see Box 1.3).

Interdependent goals are an important aspect of negotiation. The structure of the interdependence between different negotiating parties determines the range of possible outcomes of the negotiation and suggests the appropriate strategies and tactics that the negotiators should use. For instance, if the interdependence is a "win-lose" situation—that is, the more one party gains, the more the other party loses—then the negotiation will focus on how to divide a fixed amount of outcomes. An example of this type of negotiation is determining the price of a major appliance or vehicle. (Such situations, known as distributive bargaining, are discussed in detail in Chapter 3.) Another type of interdependence occurs in a "win-win" situation—that is, solutions exist so that both parties can do well in the negotiation. An example of this type of negotiation is determining the relationship between two companies in a joint venture. (Such situations, known as integrative negotiation, are discussed in detail in Chapter 4.) The type of interdependence between the negotiating parties will determine both the range of possible negotiation solutions and the type of strategies the negotiators should use.

The interdependence of people's goals is the basis for much social interaction. By examining the ways in which the goals are interdependent, we can estimate what type of behavior is most likely to emerge. When the goals of two or more people are interconnected so that only one can achieve the goal—such as winning a gold medal in a race—we have a competitive situation, also known as a zero-sum or distributive situation, in

BOX 1.3
Perspective

I have been representing athletes for almost a quarter century, longer than some of them have been alive. During the course of that time, I have developed deep relationships—friendships and partnerships—with many of the executives with whom I do business. We have done dozens of deals with one another over the years. There has been contention and struggle. There have been misunderstandings at times. But in the end, not unlike a marriage, we have stayed together, moved forward, and grown. That kind of shared relationship over time results in a foundation of trust and respect that is immeasurably valuable.

But that kind of trust must be earned. I understood this when I did my first deal 23 years ago. A basic premise of my entire career has been the knowledge that I will be working with the same people again and again. That means that I am always thinking about the deal I am making right now but also about a given player's future deals. It means I see the other party as a potential partner, not as a foe to be vanquished.

If it were not for the team owners, I would not have a profession. If they did not feel that they could operate at a profit, we would not have an industry. I may believe that a player deserves every penny he is paid, but that is only half the equation. The other half depends upon whether the *owner* believes he can profit by making that payment.

These are not showdowns. In the end they are collaborations. We each have an interest in the success and health of the other. I need and want professional sports to survive and thrive. The various leagues need a steady supply of quality players who are quality people. Each side has something to offer the other. Each side depends on the other.

In any industry in which repeat business is done with the same parties, there is always a balance between pushing the limit on any particular negotiation and making sure the other party—and your relationship with him—survives intact. This is not to suggest that you subordinate your interests to his. But sometimes it is in your best long-term interest to leave something on the table, especially if the other party has made an error that works to your advantage.

No one likes being taken advantage of. We are all human beings. We all have the potential to make a mistake. No matter how much each side stresses preparation, there is no way to consider every factor in a negotiation. There may be times during the process where one party realizes he has made an error in calculation or in interpretation and may ask that that point be revised. There may be times where terms have been agreed to but the other party then sees a mistake and asks you to let him off the hook. You don't have to do it. You could stick him on that point. But you need to ask yourself, Is it worth it? Is what I have to gain here worth what I will lose in terms of this person's willingness to work with me in the future? In most cases, the long-term relationship is much more valuable than the short-term gain.

Sometimes the other party may make a mistake and not *know* it. There are times when the GM or owner I am dealing with makes a major error in his calculations or commits a major oversight, and I can easily take advantage of that and just nail him.

which "individuals are so linked together that there is a negative correlation between their goal attainments" (Deutsch, 1962, p. 276). To the degree that one person achieves his or her goal, the other's goal attainment is blocked. In contrast, when parties' goals are linked so that one person's goal achievement *helps* others to achieve their goals, we

---

BOX 1.3 (*Concluded*)
Perspective

But I don't. He shows me his jugular, and instead of slashing it, I pull back. I might even point out his error. Because if I do crush him, he will eventually realize it. And although I might make a killing on that particular deal, I will also have killed our relationship and, very likely, any possibility of future agreements. Or it might be that the person's mistake costs him his job, in which case someone else might take his place—who is much rougher to deal with and is intent on paying me back for taking his predecessor to the cleaners.

SOURCE: Leigh Steinberg, *Winning with Integrity* (New York: Random House, 1998), pp. 217–18. Used with permission.

---

have a mutual-gains situation, also known as a non-zero-sum or integrative situation, where there is a positive correlation between the goal attainment of both parties. The nature of the interdependence will have a major impact on the nature of the relationship, the way negotiations are conducted, and the outcomes of a negotiation (Neslin and Greenhalgh, 1983; Raiffa, 1982).

Fisher, Ury, and Patton (1991), in their popular book *Getting to Yes: Negotiating Agreement without Giving In,* also stress the importance of understanding the nature of interdependence. They suggest that knowing and developing alternatives to reaching an agreement with the other party in a negotiation is an important source of power. They note that, "whether you should or should not agree on something in a negotiation depends entirely upon the attractiveness to you of the best available alternative" (p. 105). They call this concept BATNA (an acronym for *B*est *A*lternative *T*o a *N*egotiated *A*greement) and suggest that each negotiator needs to understand both parties' BATNAs when they negotiate (see Box 1.4). The value of a person's BATNA is always relative to the possible settlements available in the current negotiation, and the possibilities within a given negotiation are heavily influenced by the nature of the interdependence between the parties.

MUTUAL ADJUSTMENT

Interdependent relationships—those in which people are mutually dependent—are complex. Both parties know that they can influence the other's outcomes and that their outcomes can, in turn, be influenced by the other (Goffman, 1969; Pruitt and Rubin, 1986; Raven and Rubin, 1973; Ritov, 1996). This mutual adjustment continues throughout the negotiation as both parties act to influence the other (Alexander, Schul, and Babakus, 1991; Donohue and Roberto, 1996; Eyuboglu and Buja, 1993; Pinkley and Northcraft, 1994). It is important to recognize that negotiation is a *process* that transforms over time, and mutual adjustment is one of the key causes of the changes that occur during a negotiation (Gray, 1994; Kolb, 1985; Kolb and Putnam, 1997).

BOX 1.4
The Used Car

"Hey, Paul, would you come on over to my place a little before three?" Orlo asked his neighbor during a phone call. "I've got someone coming over to look at the old Cadillac, and I need some competition . . . just act interested."

When the prospect showed up, he saw two men poking around under the hood. Orlo greeted him, and introduced him to Paul who glanced up and grunted. After a quick tour of the car, the prospect was obviously interested. "You mind if I take it for a spin?" he ventured.

Orlo looked at Paul. Paul shrugged his shoulders, "Sure. Remember, I was here first."

The prospect returned, impressed with the roominess and comfortable ride. "Okay, how much do you want?"

Orlo quoted the price listed in the newspaper, and Paul objected, "Hey!"

The prospect stuck out his hand. "I'll take it!"

Orlo looked sheepishly at Paul and shook the now-buyer's hand.

After the new owner left, Paul said, "I can't believe that he paid you that much for that old car!"

SOURCE: Leigh Steinberg, *Winning with Integrity* (New York: Random House, 1998), p. 47.

Let us explore Sue Carter's job situation in more detail. Rather than accepting a layoff or reduced pay, Sue would like to leave her present employer and take a job that is available in a large multinational bank in her town. Her prospective manager, Bob, perceives Sue as a desirable candidate for the position and is ready to offer her the job. Bob and Sue are now attempting to establish Sue's salary. The job description announced the salary as "competitive." Sue has, privately, identified a salary below which she will not work ($40,000) but suspects she may be able to get considerably more. Because the bank has a reputation for running "hard and lean," Sue has decided not to state her minimally acceptable salary; she suspects that the bank will pay no more than necessary and that her minimum would be accepted quickly. Moreover, she knows that it would be difficult to raise the level if it should turn out that $40,000 was considerably below what Bob would pay. Sue has thought of stating her ideal salary ($45,000), but she suspects that Bob will view her as either presumptuous or rude for asking that much (see Box 1.5). If this happened, then the interview would probably end with Bob viewing her negatively and making it harder for her to get the best possible salary.

Let's take a closer look at what is happening here. Sue is making her decision based on how she *anticipates* Bob will react to her actions. Sue recognizes that her actions will affect Bob. Sue also recognizes that the way Bob acts toward her in the future will be influenced by the way her actions affect him now. As a result, Sue is assessing the *indirect* impact of her behavior on herself. Further, she also knows that Bob is alert to all this and will look upon any statement by Sue as reflecting a preliminary position on salary rather than a final one. To counter this expected view, Sue will

---

BOX 1.5
The Importance of Aligning Perceptions

Having information about your negotiation partner's perceptions is an important element of negotiation success. When your expectations of a negotiated outcome are based on faulty information, it is likely that you will not be taken seriously by the other party. Take, for example, the following story told to one of the authors:

> At the end of a job interview, the recruiter asked the enthusiastic MBA student, "And what starting salary were you looking for?"
>
> The MBA candidate replied, "I would like to start in the neighborhood of $125,000 per year, depending on your benefits package."
>
> The recruiter said, "Well, what would you say to a package of five weeks' vacation, 14 paid holidays, full medical and dental coverage, company matching retirement fund up to 50 percent of your salary, and a new company car leased for your use every two years . . . say, a red Corvette?"
>
> The MBA sat up straight and said, "Wow! Are you kidding?"
>
> "Of course," said the recruiter. "But you started it."

---

probably try to find some way to state a number as close to her desired final salary as possible. For example, she could refer to salaries that she knows other people with similar qualifications have received in other banks. Sue is choosing among behavioral options with a thought not only to how they will affect Bob but also to how they will then lead Bob to act toward Sue. Further, Sue knows that Bob believes she will act in this way and makes her decision on the basis of this belief.

One may wonder if people really pay attention to all this complexity, or think in such detail in their relationships with others. Certainly people don't do this most of the time, or they would be frozen in inactivity while they tried to think through the possibilities. However, when people face complex, important, or novel situations, they are more likely to think in this way. The effective negotiator needs to understand how people will adjust and readjust what they say during negotiations based on what the other party does and is expected to do.

Behavior in an interdependent relationship is frequently calculated on the premise that the more information one has about the other person, the better. There is the possibility, however, that too much knowledge only confuses (Beisecker, Walker, and Bart, 1989; Raven and Rubin, 1973), or it may accentuate differences in perceived fairness (Camerer and Loewenstein, 1993). For example, suppose Sue knows the average salary ranges for clerical, supervisory, and managerial positions for local, national, and multinational banks in her county, state, and country. Does all this help Sue determine her actions or does it only confuse things? In fact, given all these complexities, Sue may not have reached a decision about what salary she should be paid, other than a minimum figure below which she will not go. This is the classic bargaining situation. Both parties have their outer limits for an acceptable settlement (how high or low they are willing to go), but within that range, neither has determined what the exact number should be. The parties have to exchange information and make an effort at influencing each other and at problem solving. They must work toward a solution that takes into account each person's requirements and, hopefully, optimizes the outcomes for both (Fisher, Ury, and Patton, 1991; Follett, 1940; Nash, 1950; Sebenius, 1992; Sen, 1970; Walton and McKersie, 1965).

Problem solving is essentially a process of specifying the elements of a desired outcome, examining the components available to produce the outcome, and searching for a way to fit them together. It is possible for a person to approach problem solving in negotiation from his or her own perspective and attempt to solve the problem by considering only the components that affect his or her own desired outcome. For instance, going back to the beginning of the Carter story, Sue could decide what was best for her vacation and ignore Joe's needs. When approaching the situation as a joint problem-solving effort, however, the outcomes desired by the other party must be taken into account. In the case of Sue's salary negotiation, Bob may be constrained by company rules that limit how far he can go in negotiating salary with Sue, but the company may allow him to be very flexible in negotiating other aspects of the employment relationship. One difficulty is that opposing parties may not be open about their desired outcomes, or they may not be clear in their own minds about what they actually want. Hence, a necessary step in all negotiation is *to clarify and share information about what both parties really want as outcomes.*

As negotiations evolve, at least some part of the combined set of desired outcomes becomes known, usually through statements of bargaining positions or needs. If the suggested outcomes don't immediately work, the negotiation continues as a series of proposals. Each party's proposals usually suggest alterations to the other party's position, and perhaps contain changes to his or her own position. When one party accepts a change in his or her position, a *concession* has been made (Pruitt, 1981). Concessions restrict the range of options within which a solution or agreement will be reached; when a party makes a concession, the bargaining range is confined closer to one or both sides' limits or resistance point. For instance, Sue would like to get a starting salary of $45,000, but she scales her request down to $43,000, thereby eliminating all possible salary options above $43,000. People may recognize that concessions are necessary for a settlement, but they obviously are reluctant to make all or most of them. Before making any concessions below $43,000, Sue probably will want to see some willingness on the part of the bank to add some combination of attractive benefits to the salary package.

Making and interpreting concessions is no easy task, especially when there is little trust between negotiators. Two of the dilemmas that all negotiators face, identified by Harold Kelley (1966), help explain why this is the case. The first dilemma, the *dilemma of honesty,* concerns how much of the truth to tell the other party. (The ethical considerations of these dilemmas are discussed in Chapter 7.) On the one hand, telling the other party everything about your situation may give that person the opportunity to take advantage of you. On the other hand, not telling the other person anything about your needs and desires may lead to a stalemate. Just how much of the truth should you tell the other party? If Sue told Bob that she would work for as little as $40,000 but would like to start at $45,000, it is quite possible that Bob would hire her for $40,000 and allocate the extra money that he might have paid her elsewhere in the budget. We are not suggesting that Bob should do this; rather, because the long-term relationship is important in this situation, Bob should ensure that both parties' needs are met (see Chapter 4 for an expanded discussion of this point). If, however, Sue did not tell Bob any information about her salary aspirations, then Bob would have a difficult time knowing how to satisfy those needs.

The second dilemma that every negotiator faces, the *dilemma of trust*, concerns how much to believe of what the other party tells you. If you believe everything that the other party says, then he or she could take advantage of you. If you believe nothing that the other party says, then you will have a great deal of difficulty in reaching an agreement. To what extent you should trust the other party depends on many factors, including the reputation of the other party, how he or she treated you in the past, and the present circumstances. If Bob told Sue that $38,000 was the maximum he was allowed to pay her for the job without seeking approval "from above," should Sue believe him or not? As you can see, sharing and clarifying information is not as easy as it first appears.

The search for an optimal solution through the processes of giving information and making concessions is greatly aided by trust and a belief that you're being treated honestly and fairly. Two efforts in negotiation help to create such trust and belief—one is based on perceptions of outcomes and the other on perceptions of the process. An outcome effort attempts to change a party's estimation of the perceived importance or value of something. If Bob convinces Sue that a lower salary for the job is relatively unimportant given the high potential for promotion associated with the position, then Sue may feel comfortable making a concession on salary.

In contrast, an effort based on the negotiating process may help convey images of equity, fairness, and reciprocity in proposals and concessions. When one party makes several proposals that are rejected by the other party and the other party makes no alternate proposal, the first party may feel improperly treated and may therefore break off negotiations. When people make a concession, they feel much more comfortable and trusting if the other party responds with a concession. In fact, the belief that concessions will occur in negotiations appears to be almost universal. During training seminars, we have asked negotiators from more than 50 countries if they expect give-and-take to occur during negotiations in their culture; all have said they do. This pattern of give-and-take is not just a characteristic of negotiation; it is also essential to joint problem solving in most interdependent relationships (Kimmel, Pruitt, Magenau, Konar-Goldband, and Carnevale, 1980; Putnam and Jones, 1982; Weingart, Thompson, Bazerman, and Carroll, 1990). Satisfaction with a negotiation is as much determined by the process through which an agreement is reached as with the actual outcome obtained. To eliminate or even deliberately attempt to reduce this give-and-take—as some labor–management negotiating strategies have attempted (Raiffa, 1982; Selekman, Fuller, Kennedy, and Baitsel, 1964)—is to short-circuit the process, and may destroy both the basis for trust and any possibility of joint decision making. Even if the strategy results in maximizing joint outcomes, the other party may express dissatisfaction with the process or with the negotiation as a whole. Following a fair process will contribute to feelings of satisfaction and success for both parties.

INTERDEPENDENCE AND PERCEPTIONS

We have been treating interdependence as a more or less objective phenomenon in negotiation. That is, we have looked at how the structure of the negotiation itself (e.g., win-lose versus win-win situation) plays an important part in determining how two negotiating parties should interact. People frequently perceive economic exchanges, such as the purchase of a new car or a commodity, as win-lose situations. At other times, however, such exchanges may be structured as win-win, in which case there are opportunities for both parties to gain. For example, two companies that are considering a merger could be in a situation where both could be more effective competing with other companies after the merger. A recent trend among consulting companies illustrates this well. Companies that are traditionally strong in one area of consulting (e.g., accounting or taxation) have been merging with companies that are traditionally strong in other areas (e.g., human resource management or corporate strategy) in order to create comprehensive consulting services across several lines of business. The challenge in negotiating in these types of situations is to find solutions where *all* parties can do well.

Understanding the nature of the interdependence of the parties is critical to successful negotiation. Unfortunately, negotiation situations do not typically present themselves with neat labels. Rather, negotiators make judgments about the nature of the interdependence in their negotiation situations, and negotiator perceptions about interdependence become as important as the actual structure of the interdependence (Bazerman, Magliozzi, and Neale, 1985; Neale and Bazerman, 1985; Neale and Northcraft, 1991; Pinkley, 1992; Thompson, 1990b).

To examine how perception and structure are critically linked, let us return to the example of the merging consulting companies. Recall that one company, which we'll call Company A, was stronger in accounting and taxation consulting, although they also offered consulting in human resource management and corporate strategy. The other company, which we will refer to as Company B, was stronger in human resource management and corporate strategy consulting, although they also did some consulting in accounting and taxation. Assume that both companies were extremely competitive in the past. If one approaches the other to suggest a merger, the receiver would be likely to view the move skeptically, perhaps even seeing it as a sign of weakness of the other company. Instead, now assume that each company had strong respect for the other company's ability in its primary consulting domain and neither competed head on with each other. In this situation, an offer to merge would likely be viewed in a very different manner.

The point here is that people bring much baggage with them to a negotiation, including past experience, personality characteristics, moods, habits, and beliefs about how to negotiate. These factors will influence how people perceive an interdependent situation, and this perception will in turn have a strong effect on the subsequent negotiation.

Considerable research has been conducted on the role of perception and cognition in negotiation (see Bazerman and Neale, 1992; Neale and Bazerman, 1991, 1992b; Thompson and Hastie, 1990a, 1990b). This research suggests that how people perceive interdependent situations has an important effect on how they will negotiate. (Perception and cognition are discussed in more detail in Chapter 5.) Leigh Thompson and Reid Hastie (1990a) suggest that negotiators' perceptions and judgments can have important influences on judgments they make about (*a*) the other party, (*b*) themselves, (*c*) the utilities of both parties, (*d*) offers and counteroffers, (*e*) negotiation outcomes, and (*f*) the negotiation process as a whole.

A classic treatise by Harold Kelley and Anthony Stahelski (1970) suggests that negotiator perceptions have a critical influence on how negotiators evaluate situations and how they subsequently behave. Kelley and Stahelski propose that there are two general types of negotiators: cooperators and competitors. Competitors enter negotiations expecting the other party to compete; thus, they compete with everyone. Cooperators will cooperate with other cooperators and compete with competitors. The consequences are fascinating. Competitors come to believe that all negotiations are competitive, and that the world contains only competitors—because all the people they negotiate with compete (natural competitors or cooperators who have adapted and compete when they are with a natural competitor). Cooperators, in contrast, understand that negotiations may be cooperative or competitive and recognize that there are both cooperators and competitors in the world; one important task for them is to identify the predisposition of the other party. In addition, each type's experiences continue to reinforce their beliefs about others, thus making these beliefs highly resistant to change.

Another line of research has sought to identify systematic biases in negotiators' initial perceptions of the nature of the interdependence between the negotiating parties. Max Bazerman, Thomas Magliozzi, and Margaret Neale (1985) labeled one such systematic bias the "mythical fixed pie." Bazerman and his colleagues suggest that most negotiators will assume that there is a fixed pie; that is, the more I get, the less you have. In a laboratory study of negotiation that investigated this hypothesis, Leigh Thompson and Reid Hastie (1990a) found that more than twice as many negotiators (68 percent) assumed their upcoming negotiations were win-lose situations rather than win-win situations (32 percent). A similar study showed this percentage to be even higher in children (Dudley, Johnson, and Johnson, 1996). Thompson and Hastie (1990a) also found that the degree to which negotiators adjusted to the situation during the first five minutes of the negotiation had an important effect on the outcome of the negotiation. Negotiators who better adjusted their assessments of the structure of the negotiation early in the process earned higher profits than those who did not adjust until later.

Researchers continue to identify other systematic perceptual biases that make negotiators less than ideal decision makers (see Chapter 5 for further discussion). It is no simple task to correct the biased perceptions that occur when negotiating, however. Most authors agree that *identifying* the systematic biases in negotiators' perceptions is an important first step. An important unsolved issue is whether the next step, reducing the effect of the biases, is best accomplished through the use of an unfreezing-change-refreezing model (Neale and Bazerman, 1991), systematic consideration of the other party's position (Thompson and Loewenstein, 1992), or some other technique.

Two potential consequences of interdependent relationships are (1) value creation and (2) conflict. Negotiation skills and subprocesses are useful in situations where one wants to create value or needs to manage conflict. There is no simple recipe, however, that guarantees positive outcomes in either situation. Negotiation is a craft that blends art and science, and positive outcomes are a consequence of knowledge, experience, careful planning, and some luck. In the next section we discuss aspects of value creation, and in the following section we examine the extensive literature on conflict management.

VALUE CREATION

At the most fundamental level interdependence has the potential to lead to synergy, which is the notion that "the whole is greater than the sum of its parts." There are numerous business, Non-Government Organizations (NGOs), and personal examples of this. For instance, the recent joint ventures in research by pharmaceutical companies are designed to increase their joint research potential beyond what companies can do individually, as well as controlling their costs. Protests against globalization by various action groups are far more effective when mutually coordinated than run independently. Each of these situations involves interdependence between two or more parties, and the potential of successful value creation is significantly increased with the appropriate application of the negotiation skills discussed throughout this book.

Lax and Sebenius (1986), in their book *The Manager as Negotiator,* describe several sources of where value may be created. One of the main sources of value creation is contained in the differences that exist between negotiators. Negotiators are seldom identical, and according to Lax and Sebenius the key differences among negotiators may include differences in interests, opinions, risk aversion, and time preferences. These differences are fundamental to creating value for each negotiator, and are discussed in turn below:

- *Differences in interests.* Negotiators seldom value all items in a negotiation equally. For instance, in a collective bargaining situation management may be more willing to concede on benefits than salary because the benefits may cost them less. A wholesaler of telephone airtime may be more interested in the total value of the deal than the number of minutes sold or the rate per minute. An advertising company may be quite willing to bend on creative control of a project, but very protective of advertising placement.

- *Differences in opinions.* People differ in their evaluation of what something is worth or the future value of an item. For instance, is a piece of property in the neighborhood a good or bad investment of your hard-earned income? Some people will imagine all types of future potential, while others will see a piece of land that will unlikely increase in value. Real estate developers work hard to identify properties where they see future potential while the current owners undervalue it.

- *Differences in risk aversion.* People differ in the amount of risk that they are comfortable assuming. A young, single-income family with two children can sustain less risk than a middle-aged, dual-income couple without children. A company with a cash flow problem can assume less risk of expanding its operations than one that is cash rich.

- *Differences in time preference.* Negotiators frequently differ in how time affects them. One negotiator may be more patient with the negotiation process than the other, one may need a resolution sooner than the other, and finally there may be differences in preference for cash now versus future investments. All of these differences in time preferences have the potential to create value in a negotiation. For instance, a car salesman may want to close a deal by the end of the month in order to be eligible for a special company bonus, while the potential buyer does not need the car for another month. Or, a potential donor to a charity may need to make the donation by year end in order to realize certain tax advantages, while the charity may need to seek board approval for engaging in the new project that the donor wants and this cannot occur until the following year.

In summary, it is important that negotiators be aware that potential differences between them may be the critical factors that they can use to reach an agreement. It is also possible, however, to create value through shared interests and through scale (Lax and Sebenius, 1986). For instance, a couple who resolve their yearly vacation dilemma after a pleasant discussion, when it frequently results in arguments and acrimony, will have created positive value in their relationship, a shared interest. Companies often enter into joint ventures to reach the scale required in order to complete a project that any individual company would have trouble reaching alone. For instance, large oil companies develop expensive long-term projects together (e.g., the Alberta Tar sands development costs well in excess of $1 billion and is being done in a joint venture), and pharmaceutical companies share capital and human resources to fund their blue sky research and development projects.

CONFLICT

The other potential consequence of interdependent relationships is conflict. Conflict can be due to the highly divergent needs of the two parties, a misunderstanding that occurs between two people, or some other, intangible factor. Conflict can occur when the two parties are working toward the same goal and generally want the same outcome, or when both parties want a very different settlement. Regardless of the cause of the conflict, negotiation can play an important role in resolving it. Because many opportunities for negotiation are a result of conflict, we present a broad overview of the key definitions, concepts, terms, and models in this area.

Definitions

Conflict may be defined as a "sharp disagreement or opposition, as of interests, ideas, etc." and includes "the perceived divergence of interest, or a belief that the parties' current aspirations cannot be achieved simultaneously" (both from Pruitt and Rubin, 1986, p. 4). Relatedly, Hocker and Wilmot (1985) suggest that conflict results from "the interaction of interdependent people who perceived incompatible goals and interference from each other in achieving those goals."

Levels of Conflict

Conflict exists everywhere. One way to classify conflict is by level, and four levels of conflict are commonly identified.

1. *Intrapersonal or intrapsychic conflict.* At this level, conflict occurs within an individual. Sources of conflict can include ideas, thoughts, emotions, values, predispositions, or drives that are in conflict with each other. We want an ice cream cone badly, but we know that ice cream is very fattening. We are angry at our boss, but

we're afraid to express that anger because the boss might fire us for being insubordinate. Depending on the source and origin of the intrapsychic conflict, this domain is traditionally studied by various fields of psychology: cognitive psychologists, personality theorists, clinical psychologists, and psychiatrists. Although we will occasionally delve into the internal states of negotiators (e.g., in Chapters 6 and 10), this book generally doesn't address intrapersonal conflict.

2. *Interpersonal conflict.* A second major level of conflict is between individual people. Conflict that occurs between bosses and subordinates, spouses, siblings, or roommates is all interpersonal conflict. Most of the negotiation theory in this book addresses the resolution of interpersonal conflict, although much of it can also be applied to the levels specified below.

3. *Intragroup conflict.* A third major level of conflict is within a small group—among team and committee members and within families, classes, fraternities and sororities, and work groups. At the intragroup level, we analyze conflict as it affects the ability of the group to resolve disputes and continue to achieve its goals effectively. Within-group negotiation is discussed in Chapter 9.

4. *Intergroup conflict.* The final level of conflict is intergroup—between unions and management, warring nations, feuding families, or community action groups and government authorities. At this level, conflict is quite intricate because of the large number of people involved and possible interactions among them. Conflict can occur within groups and among groups simultaneously. Negotiations at this level are also the most complex. We will discuss the nature of intergroup negotiations throughout the book, particularly in Chapters 8 and 9.

Functions and Dysfunctions of Conflict

Most people initially think that conflict is bad or dysfunctional. This notion has two aspects: first, that conflict is an indication that something is wrong or that a problem needs to be fixed and, second, that conflict creates largely destructive consequences. Deutsch (1973) and others (Folger, Poole, and Stutman, 1993; Hocker and Wilmot, 1985) have elaborated on many of the elements that contribute to conflict's destructive image:

1. *Competitive processes.* Parties compete against each other because they believe that their goals are in opposition and that the two of them cannot both achieve their objectives. (As mentioned earlier, however, the goals may not actually be in opposition, and the parties need not compete.) In addition, competitive processes often have their own side effects; thus, the conflict that created the competition may lead to further escalation.

2. *Misperception and bias.* As conflict intensifies, perceptions become distorted. People tend to view things consistently with their own perspective on the conflict. Hence, they tend to interpret people and events as being either on their side or on the other side. In addition, thinking tends to become stereotypical and biased—parties in conflict endorse people and events that support their position and reject outright those that they suspect oppose their position.

3. *Emotionality.* Conflicts tend to become emotionally charged as the parties become anxious, irritated, annoyed, angry, or frustrated. Emotions tend to dominate thinking, and the parties may become increasingly emotional and irrational as the conflict escalates.

4. *Decreased communication.* Communication declines. Parties communicate less with those who disagree with them, and more with those who agree. What communication does occur between disputing parties may be an attempt to defeat, demean, or debunk the other's view or to add additional weight to one's own prior arguments.

5. *Blurred issues.* The central issues in the dispute become blurred and less well defined. Generalizations abound. New, unrelated issues are drawn in as the conflict becomes a vortex that attracts both related issues and innocent bystanders. The parties become less clear about how the dispute started, what it is "really about," or what it will take to solve it.

6. *Rigid commitments.* The parties become locked into positions. As the other side challenges them, parties become more committed to their points of view and less willing to back down from them for fear of losing face and looking foolish. Thinking processes become rigid, and the parties tend to see issues as simple and "either/or" rather than as complex and multidimensional.

7. *Magnified differences, minimized similarities.* As parties lock into commitments and issues become blurred, they tend to see each other—and each other's positions—as polar opposites. Factors that distinguish and separate them from each other become highlighted and emphasized, while similarities and commonalities that they share become oversimplified and minimized. This perceptual distortion leads the parties to believe they are farther apart from each other than they really may be, and hence they work harder to "win" the conflict and work less hard at finding common ground.

8. *Escalation of the conflict.* As the above points suggest, each side becomes more entrenched in its own view, less tolerant and accepting of the other, more defensive and less communicative, and more emotional. The net result is that both parties attempt to win by increasing their commitment to their position, increasing the resources they are willing to put up to "win," and increasing their tenacity in holding their ground under pressure. Both sides believe that by adding a little more pressure (resources, commitment, enthusiasm, energy, etc.), they can force the other to capitulate and admit defeat. As most destructive conflicts tell us, however, nothing could be further from the truth! Still, escalation of the level of the conflict and commitment to winning can increase to levels so high that the parties destroy their ability to resolve the dispute or ever to deal with each other again.

These are the processes that are commonly associated with conflict, but they are characteristic only of *destructive* conflict. In fact, as some authors have suggested (Coser, 1956; Deutsch, 1973), conflict can be productive. In Figure 1.1, Dean Tjosvold (1988) outlines some *productive* aspects of conflict. In this model conflict is not simply destructive or productive, it is both. The objective is not to eliminate conflict but to learn how to manage it so that the destructive elements are controlled while the productive aspects are enjoyed. Negotiation is a strategy for productively managing conflict.

FIGURE 1.1   Functions and Benefits of Conflict

- Discussing conflict makes organizational members more aware and able to cope with problems. Knowing that others are frustrated and want change creates incentives to try to solve the underlying problem.
- Conflict promises organizational change and adaptation. Procedures, assignments, budget allocations, and other organizational practices are challenged. Conflict draws attention to those issues that may interfere with and frustrate employees.
- Conflict strengthens relationships and heightens morale. Employees realize that their relationships are strong enough to withstand the test of conflict; they need not avoid frustrations and problems. They can release their tensions through discussion and problem solving.
- Conflict promotes awareness of self and others. Through conflict, people learn what makes them angry, frustrated, and frightened and also what is important to them. Knowing what we are willing to fight for tells us a lot about ourselves. Knowing what makes our colleagues unhappy helps us to understand them.
- Conflict enhances personal development. Managers find out how their style affects their subordinates through conflict. Workers learn what technical and interpersonal skills they need to upgrade themselves.
- Conflict encourages psychological development. Persons become more accurate and realistic in their self-appraisals. Through conflict, persons take others' perspectives and become less egocentric. Conflict helps persons to believe that they are powerful and capable of controlling their own lives. They do not simply need to endure hostility and frustration but can act to improve their lives.
- Conflict can be stimulating and fun. Persons feel aroused, involved, and alive in conflict, and it can be a welcome break from an easygoing pace. It invites employees to take another look and to appreciate the intricacies of their relationships.

SOURCE: Reprinted with the permission of Lexington Books, an imprint of The Rowman and Littlefield Publishing Group from *Working Together to Get Things Done: Managing for Organizational Productivity* by Dean Tjosvold. Copyright ©1986 by Lexington Books.

Factors That Make Conflict Difficult to Manage

Greenhalgh (1986) listed several useful criteria for analyzing a dispute and determining how easy or difficult it will be to resolve. Figure 1.2 presents the most important ones. Conflicts with more of the characteristics in the middle column will be much more difficult to resolve. Those that have more characteristics in the right-hand column will be easier to resolve.

CONFLICT MANAGEMENT

One of the most popular areas of conflict management research and practice has been to define the different ways that the parties themselves can manage conflict. Many approaches to managing conflict have been suggested, and inventories have been constructed to measure negotiators' tendencies to use these approaches (Filley, 1975; Hall, 1969; Rahim, 1983, 1992; Thomas, 1992; Thomas and Kilmann, 1974). Each approach

FIGURE 1.2 Conflict Diagnostic Model

Dimension	Viewpoint Continuum	
	Difficult to Resolve	*Easy to Resolve*
Issue in question	Matter of "principle"—values, ethics, or precedent a key part of the issue	Divisible issue—issue can be easily divided into small parts, pieces, units
Size of stakes—magnitude of what can be won or lost	Large—big consequences	Small—little, insignificant consequences
Interdependence of the parties—degree to which one's outcomes determine the other's outcomes	Zero sum—what one wins, the other loses	Positive sum—both believe that *both* can do better than simply distributing current outcomes
Continuity of interaction—will they be working together in the future?	Single transaction—no past or future	Long-term relationship—expected interaction in the future
Structure of the parties—how cohesive, organized they are as a group	Disorganized—uncohesive, weak leadership	Organized—cohesive, strong leadership
Involvement of third parties—can others get involved to help resolve the dispute?	No neutral third party available	Trusted, powerful, prestigious third party available
Perceived progress of the conflict—balanced (equal gains and equal harm) or unbalanced (unequal gain, unequal harm)?	Unbalanced—one party feels more harm and will want revenge and retribution whereas stronger party wants to maintain control	Balanced—both parties suffer equal harm and equal gain; both may be more willing to call it a "draw"

SOURCE: Reprinted from "Managing Conflict" by L. Greenhalgh, *Sloan Management Review* (Summer 1986), pp. 45–51, by permission of the publisher. Copyright © 1986 by the Sloan Management Review Association. All rights reserved.

FIGURE 1.3   The Dual Concerns Model

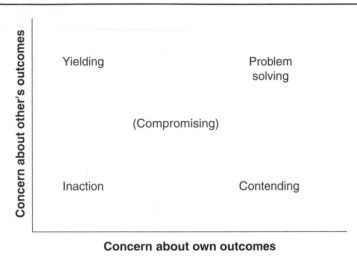

SOURCE: Reprinted from *Social Conflict: Escalation, Stalemate and Settlement* (2nd ed.) by J. Rubin, D. Pruitt and S. H. Kim by permission of the publisher. Copyright © 1994 by The McGraw-Hill Companies.

begins a fundamentally similar two-dimensional framework and then applies different labels and descriptions to five key points. We will describe these different approaches using the framework proposed by Dean Pruitt and Jeffrey Rubin (1986).

The two-dimensional framework is represented in Figure 1.3 as the dual concerns model. The model postulates that individuals in conflict have two independent levels of concern: *concern about their own outcomes* (shown on the horizontal dimension of the figure) and *concern about the other's outcomes* (shown on the vertical dimension of the figure). These concerns can be represented at any point from none (representing very low concern) to high (representing very high concern). The vertical dimension is often referred to as the cooperativeness dimension, and the horizontal dimension as the assertiveness dimension. The stronger their concern for their own outcomes, the more likely people will be to pursue strategies located on the right side of the figure, whereas the weaker their concern for their own outcomes, the more likely they will be to pursue strategies located on the left side of the figure. Similarly, the stronger their concern for permitting, encouraging, or even helping the other party achieve his or her outcomes, the more likely people will be to pursue strategies located at the top of the figure. The weaker their concern for the other party's outcomes, the more likely they will be to pursue strategies located at the bottom of the figure.

Although we can theoretically identify an almost infinite number of points within the two-dimensional space based on the level of concern for pursuing one's own and the other's outcomes, five major strategies for conflict management have been commonly identified in the dual concerns model:

"My concession speech will be brief. You win."

1. *Contending* (also called *competing* or *dominating*) is the strategy in the lower right-hand corner. Actors pursuing the contending strategy pursue their own outcomes strongly and show little concern for whether the other party obtains his or her desired outcomes. As Pruitt and Rubin (1986) state, "[P]arties who employ this strategy maintain their own aspirations and try to persuade the other party to yield" (p. 25). Threats, punishment, intimidation, and unilateral action are consistent with a contending approach.

2. *Yielding* (also called *accommodating* or *obliging*) is the strategy in the upper left-hand corner. Actors pursuing the yielding strategy show little interest or concern in whether they attain their own outcomes, but they are quite interested in whether the other party attains his or her outcomes. Yielding involves lowering one's own aspirations to "let the other win" and gain what he or she wants. Yielding may seem like a strange strategy to some, but it has its definite advantages in some situations.

3. *Inaction* (also called *avoiding*) is the strategy in the lower left-hand corner. Actors pursuing the inaction strategy show little interest in whether they attain their own outcomes, as well as little concern about whether the other party obtains his or her outcomes. Inaction is often synonymous with withdrawal or passivity; the party prefers to retreat, be silent, or do nothing.

4. *Problem solving* (also called *collaborating* or *integrating*) is the strategy in the upper right-hand corner. Actors pursuing the problem-solving strategy show high concern for attaining their own outcomes *and* high concern for whether the

other party attains his or her outcomes. In problem solving, the two parties actively pursue approaches to maximize their joint outcome from the conflict, so that both sides "win."

5. *Compromising* is the strategy located in the middle of Figure 1.3. As a conflict management strategy, it represents a moderate effort to pursue one's own outcomes and a moderate effort to help the other party achieve his or her outcomes. Pruitt and Rubin (1986) do *not* identify compromising as a viable strategy; they see it "as arising from one of two sources—either lazy problem solving involving a half-hearted attempt to satisfy the two parties' interests, or simple yielding by both parties" (p. 29). However, because other scholars (see references above) who use versions of this model believe that compromising represents a valid strategic approach to conflict, we have inserted it in Pruitt and Rubin's framework in Figure 1.3.

Many researchers have suggested that much of the writing on conflict—particularly the work in the 1960s and 1970s—had a strong normative value bias against conflict and toward cooperation (Lewicki, Weiss, and Lewin, 1992). Although the various models of conflict suggested at least five viable strategic approaches to managing conflict, the same works also suggested that problem solving was the distinctly preferred approach. These writings highlighted the virtues of problem solving, advocated using it, and described how it could be pursued in almost any dispute.

More authors in the field (see Lewicki, Weiss, and Lewin, 1992, for a review), although still strongly committed to problem solving, have also been careful to stress that each conflict management strategy has its advantages and disadvantages, and is *more or less appropriate given the type of conflict* and situation in which the dispute occurs. Thus, conflict theory and research have moved away from a normative, prescriptive approach advocating problem solving regardless of the situation and toward a contingency approach advocating that the strategy selected should be based on the objectives of the parties and the nature of their dispute. Although a full-fledged contingency approach to conflict management has yet to be articulated and supported by research, much work has been done to delineate some of the conditions under which each strategy is appropriate or inappropriate (see Figure 1.4).

OVERVIEW OF THE CHAPTERS IN THIS BOOK

The book is organized into four parts with 13 chapters, and can be viewed schematically in Figure 1.5. Part 1, Negotiation Fundamentals, contains three chapters in addition to this introductory chapter and examines the basic processes of negotiation. In Part 2, Negotiation Subprocesses, three chapters examine the key subprocesses of negotiation to help explain why negotiations unfold as they do. Part 3, Negotiation Contexts, contains four chapters that place negotiations in broader contexts. The book concludes with Part 4, Negotiation Remedies, which contains two chapters that explore individual and third-party approaches to managing difficult negotiations.

Negotiation Fundamentals continues with Chapter 2, in which we explore strategizing in negotiation and the key role that planning and preparation play in making negotiation

FIGURE 1.4   Styles of Handling Interpersonal Conflict and Situations Where They Are Appropriate or Inappropriate

Conflict Style	Situations Where Appropriate	Situations Where Inappropriate
Integrating	1. Issues are complex. 2. Synthesis of ideas is needed to come up with better solutions. 3. Commitment is needed from other parties for successful implementation. 4. Time is available for problem solving. 5. One party alone cannot solve the problem. 6. Resources possessed by different parties are needed to solve their common problems.	1. Task or problem is simple. 2. Immediate decision is required. 3. Other parties are unconcerned about outcome. 4. Other parties do not have problem-solving skills.
Obliging	1. You believe that you may be wrong. 2. Issue is more important to the other party. 3. You are willing to give up something in exchange for something from the other party in the future. 4. You are dealing from a position of weakness. 5. Preserving relationship is important.	1. Issue is important to you. 2. You believe that you are right. 3. The other party is wrong or unethical.
Dominating	1. Issue is trivial. 2. Speedy decision is needed. 3. Unpopular course of action is implemented. 4. Necessary to overcome assertive subordinates. 5. Unfavorable decision by the other party may be costly to you. 6. Subordinates lack expertise to make technical decisions. 7. Issue is important to you.	1. Issue is complex. 2. Issue is not important to you. 3. Both parties are equally powerful. 4. Decision does not have to be made quickly. 5. Subordinates possess high degree of competence.
Avoiding	1. Issue is trivial. 2. Potential dysfunctional effect of confronting the other party outweighs benefits of resolution. 3. Cooling off period is needed.	1. Issue is important to you. 2. It is your responsibility to make decision. 3. Parties are unwilling to defer; issue must be resolved. 4. Prompt attention is needed.
Compromising	1. Goals of parties are mutually exclusive. 2. Parties are equally powerful. 3. Consensus cannot be reached. 4. Integrating or dominating style is not successful. 5. Temporary solution to a complex problem is needed.	1. One party is more powerful. 2. Problem is complex enough to need a problem-solving approach.

SOURCE: Modified and reproduced by special permission of the publisher, Consulting Psychologists Press, Inc., Palo Alto, CA 94303 from *Rahim Organizational Conflict Inventories: Professional Manual* by M. A. Rahim, Copyright © 1990 by Consulting Psychologists Press, Inc. All rights reserved. Further reproduction is prohibited without the publisher's written consent.

FIGURE 1.5   Schematic Overview of Chapters in This Book

Part 1: Negotiation Fundamentals	Part 2: Negotiation Subprocesses	Part 3: Negotiation Contexts	Part 4: Negotiation Remedies
1. The Nature of Negotiation	5. Perception, Cognition, and Communication	8. The Social Context of Negotiation	12. Managing Difficult Negotiations: Individual Approaches
2. Negotiation: Strategizing, Framing, and Planning	6. Finding and Using Negotiation Leverage	9. Coalitions, Multiple Parties, and Teams	13. Managing Difficult Negotiations: Third-Party Approaches
3. Strategy and Tactics of Distributive Bargaining	7. Ethics in Negotiation	10. Individual Differences	
4. Strategy and Tactics of Integrative Negotiating		11. Global Negotiation	

successful. This chapter first examines the broad nature and role of strategy as a process planning tool. We present a general model of strategic choice and identify the key factors that affect how a strategy is designed. We then move to the more specific elements of adequate and effective planning for negotiation. Planning and preparation are the most important steps in negotiation, yet many negotiators neglect or even completely ignore them. Effective planning requires (*a*) a thorough understanding of the negotiation process so the negotiator has a general idea of what will happen and how things will evolve; (*b*) a clear formulation of goals and aspirations; (*c*) research—gathering information and arguments to support and defend desired goals; and (*d*) knowledge of the other party, his or her goals, and the ability to use that knowledge to design a strategy to reach an effective resolution. The chapter includes a series of diagnostic questions negotiators may use in planning for any negotiation.

Researchers have defined several major strategies or approaches to negotiation. Negotiation strategies and tactics should be chosen to achieve one's needs in the situation. For example, in Joe and Sue Carter's negotiations, Joe could choose one strategy to negotiate for the car: distributive (win-lose) bargaining. Joe and Sue could use a different strategy for negotiating with each other over their vacation plans: integrative (win-win) negotiation. We believe that effective negotiators make conscious choices about whether they are in a distributive or an integrative negotiation situation, and that they actively prepare strategies and tactics that match this judgment. Of course, effective negotiators are also prepared to update their judgment as the negotiation unfolds; information received during the negotiation may cause negotiators to change their perception of the structure of the negotiation situation.

Chapter 3 describes and evaluates the strategies and tactics that characterize the competitive (win-lose) distributive bargaining process. This chapter also reviews the tactics most commonly associated with distributive bargaining and evaluates the consequences of using them. The chapter concludes with a section on how to close negotiations, an aspect that many negotiators neglect in their preparation process.

Chapter 4 describes and evaluates the basic strategies and tactics common to the cooperative (win-win) integrative bargaining process. Integrative negotiation is significantly different from distributive bargaining. Whereas distributive bargaining is often characterized by mistrust and suspicion and by strategies designed to beat the other party, integrative negotiation tends to be characterized by trust and openness and by tactics designed to achieve the best possible solution for all parties involved. Integrative negotiation often resembles the process of problem solving.

Part 2, Negotiation Subprocesses, contains Chapters 5, 6, and 7. Chapter 5 explores the dynamics of perception and communication in negotiation. Negotiation is, fundamentally, a communication process involving the exchange of views, ideas, and perspectives. The chapter begins with a discussion of perception and cognition, emphasizing the miscommunication that results from perceptual and cognitive biases. We then describe the communication process and analyze its role in negotiation. The chapter concludes with a discussion of how to improve communication in negotiation and a discussion of special communication considerations at the close of negotiations.

Chapter 6 examines the sources of leverage available to negotiators. The chapter begins by defining the different sources of power that negotiators have (the tools they can potentially use to get what they want) and strategies and tactics of influence (how these tools are put to use to achieve their desired ends). Finding and using leverage in negotiation is a critical skill for all negotiators to understand and master. This chapter discusses several different sources of leverage and describes how they can work for and against negotiators.

Chapter 7 addresses the topic of ethics in negotiation. As discussed in Chapter 6, negotiation is a process in which each party engages in all manner of tactics to persuade the other. Sometimes these tactics will lead negotiators over the line of appropriate, proper, or even ethical behavior to unfair, inappropriate, unethical, or even illegal activities. Negotiators may conceal information, bluff, or tell outright lies. They may spy on other negotiators to learn about their strategies. Negotiators may decide that it is worth doing something unethical or illegal in order to achieve their goals. All these tactics fall within the category of unethical behavior. We will discuss what types of conduct are generally viewed as unethical and explore the dimensions of these behaviors in negotiation. Increasing attention has been given to ethical and unethical behavior in negotiation, and this work is discussed in detail in Chapter 7.

Part 3, Negotiation Contexts, contains Chapters 8 to 11. Chapter 8 examines the impact of the broader social context on the negotiation process. Joe and Sue Carter must deal with others who are representing their own department, organization, or political constituency. Sometimes negotiators argue not for their own interests, but for someone else's. A lawyer advocates for a client; a salesperson makes a deal for the company that must be approved by senior management; a labor leader negotiates for the union rank and file. When parties represent the interests of others and are accountable to those others, a whole new dimension of complexity is added to negotiation. This chapter also explores the role played by audiences to negotiation (observers, third parties, and the media), and shows how they affect the behavior of the negotiators and fundamentally change the negotiation dynamics.

Chapter 9 examines how negotiations change when they involve multiple parties and teams. Negotiations frequently involve more than two parties, such as a task force deciding on a new product strategy for a manufacturing organization. We devote significant attention to understanding the role of coalitions in situations involving multiple parties, and to unpacking how the dynamics of negotiation change as we move from two negotiators to multiple negotiators participating in the same negotiation. We also examine the dynamics of negotiations between teams, where the parties on each side of the table are groups of individuals rather than a single individual.

In Chapter 10, we investigate the role that individual differences among negotiators may play in enhancing or diminishing their effectiveness. Our discussion in the earlier chapters of the book implies that with planning and practice, anyone can negotiate effectively. A question that researchers have frequently investigated, however, is whether some individuals are better negotiators because of their personalities, abilities, backgrounds, or other essentially immutable characteristics. While this may seem like a simple question, it has in fact proven quite difficult for researchers to answer definitively. While most people believe that some negotiators are better than others, precisely documenting the characteristics of superior negotiators has been difficult. Chapter 10 reviews the research on this question and explores several individual attributes that appear likely to affect someone's ability to negotiate effectively.

Chapter 11 examines the role that international and cultural differences play in negotiation. In many ways, international and cultural factors operate much like the social structure dimensions we describe in Chapter 8; that is, they are a context that tempers, modifies, or changes negotiation dynamics. Because this book is being written by four white, upper-middle-class North American authors, its descriptions of typical and atypical behaviors are affected by certain cultural biases. If the book were being written by three Chinese or three Argentinean authors (or by three authors of different cultural or ethnic backgrounds), its definitions of typical and atypical behavior might be quite different. Effective research on international differences in negotiation has increased exponentially in the past five to ten years. This research attempts to determine what factors are central to all negotiations regardless of culture and which factors and dimensions are strongly shaped by national and cultural style. We will present a current perspective on this important emerging area of negotiation research.

Part 4, Negotiation Remedies, contains Chapters 12 and 13. Chapter 12 examines what negotiators can do when negotiation strategies and tactics do not work the way they were intended to. Most commonly, negotiations break down because the conflict dynamics get out of control or because poor communication interferes with the parties' ability to reach an agreement. (Recall Joe's problem with the purchasing department and Ed Laine, and Sue's problem with the bank's upper management.) This may occur in a number of ways: parties dig in to their positions and refuse to yield, communication becomes unproductive, the parties cannot find common ground or invent a solution to the problem, anger and frustration drive out effective reasoning and listening. In Chapter 12, we describe how negotiators can help put derailed negotiations back on track; most of the tactics we explore are those that negotiators can use themselves to keep a conflict from becoming increasingly destructive. We also discuss the cognitive traps negotiators sometimes lay for themselves and techniques negotiators can use to deal with difficult processes and other parties. Finally, we present a basic plan for building and maintaining productive negotiating relationships.

Chapter 13 discusses another way to get negotiations back on track by using other people—called third parties—to bring the principal negotiators back together. We encourage negotiators to approach third parties when their own efforts to put things back on track are not fruitful. We explore various types of third-party strategies that can be used to resolve breakdowns in negotiation: arbitration, mediation, process facilitation, and some additional hybrid forms.

CHAPTER 2

Negotiation: Strategizing, Framing, and Planning

In this chapter, we discuss what negotiators should do before opening negotiations. We believe that effective strategizing, planning, and preparation are the most critical precursors for achieving negotiation objectives. With effective planning and target setting, most negotiators can achieve their objectives; without them, results occur more by chance than by negotiator effort.

Regrettably, systematic planning is not something that most negotiators do willingly. Many managers, for example, are much more inclined to take action than to spend time reflecting about the future and planning for it (Mintzberg, 1973; Sheppard, Blumenfeld-Jones, Minton, and Hyder, 1994). Although time constraints and work pressures may make it difficult to set aside the time to plan adequately, the problem is that, for many of us, planning is simply boring and tedious, easily put off in favor of getting into the action quickly. Devoting insufficient time to planning is one weakness that may cause negotiators to fail; several other weaknesses include:

- Negotiators fail to set clear objectives that can serve as standards for evaluating offers and packages. When something has to give, or when the other party makes a proposal that rearranges the component elements of a settlement, a negotiator who does not have clear objectives is not in a position to evaluate the new possibilities quickly and accurately. As a result, that negotiator may agree to something that is not to his or her advantage. Alternatively, the negotiator may become confused or defensive and thereby delay the process, causing the other party to lose patience.

- If negotiators have not done their homework, they may not understand the strengths and weaknesses of their own positions or recognize weaknesses in the other party's arguments. As a result, they may not be able to formulate convincing arguments to support their own position or rebut the other party's arguments.

- Negotiators cannot simply depend upon being quick and clever during the give-and-take of negotiation. Should the other party plan to win by stalling and delaying, or holding to a position to wear the negotiator down, a new approach will be necessary. Negotiators often find that being glib or articulate in presenting their position is not helpful when the other party assails that position as illegal, inefficient, or ineffective.

Identifying potential shortcomings in the planning process is necessary, but it's not enough. Moreover, it is ironic that most people who teach about negotiation believe strongly in the efficacy of planning in negotiation, but there is *little direct, verifiable evidence that planning actually improves negotiation effectiveness*. On the one hand, almost

FIGURE 2.1　Relationship between Key Steps in the Planning Process
(Overview of Chapter 2)

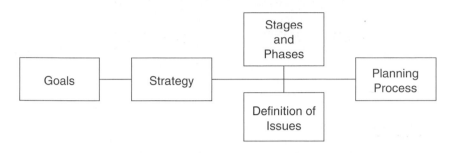

every popular book on negotiation devotes at least one or two chapters to planning (e.g., Freund, 1993; Lewicki and Hiam, 1999; Schapiro, 1993; Shell, 1999); indeed, there are books that are wholly devoted to how to plan and prepare effectively (e.g., Fisher and Ertel, 1995). Yet there is scant empirical evidence on planning activities. One study of successful negotiators, performed over 20 years ago (Rackham, 1980), suggested that during planning (compared to "average" negotiators), skilled negotiators (*a*) explored a wider range of options for action; (*b*) worked harder to find common ground with the other party; (*c*) spent more time considering the long-term implications of the issues; and (*d*) were significantly more likely to set upper and lower limits, or a "range" of acceptable settlements. While these findings appear reasonable and logical, the profession needs more hard research evidence to confirm the effectiveness of the strategizing and planning process described in this chapter.

The discussion of planning and strategizing begins by exploring the broad process of strategy development, starting with defining the negotiator's goals/objectives. We then move to understanding the process of developing a strategy to achieve those goals, discussion of the issues at stake, and exploration of how the definition of those issues may change over the course of a negotiation. Next, we address the typical stages and phases of an evolving negotiation, and how understanding them may affect planning. Finally, the critical steps involved in creating a plan to execute a strategy are discussed. Figure 2.1 shows how these elements are related. Although this model suggests that the relationships are linear—that is, goals lead to strategy leads to planning, influenced by the definition of the issues and the evolution of the negotiation—in fact, parties often begin at any point in this sequence and work their way "backward/forward" until the preparation process is aligned.

GOALS—THE OBJECTIVES THAT DRIVE A NEGOTIATION STRATEGY

The first step in developing and executing a negotiation strategy is to determine one's goals. Negotiators must anticipate what they want to achieve in a negotiation and prepare for these events in advance. The preparation must include attention to substantive items—including *goals, goal priorities,* and *multigoal packages*—as well as to procedural concerns dealing with *agendas* and *bargaining histories.* Effective prepara-tion requires a thorough, thoughtful approach to these items; negotiators should spec-ify their goals and objectives clearly. This includes stating all goals they wish to achieve in the negotiation, determining the priority among these goals, identifying potential multigoal packages, and evaluating possible trade-offs among them. As noted in Chapter 1, goals are usually *tangibles*—rate, price, specific terms, contract language, fixed packages, and so on—but they can also include *intangibles,* such as maintaining a certain precedent, defending a principle, or getting an agreement regardless of cost.

Direct Effects of Goals on Choice of Strategy

When entering a bargaining relationship, people generally have some idea of what they would like the outcome to be. They often say, "I'd be happy if . . ." and then state something they would really like to have, for example, ". . . I could buy a new car at a price that wouldn't require all of my paycheck as the loan payment." That's not bad as a *wish,* but it's not very good as a goal for negotiation. Four aspects of how goals affect negotiation are important to understand:

1. *Wishes are not goals,* especially in negotiation. Wishes may be related to interests or needs that motivate goals (see Chapter 4), but they are not goals them-selves. A wish is a fantasy, a hope that something might happen; a goal is a spe-cific, focused, realistic target that one can specifically plan to achieve.

2. *Our goals are often linked to the other party's goals.* The linkage between the two parties' goals defines an *issue* to be settled (see the discussion of issues later in this chapter). My goal is to get a car cheaply, and the dealer's goal is to sell it at the highest possible price (and profit); thus, the "issue" is the price I will pay for the car. If I could achieve my goal by myself, without the other party, I proba-bly wouldn't need to negotiate. Goals that are not linked to each other often lead the parties either to talk past each other or to intensify the conflict.

3. *There are boundaries or limits to what our goals can be* (see the discus-sion of alternatives later in this chapter). If what we want exceeds these limits (i.e., what the other party is capable of or willing to give), we must either change our goals or end the negotiation—goals must be reasonably attainable. If my goal—"to buy this car at a cheap price"—isn't possible because the dealer won't sell the car cheaply, I'm going to either change my goal or find a cheaper car to buy (per-haps from a different dealer).

4. *Effective goals must be concrete or specific,* and preferably *measurable.* The less concrete and measurable our goals are, the harder it is (*a*) to communi-cate to the other party what we want, (*b*) to understand what he or she wants, and (*c*) to determine whether any particular outcome satisfies our goals. "To get a price on a car so that the loan payment does not use all of my paycheck" is not a very clear goal. Is this every week's paycheck or only one check a month? Do I want the payment to be just under 100 percent of the paycheck, or about 50 percent, or perhaps even 25 percent? Today's paycheck only, or the paychecks expected over

the life of the loan? One has to determine exactly how much money can comfortably come out of his or her paycheck at present interest rates and add to that what is available for a down payment in order to be able to negotiate exactly what he or she will pay every week or month. Even this figure is not totally clear. Is this number the largest amount she thinks that she can possibly pay? Is it the amount that could be paid with little or no inconvenience? Or is it the amount calculated after recalling that one shouldn't pay more than a stated amount (say 15 percent) of one's monthly salary for a car payment?

The goals discussed in the preceding paragraph are all quite tangible, and they address directly the questions of the purchase price and the buyer's cash flow. No less important are the many *intangible* goals that typically arise in any negotiation. In the example of the car purchase, intangible goals might include the following: to enhance one's reputation among one's friends by owning and driving an expensive, powerful car; to maintain one's friends' image of oneself as a shrewd, pennywise negotiator; or to pay any price to ensure convenient, reliable transportation. In other negotiations, intangible goals might include: to maintain a reputation as a tough but principled negotiator, to establish a precedent for future negotiations, or to conduct the negotiations in a manner that is fair to all sides and assures each party fair treatment. (Refer back to Chapter 1 for further discussion of intangible goals.)

Which of these many criteria should we use? The answer is that *all* are probably important, for different reasons, and defining them is essential to moving toward a strategy and developing a plan.

Indirect Effects of Goals on Choice of Strategy

Simple and direct goals can often be attained in a single negotiation session. Because such goals may also be pursued infrequently (such as when we buy a car or a home), we tend to view the negotiation as a single episode—a single defined event, without future consequences. This "episodic assumption" affects our choice of strategy; in developing and framing our goals, we may ignore the present or future relationship with the other party in favor of a simplistic concern for achieving *only* the substantive outcome. Thus, the pursuit of a singular, substantive goal often tends to support the choice of a competitive strategy (refer back to the dual concerns model described in Chapter 1).

Other negotiation goals—those that are complex or difficult to define—may require initiating a sequence of negotiation episodes. In these cases progress will be made incrementally, and may depend on establishing a strong relationship with the other party. Examples here include a substantial increase in one's line of credit with a bank or credit union, or the establishment of a privileged status with an important trading partner. Such relationship-oriented goals should motivate the negotiator toward a strategy choice in which the relationship with the other party is valued as much as (or even more than) the substantive outcome. Thus, relational goals tend to support the choice of a collaborative or integrative strategy (refer back to the dual concerns model described in Chapter 1).

STRATEGY—THE OVERALL PLAN TO ACHIEVE ONE'S GOALS

After negotiators articulate goals, they move to the second element in the sequence: selecting and developing a strategy. Henry Mintzberg and J. Brian Quinn (1991), experts on business strategy, define strategy as "the pattern or plan that integrates an organization's major targets, policies, and action sequences into a cohesive whole." Applied to negotiations, strategy refers to the overall plan to accomplish one's goals in a negotiation, and the action sequences that will lead to the accomplishment of those goals.

Strategy, Tactics, or Planning?

How are strategy and tactics related? Although the line between strategy and tactics may seem indistinct, one major difference is that of scale, perspective, or immediacy (Quinn, 1991). Tactics are short-term, adaptive moves designed to enact or pursue broad (or higher-level) strategies, which in turn provide stability, continuity, and direction for tactical behaviors. For example, your negotiation *strategy* might be integrative, designed to build and maintain a productive relationship with the other party while using a joint problem-solving approach to the issues. In pursuing this strategy, appropriate *tactics* include maintaining reliable, predictable preferences (to build the other's trust in you) and using open-ended questions and active listening (to foster communication). Tactics, then, are subordinate to strategy; they are structured, directed, and driven by strategic considerations.

How are strategy and planning related? Planning is an integral part of the strategy process—the "action" component. The *planning process* takes in all the considerations and choices that parties in a negotiation make about tactics, resource use, and contingent responses in pursuit of the overall *strategy*—how they plan to proceed, to use what they have to get what they want, subject to their strategic guidelines. We address planning in detail later in this chapter.

Strategic Options—Vehicles for Achieving Goals

In the strictest sense, a unilateral choice of strategy would be wholly one-sided and intentionally ignorant of any information about the other negotiator. In our use of the term, however, a *unilateral* choice is one that is made without the *active* involvement of the other party. A reasonable effort to gain information about the other party and to incorporate that information into the choice of a negotiation strategy is always useful. In Chapter 1, the dual concerns model (Pruitt and Rubin, 1986) was used to describe the basic orientation that people take toward conflict. This model proposes that individuals in conflict have two levels of related concerns: a level of concern for their own outcomes, and a level of concern for the other's outcomes (refer back to Figure 1.3). Savage, Blair, and Sorenson (1989) propose a similar model for the choice of a negotiation strategy. According to this model, a negotiator's unilateral choice of strategy is reflected in the answers to two simple questions: (1) How much concern does the actor have for achieving the *substantive outcomes* at stake in this negotiation (substantive

FIGURE 2.2   The Dual Concerns Model

Substantive outcome important?

		Yes	No
Relational outcome important?	**Yes**	Collaboration	Accommodation
	No	Competition	Avoidance

SOURCE: ACADEMY OF MANAGEMENT EXECUTIVE by NEWSOM, WALTER B. Copyright 1989 by ACAD OF MGMT. Reproduced with permission of ACAD OF MGMT in the format Textbook via Copyright Clearance Center.

goals)? and (2) How much concern does the negotiator have for the current and future quality of the *relationship* with the other party (relationship goals)? The answers to these questions result in the mix of strategic alternatives presented in Figure 2.2.

Alternative Situational Strategies.   The power of this model lies in requiring the negotiator to determine the relative importance and priority of the two dimensions in the desired settlement. As Figure 2.2 shows, answers to these two simple questions suggest at least four types of initial strategies for negotiators: competition, collaboration, accommodation, and avoidance. A strong interest in achieving only substantive outcomes—getting *this* deal, winning *this* negotiation, with little or no regard for the effect on the relationship or on subsequent exchanges with the other party—tends to support a competitive (distributive) strategy. A strong interest in achieving only the relationship outcomes—building, preserving, or enhancing a good relationship with the other party—suggests an accommodation strategy. If both substance and relationship are important, the negotiator should pursue a collaborative (integrative) strategy. Finally, if achieving neither substantive outcomes nor an enhanced relationship is important, the party might be best served by avoiding negotiation. Each of these different strategic approaches also has different implications for negotiation planning and preparation (see also Johnston, 1982). Avoidance and accommodation strategies are discussed below; competitive (distributive) and collaborative (integrative) strategies will be extensively addressed in Chapters 3 and 4.

Avoidance: The Nonengagement Strategy.   *Avoidance* may serve a number of strategic negotiation purposes. In fact, there are many reasons why negotiators might choose not to negotiate (similar to the reasons for conflict avoidance discussed in Chapter 1). First, if one is able to meet one's needs without negotiating at all, it may make sense to use an avoidance strategy. The other party may not be willing to "cut you in," based on a simple request, or your relationship with the other may be so poor that it is not even worth asking for anything. Second, it simply may not be worth the time and effort to negotiate (although there are sometimes reasons to negotiate in such situations; see the section on accommodation below). Third, the decision to negotiate is closely related to the desirability of available alternatives—the outcomes that can be achieved if negotiations don't work out.

Alternatives—that is, the outcomes that can be obtained if this negotiation fails— are a source of power in negotiation. A negotiator with very strong alternatives has considerable power, because he or she doesn't need this negotiation to succeed in achieving at least a satisfactory outcome. But having weak alternatives puts negotiators at a disadvantage. The presence of an alternative can cut both ways in the decision about whether to avoid negotiation. First, if one has a strong alternative, one may wish to avoid negotiation strictly on efficiency grounds—it is simply quicker and easier to take the alternative than to get involved in a negotiation. But having a weak alternative may also suggest that one should avoid negotiation—once negotiations begin, the pressure of the negotiation process may lead one to a poor outcome, which one may feel obligated to accept because the alternative is also very poor. We discuss alternatives later in this chapter. Finally, avoidance may be appropriate when the negotiator is responsible for developing others (such as subordinates) into becoming better negotiators. Negotiating, like any other skill, is built by doing it. A senior executive, for example, may choose not to engage in negotiation personally but instead to delegate the task to a manager who needs the exposure and experience. In such situations, though, it is usually appropriate to assist the novice negotiator in strategy preparation and to provide some level of advisory oversight as the negotiation unfolds.

Active-Engagement Strategies: Competition, Collaboration, and Accommodation.   Competition and collaboration are described extensively in the next two chapters. *Competition* is described throughout this book as distributive or win-lose bargaining, and *collaboration* as integrative or win-win negotiation. *Accommodation* is as much a win-lose strategy as competition, although it has a decidedly different image— it involves an imbalance of outcomes, but in the opposite direction ("I lose, you win" as opposed to "I win, you lose"). As Figure 2.2 shows, an accommodative strategy may be appropriate when the negotiator considers the relationship outcome more important than the substantive outcome. In other words, the negotiator wants to let the other win, keep the other happy, or not endanger the relationship by pushing hard to achieve some goal on the substantive issues. This strategy is often used when the primary goal of the exchange is to build or strengthen the relationship (or the other party) and the negotiator is willing to sacrifice the outcome. An accommodative strategy may also be necessary if the negotiator expects the relationship to extend past a single negotiation episode. The idea is that if "I lose and you win" this time, over multiple negotiations in the relationship the win-lose accounts will balance. In any long-term social relationship, it is probably healthy for one negotiator or the other to accept a suboptimal outcome in a given negotiation while expecting reciprocal accommodation (tit for tat) from the other negotiator in the future (Homans, 1961). Such reciprocity has been called the glue that holds social groups together (e.g., Cialdini, 2001).

How do these three strategies—competition, collaboration, and accommodation—differ? Table 2.1 summarizes the three types of strategies (distributive, integrative, and accommodative), and compares and contrasts them across a number of different dimensions (adapted from Johnston, 1982).

In addition to their positive characteristics, as described in the table, each of these three types of negotiation strategies also has certain predictable drawbacks if applied blindly, thoughtlessly, or inflexibly. Distributive strategies tend to create "we-they" or "superiority-inferiority" patterns, which often lead to distortions in judgment regarding the other side's contributions and efforts, and to distortions in perceptions of the other side's values, needs, and positions (see the discussion of cognitive framing biases in Chapter 5). Integrative strategies can also be problematic if used blindly or exclusively. If a negotiator pursues a collaborative strategy without regard to the other's behavior, then the other can manipulate and exploit the collaborator and take advantage of the good faith and goodwill being demonstrated. Excessive integration can also lead negotiators to cease being accountable to their constituencies in favor of pursuit of the negotiation process for its own sake (see Chapter 8 for a discussion of negotiator–constituency dynamics). For example, negotiators who approach the process with an aggressive "we can solve it" attitude may produce an agreement that is unacceptable to their constituency (e.g., their companies). Finally, accommodative strategies also may have drawbacks. They may generate a pattern of constantly giving in to keep the other happy or to avoid a fight. This pattern establishes a precedent that is hard to break. It could also lead the other to a false sense of well-being due to the satisfaction that comes with the "harmony" of a good relationship, which may completely ignore all the giveaways on substance. Over time, this imbalance is unlikely to perpetuate, but efforts to stop the giving or restore the balance may be met with surprise and resentment.

It is also useful to remember that in presenting these strategies we are describing pure forms, typically at odds with the mixture of issues and motivations that actually characterize the evolution of most actual negotiation strategies (Lax and Sebenius, 1986). Just as most conflicts are neither purely competitive nor purely cooperative, most negotiation strategies reflect a variety of goals, intentions, and situational constraints.

In this section, we have described the major approaches to negotiation strategy. Two of these—competitive and collaborative—will be more fully explained in the next two chapters, while the other two—accommodative and avoidance—were described briefly here. We now turn to understanding how issues are framed in negotiation.

DEFINING THE ISSUES—THE PROCESS OF "FRAMING" THE PROBLEM

The next step in the planning process is determining what issues are at stake. This process is called *framing* the negotiation. Framing is about focusing, shaping, and organizing the world around us. It is about making sense of a complex reality and defining it in terms that are meaningful to us. Frames define a person, event, or process and separate it from the complex world around it. Frames "impart meaning and significance to elements within the frame and set them apart from what is outside the frame" (Buechler, 2000, p. 41). Two people walk into a room full of people and see different things: one (the extrovert) sees a great party, the other (the introvert) sees a scary and

TABLE 2.1 Characteristics of Different Engagement Strategies

Aspect	Competition (Distributive Bargaining)	Collaboration (Integrative Negotiation)	Accommodative Negotiation
Payoff structure	Usually a fixed amount of resources to be divided	Usually a variable amount of resources to be divided	Usually a fixed amount of resources to be divided
Goal pursuit	Pursuit of own goals at the expense of those of others	Pursuit of goals held jointly with others	Subordination of own goals in favor of those of others
Relationships	Short-term focus; parties do not expect to work together in the future	Long-term focus; parties expect to work together in the future	May be short term (let the other win to keep the peace) or long term (let the other win to encourage reciprocity in the future)
Primary motivation	Maximize own outcome	Maximize joint outcome	Maximize others' outcome or let them gain to enhance relationship
Trust and openness	Secrecy and defensiveness; high trust in self, low trust in others	Trust and openness, active listening, joint exploration of alternatives	One party relatively open, exposing own vulnerabilities to the other
Knowledge of needs	Parties know own needs but conceal or misrepresent them; neither party lets the other know real needs	Parties know and convey real needs while seeking and responding to needs of the other	One party is overresponsive to other's needs so as to repress own needs
Predictability	Parties use unpredictability and surprise to confuse other side	Parties are predictable and flexible when appropriate, trying not to surprise	One party's actions totally predictable, always catering to other side

Aggressiveness	Parties use threats and bluffs, trying to keep the upper hand	Parties share information honestly, treat each other with understanding and respect	One party gives up on own position to mollify the other
Solution search behavior	Parties make effort to appear committed to position, using argumentation and manipulation of the other	Parties make effort to find mutually satisfying solutions, using logic, creativity, and constructiveness	One party makes effort to find ways to accommodate the other
Success measures	Success enhanced by creating bad image of the other; increased levels of hostility and strong in-group loyalty	Success demands abandonment of bad images and consideration of ideas on their merit	Success determined by minimizing or avoiding conflict and soothing all hostility; own feelings ignored in favor of harmony
Evidence of unhealthy extreme	Unhealthy extreme reached when one party assumes total zero-sum game; defeating the other becomes a goal in itself	Unhealthy extreme reached when one party subsumes all self-interest in the common good, losing self-identity and self-responsibility	Unhealthy extreme reached when abdication to other is complete, at expense of personal and/or constituent goals
Key attitude	Key attitude is "I win, you lose"	Key attitude is "What's the best way to address the needs of all parties?"	Key attitude is "You win, I lose"
Remedy for breakdown	If impasse occurs, mediator or arbitrator may be needed	If difficulties occur, a group dynamics facilitator may be needed	If behavior becomes chronic, party becomes negotiationally bankrupt

SOURCE: Adapted and expanded from Robert W. Johnston, "Negotiation Strategies: Different Strokes for Different Folks," *Personnel* 59 (March–April 1982), pp. 38–39. Used with permission of the author.

intimidating unfriendly crowd. Because people have different backgrounds, experiences, expectations, and needs, they frame people, events, and processes differently. Moreover, these frames can change depending on perspective, or can change over time. What starts out as a game of tag between two boys may turn into an ugly fistfight. A favorite football quarterback is a "hero" when he throws a touchdown, but a "loser" when he throws an interception.

Framing has become a popular concept among social scientists who study cognitive processes, decision making, persuasion, and communication. The popularity of framing has come with the recognition that often two or more people who are involved in the same situation or in a complex problem see it or define it in different ways (Thompson, 1998). Researchers link frames and experience as follows:

> Disputes, like other social situations, are ambiguous and subject to interpretation. People can encounter the same dispute and perceive it in very different ways as a result of their backgrounds, professional training or past experiences. One label that has been placed on this form of individualized definition of a situation based on an interplay of past experiences and knowledge, and the existing situation, is a "frame." (Roth and Sheppard, 1995, p. 94)

Another view of frames is that of noted management theorist Mary Parker Follett (1942; Kolb, 1995), who was one of the first to write about integrative (win-win) negotiation in organizations. In describing the process by which parties with different views about an issue arrive at a joint agreement, Follett suggests that the parties achieve some form of unity, "not from giving in [compromise] but from 'getting the desires of each side into one field of vision'" (Follett, 1942, quoted in Putnam and Holmer, 1992). Thus, frames emerge as the parties talk about their preferences and priorities; they allow the parties to begin to develop a shared or common definition of the issues related to a situation, and a process for resolving them.

Why Frames Are Critical to Understanding Strategy

While researchers have only begun to study frames and framing dynamics in depth, there is general agreement that people often use frames to define problems, and that the effects of frames can be identified as we observe negotiations. Whether a frame is "a conception of the acts, outcomes and contingencies associated with a particular choice," an "individualized definition of a situation," or a "field of vision," how parties frame and define a negotiating issue or problem is a clear and strong reflection of what they define as central and critical to negotiating objectives, what their expectations and preferences are for certain possible outcomes, what information they seek and use to argue their case, the procedures they use to try to present their case, and the manner in which they evaluate the outcomes actually achieved.[1] Frames are inevitable; one cannot "avoid"

---

[1] Note that frames themselves cannot be "seen." They are abstractions, perceptions, and thoughts that people use to define a situation, organize information, determine what is important, what is not, and so on. We can infer other people's frames by asking them directly about their frames, by listening to their communication, and by watching their behavior. Similarly, we can try to understand our own frames, by thinking about what aspects of a situation we should pay attention to, emphasize, focus on, or ignore—and by observing our own words and actions. One cannot see or directly measure a frame, however.

framing. By choosing to define and articulate an aspect of a complex social situation, one has already implicitly "chosen" to use certain frames and to ignore others. This process often occurs without any real intentionality on the part of the negotiator; one can frame a problem because of deeply buried past experiences, deep-seated attitudes and values, or strong emotions. Frames can also be shaped by the type of information that is chosen, or the setting and context in which the information is presented. Understanding framing dynamics helps negotiators to elevate the framing process to one that is more conscious and more under control than it would otherwise be; negotiators who understand how they are framing a problem may be able to understand more completely what they are doing, what the other party is doing, and how to have more control over the negotiation process. Finally, both current theory and a stream of supportive empirical research show that frames may be malleable and, if so, can be shaped or reshaped as a function of information and communication during negotiation (i.e., a third perspective, frames as issue development). The approach here is to introduce the negotiator to the power and prevalence of frames, such that he or she can understand

- Different types of frames.
- How certain frames may be invoked or ignored in a given situation.
- The consequences of framing a conflict in a particular way.
- Approaches that negotiators can use to manage frames more effectively.

Types of Frames

Several researchers have studied different types of frames in different contexts. One area where framing has been extensively studied is environmental disputes (Gray, 1997; Gray and Donnellon, 1989; Lewicki, Gray, and Elliott, 2003). These works explore different frames that parties use in disputes. Examples include:

1. *Substantive*—what the conflict is about. Parties taking a substantive frame have a particular disposition about the key issue or concern in the conflict.

2. *Outcome*—what predispositions the party has to achieving a specific result or outcome from the negotiation. To the degree that a negotiator has a specific, preferred outcome he or she wants to achieve, the dominant frame may be to focus all strategy, tactics, and communication toward getting that outcome. Parties who have a strong outcome frame are more likely to engage primarily in distributive (win-lose or lose-lose) negotiations than in other types of negotiations.

3. *Aspiration*—what predispositions the party has toward satisfying a broader set of interests or needs in negotiation. Rather than focusing on a specific outcome, the negotiator tries to ensure that his or her basic interests, needs, and concerns are met. Parties who have a strong aspiration frame are more likely to be primarily engaged in integrative (win-win) negotiation than in other types.

4. *Conflict management process*—how the parties will go about resolving their dispute. Negotiators who have a strong process frame are less likely than others to be concerned about the specific negotiation issues but more concerned about how the deliberations will proceed, or how the dispute should be managed. When the major concerns are largely procedural rather than substantive, process frames will be strong.

5. *Identity*—how the parties define "who they are." Parties are members of a number of different social groups—gender (male), religion (Roman Catholic), ethnic origin (Italian), place of birth (Brooklyn), current place of residence (Cleveland), etc. These are only a few of the categories people can use to define themselves and distinguish themselves from others.

6. *Characterization*—how the parties defines the other parties. A characterization frame can clearly be shaped by experience with the other party, by information about the other party's history or reputation, or by the way the other party comes across early in the negotiation experience. In conflict, identity frames (of self) tend to be positive, characterization frames (of others) tend to be negative.

7. *Loss–gain*—how the parties view the risk associated with particular outcomes. A loss–gain frame is similar to a cognitive-bias frame toward issues of risk but may be more likely to shift as a function of experience and interaction with the other party. This is discussed in more detail in Chapter 5.

Communication plays a central role in the categories-of-experience approach to frames. Researchers argue that the language a party chooses to use is a strong reflection of his or her beliefs, experience, and perception of the negotiation (Gray, 1991, 1997; Lewicki, Gray, and Elliott, 2003). Linguistic analysis of negotiation transcripts has shown a number of important insights about frames:

1. Negotiators can use more than one frame. A land developer discussing a conflict over a proposed golf course that will fill in a wetland can speak about the golf course (the substantive issue), his preferences for how the land should be filled in (an outcome frame), and how much input neighborhood and environmental groups should be able to have in determining what happens to that wetland on his private property (a procedural frame), as well as whether he views these groups favorably or unfavorably (a characterization frame).

2. Mismatches in frames between parties are sources of conflict. Two negotiators may be speaking to each other from different frames (e.g., one has an outcome frame and the other has a procedural frame); using different content in the same frame (e.g., they both have a procedural frame but have strong preferences for different procedures); or using different levels of abstraction (e.g., a broad aspiration frame vs. a specific outcome frame). Such mismatches cause conflict and ambiguity, which may either create misunderstanding, lead to conflict escalation and even stalemate, or lead one or both parties to "reframe" the conflict into frames that are more compatible and that may lead to resolution. For highly polarized disputes, mutual reframing may not occur without the help of a third party. (See Box 2.1 for a discussion of mismatched frames in the Middle East.)

3. Particular types of frames may lead to particular types of agreements. For example, parties who achieve integrative agreements may be likely to use aspiration frames and to discuss a large number of issues during their deliberations. In contrast, parties who use outcome or negative characterization frames may be likely to hold negative views of the other party and a strong preference for specific outcomes, both of which may lead to an intensified conflict with the other.

BOX 2.1
Middle East Experience Frames

Some of the world's most intractable ongoing disputes take place in the Middle East. For many onlookers, the battles are merely political squabbles over land and power. This perspective, however, fails to account for the beliefs and experiences that have shaped the frames of conflict participants. For them, struggles with neighbors are based on deep-seated, long-held beliefs about themselves, their religion, and their rightful entitlements in the region. This intertwining of the daily and the divine is a volatile mix.

Take, for example, the battle between Israelis and Palestinians over land on the West Bank of Israel. Israeli leaders believe their presence in the West Bank has been sanctified because Abraham, the father of the Jewish religion, had intimate connections in the area. Palestinians, meanwhile, argue that they are descended from the Canaanites, who laid claim to the area before Abraham's time. While the dispute is undoubtedly more complex than this brief historical explanation portends, it is important for those attempting to negotiate peace in the area to understand the rationale behind each side's claims.

Religious beliefs in general tend to be strongly held. They create frames and truth perspectives through which believers view the world. When conflict arises, those who view it through a religious framework tend to believe that any compromise on their part represents a compromise of their religious beliefs, which is unacceptable. In these cases, it is important for those attempting to negotiate a peaceful settlement to provide ways for the combatants to shift their frames. They can encourage the disputants to see battles as political struggles, minimizing the religious elements so that compromise can be achieved. However, in places like the Middle East where disputes over land are inherently linked to historical religious claims, such frame shifting is difficult, if not impossible. Understanding the power of religious frames as truth perspectives provides insight into one of the most volatile regions of the world.

SOURCE: Adapted from A. Marcus, "In Mideast Politics, Controlling the Past Is Key to the Present," *The Wall Street Journal,* 77, 244, pp. 1, 13.

---

4. Specific frames may be likely to be used with certain types of issues. Parties talking about salary may be likely to use outcome frames, while parties talking about relationship issues may be likely to use characterization frames.

5. Parties are likely to assume a particular frame because of various factors. Value differences between the parties, differences in personality, power differences, and differences in the background and social context of the negotiators may lead the parties to adopt different frames. Many of these differences are discussed throughout this book, particularly in Chapter 6 (on leverage), Chapter 8 (on social context), Chapter 10 (on individual differences), and Chapter 11 (on cultural differences). As an example, see Box 2.2.

While the concept of frames seems compelling to those who have witnessed many negotiations, research in this area is difficult to conduct and is still in its infancy. As noted earlier (footnote 1), it is difficult to know what frame a party is using without having

---

BOX 2.2
Chinese Negotiation Frames

While skilled negotiators know that their and their opponents' negotiation frames are shaped through experience and culture, few stop to critically examine the cultural elements that shape others' perceptions about conflict. For example, Catherine Tinsley of Georgetown University has identified the five concepts from Chinese culture that should be recognized by those attempting to negotiate in China:

- *Social linkage.* The Chinese believe that people should be viewed in the context of their larger social groups rather than as isolated individuals.
- *Harmony.* Because people are inherently imbedded in their social network, peaceful coexistence is highly valued.
- *Roles.* In order to maintain social harmony, people must understand and abide by the requirements of their role in the relationship network. Roles specify duties, power, and privileges while specifying where in the relational hierarchy an individual falls.
- *Reciprocal obligations.* Each role specifies the obligations that people expect to fulfill and receive within the social network. These obligations persist over time, solidifying the relational network across generations.
- *Face.* The value the Chinese place on saving "face" is central to their perception of social interaction. Face is lost if an individual acts in a manner that is inconsistent with his or her role, or fails to fulfill reciprocal obligations. Face is so valued that the threat of losing it is the primary force that ensures fulfillment of obligations and, consequently, continuance of the relational hierarchy.

Negotiators approaching discussions with the Chinese would do well to consider the perspective on conflict that these cultural realities have created. For example, individual negotiators often rely on the power of their personal network to achieve desired ends. This perspective, called the "relational bargaining frame" by Tinsley, encourages parties to augment their power by both soliciting the support of powerful people and arguing for the social legitimacy of their position. While those from a more individualistic culture might reject out of hand the argument that a proposed settlement would be unpopular, such an argument would have great power in the more collectivist Chinese culture. Similarly, parties in the relational frame would be more likely to solicit outside opinions. A powerful strategy might be to encourage parties to align their positions to be compatible with the goals of a greater social collective.

SOURCE: Tinsley, C. H. (1997) "Understanding Conflict in a Chinese Cultural Context," in R. Bies, R. Lewicki, & B. Sheppard (Eds.), *Research on Negotiation in Organizations,* 6: 209–225. Stamford CT: JAI.

---

that party tell you (or listening to or reading his or her exact words), or by making inferences from the party's behavior. Even then, such inferences and interpretations may be difficult and loaded with error. In addition, the frames of those who hear or interpret communication may create biases of their own. For example, researchers who are coding the messages of parties in a dispute may have their own frames, which may bias their judgment about the negotiators' frames. Transcript coding is tedious, time-consuming work in which reasonable people can often disagree about whether a particular exchange matches the definition of one frame or another. Nevertheless, researchers continue to pursue this approach to frames because it offers great promise for understanding how parties define what a negotiation is about, how they use communication to argue for their own frame or frames and try to shape the other's orientation, and how they resolve differences when they are clearly operating from different frames.

Another Approach to Frames: Interests, Rights, and Power

Another approach to framing disputes was proposed by Ury, Brett, and Goldberg (1988). They suggested that parties in conflict use one of three frames:

Interests. People are often concerned about what they need, desire, or want. People talk about their "positions," but often what is at stake is their underlying interests. A person says he "needs" a new text messaging cell phone, but what he really *wants* is a new electronic toy because all his friends have one. Parties who focus on interests in a dispute are often able to find ways to resolve that dispute.

Rights. People may also be concerned about who is "right"—that is, who has legitimacy, who is correct, or what is fair. Disputes about rights are often resolved by helping the parties find a fair way to determine who is "right," or that they can both be "right." This resolution often requires the use of some standard or rule such as "taking turns", "split it down the middle" or "age before beauty" to settle the dispute. Disputes over rights are often referred to formal or informal arbitrators to decide whose standards or rights are more appropriate (see Chapter 13).

Power. People may also wish to resolve a negotiation on the basis of power. Negotiations resolved by power are sometimes based on who is physically stronger or is able to coerce the other, but more often, it is about imposing other types of costs—economic pressures, expertise, legitimate authority, etc. Disputes settled by power usually create clear winners and losers, with all the consequences that come from polarizing the dispute and resolving it in this manner.

Parties have a choice about how they approach a negotiation in terms of interests versus rights versus power; the same negotiation can be "framed" in different ways and will probably lead to different consequences. For example, consider the situation of a student who has a dispute with a local car repair shop near campus over the cost of fixing an automobile. The student thinks she was dramatically overcharged for the work—the garage did more work than was requested, used the most expensive replacement parts, and didn't give her the chance to review the bill before the work was done. The student might "frame" the dispute using one of these three frames:

1. *Interests*. The student might argue, "Well, small businesses have a right to charge a fair price for good quality work. I will go in and try to understand the shop owner's system for pricing repair work; we will talk about what is a fair price for the work and I will pay it, and I will probably go back to the shop again."

2. *Rights.* The student worked in a garage herself one summer and knows that car repairs are priced on what standard manuals state it will generally cost for the labor (hours of work × payment per hour), plus the cost of the parts. "I will ask to see the manual and the invoice for the parts. I will also go to the garage where I worked myself and ask the owner of that garage if he thinks this bill is out of line. I'll propose to pay for the parts at cost and the labor based on the mechanic's hourly pay rate."

3. *Power.* "I'll go in and start yelling at the owner about gouging, and I'll also threaten to tell all my friends not to use this garage. I'll write letters to the student newspaper about how bad this repair shop is. My dad is a lawyer and I'll have him call the owner. I'll teach them a thing or two!"

Note that the different frames are likely to lead to very different processes of discussion between the student and the garage owner. Moreover, the way the student approaches the problem with the garage owner will probably influence how the garage owner responds. The more the student uses power, the more likely the garage owner is to respond with power of his own (e.g., keep the car until the student pays and not reduce the price at all, and call his own lawyer); the confrontation could become angry and lead the parties into small claims court. In contrast, the more the student uses interests, the more the garage owner may be likely to use interests. The parties will have a discussion about what is fair given the services rendered; while the student may wind up paying more (than if she "won" the power argument), the tone of the discussion is likely to be far different, and the student may be in a much better position to get discounts or considerations in the future.

The Frame of an Issue Changes as the Negotiation Evolves

A final approach to framing argues that the definition of the issues often changes as the conflict evolves. Rather than focus only on the dominant frames that parties hold at the beginning of a negotiation, the issue development approach focuses on the *patterns of change* (transformation) that occur in the issues as parties communicate with each other. For example, in a classic study of legal disputes and grievances, Felstiner, Abel, and Sarat (1980–81) suggested that these disputes tend to be transformed through a process of "naming, blaming, and claiming." Naming occurs when parties in a dispute label or identify a problem and characterize what it is about. Blaming occurs next, as the parties try to determine who or what caused the problem. Finally, claiming occurs when the individual who has the problem decides to confront, file charges, or take some other action against the individual or organization that caused the problem. Thus, as one review of this approach points out,

> Although each side enters the negotiation with some conception or interpretation of an agenda item, the way people talk about a problem influences the way they define it. Frames, then, are not simply features of individual cognition, they are constructed in the ways that bargainers define problems and courses of action jointly through their talk. (Putnam and Holmer, 1992, p. 138)

Those who focus on issue development note that several factors shape a frame. First, the *negotiation context* clearly affects the way both sides define the issue. For example, in a union–management dispute, the issue will be framed by the history of relations between the parties—grievances, personnel practices, quality of relationships between the chief negotiators, and so on. Second, frames can also be shaped by the *conversations* that the parties have with each other about the issues in the bargaining mix. Although both parties may approach the discussion with initial frames that resemble the categories described earlier, the ongoing interaction between them shapes the discussion as each side attempts to argue from his or her own perspective or counterargue against the other's perspective. At least four factors can affect how the conversation is shaped:

1. Negotiators tend to argue for *stock issues,* or concerns that are raised every time the parties negotiate. For example, wage issues or working conditions may always be on the table in a labor negotiation; thus, the union always raises them, and management always expects them to be raised and is ready to respond. Jensen (1995) reports that negotiations over stock issues can be restructured to include more or fewer issues, increasing the likelihood that a resolution can be found. Discussing international negotiations, Spector (1995) suggests that conflicts framed as "nationalist, ethnic, or ideological" may be quite difficult to resolve, and a major task for mediators in these types of disputes is to provide creative new frames (see Chapter 13).

2. Each party attempts to make the *best possible case* for his or her preferred position or perspective. One party may assemble facts, numbers, testimony, or other compelling evidence to persuade the other party of the validity of his or her argument or perspective. Early in a negotiation, as each party presents his or her case, it is not uncommon for the parties to "talk past each other," with each trying to impose a certain perspective as the dominant conversation rather than listening to the other's case and trying to refute it. Each party is interested in controlling the conversation by controlling the focus; however, each party's argument eventually begins to shift as they both focus on either refuting the other's case or modifying their own arguments on the basis of the other's arguments (Putnam and Wilson, 1989; Putnam, Wilson, and Turner, 1990).

3. In a more "macro" sense, frames may also define major *shifts and transitions* in the overall negotiation. Ikle (1964), discussing diplomatic negotiations, suggested that successful bargaining results from a two-stage process he called "formula/detail." Lewicki, Weiss, and Lewin (1992) describe this process as follows: "Parties first seek a compromise that establishes some formula or framework of broad objectives and principles. Then they draw out a number of detailed points of agreement. The framework defines the subset of points that is debatable, while the detail phase permits the debate and 'packaging' of specific issues to construct a settlement acceptable to both sides" (p. 225). Zartman and his colleagues (Zartman, 1977; Zartman and Berman, 1982) elaborated on the formula-detail model to create three stages: (*a*) *diagnosis,* in which the parties recognize the need for change or improvement, review relevant history, and prepare positions; (*b*) *formula,* in which the parties attempt to develop a shared perception of the conflict, including common terms, referents, and fairness criteria; and (*c*) *detail,* in which the parties work out operational details consistent with the basic formula.

**"Now, when we explain this to Mom and Dad,
let's make sure we give it the right spin."**

In actual use, the model may be more flexible than this description suggests; in some cultures, the stages may even be pursued in a different order. An excellent example of this approach is found in the negotiations over Israeli and Palestinian rights and interests in the Middle East that led to the signing of a statement of mutual recognition in September 1993. Progress in this protracted confrontation was largely the result of a clear diagnosis (continued disagreement was in the interest of neither party); a shared formula (including complementary statements by each side regarding the other's right to existence, security, and autonomy); and the ability to resolve the complex details (i.e., given this shared vision, what must be done to sustain an appropriate environment of rights, responsibilities, and assurances for all parties).

4. Finally, *multiple agenda items* operate to shape the issue development frames. Although parties usually have one or two major objectives, priorities, or core issues, there are often a number of lesser or secondary items. When brought into the conversation, these secondary concerns often transform the conversation about the primary issues (Putnam and Geist, 1985). In her careful analysis of teacher negotiations in two school districts, Putnam (1994) showed how issues became transformed throughout a negotiation. For instance, an issue of scheduling was reframed as an issue of teacher preparation time, and an issue on the cost of personal insurance became transformed into an issue about the extent of insurance benefits (Putnam, 1994). Issues are shaped by several things, including (*a*) arguments attacking the significance or stability of problems or the feasibility of solutions; (*b*) the ways parties "make a case" to others concerning the logic of needs or positions; and (*c*) the management and interaction (e.g., addition, deletion, packaging) of multiple issues on the negotiation agenda (Putnam and Holmer, 1992).

One of the most important aspects of framing as issue development is the process of *reframing,* or the manner in which the thrust, tone, and focus of a conversation change as the parties engage in it. Putnam and Holmer (1992) note that "reframing occurs through challenging the way that a party conceives of an issue, or through

BOX 2.3
Transforming the Conversation through Frames

An independent insurance agent in a small town discussed the difficulty of moving some of his agency staff from a straight salary compensation system (at a level of $30,000 per year) to a base salary of $25,000 and performance pay beyond that, with no limits to the amount they could make. The agent was surprised to discover a lot of resistance among the sales representatives. The representatives were afraid of losing the guaranteed base pay and not knowing how much money they would really make under the new system.

One of the authors of this book devised two ways of trying to "sell" the idea: First, the author said, rather than impose the system immediately, phase it in over a multiyear period. Another agent had done this, and stated that as soon as his employees began to trust the system and their ability to earn at-risk income, they not only accepted the plan but began to ask that the transition be completed even before they were finished with the phasing-in process. Second, the author said, maintain the old system but also keep a new set of records, as if you were already on the new system. During this time the staff could see actual results and compare the two systems for actual earned amounts, to allay their fears.

By introducing the system gradually and keeping a comparative set of books, the head agent was able to change the conversation about compensation in that office and to gain rapid acceptance for his new plan.

SOURCE: Adapted from G. T. Savage, J. D. Blair, and R. J. Sorenson, "Consider Both Relationship and Substance When Negotiating Strategically," *Academy of Management Executive* 3 (1989), pp. 37–48.

demonstrating that a current frame is ineffectual" (p. 140). Reframing is a dynamic process that may occur many times in a conversation. It comes as parties challenge each other, as they present their own case or refute the other's, or as they search for ways to reconcile seemingly incompatible perspectives. Reframing can also occur as one party uses metaphors, analogies, or specific cases to illustrate a point, leading the other to use the metaphor or case as a new way to define the situation. Reframing may be done intentionally by one side or the other, or it may emerge from the conversation as one person's challenges fuel the other's creativity and imagination. In either case, the parties often propose a new way to approach the problem (see Box 2.3).

Summary.   In this section, we have presented three ways to understand frames: as categories of experience; as interests, rights, and power; and as a process of issue development. Research on frames and their impact on negotiation continues to emerge. The way a negotiation problem is defined, and the manner in which a conversation between negotiators leads to a reframing of the issues, are critical elements to consider as negotiators develop a strategy and a plan. We can offer the following prescriptive advice about problem framing for the negotiator:

   • Frames shape what the parties define as the key issues and how they talk about them. To the degree that the parties have preferences about the issues to be covered, outcomes to be achieved, or processes to be addressed, they should work to ensure that their own preferred frames are accepted and acknowledged by the others.

- Both parties have frames. When the frames match, the parties are more likely to focus on common issues and a common definition of the situation; when they do not match, communication between the parties is likely to be difficult and incomplete. Negotiators who are communicating from different frames should first recognize that they may be talking "past each other," raise the issue with each other, and have one or both parties reframe their dialogue so that they are effectively communicating "on the same wavelength."

- Frames are probably controllable, at least to some degree. If negotiators understand what frame they are operating from, and what frame the other party is operating from, they may be able to shift conversation toward the frame they would like to have the other espouse.

- Conversations change and transform frames in ways negotiators may not be able to predict but may be able to control. As parties discuss an issue, introduce arguments and evidence, and advocate a course of action, the conversation changes, and the frame of the problem may change as well. It will be critical for negotiators to track this shift and understand where it might lead.

- Certain frames are probably more likely than others to lead to certain types of processes and outcomes. All of the possible combinations are beyond the scope of this review. But, for example, parties who are competitive are likely to have positive identity frames of themselves, negative characterization frames of each other, and a preference for more win-lose processes of resolving their dispute. Recognizing these biases may empower the parties to be able to reframe their views of themselves, the other, or the dispute resolution mechanism in order to pursue a process that will resolve the conflict more productively.

Understanding frames—which means understanding how parties define the key issues and how conversations can shift and transform those issues—is the first step in effective planning.

UNDERSTANDING THE FLOW OF NEGOTIATIONS: STAGES AND PHASES

Several researchers who have studied the flow of negotiations over time have confirmed that negotiation, like communication in problem-solving groups and in other forms of ritualistic social interaction, proceeds through distinct phases or stages (Douglas, 1962; Greenhalgh, 2001; Morley and Stephenson, 1977). These phases or stages may be much like the third type of framing dynamics we described at the beginning of this chapter, in which conversations change and transform over time. We will return to this point.

Phase Models of Negotiation

Holmes (1992), examining work by others (e.g., Douglas, 1962; Gulliver, 1979; Morley and Stephenson, 1977), states that "phase models provide a narrative explanation of negotiation process; that is, they identify sequences of events that constitute the story of a negotiation . . . [A] *phase* is a coherent period of interaction characterized by a dominant constellation of communicative acts" that "serves a set of related functions

TABLE 2.2   Phase Models of Negotiation: Labels and Descriptions

Phases	Prescriptive Models	Descriptive Models
Initiation	Exploration[1] Preliminaries[2] Diagnostic[3] Introduction and relationship development[4]	Establishing the range[5] Search for arena, agenda, and issue identification[6] Agenda definition and problem formulation[7]
Problem solving	Expectation structuring, movement, and solution development[1] Positioning, bargaining, exploration[2] Formulation[3] Problem clarification and relationship development, problem solving[4]	Reconnoitering the range[5] Exploring the range, narrowing the range, preliminaries to final bargaining[6] Narrowing differences[7]
Resolution	Conclusion[1] Settlement[2] Details[3] Resolution structuring[4]	Precipitating the decision-making crisis[5] Final bargaining, ritualization, execution[6] Testing, agreement, and implementation[7]

1. Atkinson (1980)
2. Carlisle and Leary (1981)
3. Zartman and Berman (1982)
4. Donohue, Kaufman, Smith, and Ramesh (1990)
5. Douglas (1962)
6. Gulliver (1979)
7. Putnam, Wilson, and Turner (1990).

SOURCE: Adapted from M. Holmes, "Phase Structures in Negotiation," in L. Putnam and M. Roloff (eds.), *Communication and Negotiation* (Newbury Park, CA: Sage, 1992), Tables 4.1 and 4.2, pp. 87–88. Reprinted by permission of Sage Publications, Inc.

in the movement from initiation to resolution of a dispute" (p. 83). Phase research typically addresses three types of questions (Holmes and Poole, 1991):

- How does the interaction between parties change over time?
- How do the interaction structures, over time, relate to inputs and outcomes?
- How do the tactics or interventions (e.g., changing actors) affect the development of the negotiation?

Recent years have seen a marked increase in work on negotiation phase modeling. This work has been both descriptive and prescriptive—some authors describe what they have observed in natural settings, whereas others advise or prescribe certain activity sequences they feel will lead to more effective negotiation (refer back to our discussion of the Zartman and Berman formula-detail model on p. 47). Much of this work is summarized in Table 2.2.

As the table shows, the various models fit nicely into a general structure of three phases, or stages: a beginning (or initiation) phase, a middle (or problem-solving) phase, and an ending (or resolution) phase. However, a cautionary note is in order here. As Holmes (1992) points out, the "descriptive models depict *successful* negotiations" in that "unsuccessful negotiations do not proceed through the orderly stages of phase models, but tend to stall interminably in the intermediate phase or cycle within or between the beginning and middle stages, without achieving successful closure" (p. 92 emphasis added). Although phase modeling of negotiation offers much potential value in enhancing our understanding of negotiation, further research is necessary before it becomes a proactive tool for improving negotiation practice. In particular, Holmes's (1992) review suggests that more research must be done about the nature of the phases themselves and about the nature of the processes that enable or drive the movement from phase to phase. Simple descriptions of the order of events in a negotiation are insufficient to improve negotiation practice.

Stages and phases may also be a reflection of the framing conversation in negotiation. Because people are in so many negotiations in their daily lives, they develop a reasonably ritualistic understanding of what should happen at each stage, and what needs to happen at the beginning and end of the process. Parties begin with the activities in the "beginning" stages; once they sense that these activities have been completed, they move on to the activities in the "middle" stage. Finally—and particularly if there is a deadline motivating one or both of the parties to complete negotiation by a certain point—they move from the middle stage to the "end" stage. These stages and phases may occur without the conscious awareness of either party, or parties may make clear, visible, systematic efforts to shape the stage movement by what they say, how they say it, and when they say it.

More recently, Greenhalgh (2001) has articulated an easy-to-visualize stage model of negotiation, particularly relevant for integrative negotiation. Greenhalgh suggests that there are seven key steps to an ideal negotiation process (see Figure 2.3):

Preparation: deciding what is important, defining goals, thinking ahead how to work together with the other party.

Relationship building: getting to know the other party, understanding how you and the other are similar and different, and building commitment toward achieving a mutually beneficial set of outcomes. Greenhalgh argues that this stage is extremely critical to satisfactorily moving the other stages forward.

Information gathering: learning what you need to know about the issues, about the other party and their needs, about the feasibility of possible settlements, and about what might happen if you fail to reach agreement with the other side.

Information using: at this stage, negotiators assemble the case they want to make for their preferred outcomes and settlement, one that will maximize the negotiator's own needs. This presentation is often used to "sell" the negotiator's preferred outcome to the other.

FIGURE 2.3   Phases of Negotiation

Phase 1	Phase 2	Phase 3	Phase 4	Phase 5	Phase 6	Phase 7
Preparation →	Relationship building →	Information gathering →	Information using →	Bidding →	Closing the deal →	Implementating the agreement

SOURCE: Reprinted with the permission of The Free Press, an imprint of Simon & Schuster Adult Publishing Group, from *Managing Strategic Relationships: The Key to Business Success* by Leonard Greenhalgh. Copyright © 2001 by Leonard Greenhalgh.

Bidding: the process of making moves from one's initial, ideal position to the actual outcome. Bidding is the process by which each party states their "opening offer," and then makes moves in that offer toward a middle ground. We describe this process extensively in Chapter 3.

Closing the deal: the objective here is to build commitment to the agreement achieved in the previous phase. Both the negotiator and the other party have to assure themselves that they reached a deal they can be happy with, or at least live with.

Implementing the agreement: determining who needs to do what once the hands are shaken and the documents signed. Not uncommonly parties discover that the agreement is flawed, key points were missed, or the situation has changed and new questions exist. Flaws in moving through the earlier phases arise here, and the deal may have to be reopened, or issues settled by arbitrators or the courts.

Greenhalgh (2001) argues that this model is largely prescriptive—that is, this is the way people ought to negotiate, and he creates a strong case for why this is the case. However, examination of the actual practice of negotiators shows that they frequently deviate from this model, and that one can track differences in their practice according to his or her home culture. For example, untrained American negotiators typically view the process more in "win-lose" terms (Chapter 1): their preparation stage is very short, they tend to skip relationship building altogether, spend a lot of time on bidding, gather and share information *after* the bidding, also tend to skip closing altogether, and then implement. In contrast, Japanese negotiators spend a great deal of time on relationship building first, then truncate the steps toward the end of the negotiation process. The influence of culture on negotiation is more thoroughly examined in Chapter 11.

We now turn to the final step in the strategizing process—creating a specific negotiating plan to implement the strategy.

GETTING READY TO IMPLEMENT THE STRATEGY: THE PLANNING PROCESS

On the surface, when one watches the drama and theatrics of tense, conflict-laden, face-to-face confrontation, one can easily get the impression that negotiation success lies in persuasiveness, eloquence, clever maneuvering, and occasional histrionics.

Although these tactics make the process interesting (and at times even entertaining), the foundation for success in negotiation is not in the game playing or the dramatics. The dominant force for success in negotiation is in the planning that takes place prior to the dialogue. While success in negotiation is affected by how one enacts the strategy, the foundation for success in negotiation is how one prepares.

Identifying potential shortcomings in the planning process is necessary, but it's not enough. Effective planning also requires hard work on several fronts:

- Defining the issues
- Assembling issues and defining the bargaining mix
- Defining interests
- Defining limits
- Defining one's own objectives (targets) and opening bids (where to start)
- Defining the constituents to whom one is accountable
- Understanding the other party and its interests and objectives
- Selecting a strategy
- Planning the issue presentation and defense
- Defining protocol—where and when the negotiation will occur, who will be there, agenda, etc.

The remainder of this chapter discusses each of these steps in detail (see also the planning guide in Table 2.3 that may be used to plan one's own negotiation). The list represents the collective wisdom of several sources, including Richardson (1977); Asherman and Asherman (1990); Burnstein (1995); Fisher and Ertel (1995); Lewicki, Hiam, and Olander (1996); Lewicki and Hiam (1999); and Greenhalgh (2001). Each has their own list of key steps, and often varies in the order of the steps. In this discussion, we assume that a single planning process can be followed for both a distributive and an integrative process. Although we have highlighted the differences between the two (and will do so more extensively in the next two chapters), we believe that with the exception of the specific tactics negotiators intend to use, one comprehensive planning process can be used for either form of negotiation. We also assume that the planning process can proceed linearly, in the order in which these steps are presented. Information often cannot be obtained and accumulated quite this simply and straightforwardly, however, and information discovered in some of the later steps may force a negotiator to reconsider and reevaluate earlier steps. As a result, the first iteration through the planning process should be tentative, and the negotiator should be flexible enough to modify and adjust previous steps as new information becomes available.

1. Defining the Issues

The first step in negotiation planning is to define the issues to be discussed. This step itself usually begins with an analysis of the overall situation. Usually, a negotiation involves one or two major issues (e.g., price or rate) and several minor issues. For

TABLE 2.3   Negotiation Planning Guide

1. What are the issues in the upcoming negotiation?

2. Based on a review of ALL of the issues, what is the "bargaining mix"? (Which issues do we have to cover? Which issues are connected to other issues?)

3. What are my interests?

4. What are my limits—what is my walkaway? What is my alternative?

5. Defining targets and openings—where will I start, what is my goal?

6. Who are my constituents and what do they want me to do?

7. What are the opposing negotiators and what do they want?

8. What overall strategy do I want to select?

9. How will I present my issues to the other party?

10. What protocol needs to be followed in conducting this negotiation?

instance, in buying a house, both parties immediately recognize that the central issues include price, date of sale, and date of occupancy. They might quickly identify other issues, such as appliances to be included or payment for the fuel oil left in the storage tank. During the purchase process, the buyer's lawyer, banker, or real estate agent might draw up a list of other things to consider: taxes to pay, escrow amounts for undiscovered problems, or a written statement that the seller must leave the house in "broom-clean" condition. Note that it does not take long to generate a fairly detailed list. In any negotiation, a complete list of the issues at stake is best derived from the following sources:

1. An analysis of the overall situation.
2. Our own experience in similar negotiations.
3. Research conducted to gather information (e.g., reading a book on how to buy a house).
4. Consultation with experts (real estate agents, bankers, attorneys, accountants, or friends who have bought a house recently).

Before considering ways to manage our list of issues, a word of caution is necessary. Note that we have used a simple, traditional example here—the purchase of a house. Many negotiations will differ markedly from this example, falling outside of traditional contracts and agreements. In addition, many negotiations are not based on quantitatively defined issues (like the price of a house). In these situations, defining the key issues may be much more complex and elusive. For example, suppose a manager gets signals from his boss that his performance is not up to par, yet whenever he tries to confront the boss to discuss the problem and secure a realistic performance appraisal, the boss won't talk directly about the problem (which raises the manager's anxiety even further). Although the conflict in this situation is evident, the "issues" are elusive. The central issue for the employee is the performance appraisal and why the boss won't give it. Maybe the boss is uncomfortable with the performance appraisal process or has a problem confronting other people about their behavior. Perhaps the boss is so preoccupied with her own job security that she doesn't even realize the impact she is having on the manager. In a situation like this one, where the issues are important but somewhat elusive, the manager needs to be clear about both what the issue is (in this case, getting a clear performance evaluation *and* getting the boss to talk about it) and how to initiate a productive discussion. Note that the more complex and ambiguous the situation, the more that the parties might "frame" the issues differently, as we noted earlier in this chapter.

2. Assembling the Issues and Defining the Bargaining Mix

The next step in planning is to assemble all the issues that have been defined into a comprehensive list. The combination of lists from each side in the negotiation determines the *bargaining mix* (see Chapter 3). In generating a list of issues, negotiators may feel that they put too much on the table at once, or raise too many issues. This may happen if the parties do not talk frequently or if they have lots of business to transact. It often turns out, however, that introducing a long list of issues into a negotiation often makes success more, rather than less, likely—provided that all the issues are real. Large bargaining mixes allow many possible components and arrangements for settlement, thus increasing the likelihood that a particular package will meet both parties' needs and therefore lead to a successful settlement (Rubin and Brown, 1975). At the same time, large bargaining mixes can lengthen negotiations because they present many possible combinations of issues to consider, and combining and evaluating all these mixes makes things very complex.

After assembling issues on an agenda, the negotiator next must prioritize them. Prioritization includes two steps:

1. *Determine which issues are most important and which are less important.* Once negotiation begins, parties can easily be swept up in the rush of information, arguments, offers, counteroffers, trade-offs, and concessions. For those who are not clear in advance about what they want (and what they can do without), it is easy to lose perspective and agree to suboptimal settlements, or to get distracted by points that are relatively unimportant. When negotiators do not have priorities, they may be more likely to yield on those points aggressively argued by the other side rather than to yield on the issues that are less important to *them.*

Priorities can be set in a number of ways. One simple way is for the negotiator to rank-order the issues by asking "What is most important?" "What is second most important?" and "What is least important?" An even simpler process is to group issues into categories of high, medium, or low importance. When the negotiator represents a constituency, it is important to involve that group in setting priorities. Priorities can be set for both interests and more specific issues.

It is also important to set priorities for both tangible and intangible issues. Intangible issues are often difficult to discuss and rank-order, yet if they remain subjective and not quantified, negotiators may tend to overemphasize or underemphasize them. It is easy to push such issues aside in favor of concrete, specific, numerical issues—and negotiators must be careful not to let the "hard bargaining" over numbers drive out abstract discussion of intangible issues and interests. However, more than one negotiator has received a rude shock when his or her constituency has rejected a settlement because it ignored the intangibles or dealt with them suboptimally in the final agreement.

In our house example, the buyer may determine that the price is the most important issue and that the closing date is secondary.

2. *Determine whether the issues are connected (linked together) or separate.* If the issues are separate, they can be easily added or subtracted; if connected, then settlement on one will be linked to settlement on the others and making concessions on one issue will inevitably be tied to some other issue. The negotiator must decide whether the issues are truly connected—for instance, whether the price he will pay for the house is dependent on what the bank will loan him—as opposed to simply being connected in his own mind for the sake of achieving a good settlement.

3. Defining Your Interests

After defining the issues, the negotiator must proceed to define the underlying interests and needs. *Positions*—an opening bid or a target point—are what a negotiator wants. *Interests* are why she wants them. $150,000 as a target point for a house would be a position; this is what the negotiator hopes to pay. The interest would be "to pay a fair market price, and one I can afford, for that two bedroom condominium." Although defining interests is more important to integrative negotiation than to distributive bargaining, even distributive discussions can benefit from one or both parties' identifying the key interests. (In Chapter 4, we will discuss in more detail the nature of interests and ways to bring them to the surface.) If issues help us define what we want, then understanding interests requires us to ask why we want it. Asking "why" questions usually brings critical values, needs, or principles that we want to achieve in the negotiation to the surface. Interests may include:

- Substantive, that is, directly related to the focal issues under negotiation.
- Process-based, that is, related to the manner in which the negotiators settle the dispute.
- Relationship-based, that is, tied to the current or desired future relationship between the parties.

Interests may also be based on the intangibles of negotiation, including principles or standards to which the parties wish to adhere, the informal norms by which they will negotiate, and the benchmarks they will use to guide them toward a settlement, to achieve a fair or reasonable deal, or to get the negotiation concluded quickly.

4. Knowing Your Limits and Alternatives

What will happen if the other party in a negotiation refuses to accept some proposed items for the agenda or states issues in such a way that they are unacceptable to you? Good preparation requires that you establish two clear points: your *limits* and your *alternatives*.

Limits are the point where you decide that you should stop the negotiation rather than continue, because any settlement beyond this point is not minimally acceptable. Limits are also referred to as resistance points or reservation prices or walkaway points (see Chapter 3). If you are the seller, your limit is the least you will take for the item you have for sale; if you are the buyer, your limit is the most you will pay for the item. Setting limits as a part of planning is critical. Most of us have been involved in buying situations where the item we wanted wasn't available, but we allowed ourselves to be talked into a more expensive model. Moreover, some competitive situations generate intense pressures to "escalate" the price. For example, in an auction, if there is a bidding war with another person, one may pay more than was planned. Gamblers, analogously, may encounter a losing streak and end up losing more money than they had wanted to. Clear limits keep people from agreeing to deals that they later realize weren't very smart.

On the other hand, *alternatives* are other deals negotiators could achieve and still meet their needs. We discussed alternatives earlier in this chapter, when we described the "avoidance" strategy, suggesting that when there are alternative ways to meet needs, it may not be necessary to engage in a negotiation. But alternatives are critical for almost all negotiating situations, not just ones where avoidance may be the best strategy. In any situation, the better your alternatives, the more power you have, because you can walk away from the deal in front of you and still know that you can have your needs and interests met. In the house-purchase example, the more a buyer has searched the real estate market and understands what other comparable houses are available, the more she knows that she can walk away from this negotiation and still have acceptable housing choices.

5. Setting Targets and Openings

After negotiators have defined the issues, assembled a tentative agenda, and consulted others as appropriate and necessary, the next step is to define two other key points: the *specific target point* (where one realistically expects to achieve a settlement) and the *asking price* or *opening bid* (representing the best deal one can hope to achieve).

There are numerous ways to set a target. One can ask, "What is an outcome that I would be comfortable with?" "At what point would I be generally satisfied?" "What have other people achieved in this same situation?" Targets may not be as firm and rigid as limits or alternatives; one might be able to set a general range, or a class of several outcomes that would be equally acceptable.

Similarly, there are numerous ways to set an opening bid. An opening may be the best possible outcome, an ideal solution, something even better than was achieved last time. However, it is easy to get overly idealistic about such a solution, and hence to set an opening that is so unrealistic that the other party immediately laughs, gets angry, or walks away before another word is spoken. While openings are usually formulated around a "best possible" settlement, it is also easy to inflate them to the point where they become self-defeating because they are too unrealistic (in the eyes of the other negotiator).

Target Setting Requires Positive Thinking about One's *Own* Objectives.   When approaching a negotiation, negotiators often attempt to become aware of the other party—how members of that party may behave, what they will probably demand, and how the bargainer feels about dealing with them. It is possible to devote too much attention to the other party, however; that is, to spend too much time trying to discern what the other side wants, how to meet those demands, and so forth. If negotiators focus attention on the other party to the exclusion of themselves, they may plan their entire strategy as a reaction to the other's anticipated conduct. Reactive strategies are likely to make negotiators feel threatened and defensive and to lessen the flexibility and creativity of their negotiating behavior. Reactive strategies can also lead to confusion, particularly if assumptions about the other party's strategy and intentions turn out to be wrong. In contrast, by defining realistic, optimistic, and pessimistic targets for themselves, negotiators can take a proactive stance in which they are aware of the range of possible outcomes. This permits them to be flexible in what they will accept and improves the likelihood of arriving at a mutually satisfactory outcome.

Target Setting Often Requires Considering How to Package Several Issues and Objectives. Most negotiators have a mixture of bargaining objectives, so they must consider the best way to achieve satisfaction across multiple issues. To package issues effectively, negotiators need to understand the definition of the issues, bargaining mix, and the other's bargaining mix. Negotiators propose settlements that will help them achieve their targets on the issues they have defined as important; they may then balance these areas by setting more conservative targets for items less important to them (see also our house-sale example in Chapter 3).

When evaluating a bargaining mix with a number of different issues, most people find that anticipating different ways to package issues in the mix is a great help in evaluating those packages against their targets. Some negotiators evaluate packages the same way we advocate evaluating individual issues—they define optimistic, realistic, and pessimistic packages to permit better planning of the negotiation and to be in a better position to evaluate the other party's proposals (Rubin and Brown, 1975). If packages involve intangible issues, or issues for which it is difficult to specify definite targets, it will be harder to evaluate and compare the packages explicitly. Evaluating the bargaining mix may also eventually require the negotiator to invent new options that will permit both parties to achieve their objectives; this process will be extensively described in Chapter 4.

Target Setting Requires an Understanding of Trade-offs and Throwaways. The discussion of packaging raises another possible problem: What does one do if the other party proposes a package that puts issues A, B, and C in one's optimistic range, puts item D in the realistic range, puts E at the pessimistic point, and does not even mention item F, which is part of one's bargaining mix? Is item F a throwaway item that can be ignored? If it is not a throwaway item, is it relatively unimportant and worth giving up in order to lock in agreement on A, B, and C in the optimal range? Now suppose the other party has proposed two packages, the one described above and a second one that places items A and E in the optimistic range, items B and F in the realistic range, and C at the pessimistic point, while it ignores D. Would the first or the second package be more attractive?

Negotiators may want to consider giving away something for nothing if such an item can be part of the transaction. Even if an issue is unimportant or inconsequential to you, it may be valuable or attractive to the other party. Awareness of the actual or likely value of such concessions can considerably enrich the value of what one offers to the other party at little or no cost to oneself. Using the house example again, the seller may have eight months left on a parking-lot pass for the same lot that the buyer wants to use. Because the money the seller paid for the pass is nonrefundable, the pass will be worthless to the seller once she leaves the area, but the buyer could see the pass as a valuable item.

To evaluate these packages, negotiators need to have some idea of what each item in the bargaining mix is worth in terms that can be compared across issues. The negotiator needs some way of establishing trade-offs. This may be a difficult thing to do because different items or issues will be of different value to the negotiator and will often be measured in different terms. When considering the purchase of a used car, a buyer needs to decide the importance of each of the following: (1) the make of the car, (2) the color, (3) the age of the car, and (4) the price.

While it may not be possible to find a common dimension (such as dollar value) to compare issues in the bargaining mix or to compare tangibles with intangibles, many negotiators find it convenient to scale all items on some common dimension. The premise is that even if the fit is not perfect, any guide is better than none. Moreover, if intangibles are a key part of the bargaining mix, negotiators must know the point at which they are willing to abandon the pursuit of an intangible in favor of substantial gains on tangibles. Translating every issue into dollars is one way to facilitate these comparisons. In labor relations, for example, most issues included in the bargaining mix are converted into dollar equivalents for easier comparison and evaluation of alternative packages. However, not everything is easy to convert into money (or other concrete) terms. Accountants experience this problem when trying to establish a book value for a business's goodwill.

Negotiators who want a different way to compare items and issues may use a point or utility scale to evaluate them. For example, if the value of the entire target package of issues is worth 500 points, then smaller, proportionate numbers of points could be assigned to each issue in the mix reflecting relative priorities and totaling 500. Obviously, such points are only meaningful to the party establishing them, and only for as long as the points reflect the basic values and targets of the negotiator in that situation. As long as they do, such scales are a useful tool for planning and assessing offers and counteroffers.

6. Assessing My Constituents

When people are negotiating for themselves—for example, buying a used racing bicycle or exercise machine—they can determine all of the previous issues on their own. But when people negotiate in a professional context, they most likely will have *constituents*—bosses, parties who make the final decision, parties who will evaluate and critique the solution achieved. Moreover, there may be a number of *observers* to the negotiation who will also watch and critique the negotiation. Finally, negotiation occurs in a context—a social system of laws, customs, common business practices, cultural norms, and political cross-pressures.

One way to assess all of the key parties in a negotiation is to complete a "field analysis." Imagine that you are the captain of a soccer team, about to play a game on the field (see Figure 2.4). Assessing constituents is the same as assessing all of the parties who are in the soccer stadium:

A. Who is, or should be, on the team on my side of the field? Perhaps it is just the negotiator (a 1:1 game). But perhaps we want other help: an attorney, accountant, or other expert assistance; someone to give us moral support or listen closely to what the other side says; a recorder or note taker.

B. Who is on the other side of the field? This is discussed in more detail in the next section.

C. Who is on the sidelines who can affect the play of the game? Who are the negotiation equivalents of coaches and trainers? This includes one's direct superior, or the person who must approve or authorize agreement that is reached.

D. Who is in the stands? Who is watching the game, is interested in it, but can only indirectly affect what happens? This might include senior managers, shareholders, competitors, financial analysts, or others.

FIGURE 2.4 A Field Analysis of Negotiation

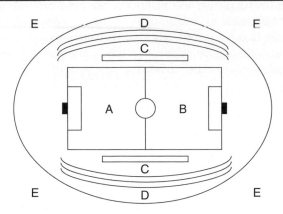

A. The direct actors (who is on the field on our side?)

B. The opposition actors (who is on the field on their side?)

C. Indirect actors (who is on the sidelines?)

D. Interested observers (who is in the stands?)

E. Environmental factors (what is going on in the broad environment of the game—outside the stadium, but shaping and defining what happens in the stadium?)

E. What is going on in the broader environment in which the negotiation takes place? As we will point out in later chapters of the book, a number of "context" issues can affect negotiation:

- What has been the history of the relationship between these parties, and how does it affect the overall expectations they bring to this negotiation (Chapter 8)?
- What kind of a relationship is expected or desired for the future, and how does it affect the current negotiation (Chapter 8)?
- How successful has this negotiator been in past deliberations with others?
- What is common and acceptable practice in the legal system in which the deal is being done?
- What is common and acceptable practice in the ethical system in which the deal is being done (Chapter 7)?
- What is common and acceptable practice given the culture in which the negotiation is occurring (Chapter 11)?

A negotiator bargaining on behalf of others (a company, union, department, club, family, etc.) must consult with them so that their concerns and priorities are included in the mix. In the house-buying illustration used earlier, let us assume that one member of a couple is doing the negotiating. If that person fails to consider his partner's concerns about the condition in which the house is left, or their children's wish that the move not occur during the school year, then the negotiated resolution may be rejected. A negotiator who is representing a constituency is accountable to that constituency and must include their wishes in proposals, subsequently either fulfilling those wishes for them through negotiation or explaining why their desires were not met. When negotiating for a large constituency, such as an entire company or a union or a community, the process of consulting with the constituency can be elaborate and exhaustive. Many times the negotiator recognizes that the constituency's wish list is unrealistic and unobtainable; the negotiator will then be required to negotiate with the constituency over what should be included on the agenda and what is realistic to expect. It is also critical to understand what happens when the two parties get close to an agreement. Does the negotiator have authority to agree on his or her own, or does the approval of the constituents have to be obtained? Constituents control negotiators by limiting how much they can decide on their own, and understanding these limits will keep one out of trouble when a deal has to be approved or ratified. (We explore these problems in detail in Chapters 3 and 9.)

7. Analyzing the Other Party

Earlier in this section, we discussed the importance of assigning priorities to one's own goals and objectives. When negotiators have the opportunity to meet with people from the other side, they may be able to learn what issues are important to them. Negotiators may also use this opportunity to discuss their priorities on those issues—which ones are most important, least important, and so on. Finally, negotiators may also have learned something about their interests—why they want what they want. Conversely, if negotiators have not had the opportunity to meet with people from the other side, then they should attempt to see the negotiation from the other party's perspective, or to gather information to learn about their issues, interests, and priorities. Negotiators might call the other party and interview them prior to the actual meeting, or try to take their perspective and anticipate what it is that you would want if you were negotiating from that point of view. Negotiators might speak to others who know the other party, or people who have been in their situation before. All this will provide a better idea of what they are likely to want. By comparing this assessment against your own, one can begin to define areas where there may be strong conflict (both parties have a high priority for the same thing), simple trade-offs (both parties want the same group of things but in differing priorities), or no conflict at all (both parties want very different things and both can easily have their objectives and interests met).

In this discussion of the planning process, we have made several references to the other party and the negotiator's history with him or her. Gathering information about the other party is a critical step in preparing for negotiation. What information does one party need about the other party in order to prepare effectively? Several key pieces of background information will be of great importance:

- The other party's current resources, interests, and needs.
- The other party's objectives.
- The other party's reputation and negotiation style.
- The other party's alternative(s).
- The other party's authority to make an agreement.
- The other party's likely strategy and tactics.

Let us now explore each of these in more detail. In theory, it would be extremely useful to have as much of this information as possible before negotiations occur. In reality, it may not be possible to obtain this information through either direct contact with the negotiator or other research sources. If not, the negotiator should plan to collect as much of this information as possible during the opening stages of the actual deliberations. (Master negotiator Bill Richardson includes gathering information about the other party in his advice to negotiators—see Box 2.4.)

The Other Party's Current Resources, Interests, and Needs. Negotiators will learn much about the other party while negotiating, but as much information as possible should be gathered in advance through research and homework. Which data are most relevant will depend on what type of negotiation will be conducted and on who the other party is. An analysis of the other party's business history or previous negotiations, successful and otherwise, might provide useful clues. Financial data about the other party might be obtained through channels such as Dun and Bradstreet, financial statements, newspapers, files, company biographies, stock reports, and public records of legal judgments. One might investigate the other party's inventories. Sometimes one can learn a great deal simply by visiting the other party or speaking to his or her friends and peers. Another way to learn is to ask questions of people who have done business with the other party (Calero and Oskam, 1983).

BOX 2.4
Bill Richardson Interview

Bill Richardson is a master negotiator. When the United States needs to negotiate with hostile governments for the release of political prisoners, they turn to Richardson, a New Mexico congressperson, to represent their interests. His former negotiation adversaries include Iraq's Saddam Hussein, Cuba's Fidel Castro, and Haiti's Raoul Cedras. Richardson offers the following tips for negotiators:

- Be a good listener. In order to negotiate, you must understand your opponent's perspective and know what motivates him or her.
- Use every negotiation technique you know. There is no single "best" strategy.
- Try to come out of every meeting with something, even if it is just a plan for a second meeting.
- Prepare for a negotiation by gathering information from those who are knowledgeable about the situation and the person you will interact with.
- Show humility, but not weakness. You can't back down or let down your guard.

SOURCE: Adapted from J. Martin, "How to Negotiate with Really Tough Guys," *Fortune,* May 27, 1996, pp. 173–74.

In addition to learning about the party's background, one also needs to get information about his or her current interests and needs (see Chapter 4). One can get this information through a variety of routes:

- Conduct a preliminary interview, including a discussion of what the other party would like to achieve in the upcoming negotiations.
- Anticipate the other party's interests.
- Ask others who know or have negotiated with the other party.
- Read what the other party says about himself or herself in the media.

The importance of the issues or interests, along with the nature of one's past relationship with the other party, will influence the depth to which one probes to get information. Although it does take some time and effort to get information, the results are usually more than worth the investment. It is too easy to neglect this step, which is unfortunate because valuable information can be gathered through a few simple phone calls or a visit.

The Other Party's Targets and Openings.   After negotiators have obtained information about the other side's resources and interests, they also need to understand his or her objectives. People often think stereotypically about the other party's interests and targets; they use their own targets and values as a guide and assume that others are like themselves and want similar things. A manager who is always after a bigger paycheck is usually surprised that some of his subordinates are more interested in having a challenging job, schedule flexibility, or increased leisure time than they are in maximizing their salary.

How can one understand and appraise the other party's targets? Although one may speculate about another's targets and objectives, most people do not gather information systematically—although they should. One of the best ways to get this information is directly from the other party. Because information about the other party's targets is so important to the strategy formulation of both parties, professional negotiators will often exchange information about targets or initial proposals days or even weeks before negotiations begin. If this does not occur, then the negotiator should plan to collect this information at the parties' first meeting.

The Other Party's Reputation and Style.   As noted earlier, the other party's past negotiating behavior is a good indication of how he or she will behave in the future. Even if a bargainer has had no previous experience with the other person, speaking to those who have dealt with that person in the past can be very valuable. There is a potential danger in drawing conclusions from this information, however. Assuming that the other party will act in the future as he or she has been described as acting in the past is just that—an assumption. People can and do act differently in different circumstances at different times. Although gathering information about the other party's past behavior is a reasonable starting point for making assumptions, keep in mind that people do change over time. One author on negotiation notes:

> Assumptions are potential hurdles that can move us in the wrong direction . . . The reality of negotiation is that we must and should make assumptions about the opposing party . . . The important thing to remember is that your assumptions are just that. They are no better than poorly educated guesses at best. Don't fall in love with your assumptions. Check them out; they are neither right nor wrong until proven so. (Karrass, 1974, p. 11)

One's impression of the other party's reputation may be based on several factors:

1. How the other party's predecessors have negotiated with you in the past.
2. How the other party has negotiated with you in the past, either in the same or in different contexts.
3. How the other party has negotiated with others in the past.

These different bases for one's assumptions have different degrees of relevance and usefulness for predicting future behavior. One can use the information to prepare, to alert oneself to what might happen; but one should also act with caution and actively look for new information that confirms or denies the validity of the assumptions. There is always the danger, however, that invalid assumptions will lead a negotiator into unfortunate self-fulfilling prophecies. That is, there is a tendency to seek and recognize information that confirms one's desires and assumptions, while failing to seek or recognize information that disconfirms or counters them.

A negotiator who assumes the other party is going to be demanding and aggressive may decide that the best defense is a good offense and therefore open with aggressive demands and belligerent behavior. The other party may take this behavior in stride or may then decide to reply in kind, even though he or she initially intended to be cooperative. Of course, when the other party does fight back, the first negotiator's assumptions seem to be confirmed. If this initial misunderstanding is all that occurs, the problem may be recognized and corrected before it escalates. However, certain expectations can trigger an escalating cycle of competitive mistrust and hostility, particularly when negotiations occur in long-standing relationships. These cycles are common in relationships between nations and between labor and management groups (see Lewicki and Alderfer, 1973; Pruitt and Rubin, 1986).

The previous paragraphs speak to the other party's reputation. One may assess the other party's style by looking at the way he or she has negotiated in the past and by categorizing various aspects of his or her personality. We describe personality factors that can affect negotiator behavior in Chapter 10, and we discuss ways to deal with problematic negotiator behavior in Chapter 12.

The Other Party's Alternative.   As part of the preparation process, we have stressed that negotiators need to understand their own alternative. The alternative offers the negotiator a viable option for agreement if the current negotiation does not yield an acceptable outcome. Similarly, negotiators should attempt to understand the quality of the other party's alternative. If the other party has a strong and viable alternative, he or she will probably be confident in negotiation, set high objectives, and be willing to push hard for those objectives. In contrast, if the other party has a weak alternative, then he or she will be more dependent on achieving a satisfactory agreement with you, and be less likely to push as hard.

The Other Party's Authority.   When negotiators represent others, their power to make agreements may be limited; in fact, their ability to carry out negotiations may be restricted in many ways. Sometimes a constituency stipulates that negotiators cannot make any agreements; often negotiators can only present proposals from the constituency or collect information and take it back to their superiors.

There are many reasons for limiting a negotiator's authority. Negotiators kept on a short leash cannot be won over by a persuasive presentation to commit their constituency to something that is not wanted. They cannot give out sensitive information carelessly. Although these limitations may actually be helpful to a negotiator, they can also be frustrating. One might ask, "Why should I speak with this person, if she cannot make a decision and may not even be well informed about what I want?" Negotiation under these circumstances can seem like an exercise in futility. When a negotiator always has to check things out with those he represents, the other party may refuse to continue until someone who has the power to answer questions and make decisions is brought to the table. Negotiating teams should therefore think seriously about sending in a negotiator with limited authority. Although that person will not be able to make unauthorized decisions, the limited authority may frustrate the other party and create an unproductive tension in the negotiating relationship (see Chapter 8). Before negotiations, it might be appropriate to ask the other party specifically about any limits to authority in the impending negotiation; the temptation to lie will be balanced against the likely personal costs and costs to the negotiation of doing so.

The Other Party's Strategy and Tactics.   Finally, it would be most helpful to gain information about the other party's intended strategy and tactics. Although it is unlikely the other party will reveal his or her strategy outright—particularly if he or she is intending to use distributive tactics—one can infer this information from whatever data one collects to answer the previous inquiries in this list. Thus, reputation, style, alternative, authority, and objectives may tell one a great deal about what strategy the other party intends to pursue. As we have noted before, one will have to gather this information on an emergent basis as the negotiation unfolds; if one's expectations have been incorrect, it will be necessary to recalibrate one's own strategic response.

8. What Strategy Do I Want to Pursue?

The five strategic alternatives represented in Figure 2.2 are a good place to start. It may well be that strategy was determined long before this point in the planning process, but by this time, the negotiator should clearly determine which strategy he/she intends to pursue.

9. How Will I Present the Issues to the Other Party?

One important aspect of actual negotiations is to present a case clearly and to marshal ample supporting facts and arguments; another is to refute the other party's arguments with counterarguments.

Because of the breadth and diversity of issues that can be included in negotiations, it is not possible to specify all the procedures that can be used to assemble information. (See Box 2.5 for specific advice about asking for a pay raise.) There are, however, some good general guides that can be used. A negotiator can ask these questions:

a. What facts support my point of view? What substantiates or validates this information as factual?

b. Whom may I consult or talk with to help me elaborate or clarify the facts? What records, files, or data sources exist that support my arguments?

c. Have these issues been negotiated before by others under similar circumstances? Can I consult those negotiators to determine what major arguments they used, which ones were successful, and which were not?

d. What is the other party's point of view likely to be? What are his or her interests? What arguments is the other party likely to make? How can I respond to those arguments and seek more creative positions that go further in addressing both sides' issues and interests?

e. How can I develop and present the facts so they are most convincing? What visual aids, pictures, charts, graphs, expert testimony, and the like can be helpful or make the best case?

In Chapter 6, we offer extensive advice to the negotiator on how to use power and how to structure the presentation of information in order to achieve maximum effectiveness.

BOX 2.5
Asking for a Pay Raise

When it comes to asking the boss for more money, even the most experienced, capable, and intelligent employees are usually scared out of their wits. Even people who negotiate for a living have difficulty wrangling the best deal for their own compensation. To address the fears that keep many deserving employees from asking to be paid more equitably, *Fortune* magazine surveyed middle managers across the United States who had successfully negotiated pay increases with their employers. These managers offered the following advice:

- *Figure out your market value.* Comparing yourself to the person in the next cubicle is ineffective, particularly if everyone in the company is underpaid. Instead, look outside the company to determine what your competitors are paying employees at your level. Some potential resources for this information are professional associations and trade organizations (some of which regularly publish salary surveys), or companies that provide salary surveys for various industries as part of their consulting services. Executive recruiters can often serve as a source for additional information.

- *Negotiate your position, not your paycheck.* Rather than simply asking for more money, talk about additional responsibilities or projects you would like to take on. Once your responsibilities have been expanded, it is easier to ask your supervisor what additional compensation you can expect for these new duties. Or, conversely, become the office "vacuum cleaner," taking on projects that your colleagues lack the time or expertise to complete. Once these endeavors are successful, you can approach your supervisor armed with information about how your contribution to the company has increased.

- *Threaten to quit.* Nothing gets the boss's attention like dangling your new job offer in front of her eyes. However, this strategy should not be used if you're not truly in possession of an offer you would legitimately accept. If you deliver this ultimatum, you have to be truly ready to walk out the door.

In general, it is recommended that you depersonalize the issue as much as possible. Rather than thinking of the negotiation as concerning "your" compensation, think of it as attempting to achieve equitable pay for the projects you manage, or for the position you currently hold. Taking the emotion out of the issue may make it easier for you, and your boss, to discuss the issue rationally and reach a solution that benefits you both.

SOURCE: Adapted from R. Henkoff, "Are You (More Than) Ready for a Pay Raise?" *Fortune*, December 8, 1997, pp. 233–38.

---

10. What Protocol Needs to Be Followed in This Negotiation?

There are a number of elements of "protocol" or process that a negotiator should consider:

- *The agenda.* A negotiator may unilaterally draw up a firm list of issues, and even establish specific goals, well before the initial negotiation meeting. This process is valuable because it forces the bargainer to think through his or her position and decide on objectives. The list of issues constitutes the agenda for negotiation. It is what the negotiator wants to discuss, and the order or priority in which he wants to discuss them.

While agendas may be proposed unilaterally by the negotiator, there is also a potential risk. If the negotiator's list differs from a preset agenda or the other side's preferred list, the negotiator may bring issues to the table that the other party is unprepared to discuss, or may define priorities that cannot be achieved realistically. Opposing negotiators do not welcome off-the-wall surprises or the embarrassment that may come when the other side raises an issue they are completely unprepared to discuss. In this situation, most experienced negotiators will ask for a recess to get information and prepare themselves on the new issue, thus creating unanticipated delays. They may even refuse to include the new item on the agenda because they haven't had time to prepare for it or they fear they cannot discuss it adequately. If the other party is also accountable to a constituency, he or she may not want to go back to reopen earlier consultations. For this reason, many professional negotiators (labor negotiators, diplomats, etc.) often exchange (and negotiate) the agenda in advance. They want first to agree to what issues will be discussed (the agenda) before actually engaging the substance of those issues.

• *The location of negotiation.* Negotiators tend to do better on their home turf—their own office, building, or city. They know the space, they feel comfortable and relaxed, they have direct access to all the amenities—secretaries, research information, expert advice, computers, and so on. In cross-cultural negotiations (see Chapter 11), language and cultural differences may come into play, and the parties may have to travel across many time zones. If negotiators want to minimize the advantage that comes with home turf, then they need to select neutral territory in which neither party will have an advantage. In addition, negotiators can choose the degree of formality of the environment. Formal deliberations are often held in conference rooms or even hotel meeting rooms; informal deliberations can be held in restaurants, cocktail lounges, or rooms that offer an array of furniture such as that found in a typical living room.

• *The time period of negotiation.* If negotiators expect long, protracted deliberations, they might want to negotiate the time and duration of sessions. When do we start? How long do we meet? When do we need to end? When can we call for coffee breaks or time to caucus with our team?

• *Other parties who might be involved in the negotiation.* Is the negotiation between the principals only (refer back to the field analysis, Figure 2.3)? Will one or both sides bring experts or advisers with them? What role will these outsiders play? Will one or both sides be represented by an agent who will negotiate for them? If so, will the principal be there, or will the agent only consult the principal later? Are the media involved, and what role might they play?

• *What might be done if negotiation fails.* What will happen if we deadlock? Will we go to a third-party neutral (see Chapter 13)? Might we try some other techniques? (See Chapter 12 for suggestions on getting negotiations back on track.)

"No, Thursday's out. How about never—is never good for you?"

- *How will we keep track of what is agreed to?* Many negotiators don't consider the importance of keeping track of exactly what was discussed and agreed to. Going back to the early days in school when we actively avoided being elected the class or club secretary, note taking is seen as a tedious and uninteresting job. However, experienced negotiators learn that the "secretarial role" is critical. First, the person with the best notes often becomes the "memory" of the session, his or her notes are later consulted to determine what was said and discussed. Second, the person with the best notes may also volunteer to draft the initial agreement; again, this person may be able to take some license in how the agreement is stated, and what points are emphasized or de-emphasized. Finally, if the agreement is highly technical or complex, one certainly wants to have the agreement reviewed by experts and specialists—attorneys, financial analysts, accountants, engineers, and so on. Moreover, if the agreement is between groups who speak different languages, the agreement should be translated and back-translated so that it says and means the same thing in each of the languages.

In new bargaining relationships, discussions about these procedural issues occur before the major substantive issues are raised. The ease or difficulty of resolving these procedural issues can often be used as tests to determine how the negotiation on the larger substantive issues will proceed. If the negotiator enjoys success in these procedural negotiations, he might expect that it may be easier to reach agreement later on the substantive issues.

Summary on the Planning Process

We believe planning to be the most important activity in negotiation. We began with a basic understanding of the concepts of framing and strategy; we then discussed various aspects of strategy and the strategy process and presented a model of negotiation strategy choice. In that model, we suggested that strategy choice is determined by the interplay of five components: targets, principles and standards, trust, episodic assumptions, and a list of driving factors that includes environments, contexts, outcomes, processes, and relationships.

Having described our model, we then discussed the various aspects of managing the planning process. We propose that negotiation success is largely a function of careful planning. A negotiator who carefully plans will make an effort to do the following:

1. Define the key issues that must be resolved in the upcoming negotiation.

2. Assemble all of the issues together and understand how the issues relate to each other.

3. Understand and define the key interests at stake that underlie the issues.

4. Define the limits—points where we will walk away—and alternatives—other deals we could do if this deal does not work out.

5. Clarify the targets and objectives to be achieved, and the points where we will begin the discussion.

6. Consult with others—constituents and possibly other parties—to shape and refine their interests, and the limits to my authority.

7. Try to understand the other party in the negotiation—their goals, issues, strategies, interests, limits, alternatives, targets, openings, and authority.

8. Select the strategy that is most likely to help me achieve my targets.

9. Plan the process by which I will present and "sell" my ideas to the other party (and perhaps to my own constituency).

10. Define the important points of protocol and process——the agenda, who will be at the table or observing the negotiation, where and when we will negotiate, and so on.

If a negotiator is able to consider and evaluate each of these factors, the negotiator will know what he or she wants and will have a clear sense of direction on how to proceed. This sense of direction, and the confidence derived from it, will be the single most important factor in affecting negotiating outcomes.

CHAPTER SUMMARY

In this chapter, we reviewed the key factors that a negotiator needs to know and understand to successfully plan for a negotiation. To recap:

1. Negotiators differ in the goals they select. Goals can be specific (to achieve a particular outcome), or they can be more general (to pursue a broader set of interests). They can also be tangible, such as a particular rate or price or financial

outcome; or they can be intangible, such as winning, beating the other, or defending a principle. Goals can shape the frames we adopt, or frames can shape the goals we pursue.

2. There are several major strategies that can be used in a negotiation. Select the strategy that is most likely to achieve one's objectives, and also take into consideration the long-term relationship with the other party. Two of these major strategies: competition and collaboration—are the focus of the next two chapters of this book.

3. Negotiators differ in how they "frame" the problem, issue, or conflict. Frames may be perspectives on outcomes and the related rewards or penalties that go with those outcomes, or they may be ways to define "the problem" in a negotiation. What is important is that how one or both parties frame the problem will lead them to select some conflict management strategies and ignore others. Therefore, a negotiator needs to attend to the way he or she is defining the problem and specifically be aware that

- There may be other ways to define it that may make the problem more or less amenable to negotiation and resolution.
- The other party may not be defining it in the same way, which may contribute to the ease or difficulty with which the parties can communicate about the problem with each other.

4. Negotiations tend to evolve over time according to certain predictable sequences. These sequences comprise the different stages or phases of a negotiation. The models indicate that negotiation is not a random process but has some predictable elements to it over time. Understanding these traditional stages or phases is also critical to helping the negotiator evaluate where things are at any point in time, and/or whether to try to move the process forward at a faster or slower pace.

5. Goals, strategies, frames, and predictable stages set the background for an effective planning process. Again, as we noted, there are a number of different planning templates, which tend to emphasize different elements in slightly different sequences. Nevertheless, we have tried to present the most important steps in the planning process. Effectively attending to each of these steps should allow a negotiator to be very well prepared for the challenges that he or she is going to face in playing out strategy and meeting the other party.

CHAPTER 3

Strategy and Tactics
of Distributive Bargaining

Eighteen months ago Larry decided to move closer to where he works. Following this decision to move, he put his house on the market and started to look for a new one—but with no results. Fourteen months later, Larry finally received an offer to buy his house and, after a brief negotiation, settled on the selling price. Because he had not yet found a house to buy, he postponed closing the sale for six months to give himself additional time to look. The buyer, Barbara, was not happy about having to wait that long because of the inconvenience and the difficulty of getting a bank to guarantee an interest rate so far in advance. Larry adjusted the price so that Barbara would accept this postponement, but it was clear that she would be much happier if he could move the date closer.

There were relatively few houses on the market in the area where Larry wanted to live, and none of them was satisfactory. He jokingly said that unless something new came on the market, he would be sleeping in a tent on the town common when the leaves turned in the fall. Two months later a house came on the market that met his requirements. The seller, Monica, set the asking price at $145,000, which was $10,000 above what Larry hoped to pay but $5,000 below the most he would be willing to pay. Larry knew that the more he paid for the house, the less he would have to make some very desirable alterations, buy draperies and some new furniture, and hire a moving company. Monica already had attractive drapes in the house. She was moving to a new house; if she could not use the drapes in the new house, Larry might be able to purchase them or ask Monica to include them with the sale. The same might be true for several rugs, hall tables, and other items. Larry also learned that Monica's new home was supposed to be finished soon, about the time Larry was to close on the sale of his present house.

This illustration provides the basic elements of a distributive bargaining situation. As we've mentioned in Chapters 1 and 2, it is also called competitive, or win-lose, bargaining. In a distributive bargaining situation, the goals of one party are usually in fundamental and direct conflict with the goals of the other party. Resources are fixed and limited, and both parties want to maximize their share of the resources. As a result, each party will use a set of strategies to maximize his or her share of the outcomes to be obtained. One important strategy is to guard information carefully—one party tries to give information to the other party only when it provides a strategic advantage. Meanwhile, it is highly desirable to get information from the other party to improve negotiation power. Distributive bargaining is basically a competition over who is going to get the most of a limited resource (often money). Whether or not one or both parties achieve their objectives will depend on the strategies and tactics they employ (Walton and McKersie, 1965).

For many, the strategies and tactics of distributive bargaining are what negotiation is all about. Images come to mind of smoke-filled rooms packed with men arguing and fighting for their points of view. Many people are attracted to this view of negotiation and look forward to learning and sharpening an array of hard-bargaining skills; many others are repelled by distributive bargaining and would rather walk away than negotiate in this manner. They argue that distributive bargaining is old-fashioned, macho, and destructive.

There are two reasons that every negotiator should be familiar with distributive bargaining. First, some interdependent situations that negotiators face *are* distributive, and to do well in them negotiators need to understand how they work. Second, because many people use distributive bargaining strategies and tactics almost exclusively, all negotiators will find it important to know how to counter their effects. While distributive strategies and tactics are useful, they can also be counterproductive and costly. Often they cause the negotiating parties to focus so much on their differences that they ignore what they have in common (Thompson and Hrebec, 1996). These negative effects notwithstanding, *distributive bargaining strategies and tactics are quite useful when a negotiator wants to maximize the value obtained in a single deal and when the relationship with the other party is not important.*

Some of the tactics discussed in this chapter will also generate ethical concerns. (The topic of ethics and negotiation is discussed in detail in Chapter 7.) Do not assume that the other party shares your ethical values when negotiating. Although you may not believe that it is ethical to use some of the tactics discussed in this chapter, other negotiators will be quite comfortable using them. Alternatively, you may be comfortable using some tactics that make other negotiators quite uneasy. Some of the tactics discussed are commonly accepted as ethical behavior when bargaining distributively (portraying your best alternative as more positive than it really is, for instance), whereas other tactics are generally considered unacceptable (see the discussion of typical hardball tactics later in this chapter).

Finally, most negotiators accept the difference between "soft" and "hard" distributive bargaining. The discussion of strategies and tactics in this chapter is intended to help negotiators understand the dynamics of distributive situations and thereby obtain a better deal. We also think that a thorough understanding of these concepts will allow negotiators who are by nature not entirely comfortable with distributive bargaining to manage distributive negotiations proactively.

THE DISTRIBUTIVE BARGAINING SITUATION

To describe how the distributive bargaining process works, we will return to our opening example of Larry's new house purchase. Several prices were mentioned: (1) Monica's asking price, (2) the price Larry would like to pay for a new house, and (3) the price above which Larry would not buy the house. These prices represent key points in the analysis of any distributive bargaining situation. Larry's preferred price is the *target point,* the point at which a negotiator would like to conclude negotiations—his optimal goal. The target is also sometimes referred to as a negotiator's *aspiration.* The price beyond which Larry will not go is the *resistance point,* a negotiator's bottom line—the most he will pay as a buyer (for a seller, it's the smallest amount she will settle for). Finally, the *asking price* is the initial price set by the seller; Larry might decide to

FIGURE 3.1   The Buyer's View of the House Negotiation

	Larry's target point			Monica's asking price	Larry's resistance point
$130,000	$135,000	$140,000		$145,000	$150,000

counter Monica's asking price with his *initial offer*—the first number he will quote to the seller. Using the house purchase as an example, we can treat the range of possible prices as a continuum (see Figure 3.1).

How does Larry decide on his initial offer? There are many ways to answer this question. Fundamentally, however, to make a good initial offer Larry must understand something about the process of negotiation. In Chapter 1, we discussed how people expect give-and-take when they negotiate, and Larry needs to factor this into his initial offer. If Larry opened the negotiation at his target point ($135,000) and then had to make a concession, this first concession would have him moving away from his target point to a price closer to his resistance point. If he really wants to achieve his target, he should make an initial offer that is lower than his target point to create some room for making concessions. At the same time, the starting point cannot be too far from the target point. If Larry made the first offer too low (e.g., $100,000), Monica might break off negotiations, believing him to be unreasonable or foolish. Although judgments about how to determine first offers can often be quite complex and can have a dramatic influence on the course of negotiation, let us stay with the simple case for the moment and assume that Larry decided to offer $133,000 as a reasonable first offer—less than his target point and well below his resistance point. In the meantime, remember that although this illustration concerns only price, all other issues or agenda items for the negotiation have starting, target, and resistance points.

Both parties to a negotiation should establish their starting, target, and resistance points, at least implicitly, if not explicitly, before beginning a negotiation. Starting points

DILBERT ©UFS. Reprinted by permission.

FIGURE 3.2   The Buyer's View of the House Negotiation (Extended)

Monica's resistance point (inferred)	Larry's initial offer (public)	Larry's target point (private)	Monica's target point (inferred)	Monica's asking price (public)	Larry's resistance point (private)
$130,000	$133,000	$135,000	$140,000	$145,000	$150,000

are usually in the opening statements each party makes (i.e., the seller's listing price and the buyer's first offer). The target point is usually learned or inferred as negotiations get under way. People typically give up the margin between their starting points and target points as they make concessions. The resistance point, the point beyond which a person will not go and would rather break off negotiations, is not known to the other party and should be kept secret (Raiffa, 1982). One party may not learn the other's resistance point even after the end of a successful negotiation. After an unsuccessful negotiation, one party may infer that the other's resistance point was near the last offer the other was willing to consider before the negotiation ended.

Two parties' starting and resistance points are usually arranged in reverse order, with the resistance point being a high price for the buyer and a low price for the seller. Thus, continuing the illustration, Larry would have been willing to pay up to $150,000 for the house Monica listed at $145,000. Larry can speculate that Monica may be willing to accept something less than $145,000 and probably would think $140,000 a desirable figure. What Larry does not know (but would dearly like to) is the lowest figure that Monica would accept. Is it $140,000? $135,000? Larry assumes it is $130,000. Monica, for her part, initially knows nothing about Larry's position but soon learns his starting point when he offers $133,000. Monica may suspect that Larry's target point is not too far away (in fact it is $135,000, but Monica doesn't know this) but has no idea of his resistance point ($150,000). This information—what Larry knows or infers about Monica's positions—is represented in Figure 3.2.

The spread between the resistance points, called the *bargaining range, settlement range,* or *zone of potential agreement,* is particularly important. In this area the actual bargaining takes place, for anything outside these points will be summarily rejected by one of the two negotiators. When the buyer's resistance point is above the seller's—he is minimally willing to pay more than she is minimally willing to sell for, as is true in the house example—there is a *positive bargaining range.* When the reverse is true—the seller's resistance point is above the buyer's, and the buyer won't pay more than the seller will minimally accept—there is a *negative bargaining range.* In the house example, if Monica would minimally accept $145,000 and Larry would maximally pay $140,000, then a negative bargaining range would exist. Negotiations that begin with a negative bargaining range are likely to stalemate. They can be resolved only if one or both parties are persuaded to change their resistance points, or if someone else forces a solution upon them that one or both parties dislike. However, because negotiators don't begin their deliberations by talking about their resistance points (they're talking about initial offers and demands instead), it is often hard to know whether a positive settlement range really exists until the negotiators get deep into the process. Both parties may realize that there was no overlap in their resistance points only after protracted negotiations have been exhausted; at that point, they will have to decide whether to end negotiations or reevaluate their resistance points, a process to be described in more detail later on.

The Role of Alternatives to a Negotiated Agreement

In addition to opening bids, target points, and resistance points, a fourth factor may enter the negotiations: an *alternative* outcome that can be obtained by completing a different deal with a different party (see Chapter 2). In some negotiations, the parties have only two fundamental choices: (*a*) reach a deal with the other party, or (*b*) reach no settlement at all. In other negotiations, however, one or both parties may have available the possibility of an alternative deal with another party. Thus, in the case of Larry and Monica, another house may come on the market in the neighborhood where Larry wishes to buy. Similarly, if Monica waits long enough (or drops the price of the house far enough), she will presumably find another interested buyer. If Larry picks an alternative house to buy, talks to the owner of that house, and negotiates the best price that he can, that price represents his alternative. For the sake of argument, let us assume that Larry's alternative house costs $142,000 and that Monica's alternative buyer will pay $134,000.

An alternative point can be identical to the resistance point, although the two do not necessarily have to be the same. If Larry's alternative is $142,000, then (taking no other factors into account) he should reject any price Monica asks above that amount. But Larry's alternative may not be as desirable for reasons other than price—let's say that he likes the neighborhood less, that the house is 10 minutes farther away from where he works, or that he likes the way Monica had fixed up her house and wants to enjoy that when he moves in. In any of these situations, Larry may maintain his resistance point at $150,000; he is therefore willing to pay Monica up to $8,000 more than his alternative (see Figure 3.3).

Alternatives are important because they give the negotiator power to walk away from any negotiation when the emerging deal is not very good. The number of realistic alternatives negotiators may have will vary considerably from one situation to another. In negotiations where they have many attractive alternatives, they can set their goals higher and make fewer concessions. In negotiations where they have no attractive alternative, such as when dealing with a sole supplier, they have much less bargaining power. Good distributive bargainers identify their realistic alternatives before beginning negotiations with the other party so that they can properly gauge how firm to be in the negotiation (Fisher and Ertel, 1995). Good bargainers also look for ways to *improve* their alternatives, even as the negotiation is under way. If Larry's negotiations with Monica are extending over a period of time, he may well keep his eye on the market for another possible (better) alternative. He may also continue to negotiate with the owner of the existing alternative house for a better deal. Both courses of action involve efforts by Larry to maintain and expand his bargaining power by improving the quality of his alternatives. (We discuss power and leverage in bargaining in detail in Chapter 6.)

FIGURE 3.3   The Buyer's View of the House Negotiation (Extended with Alternatives)

Monica's resistance point (inferred)	Larry's initial offer (public)	Monica's alternative buyer (private)	Larry's target point (private)	Monica's target point (inferred)	Larry's alternative house (private)	Monica's asking price (public)	Larry's resistance point (private)
$130,000	$133,000	$134,000	$135,000	$140,000	$142,000	$145,000	$150,000

Settlement Point

The fundamental process of distributive bargaining is to reach a settlement within a positive bargaining range. The objective of both parties is to obtain as much of the bargaining range as possible—that is, to get the settlement as close to the other party's resistance point as possible.

Both parties in distributive bargaining know that they might have to settle for less than what they would prefer (their opening or target point), but they hope that the settlement point will be better than their own resistance point. In order for agreement to occur, both parties must believe that the settlement point, although perhaps less desirable than they would prefer, is the best that they can get. This belief is important, both in reaching agreement and in ensuring support for the agreement after the negotiations. Parties who do not think they got the best agreement possible, or who believe that they lost something in the deal, frequently try to get out of the agreement later or find other ways to recoup their losses. If Larry thinks he got the short end of the deal, he could make life miserable and expensive for Monica by making extraneous claims later on—claiming that the house had hidden damages, that the fixtures that were supposed to come with the house were defective, and so on. Another factor that will affect satisfaction with the settlement point is whether the parties will ever see each other again. If Monica was moving out of the region, then Larry may be unable to contact her later for any adjustments and should therefore ensure that he evaluates the current deal very carefully.

Bargaining Mix

In the house-purchase illustration, as in almost all negotiations, agreement is necessary on several issues: the price, the closing date of the sale, renovations to the house, and the price of items that could remain in the house (such as drapes and appliances). This package of issues for negotiation is the *bargaining mix*. Each item in the mix has its own starting, target, and resistance points. Some items are of obvious importance to both parties; others are of importance to only one party. Negotiators need to know what is important to them and to the other party, and they need to make sure they take these priorities into account during the planning process. (See Chapter 2 for a detailed discussion of planning.)

For example, in the negotiation that we are describing, a secondary issue important to both parties is the closing date of the sale—the date when the ownership of the house will actually be transferred. The date of sale is part of the bargaining mix. Larry learned when Monica's new house was going to be completed and anticipated that she would want to transfer ownership of her old house to Larry shortly after that point. Larry asked for a closing date very close to when Monica would probably want to close; thus, the deal looked very attractive to her. As it turned out, Larry's closing date on his old house—his old target point—was close to this date as well, thus making the deal attractive for both Larry and Monica. If Larry and Monica had wanted different selling dates, then the closing date would have been a more contentious issue in the bargaining mix (although if Larry could have moved the closing date up, he might have been able to strike a better deal with Barbara, the buyer of his house).

FUNDAMENTAL STRATEGIES

The prime objective in distributive bargaining is to maximize the value of *this single deal*. In our example, the buyer has four fundamental strategies available:

1. To push for a settlement close to the seller's (as yet unknown) resistance point, thereby yielding for the buyer the largest part of the settlement range. The buyer may attempt to influence the seller's view of what settlements are possible by making extreme offers and small concessions.

2. To get the seller to change her resistance point by influencing the seller's beliefs about the value of the house. The buyer may try to convince the seller to reduce her resistance point (e.g., by telling her that the house is overpriced) and thereby increase the bargaining range.

3. If a negative settlement range exists, to get the seller to reduce her resistance point to create a positive settlement range or to modify his own resistance point to create an overlap. Thus, Monica could be persuaded to accept a lower price, or Larry could decide he has to pay more than he wanted to.

4. To get the seller to think that this settlement is the best that is possible—not that it is all she can get, or that she is incapable of getting more, or that the buyer is winning by getting more. The distinction between a party believing that an agreement is the best possible (and not the other interpretations) may appear subtle and semantic. However, in getting people to agree it is important that they feel as though they got the best possible deal. Ego satisfaction is often as important as achieving tangible objectives (recall the discussion of tangibles and intangibles in Chapter 1).

In all these strategies, the buyer is attempting to influence the seller's perceptions of what is possible through the exchange of information and persuasion. Regardless of the general strategy taken, two tasks are important in all distributive bargaining situations: (1) discovering the other party's resistance point, and (2) influencing the other party's resistance point.

Discovering the Other Party's Resistance Point

Information is the life force of negotiation. The more you can learn about the other party's outcome values, resistance point, motives, feelings of confidence, and so on, the more able you will be to strike a favorable agreement (see Box 3.1). At the same time,

---

BOX 3.1
The Piano

When shopping for a used piano, Orvel Ray answered a newspaper ad. The piano was a beautiful upright in a massive walnut cabinet. The seller was asking $1,000, and it would have been a bargain at that price, but Orvel had received a $700 tax refund and had set this windfall as the limit that he could afford to invest. He searched for a negotiating advantage.

He was able to deduce several facts from the surroundings. The furnished basement where the piano sat also contained a set of drums, and an upright acoustic base stood in the corner. Obviously the seller was a serious musician, and probably played jazz. There had to be a compelling reason for selling such a beautiful instrument.

Orvel asked the first, obvious question, "Are you buying a new piano?"

The seller hesitated. "Well, I don't know yet. See, we're moving to North Carolina, and it would be very expensive to ship this piano clear across the country."

"Did they say how much extra it would cost?" Orvel queried.

"They said an extra $300 or so."

"When do you have to decide?"

"The packers are coming this afternoon."

Now Orvel knew where the seller was vulnerable. He could ship the piano cross-country, or sell it for $700 and still break even. Or he could hold out for his asking price and take his chances. "Here's what I can do: I can give you $700 in cash, right now," Orvel said as he took seven $100 bills out of his pocket and spread them on the keyboard. "And I can have a truck and three of my friends here to move it *out of your way* by noon today."

The seller hesitated, then picked up the money. "Well, I suppose that would work. I can always buy a new piano when we get settled."

Orvel left before the seller could reconsider. By the time the group returned with the truck, the seller had received three other offers at his asking price, but because he had accepted the cash, he had to tell them that the piano had already been sold.

If the seller had not volunteered the information about the packers coming that afternoon, Orvel might not have been able to negotiate the price.

SOURCE: From J. C. Levinson, M. S. A. Smith, and O. R. Wilson, *Guerrilla Negotiating* (New York: John Wiley, 1999), pp. 15–16.

---

you do not want the other party to have certain information about you. Your real resistance point, some of the outcome values, and confidential information about a weak strategic position or an emotional vulnerability are best concealed (Stein, 1996). Alternatively, you may want the other party to have certain information—some of it factual and correct, some of it contrived to lead the other party to believe things that are favorable to you. Because each side wants to obtain some information and to conceal other information, and because each side knows that the other also wants to obtain and conceal information, communication can become complex. Information is often conveyed in a code that evolves during negotiation. People answer questions with other questions or with incomplete statements; yet for either side to influence the other's perceptions, they must both eventually establish some points effectively and convincingly.

Influencing the Other Party's Resistance Point

Central to planning the strategy and tactics for distributive bargaining is effectively locating the other party's resistance point and the relationship of that resistance point to your own. The resistance point is established by the value expected from a particular outcome, which in turn is the product of the worth and costs of an outcome. Larry sets his resistance point based on the amount of money he can afford to pay (in total or in monthly mortgage payments), the estimated market value or worth of the house, and other factors in his bargaining mix (closing date, curtains, etc.). A resistance point will also be influenced by the cost an individual attaches to delay or difficulty in negotiation (an intangible) or in having the negotiations aborted. If Larry, who had set his resistance point at $150,000, were faced with the choice of paying $151,000 or living on the town common for a month, he might well reevaluate his resistance point. The following factors are important in attempting to influence the other person's resistance point: (1) the value the other attaches to a particular outcome, (2) the costs the other attaches to delay or difficulty in negotiations, and (3) the cost the other attaches to having the negotiations aborted.

A significant factor in shaping the other person's understanding of what is possible—and therefore the value he or she places on particular outcomes—is the other's understanding of your own situation. Therefore, when influencing the other's viewpoint, you must also deal with the other party's understanding of your value for a particular outcome, the costs you attach to delay or difficulty in negotiation, and your cost of having the negotiations aborted.

To explain how these factors can affect the process of distributive bargaining, we will make four major propositions (refer to Walton and McKersie, 1965, pp. 59–82, for a more extensive treatment of this subject):

1. *The other party's resistance point will vary directly with his or her estimate of the cost of delay or aborting negotiations.* If the other party sees that you need a settlement quickly and cannot defer it, he or she can seize this advantage and press for a better outcome. Therefore, expectations will rise and the other party will set a more demanding resistance point. The more you can convince the other that your costs of delay or aborting negotiations are low (that you are in no hurry and can wait forever), the more modest the other's resistance point will be.

2. *The other's resistance point will vary inversely with his or her cost of delay or aborting.* The more a person needs a settlement, the more modest he or she will be in setting a resistance point. Therefore, the more you can do to convince the other party that delay or aborting negotiations will be costly, the more likely he or she will be to establish a modest resistance point. In contrast, the more attractive the other party's alternatives, the more that person can hang tough with a high resistance point. If negotiations are unsuccessful, the other party can move to an attractive alternative. In the earlier example, we mentioned that both Larry and Monica have satisfactory alternatives.

3. *A resistance point will vary directly with the value the other party attaches to that outcome.* Therefore, the resistance point may become more modest as the person reduces how valuable he or she considers that outcome. If you can convince

the other party that a present negotiating position will not have the desired outcome or that the present position is not as attractive because other positions are even more attractive, then he or she will adjust the resistance point.

4. *The other's resistance point varies inversely with the perceived value the first party attaches to an outcome.* Knowing that a position is important to the other party, you will expect the other to resist giving up on that issue; thus, there should be less possibility of a favorable settlement in that area. As a result, you may lower your expectations to a more modest resistance point. Hence, the more you can convince the other that you value a particular outcome outside the other's bargaining range, the more pressure you put on the other party to set a more modest resistance point with regard to that outcome.

TACTICAL TASKS

From the above assessment of the fundamental strategies of distributive bargaining, four important tactical tasks emerge for a negotiator in a distributive bargaining situation: (1) to assess the other party's outcome values and the costs of terminating negotiations, (2) to manage the other party's impression of the negotiator's outcome values, (3) to modify the other party's perception of his or her own outcome values, and (4) to manipulate the actual costs of delaying or aborting negotiations. Each of these tasks is discussed in more detail below.

Assess Outcome Values and the Costs of Termination

An important first step for a negotiator is to get information about the other party's outcome values and resistance points. The negotiator can pursue two general routes: getting information *indirectly* about the background factors behind an issue (indirect assessment) or getting information *directly* from the other party about outcome values and resistance points (direct assessment). (See Box 3.2 for some advice on gathering information.)

Indirect Assessment.   The process by which an individual sets a resistance point may include many factors. For example, how do you decide how much rent or mortgage payment you can afford each month? Or how do you decide what a house is really worth? There are lots of ways to go about doing this. Indirect assessment is aimed at determining what information an individual probably used to set target and resistance points and how he or she interpreted this information. For example, in labor negotiations, management may infer whether or not a union is willing to strike by how hard the union bargains or by the size of its strike fund. The union decides whether or not the company can afford a strike based on the size of inventories, market conditions for the company's product, and the percentage of workers who are members of the union. In a real estate negotiation, how long a piece of property has been on the market, how many other potential buyers actually exist, how soon a buyer needs the property for business or living, and the financial health of the seller will be important factors. An automobile buyer might

---

BOX 3.2
Sources of Negotiation Information

John Patrick Dolan, author of *Negotiate Like the Pros,* suggests that gathering information before you go to the negotiating table is one of the most critical elements of achieving successful negotiation outcomes. In addition to being informed of the current market value of items under discussion and other items directly related to the negotiation topic, Dolan says, you should also find out as much as you can about the people with whom you'll be interacting. He notes the following sources of information:

1. *The Internet.* Look on-line for articles about the people, their company, and their product. Newsgroups or related on-line chat groups may also be sources of information.

2. *The library.* Articles and other information about the company may be available. Public companies, for example, should have their annual report on file at the local library in cities where they do business. Also look for directories like *Who's Who* and search industry trade journals.

3. *The telephone.* Potential customers are routinely given product and company information upon request. Call and ask that background information about the company be mailed to you.

Also, Dolan recommends that once face-to-face interaction is under way, you listen more than you talk. Asking open-ended questions, which usually begin with what, why, where, when, or how, can encourage your negotiation partner to volunteer potentially valuable information. The more you know about your negotiation partner's agenda, the better you will be able to craft the most mutually acceptable negotiated solution.

SOURCE: Adapted from J. Slutsky and M. Slutsky, "Learning Others' Goals Is Important in Successful Negotiations," *The Columbus (Ohio) Dispatch,* February 23, 1998, p. 9.

---

view the number of new cars in inventory on the dealer's lot, refer to newspaper articles on automobile sales, read about a particular car's popularity in consumer buying guides (i.e., the more popular the car, the less willing they may be to bargain on the price), or consult reference guides to find out what a dealer pays wholesale for different cars.

One can use a variety of information sources to assess the other party's resistance point. Making direct observations, consulting readily available documents and publications, or talking to knowledgeable experts are some methods. It is important to note, however, that these are indirect indicators. One person may interpret a given set of data very differently from another person. Having a large inventory of automobiles may make a dealer willing to reduce the price of a car. However, the dealer may expect the market to change soon, may have just started a big promotional campaign that the buyer does not know about, or may see no real need to reduce prices and instead intend to wait for a market upturn. Thus, indirect measures provide valuable information that may reflect a reality the other person will eventually have to face. It is important to remember, however, that the same piece of information may mean different things to different people and hence may not tell you exactly what you think it does.

Direct Assessment.   In bargaining, the other party does not usually reveal accurate and precise information about his or her outcome values, resistance points, and expectations. Sometimes, however, the other party will provide accurate information. When pushed to the absolute limit and in need of a quick settlement, the other party may explain the facts quite clearly. If company executives believe that a wage settlement above a certain point would drive the company out of business, they may choose to state that absolute limit very clearly and go to considerable lengths to explain how it was determined. Similarly, a house buyer may tell the seller what his absolute maximum price is and support it with an explanation of income and other expenses. In these instances, of course, the party revealing the information believes that the settlement being proposed is within the settlement range—and that the other party will accept the offered information as true rather than see it as a bargaining ploy. An industrial salesperson may tell the purchaser about product quality and service, alternative customers who want to buy the product, and the time required to manufacture special orders.

Most of the time, however, the other party is not so forthcoming, and the methods of getting direct information are more complex. In international diplomacy, various means are used to gather information. Sources are cultivated, messages are intercepted, and codes broken. In labor negotiations, companies have been known to recruit informers or bug union meeting rooms, and unions have had their members collect papers from executives' wastebaskets. In real estate negotiations, sellers have entertained prospective buyers with abundant alcoholic beverages in the hope that tongues will be loosened and information revealed. Additional approaches involve provoking the other party into an angry outburst or putting the other party under pressure designed to cause him or her to make a slip and reveal valuable information. One party may simulate exasperation and angrily stalk out of negotiations in the hope that the other, in an effort to avoid a deadlock, will reveal what is really wanted.

Manage the Other Party's Impressions

Because each side attempts to get information about the other party through direct and indirect sources, an important tactical task for you as a negotiator may be to prevent the other party from getting accurate information about your position, while simultaneously guiding him or her to form a preferred impression of it. Your tasks, then, are to screen actual information about positions and to represent them as you would like the other to believe them. Generally speaking, screening activities are more important at the beginning of negotiation, and direct action is more useful later on. This sequence gives you time to concentrate on gathering information from the other party, which will be useful in evaluating your own resistance point, and on determining the best way to provide information to the other party about your own position.

Screening Activities.   The simplest way to screen a position is to say and do as little as possible. Silence is golden when answering questions; words should be invested in asking questions instead. Selective reticence reduces the likelihood of making verbal slips or presenting any clues that the other side could use to draw conclusions. A look of disappointment or boredom, fidgeting and restlessness, or probing with interest all can give clues about the importance of the points under discussion. Concealment is the most general screening activity.

Another approach, possible when group negotiations are carried on through a representative, is calculated incompetence. Here, the constituents do not give the negotiating agent all of the necessary information, making it impossible for the agent to leak that information. Instead, the negotiator is sent with the task of simply gathering facts and bringing them back to the group. This strategy can make negotiations complex and tedious, and it often causes the other party to protest vigorously at the negotiator's inability to divulge important data or to make agreements. Lawyers, real estate agents, and investigators are frequently used to perform this role. Representatives may also be limited (or limit themselves) in their authority to make decisions. For example, a man buying a car may claim that he must consult his wife before making a final decision.

When negotiation is carried out by a team—as is common in diplomacy, labor–management relations, and many business negotiations—channeling all communication through a team spokesperson reduces the inadvertent revelation of information (team negotiations are discussed more extensively in Chapter 9). In addition to reducing the number of people who can actively reveal information, this allows other members of the negotiating team to observe and listen carefully to what the other party is saying so they can detect clues and pieces of information about the other party's position. Still another screening activity is to present a great many items for negotiation, only a few of which are truly important to the presenter. In this way, the other party has to gather so much information about so many different items that it becomes difficult to detect which items are really important. This tactic, called the snow job or kitchen sink, may be considered a hardball tactic (discussed later in this chapter) if carried to an extreme (Karrass, 1974).

Direct Action to Alter Impressions.   Negotiators can take many actions to present facts that will directly enhance their position or at least make it appear stronger to the other party. One of the most obvious methods is *selective presentation,* in which negotiators reveal only the facts necessary to support their case. Negotiators can also use selective presentation to lead the other party to form the desired impression of their resistance point or to open up new possibilities for agreement that are more favorable to the presenter than those that currently exist. Another approach is to explain or interpret known facts to present a logical argument that shows the costs or risks to oneself if the other party's proposals were implemented. An alternative is to say, "If you were in my shoes, here is the way these facts would look in light of the proposal you have presented." These arguments are most convincing when you have gathered the facts from a neutral source because then the other party will not see them as biased by your preferred outcome. However, even with facts that you provide, selectivity can be helpful in managing the other party's impression of your preferences and priorities. It is not necessary for the other to agree that this is the way things would look if he or she were in your position. Nor must the other agree that the facts lead only to the conclusion you have presented. As long as the other party understands how you see things, then his or her thinking is likely to be influenced.

Displaying *emotional reaction* to facts, proposals, and possible outcomes is another form of direct action negotiators can take to provide information about what is important to them. Disappointment or enthusiasm usually suggests that an issue is important, whereas boredom or indifference suggests it is trivial or unimportant. A loud, angry outburst or an eager response suggests the topic is very important and may give it a prominence that will shape what is discussed. Clearly, however, emotional reactions can be real or feigned. (We discuss emotions in more detail in Chapter 5.) The length of time and amount of detail used in presenting a point or position can also convey importance. Carefully checking through the details the other side has presented about an item, or insisting on clarification and verification, can convey the impression of importance. Casually accepting the other party's arguments as true can convey the impression of disinterest in the topic being discussed.

Taking direct action to alter another's impression raises a number of hazards. It is one thing to select certain facts to present and to emphasize or de-emphasize their importance accurately, but it is a different matter to fabricate and lie. The former is expected and understood in distributive bargaining; the latter, even in hardball negotiations, is resented and often angrily attacked if discovered. Between the two extremes, however, what is said and done as skillful puffery by one may be perceived as dishonest distortion by the other. (The ethical considerations are explored in detail in Chapter 7.) Other problems can arise when trivial items are introduced as distractions or minor issues are magnified in importance. The purpose is to conceal the truly important and to direct the other's attention away from the significant, but there is a danger: The other person may become aware of this maneuver and, with great fanfare, concede on the minor points, thereby gaining the right to demand equally generous concessions on the central points. In this way the other party can defeat the maneuverer at his or her own game.

Modify the Other Party's Perceptions

A negotiator can alter the other party's impressions of his or her own objectives by making the outcomes appear less attractive or by making the cost of obtaining them appear higher. The negotiator may also try to make demands and positions appear more attractive or less unattractive to the other party.

There are several approaches to modifying the other party's perceptions. One approach is to interpret for the other party what the outcomes of his or her proposal will really be. A negotiator can explain logically how an undesirable outcome would result if the other party really did get what he or she requested. This may mean highlighting something that has been overlooked. For example, in union–management negotiations, management may demonstrate that a union request for a six-hour workday would, on the one hand, not increase the number of employees because it would not be worthwhile to hire people for two hours a day to make up for the hours taken from the standard eight-hour day. On the other hand, if the company were to keep production at the present level, it would be necessary to use the present employees on overtime, thereby increasing the total labor cost and, subsequently, the price of the product. This rise in cost would reduce demand for the product and, ultimately, the number of hours worked or the number of workers.

"Mr. Mosbacher, are you expecting anything via U.P.S.?"

Another approach to modifying the other's perceptions is to conceal information. An industrial seller may not reveal to a purchaser that certain technological changes are going to reduce significantly the cost of producing the products. A seller of real estate may not tell a prospective buyer that in three years a proposed highway will isolate the property being sold from attractive portions of the city. Concealment strategies may enter into the same ethical hazards mentioned earlier (also see Chapter 7).

Manipulate the Actual Costs of Delay or Termination

Negotiators have deadlines. A contract will expire. Agreement has to be reached before a large meeting occurs. Someone has to catch a plane. Extending negotiations beyond a deadline can be costly, particularly to the person who has the deadline, because that person has to either extend the deadline or go home empty-handed. At the same time, research and practical experience suggest that a large majority of agreements in distributive bargaining are reached when the deadline is near (Lim and Murnighan, 1994; Roth, Murnighan, and Schoumaker, 1988; Walton and McKersie, 1965). Manipulating a deadline or failing to agree by a particular deadline can be a powerful tool in the hands of the person who does not face deadline pressure. In some ways, the ultimate weapon in negotiation is to threaten to terminate negotiations, denying both parties the possibility of a settlement. One side then will usually feel this pressure more acutely than the other, and thus it presents a potent weapon. There are three ways to manipulate the costs of delay in negotiation: (1) plan disruptive action, (2) form an alliance with outsiders, and (3) manipulate the scheduling of negotiations.

Disruptive Action.   One way to encourage settlement is to increase the costs of not reaching a negotiated agreement. In one instance, a group of unionized food-service workers negotiating with a restaurant rounded up supporters, had them enter the restaurant just prior to lunch, and had each person order a cup of coffee and drink it leisurely. When regular customers came to lunch, they found every seat occupied (Jacobs, 1951). In another case, people dissatisfied with automobiles they purchased from a certain dealer had their cars painted with large, bright yellow lemons and signs bearing the dealer's name, and then drove them around town in an effort to embarrass the dealer into making a settlement. Public picketing of a business, boycotting a product or company, and locking negotiators in a room until they reach agreement are all forms of disruptive action that increase the costs to negotiators for not settling and thereby bring them back to the bargaining table. Such tactics can work, but they may also produce anger and escalation of the conflict.

Alliance with Outsiders.   Another way to increase the costs of delay or terminating negotiations is to involve other parties in the process who can somehow influence the outcome. In many business transactions, a private party may profess that, if negotiations with a merchant are unsuccessful, he or she will go to the Better Business Bureau and protest the merchant's actions. Individuals who are dissatisfied with the practices and policies of businesses or government agencies form task forces, political action groups, and protest organizations to bring greater collective pressure on the target. For example, professional schools within universities often enhance their negotiation with higher management on budget matters by citing required compliance with external accreditation standards to substantiate their budget requests.

Schedule Manipulation.   The negotiation scheduling process can often put one party at a considerable disadvantage. Businesspeople going overseas to negotiate with customers or suppliers often find that negotiations are scheduled to begin immediately after their arrival, when they are still suffering from the fatigue of travel and jet lag. Alternatively, a host party can use delay tactics to squeeze negotiations into the last remaining minutes of a session in order to extract concessions from the visiting party (Cohen, 1980). Automobile dealers will probably negotiate differently with the customer a half hour before quitting time on a Saturday night than at the beginning of the workday on Monday. Industrial buyers have a much more difficult negotiation when they have a short lead time because their plants may have to sit idle if they cannot secure a new contract for raw materials in time.

The opportunities to increase or alter the timing of negotiation vary widely from field to field. In some industries it is possible to stockpile raw materials at relatively low cost or to buy in large bulk lots; in other industries, however, it is essential that materials arrive at regular intervals because they have a short shelf life (as many manufacturing firms move to just-in-time inventory procedures, this becomes increasingly true). Thus, the opportunity to vary the scheduling of negotiations differs across industries. There are far fewer opportunities for an individual to create costly delays when negotiating a home purchase than when negotiating a huge bulk order of raw materials. Nonetheless, the tactic of increasing costs by manipulating deadlines and time pressures is an option that can both enhance your own position and protect you from the other party's actions (Camerer and Loewenstein, 1993; Stuhlmacher, Gillespie, and Champagne, 1998).

POSITIONS TAKEN DURING NEGOTIATION

Effective distributive bargainers need to understand the process of taking a position during bargaining (the opening offer or opening stance) and the role of making concessions during the negotiation process (see Tutzauer, 1992). At the beginning of negotiations, each party takes a position. Typically, one party will then change his or her position in response to information from the other party or in response to the other party's behavior. The other party's position will also typically change during bargaining. Changes in position are usually accompanied by new information concerning the other's intentions, the value of outcomes, and likely zones for settlement. Negotiation is iterative. It provides an opportunity for both sides to communicate information about their positions that may lead to changes in those positions.

Opening Offer

When negotiations begin, the negotiator is faced with a perplexing problem. What should the opening offer be? Will the offer be seen as too low or too high by the other and therefore contemptuously rejected? An offer seen as modest by the other party could perhaps have been higher, either to leave more room to maneuver or to achieve a higher eventual settlement. Should the opening offer be somewhat closer to the resistance point, suggesting a more cooperative stance? These questions become less perplexing as the negotiator learns more about the other party's limits and planned strategy. While knowledge about the other party helps negotiators set their opening offers, it does not tell them exactly what to do. The fundamental question is whether the opening offer should be exaggerated or modest. Studies indicate that negotiators who make exaggerated opening offers get higher settlements than do those who make low or modest opening offers (Brodt, 1994; Chertkoff and Conley, 1967; Donohue, 1981; Hinton, Hamner, and Pohlan, 1974; Komorita and Brenner, 1968; Liebert, Smith, and Hill, 1968; Pruitt and Syna, 1985; Ritov, 1996; Weingart, Thompson, Bazerman, and Carroll, 1990).

There are at least two reasons that an exaggerated opening offer is advantageous (see Pruitt, 1981, and Tutzauer, 1991, for further discussion of these points). First, it gives the negotiator room for movement and therefore allows him or her time to learn about the other party's priorities. Second, an exaggerated opening offer acts as a metamessage and may create, in the other party's mind, the impression that (1) there is a long way to go before a reasonable settlement will be achieved, (2) more concessions than originally intended may have to be made to bridge the difference between the two opening positions, and (3) that the other may have been wrong in estimating their resistance point (Putnam and Jones, 1982; Yukl, 1974). Two disadvantages of an exaggerated opening offer are (1) that it may be summarily rejected by the other party, and (2) that it communicates an attitude of toughness that may be harmful to long-term relationships. The more exaggerated the offer, the greater the likelihood that it will be summarily rejected by the other side. Therefore, negotiators who make exaggerated opening offers should also have viable alternatives that they can employ if the opposing negotiator refuses to deal with them.

Opening Stance

A second decision to be made at the outset of distributive bargaining concerns the stance or attitude to adopt during the negotiation. Will you be competitive (fighting to get the best on every point) or moderate (willing to make concessions and compromises)? Some negotiators take a belligerent stance, attacking the positions, offers, and even the character of the other party. In response, the other party may mirror the initial stance, meeting belligerence with belligerence. Even if the other party does not directly counter a belligerent stance, he or she is unlikely to respond in a warm and open manner. Some negotiators adopt a position of moderateness and understanding, seeming to say, "Let's be reasonable people who can solve this problem to our mutual satisfaction." Even if the attitude is not mirrored, the other's response is likely to be constrained by such a moderate opening stance.

To communicate effectively, a negotiator should try to send a consistent message through both opening offer and stance (Eyuboglu and Buja, 1993). A reasonable bargaining position is usually coupled with a friendly stance, and an exaggerated bargaining position is usually coupled with a tougher, more competitive stance. When the messages sent by the opening offer and stance are in conflict, the other party will find them confusing to interpret and answer. (Timing also plays a part—see Box 3.3; communication in negotiation is discussed in more detail in Chapter 5.)

Initial Concessions

An opening offer is usually met with a counteroffer, and these two offers define the initial bargaining range. Sometimes the other party will not counter offer but will simply state that the first offer (or set of demands) is unacceptable and ask the opener to come back with a more reasonable set of proposals. In any event, after the first round of offers, the next question is, what movement or concessions are to be made? You can choose to make none, hold firm and insist on the original position, or you can make some concessions. Note that it is not an option to escalate one's opening offer, that is, to set an offer further away from the other party's target point than the first. This would be uniformly met with disapproval from the other party. If concessions are to be made, the next question is, how large should they be? It is important to note that the first concession conveys a message, frequently a symbolic one, to the other party about how you will proceed.

Opening offers, opening stances, and initial concessions are elements at the beginning of negotiations that parties can use to communicate how they intend to negotiate. An exaggerated original offer, a determined opening stance, and a very small opening

---

BOX 3.3
The Power of the First Move

In 1997, Mississippi was one of 40 states that initiated legal action against tobacco companies to recover money they spent on health care problems associated with smoking. In July of that year, Mississippi announced that it had reached a settlement with the four largest tobacco companies, guaranteeing that the state would receive $3.6 billion over 25 years and $136 million per year thereafter.

The settlement was a personal battle for Mississippi attorney general Michael Moore, who single-handedly began an effort in 1994 to recoup his state's losses from tobacco-related illness. Over the next three years, he convinced 39 other states and Puerto Rico to join Mississippi in the suit. Their efforts led to a national-level settlement that banned billboard advertising and also forced tobacco companies to include stronger warning labels on cigarettes.

Moore parlayed his efforts into the first successful settlement with the tobacco companies, guaranteeing payment even before federal action was taken. By acting first, he ensured that Mississippi would receive adequate compensation for its losses.

SOURCE: Adapted from M. Geyelin, "Mississippi Becomes First State to Settle Suit against Big Tobacco Companies," *The Wall Street Journal,* July 7, 1997.

---

concession signal a position of firmness; a moderate opening offer, a reasonable, cooperative opening stance, and a generous initial concession communicate a basic stance of flexibility. By taking a firm position, you attempt to capture most of the bargaining range for yourself so that you maximize your final outcome or you preserve maximum maneuvering room for later in the negotiation. Firmness also creates a climate in which the other party may decide that concessions are so meager that he or she might as well capitulate and settle quickly rather than drag things out. Paradoxically, firmness may actually shorten negotiations (see Ghosh, 1996). There is also the very real possibility, however, that firmness will be reciprocated by the other. One or both parties may become either intransigent or disgusted and withdraw completely.

There are several good reasons for adopting a flexible position (Olekalns, Smith, and Walsh, 1996). First, when taking different stances throughout a negotiation, you can learn about the other party's outcome values and perceived possibilities by observing how he or she responds to your proposals. You may want to establish a cooperative rather than a combative relationship, hoping to get a better agreement. In addition, flexibility keeps the negotiations going; the more flexible you seem, the more the other party will believe that a settlement is possible.

Role of Concessions

Concessions are central to negotiation. Without them, in fact, negotiations would not exist. If one side is not prepared to make concessions, the other side must capitulate or the negotiations will deadlock.

People enter negotiations expecting concessions. Good distributive bargainers will not begin negotiations with an opening offer too close to their own resistance point, but rather will ensure that there is enough room in the bargaining range to make some concessions. It appears that people will generally accept the first or second offer that is better than their target point (see Rapoport, Erev, and Zwick, 1995), so negotiators should try to identify the other party's target point accurately and avoid conceding too quickly to that point.

Negotiators also generally resent a take-it-or-leave-it approach; an offer that may have been accepted had it emerged as a result of concession making may be rejected when it is thrown on the table and presented as a *fait accompli*. This latter approach, called Boulwarism,[1] has been illustrated many times in labor relations. In the past, some management leaders objectively analyzed what they could afford to give in their upcoming contract talks and made their initial offer at the point they intended for their final offer (i.e., they set the same opening offer, target point, and resistance point). They then insisted there were no concessions to be made because the initial offer was fair and reasonable based on their own analysis. Unions bitterly fought these positions and continued to resent them years after the companies abandoned this bargaining strategy (Northrup, 1964; Selekman, Selekman, and Fuller, 1958).

There is ample data to show that parties feel better about a settlement when the negotiation involved a progression of concessions than when it didn't (Baranowski and Summers, 1972; Crumbaugh and Evans, 1967; Deutsch, 1958; Gruder and Duslak, 1973). Rubin and Brown (1975) suggest that bargainers want to believe they are capable of shaping the other's behavior, of causing the other to choose as he or she does (pp. 277–78).

Because concession making indicates an acknowledgment of the other party and a movement toward the other's position, it implies a recognition of that position and its legitimacy. The intangible factors of status and recognition of the right to a position may be as important as the tangible issues themselves. Concession making also exposes the concession maker to some risk. If the other party does not reciprocate, the concession maker may appear to be weak. Thus, not reciprocating a concession may send a powerful message about firmness and leaves the concession maker open to feeling that his or her esteem has been damaged or reputation diminished.

A reciprocal concession cannot be haphazard. If one party has made a major concession on a significant point, it is expected that the return offer will be on the same item or one of similar weight and somewhat comparable magnitude. To make an additional concession when none has been received (or when the other party's concession was inadequate) can imply weakness and can squander valuable maneuvering room. After receiving an inadequate concession, you as a negotiator may explicitly state what you expect before offering further concessions: "That is not sufficient; you will have to give up X before I consider offering any further concessions."

---

[1] The term *Boulwarism* is named after the chief labor negotiator for the General Electric Company in the 1950s. Rather than let the union present its contract demands first, the company placed a single "fair" offer on the table and refused to negotiate further. The National Labor Relations Board eventually ruled against G.E. by stating that this practice was unfair because management did not engage in "good faith bargaining."

To encourage further concessions from the other side, negotiators sometimes link their concessions to a prior concession made by the other. They may say, "Since you have reduced your demand on X, I am willing to concede on Y." A powerful form of concession making involves wrapping a concession in a package, sometimes described as logrolling (see Pruitt, 1981). For example, "If you will give A and B, I will give C and D." Packaging concessions also leads to better outcomes for a negotiator than making concessions singly on individual issues (Froman and Cohen, 1970; Neale and Bazerman, 1991; Pruitt, 1981). This tactic is discussed as *logrolling* in Chapter 4.

Pattern of Concession Making

The pattern of concessions a negotiator makes contains valuable information, but it is not always easy to interpret. When successive concessions get smaller, the most obvious message is that the concession maker's position is getting firmer and that the resistance point is being approached. This generalization needs to be tempered, however, by pointing out that a small concession late in negotiations may also indicate that there is little room left to move. When the opening offer is exaggerated, the negotiator has considerable room available for packaging new offers, making it relatively easy to give fairly substantial concessions. When the offer or counteroffer has moved closer to a negotiator's hoped-for settlement point, giving a concession the same size as the initial one may take a negotiator past the resistance point. Suppose a negotiator makes a first offer $100 below the other's target price; an initial concession of $10 would reduce the maneuvering room by 10 percent. When negotiations get to within $10 of the other's target price, a concession of $1 gives up 10 percent of the remaining maneuvering room. A negotiator cannot always communicate such mechanical ratios in giving or interpreting concessions, but this example illustrates how the receiver might construe the meaning of concession size, depending on where it occurs in the negotiating sequence.

The pattern of concession making is also important. Consider the pattern of concessions made by two negotiators, Sandra and Linda, shown in Figure 3.4. Assume that the negotiators are discussing the unit price of a shipment of computer parts, and that each is dealing with a different client. Linda makes three concessions, each worth $4 per unit, for a total of $12. In contrast, Sandra makes four concessions, worth $4, $3, $2, and $1 per unit, for a total of $10. Both Linda and Sandra tell their counterparts that they have conceded about all that they can. Sandra is more likely to be believed when she makes this assertion because she has signaled through the pattern of her concession making that there is not much left to concede. When Linda claims to have little left to concede, her counterpart is less likely to believe her because the pattern of Linda's concessions (three concessions worth the same amount) suggests that there is plenty left to concede, even though Linda has actually conceded more than Sandra (see Yukl, 1974). Note that we have not considered the words spoken by Linda and Sandra as these concessions were made. Behaviors are interpreted by the other party when we negotiate; it is important to signal to the other party with both our actions and our words that the concessions are almost over.

FIGURE 3.4   Pattern of Concession Making for Two Negotiators

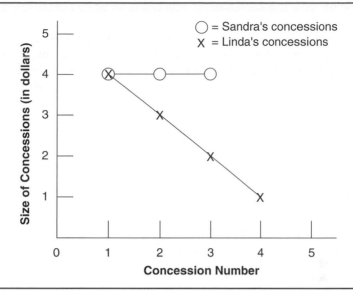

In multi-issue negotiations, skilled negotiators will also suggest different forms of a potential settlement that are worth about the same to them. They recognize that not all issues are worth the same amount to both parties. For example, a negotiator in a purchasing agreement may be interested solely in the total revenue of a package and not care whether it is paid in full within one month without interest or over six months with a financing fee at current interest rates. The length of the repayment period may, however, be critical to the other party who has a cash flow problem; that party may be willing to pay the financing fee for the right to spread the payments over six months. In fact, different combinations of principal, interest rate, and payback period may have the same value for one party but quite a different value for the other. After trying out different proposals that are worth about the same to them, skilled distributive negotiators will frequently save a final small concession for near the end of the negotiation to sweeten the deal.

Final Offer

Eventually a negotiator wants to convey the message that there is no further room for movement—that the present offer is the final one. A good negotiator will say, "This is all I can do" or "This is as far as I can go." Sometimes, however, it is clear that a simple statement will not suffice; an alternative is to use concessions to convey the point. A negotiator might simply let the absence of any further concessions convey the message in spite of urging from the other party. The other party may not recognize at first that the last offer was the final one and might volunteer a further concession to get the other to respond. Finding that no further concession results, the other party may feel betrayed and perceive that the pattern of concession–counterconcession was violated. The resulting bitterness may further complicate negotiations.

One-way negotiators may convey the message that an offer is the last one is to make the last concession substantial. This implies that the negotiator is throwing in the remainder of the negotiating range. The final offer has to be large enough to be dramatic yet not so large that it creates the suspicion that the negotiator has been holding back and that there is more available on other issues in the bargaining mix (Walton and McKersie, 1965). A concession may also be personalized to the other party ("I went to my boss and got a special deal just for you"), which signals that this is the last concession the negotiator will make.

COMMITMENT

A key concept in creating a bargaining position is that of *commitment.* One definition of commitment is the taking of a bargaining position with some explicit or implicit pledge regarding the future course of action (Walton and McKersie, 1965, p. 82). An example would be a sports agent who, during negotiation, says to the general manager of a professional sports team, "If we do not get the salary we want, my player will sit out next year." Such an act identifies the negotiator's bargaining position and a pledge of future action if that position is not reached. The purpose of a commitment is to remove ambiguity about the actor's intended course of action. By making a commitment, a negotiator signals his or her intention to take this course of action, make this decision, or pursue this objective—the negotiator says, "If you pursue your goals as well, we are likely to come into direct conflict; either one of us will win or neither of us will achieve our goals." Commitments also reduce the other party's options; they are designed to constrain the other party to a reduced portfolio of choices.

A commitment is often interpreted by the other party as a threat—if the other doesn't comply or give in, some set of negative consequences will occur. Some commitments can be threats, but others are simply statements of intended action that leave the responsibility for avoiding mutual disaster in the hands of the other party. A nation that publicly states that it is going to invade another country and that war can be averted only if no other nation tries to stop the action is making a bold and dramatic commitment. Commitments can also involve future promises, such as, "If we get this salary increase, we'll agree to have all other points arbitrated as you request."

Because of their nature, commitments are statements that usually require a follow-through in action. A negotiator who threatens consequences (e.g., the player will sit out next year), subsequently fails to get what he or she wanted with the threat, and then does not enact the consequences (e.g., the player reports to training camp) is not going to be believed in the future. In addition, a person will likely suffer a loss to self-image after not following through on a publicly made commitment. Hence, once a negotiator makes a commitment, there is strong motivation to hold to it. Because the other party probably will understand this, a commitment, once accepted, will often have a powerful effect on what the other party believes to be possible (Pruitt, 1981).

Tactical Considerations in Using Commitments

Like many tools, commitments are two-edged. They may be used to gain the advantages described above, but they may also fix a negotiator to a particular position or point. Commitments exchange flexibility for certainty of action, but they create difficulties if you want to move to a new position. For example, suppose that after committing yourself to a course of action, you find additional information indicating that a different position is desirable, such as later statements showing that an earlier estimate of the other party's resistance point was inaccurate and that there is actually a negative negotiating range. It may be desirable or even necessary to shift positions after making a commitment. For these reasons, when you make commitments you should also make contingency plans that allow you to get out of them if you have to. For the original commitment to be effective the contingency plans must be secret. For example, the player's agent might have planned to retire shortly after the expected completion of negotiations. By advancing retirement, the agent can thereby cancel the commitment and leave a new negotiator unencumbered. A purchaser of a house may be able to back away from a commitment to buy by discovering the hitherto unnoticed cracks in the plaster in the living room or being unable to obtain financing from the bank. (In Box 3.4, see examples of how to avoid premature commitments in salary negotiations.)

Commitments may be useful to you as a negotiator, but you will find it advantageous to keep the other party from becoming committed. Further, if the other party should take a committed position, it is to your advantage to keep open one or more ways for the other party to get out of the commitment. The following sections examine these tactical issues in more detail.

Establishing a Commitment

Given that strong, passionate statements—some of which are pure bluff—are made during negotiation, how does a negotiator establish that a statement is to be understood as a commitment?

A commitment statement has three properties: a high degree of *finality,* a high degree of *specificity,* and a clear statement of *consequences* (Walton and McKersie, 1965). A buyer could say, "We are going to get a volume discount, or there will be trouble." This statement is far less powerful than "We must have a 10 percent volume discount in the next contract, or we will sign with an alternative supplier next month." The latter statement communicates finality (how and when the volume discount must be granted), specificity (how much of a volume discount is expected), and a clear statement of consequences (exactly what will happen if the discount is not given). It is far stronger than the first statement and much more difficult to get released from. Several ways to create a commitment are discussed below.

Public Pronouncement.   A commitment statement increases in potency when more people know about it. The sports agent's statement about sitting out the season would have a different impact if given during a television sportscast than if given only at the bargaining table. Some parties in negotiations have called press conferences or

BOX 3.4
Salary Negotiation Tips

Myron Liebschutz, writing in *The Wall Street Journal,* offers these tips for success when job applicants must negotiate a salary package with a prospective employer:

- Delay discussion of compensation until after you have been offered the job.
- After the employer presents the offer and quotes the salary range, remain silent for about 30 seconds. By remaining quiet, you invite the other person to mention a higher figure or talk about flexibility. Then negotiations can begin.
- Don't comment on the salary offer immediately. Instead, clarify some other aspect of the job's responsibilities and reaffirm where and how you believe you can benefit the organization.
- Then say that the offer is a bit on the conservative side, though the position is still very attractive. Say you would like to think it over and talk again the next day.
- Don't discuss benefits before salary. Get agreement on salary first, then negotiate the fringe benefits.
- Be aware of over-negotiating. Asking for too much, even if you get it, may cause you to be viewed with resentment and can hinder you in future salary reviews.
- Whatever the offer, do not accept it on the spot. Express interest, but again ask for a day to think it over. The job won't go away, and the employer may be able to come up with a better offer given some additional time to get approval.
- If the company cannot meet your annual salary requirements, look for other options such as a one-time, up-front bonus, extended vacation, or specific monetary rewards for performance goals.

Typically, there is little room for negotiation when you are applying for a low-level job, when the company is highly bureaucratic, or when the labor supply exceeds demand. There are more opportunities to negotiate when you are applying for a new or high-level, high-profile position, and when you possess multiple or unique skills.

SOURCE: Adapted from Myron Liebschutz, "Negotiating the Best Deal Requires a Poker Strategy," *The Wall Street Journal,* June 8, 1997, p. B1.

placed ads in newspapers or other publications stating what they want and what will or will not happen if they don't get it. In each of these situations, the wider the audience, the less likely it is that the commitment will be changed. The effect of the broader social context on negotiations is discussed further in Chapter 8.

Linking with an Outside Base.   Another way to strengthen a commitment is to link up with one or more allies. Employees who are dissatisfied with management can form a committee to express their concerns. Industry associations may coalesce to set standards for a product. A variation of this process occurs when negotiators create conditions that make it more difficult for them to break a commitment they have made. For example, by encouraging dedicated colonists to settle on the West Bank near Jerusalem, the Israeli government made it more difficult for Israel to concede this land to the Palestinians, a point the Israelis initially wanted to reinforce.

Increase the Prominence of Demands.   Many things can be done to increase the prominence of commitment statements. If most offers and concessions have been made orally, then writing out a statement may draw attention to the commitment. If prior statements have been written, then using a different size typeface or a different color paper will draw attention to the new one. Repetition is one of the most powerful vehicles for making a statement prominent. Using different communication channels to convey a commitment hammers a point home—for example, telling the other party of a commitment; then handing over a written statement; then reading aloud the statement; then circulating the commitment to others.

Reinforce the Threat or Promise.   When making a threat, there is the danger of going too far—stating a point so strongly that you look weak or foolish rather than threatening. Statements like "If I don't get a concession on this point, I'll see that you don't stay in business another day!" are more likely to be greeted with annoyance or dismissal than with concern or compliance. Long, detailed statements that are highly exaggerated undermine credibility. In contrast, simple, direct statements of demands, conditions, and consequences are more effective.

Several things can be done to reinforce the implicit or explicit threat in a commitment. One is to review similar circumstances and their consequences; another is to make obvious preparations to carry out the threat. Facing the prospect of a strike, companies build up their inventories and move cots and food into their factories; unions build strike funds and give advice to their members about how to get by with less income should there be a strike. Another route is to create and carry out minor threats in advance, thereby leading the other party to believe that major threats will be fulfilled. For example, a negotiator could say, "If the progress of these negotiations does not speed up, I am not going to return to the negotiation table after lunch," and then do just that.

Finally, research on threats in negotiation (see de Dreu, 1995; Shapiro and Bies, 1994) suggests that negotiators who make threats are perceived as more powerful than negotiators who do not make threats. This perception of greater power does not appear to translate into higher negotiation outcomes for threat users, however (de Dreu, 1995; Shapiro and Bies, 1994). In fact, threat users are also perceived as less cooperative, and their outcomes in integrative situations seem to be lower than those of negotiators who do not use threats (Shapiro and Bies, 1994). (Integrative negotiations will be discussed in greater detail in Chapter 4.)

Preventing the Other Party from Committing Prematurely

All the advantages of a committed position work against a negotiator when the other party becomes committed. Therefore, a general strategy is to try to keep the other from becoming committed. People commonly take committed positions when they become angry or feel pushed to the limit; these commitments are often unplanned and can work to the disadvantage of both parties. Consequently, negotiators should pay careful attention to the other party's level of irritation, anger, and impatience.

Good, sound, deliberate commitments take time to establish, for the reasons already discussed. One way to prevent the other party from establishing a committed position is to deny him or her the necessary time. In a real estate deal with an option about to run out, a seller may use up the time by being unavailable or requiring extensive checking of deeds and boundaries, thereby denying time to a potential buyer to make a case (if, say, another buyer who would pay more had entered into negotiations). Another approach to keep the other party from taking a committed position is to ignore or downplay the threat by not acknowledging the other's commitment, or even by making a joke about it. A negotiator might lightheartedly say, "You don't really mean that," or "I know you can't be serious about really going through with that," or simply move negotiations along as though the commitment statement was not heard or understood. If the negotiator can pretend not to hear the other party's statement or not to consider it significant, the statement can be ignored at a later point without incurring the consequences that would have ensued had it been taken seriously. Although the other side can still carry out the threat, the belief that it must be carried out (that control of the situation has been given up) may be reduced.

There are times, however, when it is to a negotiator's advantage for the other party to become committed. When the other party takes a position on an issue relatively early in a negotiation, it may be very much to a negotiator's advantage to pin down that position so it will not be changed as the negotiation on other issues progresses. A negotiator may handle this situation in one of two ways: by pointing out the significance of a commitment when it is made, or by taking notes and keeping track of the other's statements. An employee might be very upset about the way a particular problem was handled but might also say that she will never get upset enough about it to resign. The manager might focus on this point at the time it is made or refer to it later when the employee is even more upset. Both actions are designed to keep the employee on the job in spite of her anger.

Finding Ways to Abandon a Committed Position

Frequently negotiators want to get the other party out of a committed position, and many times that party will also want a way out. How can this be done? We suggest four avenues for escaping commitments.

Plan a Way Out.   One method has already been noted: When establishing a commitment, a negotiator should simultaneously plan a private way out. The negotiator may also reword a commitment to indicate that the conditions under which it applied have changed. Sometimes information provided by the other party during negotiations can permit a negotiator to say, "Given what I've learned from you during this discussion, I see I am going to have to rethink my earlier position." The same could be done for the other party. A negotiator, wanting to make it possible for the other to abandon a committed position and yet not lose credibility, might say, "Given what I've told you about the facts of the situation [or given this new information], maybe I can help you see that your earlier position no longer holds." Needless to say, the last thing a negotiator wants to do is to embarrass the other party or make judgmental statements about the shift in position; rather, the other party should be given every opportunity to retreat with dignity and without losing face.

Let It Die Silently.   A second way to abandon a commitment is to let the matter die silently. After a lapse of time, a negotiator can make a new proposal in the area of the commitment without mentioning the earlier one. A variation on this process is to make a tentative step in a direction previously excluded by the other's commitment. For example, an employee who has said that he would never accept a certain job assignment may be asked to consider the benefits to his career of a "temporary" placement in that job. If the other party, in response to either of these variations, indicates through silence or verbal comment a willingness to let things move in that direction, the negotiation should simply be allowed to progress.

Restate the Commitment.   A third route is to restate the commitment in more general terms. The party that wants to abandon a commitment will make a new proposal, changing some of the details to be more in line with his or her current needs, while ostensibly still living with the general principles of the earlier wording. For example, the purchasing agent who demanded a 10 percent volume discount may rephrase this statement later to say simply that a significant volume discount is needed. The other party can then explore what level this "significant" discount could be.

Minimize the Damage.   Finally, if the other party backs off from a committed position, it is important to minimize any possible damage to his or her self-esteem or to constituent relationships. One strategy to use in this instance is to make a public attribution about the other party's move to some noble or higher outside cause. Diplomats can withdraw from a committed position because of their deep concern for peace and humankind. A buyer or seller can back off from a point during a real estate transaction to support the economic well-being of the community. Managers can leave a committed position for the good of the company.

A committed position is a powerful tool in negotiation; it is also a rigid tool and must therefore be used with care. As with any other tool, we must be as alert to ways of denying it to the other party as we are to ways we can use it for ourselves. Unfortunately, far more commitments are made as a result of anger and the desire to stop making concessions than as a result of clearly thought-out tactical planning. In either case, the essential property of a committed position is to arrange the consequences of an action so that at some point it is no longer an item of discussion or can only be negotiated at grave risk to one or both parties. The events or consequences become inevitable unless stopped at serious risk to one or both sides. The committed position has to be believable, and what has to be believed is that nothing can be done to change the conditions—if X happens, Y is inevitable. Convincing the other party that fate is sealed on the matter at hand is a demanding task and requires preparation, time, and skill. Consequently, getting out of a committed position is not easy, but the process is made simpler by planning a secret means of escape at the time the commitment is being established. Many of the steps a negotiator can use to get out of a commitment can also be used to help the other party get out of a committed position or, even better, to keep him or her from establishing one in the first place.

CLOSING THE DEAL

After negotiating for a period of time, learning about the other party's needs, positions, and perhaps resistance point, the next challenge for a negotiator is to close the agreement. There are several tactics available to negotiators for closing a deal (see Cellich, 1997; Girard, 1989); choosing the best tactic for a given negotiation is as much a matter of art as science.

Provide Alternatives.   Rather than making a single final offer, negotiators can provide two or three alternative packages for the other party that are more or less equivalent in value. People like to have choices, and providing a counterpart with alternative packages can be a very effective technique for closing a negotiation. This technique can also be used when a task force cannot decide on which recommendation to make to upper management. If in fact there are two distinct, defensible possible solutions, then the task force can forward both with a description of the costs and benefits of each.

Assume the Close.   Salespeople use an assume-the-close technique frequently. After having a general discussion about the needs and positions of the buyer, often the seller will take out a large order form and start to complete it. The seller usually begins by asking for the buyer's name and address before moving on to any potentially contentious issues (e.g., price, model). When using this technique, negotiators do not ask the other party if he or she would like to make a purchase. Rather, they act as if the decision to purchase something has already been made so they might as well start to get the paperwork out of the way (see Girard, 1989).

Split the Difference.   Splitting the difference is perhaps the most popular closing tactic. The negotiator using this tactic will typically give a brief summary of the negotiation ("We've both spent a lot of time, made many concessions, etc.") and then suggest that, because things are so close, "why don't we just split the difference?" While this can be an effective closing tactic, it does presume that the parties started with fair opening offers. A negotiator who uses an exaggerated opening offer and then suggests a split-the-difference close is using a hardball tactic (see below).

Exploding Offers.   An exploding offer contains an extremely tight deadline in order to pressure the other party to agree quickly. For example, a person who has interviewed for a job may be offered a very attractive salary and benefits package, but also be told that the offer will expire in 24 hours. The purpose of the exploding offer is to convince the other party to accept the settlement and to stop considering alternatives. This is particularly effective in situations where the party receiving the exploding offer is still in the process of developing alternatives that may or may not turn out to be viable (such as the job candidate who is still interviewing with other firms). People can feel quite uncomfortable about receiving exploding offers, however, because they feel as if they're under unfair pressure. Exploding offers appear to work best for organizations that have the resources to make an exceptionally attractive offer early in a negotiation in order to prevent the other party from continuing to search for a potentially superior offer.

Sweeteners.   Another closing tactic is to save a special concession for the close. The other negotiator is told, "I'll give you X if you agree to the deal." For instance, when selling a house the owner could agree to include the previously excluded curtains, appliances, or light fixtures to close the deal. To use this tactic effectively, however, negotiators need to include the sweetener in their negotiation plans or they may concede too much during the close.

HARDBALL TACTICS

Many popular books of negotiation discuss using hardball negotiation tactics to beat the other party (see Aaronson, 1989; Brooks and Odiorne, 1984; Cohen, 1980; Levinson, Smith, and Wilson, 1999; Schatzski, 1981). Such tactics are designed to pressure targeted parties to do things they would not otherwise do, and their presence usually disguises the user's adherence to a decidedly distributive bargaining approach. It is not clear exactly how often or how well these tactics work, but they work best against poorly prepared negotiators. They also can backfire. Many people find hardball tactics offensive and are motivated for revenge when such tactics are used against them. Many negotiators consider these tactics out-of-bounds for any negotiation situation (see Chapter 7 for a discussion of negotiation ethics). We do not recommend the use of any of the following techniques. In fact, it has been our experience that these tactics do more harm than good in negotiations. They are much more difficult to enact than they are to read about, and each tactic involves risk for the person using it, including harm to reputation, lost deals, negative publicity, and the other party's revenge. But it is important that negotiators understand hardball tactics and how they work so that they can recognize and understand them if they are the targeted recipients.

Dealing with Typical Hardball Tactics

The negotiator dealing with a party who uses hardball tactics has many choices about how to respond. A good strategic response to these tactics requires that the negotiator identify the tactic quickly and understand what it is and how it works. Most of the tactics are designed either to enhance the appearance of the bargaining position of the person using the tactic or to detract from the appearance of the options available to the other party. How best to respond to a tactic depends on your goals and the broader context of the negotiation (who are you negotiating with; what are your alternatives?). No one response will work in all situations. We now discuss four main options that negotiators have for responding to typical hardball tactics (see Fisher, Ury, and Patton, 1991; Ury, 1991 for an extended discussion of these points; more generally see Adler, Rosen, and Silverstein, 1996).

Ignore Them.   Although ignoring a hardball tactic may appear to be a weak response, it can in fact be very powerful. It takes a lot of energy to use some of the hardball tactics described below, and while the other side is using energy to play these games, you can be using your energy to work on satisfying your needs. Not responding to a threat is often the best way of dealing with it. Pretend you didn't hear it. Change the subject and get the other party involved in a new topic. Call a break and, upon returning, switch topics. All these options can deflate the effects of a threat and allow you to press on with your agenda while the other party is trying to decide what trick to use next.

Discuss Them.   Fisher, Ury, and Patton (1991; also see Ury, 1991) suggest that a good way to deal with hardball tactics is to discuss them—that is, indicate to the other party that you know what they are doing and that you even know what the tactic is (e.g., good cop/bad cop, which we discuss below). Then offer to negotiate the negotiation process (how you are to conduct the negotiations) before continuing on to the substance of the talks. Propose a shift to less aggressive methods of negotiating. Explicitly acknowledge that the other party is a tough negotiator and that you can be tough too. Then suggest that you both change to more productive methods that can allow you both to gain. Fisher, Ury, and Patton suggest that negotiators separate the people from the problem and then be hard on the problem, soft on the people. It doesn't hurt to remind the other negotiator of this from time to time during the negotiation.

Respond in Kind.   It is always possible to respond to a hardball tactic with one of your own in turn. Although this response can frequently result in chaos and hard feelings, it is not an option that should be dismissed out of hand. Once the smoke clears, both parties will realize that they are skilled in the use of hardball tactics and may recognize that it is time to try something different. Responding in kind may be most useful when dealing with another party who is testing your resolve or as a response to exaggerated positions taken in negotiations. A participant in a negotiation seminar told one of the authors the following story about bargaining for a carpet in a northern African country:

> I knew that the value of the carpet was about $2,000 because I had been looking at carpets throughout my trip. I found the carpet that I wanted and made sure not to appear too interested. I discussed some other carpets with the vendor before moving on to the carpet that I really wanted. When I asked him the price of this carpet, he replied $9,000. I replied that I would give him *negative* $5,000. We bargained for a while and I bought the carpet for $2,000.

The purchaser in this negotiation clearly responded to a hardball tactic with one of his own. When asked if he felt comfortable with his opening bid, he responded:

> Sure. Why not? The seller knew the value of the carpet was about $2,000. If anything, he seemed to respect me when I bargained this way. If I had opened with a positive number I would have ended up having to pay more than the carpet was worth. And I really wanted the carpet.

Co-Opt the Other Party.   Another way to deal with negotiators who are known to use aggressive hardball tactics is to try to befriend them before they use the tactics on you. This approach is built on the theory that it is much more difficult to attack a friend than an enemy. If you can stress what you have in common with the other party and find another element upon which to place the blame (the system, foreign competition), you may then be able to sidetrack the other party and thereby prevent the use of any hardball tactics.

Typical Hardball Tactics

We will now discuss some of the more frequently described hardball tactics and their weaknesses.

Good Cop/Bad Cop.   The good cop/bad cop tactic is named after a police interrogation technique in which two officers (one kind, the other tough) take turns questioning a suspect; it can frequently be seen in episodes of popular television series such as *Law and Order,* and *NYPD Blue.* The use of this tactic in negotiations typically goes as follows: The first interrogator (bad cop) presents a tough opening position, punctuated with threats, obnoxious behavior, and intransigence. The interrogator then leaves the room to make an important telephone call or to cool off—frequently at the partner's suggestion. While out of the room, the other interrogator (good cop) tries to reach a quick agreement before the bad cop returns and makes life difficult for everyone. A more subtle form of this tactic is to assign the bad cop the role of speaking only when the negotiations are headed in a direction that the team does not want; as long as things are going well, the good cop does the talking. Although the good cop/bad cop tactic can be somewhat transparent, it often leads to concessions and negotiated agreements (Hilty and Carnevale, 1993).

There are many weaknesses to this tactic. As mentioned above, it is relatively transparent, especially with repeated use. It can be countered by openly describing what the negotiators are doing. A humorously delivered statement like "You two aren't playing the old good cop/bad cop game with me, are you?" will go a long way to deflating this tactic even if both of the other parties deny it self-righteously. The good cop/bad cop tactic is also much harder to use than it is to read about; it typically alienates the targeted party and frequently requires negotiators to direct much more energy toward making the tactic work smoothly than toward accomplishing the negotiation goals. Negotiators using this tactic can become so involved with their gaming and acting that they fail to concentrate on obtaining their negotiation goals.

Lowball/Highball.   Negotiators using the lowball (highball) tactic start with a ridiculously low (or high) opening offer that they know they will never achieve. The theory is that the extreme offer will cause the other party to reevaluate his or her own opening offer and move closer to the resistance point. The risk of using this tactic is that the other party will think negotiating is a waste of time and will therefore halt the process. Even if the other party continues to negotiate after receiving a lowball (highball) offer, however, it takes a very skilled negotiator to be able to justify the extreme opening offer and to finesse the negotiation back to a point where the other side will be willing to make a major concession toward the outrageous bid.

The best way to deal with a lowball (highball) tactic is not to make a counteroffer. The reason is that this tactic works in the split second between hearing the other party's

opening offer and the delivery of your first offer. If you give in to the natural tendency to change your opening offer because it would be embarrassing to start negotiations so far apart, or because the other party's extreme opening makes you rethink where the bargaining zone may lie, then you have fallen victim to this tactic. When that happens, you have been "anchored" by the other party's extreme first offer. Good preparation for the negotiation is a critical defense against this tactic. Proper planning will help you know the general range for the value of the item under discussion and allow you to respond verbally with one of several different strategies: (1) insisting that the other party start with a reasonable opening offer and refusing to negotiate further until he or she does; (2) stating your understanding of the general market value of the item being discussed, supporting it with facts and figures, and by doing so, demonstrating to the other party that you won't be tricked; (3) threatening to leave the negotiation, either briefly or for good, to demonstrate dissatisfaction with the other party for using this tactic; and (4) responding with an extreme counteroffer to send a clear message you won't be anchored by an extreme offer from the other party.

Bogey.   Negotiators using the bogey tactic pretend that an issue of little or no importance to them is quite important. Later in the negotiation this issue can then be traded for major concessions on issues that are actually important to them. This tactic is most effective when negotiators identify an issue that is quite important to the other side but of little value to themselves. For example, a seller may have a product in the warehouse ready for delivery. When negotiating with a purchasing agent, however, the seller may ask for large concessions to process a rush order for the client. The seller can reduce the size of the concession demanded for the rush order in exchange for concessions on other issues, such as the price or the size of the order. Another example of a bogey is to argue as if you wanted a particular work assignment or project (when in fact you don't prefer it) and then, in exchange for large concessions from the other party, accept the assignment you actually preferred (but had pretended not to).

This tactic is fundamentally deceptive, and as such can be a difficult tactic to enact. Typically, the other party will negotiate in good faith and take you seriously when you are trying to make a case for the issue that you want to bogey. This can lead to a very unusual situation, one in which both negotiators may be arguing against their true wishes (the other party is asking for large concessions on other issues to give you the bogey issue that you really don't want, and you are spending time evaluating offers and making arguments for an issue that you know you do not want). It can also be very difficult to change gracefully and accept an offer in completely the opposite direction. If this maneuver cannot be done, however, then you may end up accepting a suboptimal deal—the bogey may be something you do not really want, and perhaps the other party doesn't either.

Recent research by O'Connor and Carnevale (1997) suggests that bogeys occur more often by omission than commission. They suggest that negotiators who wish to use the bogey should "get the other person to state his or her preferences on all the issues first and look for common value" (p. 513). This presumes that the other person will state the preferences in the correct direction, which is not always true—negotiators may deliberately misstate their true preferences to try to set up a bogey. O'Connor and Carnevale do suggest that the tactic may be harmful to relationships, however, if the other party reacts strongly to being misled. We explore ethical issues involved in the use of this and other deceptive tactics in Chapter 7.

Although the bogey is a difficult tactic to defend against, being well prepared for the negotiation will make you less susceptible to it. When the other party takes a position completely counter to what you expected, you may suspect that a bogey tactic is being used. Probing with questions about why the other party wants a particular outcome may help you reduce the effectiveness of a bogey. Finally, you should be very cautious about sudden reversals in positions taken by the other party, especially late in a negotiation. This may be a sign that the bogey tactic has been in use. Again, questioning the other party carefully about why the reverse position is suddenly acceptable and not conceding too much after the other party completely reverses a position may significantly reduce the effectiveness of the bogey.

The Nibble.   Negotiators using the nibble tactic ask for a proportionally small concession (for instance, 1 to 2 percent of the total profit of the deal) on an item that hasn't been discussed previously in order to close the deal. Herb Cohen (1980) describes the nibble as follows: After trying many different suits in a clothing store, tell the clerk that you will take a given suit if a tie is included for free. The tie is the nibble. Cohen claims that he usually gets the tie. In a business context, the tactic occurs like this: after a considerable amount of time has been spent in negotiation, when an agreement is close, one party asks to include a clause that hasn't been discussed previously and that will cost the other party a proportionally small amount. This amount is too small to lose the deal over, but large enough to upset the other party. This is the major weakness with the nibble tactic—many people feel that the party using the nibble did not bargain in good faith (as part of a fair negotiation process, all items to be discussed during the negotiation should be placed on the agenda early). Even if the party claims to be very embarrassed about forgetting this item until now, the party who has been nibbled will not feel good about the process and will often seek revenge in future negotiations.

According to Landon (1997), there are two good ways to combat the nibble. First, respond to each nibble with the question "What else do you want?" This should continue until the other party indicates that all issues are in the open; then both parties can discuss all of the issues simultaneously. Second, have your own nibbles prepared to offer in exchange. When the other party suggests a nibble on one issue, you can respond with your own nibble on another.

Chicken.   The chicken tactic is named after the 1950s challenge, portrayed in the James Dean movie *Rebel Without a Cause,* of two people driving cars at each other or toward a cliff until one person swerves to avoid disaster. The person who swerves is labeled a chicken, and the other person is treated like a hero. Negotiators who use this tactic combine a large bluff with a threatened action to force the other party to chicken out and give them what they want. In labor–management negotiations, management may tell the union representatives that if they do not agree to the current contract offer the company will close the factory and go out of business (or move to another state or country). Clearly this is a high-stakes gamble. On the one hand, management must be willing to follow through on the threat—if the union calls their bluff and they do not follow through, they will not be believed in the future. On the other hand, how can the union take the risk and call the bluff? If management is telling the truth, the company may actually close the factory and move elsewhere.

The weakness of the chicken tactic is that negotiation is turned into a serious game in which one or both parties find it difficult to distinguish reality from postured negotiation positions. Will the other party really follow through on his or her threats? We frequently cannot know for sure, because the circumstances must be grave in order for this tactic to be believable; but it is precisely when circumstances are grave that a negotiator may be most tempted to use this tactic. For example, President William Clinton of the United States and President Saddam Hussein of Iraq played chicken over the United Nations inspection program, designed to inspect Iraq for suspected biological and chemical warfare factories (see Box 3.5). Occasionally, this high-stakes game resulted in actual missile attacks on Iraq.

The chicken tactic is very difficult for a negotiator to defend against. To the extent that the commitment can be downplayed, reworded, or ignored, however, it could lose its power. Perhaps the riskiest response is to introduce one's own chicken tactic. At that point neither party may be willing to back down in order not to lose face. Preparation and a thorough understanding of the situations of both parties are absolutely essential for trying to identify where reality ends and the chicken tactic begins. Use of external experts to verify information or to help to reframe the situation is another option.

BOX 3.5
Playing Chicken in International Relations

It was 4 P.M. on Saturday, November 14, 1998, in Iraq and still morning back in the United States. Prekash Shah, the United Nations special envoy to Iraq, was in his office in Baghdad waiting for a letter from Tariq Aziz, Iraq's deputy prime minister. Two weeks earlier, Iraqi leader Saddam Hussein had stopped the United Nations weapons inspection program in Iraq. The United States had previously announced that if the inspectors could not continue their inspections without restrictions, the United States would resume bombing of suspected chemical and biological warfare factories in the country. Kofi Annan, Secretary General of the United Nations, had been conducting diplomatic initiatives to stop the attack and resume the inspections.

What Shah did not know was that B-52 bombers with air-launched cruise missiles were already in the air headed toward Iraq, while U.S. warships with sea-launched cruise missiles were on standby in the Persian Gulf. Once the missiles were launched, they could not be recalled.

Shah received word that a letter from the Iraqis had been received, but it needed to be translated from Arabic to English. Shah, sensing that time was of the essence, sent his deputy minister to drive across town (a twenty-minute trip) to pick up the letter at 4:45 P.M. But rather than drive it back, he had his deputy call him and read it over the phone. Shah rapidly took notes and had his secretary standing by to type them up and fax them to Annan in New York. Just before 6 P.M., Shah talked to Annan on the phone; a few minutes later, he called a news conference to announce that Iraq would permit the inspections to continue. The attack was called off minutes before the missiles were fired.

Wamidh Nadhimi, a political scientist at Baghdad University, was quoted as saying that "He (Saddam) behaved very quickly, as though he knew a strike was coming, as though he knew he was racing against time. It was irrational escalation on the part of the Iraqis and an even more irrational escalation on the American side."

Four weeks later, when Iraq again refused to permit the inspectors free access to suspected sites, the United States initiated a major four-day bombing attack on military targets.

SOURCE: B. Demick, "Saddam, United States Play High-Stakes Chicken," *Columbus Dispatch,* November 16, 1998, pp. 1A, 2A.

Intimidation.   Many tactics can be gathered under the general label of intimidation. What they have in common is that they all attempt to force the other party to agree by means of an emotional ploy, usually anger or fear. For example, the other party may deliberately *use anger* to indicate the seriousness of a position. One of the authors of this book had the following experience:

> Once while I was negotiating with a car salesman he lost his temper, destroyed his written notes, told me to sit down and listen to him, and went on to explain in a loud voice that this was the best deal in the city and if I did not accept it that evening I should not bother returning to that dealership and wasting his time. I didn't buy the car and I haven't been back, nor I suspect have any of the students in my negotiation classes, to whom I relate this story

every year! I suspect that the salesman was trying to intimidate me into agreeing to the deal and realized that if I went elsewhere his deal would not look as good. What he didn't realize was that I had asked the accountant at the dealership for further information about the deal and had found that he had lied about the value of a trade-in; he really lost his cool when I exposed the lie!

Another form of intimidation includes increasing the *appearance of legitimacy*. When there is a high degree of legitimacy, there are set policies or procedures for resolving disputes. Negotiators who do not have such policies or procedures available may try to invent them and then impose them on the other negotiator while making the process appear legitimate. For example, policies that are written in manuals or preprinted official forms and agreements are less likely to be questioned than those that are delivered verbally (Cohen, 1980); long and detailed loan contracts used by banks for consumer loans are seldom read completely (Hendon and Hendon, 1990). The greater the appearance of legitimacy, the less likely the other party will be to question the process being followed or the contract terms being proposed.

Finally, *guilt* can also be used as a form of intimidation. Negotiators can question the other party's integrity or the other's lack of trust in them. The purpose of this tactic is to place the other party on the defensive so that they are dealing with the issues of guilt or trust rather than discussing the substance of the negotiation.

To deal with intimidation tactics, negotiators have several options. Intimidation tactics are designed to make the intimidator feel more powerful than the other party and to lead people to make concessions for emotional rather than objective reasons (e.g., a new fact). When making any concession, it is important for negotiators to understand why they are doing so. If one starts to feel threatened, assumes that the other party is more powerful (when objectively he or she is not), or simply accepts the legitimacy of the other negotiator's "company policy," then it is likely that intimidation is having an effect on the negotiations.

If the other negotiator is acting aggressively, then discussing the negotiation process with him or her is a good option. You can explain that your policy is to bargain in a fair and respectful manner, and that you expect to be treated the same way in return. Another good option is to ignore the other party's attempts to intimidate you, because intimidation can only have an effect on you if you let it. While this may sound too simple to be realistic, you can think about why some people you know are intimidated by authority figures and others are not—the reason often lies in the perceiver, not the authority figure.

Another effective strategy for dealing with intimidation is to use a team to negotiate with the other party. Teams have at least two advantages over individuals in acting against intimidation. First, people are not always intimidated by the same things; while you may be intimidated by one particular negotiator, it is quite possible that other members on your team won't be. In an ongoing negotiation in China when he was younger, one of the authors of this book found that his Chinese counterparts were frequently changing their team members so that older and older members appeared in each subsequent negotiation session. He decided to bring a senior colleague of his own to subsequent meetings in order not to be intimidated by the age and experience of the counterparts on the other negotiating team. The second advantage of using a team is that the team members can discuss the tactics of the other negotiators and provide mutual support if the intimidation starts to become increasingly uncomfortable.

Aggressive Behavior.   A group of tactics similar to those described under intimidation include various ways of being aggressive in pushing your position or attacking the other person's position. Aggressive tactics include a relentless push for further concessions ("You can do better than that"), asking for the best offer early in negotiations ("Let's not waste any time. What is the most that you will pay?"), and asking the other party to explain and justify his or her proposals item by item or line by line ("What is your cost breakdown for each item?"). The negotiator using these techniques is signaling a hard-nosed, intransigent position and trying to force the other side to make many concessions to reach an agreement.

When faced with another party's aggressive behavior tactics an excellent response is to halt the negotiations in order to discuss the negotiation process itself. Negotiators can explain that they will reach a decision based on needs and interests, not aggressive behavior. Again, having a team to counter aggressive tactics from the other party can be helpful for the same reasons discussed above under intimidation tactics. Good preparation and understanding both one's own and the other party's needs and interests together make responding to aggressive tactics easier because the merits to both parties of reaching an agreement can be highlighted.

Snow Job.   The snow job tactic occurs when negotiators overwhelm the other party with so much information that he or she has trouble determining which facts are real or important, and which are included merely as distractions. Governments use this tactic frequently when releasing information publicly. Rather than answering a question briefly, they release thousands of pages of documents from hearings and transcripts that may or may not contain the information that the other party is seeking. Another example of the snow job is the use of highly technical language to hide a simple answer to a question asked by a nonexpert. Any group of professionals—such as engineers, lawyers, or computer network administrators—can use this tactic to overwhelm ("snow") the other party with so much information that they cannot make sense of the answer. Frequently, in order not to be embarrassed by asking "obvious" questions, the recipient of the snow job will simply nod his or her head and passively agree with the other party's analysis or statements.

Negotiators trying to counter a snow job tactic can choose one of several alternative responses. First, they should not be afraid to ask questions until they receive an answer they understand. Second, if the matter under discussion is in fact highly technical, then negotiators may suggest that technical experts get together to discuss the technical issues. Finally, negotiators should listen carefully to the other party and identify consistent and inconsistent information. Probing for further information after identifying a piece of inconsistent information can work to undermine the effectiveness of the snow job. For example, if one piece of incorrect or inconsistent information is discovered in the complete snow job package, the negotiator can question the accuracy of the whole presentation (e.g., "Since point X was incorrect, how can I be sure that the rest is accurate?"). Again, strong preparation is very important for defending effectively against the snow job tactic.

CHAPTER SUMMARY

In this chapter we examined the basic structure of competitive or distributive bargaining situations and some of the strategies and tactics used in distributive bargaining. Distributive bargaining begins with setting your own opening, target, and resistance points. You soon learn the other party's starting points and find out his or her target points directly or through inference. Usually you won't know the resistance points, the points beyond which a party will not go, until late in negotiation because the other party often carefully conceals them. All points are important, but the resistance points are the most critical. The spread between the parties' resistance points defines the bargaining range. If positive, it defines the area of negotiation within which a settlement is likely to occur, with each party working to obtain as much of the bargaining range as possible. If negative, successful negotiation may be impossible.

It is rare that a negotiation includes only one item; more typically, there is a set of items, referred to as a bargaining mix. Each item in a bargaining mix can have opening, target, and resistance points. The bargaining mix may provide opportunities for bundling issues together, trading off across issues, or displaying mutually concessionary behavior.

Examining the structure of distributive bargaining reveals many options for a negotiator to achieve a successful resolution, most of which fall within two broad efforts: to influence the other party's belief about what is possible and to learn as much as possible about the other party's position, particularly about the resistance points. The negotiator's basic goal is to reach a final settlement as close to the other party's resistance point as possible. To achieve this goal, negotiators work to gather information about the opposition and its positions; to convince members of the other party to change their minds about their ability to achieve their own goals; and to promote their own objectives as desirable, necessary, or even inevitable.

Distributive bargaining is basically a conflict situation, wherein parties seek their own advantage—in part through concealing information, attempting to mislead, or using manipulative actions. All these tactics can easily escalate interaction from calm discussion to bitter hostility. Yet negotiation is the attempt to resolve a conflict without force, without fighting. Further, to be successful, both parties to the negotiation must feel at the end that the outcome was the best that they could achieve and that it is worth accepting and supporting. Hence, effective distributive bargaining is a process that requires careful planning, strong execution, and constant monitoring of the other party's reactions.

CHAPTER 4

Strategy and Tactics
of Integrative Negotiation

INTRODUCTION

Even well-intentioned negotiators often make one or more of three mistakes: failing to negotiate when they should, negotiating when they should not, or negotiating when they should but picking an inappropriate strategy. As suggested by the dual concerns model described in Chapter 1, being committed to the other party's interests as well as to one's own makes problem solving the strategy of choice. In many negotiations, there need not be winners and losers; all parties can gain. Rather than assume that all conflicts are win-lose events, negotiators can look for win-win solutions—and usually they will find them. Integrative negotiation—variously known as cooperative, collaborative, win-win, mutual gains, or problem solving—is the focus of this chapter.

In distributive bargaining, the goals of the parties are initially at odds—or at least appear that way to some or all of the parties. Central to such conflict is the belief that there is a limited, controlled amount of key resources to be distributed—a "fixed-pie" situation. Both parties may want to be the winner; both may want more than half of what is available. For example, both management (on behalf of the stockholders) and labor (on behalf of the rank and file) may believe that they deserve the larger share of the company's profits. Both may want to win on the same dimension, such as the financial package or control of certain policy decisions. In these situations, their goals are mutually exclusive and hence lead to conflict.

In contrast, in integrative negotiation the goals of the parties are not mutually exclusive. If one side achieves its goals, the other is not necessarily precluded from achieving its goals. One party's gain is not necessarily at the other party's expense. The fundamental structure of an integrative negotiation situation is such that it allows both sides to achieve their objectives (Walton and McKersie, 1965). Although the conflict may appear initially to be win-lose to the parties, discussion and mutual exploration will usually suggest win-win alternatives. A description of the efforts and tactics by which negotiators discover these alternatives accounts for the major part of this chapter. Our descriptions will draw heavily on the writings of several authors who have studied the integrative process in great detail (Carnevale and Pruitt, 1992; Filley, 1975; Fisher, Ury, and Patton, 1991; Pruitt, 1981, 1983; Pruitt and Carnevale, 1993; Walton and McKersie, 1965). In addition, we will note recent research findings that have affirmed the validity of particular strategies and tactics.

What Makes Integrative Negotiation Different?

In Chapter 1, we listed elements common to all negotiations. For a negotiation to be characterized as integrative, negotiators must also:

- Focus on commonalties rather than differences.
- Attempt to address needs and interests, not positions.
- Commit to meeting the needs of all involved parties.
- Exchange information and ideas.
- Invent options for mutual gain.
- Use objective criteria for standards of performance.

These requisite behaviors and perspectives are the main components of the integrative process (see Box 4.1).

AN OVERVIEW OF THE INTEGRATIVE NEGOTIATION PROCESS

Past experience, biased perceptions, and the truly distributive aspects of bargaining often make it remarkable that integrative agreements occur at all. But they do, largely because negotiators work hard to overcome inhibiting factors and assertively search for common ground. Our presentation of the integrative process is analogous to much of the managerial advice on motivating others. Those wishing to achieve integrative results find that they must manage both the context and the process of the negotiation in order to gain the willing cooperation and commitment of all parties (e.g., Ury, 1991). The following processes tend to be central to achieving almost all integrative agreements.

Creating a Free Flow of Information

Ample research evidence indicates that effective information exchange promotes the development of good integrative solutions (Butler, 1999; Pruitt, 1981; Thompson, 1991). Researchers have shown that the failure to reach integrative agreements is often linked to the failure to exchange enough information to allow the parties to identify integrative options (Butler, 1999; Kemp and Smith, 1994). For the necessary exchange to occur, negotiators must be willing to reveal their true objectives and to listen to each other carefully. In short, negotiators must create the conditions for a free and open discussion of all related issues and concerns. Willingness to share information is not a characteristic of distributive bargaining situations, in which the parties distrust one another, conceal and manipulate information, and attempt to learn about the other for their own competitive advantage.

Creating a free flow of information may also require both parties to know and share their alternatives. A study by Pinkley (1995) involving a simulated salary negotiation indicated that when both parties were aware of each other's alternatives to a negotiated agreement, they made their resistance points less extreme, made better

---

BOX 4.1
Characteristics of the Interest-Based Negotiator

A successful interest-based negotiator models the following traits:

Honesty and integrity. Interest-based negotiating requires a certain level of trust between the parties. Actions that demonstrate interest in all players' concerns will help establish a trusting environment.

Abundance mentality. Those with an abundance mentality do not perceive a concession of monies, prestige, control, and so on, as something that makes their slice of the pie smaller, but merely as a way to enlarge the pie. A scarcity or zero-sum mentality says, "anything I give to you takes away from me." A negotiator with an abundance mentality knows that making concessions helps build stronger long-term relationships.

Maturity. In his book *Seven Habits of Highly Effective Leaders*, Stephen Covey refers to maturity as having the courage to stand up for your issues and values while being able to recognize that others' issues and values are just as valid.

Systems orientation. Systems thinkers will look at ways in which the entire system can be optimized, rather than focusing on suboptimizing components of the system.

Superior listening skills. Ninety percent of communication is not in one's words but in the whole context of the communication, including mode of expression, body language, and many other cues. Effective listening also requires that one avoid listening only from his or her frame of reference.

SOURCE: Chris Laubach, "Negotiating a Gain-Gain Agreement," *Healthcare Executive* (Jan/Feb 1997), p. 14.

---

negotiating trade-offs, and increased the size of the resource pie compared to when one or both were not aware of the alternatives. Pinkley expressed the importance of this result, saying that "it is the negotiator with the alternative who is responsible for expanding the pie, but both members of the dyad determine its distribution" (p. 409). Negotiators who did not reveal the availability of a good alternative received some benefits to themselves, but those who did share information about their alternatives received additional benefits.

Attempting to Understand the Other Negotiator's Real Needs and Objectives

As we noted earlier, negotiators differ in their values and preferences. What one side needs and wants may or may not be what the other side needs and wants. If you are to help satisfy another's needs, you must first understand them. Research has shown that one party's simply being aware of the possibility that the other's priorities are not the same as his or her own is sufficient to stimulate the parties to exchange more information, understand the nature of the negotiation better, and achieve higher joint profits (Kemp and Smith, 1994). Similarly, integrative agreements are facilitated when the parties exchanged information about their priorities for particular issues, but not necessarily about their positions on those issues (Olekalns, Smith, and Walsh, 1996). Hence, throughout the process of sharing information about preferences and priorities, the parties must make a true effort to understand what the other side really wants to achieve. Again, this is in contrast to distributive bargaining, where the negotiator either makes no effort to understand the other side's needs and objectives or does so only to challenge, undermine, or even deny the other party the opportunity to have those needs and objectives met. It should be noted that the communicative aspects of information flow and understanding, while critical to integrative negotiation, require that Kelley's (1966) dilemmas of trust and honesty be managed (see Chapter 1). Also, parties may differ in their ability to differentiate needs and interests from positions, as when one party knows and applies a truly integrative process while the other party is unskilled or naive about negotiations. In such situations, the more experienced party may come to assist the less experienced party in discovering his or her underlying needs and interests.

Emphasizing the Commonalities between the Parties and Minimizing the Differences

To sustain a free flow of information and an effort to understand the other's needs and objectives, negotiators may require a different outlook or frame of reference (see Chapter 2 for a discussion of framing). Individual goals may need to be redefined as best achievable through collaborative efforts directed toward a collective goal. Sometimes the collective goal is clear and obvious. For example, politicians in the same party may recognize that their petty squabbles must be put aside to ensure the party's victory at the polls. The saying "politics makes strange bedfellows" suggests that the quest for victory can unite political enemies. Similarly, managers who are quarreling over cutbacks in their individual department budgets may need to recognize that unless all departments sustain appropriate budget cuts, they will be unable to change an unprofitable firm into a profitable one. At other times, the collective goal is not so clear, nor so easy to keep in sight. For example, one of the authors worked as a consultant to a company that was closing down a major manufacturing plant while at the same time, opening several other plants in different parts of the country. The company was perfectly willing to transfer employees to new plants and let them take their seniority with them up to the time of the announced move; the union agreed to this arrangement. However, conflict developed over the transfer issue. Some employees were able to transfer immediately, whereas others—those who were needed to close and dismantle the old plant—could not. Because workers acquired seniority in the new plants based on the date they arrived, those who stayed to close the old plant would have comparatively less seniority once they arrived at the new plants. The union wanted everyone to go at the same time to avoid this inequity. Management adamantly maintained that this was unworkable. In the argument that resulted, both parties lost sight of the larger goal—to transfer all willing employees to the new plants with their seniority intact. Only by constantly stressing this larger goal were the parties able to maintain a focus on commonalities that eventually led to a solution; management allowed the workers to select their new jobs in advance and transferred their seniority to those jobs when the choice was made, not when the physical move actually occurred.

Searching for Solutions That Meet the Goals and Objectives of Both Sides

The success of integrative negotiation depends on a search for solutions that meet the objectives and needs of both (or all) sides. In this process, negotiators must be firm but flexible (Fisher, Ury, and Patton, 1991; Pruitt and Rubin, 1986)—firm about their primary interests and needs, but flexible about the manner in which these interests and needs are met. When the parties are used to taking a combative, competitive orientation toward each other, they are prone to be concerned only with their own objectives. In such a competitive interaction, a low level of concern for the other's objectives may drive one of two forms of behavior. The first is making sure that what the other obtains does not take away from one's own accomplishments. The second is attempting to block the other from obtaining his or her objectives because of a strong desire to win or to "defeat the opponent." In contrast, successful integrative negotiation requires each negotiator not only to define and pursue his or her own goals but also to be mindful of the other's goals and to search for solutions that satisfy both sides. Outcomes are measured by the degree to which they meet both negotiators' goals. They are not measured by determining whether one party is doing better than the other. If the objective of one party is simply to get more than the other, integrative negotiation is difficult at best; if both strive to get more than the other, integrative negotiation may be impossible.

In summary, integrative negotiation requires a process fundamentally different from that of distributive bargaining. Negotiators must attempt to probe below the surface of the other party's position to discover his or her underlying needs. They must create a free and open flow of information, and they must use their desire to satisfy both sides as the perspective from which to structure their dialogue. If negotiators do not have this perspective—if they approach the problem and their "opponent" in win-lose terms—integrative negotiation cannot occur.

KEY STEPS IN THE INTEGRATIVE NEGOTIATION PROCESS

There are four major steps in the integrative negotiation process: identify and define the problem, understand the problem and bring interests and needs to the surface, generate alternative solutions to the problem, and evaluate those alternatives and select among them.

Identify and Define the Problem

The problem identification step is often the most difficult one; this is even more challenging when several parties are involved. Consider the following example: In a large electronics plant, considerable difficulty with one of the subassemblies occurred in the final assembly department. Various pins and fittings that held the subassembly in place were getting bent and distorted. When this happened, the unit would be laid aside as a reject. At the end of the month, the rejects would be returned to be reworked, often arriving at the subassembly department just when workers there were under pressure to meet end-of-the-month schedules and were also low on parts. As a result, the reworking effort had to be done in a rush and on overtime. The extra cost of overtime did not fit into the standard cost allocation system. The manager of the subassembly department did not want the costs allocated to his overhead charge. The manager of the final assembly department insisted that he should not pay the additional cost; he argued that the subassembly department should bear the cost because its poor work originally caused the problem. The subassembly department manager countered that the parts were in good condition when they left his area and that it was the poor workmanship in the final assembly area that created the damage. The immediate costs were relatively small. What really concerned both parties was setting a long-term precedent for handling rejects and for paying the costs.

Eventually an integrative solution was reached. During any given month, the subassembly department had a number of short slack-time periods. Arrangements were made for the final assembly department to return damaged subassemblies in small batches during those slack periods. It also became clear that many people in the final assembly department did not fully understand the parts they were handling, which may have contributed to some of the damage. These people were then temporarily transferred to the subassembly department during assembly department slack periods to learn more about subassembly and to process some of the rush orders in that department. This example helps us identify a number of key aspects of the problem definition process (see Filley, 1975, and Shea, 1983, for fuller treatments of these points).

Define the Problem in a Way That Is Mutually Acceptable to Both Sides. Ideally, parties should enter the integrative negotiation process with few if any preconceptions about the solution and with open minds about each other's needs. As a problem is defined jointly, it should accurately reflect both parties' needs and priorities. Regrettably, this is not what we usually encounter. An understandable and widely held fear about integrative negotiation is that during the problem definition process, the other party is manipulating information to state the problem to his or her own advantage (see Chapter 2). For positive problem solving to occur, both parties must be committed to stating the problem in neutral terms. The problem statement must be mutually acceptable to both sides and not worded so that it lays blame or favors the preferences or priorities of one side over the other. The parties may be required to work the problem statement over several times until they agree on its wording. It is critical to note that problem definition is, and should be, separate from any leap to judgment that might be expected from parties impatient with careful integrative negotiation. It is critical, though, to define problems clearly at this stage, if only to accomplish an initial structure within which parties "agree to disagree," albeit on a common, distinct issue.

State the Problem with an Eye toward Practicality AND Comprehensiveness. The major focus of an integrative agreement is to solve the core problem(s). Anything which distracts from this focus should be removed or streamlined in order to ensure that this objective is achieved. As a result, one might argue that the problem statements should be as clear as possible. Yet if the problem is, indeed, complex and multifaceted, and the statement of the problem does not reflect that complexity, then efforts at problem solving will be incomplete. In fact, if the problem is complex, the parties may not even be able to agree on a statement of the problem. So the objective here should be to state the problem as succinctly as possible, while at the same time ensuring that the most important dimensions and elements are included in the definition. This approach is in stark contrast to the distributive bargaining process (see Chapter 3), in which the parties are encouraged to beef up their positions by bringing in a large number of secondary issues and concerns so they can trade these items off during the hard-bargaining phase. If there are several issues on the table in an integrative negotiation, the parties may want to clearly identify the link among them and decide whether they will be approached as separate problems (which may be packaged together later) or as one larger problem.

State the Problem as a Goal and Identify the Obstacles to Attaining This Goal.   The parties should define the problem as a specific goal to be attained (what we want to achieve) rather than as a solution process (how we are going to achieve it). They should then proceed to specify what obstacles must be overcome for the goal to be attained. For example, in the previous example, the goal might have been "to minimize the number of rejects." A clearer and more explicit definition would be "to cut the number of rejects in half." After specifying the goal, the parties would then specify what they need to know about how the product is made, how defects occur, what must be done to repair the defects, and so on.

One key issue here is whether the obstacles specified are amenable to corrective efforts on the parts of the negotiating parties. If the parties cannot address the obstacles effectively, given limited time or other resources, the obstacles then become boundary markers for the negotiation playing field. A clear understanding of which obstacles are addressable and which are not can be just as critical to realistic integrative negotiation as an explicit awareness of what is negotiable and what is not.

Depersonalize the Problem.   As we pointed out earlier, when parties are engaged in conflict, they tend to become evaluative and judgmental. They view their own actions, strategies, and preferences in a positive light and the other party's actions, strategies, and preferences in a negative light. Such evaluative judgments can get in the way of clear and dispassionate thinking. (See Chapter 12 for a discussion of depersonalizing the issues.) Saying "Your point of view is wrong and mine is right" inhibits the integrative negotiation process because you cannot attack the problem without attacking the person who owns the problem. In contrast, depersonalizing the definition of the problem—stating, for example, "We have different viewpoints on this problem"—allows both sides to approach the issue as a problem "out there" rather than as a problem that belongs to one side only.

Separate the Problem Definition from the Search for Solutions.   Finally, we will repeat the advice included in almost every discussion of problem solving: Don't jump to solutions until the problem is fully defined. In distributive bargaining, negotiators are encouraged to state the problem in terms of their preferred solution and to make concessions based on this statement. In contrast, parties attempting integrative negotiation should avoid stating solutions that favor one side or the other until they have fully defined the problem and examined as many alternative solutions as possible.

Instead of premature solutions, negotiators should develop standards by which potential solutions will be judged for goodness of fit. These standards can be assembled by asking interested parties questions such as the following:

- How will we know the problem has been solved?
- How would we know that our goal has been attained?
- How would a neutral third party know that our dispute has been settled?
- Is there any legitimate interest or position that remains unaddressed (or disenfranchised) by our outcome?

Developing standards in this way and using them as measures for evaluating alternatives will help negotiators avoid a single-minded, tunnel-vision approach and allow them to differentiate a particular favorite alternative from one that may be less favorable individually but that will accomplish a collaborative, integrative resolution.

Understand the Problem Fully—Identify Interests and Needs

Many writers on negotiation—most particularly, Roger Fisher, William Ury, and Bruce Patton in their popular book, *Getting to Yes* (1991)—have stressed that a key to achieving an integrative agreement is the ability of the parties to understand and satisfy each other's *interests*. Thus, we consider identifying interests an important second step in the integrative negotiation process. Interests are different from positions in that interests are the underlying concerns, needs, desires, or fears that motivate a negotiator to take a particular position. Fisher, Ury, and Patton argue that although negotiators may have difficulty satisfying each other's specific positions, an understanding of underlying interests may permit them to invent solutions that meet those interests. In this section, we will first define interests more fully and then discuss how understanding them may be critical to effective integrative negotiation.

An example reveals the essence of the difference between interests and positions:

> Consider the story of two men quarreling in a library. One wants the window open and the other wants it closed. They bicker back and forth about how much to leave it open: a crack, halfway, three-quarters of the way. No solution satisfied them both. Enter the librarian. She asks one why he wants the window open. "To get some fresh air." She asks the other why he wants it closed. "To avoid the draft." After thinking a minute, she opens wide a window in the next room, bringing in fresh air without a draft. (Fisher, Ury, and Patton, 1991, p. 40; originally told by Follett, 1940)

As Fisher, Ury, and Patton identify, this is a classic example of negotiating over positions and failing to understand underlying interests. The positions are "window open" and "window closed." If they continue to pursue positional bargaining, the set of possible outcomes can include only a victory for the one who wants the window open, a victory for the one who wants it shut, or some compromise in which neither gets what he wants. Note that a compromise here is more a form of lose-lose than win-win for these bargainers because one party believes that he won't get enough fresh air with the window partially open and the other believes that any opening is unsatisfactory. The librarian's questions transform the dispute by focusing on *why* each man wants the window open or closed: to get fresh air, to avoid a draft. Understanding these interests enables the librarian to invent a solution that meets the interests of both sides—a solution that was not at all apparent when the two men were arguing over their positions.

In this description, the key word is *why*—why they want what they want. When two parties begin negotiation, they usually expose their position or demands; and as we have pointed out, this position or these demands have emerged from a planning process in which the parties decided *what* they wanted and then specified opening bids, targets, and resistance points. In distributive bargaining, negotiators trade these points and positions back and forth, attempting to achieve a settlement as close to their targets as possible. However, in integrative negotiation, each negotiator needs to pursue the other party's thinking and logic to determine the factors that motivated him or her to arrive at those points. The presumption is that if both parties understand the motivating factors for the other, they may recognize possible compatibilities in interests that permit them to invent new options that both will endorse. Consider the following dialogue between a company recruiter and a job applicant over starting salary:

Recruiter:

What were you thinking about as a starting salary?

Applicant:

I would like $40,000.

Recruiter:

We can only offer $35,000.

Applicant:

That's not acceptable.

Thus far, the parties have only exposed their positions. They are $5,000 apart. Moreover, the applicant may be afraid to bargain positionally with the recruiter, whereas the recruiter may be afraid that the applicant—whom she very much wants to hire—will walk out. Now let us extend their dialogue to help them focus on interests.

Recruiter:

$40,000 is a problem for our company. Can you tell me why you decided you wanted $40,000?

Applicant:

Well, I have lots of education loans to pay off, and I will need to pay for a few more courses to finish my degree. I can't really afford to pay these bills and live comfortably for less than $40,000.

Recruiter:

Our company has a program to help new employees refinance their education loans. In addition, we also have a program to provide tuition assistance for new courses if the courses you need to take are related to your job. Would these programs help you with your problem?

Applicant:

Yes!

Bringing the applicant's interests—paying off education loans and future education costs—to the surface allows the recruiter to offer a financial package that meets the needs of both the company and the applicant. Similarly, the applicant might have asked why the company could pay only $35,000 and discovered that it was company policy not to offer more than this to any applicant with the same qualifications. However, the question might also have revealed that the company can pay performance bonuses and would be willing to review the salary after six months. Thus, the applicant may well make $40,000 by the end of the first year and so have his financial goal met.

Types of Interests.   Lax and Sebenius (1986) have suggested that several types of interests may be at stake in a negotiation and that each type may be intrinsic (the parties value it in and of itself) or instrumental (the parties value it because it helps them derive other outcomes in the future).

Substantive interests are the types of interests we have just been discussing; they are like the tangible issues we mentioned in Chapter 1. Substantive interests relate to the focal issues under negotiation—economic and financial issues such as price or rate, or the substance of a negotiation such as the division of resources. These interests may be intrinsic or instrumental or both; we may want something because it is intrinsically satisfying to us and/or we may want something because it helps us achieve a long-range goal. Thus, the job applicant may want $40,000 both because the salary affirms his intrinsic sense of personal worth in the marketplace and because it instrumentally contributes toward paying off his education loans.

Process interests are related to the way a dispute is settled. One party may pursue distributive bargaining because he enjoys the competitive game of wits that comes from nose-to-nose, hard-line bargaining. Another party may enjoy negotiating because she believes she has not been consulted in the past and wants to have some say in how a key problem is resolved. In the latter case, the negotiator may find the issues under discussion less important than the opportunity they allow for her to voice her opinions at the negotiating table. (See Chapter 5 of Sheppard, Lewicki, and Minton, 1992, for a more complete discussion of the role of "voice" in organizations.) Process interests can also be both intrinsic and instrumental. Thus in the voice example, having a say may be intrinsically important to a group—it allows them to affirm their legitimacy and worth, and highlights the key role they play in the organization; it can also be instrumentally important, in that if they are successful in gaining voice in this negotiation, they may be able to demonstrate that they should be invited back into the negotiation on other, related issues in the future.

Relationship interests indicate that one or both parties value their relationship with each other and do not want to take actions that will damage it. Intrinsic relationship interests exist when the parties value the relationship both for its existence and for the pleasure or fulfillment that sustaining it creates. Instrumental relationship interests exist when the parties derive positive benefits from the relationship and do not wish to endanger future benefits by souring it.

Finally, Lax and Sebenius (1986) point out that the parties may have *interests in principle.* Certain principles—concerning what is fair, what is right, what is acceptable, what is ethical, or what has been done in the past and should be done in the future—may be deeply held by the parties and serve as the dominant guides to their action. (These principles often involve the intangibles we described in Chapter 1.) Interests in principles can also be intrinsic (valued because of their inherent worth) or instrumental (valued because they can be applied to a variety of future situations and scenarios). Bringing their interests in principles to the surface will lead the parties to discuss explicitly the principles at stake and to invent solutions consistent with them. For example, suppose three students (who are also good friends) collaborate on an essay, enter it in a competition, and win a prize of $300. The issue is how to split the prize money. Obviously, one way to split it is for each to take $100. But two of the students contributed equally, and together they did 90 percent of the work, so if they split it based on what they each contributed, the two hardworking students would get $135 each and the third student would get $30. However, separately or together, they may also decide that it is not worth fighting over the workload, that they don't want to alienate their third friend, or that the difference in money is trivial—and so simply decide to split the prize into $100 parts after all. Only by discussing the interests at stake—principles about what is fair in this situation and about their relationship—can they arrive at a solution that divides the prize, minimizes animosity, and maintains their relationship.

Some Observations on Interests.   Based on the preceding discussion, we may make several observations about interests and types of interests:

1. There is almost always more than one type of interest in a dispute. Parties can have more than substantive interests about the issues. They can also care deeply about process, the relationship, or the principles at stake. Note that interests in principles effectively cut across substantive, procedural, and relationship interests as well, so that the categories are not necessarily exclusive.

2. Parties can have different types of interests at stake. One party may care deeply about the specific issues under discussion while the other cares about how the issues are resolved—questions of principle or process. Bringing these different interests to the surface may enable the parties to see that in fact they care about very different things, and thus to invent a solution that addresses the interests of both sides.

3. Interests often stem from deeply rooted human needs or values. Several authors have suggested that frameworks for understanding basic human needs and values are helpful for understanding interests. According to these frameworks, needs are hierarchical and satisfaction of the basic or lower order needs will be more important in negotiation than that of higher order needs. For example, Nierenberg (1976) proposed a need theory of negotiation based on Maslow's well-known

hierarchy of needs. In this hierarchy, basic physiological and safety (security) needs will take precedence over higher order needs such as recognition, respect, affirmation, and self-actualization. Similarly, Burton (1984) has suggested that the intensity of many international disputes reflects deep underlying needs for security, protection of ethnic and national identity, and other such fundamental needs.

4. Interests can change. Like positions on issues, interests can change over time. What was important to the parties last week—or even 20 minutes ago—may not be important now. Interaction between the parties can put some interests to rest, but it may raise others. Thus, the parties must continually be attentive to changes in their own interests and the interests of the other side. When one party begins to talk about things in a different way—when the language or emphasis changes—the other party may look for a change in interests.

5. Getting at interests. There are numerous ways to get at interests. Sometimes people are not even sure of their own interests. Negotiators should not only ask themselves "What do I want from this negotiation?" but also "Why do I want that?" "Why is that important to me?" "What will achieving that help me do?" and "What will happen if I don't achieve my objective?" Listening to your own inner voices—fears, aspirations, hopes, desires—is important in order to bring your own interests to the surface.

The same dialogue is essential in clarifying the other party's interests. Asking probing questions ("why" questions; e.g., see Chapter 5) and paying careful attention to the other party's language, emotions, and nonverbal behavior are essential keys to the process. You might also want to distinguish between intrinsic interests—which need to be satisfied as ends in themselves—and instrumental interests—which help one get other outcomes. In both cases, once these interests are understood, it may be possible to invent a variety of ways to address them. The result is a mutually satisfactory solution.

6. Getting at interests is not always easy or to one's best advantage. Critics of the "interests approach" to negotiation have often identified the difficulty of defining interests and taking them into consideration. Provis (1996) has noted that it is often not easy to define interests and that trying to focus on interests alone often oversimplifies or conceals the real dynamics of a conflict. Provis also notes that in some cases parties do not pursue their own best objective interests but instead focus on one or more subjective interests, which may mislead the other party. Thus, a car buyer may prefer a fast, flashy car (his subjective interest) even though his objective interest is to buy a safe, conservative one.

7. Finally, focusing on interests can be harmful to a group of negotiators whose consensus on a particular issue is built around a unified position rather than a more generalized set of interests. If a coalition is held together by a commitment to pursue a specific objective in negotiation, then encouraging the chief negotiator to discuss interests rather than to drive for the specific objective is clearly encouraging him or her to deviate from the coalition's purpose.

Generate Alternative Solutions

The search for alternatives is the creative phase of integrative negotiations. Once the parties have agreed on a common definition of the problem and understood each other's interests, they generate a variety of alternative solutions. The objective is to create a list of options or possible solutions to the problem; evaluating and selecting from among those options will be their task in the final phase.

A number of techniques have been suggested to help negotiators generate alternative solutions. These techniques fall into two general categories. The first requires the negotiators to redefine, recast, or reframe the problem (or problem set) so as to create win-win alternatives out of what earlier appeared to be a win-lose problem (see Box 4.2). The second takes the problem as given and creates a long list of options from which the parties can choose. In integrative negotiation over a complex problem, both types of techniques may be used and even intertwined.

Inventing Options: Generating Alternative Solutions by Redefining the Problem or Problem Set.   The techniques in this category call for the parties to define their underlying needs specifically and to develop alternatives to meet them. At least five different methods for achieving integrative agreements have been proposed (see Neale and Bazerman, 1991; Pruitt, 1981, 1983; Pruitt and Carnevale, 1993; Pruitt and Lewis, 1975). Each of these methods not only refocuses the issues under dispute, but also requires progressively more information about the other side's true needs; thus, solutions move from simpler, distributive to more complex (and comprehensive), integrative ones. Accordingly, they are presented in order of increasing "cost" and difficulty. We suggest that parties begin with the easiest and least costly ("expand the pie") and progress to the more costly approaches only in the event that the simpler remedies fail. Each approach will be illustrated by the example of a husband and wife attempting to decide where to spend their two-week vacation. The husband wants to go to the mountains for the entire two weeks, and the wife wants to go to the coast for the entire two weeks. A compromise solution—to spend a week at each place—is possible, but the husband and wife want to determine whether other solutions are possible as well.

Expand the Pie.   Many negotiations begin with a shortage of resources in which it is not possible for both sides to satisfy their interests or obtain their objectives under the current allocation. A simple solution is to add resources—expand the pie—in such a way that both sides can achieve their objectives. If the married couple could persuade their employers to give them four weeks for their vacation, they could go to the mountains and the beach for two weeks each. In expanding the pie, one party requires no information about the other party except her interests; it is a simple way to solve resource shortage problems. In addition, the approach assumes that simply enlarging the resources will solve the problem. Thus, having four weeks of vacation would be a very satisfactory solution if the husband and wife both liked the mountains and the beach but each simply wanted one or the other this particular year. However, expanding the pie would not be a satisfactory solution if their conflict were based on other

BOX 4.2
The Art of Win-Win Negotiations

Most people see negotiation as a game in which the gains of one come at the expense of another. Winning means getting six pieces from a 10-piece pie. But negotiation has the potential to be a win-win process by which both parties cooperate to create a bigger, better tasting pie. The basic principle of win-win negotiating is that there is always a bigger, better deal. Only after searching and finding that deal do they worry about how to share it. Some avenues to explore:

Taxes. It's safe to assume that the parties to a negotiation have different tax needs. Accountants might be able to point out some unseen opportunities (particularly in foreign transactions).

Payment terms. Some sellers need quick payment; others might prefer a deferred payment (for tax or other reasons). There are many win-win variations.

Specifications. A better deal may be possible if changes can be made to balance the buyer's end-use requirements against the seller's specific production capabilities.

Transportation. Transportation costs can often be reduced at no expense to either party. Perhaps the buyer's empty trucks will pass the seller's facility. Or maybe the seller has access to low bulk rates.

Delivery date or performance specifications. The reality is this: A buyer's delivery requirements never represent the seller's optimum production economics.

Quantity. One of the best win-win strategies I know is to close a spice gap by changing quantity.

Processes. In my experience, the surest path to finding a better way to do anything is to study the detailed production and paperwork processes.

Risk and contract type. All business involves risk. Incentives might be used to balance the seller's risk with potential for earning greater profit.

Like successful entrepreneurs everywhere, win-win negotiators find hidden opportunities in what each could do for the other. Win-win raises the stakes in a negotiation. It raises the level and content of the relationship between the bargainers. It also reduces the tensions inherent in bargaining. There are a few phrases that more quickly capture the attention of the other party than, "Let's find a better deal for both of us."

SOURCE: Chester L. Karrass, "The Art of Win-Win Negotiations," *Purchasing*, May 6, 1999, p. 28.

grounds—if, for example, the husband couldn't stand the beach or the wife wouldn't go to the mountains under any conditions. In addition, to the extent that the negotiation increases the costs of a person or organization not directly involved in the negotiation (e.g., the employers in this example), the solution may be integrative for the negotiators but parasitic to other stakeholders (Gillespie and Bazerman, 1997).

Logroll.   Successful logrolling requires the parties to establish (or find) more than one issue in conflict; the parties then agree to trade off among these issues so that one party achieves a highly preferred outcome on the first issue and the other person achieves a highly preferred outcome on the second issue. If the parties do in fact have different preferences on different issues and each party gets his or her most preferred outcome on a high-priority issue, then each should be happy with the overall agreement. Thus, suppose that the husband and wife disagree not only about where to take their vacation but also about the kind of accommodations. The husband prefers informal housekeeping cabins whereas the wife prefers a luxury hotel. If the wife decides that the formality of the accommodations is more important to her than the location, the couple may be able to agree on a luxury hotel in the mountains as a way to meet both their needs.

Logrolling is frequently done by trial and error—as the parties experiment with various packages of offers that will satisfy everyone involved. The parties must first establish which issues are at stake and then decide their individual priorities on these issues. If there are already at least two issues on the table, then any combination of two or more issues may be suitable for logrolling. If it appears initially that only one issue is at stake, the parties may need to engage in "unbundling" (Lax and Sebenius, 1986) or "unlinking" (Pruitt, 1981), which is the process of separating a single issue into two or more issues so that the logrolling may begin. Additional issues of concern may also be generated through the brainstorming processes described below.

Finally, logrolling may be effective when the parties can combine two issues, but not when the parties take turns in successive negotiations—that is, when one party gets what he wants this time, while the other gets what she wants next time. Research by Mannix, Tinsley, and Bazerman (1995) shows that when parties do not expect to negotiate with the other person in the future, they are less likely to employ logrolling over time and hence may reach a suboptimal agreement in the current negotiation.

Use Nonspecific Compensation.   A third way to generate alternatives is to allow one person to obtain his objectives and pay off the other person for accommodating his interests. The payoff may be unrelated to the substantive negotiation, but the party who receives it nevertheless views it as adequate for acceding to the other party's preferences. Such compensation is "nonspecific" in that it is not directly related to the substantive issues being discussed. In the vacation example, the wife could tell the husband that if he agrees to go to the coast, she will buy him a new camera or set of golf clubs. For nonspecific compensation to work, the person doing the compensating needs to know what is valuable to the other person and how seriously he is inconvenienced (i.e., how much compensation is needed to make him feel satisfied). The wife might need to test several different offers (types and amounts of compensation) to find out how much it will take to satisfy her husband. This discovery process can turn into a distributive bargaining situation itself, as the husband may choose to set very high demands as the price for going along to the beach while the wife tries to minimize the compensation she will pay.

Cut the Costs for Compliance.   Through cost cutting, one party achieves her objectives and the other's costs are minimized if he agrees to go along. In the vacation example, suppose that the husband really likes a quiet and peaceful vacation and dislikes the beach because of the crowds, whereas the wife really likes the beach because of all the activity. If peace and quiet is what the husband really wants, then he may be willing to go to the beach if the wife assures him that they will stay in a secluded place far away from the other resorts. Unlike nonspecific compensation, where the compensated party simply receives something for going along, cost cutting is specifically designed to minimize the other party's costs and suffering. The technique is thus more sophisticated than logrolling or nonspecific compensation because it requires a more intimate knowledge of the other party's real needs and preferences (the party's interests, what really matters to him, how his needs can be specifically met).

Find a Bridge Solution.   Finally, by "bridging," the parties are able to invent new options that meet their respective needs. Thus, if the husband reveals that he really wants to hunt and fish on his vacation, whereas the wife wants to swim, go shopping, and enjoy the nightlife, they may be able to discover a resort area that will allow both to have what they want. Successful bridging requires a fundamental reformulation of the problem such that the parties are no longer squabbling over their positions; instead, they are disclosing sufficient information to discover their interests and needs and then inventing options that will satisfy those needs (Butler, 1996). Bridging solutions do not always remedy all concerns; the wife may not get the salt sea air at the resort, and the husband may spend more money than he wanted to, but both have agreed that taking their vacation together is more desirable than taking it separately (i.e., they have committed themselves to interdependence) and have worked to invent a solution that meets their most important needs. If negotiators fundamentally commit themselves to a win-win negotiation, bridging solutions are likely to be highly satisfactory to both sides.

As we stated earlier, the successful pursuit of these five strategies requires a meaningful exchange of information between the parties. The parties must either volunteer information or ask each other questions that will generate sufficient information to reveal win-win options. Table 4.1 presents a series of refocusing questions (Pruitt and Carnevale, 1993; Pruitt and Rubin, 1986) that may reveal these possibilities.

Generating Alternative Solutions to the Problem as Given.   In addition to the techniques mentioned above, there are a number of other approaches to generating alternative solutions. These approaches can be used by the negotiators themselves or by a number of other parties (constituencies, audiences, bystanders, etc.). Several of these approaches are commonly used in small groups. Groups of people are frequently better problem solvers than single individuals, particularly because groups provide a wider number of perspectives and hence can invent a greater variety of ways to solve a given problem. However, groups also should adopt procedures for defining the problem, defining interests, and generating options lest the group process degenerate into a win-lose competition or a debating event.

Brainstorming.   In brainstorming, small groups of people work to generate as many possible solutions to the problem as they can. Someone records the solutions, without comment, as they are identified. Participants are urged to be spontaneous, even impractical, and not to censor anyone's ideas (including their own). Moreover, participants are required not to discuss or evaluate any solution as it is proposed, so they do not stop the free flow of new ideas. The success of brainstorming depends on the amount of intellectual stimulation that occurs as different ideas are tossed around. Therefore, the following rules should be observed:

TABLE 4.1   Refocusing Questions to Reveal Win-Win Options

Expanding the Pie

---

1. How can both parties get what they want?
2. Is there a resource shortage?
3. How can resources be expanded to meet the demands of both sides?

Logrolling

---

1. What issues are of higher and lower priority to me?
2. What issues are of higher and lower priority to the other?
3. Are there any issues of high priority to me that are of low priority for the other, and vice versa?
4. Can I "unbundle" an issue—that is, make one larger issue into two or more smaller ones that can then be logrolled?
5. What are things that would be inexpensive for me to give and valuable for the other to get that might be used in logrolling?

Nonspecific Compensation

---

1. What are the other party's goals and values?
2. What could I do that would make the other side happy and simultaneously allow me to get my way on the key issue?
3. What are things that would be inexpensive for me to give and valuable for the other to get that might be used as nonspecific compensation?

Cost Cutting

---

1. What risks and costs does my proposal create for the other?
2. What can I do to minimize the other's risks and costs so that he or she would be more willing to agree?

Bridging

---

1. What are the other's real underlying interests and needs?
2. What are my own real underlying interests and needs?
3. What are the higher and lower priorities for each of us in our underlying interests and needs?
4. Can we invent a solution that meets the relative priorities, underlying interests, and needs of both parties?

---

    1. *Avoid judging or evaluating solutions.* Criticism inhibits creative thinking. Creative solutions often come from ideas that initially seem wild and impractical. No idea should be evaluated or eliminated until the group is finished generating options.

    2. *Separate the people from the problem.* Group discussion and brainstorming processes are often constrained because the parties take ownership of preferred solutions and alternatives (Filley, 1975; Fisher, Ury, and Patton, 1991; Walton and McKersie, 1965). Since competitive negotiators assume an offensive posture toward the other party, they are unlikely to see the merits of a suggested alternative that comes from that party or appears to favor that party's position. It is often

not possible to attack the problem without attacking the person who owns it. Therefore, for effective problem solving to occur, negotiators must concentrate on depersonalizing the problem and treating all possible solutions as equally viable, regardless of who initiated them. For example, collectively listing suggestions on a blackboard or flip chart will help parties depersonalize any particular idea, and will allow them to pick the solution that best solves the problem without regard to which side originated it. Techniques for generating options that ensure anonymity may minimize the likelihood that interpersonal conflict will escalate.

3. *Be exhaustive in the brainstorming process.* Many times the best ideas come after a meeting is over or after a problem is solved. Sometimes this happens because the parties were not persistent enough. Research has shown that when brainstormers work at the process for a long time, the best ideas are most likely to surface during the latter part of the activity. As Shea (1983) notes, "Generating a large number of ideas apparently increases the probability of developing superior ideas. Ideas, when expressed, tend to trigger other ideas. And since ideas can be built one upon the other, those that develop later in a session are often superior to those without refinement or elaboration. What difference does it make if a lot of impractical ideas are recorded? They can be evaluated and dismissed rapidly in the next step of the win-win process. The important thing is to ensure that few, if any, usable ideas are lost" (p. 57).

4. *Ask outsiders.* Often people who know nothing about the history of the negotiation, or even about the issues, can suggest options and possibilities that have not been considered. Outsiders can provide additional input to the list of alternatives, or they can help orchestrate the process and keep the parties on track.

Nominal Groups.   In the nominal group technique (Delbecq and Van de Ven, 1971), negotiators must start with the problem as defined, then individually prepare a written list of possible solutions. Participants are encouraged to list as many solutions as they can. Then they meet in small groups and read their solutions aloud while a recorder writes them on flip charts or a blackboard. Particularly in a large group, this approach can generate a great number of options in a short time. All those working on the problem can then examine these solutions.

Surveys.   The disadvantage of nominal groups is that they do not solicit the ideas of those who are not present at the negotiation. In addition, the nominal group technique can be time-consuming. A different approach is to distribute a written questionnaire to a large number of people, stating the problem and asking them to list all the possible solutions they can imagine. This process can be conducted in a short time. The liability, however, is that the parties cannot benefit from seeing and hearing the other people's ideas, a key advantage of the nominal group technique.

Summary.   Our discussion of the two basic approaches to generating alternative solutions—generating options to the problem as given and generating options by redefining the problem—may give the impression that if bargainers simply invent enough different options, they will find a solution to solve their problem rather easily. Although identifying options sometimes leads to a solution, solutions are usually attained through hard work and pursuit of several related processes: information exchange, focusing on interests rather than positions, and firm flexibility (Fisher, Ury, and Patton, 1991; Pruitt, 1983). Information exchange will allow the parties to maximize the amount of information available. Focusing on interests will allow the parties to move beyond opening positions and demands to determine what the parties really want— what needs truly must be satisfied. Finally, firm flexibility will allow the parties to be firm with regard to what they want to achieve (i.e., interests) while remaining flexible on the means by which they achieve it. Firm flexibility recognizes that negotiators have one or two fundamental interests or principles, although a wide variety of positions, possible solutions, or secondary issues may get drawn into the negotiations. Thus, among the many viable alternatives that will satisfy a negotiator, the important ones directly address the bottom line or the top priorities. Negotiators need to be able to signal to the other side the positions on which they are firm and the positions on which they are willing to be flexible. Pruitt (1983) and Fisher, Ury, and Patton (1991) suggest several tactics to communicate firm flexibility to the other negotiator:

1. Use contentious (competitive) tactics to establish and defend basic interests rather than to demand a particular position or solution to the dispute. State what you want clearly.

2. Send signals of flexibility and concern about your willingness to address the other party's interests. Openly express concern for the other's welfare and "acknowledge their interests as part of the problem" (Fisher, Ury, and Patton, 1991, p. 55). In doing so, you communicate that you have your own interests at stake but are willing to try to address the other's as well.

3. Indicate a willingness to change your proposals if a way can be found to bridge the two parties' interests.

4. Demonstrate problem-solving capacity. For example, use experts on a negotiating team or bring them in as consultants based on their expertise at generating new ideas.

5. Maintain open communication channels. Do not eliminate opportunities to communicate and work together, if only to demonstrate continually that you are willing to work with the other party.

6. Reaffirm what is most important to you through the use of clear statements—for example, "I need to attain this; this is a must; this cannot be touched or changed." These statements communicate to the other party that a particular interest is fundamental to your position, but it does not necessarily mean that the other's interests can't be satisfied as well.

7. Reexamine any aspect of your interests that are clearly unacceptable to the other party and determine if they are still essential to your fundamental position. It is rare that negotiators will find that they truly disagree on basic interests.

8. Separate and isolate contentious tactics from problem-solving behavior to better manage the contentious behavior. This may be accomplished by clearly specifying a change in the negotiation process, by separating the two processes with a break or recess, or, in team negotiations, by having one party act contentiously and then having a second negotiator offer to engage in problem solving. This last approach, called "good cop/bad cop" or "black hat/white hat," is also frequently used as a

purely distributive bargaining tactic, as we discussed in Chapter 3. In this situation, however, separate the competitive from the collaborative elements of the process by changing the individuals who represent those positions.

Evaluation and Selection of Alternatives

The fourth stage in the integrative negotiation process is to evaluate the alternatives generated during the previous phase and to select the best ones to implement. When the problem is a reasonably simple one, the evaluation and selection steps may be effectively combined into a single step. For those new to or uncomfortable with the integrative process, though, we suggest a close adherence to a series of distinct steps: definitions and standards, alternatives, evaluation, and selection. Following these distinct steps is also a good idea for those confronted with complex problems or a large number of alternative options. Negotiators will need to weigh or rank-order each option against the criteria. If no option or set of options appears suitable and acceptable, this is a strong indication that the problem was not clearly defined (return to definitions), or that the standards developed earlier are not reasonable, relevant, and/or realistic (return to standards). Finally, the parties will be required to engage in some form of decision-making process, in which they debate the relative merits of each side's preferred options and come to agreement on the best options. The following guidelines should be used in evaluating options and reaching a consensus (Filley, 1975; Pruitt and Carnevale, 1993; Shea, 1983; Walton and McKersie, 1965).

Narrow the Range of Solution Options.   Examine the list of options generated and focus on those that are strongly supported by one or more negotiators. This approach is more positive than allowing people to focus on negative, unacceptable criteria and options. Solutions not strongly advocated by at least one negotiator should be eliminated.

Evaluate Solutions on the Basis of Quality, Acceptability, and Standards. Solutions should be judged on two major criteria: how good they are, and how acceptable they will be to those who have to implement them. These are the same two dimensions that research has revealed to be critical in effective participative decision making in organizations (Vroom and Yetton, 1973). Negotiators will evaluate the quality dimension by determining what is best, what is most rational, what is most logical. To the degree that parties can support their arguments with statements of hard fact, logical deduction, and appeals to rational criteria, their arguments will be more compelling in obtaining the support of others. Fisher, Ury, and Patton (1991) suggest that the parties appeal to *objective standards* for making decisions. This suggests that the parties are more likely to accept a solution they perceive as fair and equitable to all concerned than one that seems biased. Thus, the parties should search for precedents, arbitration decisions, or other objectively fair outcomes and processes that can be used as benchmarks for legitimizing the fairness of the current settlement. These criteria may be different from what the negotiators judge to be most rational or the best solution. Those evaluating the solution options may also have to be prepared to make trade-offs to ensure that the criteria of both quality and acceptability (fairness) are met.

Agree to the Criteria in Advance of Evaluating Options.   Ideally, negotiators should agree to the criteria for evaluating potential integrative solutions early in the process (Fisher, Ury, and Patton, 1991). Negotiators can use these criteria when they have to narrow the choice of options down to a single alternative—for example, one candidate for a new job or to select the option most likely to succeed. If the parties first debate their criteria and determine which ones are most important, they will be able to decide on criteria independent of the consideration of any particular candidate or option. Then, when they consider the individual candidates or options, they will pick the best one based on these criteria, not on the individual preferences of one side or the other. If the parties agree, they may revise their criteria later to improve their choice, but this should be done only by the agreement of all negotiators. In fact, it is not a bad idea to check criteria periodically and determine whether each negotiator places the same priority on them as before. Discussion of alternatives frequently leads negotiators to revise their preferences, as well as their estimates of the probability of success and the cost of particular options.

Be Willing to Justify Personal Preferences.   People often find it hard to publicly explain why they like what they like, or dislike what they dislike. "Why do you like that?" "I don't know, I just do," is usually the reply. Moreover, negotiators gain little by pressing opponents to justify themselves—doing so usually just makes them angry and defensive; they may feel that a simple statement of preference is not viewed as sufficient. For example, if the topic under negotiation is what to have for dinner, and one party states that she hates clam chowder, no amount of persuasive effort is likely to induce her to eat clam chowder. Instead, the parties would be more productive if they accepted this information and attempted to explore other options for dinner. Yet what people prefer often has a deep-seated rationale—recall our discussion of how interests, values, and needs often underlie positions. Thus, inquiries from one party about the other party's preferences may be an effort to probe behind a position and identify underlying interests and needs. If the other party elicits a little defensiveness in response to a why question, the negotiator should explain that the intent is to probe for possible underlying interests that might facilitate a collaborative settlement rather than to produce defensiveness.

Be Alert to the Influence of Intangibles in Selecting Options.   One side may favor an option because it helps satisfy some intangible—gaining recognition, looking strong or tough to a constituency, feeling like a winner, and so on. Intangibles or principles can serve as strong interests for a negotiator. Intangibles can lead the negotiator to fight harder to attain a particular solution if that option satisfies both tangibles and intangibles. Some parties may be uncomfortable with discussing intangibles, or even unaware of their nature and power in negotiation process. In spite (or possibly because) of this, it is often good practice to help the other party identify those intangibles and make them public as part of the evaluation process. The other party is likely to prefer options that satisfy those intangibles, and to the degree that you can accept them, agreeing to those options may be important concessions.

Use Subgroups to Evaluate Complex Options.   Small groups may be particularly helpful when many complex options must be considered or when many people will be affected by the solution. Groups of six to eight people, composed of representatives from each faction, side, or subgroup, will be able to work more effectively than a large group. (See our earlier discussion of nominal groups for deciding on options.) As with other areas in this chapter that address group processes, additional insight can be found in Chapter 9.

Take Time Out to Cool Off.   Even though the parties may have completed the hardest part of the process—generating a list of viable options—they may become upset if communication breaks down, they feel their preferences are not being acknowledged, or the other side pushes too hard for a particular option. If the parties become angry, they should take a break. They should make their dissatisfaction known and openly discuss the reasons for it. The parties should feel that they are back on an even emotional keel before continuing to evaluate options. Finally, they should work as hard as possible to keep discussions on the specifics of the proposals, not on the people advocating them. The parties should depersonalize the discussion as much as possible so that the options for settlement are not associated with the people who advocated them.

Explore Different Ways to Logroll.   Earlier we discussed a variety of ways to invent options. The strategy of logroll is effective not only in inventing options but also as a mechanism to combine options into negotiated packages. Neale and Bazerman (1991) identify a variety of approaches in addition to simply combining several issues into a package. Three of these, in particular, relate to the matters of outcome, probabilities, and timing—in other words, *what* is to happen, the *likelihood* of it happening, and *when* it happens.

Exploit Differences in Risk Preference.   Suppose two partners are discussing a future business venture. One has little to risk at the moment and everything to gain from the future; the other has a lot on the line now that he does not want to risk losing if the future is bad. If the partners simply agree to split profits in the future, the one with a large amount of current risk may feel vulnerable. Logrolling around these interests can create a solution that protects one partner's current investment first while providing long-term profits for the other partner as well.

Exploit Differences in Expectations.   In the same example, the person with a lot to lose may also have pessimistic expectations about the future of the joint venture, whereas the person with little to lose may be more optimistic about it. The optimist may thus be willing to gamble more on the future profitability and payout, whereas the pessimist may be willing to settle for a smaller but more assured payment. As with differences in risk, simple differences in expectations about what will happen can permit the parties to invent a solution that addresses the needs of both parties.

Exploit Differences in Time Preferences.   Negotiators may have different time preferences—one may be concerned about meeting short-term needs while the other may be interested in the long-term rewards of their relationship. Parties with short-term interests will need immediate gratification, whereas parties who look for long-term rewards may be willing to make immediate sacrifices to ensure a future payoff. Parties with different time preferences can invent solutions that address both their interests.

Keep Decisions Tentative and Conditional Until All Aspects of the Final Proposal Are Complete.   Even though a clear consensus may emerge about the solution option(s) that will be selected, the parties should talk about the solution in conditional terms—a sort of "soft bundling." Maintaining a tentative tone allows any side to change or revise the final package at any time. Points agreed upon in earlier discussions are not firm until the entire package is determined. Parties do not have to feel that because they gave up an earlier option they have burned their bridges behind them; rather, nothing should be considered final until everything is final.

Minimize Formality and Record Keeping Until Final Agreements Are Closed. Parties usually do not want to lock themselves into any specific language or written agreement until they are close to a consensus. They want to make sure that they will not be held to any comments recorded in notes or transcripts. In general, the fewer the written records during the solution generating phase, the better. In contrast, when the parties are close to consensus, one side should write down the terms of the agreement. This document may then be used as a "single text" (Fisher, Ury, and Patton 1991), to be passed around from party to party as often as necessary until all sides agree to the phrasing and wording of their agreement.

We strongly urge groups to avoid the apparent expediency of "voting" on final agreements or packages, if at all possible. This accomplishes only the relative disenfranchisement of the losing party and makes it more likely that "losers" will be less committed than desirable for the implementation and attainment of the negotiated outcome.

FACTORS THAT FACILITATE SUCCESSFUL INTEGRATIVE NEGOTIATION

We have stressed that successful integrative negotiation can occur if the parties are predisposed to finding a mutually acceptable joint solution. Many other factors contribute to a predisposition toward problem solving and a willingness to work together to find the best solution. These factors are also the preconditions necessary for more successful integrative negotiations (Filley, 1975; Pruitt, 1981, 1983). In this section, we will review in greater detail these factors: the presence of a common goal, faith in one's own problem-solving ability, a belief in the validity of the other party's position, the motivation and commitment to work together, trust, clear and accurate communication, and an understanding of the dynamics of integrative negotiation.

Some Common Objective or Goal

When the parties believe that they are likely to benefit more from working together than from competing or working separately, the situation offers greater potential for successful integrative negotiation. Three types of goals—common, shared, and joint—may facilitate the development of integrative agreements (see Table 4.2).

TABLE 4.2   Goal Typology

Type of Goal	Goal Characteristics
Common	Same goal, same (equal) benefit
Shared	Same goal, different benefits
Joint	Different goals (combined), different benefits

A common goal is one that all parties share equally, each one benefiting in a way that would not be possible if they did not work together. A town government and an industrial manufacturing plant may debate the amount of taxes owed by the plant, but they are more likely to work together if the common goal is to keep the plant open and employ half the town's workforce.

A shared goal is one that both parties work toward but that benefits each party differently. For example, partners can work together in a business but not divide the profits equally. One may get a larger share of the profit because she contributed more experience or capital investment. Inherent in the idea of a shared goal is that parties will work together to achieve some output that will be divided among them. The same result can also come from cost cutting, by which the parties can earn the same outcome as before by working together, but with less effort, expense, or risk. This is often described as an "expandable pie" in contrast to a "fixed pie" (see Chapter 5).

A joint goal is one that involves individuals with different personal goals agreeing to combine them in a collective effort. For example, people joining a political campaign can have different goals: One wants to satisfy personal ambition to hold public office, another wants to serve the community, and yet another wants to benefit from policies that will be implemented under the new administration. All will unite around the joint goal of helping the new administration get elected.

The key element of an integrative negotiation situation is the belief that all sides can benefit. Whether the sides attain the same outcome or different outcomes, all sides must believe that they will be better off by working in cooperation than by working independently or competing.

Faith in One's Problem-Solving Ability

Parties who believe they can work together usually are able to do so. Those who do not share this belief in themselves (and others) are less willing to invest the time and energy in the potential payoffs of a collaborative relationship and more likely to assume a contending or accommodating approach to conflict. Expertise in the focal problem area strengthens the negotiator's understanding of the problem's complexity, nuances, and possible solutions. Neale and Northcraft (1986) demonstrated in a real estate problem that expert negotiators—corporate real estate executives—achieved significantly better integrative agreements than amateurs did. Expertise increases both the negotiator's knowledge base and his or her self-confidence, both of which are necessary to approach the problem at hand with an open mind. Similarly, direct experience in negotiation increases the negotiator's sophistication in understanding the bargaining process and approaching it more creatively (Thompson, 1990a). Finally, there is also evidence that knowledge of integrative tactics leads to an increase in integrative behavior (Weingart, Prietula, Hyder, and Genovese, 1999). Taken together, these results suggest that a faith in one's ability to negotiate integratively is positively related to successful integrative negotiations.

A Belief in the Validity of One's Own Position and the Other's Perspective

In distributive bargaining, negotiators invest time and energy in inflating and justifying the value of their own point of view and debunking the value and importance of the other's perspective. In contrast, integrative negotiation requires negotiators to accept both their own and the other's attitudes, information, and desires as valid (Fisher, Ury, and Patton, 1991). First, you must believe in the validity of your own perspective—that what you believe is worth fighting for and should not be compromised. Research by Kemp and Smith (1994) showed that negotiators who were firmer about insisting that their own point of view become incorporated into the group solution achieved more integrative agreements than those who were less firm. But one must also accept the validity of the other party's perspective. If you challenge the other party's views, he or she may become angry, defensive, and hence unproductive in the problem-solving process. The purpose of integrative negotiation is not to question or challenge the other's viewpoint, but to incorporate it into the definition of the problem and to attend to it as the parties search for mutually acceptable alternatives. In addition, the other party's views should be valued no less (and no more) than the negotiator's own position and viewpoint. The Kemp and Smith study also showed that parties who were able to take the perspective of the other appeared to make better agreements than those who were less able to do so.

The Motivation and Commitment to Work Together

For integrative negotiation to succeed, the parties must be motivated to collaborate rather than to compete. They need to be committed to reaching a goal that benefits both of them rather than to pursuing only their own ends. They must adopt interpersonal styles that are more congenial than combative, more open and trusting than evasive and defensive, more flexible (but firm) than stubborn (but yielding). Specifically, they must be willing to make their own needs explicit, to identify similarities, and to recognize and accept differences. They must also tolerate uncertainties and unravel inconsistencies.

It might seem that, for successful integrative negotiation to occur, each party should be just as interested in the objectives and problems of the other as he is in his own—that each must assume responsibility for the other's needs and outcomes as well as for his own. This is an incorrect interpretation; in fact, such a position is more likely to be dysfunctional than successful. Parties who are deeply committed to each other and each other's welfare often do not work out the best solution (Fry, Firestone, and Williams, 1979; Kelley and Schenitzki, 1972), for several reasons. First, as close as the parties may feel to each other, they still may not fully understand each other's needs, objectives, and concerns, and thus they can fall into the trap of not meeting each other's objectives while thinking that they are (Rubin and Brown, 1975). Further, parties strongly committed to each other are likely to yield more than they would otherwise; the result is that they may arrive at a joint outcome that is less satisfactory than one they would have reached had they remained firm in pursuing their own objectives. Parties in negotiation maximize their outcomes when they assume a healthy, active self-interest in achieving their own goals while also recognizing that they are in a collaborative, problem-solving relationship (Kelley and Schenitzki, 1972). Maximizing outcomes may also be negatively correlated with one party's ability to punish the other party. De Dreu, Giebels, and van de Vliert (1998) showed that even cooperatively motivated negotiators have less trust, exchange less information about preferences and priorities, and achieve agreements of lower joint profit when they can punish the other party than when they do not have this capability.

Motivation and commitment to problem solving can be enhanced in several ways:

1. The parties can come to believe that they share a common fate; to quote Ben Franklin, "If we do not hang together, we will surely hang separately."

2. The parties can demonstrate to each other that there is more to be gained by working together (to increase the payoffs or reduce the costs) than by working separately. The parties can emphasize that they may have to work together after the negotiations are over and will continue to benefit from the relationship they have created. In spite of these efforts, competitive and contentious behavior may persist. In Chapter 12, we will elaborate on approaches that may be used to enhance the parties' predisposition toward cooperation and problem solving.

3. The parties can engage in commitments to each other before the negotiations begin; such commitments have been called *presettlement settlements* (Gillespie and Bazerman, 1998) and are distinguished by three major characteristics:

    a. The settlement results in a firm, legally binding written agreement between the parties (it is more than a "gentlemen's agreement").

    b. The settlement occurs in advance of the parties undertaking full-scale negotiations, but the parties intend that the agreement will be replaced by a more clearly delineated long-term agreement which is to be negotiated.

    c. The settlement resolves only a subset of the issues on which the parties disagree and may simply establish a framework within which the more comprehensive agreement can be defined and delineated.

See Box 4.3 for an example of a presettlement settlement.

Trust

Although there is no guarantee that trust will lead to collaboration, there is plenty of evidence to suggest that mistrust inhibits collaboration. People who are interdependent but do not trust each other will act tentatively or defensively. Defensiveness usually means that they will not accept information at face value but instead will look for hidden, deceptive meanings. When people are defensive, they withdraw and withhold

BOX 4.3
Presettlement Settlements: An Example

In their description of the advantage of presettlement settlements (PreSS), authors James Gillespie and Max Bazerman offer the following example:

> In the international arena, perhaps the most prominent recent example of a presettlement settlement is the 1993 Oslo accords between Israel and the Palestinians. The Oslo accords sought to establish an incremental process of negotiation and reciprocation that would lead to what both parties termed "final status talks." The parties agreed to reserve the most difficult issues (e.g., borders, settlements, Jerusalem) until the final status talks. In the meantime, the Israelis and Palestinians sought to resolve less difficult issues, thereby establishing a political dialogue and working toward normalized relations. The Israelis agreed to release female prisoners, transfer disputed money, and withdraw from Hebron. The Palestinians agreed to revise their national charter, transfer suspected terrorists, and limit the size of the Palestinian police force. . . .
>
> The Oslo accords contained all three elements of a PreSS. Israel and the Palestinians signed a formal agreement containing very specific terms. Since sovereign parties were involved, the agreement was not strictly binding, but it did create obligations on both sides that would be politically costly to reduce unilaterally. The Oslo accords were intended as an initial step in a political and negotiating process leading to a comprehensive resolution of the Israeli–Palestinian dispute. Finally, this PreSS was partial because the parties deferred extremely difficult issues such as Jerusalem until the final-status talks. (p. 151)

The researchers go on to note that by 1998, the framework set out in the Oslo accords had subsequently floundered because of heated rhetoric and escalating violence, and a PreSS no longer exists between Israel and the Palestinians.

SOURCE: James Gillespie and Max Bazerman, "Pre-settlement Settlement (PreSS): A Simple Technique for Initiating Complex Negotiations," *Negotiation Journal* (April 1998), pp. 149–59.

information. Defensive people also attack their opponent's statements and position, seeking to defeat their position rather than to work together. Either of these responses is likely to make the negotiator hesitant, cautious, and distrustful of the other, undermining the negotiation process (Gibb, 1961).

Generating trust is a complex, uncertain process; it depends in part on how the parties behave and in part on the parties' personal characteristics. When people trust each other, they are more likely to share information, communicate accurately their needs, positions, and the facts of the situation (Butler, 1999; Tenbrunsel, 1999). In contrast, when people do not trust each other, they are more likely to engage in positional bargaining, use threats, and commit themselves to tough positions (Kimmel, Pruitt, Magenau, Konar-Goldband, and Carnevale, 1980). As with defensiveness, mistrust is likely to be reciprocated and to lead to unproductive negotiations. To develop trust effectively, each negotiator must believe that both she and the other party choose to behave in a cooperative manner; moreover, each must believe that this behavior is a signal of the other's honesty, openness, and a similar mutual commitment to a joint solution (see also Chapter 8).

Trust in itself is not sufficient to create good problem solving; it must be linked to several other behaviors on the part of both negotiators. The first is a firm commitment to one's own position. If a negotiator is trustworthy but very willing to yield his or her own position to the other party in negotiations, the other will be likely to take advantage of it. Although trust may exist, the negotiator's willingness to yield may lead the other party to take a tough, firm position. In contrast, if the other party is firmly committed to a position, the negotiator must work hard to find alternatives that will meet both parties' needs. Thus, good problem solving is likely to come from a combination of trust and firmness (Michener, Vaske, Schleiffer, Plazewski, and Chapman, 1975; Wall, 1977). The second key behavior is support in the solution-exploration process. A person brainstorming about ways to solve a problem will respond differently if met with ridicule or silence than if met with interest and respect. A person whose ideas are accepted and developed by someone will be encouraged to continue.

A number of key factors contribute to the development of trust between negotiators. First, people are more likely to trust someone they perceive as similar to them or as holding a positive attitude toward them. Second, people often trust those who depend on them; being in a position to help or hurt someone (who can do the same in return) fosters mutual trust (Solomon, 1960). Third, people are more likely to trust those who initiate cooperative, trusting behavior. Acting in a cooperative, trusting manner serves as an invitation to others, especially if the invitation is repeated despite initially contentious behavior from the opponent (Bonoma, Horai, Lindskold, Gahagan, and Tedeschi, 1969; Gahagan, Long, and Horai, 1969; Gruder and Duslak, 1973; Heller, 1967; Kleinke and Pohlan, 1971). Fourth, there is some evidence that giving a gift to the other negotiator may lead to increased trust (Large, 1999). Finally, people are more likely to trust those who make concessions. The more other people's behavior communicates that they are holding firm in their fundamental commitment to their own needs at the same time as they are working toward a joint solution, the more negotiators are likely to find their conduct trustworthy, in the spirit of the best joint agreement (Rubin and Brown, 1975).

Given that trust has to be built during the negotiation, tone-setting and other opening moves are crucial. The more cooperative, open, and nonthreatening the opening statements and actions of a party are, the more trust and cooperation are engendered in the other party (Crumbaugh and Evans, 1967; Michelini, 1971; Oskamp, 1970; Sermat and Gregovich, 1966). (See Box 4.4 for how parties from different cultures may interpret cooperation.) Once a cooperative position is established, it is more likely to persist. If cooperative behavior can be established at the very beginning, there is a tendency for parties to lock in to this cycle and make it continue (Pilisuk and Skolnick, 1978). Finally, opening moves not only help set the tone for the negotiation but also begin the momentum. The longer the cycle of trust and cooperation continues, the easier it would be to reestablish it should the cycle break down (Komorita and Mechling, 1967; Sermat, 1967; Swinth, 1967).

Clear and Accurate Communication

Another precondition for high-quality integrative negotiation is clear and accurate communication. First, negotiators must be willing to share information about themselves (Neale and Bazerman, 1991). They must be willing to tell what they want and, more important, must be willing to state why they want it in specific, concrete terms, avoid-

BOX 4.4
What Does *Cooperation* Mean to You?

Researchers in international organizational behavior often define *culture* in terms of how citizens of each group differ in their perspective of the world and their place in it. For example, cultures can be placed on a continuum of individualism and collectivism. In the United States, citizens tend to look at things from an individual perspective and see events in terms of personal impact. In contrast, citizens of countries such as Japan tend toward collectivism, meaning that they place greater importance on how events affect the groups to which they belong rather than how things affect them personally.

Recently, negotiation scholars have begun to recognize that cultural differences also color how individuals view the notion of cooperation. Chen, Chen, and Meindl (1998) have highlighted two ways that differing views of cooperation affect negotiation strategy:

- *Goal interdependence versus goal sharing.* When faced with the task of consolidating resources to reach a shared or superordinate goal, members of collectivist and individualistic societies will view that overarching goal differently. Those from an individualistic culture see their goals as interdependent with the other party's, meaning that they cooperate because they need the other side's cooperation to achieve their own ends. People in collectivist cultures view overarching goals as shared and see a settlement as linking their fate or destiny to the other party's to achieve a greater good. Negotiators who understand this distinction use appropriate strategies to "sell" goals to their negotiating partners. For individualists, the negotiator should emphasize the instrumentality of the agreement: "Cooperating with me offers you the following tangible rewards . . ." For collectivists, the negotiator should appeal to notions of self-sacrifice for a collective good: "Think of what this settlement will allow us to achieve."

- *Accountability.* As you would expect, individualists see themselves as personally responsible for outcomes they negotiate, while collectivists look primarily at the impact a proposed settlement might have on groups with which they affiliate. When encouraging an individualist to accept a proposal, the negotiator should emphasize the personal gains the other party might achieve: "Think of how your constituents will cheer you when you come back to them having averted a strike." In contrast, collectivists need to be convinced of the value of the settlement to their group: "When this settlement is announced to the press, your organization will profit from the positive publicity."

As these two examples demonstrate, people from different cultures choose to cooperate for different reasons. Understanding where on the continuum your negotiating partner falls will enable you to be more persuasive in presenting potential settlements.

SOURCE: Adapted from C. C. Chen, X. Chen, and J. R. Meindl (1998), "How Can Cooperation Be Fostered? The Cultural Effects of Individualism-Collectivism," *Academy of Management Review,* 23, 285–304.

ing generalities and ambiguities. Second, the other negotiators must understand the communication. At a minimum, they must understand the meaning they each attach to their statements; hopefully, the parties each interpret the facts in the same way. Others at the negotiating table can frequently identify ambiguities and breakdowns in communication.

If someone on a bargaining team makes a confusing statement, others can address it and try to clarify it. When one person on the other side does not grasp a difficult point, someone else from the same side will often be able to find the words or illustrations to bring out the meaning. Still, mutual understanding is the responsibility of both sides. The communicator must be willing to test whether the other side has received the message that was intended. Similarly, the listener must engage in active listening, testing to make sure that what he or she received and understood is the message that the sender intended.

Using multiple communication channels (i.e., opportunities for the two sides to communicate in ways other than formally across the negotiation table) will help negotiators clarify the formal communication or get information through if the formal channels break down. Conversations over coffee breaks, separate meetings between chief negotiators outside the formal sessions, and off-the-record contacts between key subordinates are all alternatives to the formal channel. The negotiators must exercise care, though, to make sure that the multiple messages and media are consistent. Sending conflicting messages in integrative negotiations can confuse the other party at best, and threaten or anger at worst.

When there are strong negative feelings or when one or more parties are inclined to dominate, negotiators may create formal, structured procedures for communication. Under these circumstances, negotiators should follow a procedure that gives everyone a chance to speak. For example, the rules of most debates limit statements to five minutes, and similar rules are often adopted in contentious open meetings or public hearings. In addition, the parties may agree to follow a previously agreed-on agenda so that everyone can be heard and their contributions noted. Other ways to ensure effective communication processes in negotiation are covered extensively in Chapters 5 and 12. In addition, in Chapter 13, we will describe how third parties can help facilitate disabled communication processes.

An Understanding of the Dynamics of Integrative Negotiation

It is possible for negotiators to have "traditional" views of negotiation that lead them to assume that the distributive bargaining process is the only way to approach negotiations. Yet several studies indicate that training in integrative negotiation enhances the ability of the parties to successfully pursue the process. For example, Weingart, Hyder, and Prietula (1996) demonstrated that training negotiators in integrative tactics—particularly in how to exchange information about priorities across issues and preferences within issues, and how to set high goals—significantly enhanced the frequency of integrative behaviors and led the parties to achieve higher joint outcomes. This study also found that using distributive tactics, such as strongly trying to persuade the other of the validity of one's own views, was negatively related to joint outcome.

Summary

We identified six fundamental preconditions for successful integrative negotiation: some form of shared or common goals, faith in one's ability to solve problems, a belief in the validity and importance of the other's position, the motivation and commitment to work together, trust in the opposing negotiator, and the ability to accurately exchange information in spite of conflict conditions. If the parties are not able to successfully meet these preconditions, they will need to resolve problems in these areas as the integrative negotiation evolves.

WHY INTEGRATIVE NEGOTIATION IS DIFFICULT TO ACHIEVE

Integrative negotiation is a collaborative process in which the parties define their common problem and pursue strategies to solve it. Unfortunately, negotiators do not always perceive situations as having integrative potential or cannot always sustain a productive integrative discussion. People frequently view conflict-laden situations with a fundamentally more distrustful, win-lose attitude than is necessary. The approach that individuals take toward conflict and negotiation is essential to understanding the differences between distributive bargaining and integrative negotiation. We have stated that the primary reason negotiators do not pursue integrative agreements is that they fail to perceive a situation as having integrative potential and are primarily motivated to achieve outcomes that satisfy only their own needs. Three additional factors contribute to this difficulty: the history of the relationship between the parties, the tendency toward black-and-white thinking, and the mixed-motive nature of most bargaining situations.

The History of the Relationship between the Parties

The more competitive and conflict-laden their past relationship, the more negotiators are likely to approach the current negotiation with a defensive, win-lose attitude. Long-term opponents are unlikely to trust each other or to believe that a cooperative gesture is not a ruse or setup for future exploitation. Since the opponent has never shown any genuine interest in cooperation in the past, why should the present be any different? Even if the parties have no history with each other, the expectation of a competitive opponent is sufficient to create defensiveness. Research suggests that the majority of people enter negotiations expecting them to be win-lose, not win-win (Thompson and Hastie, 1990a). Although people's perceptions are often loaded with self-serving rationalizations—negotiators expect competition from their opponents to justify their own strategies—the perceptions nevertheless deter them from initiating an integrative negotiation process. (See Box 4.5 for a description of two researchers' attempts to remedy such a situation.)

A Belief That an Issue Can Only Be Resolved Distributively

We have noted several times that conflict dynamics tend to lead negotiators to polarize issues or see them only in win-lose terms. In addition, negotiators may be prone to a number of cognitive biases or heuristic decision rules (Neale and Bazerman, 1985, 1991) that systematically allow them to bias their perception of the situation, the range of possible outcomes, and the likelihood of achieving possible outcomes, all of which tend to preclude negotiators from engaging in the behaviors necessary for integrative

BOX 4.5
Using Integrative Negotiation to Enhance Collective Bargaining

Union–management collective bargaining has often been used as a classic example of the distributive bargaining process. Often, the tendency for the parties to use collective bargaining rests on a long history of perceived abuse and mistrust on both sides of the table. But recent work shows that integrative negotiation can be successful even in this context. Post and Bennett (1994) report the results of a five-step process that was introduced into a union–management negotiation that successfully reduced grievances from 40 per year under the previous contract to 2 in 18 months under the new contract, significantly reduced anger and hostility between the parties, and significantly enhanced the spirit of cooperation in the plant. The five steps were as follows:

1. A *commitment phase,* occurring 12 and 6 months before the expiration of the current contract, during which the parties committed to participate in a collaborative process, including commitments to harmonize negotiation philosophy, harmonize the negotiation process, and articulate the respective interests of the parties.

2. An *explanation phase,* occurring one month before contract expiration, during which the parties hold their first meeting, present their respective proposals to each other, introduce supporting documentation, and set a timetable for remaining meetings.

3. A *validation phase,* occurring two to four weeks prior to contract expiration, in which the parties gather information from employees and employers about the validity of the interests expressed in the opening statements. This information is used to generate a collective consensus about the relative importance and priority of the interests to the constituencies of both groups.

4. A *prioritization phase,* occurring two weeks prior to contract expiration, in which the parties work together to develop a joint list of priorities based on the data. This process is often facilitated by a mediator, who uses the commitments generated in the commitment phase to help the parties represent their priorities genuinely and candidly.

5. A *negotiation phase,* occurring one week prior to the contract expiration, in which the parties meet in a series of frequent and intensive gatherings to negotiate a resolution to the prioritized list of interests. Once again, this process is often facilitated by a mediator, whose role is to vigorously ask questions of the parties, hold them to their agenda, and ensure that the negotiations proceed in an open and trusting atmosphere.

Note that this process requires the ongoing participation of a mediator, who acts as a referee and as a monitor of the parties' commitment to stay with an integrative process. Whether the parties could learn to trust each other to sustain such a process without an active third-party role is still a matter of debate.

SOURCE: Adapted from F. R. Post and R. J. Bennett, "Use of Collaborative Collective Bargaining Processes in Labor Negotiations," *The International Journal of Conflict Management,* 5 (1994), pp. 34–61.

negotiation. We will describe these biases at length in Chapter 5. For example, unions and management have historically clashed over the introduction of new procedures or technology that "de-skills" labor or replaces workers with machines. Labor usually pursues job security, believing that the new machines will eliminate workers, whereas management takes the position that the new machines will increase efficiency, quality, and profit, and that it is management's right to make decisions regarding these issues. On the surface, the two positions seem irreconcilable: Either the workers pressure the company to keep employees at the expense of machines, or management makes the decisions about how to introduce new technology. However, recent experience shows that labor and management have devised a number of ways to solve the problem to both sides' satisfaction—such as retraining and reallocating employees, or reducing employees through attrition rather than layoff.

The Mixed-Motive Nature of Most Negotiating Situations

Purely integrative or purely distributive negotiation situations are rare. Most situations are mixed-motive, containing some elements that require distributive bargaining processes and others that require integrative negotiation. For example, when people become partners in a business, the common goal of making a profit provides a basis for their collaboration. How to allocate the profits becomes a different matter, however, and is much more likely to create conflict. In this example, the parties must recognize that the integrative element is more important; that is, there must be a business before there can be profits to divide. Nevertheless, their competitiveness over profit distribution may make it hard for them to stay in business at all. As a general rule, conflict and competitiveness drive out cooperation and trust, making it more difficult for the parties to find common ground.

One of the most fundamental problems in integrative negotiation is that parties fail to recognize (or search for) the integrative potential in a negotiation problem. The primary cause of this failure is the desire to satisfy one's own concerns without regard to the other's concerns. Negotiators too often assume that the other party has the same objectives and goals as they do, and accordingly they fail to search for information about the other party's preferences and priorities (Kemp and Smith, 1994). Negotiators may also be led to this assumption when they are closely accountable to someone else for their performance, when the parties have had a history of conflict, and when the issues are too complex to disentangle and are easily interpreted in simple win-lose terms. As a result, negotiators fail to invest the time and energy necessary to search for and find integrative options (Cyert and March, 1963).

CHAPTER SUMMARY

In this chapter, we have reviewed the strategy and tactics of integrative negotiation. The fundamental structure of integrative negotiation is one within which the parties are able to define goals that allow both sides to achieve their objectives. Integrative negotiation is the process of defining these goals and engaging in a set of procedures that permit both sides to maximize their objectives.

The chapter began with an overview of the integrative negotiation process. A high level of concern for both sides achieving their own objectives propels a collaborative, problem-solving approach. Negotiators frequently fail at integrative negotiation because they fail to perceive the integrative potential of the negotiating problem. However, breakdowns also occur due to distributive assumptions about the negotiating problem, the mixed-motive nature of the issues, or the negotiators' previous relationship with each other. Successful integrative negotiation requires several processes. First, the parties must understand each other's true needs and objectives. Second, they must create a free flow of information and an open exchange of ideas. Third, they must focus on their similarities, emphasizing their commonalities rather than their differences. Finally, they must engage in a search for solutions that meet the goals of both sides. This is a very different set of processes from those in distributive bargaining, described in Chapter 3.

The four key steps in the integrative negotiation process are identifying and defining the problem, identifying interests and needs, generating alternative solutions, and evaluating and selecting alternatives. For each of these steps, we proposed techniques and tactics to make the process successful.

We then discussed various factors that facilitate successful integrative negotiation. First, the process will be greatly facilitated by some form of common goal or objective. This goal may be one that the parties both want to achieve, one they want to share, or one they could not possibly attain unless they worked together. Second, they must share a motivation and commitment to work together, to make their relationship a productive one. Third, the parties must be willing to believe that the other's needs are valid. Fourth, they must be able to trust each other and to work hard to establish and maintain that trust. Finally, there must be clear and accurate communication about what each one wants and an effort to understand the other's needs. Instead of talking the other out of his or her needs or failing to acknowledge them as important, negotiators must be willing to work for both their own needs and the other's needs to find the best joint arrangement.

In spite of all of these suggestions, the process is not as easy as it seems for parties who are locked in conflict, defensiveness, and a hard-line position. Only by working to create the necessary conditions for integrative negotiation can the process occur with relative ease and success. In Chapters 12 and 13 we will discuss a number of ways that parties can defuse hostility, defensiveness, and the disposition toward hard-line negotiating to create the conditions for successful integrative negotiation.

CHAPTER 5

Perception, Cognition, and Communication

Perception, cognition, and communication are fundamental processes that govern how individuals construct and interpret the interaction that takes place in a negotiation. Reduced to its essence, negotiation is a form of interpersonal communication, which itself is a subset of the broader category of human perception and communication. Perception and cognition are the basic building blocks of all social encounters, including negotiation, in the sense that our social actions are guided by the way we perceive and analyze the other party, the situation, and our own interests and positions. A sound understanding of how humans perceive and communicate in general will help negotiators understand why people behave the way they do during negotiations. Communication, which grows out of our perceptions and cognitions, is the central process by which a negotiator's planning, preparation, and strategizing are enacted. Communication processes, both verbal and nonverbal, are critical to achieving negotiation goals and to resolving conflicts. According to Putnam and Poole (1987),

> . . . the activity of having or managing a conflict occurs through communication. More specifically, communication undergirds the setting and reframing of goals; the defining and narrowing of conflict issues; the developing of relationships between disputants and among constituents; the selecting and implementing of strategies and tactics; the generating, attacking, and defending of alternative solutions; and the reaching and confirming of agreements. (p. 550)

We begin the chapter by examining how psychological perception is related to the process of negotiation, with particular attention to forms of perceptual distortion that can cause problems of understanding and meaning making for negotiators. We then look at how negotiators use information to make decisions about tactics and strategy—the process of cognition. Our focus here is on the various kinds of systematic errors, or "cognitive biases," in information processing that negotiators are prone to make and that may compromise negotiator performance. This section will also consider how negotiators can manage misperceptions and cognitive biases in order to maximize strategic advantage and minimize their adverse effects.

Following these sections on perception and cognition, we turn to the process by which negotiators communicate their own interests, positions, and goals—and in turn make sense of those of the other party and of the negotiation as a whole. Clearly, communication pervades the negotiation process, and "communication scholarship sets forth a perspective for understanding the negotiation process, for examining bargaining interaction as a system, and for exploring the micro elements and subtleties that frequently alter the course of negotiations" (Chatman, Putnam, and Sondak, 1991, p. 159).

Following a discussion of the basic mechanisms through which messages are encoded, sent, received, and decoded, we will consider in some depth *what* is communicated in a negotiation, and *how* people communicate in negotiation. The chapter ends with discussions of how to improve communication in negotiation, the effect of moods and emotions on communication, and special communication considerations at the close of negotiations.

PERCEPTION AND NEGOTIATION

The Role of Perception

In this section, we examine some of the psychological principles of perception and communication, and draw examples to the negotiation domain. Negotiators approach each negotiation guided by their perceptions of past situations and current attitudes and behaviors. Their expectations of the future behaviors of other parties and subsequent outcomes are based in large part on their cognitive information, gained through direct or vicarious experience and observations.

Perception is the process by which individuals connect to their environment. The process of ascribing meaning to messages received is strongly influenced by the receiver's current state of mind, role, and understanding or comprehension of earlier communications (Babcock, Wang, and Loewenstein, 1996; de Dreu and van Lange, 1995; Thompson, 1995; Thompson and Hastie, 1990a). Other parties' perceptions, the environment, and the receiver's own dispositions all affect how meanings are ascribed, and whether the receiver can determine exactly what the other party is saying, and what is meant. We will now examine in more detail how perceptions are created and how they affect the success of communication.

Perception is a complex physical and psychological process. It has been defined as "the process of screening, selecting, and interpreting stimuli so that they have meaning to the individual" (Steers, 1984, p. 98). Perception is a "sense-making" process; people interpret their environment so that they can respond appropriately (see Figure 5.1). Most environments are extremely complex—they present a large number and variety of stimuli, each having different properties such as magnitude, color, shape, texture, and relative novelty. The sheer complexity of such environments makes it impossible to process all of the available information, so perception becomes selective, focusing on some stimuli while tuning out others. As a result, people have several shortcuts in their perceptual systems that allow them to process information more readily. Unfortunately, these shortcuts come with a cost—perceptual errors, which typically occur without people being aware that they are happening.

Perceptual Distortion in Negotiation

In any given negotiation, the perceiver's own needs, desires, motivations, and personal experiences may create a predisposition about the other party. Such predispositions are most problematic when they lead to biases and errors in perception and subsequent communication. Research on perception and communication goes back several decades

FIGURE 5.1   The Perceptual Process

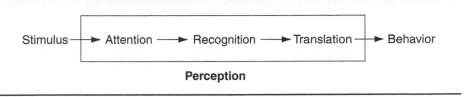

Perception

(e.g., Bruner and Tagiuri, 1954), with attention to this topic in the negotiation domain coming much later (e.g., Thompson, 1995). Although we can extend some concepts and examples from the general study of perception to the context negotiation, further research needs to be conducted to delineate the extent to which these perceptual distortions influence negotiations.

We will discuss four major perceptual errors: stereotyping, halo effects, selective perception, and projection. Stereotyping and halo effects are examples of perceptual distortion by *generalization:* small amounts of perceptual information are used to draw large conclusions about individuals. Selective perception and projection are, in contrast, examples of perceptual distortion by the *anticipation* of encountering certain attributes and qualities in another person. In each case, the perceiver filters and distorts information to arrive at a consistent view.

Stereotyping is a very common distortion of the perceptual process. Stereotyping occurs when one individual assigns attributes to another solely on the basis of the other's membership in a particular social or demographic group. Stereotypes are formed about a wide variety of different groups, for example, the younger generation; males or females; Italians or Germans; or people of different races, religions, or sexual orientations. In each case, stereotypes tend to be formed in the same way. People assign an individual to a group based on one piece of perceptual information (e.g., the individual is young or old); then they assign a broad range of other characteristics of the group to this individual (e.g., "Old people are conservative; this person is old and therefore is conservative" or "Young people are disrespectful; this person is young and therefore is disrespectful"). There may be no factual basis for the conclusion that this particular older individual is conservative; the conclusion is based on the generalization of qualities that have been ascribed to the larger group. Applying other traits associated with the category to this particular individual further compounds the error. Moreover, stereotypes, once formed, are often highly resistant to change. In organizations, problems of age, race, and gender stereotyping have received much attention, yet they persist. The simple process of using a single criterion—even an arbitrary one—to divide people into groups encourages group members to begin to define themselves as "we" and the other group as "they," and then to make evaluative comparisons between them. Direct competition for resources among groups, or a conflict of values and ideologies, significantly enhances the stereotyping process (Sherif, Harvey, White, Hood, and Sherif, 1988).

Halo effects in perception are similar to stereotypes. Rather than using a person's group membership as a basis for classification, halo effects occur when people generalize about a variety of attributes based on the knowledge of one attribute of an individual

(Cooper, 1981). A smiling person is judged to be more honest than a frowning or scowling person, even though there is no consistent relationship between smiling and honesty. Halo effects may be positive or negative. A good attribute may be generalized so that people are seen in a very positive light, whereas a negative attribute has the reverse effect. The more prominent the attribute is in influencing the overall judgment about an individual, the more likely that it will be used to cast further information into a perspective consistent with the initial judgment. Research shows that halo effects are most likely to occur in perception (1) when there is very little experience with a person along some dimension (and hence generalization occurs about that person from knowledge of him or her in other contexts), (2) when the person is well known, and (3) when the qualities have strong moral implications (Bruner and Tagiuri, 1954).

Halo effects are as common as stereotypes in negotiation. Negotiators are likely to form rapid impressions of each other based on very limited initial information, such as appearance, group membership, or initial statements. Negotiators tend to maintain these judgments as they get to know each other better, fitting each piece of new information into some consistent pattern. Finally, as Bruner and Tagiuri suggest, the mere suggestion that the other party can be viewed in moral terms—for example, honest or dishonest, ethical or unethical—is likely to affect the perception of a wide variety of their other attributes.

Selective perception occurs when the perceiver singles out certain information that supports or reinforces a prior belief, and filters out information that does not confirm that belief. Selective perception has the effect of perpetuating stereotypes or halo effects—negotiators not only form quick judgments about individuals on the basis of limited information but also filter out further evidence that might disconfirm the judgment. An initial smile from the other party, which leads the negotiator to believe that he or she is honest, might also lead the negotiator to downplay any of that party's statements that demonstrate an intention to be competitive and aggressive. If the negotiator perceives the same initial smile as a smirk, then the negotiator may downplay the other party's offers to establish an honest and cooperative relationship. In both cases, the negotiator's own biases—the predisposition to view the smile as honest or dishonest—are likely to affect how the other party's behavior is perceived and interpreted.

Projection occurs when people ascribe to others the characteristics or feelings that they possess themselves. Projection usually arises out of a need to protect one's own self-concept. People have a need to see themselves as consistent and good. Negotiators tend to assume that the other party would respond in the same manner they would if they were in the same situation. For instance, if a negotiator feels that he would be frustrated if he were in the other party's position, then he is likely to perceive that the other party is frustrated. People respond differently to similar situations, however, and projecting one's own feelings and beliefs onto the other negotiator may be incorrect. For instance, if a negotiator is really bothered by delays in negotiations but needs to tell the other party that there will be an unavoidable delay, the negotiator may expect the other party to exhibit frustration at the announcement. While it is possible that the other party will be frustrated, it is also possible that he or she will welcome the delay as an opportunity to complete work on a different project, and that any frustration was only a projection from the negotiator's mind.

Perceptions can influence many aspects of the negotiation process and can be quite persistent once they are formed. The influence of perceptions on cognition will be discussed later in this chapter, as will methods for managing the effects of misperception in communication and negotiation.

Framing

Another key issue in perception and negotiation is *framing*. A frame is the subjective mechanism through which people evaluate and make sense out of situations, leading them to pursue or avoid subsequent actions (Bateson, 1972; Goffman, 1974). Framing helps explain "how bargainers conceive of ongoing sets of events in light of past experiences"; framing and reframing, along with reevaluation of information and positions, "are tied to information processing, message patterns, linguistic cues, and socially constructed meanings" (Putnam and Holmer, 1992, p. 129). As we explained in Chapter 2, framing is about focusing, shaping, and organizing the world around us—making sense of complex realities and defining it in ways that are meaningful to us. We discussed at length in Chapter 2 the different type of frames that exist and their importance for understanding strategic choices in negotiation.

An important aspect of framing for our discussion in this chapter is the *cognitive heuristics* approach, which examines the ways in which negotiators make systematic errors in judgment when they process information. The foundations of this approach are in behavioral decision theory and the prospect theory of human judgment and decision making (e.g., Bazerman, 1998; Neale and Bazerman 1991; Tversky and Kahnemann, 1981). Decision theorists have been interested in the development of decision heuristics (or shortcuts) because such heuristics often lead parties to make decisions that are less than optimal or even irrational. For example, when faced with a situation where they can make decisions based only on easily available information, negotiators often fail to search for additional information that may be hard to access or understand, and thus they may frame the decision in a manner that gives the other party an advantage.

In Chapter 2, we discussed the dynamic nature of frames—the notion that the thrust and tone of a conversation changes as parties engage in interaction, reveal interaction, and seek to reconcile seemingly competing perspectives. In contrast, the cognitive heuristic approach to framing can be seen as static rather than dynamic (Putnam and Holmer, 1992), in that it focuses on how a party perceives and shapes the outcome (particularly with regard to risk), and how the party's frame tends to persist regardless of the events and information that follow it. We treat this type of frame as a *cognitive bias* that may shape the negotiator's decision-making process in evaluating outcomes and alternatives; we will explore cognitive biases in depth in the next section of this chapter.

Section Summary

Stereotypes, halo effects, selective perceptions, and projection all can distort the information that people receive. These distortions affect expectations about the other party and lead to assumptions about his or her position, willingness to cooperate or make concessions, and so on. These assumptions, in turn, may cause negotiators to assume a competitive, defensive stance early in a negotiation. The problem with this chain of events is that if the initial assumptions are incorrect, then negotiators may not be able to reverse their effects; by the time negotiators are in a position to judge the predisposition of the other party accurately, the other party may have interpreted the initial competitive mood and defensive posture of the negotiator as offensive and antagonistic. This problem may be most acute between groups that have long-standing hostile relationships: unions and management that have been plagued by bitter strikes, ethnic groups with ongoing disagreements, or marital partners in divorce proceedings. To break this self-fulfilling spiral, individual negotiators and their constituencies must take specific public actions to signal to their adversaries a desire to change to cooperative behavior. Detailed strategies for doing this will be discussed in Chapters 12 and 13.

COGNITIVE BIASES IN NEGOTIATION

In the last section, we examined how information is perceived and potentially distorted in the perception process. In this section, we look at how negotiators use that information to make decisions during the negotiation. Rather than being perfect processors of information, it is quite clear that negotiators have a tendency to make systematic errors when they process information (for reviews see Bazerman and Carroll, 1987; Neale and Bazerman, 1992b; Thompson and Hastie, 1990b).[1] These errors, collectively labeled *cognitive biases,* tend to impede negotiator performance; they include (1) the irrational escalation of commitment, (2) the mythical belief that the issues under negotiation are all fixed-pie, (3) the process of anchoring and adjustment in decision making, (4) issue and problem framing, (5) the availability of information, (6) the winner's curse, (7) negotiator overconfidence, (8) the law of small numbers, (9) self-serving biases, (10) the endowment effect, (11) the tendency to ignore others' cognitions, and (12) the process of reactive devaluation. We will discuss each of these in more detail below.

1. Irrational Escalation of Commitment

Negotiators sometimes maintain commitment to a course of action even when that commitment constitutes irrational behavior on their part. This is an example of a broader psychological phenomenon known as "escalation of commitment," which is the tendency for an individual to make decisions that stick with a failing course of action (Brockner, 1992; Staw, 1981; Teger, 1980). Classic examples include a country that continues to pour military resources into an unwinnable armed conflict, or an investor who continues to put more money into a declining stock in hopes its fortunes will turn ("throwing good money after bad," as escalation of commitment is sometimes colloquially described). Escalation of commitment situations is defined by "repeated (rather

---

[1] Whether negotiators misperceive information or misprocess information remains a technical debate in the communication and negotiation literature that is beyond the scope of this book.

than one-shot) decision making in the face of negative feedback about prior resource allocations, uncertainty surrounding the likelihood of goal attainment, and choice about whether to continue" (Brocker, 1992, p. 40).

In negotiation (as elsewhere), escalation of commitment is due in part to biases in individual perception and judgment. Once a course of action is decided, negotiators often seek supportive (confirming) evidence for that choice, while ignoring or failing to seek disconfirming evidence. Initial commitments become set in stone (see the section on anchoring and adjustment, below), and a desire for consistency prevents negotiators from changing them. This desire for consistency is often exacerbated by a desire to save face and to maintain an impression of expertise or control in front of others (see Chapter 8). No one likes to admit error or failure, especially when the other party may perceive doing so as a weakness. Escalation of commitment is common when a union goes on strike and expects management to capitulate eventually, in competitive bidding or auction situations, or when negotiators make a threat in anger and then find that they have to follow through on it. One way to combat these tendencies is to have an advisor serve as a reality checkpoint—someone who is not consumed by the "heat of the moment" and who can warn negotiators when they inadvertently begin to behave irrationally.

2. Mythical Fixed-Pie Beliefs

Many negotiators assume that all negotiations (not just some) involve a fixed pie (Bazerman, Magliozzi, and Neale, 1985; Bazerman and Neale, 1983; Thompson, 1990b). Negotiators often approach integrative negotiation opportunities as zero-sum games or win-lose exchanges. Those who believe in the mythical fixed pie assume that the possibility for integrative settlements and mutually beneficial trade-offs doesn't exist, and they suppress efforts to search for such settlements or trade-offs (see Pinkley, Griffith, and Northcraft, 1995; Thompson and Hastie, 1990a, 1990b). In the salary negotiations we have frequently used as an example, the job applicant who assumes that salary is the only issue may insist on $35,000 when the company is offering $32,000. Only when the two parties discuss the possibilities further do they discover that moving expenses and starting date can also be negotiated, which may make the resolution of the salary issue far easier.

The tendency to see negotiation in fixed-pie terms seems to vary depending on how people view the nature of a given conflict situation. This was shown in a clever experiment by Harinck, de Dreu, and Van Vianen (2000) involving a simulated negotiation between prosecutors and defense lawyers over jail sentences. Some participants were told to view their goals in terms of personal *interests* (e.g., arranging a particular jail sentence will help your career), others were told to view their goals in terms of *effectiveness* (a particular sentence is most likely to prevent recidivism), and still others were told to focus on *values* (a particular jail sentence is fair and just). Negotiators focusing on personal interests were most likely to come under the influence of fixed-pie beliefs and approach the situation competitively. Negotiators focusing on values were least likely to see the problem in fixed-pie terms, and more inclined to approach the situation cooperatively. Fixed-pie beliefs may also vary with cultural values that negotiators bring to the exchange (see Box 5.1).

BOX 5.1
Cultural Effects on Fixed-Pie Perceptions

Michele Gelfand and Sophia Christakopoulou (1999) investigated whether the tendency to view negotiations in fixed-pie terms might vary according to cultural values held by negotiators. They argued that fixed-pie judgments are probably commonly experienced across cultures at the start of negotiations, but are stronger in some cultures than others by the end of a negotiation encounter. Gelfand and Christakopoulou compared negotiators in an *individualistic* culture, where cultural norms emphasize individual rights, accomplishments, and competition, with negotiators in a *collectivistic* culture, where the emphasis is on group accomplishment, interdependence, and harmony. They predicted that negotiators from individualistic cultures would focus more on their own interests and priorities, which may diminish the negotiator's ability to accurately gauge the other party's interests, leading to persistent assumptions that the pie is fixed.

Gelfand and Christakopoulou tested this prediction in a simulated business negotiation involving students from an American university (a highly individualistic culture) and students from a university in Greece (a highly collectivistic culture). Participants were asked both before and after the negotiation, which took place via e-mail, to record their judgments of the other party's interests and desires. With this method, fixed-pie perceptions are present to the extent that an individual regards the other party's interests as directly opposed to his or her own interests. (Such perceptions were erroneous in this study because the negotiation task did incorporate some integrative potential.)

As expected, the researchers found that there was no difference in the level of fixed-pie error between U.S. and Greek negotiators at the *start* of the negotiations. *After* the negotiation, however, Americans were significantly more likely than Greeks to make errors in judging the other party's interests, indicating a bias toward assuming a fixed pie. Transcripts of the negotiations revealed that Greek negotiators made more statements about insight into and awareness of the other party's interests. Curiously, although American negotiators made more judgment errors, they expressed more confidence after the negotiation than Greek negotiators that their understanding of the other party's interests was accurate!

SOURCE: Adapted from M. J. Gelfand and S. Christakopoulou, "Culture and Negotiator Cognition: Judgment Accuracy and Negotiation Processes in Individualistic and Collectivistic Cultures," *Organizational Behavior and Human Decision Processes* 79 (1999), pp. 248–69.

In Chapter 4 we provided advice on minimizing this fixed-pie belief through procedures for inventing options. A recent study by de Dreu, Koole, and Steinel (2000) showed that fixed-pie perceptions can also be diminished by holding negotiators accountable for the way that they negotiate. In their experiment, some negotiators were told that they would be interviewed afterwards by experts to discuss what happened. Fixed-pie perceptions were weaker for these negotiators compared to negotiators who were not expecting an "accountability interview." Negotiators operating under accountability also reached agreements having higher joint value for the two parties. It appears that introducing accountability into the negotiation context is one way to increase the chances that individuals will overcome fixed-pie beliefs and reach more integrative agreements.

3. Anchoring and Adjustment

Cognitive biases in anchoring and adjustment are related to the effect of the standard (or anchor) against which subsequent adjustments (gains or losses) are measured during negotiation. The choice of an anchor (e.g., an initial offer or an intended goal) might well be based on faulty or incomplete information and thus be misleading in and of itself. However, once the anchor is defined, parties tend to treat it as a real, valid benchmark by which to adjust other judgments, such as the size of one side's opening offer (Diekmann, Tenbrunsel, Shah, Schroth, and Bazerman, 1996; Kristensen and Garling, 1997; Ritov, 1996). For example, Northcraft and Neale (1987) report a study in which real estate agents appraising the value of a house were very strongly affected by its asking price (also see Diekmann et al., 1996). The asking price served as a convenient anchor to use in appraising the value of the house. Goals in negotiation—whether set realistically or carelessly—can also serve as anchors. These anchors may be visible or invisible to the other party (a published market price versus an uncommunicated expectation), and, similarly, the person who holds them may do so consciously or unconsciously (a specific expectation versus an unexamined, unquestioned expectation or norm). Thorough preparation, along with the use of a devil's advocate or reality check, can help prevent errors of anchoring and adjustment.

4. Framing

In decision theory terms (Tversky and Kahneman, 1981), a frame is a perspective or point of view that people use when they gather information and solve problems (again, see Chapter 2). The framing process can cause people to exhibit certain types of behavior while ignoring or avoiding others. What is of most interest here is that frames can particularly lead people to seek, avoid, or be neutral about risk in decision making and negotiation. It is in evaluating risk that framing has a strong influence on negotiators. The way that a negotiation is framed can make negotiators more or less risk averse (or risk seeking). For instance, people respond quite differently when they are negotiating to "gain" something rather than to "not lose" something (Bazerman, Magliozzi, and Neale, 1985; de Dreu, Carnevale, Emans, and van de Vliert, 1994; Neale, Huber, and Northcraft, 1987; Schurr, 1987), although the exact nature of how framing and risk propensity influence negotiation outcomes seems to be influenced by the negotiation task (Bottom, 1998; Bottom and Studt, 1993).

The way a negotiation issue is framed appears to influence the ways in which negotiators perceive risk and behave in relation to it. Neale and Bazerman (1992a) suggest two things regarding the effect of frames on risk aversion in negotiation: (1) negotiators are not usually indifferent to risk, but (2) they should not necessarily trust their intuitions regarding it. In other words, negotiators may overreact to a perceived loss when they might react more positively to the same situation if it is framed as a perceived gain. Hence, as a negotiator you must "avoid the pitfalls of being framed while, simultaneously, understanding positively and negatively framing your opponent" (Neale and Bazerman, 1992a, p. 50). When negotiators are risk averse, they are likely to accept any viable offer put on the table simply because they are afraid of losing. In contrast, when negotiators are risk seeking, they are likely to pass up an offer, choosing instead to wait for a better offer or for possible future concessions.

The tendency to either seek or avoid risk may be based on the reference point against which offers and concessions are judged (see the preceding section on anchoring and adjustment). In a typical salary negotiation, a number of reference points are possible (adapted from Bazerman and Neale, 1992):

1. Your current salary ($30,000).
2. Your potential employer's initial offer to you ($35,000).
3. The least amount you are willing to accept ($38,000).
4. Your estimate of the most the company is willing to offer to you ($40,000).
5. Your initial salary request ($45,000).

At each point on this list from the first to the fifth, the suggested frame (through which you will evaluate negotiation progress and define success) changes from positive to negative. Thus, a settlement of $35,000, which would be judged as a gain with regard to your current salary, becomes progressively framed as a loss when the standard of comparison moves down the list. The same settlement of $35,000 is a significant loss when compared against the initial request of $45,000.

This positive/negative framing process is not inconsequential. Negotiations in which the outcomes are negatively framed tend to produce fewer concessions, reach fewer agreements, and perceive outcomes as less fair than negotiations in which the outcomes are positively framed (Bazerman and Neale, 1992, p. 39). Remedies for framing effects are similar to those mentioned above (e.g., sufficient information, thorough analysis, and reality checks) but are more difficult to achieve because frames are often tied to deeply held values and beliefs or to other anchors that are hard to detect.

5. Availability of Information

Negotiators must also be concerned with the potential bias caused by the availability of information or how easy information is to retrieve—that is, how easily it can be recalled and used to inform or evaluate a process or a decision. In negotiation, the availability bias operates when information that is presented in vivid, colorful, or attention-getting ways becomes easy to recall, and thus also becomes central and critical in evaluating events and options. Information presented through a particularly clear chart, diagram, or formula (even one that is oversimplified) might be used or believed more readily than information presented in a confusing or detailed format—regardless of the accuracy of each.

The availability of information also affects negotiation through the use of established search patterns. If negotiators have a favorite way of collecting information, or looking for key signals, they will use these patterns repeatedly and hence overvalue the information that comes from them. In Chapter 2, we noted that many negotiators fail to plan, and that the planning they do tends to focus on a limited subset of information that is easily available. Negotiators who do not plan properly run the risk of being overwhelmed by the availability bias and thus losing the benefits of thorough analysis.

6. The Winner's Curse

The winner's curse refers to the tendency of negotiators, particularly in an auction setting, to settle quickly on an item and then subsequently feel discomfort about a negotiation win that comes too easily (Ball, Bazerman, and Carroll, 1991; Bazerman and Samuelson, 1983; Foreman and Murnighan, 1996). If the other party capitulates too quickly, the negotiator is often left wondering, "Could I have gotten this for less?" or asking "What's wrong with the item/product/option?" The negotiator may suspect that the other party knows too much or has insight into an unseen advantage; thus, either "I could have done better" or "This must be a bad deal."

For example, in an antique store several years ago one of the authors of this book saw a clock that he and his wife fell in love with. After spending the afternoon in the neighborhood deciding on a negotiation strategy (opening offer, bottom line, timing, feigned disinterest, the good guy/bad guy tactic), the author and his wife returned to the store to enact their strategy. The storeowner accepted their first offer. Upon arriving home, suffering from the winner's curse, they left the clock in the garage, where it remains collecting dust.

The best remedy for the winner's curse is to prevent it from occurring. Thorough investigation and preparation can provide negotiators with independent verification of the proper settlement point. Negotiators can also try to secure performance or quality guarantees from the other party to make sure the outcome is not faulty or defective.

7. Overconfidence

Overconfidence is the tendency of negotiators to believe that their ability to be correct or accurate is greater than is actually true. Overconfidence has a double-edged effect: (1) it can solidify the degree to which negotiators support positions or options that are incorrect or inappropriate, and (2) it can lead negotiators to discount the worth or validity of the judgments of others, in effect shutting down other parties as sources of information, interests, and options necessary for a successful integrative negotiation. For instance, Neale and Bazerman (1983) found that negotiators who were not trained to be aware of the overconfidence heuristic tended to overestimate their probability of being successful, and they were significantly less likely to compromise or reach agreements than trained negotiators.

More recently, Lim (1997) also studied overconfident negotiators. Before negotiations began, those negotiators who had been identified as overconfident estimated that agreements would be more likely and that they would have higher profits than did realistically confident negotiators. Lim also reported that the overconfident individuals were more persistent and were more concerned about their own outcomes than were the realistically confident negotiators. (Lim did not find a strong effect of overconfidence on negotiation outcomes, but this may have been due to the ease of the negotiation task used in the experiment.)

In summary, it appears that negotiators have a tendency to be overconfident about their own abilities, and that this overconfidence affects a wide variety of perceptions and behavior during negotiations (see Box 5.2). In particular, overconfidence can

---

BOX 5.2
Confident or Overconfident?

We came to Iceland to advance the cause of peace . . . and though we put on the table the most far-reaching arms control proposal in history, the General Secretary rejected it.

President Ronald Reagan to reporters, following
completion of presummit arms control discussions in
Reykjavik, Iceland, on October 12, 1986.

I proposed an urgent meeting here because we had something to propose . . . The Americans came to this meeting empty handed.

Secretary General Mikhail Gorbachev,
describing the same meeting to reporters.

Researchers Roderick Kramer, Elizabeth Newton, and Pamela Pommerenke (1993) have investigated the role played by positive mood and high levels of self-esteem on the cognitive biases held by negotiators. Their research has shown that negotiators with very high self-esteem and positive mood were more likely to be overconfident in their judgments prior to negotiation, as well as after the negotiation is over.

SOURCE: Adapted from Roderick Kramer, Elizabeth Newton, and Pamela Pommerenke, "Self-Enhancement Biases and Negotiator Judgment: Effects of Self-Esteem and Mood," *Organizational Behavior and Human Decision Processes* 56 (1993), pp. 110–33.

---

undermine the prospects for finding and exploiting integrative potential. This does not mean, however, that negotiators should always seek to suppress confidence or optimism. Bottom and Paese (1999) in a study of distributive bargaining found that negotiators biased toward optimism achieved more profitable settlements compared to negotiators with accurate perceptions or a bias toward pessimism. Clearly, more research is needed on the interplay of optimism, overconfidence, and negotiation outcomes.

8. The Law of Small Numbers

In decision theory, the law of small numbers refers to the tendency of people to draw conclusions from small sample sizes. In negotiation, the law of small numbers applies to the way negotiators learn and extrapolate from their own experience. If that experience is limited in time or in scope (e.g., if all of one's prior negotiations have been hard-fought and distributive), the tendency is to extrapolate prior experience onto future negotiations (e.g., all negotiations are distributive). This tendency will often lead to a self-fulfilling prophecy, as follows: People who expect to be treated in a distributive manner will (1) be more likely to perceive the other party's behavior as distributive, and (2) treat the other party in a more distributive manner. The other party will then be likely to interpret the negotiator's behavior as evidence of a distributive tendency, and will therefore respond in kind. The smaller the prior sample (i.e., the more limited the negotiation experience), the greater the possibility that past lessons will be erroneously used to infer what will happen in the future. Styles and strategies that worked in the past may not work in the future, and certainly will not work if future negotiations differ significantly from past experiences.

9. Self-Serving Biases

People often explain another person's behavior by making attributions, either to the person (i.e., the behaviors were caused by internal factors such as ability, mood, or effort) or to the situation (i.e., the behaviors were caused by external factors such as the task, other people, or fate) (Heider, 1958). In "explaining" another person's behavior, the tendency is to overestimate the causal role of personal or internal factors and underestimate the causal role of situational or external factors. This tendency is known as the *fundamental attribution error* (Ross, 1977). An an example, consider the student who arrives late for a morning class. Perhaps she is lazy (an internal, dispositional explanation), or perhaps she had a flat tire driving to campus (an external, situational explanation). The fundamental attribution error suggests a tendency for the professor, absent other information, to be biased toward the internal explanation (she's lazy). Perceptual biases are often exacerbated by the *actor-observer effect*, in which people tend to attribute their own behavior to situational factors, but attribute others' behaviors to personal factors (Jones and Nisbett, 1976), saying in effect, "If I mess up, it's bad luck (the situation, someone else's fault, etc.); if you mess up, it's your fault!"

Recent research has documented the effects of self-serving biases on the negotiation process. For instance, Babcock, Wang and Loewenstein (1996) found that negotiators in different school districts chose comparison school districts in a self-serving way; that is, the districts they chose as comparison standards for their own district's activities were those that made their districts look most favorable. In another example, de Dreu, Nauta, and van de Vliert (1995) found that negotiators believed that they used more constructive tactics than their counterparts (also see Kramer, Newton, and Pommerenke, 1993), and that the strength of this self-serving bias increased with the strength of the conflict between the parties. Finally, Thompson (1995) found that participants in a negotiation were less accurate in estimating the other party's preferred outcomes than were nonpartisan observers watching the negotiation. Thompson also found that for partisan observers, involvement in the negotiation reduced the accuracy of their perceptions of the other party's preferences while it increased the perceptual accuracy of nonpartisan observers. Thompson's sobering finding reveals that when people "know" they are right, confidence is not related to perceptual accuracy.

Perceptual error may also be expressed in the form of biases or distortions in the evaluation of data. For instance, the false-consensus effect is a tendency to overestimate the degree of support and consensus that exists for one's own position, opinions, or behaviors (Ross, Greene, and House, 1977). If consensus information is available, but expressed in numerical probabilities (e.g., one chance in a hundred), many observers neglect to use the information, falling subject to a bias called the base rate fallacy (Bar-Hillel, 1980). Either of these biases can seriously damage a negotiation effort—negotiators subject to them would make faulty judgments regarding tactics or outcome probabilities.

10. Endowment Effect

The endowment effect is the tendency to overvalue something you own or believe you possess. Kahneman, Knetsch, and Thaler (1990) demonstrated the existence of the endowment effect rather dramatically in a series of experiments involving coffee mugs. In one experiment, some participants were asked whether they would prefer a sum of money or the mug at various possible dollar levels. Based on their responses, it could be determined that they assigned an average value of just over $3.00 to the mug. Other participants were asked to value the mug as a potential buyer; the average value they assigned to the mug was just under $3.00. Members of a third group were actually given the mug, and then asked if they would sell the mug for various amounts. Their answers indicated that they placed a value of more than $7.00 on the mug! (In a replication, Kahneman and his colleagues left the price tags on the mugs, making the objective value of the mug clearly visible to participants. Nonetheless, results were consistent with those just described.) Thus, the simple act of possessing something seems to induce people to elevate its perceived value, even when its actual value is known.

In negotiation, the endowment effect can lead to inflated estimations of value that interfere with reaching a good deal. Bazerman, Moore, and Gillespie (1999) discussed endowment effects in the context of negotiations over environmental issues. Viewing the endowment effect as an inflated personal attachment to the status quo, Bazerman and colleagues argued that the status quo serves as a "potentially dysfunctional anchor point, making mutually beneficial trades more difficult" (p. 1288). They illustrate with a hypothetical environmentalist who places excessive value on preserving existing wilderness at the expense of pursing opportunities to protect or restore other lands. "The result," say Bazerman et al., "is likely to be a steep, sticky slope in which environmentalists will fight to preserve natural areas they perceive as being pristine but in which, once lost, wilderness is unlikely to be restored" (p. 1288).

11. Ignoring Others' Cognitions

Negotiators often just don't bother to ask about the other party's perceptions and thoughts, which leaves them to work with incomplete information, and thus produces faulty results. Failure to consider others' cognitions allows negotiators to simplify their thinking about otherwise complex processes; this usually leads to a more distributive strategy and causes a failure to recognize the contingent nature of both sides' behaviors and responses. Although this "failure to consider" might be attributed to some basic, underlying bias against the other party, research suggests that it is more often a way "to make decision making under uncertainty more manageable" (Carroll, Bazerman, and Maury, 1988). Research also suggests that training and awareness of this trap reduces its effects only modestly (Carroll, Delquie, Halpern, and Bazerman, 1990). The emotional drives at work here can be very deep-seated, and they can be avoided only if negotiators explicitly focus on accurately understanding the other party's interests, goals, and perspectives.

12. Reactive Devaluation

Reactive devaluation is the process of devaluing the other party's concessions simply because the other party made them (Stillenger, Epelbaum, Keltner, and Ross, 1990). Such devaluation may be based in emotionality ("I just don't like that so-and-so") or on distrust fostered by past experience. Reactive devaluation leads negotiators to minimize the magnitude of a concession made by a disliked other, to reduce their willingness to respond with a concession of equal size, or to seek even more from the other party once a concession has been made (see Neale and Bazerman, 1992b). Reactive devaluation may be minimized by maintaining an objective view of the process, or assigning a colleague to do this task; by clarifying each side's preferences on options and concessions before any are made (Stillenger et al., 1990); or by using a third party to mediate or filter concession-making processes (see Chapter 13).

MANAGING MISPERCEPTIONS AND COGNITIVE BIASES IN NEGOTIATION

Misperceptions and cognitive biases arise automatically and out of conscious awareness as negotiators gather and process information. The more complex the situation, the more opportunities that exist for information bias and distortion to hinder judgment and decision making (Hammond, Keeney, and Raiffa, 1998). The result for negotiators can be overreliance on faulty assumptions, leading to deals that are suboptimal.

The question of how best to manage the negative consequences of misperception is very difficult to answer. Certainly the first level of managing such distortions is to be aware that they can occur. However, awareness by itself may not be enough; research evidence shows that simply telling people about misconceptions and cognitive biases does little to counteract their effects (Babcock and Loewenstein, 1997; Foreman and Murnighan, 1996; Thompson and Hastie, 1990a). For instance, Foreman and Murnighan tried to teach students to avoid the winner's curse in a series of auction simulations. They told students about the results of 128 auctions over a four-week period but found that the training had little impact on reducing the winner's curse.

Whyte and Sebenius (1997) took a different approach to trying to reduce the effects of the anchoring and adjustment bias. They had negotiators participate in a group discussion to see if the group process reduced the use of inappropriate anchors to set initial offers, aspiration levels, and bottom lines for an upcoming real estate negotiation. The results showed that both individuals and groups used inappropriate anchors to set their initial offers, aspiration levels, and bottom lines, and that groups were as susceptible to the effects of anchoring and adjustment as were individuals. This suggests that merely discussing how to set opening offers, aspiration levels, and bottom lines with team members will not reduce the effects of anchoring and adjustment.

"Careful—it might be a trap!"

Clearly, then, merely telling people about a perceptual or cognitive bias, or having them discuss things in a group setting, does not make the bias go away. Unfortunately, there has been little other research done on managing perceptual biases. An exception is a study by Arunachalam and Dilla (1995), who had subjects participate in a simulated negotiation to set transfer prices between two divisions of the same company, in either an unstructured or a structured communication condition. In the unstructured communication condition, participants were given their role-play information and asked to prepare for the negotiation. Before bargaining in the structured communication condition, however, participants were also asked to complete a questionnaire asking them to identify what they thought their counterpart's priorities were in the negotiation. They then received training on how to identify and discuss issues and priorities in negotiation effectively. Finally, participants in both conditions negotiated either face-to-face or via computer terminals. Arunachalam and Dilla found that (1) negotiators in the structured communication condition negotiated higher profit outcomes and made fewer fixed-pie errors than negotiators in the unstructured communication condition, and (2) negotiators in the face-to-face condition negotiated higher profits and had fewer fixed-pie errors than negotiators in the computer terminal condition. The authors concluded that both problem definition and problem evaluation are important components of reducing fixed-pie bias. Careful discussion of the issues and preferences by both negotiators may reduce the effects of perceptual biases. Arunachalam and Dilla did not study the consequences of only one negotiator following this strategy, however, so it is not clear what would happen if both negotiators did not agree to participate in the decision-making process.

In conclusion, more research needs to be conducted to provide negotiators with advice about how to manage the negative effects of misperception and cognitive biases in negotiation. Until then, the best advice that negotiators can follow is simply to be aware of the negative aspects of these effects, and to discuss them in a structured manner within their team and with their counterparts. Given the strength of the biases, this advice is weak, and we hope that researchers will be able to identify other useful techniques for managing misperceptions and biases.

Reframing

It is likely that negotiators will apply several different frames to the same negotiation. When different negotiators apply different, or mismatched, frames, they will find the bargaining process ambiguous and frustrating. In such situations, it may become necessary to reframe the negotiation systematically, to assist the other party in reframing the negotiation, or to establish a common frame or set of frames within which the negotiation may be conducted more productively. Reframing might involve any of a number of approaches. For instance, rather than perceiving a particular outcome as a loss, the negotiator might reframe it as an opportunity to gain (e.g., Kahneman and Tversky, 1979), that is, as a bright-side alternative to approaching a given situation. For instance, when a company loses a contract bid (a loss), those involved may use this information to reexamine their cost structure.

Negotiators can also reframe by trying to perceive or understand the situation in a different way or from a different perspective. For instance, they can constructively reframe a problem by defining it in terms that are broader or narrower, bigger or smaller, riskier or less risky, or subject to a longer or shorter time constraint. We discussed how this could be done in Chapter 4, in our review of ways in which the parties could creatively invent options to ensure mutual gain. Because reframing requires negotiators to be flexible during the negotiation itself, during the planning phase, they should plan for multiple contingencies to occur during negotiations. The ebb and flow of the framing and issue development processes means that negotiators cannot completely plan the sequence of a negotiation at the outset but rather need to be prepared for shifts in the discussion.

COMMUNICATION IN NEGOTIATION

Most analyses of communication begin with a basic model of the communication process, and we do so here. An early and influential model developed by Shannon and Weaver (1948) conceptualizes communication as an activity that occurs between two people: a *sender* and a *receiver*.[2] A sender has a thought or meaning in his or her mind. The sender encodes this meaning into a message that is to be transmitted to a receiver. For instance, the thought could be about the sender's preference for a particular outcome in a negotiation. The message may be encoded into verbal language (e.g., words and sentences); nonverbal expression (e.g., facial gestures, hand waving, and finger pointing); or both. Once encoded, the message is then transmitted (e.g., via voice, facial expression,

---

[2] Clearly communication can occur among more than two people, but the same general processes are expected to apply as to the two-person case, albeit with more complexity. For the sake of clarity, we will restrict our discussion to the two-person case in this chapter. The complexity of negotiations involving more than two parties is examined in detail in Chapter 9.

or written statement) through a channel (e.g., face-to-face interaction, telephone, e-mail, letter) to the receiver. The receiver's receptors—eyes and ears—receive the transmission and then the brain decodes it, giving meaning and understanding to the receiver.

In one-way communication, from sender to receiver, this process would constitute a complete transmission. A sender who writes a message, reads it over to check its clarity, and sends it by e-mail to the receiver generally assumes that the message is received and understood. However, most communication, particularly in negotiation, involves dialogue and discussion. As a result, the receiver takes an active role in the communication process, first, by providing the sender information about how the message was received and, second, by becoming a sender and responding to, building on, or rebutting the message of the original sender. For the current discussion, we shall refer to both of these processes as *feedback*. In the feedback process, receivers decode the message and reach their own understanding of what the sender said. They may also ascribe meaning to the message by interpreting its information content as well as the motives that the sender may have had for transmitting that content.

Receivers then become senders of communication back to the original sender. The encoded feedback message may take multiple forms: questions or other communications intended to obtain clarification of the original message, emotional reactions to the content or context of the message, or rebuttals to the statements in the message. All these forms of encoded feedback can be transmitted through various channels, received, and decoded by the original source. The entire sequence may range from something as simple as a question by one person ("Want to go for a cup of coffee?") and an affirmative nod by another, to complex statements of fact and opinion, and equally complex responses as negotiators shape a multilevel, comprehensive agreement that will have to be accepted by several contentious parties.

Having sketched this basic model of the communication process between two parties, we next consider two key implications for negotiation: first, the distortions that can occur in communication, and second, how communication in negotiation can be viewed in phases or stages.

Distortion in Communication

Communication works to the degree that a wide variety of information—facts, opinions, feelings, preferences, and experiences—is completely and thoroughly shared among the parties, and mutual understanding is reached. As most of us know from experience, human communication systems seldom perform to the highest possible degree. Rather, the elements of the model and the linkages among them are subject to external factors that distort messages and their meaning, preventing them from being understood completely. In the following paragraphs, we will explore how distortions occur in communication by looking at the individual elements that comprise the communication sequence in the Shannon and Weaver (1948) model.

1. *Senders* and *receivers* each have goals and objectives, things that they want to accomplish. The sender may want to change the receiver's mind or secure concessions toward a negotiated agreement. A receiver may not want to have his

or her mind changed or to make concessions; moreover, the receiver is likely to want the sender to change or make concessions. The more diverse the goals of the sender and receiver, or the more antagonistic they are in their relationship, the greater the likelihood that distortions and errors in communication will occur (de Dreu, Nauta, and van de Vliert, 1995). Similarly, senders and receivers differ in their individual characteristics—each is likely to have different personal values, attitudes toward certain issues and objectives, previous experiences, life history, and personality characteristics. Each of these elements contributes to a different way of viewing the world.

2. *Transmitters* and *receptors* are the means through which information is sent and received. Information can be transmitted verbally—by speaking or by writing—and nonverbally—by body posture, hand and facial gestures, tone of voice, and the like. The choice of transmitter can affect outcomes. Some messages may be better spoken, whereas others need to be written. Moreover, when presenting information face-to-face, the congruence or incongruence between multiple transmission channels is often a problem. If a parent says to a child, "Don't do that!" but simultaneously smiles or laughs, the incongruity of the messages can lead to confusion ("Do I stop, or do I keep doing it?"). On the receiver's end, poor eyesight, faulty hearing, or a distracted mental state may similarly diminish the ability to receive a message accurately.

3. *Messages* are the symbolic forms by which information is communicated. Humans are unique in their ability to use symbols—primarily written or spoken language—to transmit information. Some messages are direct expressions of meaning (e.g., I lean over the table and take the pencil I want) whereas others are symbolic representations (e.g., I say to the person seated across the table, "Please pass me the pencil"). The more prone we are to use symbolic communication, the more likely it is that the symbols we choose may not accurately communicate the meaning we intend. In the pencil example, if the other person does not understand English, or if there are several different pencils on the table, the communication will be less effective.

4. *Encoding* is the process by which messages are put into symbolic form. The encoding process will be affected by varying degrees of skill in encoding (e.g., fluency in language, skill at written and oral expression). It will also be affected by earlier communication, including what both parties want to communicate and how they have reacted to earlier communications. Senders are likely to encode messages in the form which receivers may not prefer. Consider two managers who want to negotiate an agreement. One may prefer to get together and discuss it over lunch, then shake hands on the deal and be done with it, whereas the other may prefer to prepare a written draft that the managers can exchange and revise until they agree on the specific wording. Thus, how the contract will be prepared may itself be a subject of negotiation.

5. *Channels* are the conduits by which messages are carried from one party to another. If we speak directly, the channels are the airwaves; if we write, they are the paper and pen or the word processor; if we speak over the telephone, they are

the telephone circuitry, cables, and microwaves. Messages are subject to distortion from channel *noise,* a broad term used to describe various forms of interference in the communication process. Messages can be transmitted more clearly in a quiet room than in a loud restaurant. The greater the sources of distraction and confusion in the communication environment, the more likely it is that noise will interfere with accurate and complete message transmission.

6. *Decoding* is the process of translating messages from their symbolic form into a form that makes sense. If the parties speak the same language or use the same common nonverbal gestures to communicate messages, the process may be reasonably simple, although it is subject to perceptual and cognitive errors (see above). When people speak different languages, decoding involves higher degrees of error. Although translators may help decode the other party's messages, full translation may not be possible; that is, it may not be possible to capture fully the other party's meaning or tone along with the words. In fact, translators introduce the possibility of additional error into the communication process.

7. *Meanings* are the facts, ideas, feelings, reactions, or thoughts that exist within individuals and act as a set of filters for interpreting the decoded messages. If one person has said to the other, "Please pass me that pencil," and the other person has said, "No," the encoded *no* is likely to stimulate a variety of reactions in the first person's search for its exact meaning: Was the *no* a direct refusal to the request? Why did the other person say no? Does he need the pencil too? Is he being obstinate and intentionally blocking me? Was it a playful joke? Answers to these questions will vary depending on other aspects of the communication sequence and the relationship between the parties, all of which lead the person to ascribe different meanings to the word *no.*

8. *Feedback* is the process by which the receiver reacts to the sender's message. Even in one-way communication, feedback is necessary to inform the sender that the message was received, encoded, and ascribed with the meaning that the sender intended. The absence of feedback can contribute to significant distortions in communication, especially when senders do not know whether their message has been received, much less understood. Those addressing a large audience may find themselves either speaking into space or directing comments to people who are nodding their heads to signify agreement, smiling, or otherwise acknowledging that the communication is being received and appreciated. The sender is unlikely to continue directing comments to receivers who are scowling, sleeping, or shaking their heads to signify disagreement, unless the comments are specifically designed to influence them to act otherwise. Feedback can, however, also distort communication in negotiation by leading negotiators to change how they negotiate or evaluate negotiation outcomes (Larrick and Boles, 1995; Thompson, Valley, and Kramer, 1995), and even by influencing the offers they make (e.g., Kristensen and Garling, 1997). It is important for negotiators to realize that feedback can play multiple roles. Some feedback is genuinely intended to improve understanding, but feedback can also be used strategically to induce negotiators to adjust their requests or

change their evaluation of the negotiation process or outcome. Finally, feedback can also play a motivational role, meaning that the results of feedback can motivate (or demotivate) the sender to change his or her behavior, either in a positive or negative direction.

Phase Models of Communication in Negotiation

A strong research tradition examining communication and negotiation has examined the process that communication follows during negotiations. In a seminal piece of work in this area, Morley and Stephenson (1977) proposed that Bales's (1950) scheme for analyzing communication in small groups could be modified to apply to negotiation communication. Bales's framework analyzes the dialogue of small-group meetings, using categories representing two major dimensions of group activity: "task" activities, in which group members focused on the nature of the problem to be solved or job to be accomplished, and "process" activities, in which group members displayed various social-emotional reactions to one another as the activity progressed. Bales's work demonstrated that communication changes as groups work on their tasks and that clear stages of group communication process could be identified.

Morley and Stephenson (1977) extended Bales's (1950) work by defining a communication content analysis mechanism (conference process analysis) for assessing negotiation deliberations. They identified three dimensions of such communication: mode, resource, and reference. The *mode* dimension indicates how information is exchanged; modes include offers, acceptances, rejections, or requests for responses from the other side. The *resource* dimension refers to the function of the information being exchanged; for instance, structuring the negotiations, as when discussing procedures; focusing on outcomes, as when discussing settlement points or limits; acknowledging others' behaviors, as with praise or criticism; and exchanging information, such as facts or supporting data. Finally, the *reference* dimension indicates who is being referred to in the information: the negotiator, a fellow team member, an opposing team member, the negotiator's organization, the opposing organization, or some combination of the above.

By applying this coding scheme to transcripts of negotiations from a complex role-play, Morley and Stephenson were able to confirm that negotiation, like communication in problem-solving groups, proceeds through distinct phases or stages (refer back to our discussion of phases and stages in Chapter 2). In the early stages, negotiators are engaged in behavior to state and defend their own position to the other party. The most important elements of this stage are building a strong case for one's own side and demonstrating power to the other side. At some point, negotiators move to a second phase during which they become less competitive and protective of their original position; they move from a more expository mode to a problem-oriented mode, searching for possible solutions within the criteria or limits that were defined earlier. Finally, in the third stage, negotiators work to achieve a joint solution. At this point, they are trying to agree on a settlement point that will satisfy each party and those they represent.

More recently, Goering (1997) used similar techniques to study the communication strategies used by labor and management negotiators at various phases of a process of collective bargaining. She found that the strategies used by each side varied depending on phase. For example, early in the negotiations, representatives of management were more likely to use offensive strategies (tactics that attack the opponent's position), while labor negotiators were more likely to use defensive or integrative strategies. In middle phases, Goering found that labor increased its use of offensive strategies, while management negotiators grew more defensive. By late stages, strategic differences between the sides mostly disappear. Goering's results and those of earlier studies suggest that negotiators frequently converge in their communication styles as the encounter progresses, especially to the extent that the tone and substance of the negotiation is shifting from a distributive to an integrative focus. (We discuss how negotiators can use reframing techniques to manage these shifts in Chapter 12.)

WHAT IS COMMUNICATED DURING NEGOTIATION?

One of the fundamental questions that researchers in communication and negotiation have examined is, What is communicated during negotiation? This work has taken several different forms but generally involves audio taping or videotaping negotiation role-plays and analyzing the patterns of communication that occur in them. For instance, Alexander, Schul, and Babakus (1991) videotaped executives who participated in a 60-minute, three-person negotiation involving two oil companies. The videotapes were classified into 6,432 verbal units, which were then coded into 24 different response categories. The researchers found that over 70 percent of the verbal tactics that buyers and sellers used during the negotiation were integrative. In addition, buyers and sellers tended to behave reciprocally—when one party used an integrative tactic, the other tended to respond with an integrative tactic.

Most of the communication during negotiation is not about negotiator preferences (Carnevale, Pruitt, and Seilheimer, 1981), and while the blend of integrative versus distributive content varies as a function of the issues being discussed (Weingart, Hyder, and Prietula, 1996), it is also clear that the content of communication is only partly responsible for negotiation outcomes (Olekalns, Smith, and Walsh, 1996). For example, one party may choose not to communicate certain things (e.g., the reason she chose a different supplier), so her counterpart (e.g., the supplier not chosen) may be unaware why some outcomes occur. In the following sections, we discuss five different categories of communication that take place during negotiations, and then consider the question of whether more communication is always better than less communication.

1. Offers and Counteroffers

According to Tutzauer (1992), "Perhaps the most important communications in a bargaining session are those that convey the disputants' offers and counteroffers" (p. 67). Tutzauer assumes that bargainers have definite preferences and exhibit rational behavior by acting in accordance with those preferences, and that the preferences can be expressed according to some numerical scale, that is, that they have different degrees of utility or worth (see also Luce and Raiffa, 1957, and refer back to Chapter 3). A communicative framework for negotiation, in turn, is based on the assumptions that (1) the communication of offers is a dynamic process (the offers change or shift over time); (2) the offer process is interactive (bargainers influence each other); and (3) various internal and external factors (e.g., time limitations, reciprocity norms, alternatives, constituency pressures) drive the interaction and "motivate a bargainer to change his or her offer" (Tutzauer, p. 73). In other words, the offer-counteroffer process is dynamic and interactive, like the reciprocal influence process described in Chapter 3, and subject to situational and environmental constraints. This process constantly revises the parameters of the negotiation, eventually narrowing the bargaining range and guiding the discussion toward a settlement point.

2. Information about Alternatives

Communication in negotiation is not limited to the exchange of offers and counteroffers, however. Another important aspect that has been studied is how sharing information with the other party influences the negotiation process. For instance, Pinkley and her colleagues (Pinkley, 1995; Pinkley, Neale, and Bennett, 1994) have examined the question of whether simply having a best alternative to a negotiated agreement (BATNA) (Fisher, Ury, and Patton, 1991) is sufficient to give a negotiator an advantage over the other party, or whether the BATNA needs to be communicated to the other person. Pinkley and her colleagues found that the existence of a BATNA changed several things in a negotiation: (1) compared to negotiators without attractive BATNAs, negotiators with attractive BATNAs set higher reservation prices for themselves than their counterparts did; (2) negotiators whose counterparts had attractive BATNAs set lower reservation points for themselves; and (3) when both parties were aware of the attractive BATNA that one of the negotiators had, that negotiator received a more positive negotiation outcome. The results of this research suggest that negotiators with an attractive BATNA should tell the other party about it if they expect to receive its full benefits.

3. Information about Outcomes

In a simulation study of negotiation, Thompson, Valley, and Kramer (1995) examined the effects of sharing different types of information, how the other party evaluated his or her success in the negotiation, and how this influenced negotiators' evaluations of their own success. The study focused on how winners and losers evaluated their negotiation outcomes (*winners* were defined as negotiators who received more points in the negotiation simulation). Thompson and her colleagues found that winners and losers evaluated their own outcomes equally when they did not know how well the other party had done, but if they found out that the other negotiator had done better, or was simply pleased with his or her outcome, then negotiators felt less positive about their own outcome. The results of this study suggest that negotiators should be careful not to share their outcomes or even their positive reactions to the outcomes with the other party, especially if they are going to negotiate with that party again in the future. In addition, the study suggested that negotiators should evaluate their own success before learning about the other party's evaluations of the outcomes.

4. Social Accounts

Another type of communication that occurs during negotiation consists of the "social accounts" that negotiators use to explain things to the other party (see Bies and Shapiro, 1987; Shapiro, 1991), especially when negotiators need to justify bad news. A review of the relevant literature by Sitkin and Bies (1993) suggests that three types of explanations are important: (1) *explanations of mitigating circumstances,* where negotiators suggest that they had no choice in taking the positions they did; (2) *explanations of exonerating circumstances,* where negotiators explain their positions from a broader perspective, suggesting that while their current position may appear negative, it derives from positive motives (e.g., an honest mistake); and (3) *reframing explanations,* where outcomes can be explained by changing the context (e.g., short-term pain for long-term gain). Sitkin and Bies suggest that negotiators who use multiple explanations are more likely to have better outcomes and that the negative effects of poor outcomes can be alleviated by communicating explanations for them.

5. Communication about Process

Lastly, some communication is about the negotiation process itself—how well it is going, or what procedures might be adopted to improve the situation. A study by Brett, Shapiro, and Lytle (1998) examined communication strategies in negotiation that are used to halt conflict spirals that might otherwise lead to impasse or less-than-ideal outcomes. One such strategy involves calling attention to the other party's contentious actions and explicitly labeling the process as counterproductive. More generally, Brett and her colleagues suggest that negotiators seeking to break out of a conflict spiral should resist the natural urge to reciprocate contentious communication from the other party.

Is More Information Always Better?

Some research has suggested that receiving too much information during negotiation may actually be detrimental to negotiators; this is sometimes called the information-is-weakness effect (e.g., Roth and Malouf, 1979; Schelling, 1960; Siegel and Fouraker, 1960) (see Box 5.3 for a discussion of ways to manage communication during a negotiation). The argument here is that negotiators who know the complete preferences of both parties will have more difficulty determining fair outcomes than will negotiators who do not have this information. Brodt (1994) conducted a study to examine how a specific type of information—namely, inside information about the other party's deadline—influenced the negotiation process. In a simulation study of a distributive negotiation over an exotic automobile, Brodt found that negotiators with inside information (1) paid less for the car, (2) were less likely to make concessions during negotiation, and (3) made more creative offers during negotiation than did negotiators without inside information. Brodt concluded that having more information enhanced the negotiator's strength, suggesting that the information-is-weakness effect may be limited to very specific circumstances.

BOX 5.3
Staying Clear-Headed at the Negotiating Table

One of the most difficult aspects of negotiation is the actual give-and-take that occurs at the table. Should I stick with this point, or is it time to fold? Should I open the bidding or wait for the other side to take the lead? It requires good judgment to make these tough decisions. While experience certainly contributes to the development of judgment, other key ingredients are the knack of analyzing situations, the courage to make concessions when they're called for, and the willingness to stick to an unpopular position when necessary. Also important are creativity, persuasiveness, and the ability to see the big picture of the exchange.

James Freund is a lawyer and experienced negotiator. He recommends the following:

- *Stay in balance.* Remember that there is a time to be aggressive and a time to concede, a time to wrap things up and a time to keep options open. It is important to strike some sort of balance in the process, even when you are in the driver's seat, to ensure that your future relationship with this negotiating partner (or your own personal reputation as a negotiator) does not suffer from this single encounter.

- *Manage appearances.* The negotiator who arrives at the meeting with bags packed and a plane ticket obtrusively in the pocket of her coat telegraphs to her counterpart, "Hey, I want to wrap this up and make my plane home." Her opponent will be motivated to slow the tempo of negotiation, expecting that she will be willing to make big concessions as the time for her departure grows closer. Cultivating an appearance that says you will wait patiently for the best deal to be negotiated is a more effective strategy.

- *Be patient.* You can learn a great deal about your counterpart's real level of desire by hanging back and watching. Does he hurry things along? Is she willing to take time to learn the details of a new but complex proposal? Patient adherence to your position provides you with gradually increasing credibility as negotiations wear on.

Freund concluded, "Patience and perseverance are most effective when clothed in a low-key style that emphasizes deliberateness rather than obstinacy. So learn how to insist on your point without being overbearing—and how to say no without seeming too negative" (p. 34).

SOURCE: Adapted from J. C. Freund, "Being a Smart Negotiator," *Directors and Boards,* 2, no. 18 (Winter 1994), pp. 33–36.

A study by O'Connor (1997), however, demonstrates that having more information does not automatically translate into better negotiation outcomes. O'Connor had subjects participate in a role-play of a union–management negotiation over an employment contract, which included both integrative issues and common-value issues (i.e., issues where both parties wanted the same outcome). Subjects negotiated in either cooperative or individualistic dyads. O'Connor found that cooperative dyads exchanged more information than individualistic dyads, but that the amount of information exchanged did not improve the overall accuracy of the parties' perceptions of each other's preferences. When cooperative and individualistic pairs were examined separately, O'Connor found the following pattern of results: For cooperative negotiators, accurate exchange of information about preferences led to more positive negotiation outcomes on integrative issues, but there was no relation between information exchange and outcomes for common-value issues. For individualistic negotiators, more information exchange led to worse negotiation outcomes on integrative issues, but there was also no relation between information exchange and outcomes on common-value issues. The results of O'Connor's study suggest that the influence of the exchange of accurate information on negotiation outcomes is not as direct as people might expect—that is, simply exchanging information does not automatically lead to better understanding of the other party's preferences or to better negotiation outcomes. Nor does it automatically result in the "information is weakness" effect. Rather, the effect of exchanging information during negotiation depends on the type of issues being discussed and the negotiators' motivation to use the information.

HOW PEOPLE COMMUNICATE IN NEGOTIATION

While it may seem obvious that how negotiators communicate is as important as what they have to say, research has examined different aspects of *how* people communicate in negotiation. We address two aspects related to the "how" of communication: the characteristics of language that communicators use, and the selection of a communication channel for sending and receiving messages.

Use of Language

Gibbons, Bradac, and Busch (1992) have proposed that negotiation "represents the exchange of information through language that coordinates and manages meaning" (p. 156). In negotiation, language operates at two levels: the *logical* level (for proposals or offers) and the *pragmatic* level (semantics, syntax, and style). The meaning conveyed by a proposition or statement is a combination of one logical, surface message and several pragmatic (i.e., hinted or inferred) messages. In other words, it is not only what is said and how it is said that matters but also what additional, veiled, or subsurface information is intended, conveyed, or perceived in reception. By way of illustration, consider threats. We often react not only to the substance of a threatening statement but also (and frequently more strongly) to its unspoken messages. Gibbons, Bradac, and Busch identify five linguistic dimensions of making threats:

1. The use of *polarized language,* in which negotiators use positive words when speaking of their own positions (e.g., generous, reasonable, or even-handed) and negative words when referring to the other party's position (e.g., tight-fisted, unreasonable, or heavy-handed).

2. The conveyance of *verbal immediacy* (a measure of intended immediacy, urgency, or relative psychological distance), either high and intended to engage or compel the other party ("Okay, here is the deal" or "I take great care to . . .") or low and intended to create a sense of distance or aloofness ("Well, there it is" or "One should take great care to . . .").

3. The degree of *language intensity,* in which high intensity conveys strong feelings to the recipient (as with statements of affirmation or the frequent use of profanity) and low intensity conveys weak feelings.

4. The degree of *lexical diversity* (i.e., the command of a broad, rich vocabulary), where high levels of lexical diversity denote comfort and competence with language, and low levels denote discomfort, anxiety, or inexperience.

5. The extent of *high-power language style,* with low power denoted by the use of verbal hedges, hesitations, or politeness to the point of deference and subordination, and high power denoted by verbal dominance, clarity and firmness of expression, and self-assurance.

Using these dimensions, Gibbons, Bradac, and Busch suggest that threats can be made more credible and more compelling by negatively polarized descriptions of the other party and his or her position, high immediacy, high intensity, high lexical diversity, and a distinctively high-power style.

Whether the intent is to command and compel, sell, persuade, or gain commitment, how parties communicate in negotiation would seem to depend on the ability of the speaker to encode thoughts properly, as well as on the ability of the listener to understand and decode the intended message(s) (see again Figure 5.1). In addition, negotiators' use of idioms or colloquialisms is often problematic, especially in cross-cultural negotiations (see Chapter 11). The meaning conveyed might be clear to the speaker but confusing to the listener (e.g., "I'm willing to stay until the last dog is hung"—a statement of positive commitment on the part of some regional Americans, but confusing at best to those with different cultural backgrounds, even within the United States). Even if the meaning is clear, the choice of a word or metaphor may convey a lack of sensitivity or create a sense of exclusion, as is often done when men relate strategic business concerns by using sports metaphors ("Well, it's fourth down and goal to go; this is no time to drop the ball"). Intentional or not, the message received or inferred by women may be that they're excluded from the club. Deborah Tannen (1990), in her aptly named book *You Just Don't Understand,* states that "male-female miscommunication may be more dangerous [than cross-cultural miscommunication] because it is more pervasive in our lives, and we are less prepared for it" (p. 281). Because people generally aren't aware of the potential for such miscommunication with someone from their own culture, they are less well prepared to deal with such miscommunication than they would be if the person were from a different culture.

Finally, a negotiator's choice of words may not only signal a position but also shape and predict it. Using language and its relation to cognitive maps—that is, "the concepts and relations [a party] uses to understand organizational situations" (Weick and Bougon, 1986, p. 106)—Simons (1993) examined the linguistic patterns of communication in negotiations and found two salient points: First, parties whose statements communicated interests in both the substance of the negotiation (i.e., things) and the relationship with the other party (i.e., people) achieved better, more integrative solutions than parties whose statements were concerned solely with either substance or relationship. Second, in support of Thompson and Hastie (1990a), "early discussion in negotiation may be critical in defining issues in a way that promotes or inhibits the discovery of integrative solutions" (Simons, p. 154). The "stage-setting" value of constructive communication is borne out by Simons's finding that "linguistic patterns from the first half of negotiation were better predictors of agreements than linguistic patterns from the second half of negotiation" (p. 139).

Selection of a Communication Channel

Communication is experienced differently when it occurs through different channels. We may think of negotiation as typically occurring face-to-face—an assumption reinforced by the common metaphor of the "negotiation table." But the reality is that people negotiate through a variety of communication media: over the telephone, in writing, and increasingly through electronic channels such as e-mail and teleconferencing systems (sometimes referred to as "virtual negotiations"). The use of a particular channel shapes both perceptions of the communication task at hand and norms regarding appropriate behavior; accordingly, channel variations are potentially important drivers of negotiation processes and outcomes (Bazerman, Curhan, Moore, and Valley, 2000; Lewicki and Dineen, 2002).

For our purposes here, the key variation that distinguishes one communication channel from another is *social presence* (Short, Williams, and Christie, 1976)—the ability of a channel to carry and convey subtle social cues from sender to receiver that go beyond the literal "text" of the message itself. For example, as an alternative to face-to-face interaction, the telephone preserves one's ability to transmit social cues through inflection or tone of voice, but forfeits the ability to communicate through facial expressions or physical gestures. In written communication, there are only the words and symbols on paper, although one's choice of words and the way they are arranged can certainly convey tone, (in)formality, and emotion.

E-mail, as an increasingly ubiquitous mode of personal and organizational communication, can be viewed as simply another form of written communication that happens to involve electronic transmission. There are, however, important distinctions between e-mail and other forms of written communication. Many users, regarding e-mail as a highly informal medium, are comfortable sending messages that are stylistically or grammatically unpolished in situations (such as on the job) where they would never send a carelessly written communication on paper. Some e-mail users incorporate text-based "emoticons" to convey emotional social cues in their messages (the notorious smiley face [:-)] is perhaps the best known emoticon). Some research on interpersonal and small-group communication through computers indicates that the lack of social cues lowers communicator inhibition and leads to more aggressive communication behavior that is unrestrained by social norms, such as "flaming" (Sproull and Kiesler, 1986). However, much of the research into computer-mediated communication has focused on anonymous interaction. It is not clear that reduced social cues have the same effect in a communication context, such as negotiation, where the parties are known to each other, and in fact may know each other quite well (Barry and Fulmer, 2001).

Treating e-mail as just another vehicle for written communication is analytically simplistic because e-mail interactions frequently substitute for communication that would otherwise occur via telephone, face-to-face, or perhaps not at all. Accordingly, it is not enough to ask how e-mail communication differs from conventional writing; we need also to understand how interaction (such as negotiation) is affected when people choose to use e-mail rather than communicate through higher social presence channels.

Researchers have been examining the effects of channels in general, and e-mail in particular, on negotiation processes and outcomes during much of the past decade. Unfortunately, there are few consistent findings that point to clear effects. We do know that interacting parties can more easily develop personal rapport in face-to-face communication compared to other channels (Drolet and Morris, 2000), and that face-to-face negotiators are more inclined to disclose information truthfully, increasing their ability to attain mutual gain (Valley, Moag, and Bazerman, 1998). There is evidence that negotiation through written channels is more likely to end in impasse than negotiation that occurs face-to-face or by phone (Valley et al., 1998), although an attempt to extend this finding to written e-mail did not yield a clear finding (Croson, 1999). There is also evidence that e-mail negotiators reach agreements that are more equal (a balanced division of resources) than face-to-face negotiators (Croson, 1999). According to Croson (p. 33), this may occur because electronic communication "'levels the playing field' between stronger and weaker negotiators." By giving the individual a chance to ponder at length the other party's message, and to review and revise one's own communication, e-mail may indeed help less interpersonally skilled parties improve their performance, especially when the alternative is negotiating spontaneously (face-to-face or by phone) with a more accomplished other party.

One recent study (Moore, Kurtzberg, Thompson, and Morris, 1999) explored reasons why e-mail negotiations sometimes end in impasse. In their experiment, students negotiated over e-mail with other students who were either at the same university (an "in-group" pairing) or at another university ("out-group" pairing). Also, some of the negotiators disclosed personal information about themselves with the other party; others did not. They found that impasse was more likely in e-mail negotiations when people negotiated with out-group parties, and when there was no mutual self-disclosure of personal information. A conclusion one can draw from this research is that negotiators using e-mail may need to work harder at building personal rapport with the other party if they are to overcome limitations of the channel that would otherwise fuel impasse. (See Box 5.4 for a list of ways to maximize effectiveness when negotiations occur in virtual enviornments.)

HOW TO IMPROVE COMMUNICATION IN NEGOTIATION

Given the many ways that communication can be disrupted and distorted, we can only marvel at the extent to which negotiators can actually understand each other. Failures and distortions in perception, cognition, and communication are the most dominant contributors to breakdowns and failures in negotiation (Bazerman and Carroll, 1987). Research cannot directly confirm this assertion because the processes of perception, cognition, and communication are so intertwined with other major factors, including commitment to one's own position and objectives, the nature of the negotiating process,

---

BOX 5.4
Top Ten Rules for Virtual Negotiation

1. Take steps to create a face-to-face relationship before negotiation, or early on, so that there is a face or voice behind the e-mail.

2. Be explicit about the normative process to be followed during the negotiation.

3. If others are present in a virtual negotiation (on either your side or theirs) make sure everyone knows who is there and why.

4. Pick the channel (face-to-face, videophone, voice, fax or e-mail, etc.) that is most effective at getting all the information and detail on the table so that it can be fully considered by both sides.

5. Avoid "flaming"; when you must express emotion, label the emotion explicitly so the other knows what it is and what's behind it.

6. Formal turn-taking is not strictly necessary, but try to synchronize offers and counteroffers. Speak up if it is not clear "whose turn it is."

7. Check out assumptions you are making about the other's interests, offers, proposals, or conduct. Less face-to-face contact means less information about the other party, and a greater chance that inferences will get you in trouble, so ask questions.

8. In many virtual negotiations (e.g., e-mail) everything is communicated in writing, so be careful not to make unwise commitments that can be used against you. Neither should you take undue advantage of the other party in this way; discuss and clarify until there is agreement by all.

9. It may be easier to use unethical tactics in virtual negotiation because facts are harder to verify. But resist the temptation: the consequences are just as severe, and perhaps more so, given the incriminating evidence available when virtual negotiations are automatically archived.

10. Not all styles work equally well in all settings. Work to develop a personal negotiation style (collaboration, competition, etc.) that is a good fit with the communication channel you are using. One of the most difficult aspects of negotiation is the actual give-and-take that occurs at the table. Should I stick with this point, or is it time to fold? Should I open the bidding or wait for the other side to take the lead? It requires good judgment to make these.

SOURCE: Adapted from R. J. Lewicki and B. R. Dineen, "Negotiation in Virtual Organizations," in R. Heneman, ed., *Human Resource Management in the Virtual Organization* (2002).

---

the use of power and power tactics, and the negotiators' personalities. Nevertheless, as we discussed above, research consistently demonstrates that even those parties whose actual goals are compatible or integrative may either fail to reach agreement or reach suboptimal agreements because of the misperceptions of the other party or because of breakdowns in the communication process.

Three main techniques have been proposed for improving communication in negotiation: the use of questions, listening, and role reversal (also see Chapter 12). Each of these will be discussed in more detail below.

The Use of Questions

One of the most common techniques for clarifying communication and eliminating noise and distortion is the use of questions. Nierenberg (1976) emphasized that questions are essential elements in negotiations for securing information; asking good questions enables negotiators to secure a great deal of information about the other party's position, supporting arguments, and needs.

Nierenberg proposed that questions could be divided into two basic categories: those that are manageable, and those that are unmanageable and cause difficulty (see Table 5.1). Manageable questions cause attention or prepare the other person's thinking for further questions ("May I ask you a question?"), get information ("How much will this cost?"), and generate thoughts ("Do you have any suggestions for improving this?"). Unmanageable questions cause difficulty, give information ("Didn't you know that we couldn't afford this?"), and bring the discussion to a false conclusion ("Don't you think we've talked about this enough?"). As you can see in Table 5.1, most of the unmanageable questions are likely to produce defensiveness and anger in the other party. Although these questions may yield information, they are likely to make the other party feel uncomfortable and less willing to provide information in the future.

Negotiators can also use questions to manage difficult or stalled negotiations. Aside from their typical uses for collecting and diagnosing information or assisting the other party in addressing and expressing needs and interests, questions can also be used tactically to pry or lever a negotiation out of a breakdown or an apparent dead end. Deep and Sussman (1993) identify a number of such situations and suggest specific questions for dealing with them (see Table 5.2). The value of such questions seems to be in their power to assist or force the other party to face up to the effects or consequences of his or her behavior, intended and anticipated or not. In addition, Ury (1991) suggests that using "why not" questions instead of "why" questions is a good way to unblock negotiations (see Chapter 12). The other party may be more prepared to discuss what's wrong with a proposal than what's right; using "why not" questions and careful listening skills can thus help negotiators identify the other party's preferences.

Listening

Active listening and *reflecting* are terms that are commonly used in the helping professions such as counseling and therapy (Rogers, 1957, 1961). Counselors recognize that communications are frequently loaded with multiple meanings and that the counselor must try to identify these different meanings without making the communicator angry or defensive. In the decades since Carl Rogers advocated this key communication dynamic, interest in listening skills, and active listening in particular, has continued to grow both generally (e.g., Austin, 1989; Bostrom, 1990; Wolff, Marsnik, Tacey,

TABLE 5.1 Questions in Negotiation

Manageable Questions	Examples
Open-ended questions—ones that cannot be answered with a simple yes or no. *Who, what, when, where,* and *why* questions.	"Why do you take that position in these deliberations?"
Open questions—invite the other's thinking.	"What do you think of our proposal?"
Leading questions—point toward an answer.	"Don't you think our proposal is a fair and reasonable offer?"
Cool questions—low emotionality.	"What is the additional rate that we will have to pay if you make the improvements on the property?"
Planned questions—part of an overall logical sequence of questions developed in advance.	"After you make the improvements to the property, when can we expect to take occupancy?"
Treat questions—flatter the opponent at the same time as you ask for information.	"Can you provide us with some of your excellent insight on this problem?"
Window questions—aid in looking into the other person's mind.	"Can you tell us how you came to that conclusion?"
Directive questions—focus on a specific point.	"How much is the rental rate per square foot with these improvements?"
Gauging questions—ascertain how the other person feels.	"How do you feel about our proposal?"

Unmanageable Questions	Examples
Close-out questions—force the other party into seeing things your way.	"You wouldn't try to take advantage of us here, would you?"
Loaded questions—put the other party on the spot regardless of the answer.	"Do you mean to tell me that these are the only terms that you will accept?"
Heated questions—high emotionality, trigger emotional responses.	"Don't you think we've spent enough time discussing this ridiculous proposal of yours?"
Impulse questions—occur "on the spur of the moment," without planning, and tend to get conversation off the track.	"As long as we're discussing this, what do you think we ought to tell other groups who have made similar demands on us?"
Trick questions—appear to require a frank answer, but really are "loaded" in their meaning.	"What are you going to do—give in to our demands, or take this to arbitration?"
Reflective trick questions—reflects the other into agreeing with your point of view.	"Here's how I see the situation—don't you agree?"

SOURCE: From Gerard Nierenberg, *Fundamentals of Negotiating* (New York: Hawthorn Books, 1973), pp. 125–26. Used with permission of the author.

TABLE 5.2   Questions for Tough Situations

The Situation	Possible Questions
"Take it or leave it" ultimatums	"If we can come up with a more attractive alternative than that, would you still want me to 'take or leave' your offer?" "Do I have to decide now, or do I have some time to think about it?" "Are you feeling pressure to bring the negotiation to a close?"
Pressure to respond to an unreasonable deadline	"Why can't we negotiate about this deadline?" "If you're under pressure to meet this deadline, what can I do to help remove some of that pressure?" "What's magical about this afternoon? What about first thing in the morning?"
Highball or lowball tactics	"What's your reasoning behind this position?" "What would *you* think I see as a fair offer?" "What standards do you think the final resolution should meet?"
An impasse	"What else can either of us do to close the gap between our positions?" "Specifically what concession do you need from me to bring this to a close right now?" "If it were already six weeks from now and we were looking back at this negotiation, what might we wish we had brought to the table?"
Indecision between accepting and rejecting a proposal	"What's your best alternative to accepting my offer right now?" "If you reject this offer, what will take its place that's better than what you know you'll receive from me?" "How can you be sure that you will get a better deal elsewhere?"
A question about whether the offer you just made is the same as that offered to others	"What do you see as a fair offer, and given that, what do you think of my current offer to you?" "Do you believe that I think it's in my best interest to be unfair to you?" "Do you believe that people can be treated differently, but still all be treated fairly?"
Attempts to pressure, control, or manipulate	"Shouldn't we both walk away from this negotiation feeling satisfied?" "How would you feel if our roles were reversed, and you were feeling the pressure I'm feeling right now?" "Are you experiencing outside pressures to conclude these negotiations?"

SOURCE: Adapted from the book *What to Ask When You Don't Know What to Say* by Sam Deep and Lyle Sussman ©1993. Used by permission of the publisher, Prentice Hall/A Division of Simon & Schuster, Englewood Cliffs, NJ.

and Nichols, 1983; Wolvin and Coakley, 1988) and in business and organizational settings (e.g., Bone, 1988; Carnevale, Gainer, Meltzer, and Holland, 1988; Lewis and Reinsch, 1988; Rogers and Roethlisberger, 1991; Wolvin and Coakley, 1991).

There are three major forms of listening:

1. *Passive listening* involves receiving the message while providing no feedback to the sender about the accuracy or completeness of reception. Sometimes passive listening is itself enough to keep a communicator sending information. Some people like to talk and are uncomfortable with long silences. Negotiators whose counterpart is talkative may find that their best strategy is to sit and listen while the other party eventually works into, or out of, a position on his or her own.

2. *Acknowledgment* is the second form of listening, slightly more active than passive listening. When acknowledging, receivers occasionally nod their heads, maintain eye contact, or interject responses like "I see," "Mm-hmm," "Interesting," "Really," "Sure," "Go on," and the like. These responses are sufficient to keep communicators sending messages, but a sender may misinterpret them as the receiver's agreement with his or her position, rather than as simple acknowledgments of receipt of the message.

3. *Active listening* is the third form of listening. When receivers are actively listening, they restate or paraphrase the sender's message in their own language. Gordon (1977) provides the following examples of active listening:

Sender:

I don't know how I am going to untangle this messy problem.

Receiver:

You're really stumped on how to solve this one.

Sender:

Please, don't ask me about that now.

Receiver:

Sounds like you're awfully busy right now.

Sender:

I thought the meeting today accomplished nothing.

Receiver:

You were very disappointed with our session.

Athos and Gabarro (1978) note that successful reflective responding is a critical part of active listening and is characterized by the following: (1) a greater emphasis on listening than on speaking; (2) responding to personal rather than abstract points (i.e., feelings, beliefs, and positions rather than abstract ideas); (3) following the other rather than leading him or her into areas that the listener thinks should be explored (i.e., allowing the speaker to frame the conversation process); (4) clarifying what the speaker has said about his or her own thoughts and feelings rather than questioning or suggesting what he or she should be thinking or feeling; and (5) responding to the feelings the other has expressed.

Active listening has generally been recommended for counseling communications, such as employee counseling and performance improvement. In negotiation, it may appear initially that active listening is unsuitable because, unlike a counselor, the receiver normally has a set position and may feel strongly about the issues. By recommending active listening we are not suggesting that receivers should automatically agree with the other party's position and abandon their own. Rather, we are suggesting that active listening is a skill that encourages people to speak more fully about their feelings, priorities, frames of reference, and, by extension, the positions they are taking. When the other party does so, negotiators will better understand his or her positions, the factors and information that support it, and the ways that the position can be compromised, reconciled, or negotiated in accordance with their own preferences and priorities.

Role Reversal

Communication may also be improved through role reversal. Rapoport (1964) suggests that continually arguing for one particular position in debate leads to a "blindness of involvement," or a self-reinforcing cycle of argumentation that prohibits negotiators from recognizing the possible compatibility between their own position and that of the other party. While discussing active listening above, we suggested that one objective was to gain an understanding of the other party's perspective or frame of reference. Active listening is, however, still a somewhat passive process. Role-reversal techniques allow negotiators to understand more completely the other party's positions by actively arguing these positions until the other party is convinced that he or she is understood. For example, someone can ask you how you would respond to the situation that he or she is in. In doing so, you can come to understand that person's position, perhaps can come to accept its validity, and can discover how to modify both of your positions to make them more compatible. A number of studies have examined the impact and success of the role-reversal technique (Johnson, 1971; Walcott, Hopmann, and King, 1977). In general, the research supports the following conclusions:

1. Role reversal is effective in producing cognitive changes (greater understanding of the other party's position) and attitude changes (perceived similarities between the two positions).

2. When the parties' positions are fundamentally compatible with each other, role reversal is likely to produce acceptable results (cognitive and attitudinal change); when the parties' positions are fundamentally incompatible, role reversal may sharpen the perceptions of incompatibility and inhibit positive attitude change.

3. Although role reversal may induce greater understanding of the other party's position and highlight possible areas of similarity, it is not necessarily effective overall as a means of inducing agreement between parties.

In sum, role reversal may be a useful tool for improving communication and the accurate understanding and appreciation of the other party's position in negotiation. However, such understanding does not necessarily lead to easy resolution of the conflict, particularly when accurate communication reveals a fundamental incompatibility in the positions of the two sides.

MOOD, EMOTION, AND NEGOTIATION

Research on negotiation has been dominated by views that have favored rational, cognitive, economic analyses of the negotiation process. These approaches have tended to analyze the rationality of negotiation, examine how negotiators make judgment errors that deviate from rationality, or assess how negotiators can optimize their outcomes. Negotiators are portrayed as rational beings who seem calculating, calm, and in control. But, as noted by Davidson and Greenhalgh (1999), Kumar (1997), and others, we have not fully explored the role played by emotions in the negotiation process. While cognitive and emotional processes have a strong relationship to each other (see Fiske and Taylor, 1991; Kumar, 1997), the emotional component and its role have received considerably less attention.

The role of mood and emotion in negotiation has been the subject of an increasing body of recent theory and research during the last decade, and there are several good reviews of this literature (see Allred, Mallozzi, Matsui, and Raia, 1997; Barry, Fulmer, and Van Kleef, 2002; Barry and Oliver, 1996; Kumar, 1997). The distinction between mood and emotion is based on three characteristics: specificity, intensity, and duration. Mood states are more diffuse, less intense, and more enduring than emotion states, which tend to be more intense and directed at more specific targets (Forgas, 1992; Parrott, 2001). Like most emerging areas of study, there are many new and exciting developments in the study of mood, emotion, and negotiation, and we can present only a limited overview here. The following are some selected findings.

Negotiations Create Both Positive and Negative Emotions.   Negotiation processes and outcomes may create both positive and negative feelings. Positive emotions can result from being attracted to the other party, feeling good about the development of the negotiation process and the progress that the parties are making (Carver and Scheir, 1990), or liking the results that the negotiations have produced. Thus, a cognitive assessment of a "good outcome" leads parties to feel happy and satisfied (Lazarus, 1991). Conversely, negative emotions can result from being turned off by the other party, feeling bad about the development of the negotiation process and the progress being made, or disliking the results. As noted by Kumar (1997), many positive emotions tend to be classified under the single term *happiness,* but we tend to discriminate more precisely among negative emotions. Some negative emotions may tend to be based in dejection while others are based in agitation. Dejection-related emotions result from feeling disappointed, frustrated, or dissatisfied, while agitation-related emotions result from feeling anxious, fearful, or threatened (Higgins, 1987). Most researchers agree that emotions tend to move the parties toward some form of action in their relationship, such as initiating a relationship, maintaining or fixing the relationship, or terminating the relationship. Dejection-related emotions may lead negotiators to act aggressively (Berkowitz, 1989), while agitation-related emotions may lead negotiators to try to retaliate or to get out of the situation.

Positive Emotions Generally Have Positive Consequences for Negotiations.
Positive emotions generally lead to three sets of consequences: improving the negotiating (decision-making) process, creating positive feelings toward the other negotiator(s), and making negotiators more persistent. Let us briefly review each:

• *Positive feelings are more likely to lead the parties toward more integrative processes.* Researchers have shown that negotiators who feel positive emotions toward each other are more likely to try, and feel successful at, shaping integrative agreements (Carnevale and Isen, 1986). In addition, negotiators who feel positive emotions are more likely to be flexible in how they arrive at a solution to a problem, and hence may be less likely to get caught up in escalating their commitment to a single course of action (Isen and Baron, 1991).

• *Positive feelings also create a positive attitude toward the other side.* When negotiators like the other party, they tend to be more flexible in the negotiations (Druckman and Broome, 1991). In addition, having a positive attitude toward the other increases concession making (Pruitt and Carnevale, 1993), lessens hostile behaviors (Baron, 1990), and promotes win-win agreements (Hollingshead and Carnevale, 1990).

• *Positive feelings promote persistence.* If negotiators feel positively attracted, they are more likely to feel confident and, as a result, to persist in trying to get their concerns and issues addressed in the negotiation, and to achieve better outcomes (Kramer, Pommerenke, and Newton, 1993).

• *Positive feelings result from fair procedures during negotiation.* Hegtvedt and Killian (1999) explored how emotional responses are related to the experience of fairness during the negotiation process. Their findings indicated that negotiators who see the process as fair experience more positive feelings and are less inclined to express negative emotions following the encounter.

• *Positive feelings may also have negative consequences.* Finally, however, positive feelings may create negative consequences as well. First, negotiators in a positive mood may be less likely to examine closely the arguments put forward by the other party. As a result, they may be more susceptible to deceptive tactics used by a competitive opponent (Bless, Bohner, Schwartz, and Strack, 1988). In addition, because negotiators with positive feelings are less focused on the arguments being made by the other party, they may end up with less-than-optimal outcomes (Kumar, 1997). Finally, if positive feelings create strong positive expectations, parties who are not able to find an integrative agreement are likely to experience the defeat more strongly and perhaps treat the other party more harshly (Parrott, 1994).

Negative Emotions Generally Have Negative Consequences for Negotiations. As positive feelings have been generally shown to have positive consequences for negotiations, so negative emotions tend to have negative consequences. As we noted above, negative feelings may be based either in dejection or in agitation, and one or both parties may feel the emotions, or the behavior of one may prompt the emotional reaction in the other. Some more specific results from studies are as follows:

• *Negative emotions may lead parties to define the situation as competitive or distributive.* Veitch and Griffith (1976) demonstrate that a negative mood increases the likelihood that the actor will increase belligerent behavior toward the other. In a negotiation situation, this negative behavior is most likely to take the shape of a more distributive posture on the issues.

• *Negative emotions may lead parties to escalate the conflict.* When the mood is negative—more specifically, when both parties are dejected, are frustrated, and blame the other—conflict is likely to become personal, the number of issues in the conflict may expand, and other parties may become drawn into the dispute (Kumar, 1997).

• *Negative emotions may lead parties to use retaliatory behavior and obtain poorer outcomes.* When the parties are angry with each other, and when their previous interaction has already led one party to seek to punish the other, the other may choose to retaliate (Allred, 1998; Bies and Tripp, 1998). Retaliatory behavior serves to increase the conflict level even more dramatically and usually leads to highly unproductive negotiations or to terminating the discussions. Negative emotions may also actually lead to less effective outcomes. The more that a negotiator holds the other responsible for destructive behavior in a previous interaction, the more anger and less compassion he or she feels for the other party. This in turn leads to less concern for the other's interests, and a lower likelihood of discovering mutually beneficial negotiated solutions (Allred, Mallozzi, Matsui, and Raia, 1997).

• *Negative emotions may result from impasse.* When a negotiation ends in impasse, negotiators are more likely to experience negative emotions such as anger and frustration compared to negotiators who successfully reach agreement (O'Connor and Arnold, 2001). These researchers found, however, that people with more confidence in their negotiating ability were less likely to experience negative emotion in the wake of impasse. This is important because impasse is not always a bad thing—the goal is outcome, not merely the reaching of an agreement.

• *Negative feelings may create positive outcomes.* Just as positive emotions can create negative outcomes, it is clear that negative emotions can create positive consequences for negotiation. First, negative emotion has information value. It alerts the parties that the situation is problematic and needs attention, which may motivate them to either leave the situation or resolve the problem (van de Vliert, 1985). An expression of anger may alert the other party that there is a problem in the relationship and lead both parties to work on fixing the problem. Anger can thus serve as a danger signal that motivates both parties to confront the problem directly and search for a resolution (Daly, 1991).

Emotions Can Be Used Strategically as Negotiation Tactics. Finally, we have been discussing emotions here as though they were genuine. Given the power that emotions may have in swaying the other side toward one's own point of view, emotions may also be used strategically and manipulatively as influence tactics within negotiation. For example, negotiators may intentionally manipulate emotion in order to get the other side to adopt certain beliefs or take certain actions. Barry (1999) asked negotiators to assess their own ability to manipulate emotions (such as anger, disgust, sympathy, enthusiasm, caring, and liking), and to judge the appropriateness of using such tactics in negotiation as a form of deception. The participants in Barry's study rated emotional manipulation as a highly appropriate tactic—more appropriate than deception about informational aspects of negotiation (such as goals or plans or bottom lines). Negotiators also expressed greater confidence in their ability to use tactics of emotional manipulation effectively compared to other forms of deception.

In addition to the strategic expression of one's own (genuine or fabricated) emotions, negotiators may also engage in the regulation or management of the emotions of the other party. Finally, as noted by Thompson, Nadler, and Kim (1999), effective negotiators are able to adjust their messages to adapt to the emotional state that they perceive is held by the other party—a process they label *emotional tuning*. Some psychologists regard the ability to perceive and regulate emotions as a stable individual difference that has come to be known as *emotional intelligence* (e.g., Mayer, Salovey, and Caruso, 2000). We will consider the potential role of emotional intelligence in negotiation within our broader treatment of individual differences in Chapter 10.

SPECIAL COMMUNICATION CONSIDERATIONS AT THE CLOSE OF NEGOTIATIONS

As negotiations come to a close, negotiators must attend to two key aspects of communication and negotiation simultaneously: the avoidance of fatal mistakes, and the achievement of satisfactory closure in a constructive manner.

Avoiding Fatal Mistakes

Achieving closure in negotiation generally concerns making decisions to accept offers, to compromise priorities, to trade off across issues with the other party, or some combination of these elements. Such decision-making processes can be broken down into four key elements: framing, gathering intelligence, coming to conclusions, and learning from feedback (Russo and Schoemaker, 1989). The first three of these elements we have discussed elsewhere; the fourth element, that of learning (or failing to learn) from feedback, is largely a communication issue, which involves "keeping track of what you expected would happen, systematically guarding against self-serving expectations, and making sure you review the lessons your feedback has provided the next time a similar decision comes along" (Russo and Schoemaker, p. 3). Russo and Schoemaker warn of 10 decision traps that can ensnare decision makers, resulting in suboptimal decisions (see Box 5.5). Although some of these traps occur in earlier stages of the negotiation, we suspect that a number of them occur at the end of a negotiation, when parties are in a hurry to wrap up loose ends and cement a deal.

Achieving Closure

Gary Karrass (1985), focusing on sales negotiations in particular, has specific advice about communication near the end of a negotiation. Karrass enjoins negotiators to "know when to shut up," to avoid surrendering important information needlessly, and to refrain from making "dumb remarks" that push a wavering counterpart away from the agreement he or she is almost ready to endorse. The other side of this is to "beware of garbage and the garbage truck" by recognizing the other party's faux pas and dumb remarks for what they are, and refusing to respond or be distracted by them. Karrass also

BOX 5.5
Decision Traps and Learning from Negotiation Feedback

1. *Plunging in* involves reaching a conclusion to a problem before fully identifying the essence or crux of the problem (e.g., forcing negotiations into the end stage prematurely by pushing for a quantitative or substantive resolution to a problem that has been incompletely defined or is basically relational).

2. *Overconfidence in one's own judgment* involves blocking, ignoring, or failing to seek factual information that might contradict one's own assumptions and opinions (e.g., strictly adhering to a unilateral strategy, regardless of other information that emerges during the course of the negotiation).

3. *Frame blindness* involves perceiving, then solving, the wrong problem, accompanied by overlooking options and losing sight of objectives because they do not fit the frame being used (e.g., forcing resolution of a complex, mixed-motive dispute into some simplistic, concrete measure of performance such as money).

4. *Lack of frame* control involves failing to test different frames to determine if they fit the issues being discussed, or being unduly influenced by the other party's frame (e.g., agreeing to a suboptimal outcome, because the other party has taken advantage of our aversion to not reaching an agreement—see Neale and Bazerman, 1992).

5. *Shortsighted shortcuts* involves misusing heuristics or rules of thumb, such as convenient (but misleading) referent points (e.g., accepting the other party's commitment to turning over a new leaf when past experience suggests that he or she is really unlikely to do so).

6. *Shooting from the hip* involves managing too much information in one's head rather than adopting and using a systematic process of evaluation and choice (e.g., proceeding on gut feelings or eye contact alone in deciding to accept a resolution, trusting that problems will not occur or that they will be easily worked out if they do).

7. *Group failure* involves not managing the group process effectively and instead assuming that smart and well-intentioned individuals can invariably produce a durable, high-quality group decision (see Janis's 1982 work on "groupthink"; e.g., in order to move stalled decisions, a group might take a vote on accepting a resolution, thereby disenfranchising the minority who do not vote for the resolution and stopping the deliberative process short of achieving its integrative possibilities).

8. *Fooling yourself about feedback* involves failing to use feedback correctly, either to protect one's ego or through the bias of hindsight (e.g., dealing with the embarrassment of being outmaneuvered by the other party because of a lack of good information or a failure to prepare rigorously).

9. *Not keeping track* involves assuming that learning occurs automatically and thus not keeping systematic records of decisions and related outcomes (e.g., losing sight of the gains and deals purchased with concessions and trade-offs made during the negotiation, or not applying the lessons of one negotiation episode to future negotiations).

10. *Failure to audit one's own decision processes* involves failing to establish and use a plan to avoid the traps mentioned here or the inability or unwillingness to fully understand one's own style, warts and all (thus, doggedly adhering to a flawed or inappropriate approach to negotiation, even in the face of frequent failures and suboptimal outcomes).

SOURCE: Adapted from Russo and Schoemaker, 1989.

BOX 5.6
Do You Have a "Good" Agreement?

Is there a preamble in which the intent of the agreement is spelled out clearly?

Are all the issues of interest to all parties addressed?

Are all the proposals workable?

Have all parties affected by the agreement been consulted?

For each point of agreement, is it crystal clear what you have agreed to, including what is to be done, by whom, by what time, and how?

Does the agreement make sense in total?

Is the agreement reasonable and equitable?

Have you considered the major barriers to fulfilling the agreement?

Do you have a vehicle for managing disagreements arising out of this agreement? Is it clear to all parties what this vehicle is and how to use it?

SOURCE: Used with permission of Blair Sheppard.

---

reminds of the need to watch out for last-minute hitches, such as nit-picking or second-guessing by parties who didn't participate in the bargaining process but who have the right or responsibility to review it. Karrass says to expect such hitches and to be prepared to manage them with aplomb. Finally, Karrass notes the importance of reducing the agreement to written form, recognizing that the party who writes the contract is in a position to achieve clarity of purpose and conduct for the deal. As for the communicative quality of the final, written agreement, Sheppard (1993) provides a good checklist, which is presented in Box 5.6.

CHAPTER SUMMARY

In this chapter we have taken a multifaceted look at the role of perception and communication in negotiation. We examined how negotiators make sense of negotiation and the role that communication processes play in negotiation processes and outcomes.

The first portion of the chapter discussed perception and negotiation, beginning with a brief overview of the perceptual process. Four types of perceptual distortions were discussed next: stereotyping, halo effects, selective perception, and projection. We ended the section on perception with a discussion of how framing influences perceptions in negotiation, and how reframing and issue development both change negotiator perceptions during negotiations.

The chapter then reviewed the research findings from one of the most important recent areas of inquiry in negotiation, that of cognitive biases in negotiation. The effects of 12 different cognitive biases were discussed: irrational escalation of commitment, mythical fixed-pie beliefs, anchoring and adjustment, framing, availability of information, the winner's curse, overconfidence, the law of small numbers, self-serving biases, endowment effects, ignoring others' cognitions, and reactive devaluation. The next section of the chapter examined ways to manage misperception and cognitive biases in negotiation, an area that has received relatively little research attention.

Our discussion then shifted to a model of the communication process. We noted that many elements of communication are prone to error and distortion. Such distortions are more likely to occur when communicating parties have conflicting goals and objectives, or strong feelings of dislike for one another. Distortion may occur as information is encoded, transmitted, and decoded. The closure of the communication loop occurs through feedback, by which the success of the intended communication can be checked. During transmission and feedback, the problem of "noise" or interference might affect the clarity with which the message and response are sent and received.

We then moved to a discussion of *what* is communicated during negotiation. Rather than simply being an exchange of preferences about solutions, negotiations can cover a wide-ranging number of topics in an environment where each party is trying to influence the other. This was followed by an exploration of two issues related to *how* people communicate in negotiation: the use of language, and the selection of a communication channel.

In the final three sections of the chapter we considered: (1) how to improve communication in negotiation, where we discussed listening skills and the use of questions; (2) mood and emotion in negotiation, where we discussed recent work on this topic; and (3) special communication considerations at the close of negotiation, where we discussed avoiding last-minute mistakes and achieving closure.

CHAPTER 6

Finding and Using
Negotiation Leverage

In this chapter, we focus on leverage in negotiation. By *leverage,* we mean the tools negotiators can use to give themselves an advantage or increase the probability of achieving their objectives. All negotiators want leverage; they want to know what they can do to put pressure on the other party, persuade the other to see it their way, get the other to give them what they want, get one up on the other, or change the other's mind. Note that, according to this definition, we have already talked about many leverage tactics in Chapters 3 and 4. The tactics of distributive bargaining and integrative negotiation are leverage tactics, used in the service of achieving the best deal for one or both parties.

In this chapter, we dissect the concept of leverage in relation to the use of *power* and *influence*. It is important to be clear about the distinction between the two. We treat power as the potential to alter the attitudes and behaviors of others that an individual brings to a given situation. Influence, on the other hand, can be thought of as power in action—the actual messages and tactics an individual undertakes in order to change the attitudes and/or behaviors of others. To put it concisely, power is potential influence, while influence is kinetic power (French and Raven, 1959).

We begin by defining the nature of power and discussing some of the dynamics of its use in negotiation. We will focus on the power sources that give negotiators the capacity for leverage. Of the many sources of power that exist (see French and Raven, 1959; Pfeffer, 1992), we will consider three major ones here: information and expertise, control over resources, and one's position in an organization or network. We then move to discussing the process for managing this power—influence—which we will view as attempts to change the other's perspective, position, or behavior. In this discussion, we consider four key elements of influence: ways in which *sources* of information can be powerful, ways in which *messages* can be structured to be more persuasive, ways in which *targets* of persuasion can enhance or reduce their power, and ways in which elements in the *social context* can exert indirect influence on the other negotiator.

LEVERAGE AS ADVANTAGE:
WHY IS POWER IMPORTANT TO NEGOTIATORS?

Leverage is often used synonymously with *power*. Most negotiators believe that power is important in negotiation, because it gives one negotiator an advantage over the other party. Negotiators who have this advantage usually want to use it to secure a greater share of the outcomes or achieve their preferred solution. Seeking leverage in negotiation usually arises from one of two perceptions:

1. The negotiator believes he or she currently has *less* leverage than the other party. In this situation, a negotiator believes the other party already has some advantage that can and will be used, so he or she seeks power to offset or counterbalance that advantage.

2. The negotiator believes he or she needs *more* leverage than the other party to increase the probability of securing a desired outcome. In this context, the negotiator believes that added power is necessary to gain or sustain an advantage in the upcoming negotiation.

Embedded in these two beliefs are significant questions of tactics and motives. The tactics may be designed to enhance the negotiator's own power or to diminish the other's power, and to create a state of either power equalization (both parties have relatively equal or countervailing power) or power difference (one's power is greater than the other's). The motive questions relate to why the negotiator is using the tactics. Most commonly, negotiators employ tactics designed to create power equalization as a way to level the playing field. Such tactics minimize the capacity for either side to dominate the relationship and often serve as the groundwork for moving discussions toward a compromising or collaborative, integrative agreement. In contrast, negotiators also employ tactics designed to create power difference as a way to gain advantage or to block the other party's power moves. Such tactics enhance the capacity for one side to dominate the relationship, and often serve as the groundwork for a competing or dominating strategy and a distributive agreement. Box 6.1 presents a framework on the merits of using power as a negotiating tactic.

BOX 6.1
Interests, Rights, and Power in Negotiation

One way of thinking about the role of power in negotiation is in relation to other, alternative strategic options. In Chapter 2 we introduced a framework developed by Ury, Brett, and Goldberg (1993) that compares three different strategic approaches to negotiation: interests, rights, and power.

- Negotiators focus on *interests* when they strive to learn about each other's interests and priorities as a way to work toward a mutually satisfying agreement that creates value.
- Negotiators focus on *rights* when they seek to resolve a dispute by drawing upon decision rules or standards grounded in principles of law, fairness, or perhaps an existing contract.
- Negotiators focus on *power* when they use threats or other means to try to coerce the other party into making concessions.

This framework assumes that all three approaches can potentially exist in a single situation; negotiators make choices about where to place their focus. But do negotiators really use all three? Should they? These questions were addressed in a study by Anne Lytle, Jeanne Brett, and Debra Shapiro (1999). They analyzed audiotapes of negotiations

BOX 6.1
(continued)

of a simulated contract dispute between two companies seeking to clarify their interdependent business relationship. Of the 50 negotiators who participated (25 tape-recorded
pairs), some were students and some were employed managers, but all had five or more
years of business experience.

Lytle and her colleagues found that most negotiators cycled through all three strategies—interests, rights, and power—during the same encounter. They also found that
negotiators tended to reciprocate these strategies. A coercive power strategy, for example,
may be met with a power strategy in return, which can lead to a negative conflict spiral
and a poor (or no) agreement. They developed some important implications for the use of
power in negotiation:

- Starting a negotiation by conveying your own power to coerce the other party could
  bring a quick settlement if your threat is credible. If the other party calls your bluff,
  however, you are left to either carry out your threat or lose face, both of which may be
  undesirable.

- To avert a conflict spiral and move toward an interests-based exchange, avoid reciprocating messages involving rights or power. Shift the conversation by asking an
  interests-related question. It may take several attempts to redirect the interaction
  successfully.

- If you can't avoid reciprocating negative behaviors (which is, after all, only natural),
  try a "combined statement" that mixes a threat with an interests-oriented refocusing
  question or statement (e.g., "yes, we could sue you as well, but that won't solve our
  problem, so why don't we try to reach an outcome that helps us both?").

- Power tactics (and rights tactics) may be most useful when the other party refuses to
  negotiate or when negotiations have broken down and need to be restarted. In these
  situations, not much is risked by making threats based on rights or power, but the
  threat itself may help the other party appreciate the severity of the situation.

- The success of power tactics (and rights tactics) depends to a great extent on *how* they
  are implemented. To be effective, threats must be specific and credible, targeting the
  other party's high-priority interests. Otherwise, the other party has little incentive to
  comply. Make sure that you leave an avenue for the other party to "turn off" the threat,
  save face, and reopen the negotiations around interests. After all, most negotiators
  who make threats really don't want to implement them. As Lytle et al. observe, "once
  you carry through with your threat, you frequently lose your source of power" (p. 48).

SOURCE: Adapted from A. L. Lytle, J. M. Brett, and D. L. Shapiro, "The Strategic Use of Interests,
Rights, and Power to Resolve Disputes," *Negotiation Journal* 15(1) (1999), pp. 31–51.

In general, negotiators who don't care about their power or who have matched
power—equally high or low—will find that their deliberations proceed with greater
ease and simplicity toward a mutually satisfying and acceptable outcome. In contrast,
negotiators who do care about their power and seek to match or exceed the other's

power are probably seeking a solution in which they either do not lose the negotiation (a defensive posture) or win the negotiation (an offensive posture).

Power is implicated in the use of many negotiation tactics, such as hinting to the other party that you have good alternatives (a strong BATNA) in order to increase your leverage. Nevertheless, relatively few research studies have focused specifically on power and influence tactics in negotiation. Many of the findings discussed in this chapter are drawn from broader studies of how managers influence one another in organizations, and how to use persuasion effectively in communication and marketing. We will apply those findings to negotiation situations as appropriate.

A DEFINITION OF POWER

In a broad sense, people have power when they have "the ability to bring about outcomes they desire" or "the ability to get things done the way [they want] them to be done" (Salancik and Pfeffer, 1977). Presumably, a party with power can induce another to do what the latter otherwise would not do (Dahl, 1957; Kotter, 1979). But there is a problem here: the definition we have developed so far seems to focus on power as absolute and coercive, which is too restrictive for understanding how power is used in negotiation. We prefer what may be called a *relational* definition of power, as defined by Deutsch (1973):

> an actor . . . has power in a given situation (situational power) to the degree that he can *satisfy the purposes (goals, desires, or wants) that he is attempting to fulfill in that situation.* Power is a relational concept; it does not reside in the individual but rather in the relationship of the person to his environment. Thus, the power of an actor in a given situation is determined by the characteristics of the situation as well as by his own characteristics. (pp. 84–85)

Deutsch (1973) notes a tendency to view power as an attribute of the actor only. This tendency ignores those elements of power that are derived from the situation or context in which the actor operates. As Deutsch suggests, the statement "A is more powerful than B" should be viewed from three distinct yet often interrelated perspectives: *environmental power,* or "A is more usually able to favorably influence his overall environment and/or to overcome its resistance than is B"; *relationship power,* or "A is usually more able to influence B favorably and/or to overcome B's resistance than B is able to do with A"; and *personal power,* or "A is usually more able to satisfy his desires than is B" (p. 85). Let us consider two examples of power that fit these views:

1. During economic downswings, labor unions can find themselves negotiating new contracts that delay wage increases or even reduce wages, which means giving hard-won concessions back to management—hardly something union officials want to do. They have usually done so when company officials have argued that unless wages go down, the firm will lay off thousands of employees, move operations to another country, drop a line of business, or take some similar action. The union officials can be seen as making a rational or calculated decision to do something they ordinarily would not do (Dahl's definition), but in this case management is simply taking advantage of the shift in power within the economic environment. As markets shift, demand for products changes; costs rise; or less expensive (nonunion) labor becomes available in other areas.

2. In contemporary organizations, heads of projects, teams, and task forces find that they must effectively influence other people without having the formal authority (direct reporting relationships) to give direct orders. As a result, managers have to master the use of "influence without authority" (Cohen and Bradford, 1989) to get their jobs done and meet group goals. The targets of this influence may be employees, peers, other managers, or the boss. Subordinates who approach their superior with a list of grievances about the job and tasks that cannot be done without the boss's help will receive scant attention. However, those who are able to use influence to get their boss's assistance without creating major problems for the boss may earn the boss's respect and accomplish their goals as well. In these kinds of situations, strong relationship and personal power skills are critical. In short, managers must learn to use relationship and personal power when environmental power, derived from a position in a formal organizational chart, is not available.

Before moving forward, we want to draw attention to the weakness of any discussion of power. It would be nice to be able to write this chapter and delineate a comprehensive review of the power sources available to negotiators, the major configurations of power bases assembled as influence strategies, and the conditions under which each should be used. Unfortunately, such a task is not just daunting but impossible, for two principal reasons. First, the effective use of power requires a sensitive and deft touch, and its consequences may vary greatly from one person to the next. In the hands of one user, the tools of power can craft a benevolent realm of prosperity and achievement, whereas in the hands of another, they may create a nightmare of tyranny and disorder.[1] Second, not only do the key actors and targets change from situation to situation, but the context in which the tools of power operate changes as well. As a result, the best we can do is to identify a few key sources of power and the major influence strategies that accompany them. Exactly how and when to use these tools, or in what combination, is beyond the scope of our current understanding (e.g., Schreisheim and Hinkin, 1990; Yukl and Tracey, 1992). (See Box 6.2 for a few relevant observations.)

SOURCES OF POWER—HOW PEOPLE ACQUIRE POWER

Understanding the different ways in which power can be exercised is best accomplished by looking first at the various sources of power. In their seminal work on power, French and Raven (1959) identified five major types: expert power, reward power, coercive power, legitimate power, and referent power. Although many contemporary discussions of power are still grounded in this typology, we will focus our attention on three specific variations: information and expertise, control over resources, and position power (see Table 6.1).

---

[1] Researchers have defined an individual difference called *communication competency* (Spitzberg and Cupach, 1984). Individuals who are high in communication competency are likely to have strong verbal ability, are able to strategize about the way they communicate from one situation to the next, and can easily take the perspective of the other party. Individuals who are high in communication competence are able to adapt to different situations and do what is most necessary and desirable in any given situation.

BOX 6.2
Some Thoughts about Power

- Power is in the eye of the beholder. For power to be effective, it does not necessarily have to be fully and completely possessed; rather, the actor must convey the *appearance* that he or she has power and can use it at will. Power is therefore somewhat self-fulfilling. If you—and others—think you have it, you have it. If you—and others—don't think you have it, you don't have it. Perceived power is what creates leverage, and many power holders go out of their way to create the image of power as the critical element of effective influence (see Sun Tsu, 1983, for an excellent exposition of this point).

- The effectiveness of power and influence is ultimately defined by the behavior of the target person. What matters most is which tools and strategies actually work on that person. Does that individual comply, do what you want, or behave the way you want him or her to behave? When designing an influence strategy, you must pay attention to what you think will work with a particular target, while also being sensitive to suggestions for alternative strategies.

- There is some indication that power is, in fact, corrupting—in Lord Acton's words, "Power tends to corrupt; absolute power corrupts absolutely." This may occur for several reasons. First, as just suggested, power is based on perception—creating the perception, or even the illusion, that you have power and can use it. In creating such an illusion, it is not uncommon for actors to deceive themselves as much as they deceive the target. Second, power can be intoxicating. This point is frequently lost on the naive and unskilled. Those who gain a great deal of power through rapid career success frequently overuse and eventually abuse it. Power brings a large resource base, privileged information, and the ability to control the fate of many others. In the hands of the unskilled, power can be dramatically destructive (Lewis, 1990; Stewart, 1992).

Power Based on Information and Expertise

Within the context of negotiation, information is perhaps the most common source of power. Information power is derived from the negotiator's ability to assemble and organize data to support his or her position, arguments, or desired outcomes. Negotiators may also use information as a tool to challenge the other party's position or desired outcomes, or to undermine the effectiveness of the other's negotiating arguments. Even in the simplest negotiation, the parties take a position and then present arguments and facts to support that position. I want to sell a used motorcycle for $1,500; you say it is worth only $1,000. I proceed to tell you how much I paid for it, point out what good condition it is in and what attractive features it has, and explain why it is worth $1,500. You point out that it is five years old, emphasize the paint chips and rust spots, and comment that the tires are worn and need to be replaced. You also tell me that you can't afford to spend $1,500. After 20 minutes of discussion about the motorcycle, we have exchanged extensive information about its original cost, age, depreciation, and current condition, as well as your financial situation and my need to raise cash. We then settle on a price of $1,300, including a "loan" of $300 I have given you. (See Box 6.3 on the power of information in buying a new car.)

TABLE 6.1   Sources of Power

Sources of Power	Description
Information and expertise	The accumulation and presentation of data intended to change the other person's point of view or position on an issue; and (for expertise) an acknowledged accumulation of information, or mastery of a body of information, on a particular problem or issue.
Control over resources	The accumulation of money, raw material, labor, time, and equipment that can be used as incentives to encourage compliance or as punishments for noncompliance.
Position	Power derived from being located in a particular position in an organizational or communication structure; leads to two different kinds of leverage: • Formal authority, derived from occupying a key position in a hierarchical organization. • Access to or control over information or supply flows, derived from location within a network.

BOX 6.3
Planning for a Car-Buying Negotiation

Before the age of electronic information, many consumers approached buying a car with the same enthusiasm as visiting the dentist. Customers knew their role was to scoff at the asking price, threaten to walk away from the vehicle, and generally engage in tough negotiation postures in order to get the best deal. Still, after they drove the car off the lot, nagging doubts remained about whether or not they paid too much for their new car.

Savvy customers have always known that they should determine their real requirements for an automobile, find several cars that meet their objectives, determine the book value of each car, contact current owners to determine their satisfaction, and keep from becoming emotionally attached to a particular automobile. These strategies certainly have helped people prepare for negotiations with their local dealer. However, customers still had to rely largely on guesswork to determine what price offers would be acceptable to the dealership.

Today, however, price information on new and used cars is readily available through the Internet and other sources. Customers can enter negotiations with car dealers armed with accurate facts and figures about the car's cost to the dealership, the actual price for various options, prices in neighboring states, and the customer and dealer incentives in place at a given time. Car buyers who take the time to gather information about "real" prices report saving hundreds or even thousands of dollars on automobiles. This wealth of information gives consumers more power in negotiations with dealers. Ultimately, that power leads to lower prices on new automobiles (Blumenstein, 1997; McGraw, 1997).

The exchange of information in negotiation is also at the heart of the concession-making process. As each side presents information, a common definition of the situation emerges. The amount and kind of information shared, and the way the negotiators share it, allow both parties to derive a common (and hopefully realistic) picture of the current condition of the motorcycle, its market worth, and the preferences of each side. Moreover, this information need not be 100 percent accurate to be effective; bluffs, exaggerations, omissions, and outright lies may work just as well. I may tell you I paid $2,200 for the bike when I paid only $2,000; I may not tell you that the clutch needs to be replaced. You may not tell me that you actually can pay $1,500 but simply don't want to spend that much, or that you plan to buy this bike regardless of what you have to pay for it. (We return to these issues of bluffing and misrepresentation in Chapter 7, when we discuss the ethics of lying and deception.)

Through the exchange of information, a common definition of the situation emerges and serves as a rationale for both sides to modify their positions and, eventually, arrive at a mutually acceptable price. Negotiators in the motorcycle example may derive feelings of satisfaction about that settlement from two sources: the price itself, and the feeling that the price is justified because of their revised view of the motorcycle and the other party. Thus, information exchange in negotiation serves as the primary medium for creating a common view of the situation, justifying one's own and the other's perspective, making concessions, and eventually explaining one's feelings about the agreement achieved.

Power derived from expertise is a special form of information power. The power that comes from information is available to anyone who assembles facts and figures to support arguments, but expert power is accorded to those who are seen as having achieved some level of command and mastery of a body of information. Experts are accorded respect, deference, and credibility based on their experience, study, or accomplishments. One or both parties in a negotiation will give experts' arguments more credibility than those of nonexperts—but only to the extent that the expertise is seen as functionally relevant to the persuasion situation (Cronkhite and Liska, 1976, 1980). For example, someone knowledgeable about cars may not be an expert on motorcycles. Thus, a negotiator who would like to take advantage of his or her expertise will often need to demonstrate that this expertise (*a*) actually exists, and (*b*) is relevant to the issues under discussion.

Power Based on Control over Resources

People who control resources have the capacity to give them to someone who will do what they want, and withhold them (or take them away) from someone who doesn't do what they want. *Resources* can be many things. Particular resources are more useful as instruments of power to the extent that they are highly valued by participants in the negotiation. In an organizational context, some of the most important resources are the following:

1. Money, in its various forms: cash, salary, budget allocations, grants, bonus money, expense accounts, and discretionary funds.
2. Supplies: raw materials, components, pieces, and parts.

3. Human capital: available labor supply, staff that can be allocated to a problem or task, temporary help.

4. Time: free time, the ability to meet deadlines, the ability to control a deadline. If time pressure is operating on one or both parties, the ability to help someone meet or move a deadline can be extremely powerful (see Chapter 3 for a discussion of deadlines).

5. Equipment: machines, tools, technology, computer hardware and software, vehicles.

6. Critical services: repair, maintenance, upkeep, installation and delivery, technical support, transportation.

7. Interpersonal support: verbal praise and encouragement for good performance or criticism for bad performance. This is an interesting resource, because it is available to almost anyone, does not require significant effort to acquire, and is quite powerful on its own.

Pfeffer and Salancik (1974), among others, stress that the ability to control and dispense resources is a major power source in organizations. Power also comes from creating a resource stockpile in an environment where resources appear to be scarce. Jeffrey Pfeffer in his book *Managing with Power* (1992) illustrated how powerful political and corporate figures build empires founded on resource control. During his early years in Congress, Lyndon Johnson took over the "Little Congress" (a speaker's bureau for clerical personnel and aides to members of Congress) and leveraged it into a major power base that led him to become Speaker of the House and eventually president. Similarly, Robert Moses, beginning as the parks commissioner of New York City, built a power empire that resulted in the successful construction of 12 bridges, 35 highways, 751 playgrounds, 13 golf courses, 18 swimming pools, and more than 2 million acres of park land in the New York metropolitan area—a base he used to become a dominant power broker in the city.

To use resources as a basis for power, negotiators must develop or maintain control over some scarce commodity that the other party wants, such as physical space, jobs, budget authorizations, or raw materials. Successful control over resources also requires that the other party must deal directly with the power holder. Finally, the power holder must be willing to allocate resources depending on the other's compliance or cooperation with the power holder's requests. The increasing scarcity of resources of all kinds has led to the new golden rule of organizations: "Whoever has the gold makes the rules."

Power Based on One's Position

We discuss two kinds of power in this section: legitimate power, and power derived from location in an organizational structure. Legitimate power is derived from occupying a particular job, office, or position in an organizational hierarchy. In this case, the power resides in the title, duties, and responsibilities of the job itself. Thus, a newly promoted vice president acquires some legitimate power merely from being a vice president. The second type of power also comes from location in an organizational structure, but not necessarily a hierarchical structure. In this case, power is derived from whatever flows through that particular location in the structure (usually information and resources, such as money). The person occupying a certain position may not have a formal title or office; his or her leverage comes from the ability to control and manage what "flows" through that position. For example, before China modernized in the 1980s, automobile chauffeurs held enormous power even though their title was not prestigious. If a chauffeur did not like a passenger or did not feel like driving to a certain location, he could make life very difficult and impose consequences in several areas (e.g., departure time, duration of trip, lunch time, and location). We will now describe each kind of power in more detail.

Legitimate Power.   There are times when people respond to directions from another, even directions they do not like, because they feel it is proper (legitimate) for the other to direct them and proper (obligatory) for them to obey. This is the effect of legitimate power.

Legitimate power is at the foundation of our social structure. When individuals and groups organize into any social system—a small business, a combat unit, a union, a political action organization, a sports team, a task force—they almost immediately create some form of structure and hierarchy. They elect or appoint a leader and may introduce formal rules about decision making, work division, allocation of responsibilities, and conflict management. Without this social order, either the group can take little coordinated action (chaos prevails), or everyone is required to participate in every decision and thus group coordination takes forever. Social structures are efficient and effective, and this fact creates the basis for legitimate power. People are willing to give up their right to participate in every decision by vesting authority in someone who can act on their behalf (a president, leader, or spokesperson). By creating a group structure that gives one person a power base, group members also create an obligation in themselves to obey that person's directives.

People can acquire legitimate power in several ways. First, it may be acquired at birth. Elizabeth II has the title of Queen of England and all of the stature the title commands. She also controls a great deal of the personal wealth of the monarchy. However, she has little actual power in terms of her ability to run the day-to-day affairs of Britain, a situation that has created controversy and resentment in recent years. Second, legitimate power may be acquired by election to a designated office: the president of the United States has substantial legitimate power derived from the constitutional structure of the American government. Third, legitimate power is derived simply by appointment or promotion to some organizational position. Thus, holding the title of director or general manager entitles a person to all the rights, responsibilities, and privileges that go with that position. Finally, some legitimate authority comes to an individual who occupies a position for which other people simply show respect. Usually, such respect is derived from the intrinsic social good or important social values of that person's position or organization. In many societies, the young listen to and obey the old. People also listen to college presidents or the members of the clergy. They follow their advice because they believe it is proper to do so. Clergy members, college presidents, and many others may have precious little they can actually give to individuals as rewards or use against them as coercive punishments, yet they have considerable legitimate power (see Cialdini, 2001, on the illusions of authority).

The effectiveness of formal authority is derived from the willingness of followers to acknowledge the legitimacy of the organizational structure and the system of rules and regulations that empowers its leaders (Barnard, 1938). In short, legitimate power cannot function without obedience, or the consent of the governed. If enough British citizens question the legitimacy of the queen and her authority—even given the hundreds of years of tradition and law on which the monarchy is founded—her continued rule will be in serious jeopardy. If enough people challenge the Pope's rulings on abortion, birth control, or other social policy, the Pope's authority will erode. If the president's cabinet and key advisers are unwilling to act on and dispatch presidential orders, then the president's effectiveness is nullified. When enough people begin to distrust the authority or discredit its legitimacy, they will begin to defy it and thereby undermine its potential as a power source.

Because legitimate power can be undermined if followers choose to no longer recognize the power holder's authority, it is not uncommon for power holders to accumulate other power sources (such as resource control or information) to fortify their power base. Resource control and information power frequently accompany a title, position, or job definition. Legitimate power is often derived from manipulating these other sources of power. Military officers have known this for a long time. All military-style organizations (soldiers, police, etc.) still drill their personnel, even though military units no longer march into battle as they once did. There are several reasons for this: A drill is an easy place to give instructions, teach discipline and obedience, closely monitor large numbers of people, and quickly punish or reward performance. Drilling gets large numbers of people used to accepting orders from a specific person, without question. Those who follow orders are rewarded, whereas those who do not are quickly and publicly punished. After a while, the need for reward and punishment drops off, and it seems natural or legitimate for the soldier to accept orders from an officer without asking why or inquiring about the consequences.

Location in an Organizational Structure.   In the last section, we focused on power derived from the legitimacy that accompanies a particular organizational position or title. Yet even without a lofty position or title, individuals can become powerful because of the way that their actions and responsibilities are embedded in a larger organization. For example, individuals who have access to a large amount of information, who are responsible for collecting vital data and resources, or who are in jobs the organization deems central to its mission may become very powerful (see Charan, 1991; Kaplan, 1984; Krackhart and Hanson, 1993). The job may not have a fancy title, a big budget, or a large corner office, but it can confer a significant amount of power by virtue of the amount of information and resource control associated with it.

Understanding power in this way is derived from conceptualizing an organization not as a hierarchy, but as a network of interrelationships. Network schematics represent key individuals as circles or nodes, and relationships between individuals as lines of transaction. See Figure 6.1 for an example of a network, as compared to an organizational hierarchy. These lines connect individuals who interact or need to interact with each other in the organization. Through information and resources as the primary focus of transactions, personal relationships and authority may also be negotiated across network lines. In formal hierarchy terms, authority is directly related to how high the position is on the

FIGURE 6.1   Comparing Organization Hierarchies and Networks

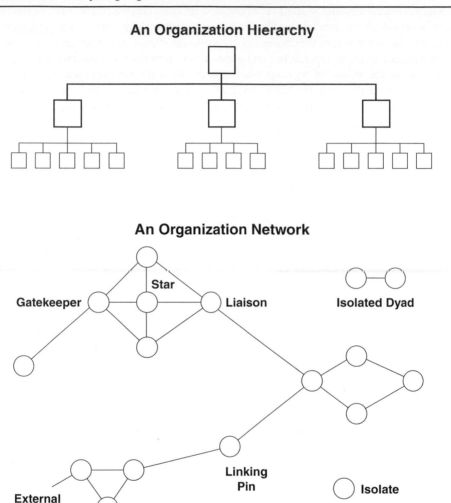

vertical organization chart and how many people report to that individual from lower levels. In network terms, in contrast, power is determined by location within the set of relationships. These key location concepts include centrality, criticality, flexibility, and visibility.

Centrality.   The more central a node is in a network of exchanges and transactions, the more power that node's occupant will have. Centrality may be determined by the amount of information that passes through a node, the number of transactions that occur through the node, or the degree to which the node is central to managing information flow. In the network depicted in Figure 6.1, the "star" has greater centrality, and therefore more power. Researchers have shown that being in the center of information flows—the workflow network, the informal communication network, and the friendship network—is particularly important to being promoted (see Brass, 1984). Centrality may also simply be determined by where one's office or parking space is located, such as in the hallway where the president walks to lunch, or near where one parks in the parking lot. Pfeffer (1992) relates a story about a new faculty colleague who became well known simply by the proximity of his office to one of the few men's rooms in the building—most colleagues got to know him on their periodic trips to the lavatory.

Criticality and Relevance.   A second source of network power is the criticality of the node. Although a node may not have a large amount of information or resources flowing through it, what does flow through it may be essential to the organization's mission, major task, or key product. People who depend highly on others may become critical to the degree that they are charged with assembling information from many locations; that is, they may be in frequent contact with many important people and may be required to integrate information from those contacts into a recommendation, action strategy, or decision. In Figure 6.1, "liaisons" and "linking pins" perform this role. Employees who want to succeed rapidly are frequently counseled to find jobs with high centrality and criticality in an organization so they can get the experience and visibility necessary for rapid promotion. Being critical—even irreplaceable—is a core part of getting and maintaining power.

Flexibility.   A third source of network power lies in the position's flexibility, or the degree to which the key individual can exercise discretion in how certain decisions are made or who gains access. Flexibility is often related to criticality (see preceding discussion). A classic example of flexibility is the role of "gatekeeper" (Figure 6.1), the person in a network who controls the access to a key figure or group. Anyone who wants to get to the star has to go through the gatekeeper. If you want to see the boss, you have to get permission and access from the secretary.

Visibility.   Finally, nodes differ in their degree of visibility—that is, how visible the task performance is to others in the organization. Visibility is not necessarily the same thing as centrality or criticality. A negotiator who deals with his or her constituency in the same room has high visibility; if the negotiator gains significant concessions from the other party while being watched, the team will give that negotiator a great deal of affirmation. A node with high centrality and criticality may not be visible, but if it is not, it is much less likely to be recognized and rewarded.

Section Summary

In this section, we considered three major sources of leverage: information and expertise, control over resources (capacity to use rewards and punishments), and structural position (formal authority and/or position in a network). Imbalances in these power sources across the table are inevitable, but effective negotiators can nevertheless take steps to alter the power dynamics before and during the negotiation. Box 6.4 offers some insights into how negotiators recognize and remedy power imbalances.

We turn next to a detailed examination of how negotiators implement these power sources through the strategies and tactics of interpersonal influence.

BOX 6.4
The Shadow Negotiation

How do negotiators manage unequal power at the bargaining table? Researchers Deborah Kolb and Judith Williams (2001) interviewed hundreds of executives about their negotiation experiences. From their interviews, Kolb and Williams came to see the existence of what they call the "shadow negotiation"—the subtle yet complex interaction lurking beneath the formal negotiation itself where issues of power imbalance, conversational tone, and influence over process are settled. They suggest that negotiators ignore these issues at their peril: the unaddressed shadow negotiation can lead to negotiations that are "blocked or stalled—undermined by hidden assumptions, unrealistic expectations, or personal histories" (p. 90). Kolb and Williams identify three strategic levers available to help people navigate the shadow negotiation:

- *Power moves* are designed to bring reluctant bargainers back to the table. They can take the form of incentives offered to help the other side recognize that they will benefit from negotiation, pressure tactics that lead the other to realize that the status quo is unacceptable, and the enlistment of allies to help the other party see the advantage of negotiating.

- *Process moves* are designed to alter the negotiation process itself through adjustments to the agenda, sequencing, decision rules, and the like. For example, a competitive mindset may favor those who talk loudest or longest, or who like bluffing and gamesmanship. A negotiator who is uncomfortable with this dynamic can try to reframe the process, for example, by redefining what was a competition of resources into a collaborative group allocation decision based on need.

- *Appreciative moves* are designed to break cycles of contentiousness that may have led to deteriorating communication, acrimony, or even silence. Examples of appreciative moves are tactics that help the other party save face in an argument, maintain dialogue and information exchange in the face of pressures to disengage, or invite new perspectives into the discussion to try to break a logjam or reverse a skid toward stalemate.

The concept of the shadow negotiation is a compelling way to think about the often hidden yet crucial power plays that occur in negotiation alongside haggling over positions and arriving at agreements. As Kolb and Williams (2001, p. 97) observe, "strategic moves in the shadow negotiation can determine the outcome of the negotiation on the issues."

SOURCE: Adapted from D. M. Kolb and J. Williams, "Breakthrough Bargaining," *Harvard Business Review* 79(2) (2001), pp. 89–97.

MANAGING POWER: INFLUENCE AND PERSUASION

During negotiations, actors frequently need to convince the other party they have offered something of value, that their offer is reasonable, and that they cannot offer more. Negotiators may also want to alter the other party's beliefs about the importance of his own objectives and convince him that his concessions are not as valuable as he first believed. Negotiators may portray themselves as likable people who should be treated decently. All these efforts are designed to use information, as well as the qualities of the sender and receiver of that information, to adjust the other party's positions, perceptions, and opinions; we call this group of tactics *influence*.

People differ widely in their ability to use influence effectively. Some observers think that the ability to persuade is something with which people are born—something they either have or don't have. Although the natural persuasive abilities of people do differ, persuasion is as much a science as a native ability; improving persuasive skills is an opportunity open to everyone.

There are two major ways in which to think about the key factors in the influence process. One is based on a traditional model of persuasion (Shannon and Weaver, 1948) that considers the characteristics of the *message,* or the content that the sender wants the receiver to believe, accept, or understand; the characteristics of the *source,* or the party attempting to persuade; and the characteristics of the *receiver,* or the party to be persuaded. The second way is based on a more contemporary understanding of how persuasion works. This approach, developed in a stream of research by Richard Petty and John Cacioppo, suggests that there are two general paths by which people are persuaded (see Chaiken, 1987; Petty and Cacioppo, 1986a, 1986b). The first path occurs consciously and involves integration of the *message* into the individual's previously existing cognitive structures (thoughts, intellectual frameworks, etc.). Petty and Cacioppo have labeled this path to persuasion the *central route,* which "occurs when motivation and ability to scrutinize issue-relevant arguments are relatively high" (Petty and Cacioppo, 1986b, p. 131). The other route to persuasion, the *peripheral route,* is characterized by subtle cues and context, with less cognitive processing of the message. Persuasion via the peripheral route is thought to occur automatically (i.e., out of conscious awareness), leading to "attitude change without argument scrutiny" (Petty and Cacioppo, 1986b, p. 132). Because the information is not integrated into existing cognitive structures, persuasion occurring via this route is likely to last a shorter time than persuasion occurring via the central route (Petty and Cacioppo, 1986b). A simple example of peripheral-route persuasion is the listener who is convinced by the impressive credentials of the speaker rather than by the arguments the speaker is actually presenting.

For clarity of presentation, we will represent elements from both paths in a single diagram (Figure 6.2). Many of the common elements used to increase leverage are part of the central route: the structure and content of the message, or the relationship between sender and receiver. However, several influence strategies are designed to persuade through the indirect or peripheral route, such as enhancing the attractiveness and credibility of the source, invoking the principle of reciprocity (you should do something for me because I did something for you), or drawing on appeals to popularity (you should think this way because many others do).[2] The remainder of this chapter will address the leverage factors presented in Figure 6.2. We organize this discussion according to the distinction between central and peripheral routes to influence.

---

[2] Researchers have disagreed as to whether the two routes to persuasion are separate systems (e.g., Petty and Cacioppo, 1986 a, b) or compensatory systems (e.g., Chaiken, 1987). That is, it is not clear if the two routes to persuasion operate separately or if they work in conjunction. Some work (e.g., O'Keefe, 1990) seems to suggest that both processes operate at all times, but one is likely to be dominant. There is also disagreement

FIGURE 6.2   Leverage: Two Routes to Influence

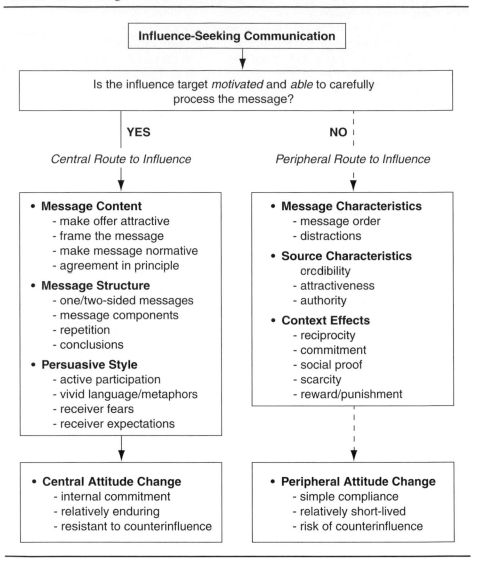

about what to label the two routes and which research findings fit more precisely into which route. For sake of clarity, we have adopted Petty and Cacioppo's labels for the two routes: central and peripheral. It is also difficult to summarize and apply some concepts of persuasion because of contradictory research findings and the complex relationships between variables. Despite these weaknesses, this model of persuasion is comprehensive and helps organize a great deal of conflicting research on persuasion. The model does *not* provide exact prescriptions about how to persuade everyone in all circumstances. It *does* provide a clear way to think about the variables that have been found to influence persuasion. It helps clarify when persuasive tactics can work, although this does not mean that these factors will work in all circumstances. In many situations, influence is achieved through a skillful blend of many persuasive techniques.

THE CENTRAL ROUTE TO INFLUENCE: THE MESSAGE AND ITS DELIVERY

Facts and ideas are clearly important in changing another person's opinions and perceptions, but the effectiveness of a persuasion effort depends on how the facts and ideas are selected, organized, and presented. There are three major issues to consider when constructing a message: the *content* of the message (the facts and topics that should be covered), *structure* of the message (how the topics and facts should be arranged and organized), and the *delivery style* (how the message should be presented).

Message Content

When constructing arguments to persuade the other party, negotiators need to decide what topics and facts they should include. In this section, we discuss four questions negotiators need to consider when constructing persuasive arguments: (1) how to make the offer attractive to the other party, (2) how to frame the message so the other party will say yes, (3) how to make messages normative, and (4) how to obtain agreements in principle.

1. Make the Offer Attractive to the Other Party.   In structuring the message, negotiators should emphasize the advantage the other party gains from accepting the proposal (Michener and Suchner, 1971). Although this may seem obvious, it is surprising how many negotiators spend more time on explaining what aspects of their offer are attractive to themselves than on identifying what aspects are likely to be attractive to the other party. Experienced negotiators ensure that the other party understands what he or she will gain by accepting an offer. To do this well, negotiators need to understand the other party's needs. Salespeople often identify a customer's needs and requirements before they get down to the details of what a particular product or service can do for the purchaser. Labor negotiators often have preliminary, unofficial meetings with management at which both parties discuss the upcoming deliberations and signal the high-priority issues for the year. With information about the other party's needs and interests, negotiators can construct offers with highly appealing features.

When negotiators are on the *receiving* end of a proposal, they frequently choose not to talk about the attractive features of an offer but rather to highlight why certain features are undesirable (Emerson, 1962). They try to argue that what the other party is trying to sell is not what they need, or is inadequate, or unsuited to their specifications. Thus, persuasion can be a struggle to define or evaluate the attractiveness of an offer. The negotiator making the offer stresses its attractive features, hoping to minimize further concessions. The receiver of the offer stresses its unattractive features, hoping to receive more concessions. The better a negotiator understands the other's real needs and concerns, the more that he or she can anticipate the other's objections and structure the presentation to counteract them.

2. Frame the Message So the Other Party Will Say "Yes."   Advertisers discovered long ago that people who agree with one statement or proposal, even though it may be minor, are likely to agree with a second, more significant statement or proposal from the same person or on the same topic (Fern, Monroe, and Avila, 1986; Freedman and Fraser, 1966; Seligman, Bush, and Kirsch, 1976). Hence, if you can get the other party to agree to something—almost anything—then you have laid the foundation for subsequent agreement. The task is to find something that the other party can agree with that puts him or her in the mind-set of saying yes. A real estate salesperson who gets potential buyers to agree that the house they are visiting is in a nice neighborhood or has a nice yard for their children has made the first step toward getting them to say yes to buying the house (even if it is not the ideal size, layout, or price).

3. Make the Message Normative.   It is easy to assume that people are driven by simple and direct self-interest. There is plenty of evidence, however, to indicate that people are motivated to behave consistently with their values, that is, their religious, social, or ethical standards. These standards become part of people's self-image, a concept in their mind of what they are really like. People will go to considerable lengths to act or say things consistent with their self-image. At times, people act politely when in fact they are feeling quite hostile. People can act generously when they are actually financially strained and feel like being greedy (Reardon, 1981). They behave this way to preserve their self-image and to convince others that they are nice people (see our discussion of face saving in Chapter 8; see also Bem, 1972).

A powerful argument in negotiation is to show the other person that by following a course of action (your proposal), she will be acting in accordance both with her values and with some higher (more noble, moral, or ethical) code of conduct. Presidents use normative messages to justify fiscal policies to promote domestic purchases (e.g., "Buy American," "Protect American Jobs"), and interest groups use normative messages to either promote their points of view or demean other points of view (e.g., "Save a Tree," "Liberal Economics"). At times, the simple statement "This is the right (or proper) thing to do" may carry considerable weight. People work hard to take responsibility for actions that lead to positive outcomes (Schlenker and Riess, 1979).

4. Suggest an "Agreement in Principle."   There are times when getting the other party to accept an "agreement in principle" may be a valuable step in a negotiation. For example, when there is bitter conflict between two parties who cannot seem to agree on anything, getting agreement on a general principle, such as a cease-fire, may be the first "yes" statement to which both parties can ascribe. In the negotiations between Israel and Egypt over the Sinai, no details were settled about the fate of the Palestinians, but an agreement on the principle of Palestinian self-rule was reached. Although an agreement in principle is desirable when other options are blocked, it still takes a great deal of work to turn such an agreement into one that contains specific details and action proposals. Principles sound good, and most people may agree with what they advocate, but there is usually great uncertainty about how a principle applies to a specific situation. For example, to return to the Middle East, even if the parties agree to the principle of trading land for peace, there is still a great deal of work to do to specify which land and what kind of peace.

Message Structure

People are influenced not only by what negotiators say but also by how they arrange the words. Any writer or speaker faces the question of how to present material in the most logical or persuasive manner. How should arguments be arranged? Should counterarguments or opposing ideas be mentioned at all? There has been a considerable amount of research on the persuasive power of different message structures. Surprisingly, many of those elements that you might expect to have an important impact, such as the structure of logic in the message, have not been clearly shown to be important. Here we discuss four aspects of message structure that do appear to contribute to persuasion through the central route: (1) one- and two-sided messages, (2) message components, (3) repetition, and (4) conclusions.

1. One- and Two-Sided Messages.   When negotiators try to persuade the other party it is because they believe that the other holds an opinion different from theirs. Many people deal with this problem by completely ignoring arguments and opinions that might support the other party's position—a *one-sided* approach. Many politicians not only do not mention their opponent's point of view but may never even mention their opponent's name. Until recently, advertisements for consumer products would never identify competing products by name or stage an open comparison; only recently have some advertisers begun to explicitly mention "the competition" and comparatively evaluate the features or qualities of both products.

An alternate approach to ignoring the competition is to mention and describe the opposing point of view, and then show how and why it is less desirable than the presenter's point of view—a *two-sided* approach.

The question then arises: Which of these approaches is most effective? In general, *two-sided messages are considered to be more effective than one-sided messages* (Jackson and Allen, 1987). More specifically, two-sided messages appear to be most effective (1) when the other party is well educated, (2) when the other party initially disagrees with the position, (3) when the other party will be exposed to people who will argue points of view different from the position advocated, and (4) when the issue discussed is already familiar. In summary, when dealing with reasonably intelligent receivers, it is a mistake to ignore the impact of counterarguments. The other party will be formulating them as you speak, and it is an advantage to refute them by using two-sided messages. In addition, two-sided arguments work best when the preferred argument is presented *last* (Bettinghaus, 1966; Zimbardo, Ebbesen, and Maslach, 1977).

2. Message Components.   Big ideas or large propositions are hard to grasp and accept, especially when they are significantly different from your own. Negotiators can help the other party understand and accept their arguments by breaking them into smaller, more understandable pieces (Fisher, 1964; Ikle, 1964). It is even better if they can show that the component parts contain statements that the other party has already accepted or agreed with. For example, a company that is having trouble getting the union to accept a whole package of rule changes could break its presentation down into separate discussions of specific rules: transfers between departments within a plant, transfers between plants, temporary changes in work classifications, and so on. In one case, for example, a union was very interested in making changes to work rules to preserve job security; having already said yes to these changes, the union seemed more receptive to management's argument for other work rule changes. In addition, it is possible that breaking down complex arguments into smaller parts will lead the parties to see the possibilities to logroll, bundle, and trade off across issues (see Chapter 4) because the issues will be seen in sharper focus.

3. Repetition.   We only have to think of the regular blitz of typical television or radio advertisements to realize the power of repetition in getting a message across. Repetition also encourages central-route processing and thus enhances the likelihood that the message will be understood (Cacioppo and Petty, 1985). However, repeating a point is effective only for the first few times. After that, additional repetition does not significantly change attitudes (McGuire, 1973) and may become annoying and lead people to react against the message.

4. Conclusions.   Sometimes writers or speakers will make an argument and then state the conclusion; other times, they will let the listeners draw their own conclusions. Letting others draw their own conclusion (as long as it is the conclusion one wants drawn) can lead to a very effective presentation. Research suggests that when negotiating with people who are very intelligent, or have not yet made up their minds, leaving the conclusion open is a good approach. In contrast, for people whose ideas are already well-formulated and strong, to leave the conclusion unstated is to leave the most important part of the persuasive effort undone. In general, do not assume that given a set of facts or arguments, the other party will reach the same conclusion you would reach; rather, draw explicit conclusions for listeners to ensure that they have understood the argument completely (Feingold and Knapp, 1977; Hovland and Mandell, 1952; McGuire, 1964).

Persuasive Style: How to Pitch the Message

When negotiators select a delivery style for the message they have constructed, they are setting the emotional tone and manner of their presentation. Some people are belligerent; others are solicitous and accommodating. Some people make speeches; others start a dialogue. Some present detailed facts and draw specific conclusions; others use metaphors and paint beautiful pictures with words. We will now consider four major elements of persuasive style and how they affect successful persuasion: (1) active participation versus passive responding, (2) use of vivid language and metaphors, (3) use of threats to incite fears, and (4) violation of the receiver's expectations.

1. Encourage Active Participation.   People are more likely to change their attitudes and beliefs for the long term when they are actively involved in the process of learning new material (Bettinghaus, 1966; Johnson and Eagly, 1989, 1990; Petty and Cacioppo, 1990). Good teachers know this—rather than lecture, they ask questions and start discussions. Teachers are even more effective when they can get students both intellectually and emotionally involved. Role-plays and cases can help negotiators make use of the power of active participation. Negotiators who can use active approaches are generally more persuasive than those who don't, since an active approach requires the receiver to exert effort, which leads to involvement, which leads to attitude change.

2. Use Vivid Language and Metaphors.   The vividness and intensity of the language negotiators use have a major effect on their persuasiveness. Saying "This is certainly the best price you will get" is more intense than saying "This is quite a good price." Similarly, the statement "I don't feel like going out tonight" is not as intense as "You could not drag me out tonight with a team of horses." The intensity of language can also be increased through the use of colorful metaphors, swear words, or a change in intonation—from quiet to loud or loud to quiet (Bowers, 1964).

You might think that the most intense language would also be the most persuasive. To the contrary, language of relatively low intensity seems to be more effective than highly intense language (Bowers, 1964). Evidence indicates that people react negatively to persuasive attempts using language they perceive as too intense (Burgoon and King, 1974). People under stress seem to be particularly receptive to messages using low-intensity language and more inclined to reject those using high-intensity language (Jones and Burgoon, 1975). The impact of language intensity is even more complex, however: Research has shown that the effect of intense language depends in part on who uses it. Sources with high credibility can use more intense language than those who are not seen as credible (Burgoon and Stewart, 1975). Hence, members of the clergy can speak with more intensity (and convincingness) about the characteristics of heaven and hell and the likelihood of someone going there than can the authors of this book. It is also the case that an effective influencer will match his or her emotional fervor to the ability of the target of influence to receive and interpret the message (Conger, 1998). In conclusion, although there is a strong temptation to use intense language to make a point, it is typically better to moderate this impulse.

Metaphors and analogies are a particularly useful way to elevate the vividness of a message in the service of persuasion (Bowers and Osborn, 1966; Burgoon and King, 1974; Conger, 1998). An auto salesperson can give the potential customer details about a car's carburetor, the miles per gallon of gasoline used at different speeds, and rates of acceleration, but can make these points just as well by saying, "This car flies like the wind and doesn't guzzle gas." The same salesperson could show a car's fine finish, point out the body undercoating, and draw attention to the immaculate condition of the engine, or he could say, "This car is as sleek as a cat." Using metaphors to excess may lead the other party to believe that you're filled with hot air (itself a metaphor for not having the facts to support arguments), but using them to summarize some facts or to establish clear visual impressions can be valuable in persuasion. Advertisers use metaphors frequently when they promote their products; Allstate's "You're in Good Hands" or State Farm's "Like a Good Neighbor . . ." are just two examples. Finally, when using metaphors, be careful to choose the correct picture. This is especially difficult when negotiating across cultures, where metaphors do not always translate well. (See Chapter 11 for more discussion of culture and negotiation.)

3. Incite Fears.   Messages that contain threats—threats of strikes by unions or lockouts by management, threats to harm the other party's reputation, or threats to break off negotiations—can be useful when a negotiator needs to underscore the absolute importance of a point being made. In essence, threats are if–then statements with serious negative consequences attached: "If you do X, then I will be forced to do Y." Negotiators must be prepared to follow through with the consequences threatened, however, or they will be perceived as making empty threats and thereby lose credibility.

Because of their dramatic nature and the emotional response they evoke, threats may be tempting to use (see Chapter 3). In fact, threats are probably used less frequently than one might expect, for several reasons. One reason is that the other person's reaction to a threat is hard to predict. A second reason is that it is hard to know how menacing the threat appears to the other party. Often threats appear more powerful to the people who make them than they do to the receivers. Third, threats put other parties in a position where they can call the bluff, forcing the negotiator to carry out the threat. Often, following through with a threat will cost more than negotiators are willing to pay (Lytle, Brett, and Shapiro, 1999). Finally, threats may produce compliance, but they do not usually produce commitment. As we have pointed out, negotiating parties often want to reach an agreement they can live with. People can find many ways to avoid or undermine arrangements they were forced to comply with but to which they are not committed.

Fear-arousing messages may be sent without issuing threats. One manager, negotiating with another about the flow of work between their two departments, may suggest that if an agreement is not reached, the other manager will be portrayed to higher management as uncooperative. Research suggests that such messages can be effective if they increase the fear level of the receiver (Boster and Mongeau, 1984; Sutton, 1982). To be most effective, this kind of message must be accompanied by both a suggested alternative action that will reduce or eliminate the feared outcome and a reassurance that the action will work (Leventhal, 1970). The manager in the example above could propose that some of his or her employees be reassigned to help the other department speed up the work flow if the other manager will provide additional storage space, and then show how these changes will eliminate the problem.

4. Violate the Receiver's Expectations.   In *All the King's Men,* Robert Penn Warren describes a scene in which Willy Stark, the demagogic, radical candidate for governor, is about to speak to a group of wealthy citizens to raise funds for his campaign. The citizens support neither his radical proposals nor his violent manner of speech. When he arrives, Stark is conservatively dressed and greets them in a quiet, relaxed manner. In a conversational tone, he proceeds to describe some modest proposals for social change, along with some sensible ways of financing them. His audience is at first surprised, then impressed, and finally won over. Stark is employing the technique of *violating expectations*. People who argue positions that are thought to be counter to their self-interest are generally more persuasive because they violate the receiver's expectation about what the sender should be advocating (O'Keefe, 1990). For instance, an automobile mechanic recently suggested that one of the authors of this book should use mid- or high-octane gas in his car to reduce fuel-injector maintenance and save money. This message was persuasive because the mechanic was arguing against his own self-interest (future car repairs) when he suggested the change in gas (his business does not sell gasoline).

Another way that receivers' expectations can be violated occurs when they expect one style of delivery from the speaker and then experience a totally different style. For example, when one expects to be subjected to intense language (loud, volatile, provocative, etc.), one prepares defenses and counterarguments. If one instead encounters moderate, casual, reasonable language, one can relax one's defenses, listen to the message less critically, and be more likely to be persuaded (Miller and Burgoon, 1979). Great orators such as Winston Churchill and Martin Luther King, Jr. have used this style, frequently changing the intensity of their voices to hold the audience's attention. Although this is not a stylistic tactic that everyone can use, strong orators have a valuable tool at their disposal. Clearly, the process may also work in reverse—an emotionally intense speaker may equally persuade audiences who expect quiet, controlled, highly rational discourse.

More generally, Barry (2001) proposed a model of interpersonal influence that revolves around violating expectations of influence targets as a way to increase one's effectiveness as an influencer. The model proposes that violated expectations will alter how the target of influence attends to an influence-seeking message. For example, if an influence seeker unexpectedly uses friendly tactics in what has up until now been a formal or aloof relationship, the target may become favorably disposed to comply and engage in diminished cognitive scrutiny of the message itself. Conversely, negative arousal created by (for example) an unexpectedly direct or assertive request may inhibit influence to the extent that the violation of expectations leads the target to scrutinize the message more closely.

Section Summary

In summary, negotiators need to take care when they construct a message to persuade the other party to their point of view. Aspects of the message content, message structure, and the delivery style can all influence the extent to which a message is persuasive. In other words, how one says something can be as important as what one has to say, and if the other party is not persuaded by the arguments, then perhaps the negotiator did not construct the message effectively. When influence does successfully occur through the "central route," the change in the target's attitudes is more likely to be long lasting and resistant to counterinfluence.

PERIPHERAL ROUTES TO INFLUENCE

Thus far, we have focused on organizing the structure and content of the message in order to create leverage through the "central" route to influence. In this section, we will consider ways that a person can influence others through the "peripheral" route. In such cases, the receiver attends less to the substance of persuasive arguments and is instead susceptible to more "automatic" influence through subtle cues. This usually occurs when the target of influence is either unmotivated or unable to attend carefully to the substance contained within a persuasive message. As we suggested earlier, persuasion that occurs through the peripheral route is less likely to bring about real attitude change, is more likely to last a shorter time, and is more vulnerable to counterinfluence.

In our discussion of peripheral routes to influence we draw in part on the work of psychologist Robert Cialdini (2001), who argues that this type of persuasion can work almost automatically, like an eye blink or a startle response. Cialdini spent many years investigating why people comply with requests that, upon further reflection, they would rather not have agreed to. His research represents a skillful blend of laboratory research and observation of "compliance experts" such as salespeople, fund-raisers, and marketing and advertising experts. The insights that emerge are useful not only for achieving successful influence in negotiation and other contexts, but also for avoiding being a "victim" of these persuasive traps.

Our discussion of peripheral routes to influence will consider three sets of strategies: message aspects, attributes of the persuader, and elements of the influence context.

Aspects of Messages That Foster Peripheral Influence

When targets of influence are unmotivated or unable to pay close attention to the influence seeker's message, they are susceptible to being influenced by message elements that exist apart from the actual arguments involved. We discuss two such elements here: the way in which the influence seeker chooses to order those arguments, and the use of distraction to interfere with the target's ability to think effortfully about the arguments in play.

Message Order.   In preparing a persuasive argument, negotiators usually have one major point, piece of information, or illustration that is particularly important or compelling. Where should it be placed in the message? At the beginning? In the middle? At the end? Research tells us one thing clearly—do not place the important point in the middle of the message (Bettinghaus, 1966). Should it be at the beginning or at the end? When the topics are familiar, interesting, or controversial to the receiver, the important points should be made early, exposing the receiver to the *primacy effect:* The first item in a long list of items is the one most likely to be remembered. Thus, the negotiator should state messages that are attractive to the receiver early, before they present something the receiver may not want to hear. In contrast, when the topic is uninteresting, unfamiliar, or not very important to the receiver, the most critical point should be placed at the end of the message to take advantage of the *recency effect:* the tendency for the last item presented to be the best remembered. The recency effect should be considered when the message is likely to be contrary to the receiver's current point of view (Clark, 1984; Rosnow and Robinson, 1967).

Distractions.   One factor that makes the persuasion process complex is that people start to defend themselves against being persuaded as soon as they suspect that someone is trying to persuade them. As they listen, part of their attention is devoted to what is being said, but a large portion is also devoted to developing counterarguments (Brock, 1963; Festinger and Maccoby, 1964). Persuasion efforts are more effective if they can reduce the other party's efforts to develop defensive counterarguments. One way to do this is to have a *distraction* occur at the same time the message is sent. Distractions apparently absorb the effort that the other party normally would put into building counterarguments and leave the listener "vulnerable to the message appeals" (Reardon, 1981, p. 192). In other words, when receivers are distracted, they are less able to engage in issue-relevant thinking (Petty and Brock, 1981), and hence may be more susceptible to processing peripheral cues that may push them toward a particular choice. For example, during an oral presentation of the economic advantages of an offer, negotiators could lay out papers with charts and graphs, hand them to the other party, and help that person turn from one chart to another as the oral presentation continues. Presumably, the charts and graphs absorb that part of the other party's attention that might normally go into formulating counterarguments. Distractions seem to inhibit the receiver's subvocalization (what people say to themselves as they hear a message). Sometimes subvocalizations are counterarguments, which occur when the receiver is opposed to or cautious about the message, but they can be supportive arguments as well. When receivers really like what is being said (such as when a friend is trying to persuade someone to take a second helping of chocolate cake), subvocalizations will encourage them to accept the offer. At that time, if the receivers want to protect themselves from temptation, they in turn should create distractions. If the friend wants to successfully convince the other person to eat the dessert, then he or she should try to eliminate any distractions (Petty, Wells, and Brock, 1976).

Source Characteristics That Foster Peripheral Influence

When the recipients of a persuasive message are unmotivated or unable to attend closely to the substance of the persuasive appeal, they become vulnerable to source effects. In other words, someone who is not paying close attention to the message may be unduly influenced by the characteristics of the person or organization delivering the message. A wide variety of source effects can potentially have an effect on the recipient of a persuasive message. We group them here into three broad categories: credibility, attractiveness, and authority.

Source Credibility.   During a negotiation, both parties exchange information, opinions, and interpretations. What, and how much, should be believed? On the one hand, there are often strong incentives for negotiators to mislead each other (see also Chapter 7, on ethics). On the other hand, negotiators have to accept and believe at least some of the information they are given, or successful negotiation is impossible (Kelley, 1966). As a negotiator, you cannot check every fact and statement. The more information one is willing to accept from the other party without independent verification, the easier that person's job will be. The reverse is also true—the more credible you are to the other party, the more persuasive you will be. Let us assume you are buying a house. The sellers tell you that they have three other parties coming to look at the house in the afternoon; two of them are being transferred to this area and have only one day to locate a house. If this is true, and you like the house, it would be to your advantage to make an offer now rather than to delay your decision and possibly find that one of the afternoon visitors has bought the house. But are the sellers' statements true? No doubt the sellers know whether or not there are other potential buyers coming that same day; hence, there is no question that they are competent or qualified to have good information. The issue is whether or not they are credible.

Source credibility depends mostly on three things: the qualifications of the source, the perceived trustworthiness of the source, and self-presentation (or source likability—see O'Keefe, 1990).

First, qualifications: When people are determining how much to believe another person, they often ask, "Is this person in a position to possess the information he or she claims to have? That is, is he or she competent and qualified?" The stronger the person's perceived qualifications and expertise, the higher the credibility (see Ostermeier, 1967; Swenson, Nash, and Roos, 1984). Second, trustworthiness: "Is this person reporting accurately what he or she knows? That is, is he or she personally believable or trustworthy?" (Berlo, Lemert, and Mertz, 1966) Third, self-presentation: People appear more or less credible because of their *presence*—the way they present themselves to others. Three components of behavior are instrumental in creating a favorable presence: composure, sociability, and extroversion (McCroskey, Jensen, and Valencia, 1973). A person who seems hesitant, confused, or uncertain when giving information is not as convincing as a person who appears calm, confident, and comfortable. A friendly, open person is easier to talk to (and therefore to believe) than someone who is distant, abrasive, or haughty. A person with a dynamic vocal style and a strong delivery is often more persuasive than one without these attributes. Trustworthiness and qualifications are more powerful characteristics in determining your perception of another's credibility than his or her self-presentation is, but all three play a critical role.

Many other factors contribute to source credibility. Below we discuss several that negotiators can control.

1. Personal Reputation for Integrity. Integrity is character—the personal values and ethics that ground your behavior in high moral principles. Integrity is the quality that assures people you can be trusted, you will be honest, and you will do as you say. If people trust you with confidential information, you will not disclose that information to others. Finally, if you make an agreement, you will abide by its terms and conditions, and follow through on it (Shapiro, Sheppard, and Cheraskin, 1992).

Conversely, people with a reputation for being dishonest or insincere have an extremely difficult time in negotiations—they tend not to be believed, even when they tell the truth. A reputation for being dishonest is very difficult to change. It is not surprising that professional negotiators work very hard to protect their reputation. While negotiators using a competitive strategy are often expected to inflate, magnify, and distort in order to present things in the best possible light for their side, a onetime success may contribute directly to future credibility problems (see also Chapter 7, on ethics). It is therefore critical for negotiators to consider the long-term consequences of their behavior if they are to be trusted by others (we introduced the role of trust in Chapter 4 and will explore it in greater depth in Chapter 8).

2. "Benefit-of-the-Doubt" First Impressions. The statement "First impressions are lasting impressions" has a great deal of validity. How people dress, behave, and speak can be enormously important in the first few minutes of meeting a stranger. When meeting others for the first time, people generally tend to evaluate them positively rather than negatively (Greenberg and Miller, 1966). People frequently remain open-minded during the first meeting; if they do form a first impression, they often err toward the positive viewpoint. Although this bias may seem to be an advantage in helping persuade someone you have recently met, keep in mind that it is probably working the other way as well.

3. Intention to Persuade.   Does a negotiator initially come across as a huckster or as cool, poised, and polished? While people may give the benefit of the doubt in their initial judgment, the more they detect that a negotiator's mission is to change their minds, the more suspicious and resistant they may become. For instance, when the phone rings unexpectedly, it is often easy to identify the telemarketer who mispronounces your name and tries to involve you in friendly chit-chat ("How are you this evening?") while she eases into her prepared sales pitch ("I'm glad you're well. Do you ever have problems with . . ."). By the time she has gotten to the sales pitch, your defenses are most likely already well fortified. In contrast, communicating with natural enthusiasm, sincerity, and spontaneity may take the edge off persuasive communication and reduce defensive reactions. Many skillful negotiators and persuaders may therefore assume a mild-mannered or even slightly confused demeanor (recall Peter Falk in the television role of Detective Columbo) to minimize the negative impact of a hard, persuasive style while giving or getting the information they need.

4. Use or Minimize Status Differences.   Status is signaled by a variety of criteria: occupation, age, education level, the neighborhood where a person lives, dress, type of automobile, and the like. A president of a major corporation, for example, has more status than a university professor, but less than a justice of the Supreme Court. High-status people generally have more influence than low-status people, in several ways. First, status gives people visibility, which allows them to get attention and be heard. It also confers prestige, lending the image that certain people are worth listening to (Bettinghaus, 1980). However, a status difference may also increase resistance, because receivers expect to be persuaded and therefore increase their defenses against the effort. Persuaders need to decide whether they should enforce a status difference (act or dress consistently with their status) or minimize the difference by acting or dressing more like the listener.

5. Appearance and Self-Presentation.   It is not an earth-shaking revelation to note that how you dress, speak, and behave will influence how credible you appear to others. What may not be as obvious is how you should adjust your appearance to increase your credibility. Often appearance and dress are tied to the status difference and intent-to-persuade issues. Should you wear a suit for an interview, even if you usually wear jeans and a T-shirt? Should you adopt some of the local speech pronunciations and drop those that are native to you? Is a member of the clergy more effective in clerical garb or in street clothes? In general, researchers have found that it is best to be "normal" (Bettinghaus, 1980), meaning to act appropriately, naturally, and unaffectedly. A Harvard-educated politician with a New England accent who tries to spice his language with "Aw, shucks" and "y'all" in the South will not appear normal; neither will a college student who drops in to buy a Porsche dressed in muddy boots and grimy work clothes.

6. Associates.   Whom you associate with also can influence how you are perceived, in terms of both status and expertise. Judicious name dropping (i.e., mentioning well-known people who are also credible and prestigious) and even arranging for introductions or endorsements by people who can add to your reputation can be useful steps.

7. Perceived Expertise. Sometimes your occupation, education, or past experiences will establish your expertise and therefore the perception of your competence (Swenson, Nash, and Roos, 1984). At other times, there are no obvious ways to make your expertise known. Stereotypes can lead others to see you as lacking the requisite expertise to be credible. Women are often seen as lacking knowledge about mechanical things, and men are seen as ignorant about childcare or cooking.

In situations where you are unknown or likely to be viewed stereotypically, you need to make an extra effort to establish your expertise. There are numerous things you can do to establish your expertise:

- Find ways to introduce your education or experience into the conversation: "When I went to law school, we were taught that . . ."
- Cite other highly credible sources of information: "According to this morning's *New York Times* . . ."
- Ask questions or draw quick conclusions that could only be derived from in-depth, firsthand knowledge or experience. Consider the example of a woman manager who was representing her department at a planning committee for a new office building. The other committee members, all men, were pointedly ignoring her until she started to ask questions about heat loss gradients through the walls and the number of foot candles of light falling on work surfaces.

8. Persistence and Tenacity. Persistence and tenacity are valuable personal qualities in a negotiator. Children are often considered great negotiators because they are so wonderfully persistent in pursuing what they want. Saying no to a child usually does not stop the child from asking; children find all kinds of creative ways to persist in trying to achieve their objective (the candy bar, the toy, watching the TV show). From watching how children persist as negotiators, we can learn that part of persistence is doggedly pursuing the objective, but that another part is finding new, unique, and creative ways to pursue the same request. The effective use of persistence doesn't mean pursuing your goals blindly and rigidly, because you can be effectively rebuffed; instead, it means to display creativity in finding new ways to pursue the objective. Persistent people are comfortable being in a contentious mode with others—they don't fear conflict and try to escape simply because of a difference of opinion or views. They are persistent, but they are also flexible, redefining strategy and approach as the times and conditions change.

Personal Attractiveness. People will treat others better when they like them than when they don't (Eagly and Chaiken, 1975). They are less likely to feel that attractive negotiators will be dishonest or attempt to coerce them (Tedeschi, Schlenker, and Bonoma, 1973). They are more likely to accept their influence, to believe them, and to trust them (Chaiken, 1986). Being nice and pleasant is a logical step to being more persuasive. It is not clear why personal attractiveness increases persuasiveness. People may have a tendency to let their guard down and trust attractive people more readily. Attractive people may receive a lot of attention, or they may cause others to imitate them in order to be more like them (Trenholm, 1989). Personal attractiveness may also increase liking, as we have noted before (O'Keefe, 1990). The following tactics are some of the many ways that an individual can enhance his or her personal attractiveness to a target of influence or a negotiating opponent.

1. Friendliness.   A critically important attribute that a negotiator can have is the ability to be friendly and outgoing and to establish personal relationships with others—particularly the other parties in the negotiation. Warmth, empathy, and simple direct, personal interest in others all help to soften the harder edges of some of the other power sources. Friendliness also involves a strong emotional component, and therefore it appeals to the other party's moods and feelings as well as to his or her intellect. Rather than immediately getting down to business, successful negotiators use friendliness to make the other party feel comfortable and at ease, to get to know the other negotiator, and to discover things that they may have in common. Friendliness, empathy, and sensitivity are all part of a larger ability to show warmth and personal interest in the other individual. They are also related to the ability to perceive others accurately, know what they are about and how they are feeling, or be aware of the personal preferences and circumstances that may dictate what they do and how they do it. Friendly, outgoing negotiators are also likely to use reward and praise to encourage and support the other party, whereas less friendly negotiators will be more likely to use criticism and verbal punishment.

2. Ingratiation.   Ingratiation involves flattering or enhancing the other's self-image or reputation through statements or actions, and thus enhancing one's own image in the same way (Jones, 1964). Ingratiation does not try to put other people down, but excessively builds them up. Handing out flattery may presumably make others like you and be more prone to accept your persuasive arguments and point of view. Flattering another person by giving compliments is perhaps the most obvious form of ingratiation. Because it is obvious, it is used often and sometimes abused. Negotiators congratulate others on their excellent and thorough preparation, their considerate suggestions, or their willingness to listen to a long and complex presentation. Compliments can be a potent means of ingratiation, not only because people like to receive them, but also because the norm of reciprocity leaves the other party with the obligation to return something for the compliment (Cialdini, 2001; Jones, 1964). But when people are complimented for attributes they do not have or actions they know they did not perform well, or when the praise seems excessive, they are likely to become wary, wondering what the flatterer is after.

3. Likability.   In negotiation, selecting members of a negotiation team that the other party will like is one way to use liking as an influence strategy. The liking principle is quite straightforward: People you like have more influence over you (see our discussion of similarity under source factors earlier in this chapter). If you like the sender, you are more likely to be persuaded by him or her, although research has shown that likability is less important than other credibility factors, such as expertise (Eagly and Chaiken, 1975).

The effects of the liking principle are insidious. Liking can occur through many different approaches, and defending against them all would be impossible. Deborah Tannen, in her well-known work on gender and communication differences (see Tannen, 1990), suggests that compared to men, women practice more "rapport-talk," in which their objective is to establish connections and negotiate the relationship, while, compared to women, men practice more "report-talk" in order to preserve status differences in some form of a hierarchical social order. Cialdini (2001) points out that it would be useless to try to prevent yourself from liking others. Rather, you should let the liking occur and then explore *why* you like the other person. If you find that you like the person more than you would typically like another person under similar circumstances, then it is time to be wary. Separating liking the other party from an evaluation of the deal should be enough to moderate the influence of the liking principle in your negotiations.

4. Helping the Other Party.   There are many ways one party can help the other party in a negotiation: by doing a favor, allowing extra time, providing confidential information, complying with a request, or helping with a constituency. Negotiators can help the other party avoid being caught by surprise. For example, an automobile salesperson may say to the customer, "In a moment I'm going to take you in to talk to the sales manager about the amount we are going to allow on your present car. You may hear me say some unfavorable things about your car. Don't let that bother you—we'll still get the figure you and I agreed on." By "helping" you with his manager, the salesperson hopes you will help him by buying a new car from him. In another example, during negotiations on the sale of a large parcel of land to a major corporation, the seller privately told the company executive handling the negotiation about a forthcoming zoning change that would benefit the company. The executive got the credit for uncovering this inside information, and the seller was not materially affected one way or the other by sharing it (but got the deal).

5. Perceived Similarity.   When meeting for the first time, people often try to find something they have in common. Perhaps they attended the same school, grew up in the same neighborhood, or have friends in common. The more similarities they find, the more bonds they establish, the better both parties feel, and more important, the more receptive they will be to each other's messages and efforts at persuasion (O'Keefe, 1990). A useful negotiating tactic, therefore, is to identify and discuss experiences, characteristics, and opinions you hold in common with the other party. If you see pictures of a yacht on an office wall, you might mention your own interest in sailing. The other party's winter suntan might cue you to mention your own trips to the tropics or the ski slopes. But if it is to your advantage to find and explore commonalities in experience, attitude, and background with the other party, it is also to your disadvantage to highlight those areas where you differ. There is no point to starting a conversation on a politically controversial topic when you know or suspect that the other holds a completely different view from yours. Thus, as we noted from Tannen's work, discussion of the relationship, along with self-disclosure to the other, is more likely to elicit reciprocity norms and promote similarity and liking (see also Lumsden and Lumsden, 1996).

6. Emotion.   We discussed emotion earlier in this chapter in connection with the use of language to construct a message, but emotion can also be a source factor. Emotion combined with persistence leads to assertiveness and determination. Used effectively, emotion may enhance a message source's attractiveness by instilling in listeners the belief that the speaker holds appealing deep-seated values (this may also enhance the speaker's credibility).

Pepper . . . and Salt

THE WALL STREET JOURNAL

STOCKHOLDERS MEETING

Ray

**"Remember, no sobbing.
It makes them jittery."**

From *The Wall Street Journal*. Used with permission of Cartoon Features Syndicate.

As we discussed in Chapter 5, expressions of fear, anger, or enthusiasm can become an integral part of negotiations—particularly over issues about which you feel strongly (see Box 6.5). Emotion can be powerful because it offers a stark contrast to the expectation that negotiation is a cool, calm, rational exchange of information, driven by logical analysis of outcome maximization and economic valuation of alternatives. Yet negotiators frequently do not behave according to the principles of logic and economic rationality. In addition, when everyone else is being rational, it is frequently the person who expresses strong feelings, gets angry, or makes an impassioned speech in favor of a proposed solution that carries the day (Henderson, 1973). Union organizers, political stump speakers, leaders of social movements, evangelists, and others whose aim is to organize and mobilize supporters all understand the importance of arousing emotion through their appeals.

Authority.   The principle of authority is quite simple: People with authority have more influence than those without authority. Researchers have long been interested in the effects of authority figures on human behavior. Stanley Milgram's (1974) classic studies of obedience to authority suggest that people will go to great lengths when their behavior is legitimized by an authority figure. Most people will obey the orders of a person wearing a uniform, even if there is no war or apparent emergency. This, too, is an effect of the principle of authority.

BOX 6.5
The Role of Anger and Compassion in Negotiation

Does the expression of emotion actually affect negotiation processes and outcomes? This is a relatively new area for systematic exploration by negotiation researchers. In one study, Keith Allred and his colleagues (Allred, Mallozzi, Matsui, and Raia, 1997) examined whether the expression of anger and compassion would exert influence on negotiation by affecting how the parties feel about each other, the outcomes each derived individually, and the amount of joint gain. The researchers found that expressing high anger and low compassion led the negotiators to have less desire to work together in the future, and to achieve fewer joint gains, but did not affect the ability of individual negotiators to yield greater gains. The authors have developed a promising approach for studying the role of emotional expression and understanding within the negotiation process.

SOURCE: Adapted from K. G. Allred, J. S. Mallozzi, F. Matsui, and C. P. Raia, "The Influence of Anger and Compassion on Negotiation Performance," *Organizational Behavior and Human Decision Processes* 70 (1997), pp. 175–87.

In negotiation, the principle of authority can be used in many ways. Herb Cohen (1980) suggests that written rules carry more weight than those given verbally. Thus, a procedure is more likely to be followed if it is in the policy manual or fine print of the contract than if it is merely expressed orally. Cialdini (2001) observes that the use of a title, such as *doctor* or *professor,* gives the user more authority and thus more influence. A friend of one of the authors uses the title *doctor* whenever ordering airline tickets. He found out early in his career that airlines would telephone doctors when there was a flight delay but would ignore the other passengers. This simple illustration shows the esteem with which some titles (or positions) are held in society. Cialdini also suggests that authority is more than position; it can further lead to attributions of expertise. He tells the story of a waiter who, regardless of what patrons order, recommends something else on the menu that is cheaper because the original dish "is not as good tonight as it normally is" (pp. 198–99). In doing so, the waiter establishes his authority for later (more expensive) advice about the meal, such as expensive desserts (and perhaps also induces diners to reciprocate his generous advice when it's time to leave a tip).

Cialdini (2001, p. 197) offers the following advice about dealing with authority figures who may have influence over you. Ask two questions: "Is this authority truly an expert?" and "How truthful can you expect this expert to be?" The first question forces you to verify that the person really does have expertise in the situation and not just the appearance (title, attire) of expertise. The second question suggests that you examine the motive of the expert who is offering advice. If someone, like the waiter described above, gives you some negative information before another suggestion, he or she may in fact be manipulating you into thinking that he or she is honest when this is not the case. (We address ethical implications in Chapter 7.)

Aspects of Context That Foster Peripheral Influence

Finally, we explore aspects of the situation beyond the message itself and the sender of the message that create opportunities to pursue the peripheral route to influence. Five strategies are discussed: reciprocity, commitment, social proof, scarcity, and reward and punishment.

Reciprocity.   The norm of reciprocity has been studied for years by philosophers, anthropologists, sociologists, and other social scientists. This norm suggests that when you receive something from another person, you should respond in the future with a favor in return. This norm is thought to be pan-cultural in that groups around the world appear to respect it (Gouldner, 1960). We alluded to the reciprocity norm in the previous section, when discussing personal attractiveness of sources and some receiver factors.

The norm of reciprocity plays an important role in negotiations. Negotiators give concessions and expect concessions in return. When they treat the other party politely, they expect a corresponding politeness. The norm can also be used to obtain compliance from another negotiator. For instance, negotiator A does a small favor for negotiator B and later asks for a larger favor from B in return. The net advantage goes to A. Although one may think that the norm of reciprocity should apply only to favors of the same size, this does not appear to be the case. In fact, many sales pitches rely on giving the consumer a small gift early in an exchange and then asking for a large concession from the consumer later. In parts of Africa, particularly Nigeria, there is a custom of giving a small gift, called *dash,* to a potential customer soon after he or she has walked into a shop— before there has ever been a chance to identify the customer's needs. The shopkeeper will claim, legitimately, that it is a gift, no strings, yours to keep even if you turn and walk out of the shop at this minute. However, knowing human nature, the shopkeeper does not really expect this to happen and is rarely disappointed. The shopkeeper knows that people like to receive gifts and will develop positive feelings toward those who give them. In a more local example, one of the authors of this book does business in a local copy shop that always gives customers a piece of candy with their change. The gift—in a small way—provides something extra that, the shop hopes, will encourage repeat patronage.

Similar opportunities exist in other negotiation situations. A compliment, such as a reference to the other party's positive behavior in a prior discussion, will make that person feel good and set the scene for him or her to act positively. Giving a quick concession on an issue that the other party wants will both please that party and create the implicit obligation for him or her to do the same. Too often negotiators begin by holding every advantage close to their chest and giving things away grudgingly, believing that this is the best way to succeed. Such rigid behavior is no more likely to lead to graceful and successful negotiation than it is to graceful and successful acting or public speaking. Flexibility and adaptability are necessary in all three.

Given the apparent powerfulness of the norm of reciprocity, how can the negotiator counter its effects? One possibility is to refuse all favors in a negotiation setting, but this would probably cause more problems than it resolves. For instance, refusing a cup of coffee from your host may remove the effects of the norm of reciprocity but at the same time may insult the host, especially if five minutes later you go out to get a cup of coffee yourself. Perhaps the other person was simply being polite. Perhaps he or she was setting a positive tone for the meeting. Or perhaps he or she was trying to use the norm of reciprocity to create a small sense of indebtedness.[3]

How should the negotiator respond to such favors? Cialdini suggests that you should respond politely to a favor and accept what is offered if it is something you want. If it becomes apparent that the favor was an attempt at manipulation, however, then you should redefine the event as a trick rather than a favor. This will remove the obligation of the rule of reciprocity because the "rule says that favors are to be met with favors; it does not require that tricks be met with favors" (Cialdini, 2001, p. 47).

Commitment.   Researchers have long recognized that once people have decided something, they can be remarkably persistent in their beliefs. This process has been labeled *commitment to a position,* and it relies heavily on the common need that people have to appear consistent, both to themselves and to others. Most people are familiar with the bait-and-switch sales technique. Unscrupulous organizations advertise merchandise for sale at an incredibly low price but "run out" of stock by the time you arrive at the store. They then try to sell you alternate merchandise at a higher price. Why does this technique work? One reason is that once you have made the decision to purchase a product (a commitment), you almost automatically follow through with the commitment (even at a higher price). Thus, even if you went to the store to buy the product at the fantastic sale price of $49.95, you will be more likely to buy the alternative product at $64.95, even though that price may never have gotten you to the store in the first place.

In his youth, one of the authors of this book decided to purchase a used MG sports car. He tells the story that follows:

> After searching the city where I lived and finding only one car within my price range ($2,400), I test-drove the car, discussed the price with the salesman, made an offer to buy the car, completed most of the paperwork, was loaned the car overnight, and came back to sign the deal the next day. At this time the salesman embarrassedly told me that he was unaware the car had "electric overdrive" until his manager had told him, and that he could not sell the car for the agreed-on price. Rather, the salesman would have to charge an additional $350 for the overdrive. Of course, he would allow me to change my mind and not buy the car. I bought the car, but after driving away I was convinced that the salesman's bargaining strategy had been a manipulation to induce compliance. I could have confronted the dealer, but there was no proof that the dealer was dishonest (and who would believe a young consumer versus an established car dealer?). The consequences of this decision cost the dealership much more than the extra $350 it received for the car. I told many of my friends to stay away from the dealer because of the way he did business. I didn't have any repairs

---

[3] Note that many public-sector bargaining laws prohibit negotiators from even buying a cup of coffee for each other. Negotiators need to be aware of the laws and norms that may have implications for compliance strategies. In addition, there are cross-cultural differences in refusing a gift, and negotiators need to prepare carefully for such instances when they negotiate across borders. (See Chapter 11 for more discussion of culture and negotiation.)

done at the dealer after the warranty on the car expired. If you think that an honest mistake occurred and the salesman really had forgotten the overdrive, his behavior during the warranty period should convince you that wasn't the case. The only repair needed under warranty was to replace the tachometer. The warranty stated that the dealer would pay for the parts and 50 percent of the labor. The salesman told me that replacing the tachometer in an MG was very difficult: the dashboard had to be removed, and many pieces under the dashboard had to be removed in order to pass the wires. He advised me that it would take six hours to install the part, and suggested that I leave the car with them for the day. I didn't believe a word the salesman said. I diligently followed the mechanic around the car until he went into the service manager's office for a brief discussion. When he returned he replaced the tachometer in 15 minutes. After paying for half of the labor cost, I drove away, never to return!

Commitment strategies are very powerful devices for making people comply. One way to increase commitment is to write things down. Cialdini (2001) notes that encyclopedia companies that have customers complete their own order forms have a far lower cancellation rate than those companies that have salespeople write out the form. Why? Writing it themselves seems to increase the commitment that the customers feel. It is as if they say to themselves, "I wouldn't have written it down if I didn't want it, would I?" Many consumer-product companies have people write testimonials about their products in order to enter a drawing for a prize. Why? Apparently, writing testimonials increases the commitment to buy the product (Cialdini, 2001). Research has shown that even signing a petition can increase your compliance with a request to do something more intrusive several days later (Freedman and Fraser, 1966). Researchers have called this the foot-in-the-door technique (Clark, 1984).

How can commitment work in a negotiation? Usually, it is incremental. Agreement to innocuous statements early in the negotiation may be used as a foundation for further and further concessions. Frequently, our own words and behaviors are used to extract further concessions. In the MG example, the buyer was more than pleased to pay the extra $350 because in the drive-around period, he had shown the car to many friends and told them about the purchase. Since the salesman had been nice enough to let the buyer take the car overnight even before signing a contract, the only fair thing to do was to let the salesman off the hook for his mistake by paying $350 more!

Commitment strategies are very difficult to combat. Frequently, one will have already been influenced and agreed to something before even realizing that the manipulation has taken place. To some extent, being forewarned about these techniques is being forearmed. Cialdini (2001) suggests that your body will send two types of warning signals when these techniques are in use. Either you will feel uncomfortable when subtle commitments are being made, or something in the deal will just not seem quite right. If you encounter these thoughts or feelings when negotiating, look out for use of a commitment strategy by the other party. At the very least, be aware of all the agreements you strike during a negotiation, even those small, innocuous ones. They may be the setup for the next move.

Social Proof.   The principle of social proof suggests that people look to others to determine the correct response in many situations. This principle suggests that people often behave in certain ways because everyone else is doing so. Cialdini (2001) suggests that this is the principle that makes laugh tracks so effective on television comedies (see Fuller and Sheehy-Skeffington, 1974). It also explains why some influence agents like to mention the names of previously satisfied customers; if other people used the product and liked it, then it must be good. Celebrities are hired to endorse products for similar reasons.

In negotiation situations, the principle of social proof can act as a powerful influence strategy. Salespeople will show lists of satisfied customers, knowing that few people will take the time to verify the list. ("If it wasn't true, why would the salesperson show me the list?") Sweepstakes advertisements highlight previous winners and feature celebrities. Negotiators will talk about how popular their new product is and how sales have really increased this year. Real estate agents will be sure that you are aware that many other people are interested in the house that you are considering buying (see Fishbein and Azjen, 1975).

The principle of social proof works because false information ("Everyone thinks this product is good") is given weight in decisions. Cialdini (2001) suggests that the way to reduce this influence is to identify the false information and give it the weight it deserves. In negotiations, this means careful preparation and being aware of "facts" about the others' advocated views that do not seem to match your preparation. When the other party offers "evidence" about the popularity of an item, do not automatically trust that the other party is being completely honest; rather, ask the other to substantiate the claims. Even when there is a shortage of an item, be sure that you are behaving in your own best interests. Frequently, a planned delay ("Let me sleep on it") will be enough to separate the influence of social proof from your own needs and interests.

Scarcity.   The principle of scarcity suggests that when things are less available, they will have more influence. Cialdini (2001) describes how common sales strategies rely on the scarcity principle. Frequently, salespeople will tell customers that they are not sure if the product the customers would like to purchase is currently in stock. Before making the trip to the stockroom they ask if they should grab one before another salesperson gets it. Typically shoppers will say yes and will feel relieved (or lucky) when the salesperson returns with the "last one" in the store. This is the scarcity principle at work; people are easier to influence when they feel that they are obtaining a scarce resource.

In negotiation situations, the scarcity influence strategy may be operating whenever there appears to be a great demand for a product. Some organizations deliberately keep their products in short supply to give the appearance that they are very popular (e.g., popular Christmas toys). Car dealers will suggest that you not wait too long before deciding on the color car you want because they have very few cars left and they are selling fast. Anytime negotiators talk about "exclusive opportunities" and "time-limited offers," they are using the scarcity principle. Censorship also results in scarcity; banning a specific book in the library is guaranteed to increase the demand for it. (See Brehm, 1976, for further discussion of this phenomenon, known as *psychological reactance*.) Finally, auctions also rely on the principle of scarcity, by selling off unique (one-of-a-kind) pieces to the highest bidder—the more scarce the item, the higher the bids.

The scarcity principle is very difficult to combat when used effectively. It creates in the victim an activity trap focused on obtaining the item and effectively suspends cognitive evaluation of the broader situation (Cialdini, 2001). Cialdini suggests that people need to be aware of the emotional trappings that this principle arouses; when confronted with a strong emotional response to obtain a scarce good, they should carefully evaluate their reasons for wanting the item in the first place.

Use of Reward and Punishment.   Earlier in this chapter, we indicated that control over resources was a strong source of power. These resources can be used in at least two major ways. First, negotiators can use exchange. Exchange is the process of offering resources, or favors (promises and assistance), to secure the other's compliance and cooperation. Some authors have said that exchange is the same as bargaining, in that the user either directly or implicitly suggests reciprocity—in short, "If I do X for you, will you do Y for me?" Exchange relies on resources as the power base, particularly resources that can be translated into rewards for the other—favors, benefits, incentives, treats, perks, and the like. Thus, exchange frequently invokes the use of promises and commitments as persuasive tools—obligations that you are willing to make in exchange for the other's cooperation, compliance, or commitment to give you what you want. Finally, exchange transactions are often negotiated so that the other party completes his or her obligation now, but chooses not to ask you to complete your obligation until some point in the future, either defined or undefined. By doing so, you and the other party leave a series of chits or obligations out in your interpersonal marketplace, which you can call back in when you need them.

In his studies of successful managers and their use of power in organizations, Kotter (1977) emphasizes that a manager must recognize, create, and cultivate dependence among those around her—subordinates, peers, and even superiors—and to convert these dependencies into obligations. Obligations may be created in several ways. Doing favors for people, recognizing and praising them for their accomplishments, helping people out, paying individual attention to them even when the job demands do not require it or they do not expect it, and dispensing extra funds for special projects in a tight-budget year are but a few examples of how resources can be controlled and measured to help people do their jobs better and to generate liking for the power holder.

A second way that negotiators attempt to use this power is through pressure—that is, by the threat of punishment. An agent can make demands, suggest consequences about what will happen if the demands are not met, engage in frequent surveillance to determine whether the demands are carried out, remind the other person frequently about what is expected, and eventually follow through with the actual punishment if the demand is not met on time. A sales manager may cut a salesperson's pay for repeatedly failing to achieve sales target projections. An executive may fire a secretary for failing to improve his or her typing skills. A father may deny his son television privileges for a week because he didn't clean up his room. A supplier may put a late charge on an overdue bill to a customer. Like reward power and the use of praise, coercive or punishment power can be as effective in the verbal form as in the withdrawal or denial of tangible resources. If the sales manager berates a salesperson for failing to make target sales quotas (rather than firing him or her), or if the father yells at his son rather than denying him television privileges, the impact may be just as great.

The conditions for the use of pressure are similar to those for the use of exchange and praise: The other party is dependent on the power holder in some way, the agent controls some form of resources that can be denied or taken away from the other party, and the punishment can be administered in a manner that will ensure the other party's compliance. The decision to use pressure versus exchange is most likely related to the power holder's perception of the willingness of the other party to comply. Kipnis (1976) states that

> *sanctions, whether positive or negative, are most likely to be involved when expectations of successful influence are lowest.* Thus, *praise and rewards* appear to be preferred when the power holder wishes to retain the good will of the target person, or when the power holder anticipates that compliance is likely to drop off in the future. *Criticism and sanctions* appear to be preferred when the good will of the target is less involved, and the influence attempts are directed at changing some behavior rather than maintaining it. (p. 104)

Kipnis proposes a number of reasons why a power holder may decide to use pressure. First, pressure may be used as a way to express anger, gain retribution, or get even for something the target person has done. Research by Goodstadt and Hjelle (1973) has shown that the use of coercive power is likely to be greatest when the "other party's resistance or influence is attributed to *motivational causes* (I refuse) rather than to a *lack of ability* (I can't)" (Kipnis, p. 105, emphasis added). Thus, if the son had said, "I can't clean my room; I've got to go to band practice this morning," the father might be more likely to accept the excuse as reasonable and less likely to resort to coercive influence. Second, pressure may be used as an expression of role behavior—the job (or role) requires it. For example, a banker forecloses on a loan "because bank rules mandate it," or a dean terminates a poorly performing student because university policy must be upheld. In these cases, pressure is tied to the use of the legitimacy influence tactic—in short, "I wouldn't ordinarily do this, but my job description says I must." Negotiators are most likely to use pressure when they expect that the other party has little or no desire to meet their expectations, does not share the same deadline, or will not comply unless directly threatened with severe negative consequences.

The few empirical studies of power use in negotiation have found that, compared to those with low power, parties with high power tend to use more pressure tactics, such as threats, and make fewer concessions (Hornstein, 1965; Michener, Vaske, Schleiffer, Plazewski, and Chapman, 1975). When the power distribution between the parties was relatively small, the low-power party also showed a high degree of threat use and power tactics, creating an escalation between the parties that usually destroyed the negotiation (see also Vitz and Kite, 1970). There is also evidence that the use of power tactics varies cross-culturally. Tinsley (2001) found that negotiators from cultures that place a higher value on social hierarchy (Japanese, in this study) were more likely to use power tactics than negotiators from cultures having a greater emphasis on individualism (Germans and Americans).

Pressure tactics produce, at best, short-term compliance with requests, but they also are likely to elicit resistance from the other party. Frequent use of pressure tactics alienates the other party and leads to very high resistance, in which case the agent must consistently escalate the severity of consequences for noncompliance and the willingness to invoke them. Pressure tactics should be used selectively and sparingly because their use is likely to corrode the relationship between the parties, and frequent use is likely to destroy it.

Section Summary

In this section, we examined several ways that persuaders can use the "peripheral route" to achieve influence. We discussed factors related to the message itself, characteristics of the message source, and aspects of the influence context that can achieve this. Influence targets are particularly susceptible to peripheral forms of influence to the extent that they are unmotivated and/or unable to pay careful attention to the argumentative substance of the influence-seeker's message. Effective negotiators realize that a big part of their task is persuading the other party to view the situation as they do. Strategies that underlie peripheral routes to influence are an important part of a negotiator's arsenal for doing just that.

THE ROLE OF RECEIVERS—TARGETS OF INFLUENCE

We now examine factors related to the person who is the target of influence. At first glance, one might think that there is not much that receivers can do to exert leverage. Not true! Just as negotiators-as-message-senders can work to increase their credibility and attractiveness, receivers can signal the sender about the general acceptability and favorableness of the message being sent, and senders can monitor the receiver's receptiveness and adapt the message accordingly. Receivers need to be conscious about the signals they send; senders need to monitor the other's receptiveness, avoid taking the "defensive/combative" stance that lets people turn off persuasive communication, and help receivers hear and understand better. Let us review a few key factors.

Attending to the Other

Much of what people communicate to one another is transmitted not only with words and sentences, but also with body language: the way they position their body, their tone of voice, their head movements. Many nonverbal acts, called *attending behaviors,* are very important in connecting with another person; they let the other know that you are listening and prepare the other party to receive your message. We will discuss three important attending behaviors: eye contact, body position, and encouraging.

Make Eye Contact.   Dishonest people and cowards are not supposed to be able to look people in the eye. Poets claim that the eye is the lens that permits us to look into a person's soul. These and other bits of conventional wisdom illustrate how important people believe eye contact to be. In general, making eye contact is one way to show others you are paying attention and listening, and that you consider them important. If people do not look at you when you are speaking, you may question whether they are listening. Of course, it is possible to listen very well even when not looking at the other person; in fact, it may be easier to look away because you can focus on the spoken words and not be confused by visual information. But the point is that by not making eye contact, you are not providing the other person with an important cue that they are listening.

In making eye contact, however, people should not keep their eyes continually fixed on the other person. Otherwise they might be accused of staring, which usually leads to suspicion rather than trust. Instead, the eyes should momentarily leave the other person. Generally, breaks in eye contact are fewer and shorter when listening actively than when speaking. When speaking, one may occasionally look away, especially when searching for a word or phrase or trying to remember a detail. Averting the gaze briefly while speaking signals to the other party that the speaker is not finished.

When persuading someone, it is important to make eye contact when delivering the most important part of the message (Beebe, 1980; Burgoon, Coker, and Coker, 1986; Kleinke, 1986). This is the equivalent of staring inside the other person, talking directly to his heart and soul. Having the verbal and nonverbal systems in parallel at this point emphasizes the importance of the message that is being sent. Also, one should maintain eye contact not only when speaking but when receiving communication as well (Kellerman, Lewis, and Laird, 1989).

It is important to recognize, however, that the patterns described above are characteristic of Western society. In other parts of the world, different patterns prevail. In the Far East, for example, to keep one's eyes down while the other is speaking is a sign of respect (Ivey and Simek-Downing, 1980).

Adjust Body Position.   Parents frequently advise their children about how to stand and sit, particularly when they are in formal settings such as school, church, or dinner parties. The command "Sit up!" is often accompanied by "And pay attention!" Here the parent is teaching the child another widely held belief—one's body position indicates whether or not one is paying attention to the other party. To ensure that others know you are attentive to them, hold your body erect, lean slightly forward, and face the other person directly (Ivey and Simek-Downing, 1980). If you accept and endorse the others' message, care needs to be taken not to show *dis*respect with body position by slouching, turning away, or placing feet on the table (Stacks and Burgoon, 1981). In contrast, crossing arms, bowing the head, furrowing the brow, and squeezing eyebrows together all can signal strong rejection or disapproval of the message (Nierenberg and Calero, 1971).

Nonverbally Encourage or Discourage What the Other Says.   One can indicate attention and interest in what another is saying through a variety of simple behaviors. A head nod, a simple hand gesture to go on, or a murmured "Unh hunh" to indicate understanding all tell the other person to continue, that you are listening. In fact, one can encourage someone to continue to speak about many subjects by simply nodding your head as he or she is speaking. Brief eye contact or a smile and a nod of the head will both provide encouraging cues. Similarly, a frown, a scowl, a shake of the head, or a grab of one's chest in mock pain will signal disapproval of the other's message.

Exploring or Ignoring the Other's Position

Negotiators frequently give very little attention to the other party's opinions and point of view. This is unfortunate, because it is very much to your advantage to understand what the other party really wants, how things look to him, and how he developed his position. One can explore the other party's perspective with questions designed to reveal his or her needs and interests (see Chapter 5). For instance, "Why are those important objectives for you?" "What would happen if you did not get everything you have asked for?" "How did you arrive at your current position?" and "Have your needs changed since the last time we talked?" bring out more detailed information about the other party's position and interests. Exploring the other person's outlook not only provides more information, which can lead you to design solutions to meet both sides' needs, but further increases the other party's feeling of being listened to and makes him or her more receptive to meeting your needs. However, questions are often used as a weapon of attack. Questions such as "How in the world can you say that?" "What possible justification can you have for that position?" and "Who in their right mind would believe that?" are likely to make the other party feel tense and combative and may make the tone of the negotiations quite negative.

Selectively Paraphrase.   Paraphrasing ensures that both parties have understood each other accurately. If you haven't understood the other party, then they have the opportunity to correct you. It is important to restate your understanding after being corrected, to make sure you have understood. Repeat in your own words what was said. In addition, vocalizing the other person's ideas helps you remember them better than simply hearing them. Do not literally repeat the other person's words; repeat the message in your own words, starting with "Let me see if I understand the point you just made." When people have an important message to get across, they will talk vigorously and at length, often emphasizing the same point over and over. Once your paraphrasing indicates that the other person has been understood, he or she will usually stop repeating the same point and move on; hence, paraphrasing can be very helpful in moving a discussion forward. You should repeat this correction process until the other person is satisfied with the way you paraphrase what was said.

You can also ask the other party to restate or paraphrase what you have said. You might say, "What I have said is very important to me, and I would appreciate it if you could restate what you understood to be my main points." This process accomplishes several things. First, it asks the other party to listen closely and recall what you have said. Second, it gives you the opportunity to check out the accuracy of his or her understanding. Third, it emphasizes the most important points of your presentation.

Reinforce Points You Like in the Other Party's Proposals.   Negotiators are frequently ineffective because they respond only to what they dislike in the other party's statement or proposal and ignore the things they like. Responding in this way ignores a powerful means of shaping and guiding what the other party is saying. Several behavioral science theories (e.g., exchange theory or learning and reinforcement theory) make the same basic point: People are more likely to repeat behavior that is rewarded than behavior that is not rewarded (Homans, 1961; Skinner, 1953).

The simplest way to reward people for what they say during a negotiation is to acknowledge and support a point that they have made: "That is an interesting point," "I had not heard that before." Give a simple "Mm-hmm" or a nod of the head. Statements and actions like these separate a key statement from other points the speaker has made. Second, compliment speakers when they make points you want emphasized, and express appreciation to them for considering your interests and needs. In a labor negotiation, for example, management might say to the union, "You raised an important point when you said that if we develop a history of bad labor relations, customers will be much less likely to give us long-term contracts. We appreciate your being aware of some of our marketing and customer image problems." A third approach is to separate particular parts of a statement that you like from those parts you don't like and to encourage the other party to develop the favorable points. In negotiating a house sale, the buyer might say, "Let me focus on one of the points you made. I think making an adjustment in price for the necessary repairs is a good idea. Please go further and explain what type of repairs you have in mind and how you might handle this adjustment." A fourth approach is to return favors. If the other party makes a concession and offers you something you want, you can reward this behavior by making a concession or offering a favor in return.

Resisting the Other's Influence

In addition to the variety of things a negotiator can do to encourage, support, or direct the other's communication, there are at least three major things that listeners can do to resist the other's influence efforts: have a best alternative to a negotiated agreement (BATNA), make a public commitment (or get the other party to make one), and inoculate yourself against the other's persuasive message.

Have a BATNA, and Know How to Use It.   Several authors identify a BATNA as a source of power (e.g., Pinkley, Neale, and Bennett, 1994). There is no question that having a BATNA enables negotiators to walk away from a given negotiation, since it means that they can get their needs met and interests addressed somewhere else. Of course, having a BATNA is a source of leverage at the negotiation table only if the other party is aware of it. To use a BATNA effectively, a negotiator must assess the other party's awareness that it exists and, if necessary, share that fact. This often must be done deftly—conveying the existence of a BATNA could be interpreted by the other party as an imminent threat to walk away. Keep in mind also that a BATNA can always be improved. Good negotiators will work to improve their BATNA before and even during an ongoing negotiation as a way to improve their leverage. (We addressed the power of a BATNA in detail in Chapter 3.)

Make a Public Commitment.   One of the most effective ways of getting people to stand firm on a position is to have them make a public commitment to that position. Union leaders have said things to their rank and file like, "I will resign before I settle for a penny less than . . ." After making that statement, the union leader faces several pressures. One is the potential loss of face with union members that would come with backing away from that position—the leader may be unceremoniously thrown out of office if he or she does not actually resign. A second pressure is that the leader's credibility with management will be sharply reduced in the future if he or she does not follow through on the commitment. Finally, the leader may have his or her own cognitive inconsistency to deal with because failing to resign will be inconsistent with his or her earlier commitment. On the other hand, negotiators usually want to prevent the other party from making public commitments to positions that counter their interests. They can do so by downplaying statements of commitment, not responding to them, or looking for a rationale to explain why the commitment does not apply at that time.

Negotiators can also get the other party to make a public commitment. If you can get the other party to make a public statement that supports something you want, that party will be hard-pressed not to stand by the statement, even though he or she may have a desire to abandon it later on. Sometimes negotiators make a statement such as "I'm committed to finding an agreement that we can both benefit from," and then invite the other party to make a similar statement. At other times the inviting statement may be more direct: "Are you interested in selling us this property or not?" or "Let's agree that we are going to work together, and then get busy on the details of how to make it happen." Even better than eliciting statements of commitment is enticing the other party to make a behavioral commitment. For example, retail merchants use down payments and layaway plans to get a behavioral commitment from customers when it is not possible to complete the total sale at that time.

Inoculate Yourself against the Other Party's Arguments.   One of the likely outcomes of listening carefully to the other party and exploring and understanding his or her point of view is that negotiators may change some of their own positions. At times they may not want to change their position, and therefore they may want to "inoculate" themselves against the other party's arguments (McGuire, 1964). For instance, managers who must support organizational policies with which they disagree may want to inoculate themselves against subordinates' arguments by preparing and rehearsing counterarguments that can be used to refute the key points the other is likely to make.

There are three approaches for inoculating against the arguments of other parties:

1. prepare supporting arguments *for your position only*.
2. develop arguments *against your position only* and then develop counterarguments, that is, find ways to refute them in the points you make.
3. develop arguments *both for your original position and against your position*, and then develop counterarguments to refute both (this is a combination approach).

To illustrate, let's take the example of a director of admissions for an MBA program who will be meeting with an applicant to the program to explain the school's decision not to accept the applicant. The admissions director could *(a)* develop arguments about why the student should not be admitted (e.g., the student's grades are not high enough); *(b)* develop arguments in favor of the student's perspective (e.g., the student took difficult courses at a very scholarly university); and *(c)* develop counterarguments to refute the student's arguments (e.g., the quality of the university and the rigor of the courses were taken into account when the admissions decision was made).

Research reveals that the best way to inoculate against being influenced is to use the combination approach (point 3 above)—developing arguments both for and against your position, and counterarguments to refute them (McGuire, 1964; Tannenbaum and Norris, 1966). Developing arguments against your position only plus counterarguments (point 2 above) is also effective, but to a lesser extent. The least effective, by a large margin, is the first approach—developing arguments in support of your position only. This research on inoculation also suggests that:

- The best way to inoculate people against attacks on their position was to involve them in developing a defense.
- The larger the number of arguments in any defense, the more effective it becomes.
- Asking people to make public statements supporting their original position increases their resistance to counterarguments.

Section Summary

Negotiators in the role of listener or target of influence can do many things to help blunt the persuasive force of an influence-seeking message that originates with the other party. By engaging in careful listening, by challenging the arguments and position set forth, and by taking steps to actively resist the influence attempt, negotiators can minimize the chance that they will be swayed by weak arguments, or be "trapped" into the kind of shortcut persuasion that occurs through the peripheral route. Some key elements of resistance include making wise decisions about how and when to wield one's BATNA, knowing when to make public commitments, and inoculating oneself against anticipated arguments. In many situations, the other party will be persuasive because his or her arguments are solid and sensible. The key is approaching influence attempts with a focused and critical mind so that one is persuaded only when the arguments merit it.

Negotiators-as-persuaders, on the other hand, can take steps to reduce the receiver's rigidity and defensiveness and to make the receiver more receptive. The most important techniques include trying to understand what the other party wants and thinks, and demonstrating that the receiver's objections will be heard. These are powerful techniques, but they do entail risks. In trying to understand the other side, one may be persuaded by their arguments, be led to abandon some initial positions, or become more willing to accept the other party's proposals. In fact, the other party's proposals may lead to a better agreement for all sides, particularly in integrative bargaining. There are times, however, when negotiators are better off preserving their own positions and avoiding the temptation of counterarguments. At times like these, inoculation makes it possible to hear others' arguments without the risk of being co-opted to their point of view.

CHAPTER SUMMARY

In this chapter, we discussed the nature of leverage in negotiation. By leverage, we mean the process of gaining or using various sources of power in order to obtain and use temporary advantage over the other negotiating party. We began by exploring the nature of power. While there are many different sources of power, we described three: information and expertise, control over resources, and the location within an organizational structure (which leads to either formal authority or informal power based on where one is located relative to flows of information or resources).

We then turned to examine a very large number of influence (leverage) tools that one could use in negotiation. These tools were considered in two broad categories: influence that occurs through the *central* route to persuasion, and influence that occurs through the *peripheral* route to persuasion. With respect to the central route, we addressed the content of the message, how messages are structured, and the style with which a persuasive message is delivered. Influence that occurs through the central route is likely to be relatively enduring and resistant to counterinfluence. With respect to the peripheral route, we considered tactics related to the construction of the message itself, as well as characteristics of the message source and elements of the influence context. When influence occurs through the peripheral route, the target may comply but will not necessarily make a corresponding attitudinal commitment; moreover, that compliance may be short-lived, and the target is generally more susceptible to counterinfluence.

In the last major section of the chapter, we considered how the receiver—the target of influence—either can shape and direct what the sender is communicating, or can intellectually resist the persuasive effects of the message. Effective negotiators are skilled not only at crafting persuasive messages, but also at playing the role of skilled "consumers" of the messages that others direct their way.

Two points should be made in closing. First, while we have many detailed elements in this chapter, it must be remembered that leverage can be highly elusive and fleeting in negotiation. Almost anything can be a source of leverage if it gives the negotiator a temporary advantage over the other party (e.g., a BATNA or a time deadline). Second, this chapter has only touched on some of the more important and well-documented aspects of influence-seeking communication that can be used in bargaining. Negotiators usually spend a great deal of time devising ways to support and document their positions; they devote less time to considering how the information is presented or how to use qualities of the source and receiver to increase the likelihood that persuasion will be successful. Careful attention to source, target, and context factors, rather than just to message factors, is likely to have a positive impact on negotiator effectiveness.

CHAPTER 7

Ethics in Negotiation

In this chapter, we explore the question of whether there are, or should be, accepted ethical standards for behavior in negotiations. This topic has received increased attention from researchers in recent years. It is our view that fundamental questions of ethical conduct arise in every negotiation. The effective negotiator must recognize when the questions are relevant and what factors must be considered to answer them.

WHY DO NEGOTIATORS NEED TO KNOW ABOUT ETHICS?

Consider the following situations:

1. You are a manager badly in need of additional clerical assistance for your office. Although work is getting done, a large and often unpredictable volume is creating periodic delays. Some of your staff members are complaining that the work flow could be managed much more effectively if another clerk were added. However, you also know that your boss is not sympathetic; she thinks that the problem could be solved if all the current clerks simply agreed to work a bit harder or volunteer a few hours of overtime. Moreover, your department's budget is very tight, and to get a new clerical position approved, you will have to demonstrate clearly to senior management (particularly your boss) that you need additional personnel. You see the following options open to you:

- Document the amount of work that each of your clerks is doing and the amount of work that is being delayed or not done properly, and make a complete report to your boss.

- Give each of your clerks a lot of extra jobs to do now, particularly ones that could really be deferred for a few months (such as cleaning out and completely reorganizing the files). Thus, you will create an artificial backlog of incomplete work that can be used to argue for more help.

- Talk to your clerks and stress that the most important standard by which they should do their jobs is to follow procedures exactly and to focus on quality rather than on getting everything done. This will probably create a slowdown and a backlog that you can then use to argue for more help.

- You've been watching the operation of the payroll office down the hall. Many of those clerks are standing around drinking coffee half the time. Talk to your boss about your observation and ask to have one of these clerks transferred to your department.

Question: Are some of these approaches more ethical than others? Which ones? Which ones would you try?

2. You are an entrepreneur interested in acquiring a business that is currently owned by a competitor. The competitor, however, has not shown any interest in either selling his business or merging with your company. To gain inside knowledge of his firm, you hired a consultant you know to call contacts in your competitor's business and ask if the company is having any serious problems that might threaten its viability. If there are such problems, you might be able to use the information to either hire away the company's employees or get the competitor to sell.

Question: Is this ethical? Would you be likely to do it if you were the entrepreneur?

3. You are a vice president of human resources, negotiating with a union representative for a new labor contract. The union has insisted that it will not sign a new contract until the company agrees to raise the number of paid holidays from six to seven. Management has calculated that it will cost approximately $150,000 for each paid holiday, and has argued to the union that the company cannot afford to meet the demand. However, you know that, in reality, money is not the issue—the company simply doesn't think the union's demand is justified. To convince the union leaders that they should withdraw their demand, you have been considering the following alternatives:

- Tell the union representatives that their request is simply unacceptable to you because they haven't justified why they need seven paid holidays.
- Tell the union that the company simply can't afford it (without explanation).
- Prepare some erroneous financial statements that show that it will cost about $300,000 per paid holiday, which you simply can't afford.
- Offer the union leaders an all-expenses-paid "working" trip to a Florida resort if they will simply drop the demand entirely.

Question: Do any of the strategies raise ethical concerns? Which ones? Why?

4. You are about to graduate from the MBA program of a leading university. You specialized in management information systems (MIS) and will be taking a job with a company that commercially develops Web pages. While you did a lot of your work on machines at the university, you owned a very powerful personal computer of your own. You have decided to sell all of your personal hardware now,

and then buy some new equipment after you see what kinds of projects your employer has you working on. So you post a note on several campus bulletin boards about the equipment for sale. You have decided not to tell prospective buyers that your hard drive acts like it is about to fail and that the computer occasionally crashes without warning.

Question: Is this ethical? Would you be likely to do this if you were this particular student?

5. You buy a new pair of shoes on sale. The printed receipt states very clearly that the shoes are not returnable. After you get them home, you wear the shoes around the house for a day and decide that they just don't fit you correctly. So you take the shoes back to the store. The clerk points to the message on the receipt; but you don't let that deter you. You start to yell angrily about the store's poor quality service, so that people in the store start to stare. The clerk calls the store manager; after some discussion, the manager agrees to give you your money back.

Question: Is this ethical? Would you be likely to do this if you were this customer?

These situations are hypothetical; however, the problems they present are real ones for negotiators. Managers are frequently confronted with important decisions about the strategies they will use to achieve important objectives, particularly when a variety of influence tactics are open to them. In this chapter, we will turn our attention to the major ethical questions that arise in negotiation. We will consider several questions:

1. What are ethics and how do they apply to negotiation?
2. What are the major ethical concerns that apply to negotiation?
3. What major types of ethical and unethical conduct are likely to occur in negotiation?
4. What factors shape a negotiator's predisposition to use unethical tactics?
5. How can negotiators deal with the other party's use of deception?

WHAT ARE ETHICS AND WHY DO THEY APPLY TO NEGOTIATION?

In this chapter, we are going to discuss the ethics of negotiation. *Ethics* are broadly applied social standards for what is right or wrong in a particular situation, or a process for setting those standards. They differ from *morals,* which are individual and personal beliefs about what is right and wrong. Ethics proceed from particular philosophies, which purport to (*a*) define the nature of the world in which we live, and (*b*) prescribe rules for living together.

We want to be clear that it is not our intention to advocate a specific ethical position for all negotiators or for the conduct of all negotiations. Many treatises on business ethics take a strongly prescriptive or normative position, advocating what a person should do. Instead, in this chapter we will simply describe the ethical issues that arise in negotiations. We will briefly identify the major ethical dimensions raised in negotiations, describe how people tend to think about these ethical choices, and provide a framework for making informed ethical decisions. Finally, we will summarize the research that has already been done in this area.

We also wish to distinguish among different criteria for judging and evaluating a negotiator's actions, particularly when questions of ethics might be involved. Many writers on business ethics (e.g., Green, 1993; Hitt, 1990; Nash, 1990) have suggested several standards. Hitt suggests that there are at least four standards for evaluating strategies and tactics in business and negotiation:

- Make the decision on the basis of expected results, or what would give us the greatest return on investment.
- Make the decision on the basis of what the law says, on the legality of the matter.
- Make the decision on the basis of the strategy and values of my organization.
- Make the decision on the basis of my own personal convictions and what my conscience told me to do. (p. 88)

Each of these approaches reflects a fundamentally different approach to ethical reasoning. The first may be called *end-result ethics,* in that the rightness of an action is determined by evaluating the pros and cons of its consequences. The second may be called *rule ethics,* in that the rightness of an action is determined by existing laws and contemporary social standards that define what is right and wrong and where the line is. The third may be called *social contract ethics,* in that the rightness of an action is based on the customs and norms of a particular society or community. Finally, the fourth may be called *personalistic ethics,* in that the rightness of the action is based on one's own conscience and moral standards.

Each of these approaches could be used to resolve the concerns we raised in the five situations at the beginning of the chapter. Going back to the clerk problem (Situation 1), if you as the manager believed in end-result ethics, then you would do whatever was necessary (lie, create an artificial overload) in order to get the boss to agree that another clerk should be hired. If you believed in rule ethics, you might believe that it is never appropriate to lie and might therefore use any tactic that does not require outright lying. If you believed in social contract ethics, you would make your decision on tactics based on what you thought was appropriate conduct for the way people behaved in your society and in your specific organization's culture; if they lie, you lie. Finally, if you believed in personalistic ethics, you would consult your conscience and decide whether the problem of getting more clerks justified using deceptive or dishonest tactics under any circumstances.

Discussions of business ethics frequently confuse ethical versus prudent versus practical versus legal criteria for judging appropriate conduct; that is, debate over these issues often confuses what is ethical (appropriate as determined by some standard of moral conduct) versus what is prudent (wise, based on trying to understand the efficacy of the tactic and the consequences it might have on the relationship with the other) versus what is practical (what a negotiator can actually make happen in a given situation) versus what is legal (what the law defines as acceptable practice) (Missner, 1980). In earlier chapters, we evaluated negotiation strategies and tactics by the prudence and practicality criteria; in this chapter, we turn to ways by which we can judge negotiation strategies and tactics by ethical criteria. In addition, other criteria come into play. For example, Lax and Sebenius (1986) suggest that some people may want to be ethical for intrinsic reasons—it feels better because behaving ethically allows them to see themselves as moral individuals or because certain principles of behavior are seen as moral absolutes. Other people may judge ethical behavior in more instrumental terms—good ethics make good business. As we will see, these criteria affect how negotiators tend to select tactics as well. But, as in our evaluation of strategies and tactics according to the other criteria, we will show that people's judgments about what is ethical or unethical in negotiation are not crystal clear. On the one hand, negotiators see some tactics as marginal—defined in shades and degrees rather than in absolutes. Reasonable people will disagree as to exactly where the line should be drawn between what is ethical and what is unethical for these tactics (e.g., bluffing). On the other hand, negotiators show remarkable agreement on whether certain other tactics are clearly ethical or clearly unethical (e.g., most agree that outright falsification of information is unethical). Thus, although it may be difficult to tell a negotiator exactly what behaviors are ethical and unethical in any one circumstance, the subject of ethics is no less important. Examining ethics encourages negotiators to examine their own decision-making processes. In addition, sharpening the questions they ask will help negotiators create the opportunity for further studies on the complexity of ethical judgments (Lewicki, 1983; Raiffa, 1982).

Having made these cautionary statements, we will now turn to a more complete consideration of the four fundamental standards identified above and their application to negotiator ethics.

WHAT ARE THE MAJOR ETHICAL CONCERNS THAT APPLY TO NEGOTIATION?

Those who write about business ethics tend to approach the subject from the perspectives of major philosophical and theological theories (see Table 7.1). Drawing on a review of the literature, we will take a brief look at the four ethical standards used to make decisions in negotiation (see also Boatright, 1993; Donaldson and Werhane, 1993; Green, 1993; and Rachels, 1986, for elaborations of these approaches): end-result ethics, rule ethics, social contract ethics, and personalistic ethics.

End-Result Ethics

Many of the ethically questionable incidents in business that upset the public involve people who argue that the ends justify the means—that is, who deem it acceptable to break a rule or violate a procedure in the service of some greater good for the individual, the organization, or even society at large. Several examples come to mind. Suppose a television network has convincing statistical evidence that a particular pickup truck was designed unsafely, so that in 1 test out of 10, it bursts into flame when hit in a side collision. To highlight this defect, the network producer decides to stage and videotape an accident. But because a collision may create a fire only 1 time in 10,

TABLE 7.1 Four Approaches to Ethical Reasoning

Ethical System	Definition	Major Proponent	Central Tenets	Major Concerns
End-result ethics	Rightness of an action is determined by considering consequences.	Jeremy Bentham (1748–1832) John Stuart Mill (1806–1873)	• One must consider all likely consequences. • Actions are more right if they promote more happiness, more wrong as they produce unhappiness. • Happiness is defined as presence of pleasure and absence of pain. • Promotion of happiness is generally the ultimate aim. • Collective happiness of all concerned is the goal.	• How does one define happiness, pleasure, or utility? • How does one measure happiness, pleasure, or utility? • How does one trade off between short-term vs. long-term happiness? • If actions create happiness for 90% of the world and misery for the other 10%, is it still ethical?
Rule ethics	Rightness of an action is determined by laws and standards.	Immanuel Kant (1724–1804)	• Human conduct should be guided by primary moral principles, or "oughts." • Individuals should stand on their principles and restrain themselves by rules. • The ultimate good is a life of virtue (acting on principles) rather than pleasure. • We should not adjust moral law to fit our actions, but adjust our actions to fit moral law.	• By what authority do we accept particular rules or the "goodness" of those rules? • What rule do we follow when rules conflict? • How do we adapt general rules to fit specific situations? • How do rules change as circumstances change? • What happens when good rules produce bad consequences? • Are there rules without any exceptions?

(Continued)

TABLE 7.1 *(Concluded)*

Ethical System	Definition	Major Proponent	Central Tenets	Major Concerns
Social contract ethics	Rightness of an action is determined by the customs and norms of a community.	Jean-Jacques Rousseau (1712–1778)	• People must function in a social, community context to survive. • Communities become "moral bodies" for determining ground rules. • Duty and obligation bind the community and the individual to each other. • What is best for the common good determines the ultimate standard. • Laws are important, but morality determines the laws and standards for right and wrong.	• How do we determine the general will? • What is meant by the "common good"? • What do we do with independent thinkers who challenge the morality of the existing social order (e.g., Jefferson, Gandhi, Martin Luther King)? • Can a state be corrupt and its people still be "moral" (e.g., Nazi Germany)?
Personalistic ethics	Rightness of an action is determined by one's conscience.	Martin Buber (1878–1965)	• Locus of truth is found in human existence. • Conscience within each person calls them to fulfill their humanness and to decide between right and wrong. • Personal decision rules are the ultimate standards. • Pursuing a noble goal by ignoble means leads to an ignoble end. • There are no absolute formulas for living. • One should follow one's group but also stick up for what one individually believes.	• How could we justify ethics other than by saying, "it felt like the right thing to do"? • How could we achieve a collective definition of what is ethical if individuals disagreed? • How could we achieve cohesiveness and consensus in a team that only fosters personal perspectives? • How could an organization assure some uniformity in ethics?

SOURCE: Derived from W. Hitt, *Ethics and Leadership: Putting Theory into Practice* (Columbus, OH: Battelle Press, 1990).

240

and the producer can't afford to destroy 10 (or more) trucks, he decides to place deto-nators near the gas tank of the truck to be used. Thus, the exploding truck viewers would see would have been designed to "simulate" what (supposedly) happens to (supposedly) 1 truck out of 10. Is this unethical, even if the producer's goal is to warn viewers about the hazards of this truck model?

Consider a second example: A pharmaceutical company is convinced, as a result of early tests, that it has developed a dramatic new miracle drug that will cure some forms of cancer. But it cannot release the drug yet because it has to comply with gov-ernment regulation that controls drug testing prior to widespread distribution, and thou-sands of lives may be lost before the government approves the drug. Is it unethical to keep the drug off the market while the regulatory testing goes on? Or is it unethical to release the drug before it has been thoroughly tested?

Those who would argue that the simulated truck test was appropriate and that the drug should be marketed argue for end-result ethics. In the negotiation context, when negotiators have noble objectives to attain for themselves or their constituencies, they will argue that they can use whatever strategies they want. They draw on a view of ethics known as *act utilitarianism.* Act utilitarians (end-result ethicists) hold that the moral worth of a particular action should be judged on the basis of the consequences it produces (see Bentham, 1789; Mill, 1962). Since they measure morality by the good-ness or badness of consequences, act utilitarians believe that the way to maximize virtue is to maximize the best consequences for the largest number of people—usually in terms of happiness, pleasure, or utility. The highest moral conduct is to maximize the greatest good for the greatest number.

Debate about end-result ethics centers on several key questions: First, how do peo-ple (and which people) define happiness or pleasure or maximum utility, and how can each be measured? Second, how do actors trade off between short-term consequences and long-term consequences, particularly when the short-term results are damaging to the long-term results (i.e., good in the short run, bad in the long run) or vice versa? Third, if people cannot create utility for everyone, is it adequate for them to create it for a large number of people, even if other people will not benefit or will even suffer? The debate on these and other questions related to end-result ethics is ongoing.

Rule Ethics

In contrast to end-result ethics, rule ethics emphasize that individuals ought to commit themselves to a series of moral rules or standards, and make decisions based on those rules. *Rule utilitarians* argue that a decision based on the utilitarian standards reviewed above leads decision makers into more trouble than benefit; instead, they argue, the best way to achieve the greatest good is to closely follow a set of rules and principles. The strongest proponent of this view was the philosopher Immanuel Kant (1963, 1964). Kant proposed a series of 10 principles (summarized into a few central tenets in Table 7.1) that serve as the standard by which each person may judge his or her own action. Kant argued that these principles are established on purely rational grounds, and that the principles can be debated (and improved upon) as we improve upon the key tenets of rational science.

For example, let us suppose that a militant subgroup within a labor union has organized in protest over what it feels are critical questions of worker safety. When their initial attempts to bring their concerns to management were rebuffed, they walked out in a
wildcat strike. Some other rank-and-file union members, who are not particularly
affected by the safety rules in question, nevertheless support the strike because they think
the strikers' concerns should be addressed by management. The strikers have presented
a series of safety demands to management—if these demands are met, the strikers will
return to work. Management agrees to meet the demands, and the strike ends. Management then immediately fires all the wildcatters for participating in the illegal strike and
takes no action on the safety issues. The union leadership accuses management of unethical negotiating. In this situation, act utilitarians would argue that management's tactic
of agreeing to meet the workers' demands—even if that agreement was in bad faith—
was necessary to end an illegal strike. (Act utilitarians in labor, obviously, would have
no trouble justifying the strike.) It is management's job (not the workers') to determine
conditions of worker safety, and it is also management's job to take action against wildcat strikes; both of these job definitions justify, in management's mind, the tactic of
falsely agreeing to meet the wildcatters' demands and then firing them. Thus, the utility
of ending the strike (the end) justified the deception (the means) in the negotiation. In
contrast, rule utilitarians might argue that management has a responsibility to adhere to
the principles of honesty and integrity—negotiating in good faith and not acting retribu-
tively against the strikers, because adhering to these principles over the long term will
produce the best results for union–management relations, and no particular end can justify dishonest means. For example, in the truck fire scenario described above (which
was, by the way, a real series of events involving an NBC network news show in 1993),
the decision to stage the collision cost NBC's news department a great deal of negative
publicity and credibility, and cost both the producer and eventually the head of the NBC
News Division their jobs—consequences that are extremely serious and may or may not
be equivalent to the possibility of lives being lost in the dangerous pickup trucks.

This scenario, and many others like it, constitute the grist of the debate between
act and rule utilitarians. When addressing means–ends questions in competition and
negotiation, observers usually focus the most attention on the question of what strategies and tactics may be seen as appropriate to achieve certain ends. Are exploitative,
manipulative, or devious tactics ever justifiable, even if they produce good ends for a
large number of people? For example, in a hostage crisis, is it ethical for a government
to agree to grant a terrorist immunity if he releases the hostages, even though the government has every intention of capturing and prosecuting the terrorist once his hostages
are released? Most people would argue that end-result ethics win out here over rule
ethics prescribing honesty and integrity, but there will also be detractors.

Clearly, rule utilitarians have their critics as well. Who makes the rules? What are the
rules that apply in all circumstances? For example, those who believe strictly in the commandment (rule) "Thou shalt not kill" will argue that the commandment is the same,
regardless of whether the subject is murder, the death penalty for a convicted murderer,
military combat, abortion (even to save the life of the mother), or euthanasia (mercy killing
of terminally ill or suffering patients).What happens when two rules conflict? For example, if there are two rules—one that says you should be considerate of others' feelings and

Pepper . . . and Salt

THE WALL STREET JOURNAL

"'Naughty or nice'—I was hoping for a little more moral relativism."

From *The Wall Street Journal.* Used with permission of Cartoon Features Syndicate.

another that says you should tell the truth—what do you do when you have to tell your best friend a truth that is painful and will hurt his or her feelings? How can the rules be adapted to specific situations, and what happens when the rules change over time? What happens when good rules produce bad circumstances? For example, in cases of physician-assisted suicide, there is moral conflict on both sides. The patient feels a moral dilemma between a right to make an autonomous decision to end his or her life with dignity and a moral prohibition against killing. Similarly, the doctor faces a moral dilemma between the mandate to save a life and the mandate to relieve undue suffering for those whose life cannot be saved. These and other questions and situations lead some to believe that a rule-oriented view of ethical conduct creates more problems than it solves.

Social Contract Ethics

A third standard of ethics holds that the rightness of an action is determined by the customs and social norms of a community. This view is best articulated in the basic writings of Jean-Jacques Rousseau (1947). Rather than arguing that the utility of ends determines the standards, or that the utility of particular rules should apply in all situations, social contract ethicists argue that societies, organizations, and cultures determine what is ethically appropriate and acceptable for themselves, and then indoctrinate new members as they are socialized into the fabric of the community. In a sense, each member of the group agrees to an implied (or even explicit) *social contract* that explains what the individual is expected to give to the community, what the individual can get back from the community, and the social rules or norms that all members are expected to follow.

Social contract ethicists focus on what individuals owe to their community (country, organization, neighborhood, etc.) and what they can or should expect in return. As applied to negotiation, social contract ethics would prescribe which behaviors are appropriate in a negotiation context, in terms of what people owe one another. For example, the context of a used-car negotiation may suggest that a buyer does not expect the truth from the salesperson, and therefore does not owe the salesperson the truth either. So when the salesperson lies about the reliability or gas mileage of the automobile that is for sale, the buyer should have no compunctions about lying about her interest in the car or her real intention to bring her friend back to take a closer look at it. In contrast, if a salesperson is establishing a multiyear contract with a customer, in this context—establishing a long-term agreement with a valued partner who should be treated honorably and fairly now and in the future—the salesperson owes it to that customer to tell her the truth when he discovers defects in his products or when he will be late in shipping due to manufacturing errors and problems (Carlisle and Parker, 1989).

As we noted in Table 7.1, social contract ethics are also not without problems. How do we decide what implicit rules should apply to a given relationship, particularly when we have not explicitly spelled out those rules? Who makes these social rules, and how are they evaluated and changed? What happens when the existing social contract becomes corrupted over time (through collusion, monopolistic practices, etc.) such that it needs to be challenged by those who seek change and reform? Are new recruits to an organization bound by a contract that is unfulfilled or violated by the organization? These critical questions pose important challenges for those who advocate a social contract view of ethical decision making.

Personalistic Ethics

A fourth standard of ethics is that, rather than attempting to determine what is ethical based on ends, or rules, or the social norms of a community, people should simply consult their own conscience. As argued most clearly by the philosopher Martin Buber (1958, 1963), the foundations for ethical behavior lie in the human conscience. Hitt (1990) offers an interesting example to highlight the tenets of this approach relative to the three earlier models:

> The setting is an outdoor hotel swimming pool on a warm July morning. At this particular time of day, there are only two persons present—a father who is fully clothed, sitting in a lounge chair beside the pool and reading the newspaper, and his five-year-old daughter, who is wading in the pool. While the father is engrossed in reading the sports page, he hears his daughter scream for help. She has waded into the deep end of the pool and is struggling to keep her head above water.
>
> At this moment, what is the *right* thing for the father to do? And what system of ethics will he use? If he chooses end-result ethics, he will compare the utilities associated with ruining his clothes, watch and billfold with those associated with saving his daughter's life. If he chooses rule ethics, he might first check to see if the hotel has posted any rules that prohibit a fully clothed person from entering the pool. And if he chooses social contract ethics, he might reflect on the social contract that he has with his family members. Obviously, he will choose none of these. He will jump into the pool immediately to rescue his daughter. (pp. 121–22)

Hitt argues that the motivation to action is clearly the conscience of the father crying, "Act now!" The very nature of human existence leads individuals to develop a personal conscience, an internal sense of what is right and what one ought to do. Ultimately, these rules remain individual and personal, although they can be influenced by the social forces that lead people to reason ethically and learn to do the right thing. Because, in this view, ethical judgments must be made by each individual, there are no absolutes. People must determine what is right and appropriate to do, on their own, and people should not impose their standards on others. Many of these forces are part of an individual's upbringing and are represented by what he or she learns at home, in school, and at religious institutions.

As applied to negotiation, personalistic ethics maintain that everyone ought to decide for themselves what is right based on their conscience (whatever it may say to them). Whether one lies, cheats, or steals, therefore, is ultimately a matter of individual conscience and not the nature of the ends, absolute rules, or narrow interpretations of the social contract. However, as you can well imagine, critics have argued that no one is as pure as Martin Buber. Individual conscience is too narrow and limited as a standard to apply to a broader social context (such as an organization). Finally, many of today's social critics would argue that the family, church, and school have all declined in their role in teaching character and developing conscience; thus, it is not clear that members of the younger generation have a strong conscience by which they can act. In addition, personalistic ethics provide no mechanism for resolving disputes when they lead to conflicting views between individuals as to what is right or proper; conflicting views among individuals would lead to teams and organizations that have tremendous value rifts within them because there is no common set of ground rules and no mechanism for resolving value-based disputes.

Summary.   In this section, we have reviewed four major approaches to ethical reasoning: end-result ethics, or the principles of act utilitarianism; rule ethics, or the principles of rule utilitarianism; social contract ethics, or the principles of community-based socially acceptable behavior; and personalistic ethics, or the principles of determining what is right by turning to one's conscience. Each of these approaches may be used by negotiators to evaluate appropriate strategies and tactics. We shall now explore some of the factors that tend to influence, if not dictate, how negotiators are disposed to deal with ethical questions.

WHAT MAJOR TYPES OF ETHICAL AND UNETHICAL CONDUCT ARE LIKELY TO OCCUR IN NEGOTIATION?

Why do some negotiators choose to use tactics that may be unethical? The first answer that occurs to many people is that such negotiators are corrupt, degenerate, or immoral. However, that answer is much too simplistic. In addition, it reflects a systematic bias in the way negotiators tend to perceive the other party and explain the reasons for his or her behavior. Simply put, this bias encourages people to attribute the causes of other people's behavior to their personalities, while attributing the causes of their own behavior to factors in the social environment (Miller and Ross, 1975). Thus, in attempting to explain why the other party used an ethically questionable negotiating tactic, a negotiator might say that this individual was unprincipled, profit-driven, or willing to use any tactic to get what he or she wanted. In contrast, when attempting to explain why you as the negotiator might use the same tactic, you would tend to say that you are highly principled but had very good reasons for deviating from those principles just this one time. Another way to describe this is in terms of the "absolutist–relativist" disparity: In general, people tend to perceive others in absolutist terms and attribute the causes of their behavior to a violation of some absolutist principles (e.g., "It is wrong to lie"), whereas they tend to perceive their own behavior in more relativistic terms and permit themselves an occasional minor transgression because they had good reasons (e.g., "The lie I told was perfectly justifiable under the circumstances").

Building in part on the material already covered in this chapter, we propose a relatively simple model to help explain how a negotiator decides whether to employ one or more deceptive tactics (see Figure 7.1). Negotiators begin by being in a situation where they must influence the other party and need to decide which tactics they will use. They then identify a range of possible influence tactics that may be effective in a given situation, but one that they might judge as deceptive, inappropriate, or marginally ethical. Once these tactics are identified, they may decide to actually use one or more of these tactics. The selection and use of this tactic decision to use this tactic is likely to be influenced by the negotiators' own motivations and their perception/judgment of the tactic's appropriateness. Once the tactic is employed, negotiators will evaluate the consequences on three standards: (1) whether the tactic worked (produced the desired result), (2) how they feel about themselves after using the tactic, and (3) how they may be judged by the other party or by neutral observers. Negative or positive conclusions on any of these three standards may lead the negotiators to try to explain or justify their use of the tactic, but will also eventually affect their decision to employ similar tactics in the future. We will now explore the components of this model in greater detail, referring to some recent research that has improved our understanding of how these components work together.

The Range of Available Influence Tactics

Little needs to be said about the wide range of influence tactics available to a negotiator. We discussed many of these tactics in Chapters 3 and 4, when we discussed distributive bargaining and integrative negotiation, and in Chapter 6, when we discussed a variety of influence and persuasion tactics. In the remainder of this chapter, we will show how deceptive tactics work to manipulate power and the persuasion processes to gain a temporary strategic advantage.

Ethics in Negotiation Is Mostly about Truth Telling.   Most of the ethics issues in negotiation are concerned with standards of truth telling—how honest, candid, and disclosing a negotiator should be. That is, individuals must decide (according to one or more of the ethical theories presented earlier) when they should tell the truth (the whole truth and nothing but the truth) as opposed to engaging in some behavior short of telling

FIGURE 7.1 A Simple Model of Ethical Decision Making

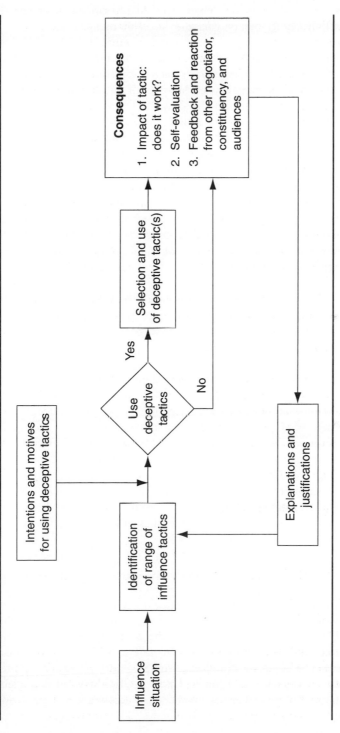

the truth. The attention here is more on what negotiators say (communicate about) what they will do (and how they say it) than on what they do (although negotiators may act unethically as well). Some negotiators may cheat (violate formal and informal rules—e.g., claiming that rules about deadlines or procedures don't apply to them) or steal (e.g., break into the other party's or competitor's database or headquarters to secure confidential documents or briefing memoranda), but most of the attention in negotiator ethics has been on lying behavior.

Most negotiators would probably place a high value on a reputation for being truthful. Yet what does *being truthful* mean? The questions about what constitutes truth telling are quite straightforward, but once again the answers are not so clear. First, how does one define *truth?* Do you follow a clear set of rules, determine what the social contract is for truth in your group or organization, or follow your conscience? Second, how does one define and classify deviations from the truth? Are all deviations *lies,* no matter how small and minor they are? Finally, one can add a relativistic dimension to these questions: Should a person tell the truth all the time, or are there times when not telling the truth is an acceptable (or even necessary) form of conduct? These are questions of major concern to negotiators who are trying to decide what they can and cannot say and still remain ethical.

A number of articles in business journals have addressed the ethical issues surrounding truth telling. For example, Carr (1968) argued in a controversial *Harvard Business Review* article that strategy in business is analogous to strategy in a game of poker. He advocated that, short of outright cheating (the equivalent of marking cards or hiding an ace up your sleeve), businesspeople ought to play the game as poker players do. Just as good poker playing often involves concealing information and bluffing (convincing others that you have the cards when you really don't), so do many business transactions. From time to time, most executives find themselves compelled, for their own interests or the interests of their companies, to practice some form of deception in their dealings with customers, suppliers, labor unions, government officials, or even other key executives. Through conscious misstatements, concealment of pertinent facts, or exaggeration—in short, bluffing—they seek to persuade others to agree with them. Carr argues that if an executive refuses to bluff periodically—if he or she feels obligated to tell the truth, the whole truth, and nothing but the truth all the time—he or she is probably ignoring opportunities permitted under the rules of business and is probably at a heavy disadvantage in business dealings (p. 144).

Carr (1968) further advocated a modified ethical act-based and rule-based relativism for standards of truth telling. Bluffing, exaggeration, and concealment or manipulation of information, he maintained, are legitimate ways for both individuals and corporations to maximize their self-interest. Such strategies may be either advantageous or disadvantageous. An executive might plead poverty in a contract negotiation with a key employee and thereby save a significant amount of money for the company. However, a similar cost-cutting focus might lead the same executive to fail to make safety or quality improvements on one of the company's products, which could have severe long-term business consequences. As you can well imagine, Carr's position sparked lively debate among *Harvard Business Review* readers. A number of critics argued that individual businesspeople and corporations should be held to higher standards of ethical conduct, and they took Carr to task for his position. For example, Koehn (1997) has challenged Carr's premise that negotiating is a game that legitimizes deceptive behavior, arguing that most games do not legitimize deception and that therefore Carr's logic is faulty.

Questions and debate regarding the ethical standards for truth telling in negotiation are ongoing. As we pointed out when we discussed interdependence (Chapter 1), negotiation is based on *information dependence* (Kelley and Thibaut, 1969)—the exchange of information regarding the true preferences and priorities of the other negotiator. Arriving at a clear, precise, effective negotiated agreement depends on the willingness of the parties to share accurate information about their own preferences, priorities, and interests. At the same time, because negotiators may also be interested in maximizing their self-interest, they may want to disclose as little as possible about their positions—particularly if they think they can do better by manipulating the information they disclose to the other party (see Chapter 3). As Kelley (1966) has pointed out, this results in two fundamental negotiation dilemmas: the dilemma of trust and the dilemma of honesty (see Chapter 1). For our purposes here, the implication of the *dilemma of trust* is that negotiators believe everything the other says and can be manipulated by his or her dishonesty. The implication of the *dilemma of honesty* is that negotiators tell the other party all about their exact requirements and limits and will therefore never do better than this minimum level. As Rubin and Brown (1975) note, "To sustain the bargaining relationship, each party must select a middle course between the extremes of complete openness toward, and deception of, the other. Each must be able to convince the other of his integrity while not at the same time endangering his bargaining position" (p. 15).

Typologies of Deceptive Tactics and Attitudes toward Their Use

Deception and disguise may take several forms in negotiation. Researchers have been working to identify the nature of these tactics, and their underlying structure, for almost 20 years (Lewicki, 1983; Lewicki and Robinson, 1998; Lewicki and Spencer, 1990; Lewicki and Stark, 1995; Robinson, Lewicki, and Donahue, 1998; Barry, Fulmer, and Long, 2001). They have extensively explored the nature and conceptual organization of marginally ethical negotiating tactics. The general approach has been to ask students and executives to rate a list of tactics on several dimensions: the appropriateness of the tactic, the rater's likelihood of using the tactic, and/or the perceived efficacy of using the tactic. Analyzing these questionnaire results, six clear categories of tactics emerged and have been confirmed by additional data collection and analysis (Robinson, Lewicki, and Donahue, 1998; Barry, Fulmer, and Long, 2000). These categories are listed in Table 7.2. It is interesting to note that of the six categories, two—emotional manipulation, and the use of "traditional competitive bargaining" tactics—are those which are viewed as generally appropriate and likely to be used. These tactics, therefore, while mildly inappropriate, are nevertheless seen as appropriate and effective in successful distributive bargaining. The other four categories—misrepresentation, bluffing, misrepresentation to opponent's network, and inappropriate information collection—generally include those tactics seen as inappropriate and unethical in negotiation.

TABLE 7.2   Categories of Marginally Ethical Negotiating Tactics

Category	Example
Traditional competitive bargaining	Not disclosing your walkaway; making an inflated opening offer
Emotional manipulation	Faking anger, fear, disappointment; faking elation, satisfaction
Misrepresentation	Distorting information or negotiation events in describing them to others
Misrepresentation to opponent's networks	Corrupting your opponent's reputation with his peers
Inappropriate information gathering	Bribery, infiltration, spying, etc.
Bluffing	Insincere threats or promises

SOURCE: Adapted from R. Robinson, R. J. Lewicki, and E. Donahue, "Extending and Testing a Five Factor Model of Ethical and Unethical Bargaining Tactics: The SINS Scale," *Journal of Organizational Behavior,* 2000, 21, 649–664; and B. Barry, I. S. Fulmer, and A. Long, *Ethically Marginal Bargaining Tactics: Sanction, Efficacy, and Performance.* Presented at the annual meeting of the Academy of Management, Toronto, August, 2000.

Summary.   The studies summarized here indicate that there are tacitly agreed-on rules of the game in negotiation. In these rules, some minor forms of untruths—misrepresentation of one's true position to the other party, bluffs, and emotional manipulations—may be seen as ethically acceptable and within the rules. In contrast, outright deception and falsification are generally seen as outside the rules. However, we must place some strong cautionary notes on these conclusions. First, these statements are based on ratings by large groups of people (mostly business students); in no way do they, or should they, predict how any one individual negotiator will perceive and use the tactics or how any one target who experiences them will rate them. (We will discuss reactions from the "victim's" perspective later in this chapter.) Second, these observations are based on what people said they would do, rather than what they actually did (see the next section for at least one study that has tried to make this link). Perceptions and reactions may well be different when the parties are making decisions in an actual negotiation, rather than rating the tactics on a questionnaire removed from any direct experience with another person in a meaningful social context. Third, by reporting these results, we do not mean to endorse the use of *any* marginally ethical tactic. Instead, our objective is to focus debate among negotiators on exactly when these tactics might be appropriate or should be used. Finally, we acknowledge that this is a very Western view, in which individuals determine what is ethically acceptable; in some other cultures (e.g., Asia), a group or organization would decide on ethics, while in other cultures (e.g., some nations with emerging free markets), ethical constraints on negotiated transactions may be minimal or hard to determine clearly, and "let the buyer beware" at all times!

Does Tolerance for Unethical Tactics Lead to Their Actual Use?

As we indicated earlier, much of the research on these tactics has asked people to respond to questionnaires about their judgment of the ethicality of certain tactics, and what they would be *likely* to do in a negotiation. One researcher (Volkema, 2001) selected five specific tactics from the larger group of unethical tactics described in the previous section and made them available to participants in a competitive buyer/seller negotiation role-play. These five tactics were exaggerating an opening offer, pretending not to be in a hurry, hiding one's own bottom line, misrepresenting factual information, and making promises that could not be kept. The researcher then measured each person's attitude toward using the tactics in general and using a specific tactic (was it appropriate or not), likelihood of using the tactics in general and using a specific tactic, and actual use of the tactic in the role play. The findings from the study suggested the following:

- There is a significant positive relationship between an attitude toward the use of each specific tactic and the intention to use it.
- There is a significant positive relationship between an attitude toward the use of a specific tactic and actually using that tactic, for four of the five tactics studied.
- There is a significant positive relationship between an intention to use a specific tactic and actually using the tactic.
- Actual measures on a specific tactic (intentions and attitudes) were better predictors of behavior than broad measures of attitudes and intentions toward the tactics in general.
- Hiding the bottom line was the tactic most frequently used, exaggerating an opening offer was the second most commonly used, followed by stalling for time and misrepresenting information. Making empty promises was only used about 10 percent of the time.
- Hiding the bottom line improved negotiator performance on the role-play. Negotiators also believed that making empty promises, misrepresenting information, and exaggerating their opening offer improved their performance, although there was no direct evidence that their performance was actually better.

INTENTIONS AND MOTIVES TO USE DECEPTIVE TACTICS

The purpose of using marginally ethical negotiating tactics is to increase the negotiator's power in the bargaining environment. As we discussed in Chapter 6, information is one of the major sources of leverage in negotiation. Information has power because negotiation is intended to be a rational activity involving the exchange of information and the persuasive use of that information. One view of negotiation is that it is primarily an exchange of facts, arguments, and logic between two wholly rational information-processing entities. Often, whoever has better information, or uses it more persuasively, stands to "win" the negotiation.

In such a view, we assume that the information is accurate and truthful. To assume otherwise—that it is not truthful—is to question the very assumptions on which daily social communication is based, and to question the honesty and integrity of the presenter of that information. We seldom have reason to raise these questions and are naturally concerned that if we did raise them, we might insult the other and reduce the implied trust we placed in them. Moreover, investigating the others' truthfulness and honesty is time and energy consuming. So any inaccurate and untruthful statements (i.e., lies) introduced into this social exchange manipulate information in favor of the introducer. A lie changes the balance of information power in the negotiating relationship, creating the image that the liar either has better information than the other party or is using it in a more persuasive and convincing manner. Through the tactics we described earlier—bluffing, falsification, misrepresentation, deception, and selective disclosure—the liar gains advantage. The receiver either accepts the information at face value or has to decide whether there is a basis for challenging the other person's accuracy, credibility, and intentions (and/or must attempt to independently verify that information). Thus, a negotiator uses inaccurate or misleading information to change the other party's preferences or priorities. In the study by Volkema (2001), cited in the previous section, negotiators who intended to be deceptive were more likely to actually use marginal tactics in the negotiation. Different types of deception can serve different purposes in negotiation. For example, O'Connor and Carnevale (1997) studied the tendency for negotiators to misrepresent their interests on a common-value issue—an issue for which both parties are seeking the same outcome. A negotiator using this tactic deceives the other party about what she wants on the common-value issue, and then (grudgingly) agrees to accept the other party's preference, which in reality matches her own. By making it look as though she has made a concession, she can seek a concession from the other party in return. Overall, 28 percent of O'Connor and Carnevale's subjects misrepresented the common-value issue in an effort to obtain a concession from the other party. The researchers discovered that negotiators used two forms of deception in misrepresenting the common-value issue: misrepresentation by omission (failing to disclose information that would benefit the other) and misrepresentation by commission (actually lying about the common-value issue).

Schweitzer (1997; Schweitzer and Croson, 1998) also examined factors that affected the tendency of negotiators to lie about material facts. Students took part in a role-play in which they had to sell a car with a defective transmission. Students could lie by omission—by simply failing to mention the defective transmission—or by commission—by denying that the transmission was defective even when asked by the other party. In both studies, far more students were willing to lie by omission (not revealing the whole truth) than by commission (falsely answering a question when asked). This finding clearly reinforces the norm of caveat emptor (let the buyer beware), suggesting that it is up to the buyer to ask the right questions and be appropriately skeptical when accepting the other's sales pitch.

In summary, negotiators use both lies and means–ends tactics to gain power. They derive power by either manipulating the information (through some form of truth distortion), gaining some form of tactical advantage over a competitor, or undermining the other party's negotiating position. Using these tactics frequently leads to consequences for the negotiator, the other party, and observers.

The Motivation to Behave Unethically

The motivation of a negotiator can clearly affect his or her tendency to use deceptive tactics. (For example, see Box 7.1 for a discussion of the motives of cheaters in running.) When we consider individual differences in Chapter 10, we will point out how motivational orientation—whether negotiators are motivated to act cooperatively, competitively, or individualistically toward the other—can affect the strategies and tactics they pursue. In the study cited earlier, O'Connor and Carnevale (1997) also manipulated the negotiators' motivational orientation to the situation, predisposing parties to either an "individualistic" or a "cooperative" orientation toward the other. Individualistic negotiators—those looking to maximize their own outcome, regardless of the consequences for the other—were more likely to use misrepresentation as a strategy.

But the impact of "motives" may not be that clear cut. In an early study on tactics, Lewicki and Spencer (1991) asked negotiators about their predisposition to use marginally ethical tactics. One part of the questionnaire explicitly instructed the respondents to assume either a competitive or a cooperative motivational orientation toward the other party, and to assume that the other party would be taking either a competitive or a cooperative motivational orientation. The authors predicted that (1) when motivated to be competitive, and when expecting the other to be competitive, the negotiator would see the marginally ethical tactics as appropriate, and (2) when both parties were competitively motivated, they would exhibit the greatest tendency to employ marginally ethical tactics. The results revealed that differences in the negotiators' own motivational orientation—cooperative versus competitive—did *not* cause differences in their view of

---

BOX 7.1
Why Do Racers Cheat?

The *Boston Globe* investigated incidents of cheating in the Boston Marathon and other similar competitions around the country. The report listed the following explanations:

1. Some cheaters were angry or disturbed, often demonstrating a pattern of erratic, unethical, or illegal behaviors.

2. More typically, cheaters were described as middle-aged males who were often successful in many parts of their lives and found it difficult not to be equally successful in racing.

3. Some people were categorized as "unintentional cheaters"; these were people who simply were caught up in the racing moment and did not fully realize what they were doing at the time.

4. Cheaters typically sought recognition rather than prize money or other material gain. Ironically, many reported that the negative publicity surrounding their cheating caused friends, neighbors, and even family members to view them negatively, even if they had never misbehaved before.

SOURCE: Larry Tye, "They're Not in It for the Long Haul," *The Columbus (Ohio) Dispatch*, April 19, 1998, p. 10E.

the appropriateness of using the tactics, but the negotiators' perception of the other's expected motivation did! In other words, negotiators were significantly more likely to see the marginally ethical tactics as appropriate if they anticipated that the other would be competitive versus cooperative. Although these findings are preliminary, they do suggest that motives and intentions may be integrally tied together. Negotiators may rationalize the use of marginally ethical tactics in anticipated defense of the other's expected conduct, rather than take personal responsibility for using these tactics in the service of their own competitive orientation. Several authors (e.g., Batson and Thompson, 2001) have indicated that people may be more motivated to appear moral, rather than to actually act morally, because to act morally (e.g., act with integrity) may have a number of costs attached to it.

The Consequences of Unethical Conduct

A negotiator who employs an unethical tactic will experience positive or negative consequences. The consequences are based on whether the tactic is effective; how the other person, constituencies, and audiences evaluate the tactic; and how the negotiator evaluates the tactic. First, consequences will occur depending on whether the tactic worked or not—that is, whether the negotiator got what he or she wanted as a result of using the tactic. A second set of consequences may result depending on how the negotiator evaluates his or her own use of the tactic—whether using the tactic creates any discomfort, personal stress, or even guilt—or, in contrast, whether the actor sees no problem in using the tactic again and even begins to consider how to use it more effectively. As we note elsewhere in this chapter, negotiators often fail to understand how the use of these tactics can seriously affect their reputation in the marketplace as a fair and ethical person. Finally, a third set of consequences may come from the judgments and evaluations of that negotiator—from the opponent, from constituencies, or from audiences that can observe the tactic. Depending on whether these parties recognize the tactic and whether they evaluate it as proper or improper to use, the negotiator may receive a great deal of feedback.

Let us first consider the consequences that occur based on whether the tactic is successful or not. It should be fairly clear that the tactic's effectiveness should have some impact on whether it is more or less likely to be used in the future (essentially, a simple learning and reinforcement process). If using the tactic allows negotiators to attain rewarding outcomes that would be unavailable to them if they behaved ethically, and if the unethical conduct is not punished by others, the frequency of unethical conduct is likely to increase because the negotiator believes he or she can get away with it. Thus, real consequences—rewards and punishments that arise from using a tactic or not using it—should not only motivate a negotiator's present behavior but also affect his or her predisposition to use similar strategies in similar circumstances in the future. (For the moment, we will ignore the consequences of these tactics on the negotiator's reputation and trustworthiness, an impact that most deceptive negotiators ignore in the short term.) These propositions have not been tested in negotiating situations, but they have been tested extensively in other research studies on ethical decision making. For example, research by Hegarty and Sims (1978) appears to support both of these assertions. In that study, when research participants expected to be rewarded for making an unethical decision by participating in a laboratory-simulated kickback scheme, they not only

participated but also were willing to participate again when a second opportunity arose. Moreover, when there were also strong pressures on the research subjects to compete with others—for example, announcing how well each person had done on the task and giving a prize to the one with the highest score—the frequency of unethical conduct increased even further.

To our knowledge, no research has been performed on the second set of consequences: the negotiator's own reactions to the use of unethical tactics. Under some conditions—such as when the other party has truly suffered—a negotiator may feel some discomfort, guilt, or remorse. On the one hand, while the use of these tactics may have strong consequences for the negotiator's reputation and trustworthiness, parties seldom appear to take these outcomes into consideration in the short term. On the other hand, and particularly if the tactic has worked, the negotiator may be able to rationalize and justify the use of the tactic. We explore these rationalizations and justifications in the next section.

A final set of consequences occurs when the negotiator experiences the reaction of the target person. If the target person is unaware that a deceptive tactic has been used, he or she shows no reaction other than disappointment at having lost the negotiation. However, if the target discovers that deception has occurred, he or she is likely to react strongly. People who discover that they have been deceived or exploited are typically angry. In addition to having lost the negotiation, they feel foolish for having allowed themselves to be manipulated or deceived by a clever ploy. As a result of both the actual loss they may have suffered in negotiations and the embarrassment they feel at having been deceived, most victims are likely to seek retaliation and revenge. Thus, although the use of unethical tactics may lead to short-term success for the negotiator, it may also create an adversary who is bent on revenge and retribution. The victim is unlikely to trust the other party again, may seek revenge from the negotiator in future dealings, and may also generalize this experience to negotiations with others. A strong experience of being exploited may thus sour a victim's perception of negotiation contexts in the future (Bies and Moag, 1986; Miller and Vidmar, 1981; Werth and Flannery, 1986).

McCornack and Levine (1990) provide some research support for these assertions. In studying people's reactions to having been deceived (in many different types of relationships, not necessarily negotiating ones), these authors found that victims had strong emotional reactions to deception when they had an intimate relationship with the subject, when the information at stake was very important, and when they saw lying as an unacceptable type of behavior for that relationship (i.e., when strong expectations of truth telling were clearly violated). In almost two-thirds of the cases reported, the discovery of the lie was instrumental in an eventual termination of the relationship with the other person, and in most cases the termination was initiated by the victim. Finally, the importance of the information that was lied about was the most significant predictor of whether the relationship would eventually terminate. If the information was about something that was serious, personal, and highly consequential for whether the parties could fundamentally trust each other or not, then the discovered deception was highly destructive to the relationship.

Explanations and Justifications

From the negotiator's perspective, as we stated earlier, the primary motivation to use a deceptive tactic is to gain a temporary power advantage. The negotiator may have made the decision to use such a tactic casually and quickly in order to seize a tactical advantage or after long and careful evaluation of the various options and their likely consequences. When a negotiator has used a tactic that may produce a reaction—as we described above—the negotiator must prepare to defend the tactic's use to himself (e.g., "I see myself as a person of integrity, and yet I have decided to do something that might be viewed as unethical"), to the victim, or to constituencies and audiences who may express their concerns. The primary purpose of these explanations and justifications is to rationalize, explain, or excuse the behavior—to verbalize some good, legitimate reason why this tactic was necessary.

There is an increasing stream of research on those who employ unethical tactics and the explanations and justifications they use to rationalize them. Most of the following rationalizations have been adapted from Bok (1978) and her excellent treatise on lying:

- *The tactic was unavoidable.* Negotiators frequently justify their actions by claiming that the situation made it necessary for them to act the way they did. The negotiator may feel that she was not in full control of her actions or had no other option, and hence should not be held responsible. Perhaps the negotiator had no intent to hurt anyone but was pressured to use the tactic by someone else.

- *The tactic was harmless.* The negotiator may say that what he did was really trivial and not very significant. People tell white lies all the time. For example, you may greet your neighbor with a cheery "Good morning, nice to see you" when, in fact, it may not be a good morning, you are in a bad mood, and you wish you hadn't run into your neighbor because you are angry about his dog barking all night. Exaggerations, bluffs, or peeking at the other party's private notes during negotiations can all be easily explained away as harmless actions. Note, however, that this particular justification interprets the harm from the actor's point of view; the victim may not agree and may have experienced significant harm or costs as a result.

- *The tactic will help to avoid negative consequences.* When using this justification, negotiators are arguing that the ends justify the means. In this case, the justification is that the tactic helped to avoid greater harm. It is okay to lie to an armed robber about where you have hidden your money in order to avoid being robbed. Similarly, negotiators may see lying (or any other means–ends tactic) as justifiable if it protects them against even more undesirable consequences should the truth be known.

• *The tactic will produce good consequences, or the tactic is altruistically motivated.* Again, the end justifies the means, but in a positive sense. As we stated earlier, a negotiator who judges a tactic on the basis of its consequences is acting in accord with the tenets of act utilitarianism—that the quality of any given action is judged by its consequences. Act utilitarians will argue that certain kinds of lies or means–ends tactics are appropriate because they may provide for the larger good—for example, Robin Hood tactics in which someone robs from the rich to make the poor better off. Another tack on this is the "I was only trying to help you . . ." explanation. In reality, most negotiators use deceptive tactics for their own advantage, not for the general good. In this case, others are likely to view these actions as less excusable than tactics that avoid negative consequences.

• *"They had it coming," or "They deserve it," or "I'm just getting my due."* All these justifications are variations on the theme of using lying and deception either against an individual who may have taken advantage of you in the past or against some generalized source of authority (i.e., "the system"). Regular polls of the U.S. population (e.g., Yankelovich , 1982) has noted the problem of a national erosion of honesty. Increasingly, people believed that it was appropriate to take advantage of the system in various ways—through tax evasion, petty theft, shoplifting, improper declaration of bankruptcy, journalistic excesses, and distortion in advertising. A decade later, newer statistical surveys show that the problem has increased dramatically on almost every front (Patterson and Kim, 1991).

• *"They were going to do it anyway, so I will do it first."* Sometimes a negotiator legitimizes the use of a tactic because he or she anticipates that the other intends to use similar tactics. When we discussed the Lewicki and Spencer (1991) study of motivational factors, we pointed out that negotiators used deceptive tactics when they expected the other party to use them. In an insightful study, Tenbrunsel (1998) also shows how the magnitude of temptation to act unethically affects both the perceptions of the other party and one's own desire to use the tactic. Research participants were given opportunities to misrepresent the value of a fictitious firm in order to win either a small prize or a large one, and competed against each other to win the prize. Individuals whose partners were more tempted to misrepresent information expected the other to be less honest than individuals whose partners were less tempted. In addition, the reverse logic also operated: The more an individual was tempted to engage in misrepresentation, the more he or she believed that the other would also misrepresent information. Thus, one's own temptation to misrepresent creates a self-fulfilling logic in which one believes one needs to misrepresent because the other is likely to do it as well. At the same time, subjects in this study consistently rated themselves as more ethical than the other party, which suggests that people experience some combination of positive illusions about themselves and their own behavior, and negative illusions about the other and the other's likely behavior.

• *The tactic is fair or appropriate to the situation.* This approach uses situational relativism as a rationale or justification. Most social situations, including negotiations, are governed by a set of generally well-understood rules of proper conduct and behavior. For example, recall the earlier arguments of Carr (1968), that business is a game and that the game has a special ethos to it that legitimizes normally unethical actions. Bowie (1993) and Koehn (1997) have countered these arguments, both to show that deceit in business is just as immoral as it is in other areas of life, and that the game analogy of business no more legitimizes unethical conduct than other analogies.

• Nevertheless, those who espouse situational ethics suggest that rules against deceit may be suspended (as we said above) in at least two cases: when others have already violated the rules (therefore legitimizing the negotiator's right to violate them as well), and when it is anticipated that others will violate the rules (and therefore the others' actions should be preempted). The first case is an example of using unethical tactics in a tit-for-tat manner, to restore balance, to give others their due. Justifications such as "An eye for an eye" or "He started it and I'm going to finish it!" are commonly heard as a defense for resorting to unethical tactics in these cases. Anticipatory justification leading to preemptive behavior (the second case) usually occurs as a result of how the actor perceives the other party and usually is a self-fulfilling prophecy. For example, negotiators use an unethical tactic because they believe the other party is likely to use one; the other party retaliates with an unethical tactic of his or her own (because the first negotiator used one), which only goes to justify to the first negotiator that the other party was likely to behave unethically anyway. (See Box 7.2 for relevant examples from the workplace.)

Pepper . . . and Salt

THE WALL STREET JOURNAL

"I swear to tell the truth, as I see it."

From *The Wall Street Journal.* Used with permission of Cartoon Features Syndicate.

BOX 7.2
When Is It Acceptable to Lie in the Office?

Most large organizations (and many smaller ones) have adopted a formal code of ethics that calls for honesty in all interactions and full accountability for opinions and behavior. However, some researchers believe that there are instances where a lack of personal accountability—and even dishonesty—may be preferable to these codified norms. These situations include the following:

- *When evaluating your boss.* Many companies have instituted a program of "360-degree feedback," in which employees provide input into their supervisors' performance evaluation. Recent research (Antonioni, 1994) suggests that employees who are asked to provide feedback on their supervisors will respond more honestly and constructively when their appraisals are anonymous. Employees who were personally accountable for their ratings evaluated their managers more positively, while providing less valuable constructive feedback.

- *When dealing with customers.* Salespeople are often at a disadvantage when they are held to strict standards of truth telling. For example, a real estate salesperson who discloses her client's interest in a home too soon in the bargaining process may negate her client's competitive advantage in future negotiations. Hamilton and Strutton (1994) have developed the following guidelines for resolving truth-telling problems in business transactions (a yes answer to any of these questions indicates that truth or full disclosure is morally required in this situation):

  Does the receiver have a right, based on legal, contractual, or human rights standards, to truth telling or full disclosure?

  Would a reasonable person expect the truth/full disclosure?

  Does the prospect/customer actually expect truth/full disclosure?

  Does the salesperson's or organization's reputation require truth telling or full disclosure in this situation?

  Should the salesperson's or organization's reputation require truth telling/full disclosure in situations such as this?

  SOURCE: Adapted from D. Antonioni, "The Effects of Feedback Accountability on Upward Appraisal Ratings," *Personnel Psychology* 47 (1994), pp. 247–56; and J. B. Hamilton and D. Strutton. "Two Practical Guidelines for Resolving Truth Telling Problems in Business Transactions," *Journal of Business Ethics* 13 (1994), pp. 899–912.

Shapiro (1991) has conducted some important research on the role these explanations and justifications play in mitigating a victim's reactions to having been deceived. Shapiro created a laboratory simulation in which experimental subjects were supposedly working together to apply for a loan to support a new business venture. In the course of the simulation, subjects were told that the loan officer had caught their partner falsifying information on the loan application. The experimenter then manipulated the severity of the consequences for being caught in the deception (how much the subject lost as a result of the partner's deception), as well as how adequately the partner explained why the deception had occurred (the deception was unintentional, or selfishly motivated, or altruistically motivated). The findings indicate that the more a subject felt that the partner's explanation was adequate for the deception, the less he or she expressed feelings of injustice, disapproval, and punitiveness toward the partner. If subjects were mildly upset, the explanations had more impact than if the subjects were strongly upset. Moreover, explanations had the most impact when the partner stated that the deception was unintentional, less impact when the deception was altruistic, and the least impact when the deception was selfishly motivated.

Summary.   Explanations and justifications are self-serving rationalizations for one's own conduct. First, they allow the negotiator to convince others—particularly the victim—that conduct that would ordinarily be wrong in a given situation is acceptable. As Shapiro's research shows, the adequacy of these explanations to others has a strong effect on mitigating the impact of deceptive behavior. In addition, explanations and justifications help people to rationalize the behavior to themselves as well. We propose that the more frequently negotiators engage in this self-serving justification process, the more their judgments about ethical standards and values will become biased, leading to a lessened ability to make accurate judgments about the truth. Moreover, although the tactics were initially used to gain power in a negotiation, the negotiators who use them frequently will experience a loss of power over time. These negotiators will be seen as having low credibility or integrity, and will be treated as people who will act exploitatively if the opportunity arises. Negotiators with these characteristics will probably be unsuccessful over time unless they are skillful at continually staying ahead of the negative reputation generated by their conduct.

WHAT FACTORS SHAPE A NEGOTIATOR'S PREDISPOSITION TO USE UNETHICAL TACTICS?

Thus far, we have talked about the use of ethically questionable tactics in terms of the simple model presented in Figure 7.1. This model describes a rational calculation process in which the negotiator selects a tactic, uses the tactic, evaluates the consequences, and attempts to manage the consequences (if the tactic is detected) through explanations and justifications. A number of other factors can moderate the sequences described in the model:

- The background and demographic characteristics of the negotiators.
- The personality characteristics and level of moral development of the negotiators.
- Elements of the social context (the situation in which the negotiators find themselves) that encourage or discourage unethical conduct.

In this section, we will briefly mention how each of these factors might influence the predisposition to use ethically questionable tactics. The factors are included in an expanded model, presented in Figure 7.2. As we discuss this model, it should be clear that the fundamental debate here is the "nature versus nurture" argument about what causes individuals to behave as they do. Many believe that making ethical decisions is

FIGURE 7.2 A More Complex Model of Decision Making

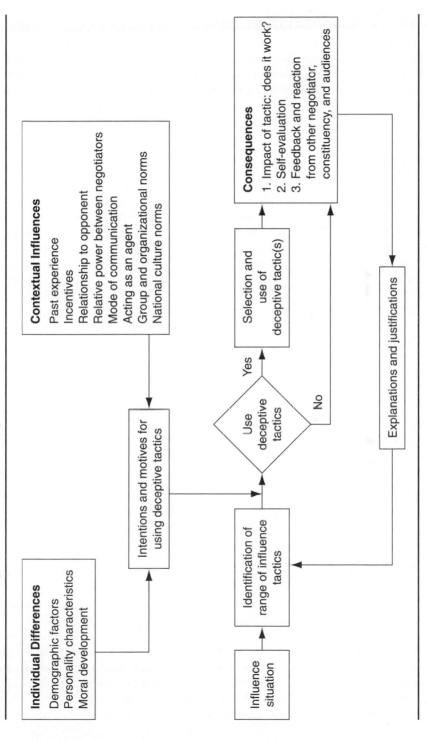

completely determined by the moral standards of the individual actor; others, however, believe that situational factors (such as group and organizational norms, accountability pressures, and reward systems) can cause even ethical people to do unethical things. We expect the debate to continue for a long time. However, when social scientists try to hold individual differences constant, or randomize them across large groups of people, it is very clear that situational influences can predispose very ethical people to do marginally ethical things.

Demographic Factors

A number of survey-oriented studies on ethical behavior have attempted to relate differences in ethical conduct to differences in individual background, religious orientation, age, gender, nationality, and education. In general, these broad demographic studies have shown that individuals who were older or had a stronger commitment to some religious philosophy would be less likely to behave unethically than younger or less religious individuals (e.g., Hassett, 1981). Several researchers have investigated the relationship between demographic factors and the use of unethical tactics in negotiation. In reporting these research findings, we do not mean to imply that all people of a particular group will necessarily act in a specified manner. Thus, for example, studies that show that young people tend to use more deceptive negotiating tactics than other people do not imply that *every* young person will use those tactics. We discuss these demographics because the trends appear to be reliable and consistent across a number of different ethical choice situations.

Sex.   A number of studies have shown that women tend to make more ethically rigorous judgments than men. For example, Volkema (1999) found that comparing Brazilian and American women, those from both cultures were significantly more ethical than men, revealing less willingness to use marginally ethical negotiation tactics. Dawson (1997) asked men and women to respond to a number of decision-making scenarios involving ethics. Half of the scenarios were relational, in that the actor's decision clearly affected the interests of others, while the other half were nonrelational, in that the consequences did not affect anyone else and were only matters of individual conscience. Dawson's results demonstrate that when making decisions about relational issues, women were significantly more ethical than men, but that there were no differences on the nonrelational situations. Hence, according to this study, women may make more ethical judgments, but only when the consequences of their decisions affect someone else.

Returning to the tactics described earlier in this chapter, Lewicki and Robinson (1998) and Robinson, Lewicki, and Donahue (1998) found that with the exception of the tactics classified as traditional competitive bargaining (where there were no gender differences in the rated use of the tactic), men were significantly more likely to use these unethical tactics than women. Recall that traditional competitive bargaining tactics included making an excessively high opening offer and stalling for time. There was no gender difference in the perceived appropriateness of these tactics.

Age and Experience.   In the Dawson (1997) and Volkema (1999) studies cited earlier, both men and women behaved more ethically as they aged. In the Anton (1990) study, where categories of deceptive tactics were rated, older parties tended to see bluffing as more acceptable and deception as less acceptable. Finally, Robinson, Lewicki, and Donahue (1998) report a strong negative correlation between age and the use of unethical negotiating tactics. Overall, older individuals were significantly more likely than younger ones to see marginally ethical tactics as inappropriate. Moreover, they reported that individuals with more general work experience, and with more direct work experience, were less likely to use unethical negotiating tactics.

Ethnicity.   Robinson, Lewicki, and Donahue (1998) investigated whether students from different ethnic backgrounds (Hispanic, Asian, etc.) rated deceptive negotiation tactics differently; no significant differences in ratings were found for the different ethnic groups.

Nationality and Cultural Background.   Lewicki and Robinson (1998) found that on the traditional competitive bargaining category, American students and those with a Middle Eastern heritage were significantly more likely to use marginally ethical tactics, and Asians, Latin Americans, and Eastern European students were less likely to use these tactics. Americans and Asians were significantly more likely to use bluffing, and Eastern Europeans were less likely to do so. On misrepresentation to opponent's network, students with a Middle Eastern heritage were more likely to use the tactics, and Americans were less likely to use the tactics. Similarly, Volkema (1997, 1998, 1999) reports on a number of cross-cultural studies of the use of marginally ethical tactics. Comparing managers from the United States and Brazil, Volkema found that while both rated traditional competitive bargaining tactics as acceptable, managers from Brazil were also more likely to rate the other marginally ethical tactics as significantly more acceptable. A follow-up study indicated that both cultures were similar in their use of tactics involving third parties (e.g., information gathering or disseminating information through a network), but that Brazilians were willing to be more deceptive in dealing with their immediate opponent. Alternatively, comparing managers from Mexico and the United States, Mexican managers saw the same tactics as less appropriate than American ones. In each study, the author interprets these results in light of differences in the culture and economic conditions in each country. We return to a richer treatment of these differences in Chapter 11.

Professional Orientation.   Anton (1990) compared ratings by MBA students, business alumni, and clergy of perceived appropriateness of categories of deceptive negotiation tactics. All groups indicated that traditional competitive bargaining and misrepresentation were ethically acceptable, but clergy were the most ethically conservative in their ratings. Deception was seen as moderately unethical, and all groups believed that outright falsification was highly unethical. Garcia, Darley, and Robinson (2001) also conducted an interesting study of district attorneys and public defenders and their use of these tactics. They found that public defenders saw the tactics as more appropriate than district attorneys, that *both* groups increased their approval of the tactics when they thought the other party was likely to use them, and that public defenders increased their approval as a "defensive move" more than district attorneys. Thus, these findings are actually more about which role a person plays—defender versus challenger of the status quo—than about the attorney role that they play.

Academic Background.   In general, students with a strong background in engineering, science, and mathematics were more likely to use marginally ethical negotiating tactics than those who majored in the arts, business, or the social sciences. In his study of lies about material facts in negotiation (disclosing a faulty transmission in a car for sale), Schweitzer (1997) found that there was no difference in lying between those who had taken a course in ethics and those who had not taken the course.

Personality Differences and Moral Development

Researchers have sought to identify dimensions of personality that would successfully predict a person's predisposition to behave unethically. Selected findings are described below.

Competitiveness versus Cooperativeness.   Lewicki and Robinson (1998) found that students who rated themselves as aggressive were significantly more likely to use bluffing, misrepresentation, and a variety of other dishonest tactics than students who rated themselves as cooperative. Similarly, Robinson, Lewicki, and Donahue (1998) report that students who rated themselves as competitive were significantly more likely to use marginally ethical tactics than those who rated themselves as cooperative.

Machiavellianism.   In Chapter 10, we will discuss the personality variable called Machiavellianism. Machiavellians adhere to a pragmatic and expedient view of human nature—"The best way to handle people is to tell them what they want to hear" or "It is hard to get ahead without cutting corners here and there." A number of studies have shown that individuals who are strongly Machiavellian are more willing and able con artists, more likely to lie when they need to, better able to tell a lie without feeling anxious about it, and more persuasive and effective in their lies (Braginsky, 1970; Christie and Geis, 1970; Exline, Thibaut, Hickey, and Gumpert, 1970; Geis and Moon, 1981). Machiavellianism thus appears to be a predictor of ethical conduct.

Locus of Control.   Individuals differ in their locus of control—that is, the degree to which they believe that the outcomes they obtain are largely a result of their own ability and effort (internal control) versus fate or chance (external control). Studies have generally predicted that individuals who are high in internal control are more likely to do what they think is right (i.e., they have a stronger personal value system or ethical code) and to feel that they had more control over producing the outcomes they wanted to achieve in a situation in which there were temptations to be unethical. Evidence from several different studies of cheating and ethical decision making has confirmed this prediction (Lefcourt, 1982; Trevino and Youngblood, 1990), although it is important to note that locus of control seems most important when individuals can also exert control over outcomes. Thus, locus of control appears to be a moderately powerful contributor to ethical decision making, although it has yet to be tested as a factor in tactic selection in negotiation. We discuss its role in negotiation more generally in Chapter 10.

Moral Development and Personal Values

Many researchers have explored the relationship of an individual's level of moral development to ethical decision making. Kohlberg (1969) proposed that an individual's moral and ethical judgments are a consequence of achieving a particular developmental level or stage of moral growth. Kohlberg proposed six stages of moral development, grouped into three levels:

1. A preconventional level (Stages 1 and 2), where the individual is concerned with concrete outcomes that meet his or her own immediate needs, particularly external rewards and punishments.
2. A conventional level (Stages 3 and 4), where the individual defines what is right on the basis of what his immediate social situation and peer group endorses or what society in general seems to want.
3. A principled level (Stages 5 and 6), where the individual defines what is right on the basis of some broader set of universal values and principles.

The higher the stage people achieve, the more complex their moral reasoning should be and the more ethical their decisions should be. In addition, there may be gender-related differences in this ethical reasoning process—as noted above, women's ethical reasoning may be more relational and less individualistic than men's (Gilligan, 1982).

Many studies have demonstrated the power of measuring ethical orientation in this way (see Trevino, 1986; Trevino and Youngblood, 1990 for reviews). The results have generally indicated that higher levels of moral development are associated with more ethical decisions, less cheating behavior, more helping behavior, and more resistance to authority figures who are attempting to dictate unethical conduct. Other studies have investigated value differences, defined more broadly. Glover, Bumpus, Logan, and Ciesla (1997) report on an extensive study of honesty/integrity and other values such as achievement, fairness, and concern for others on ethical decision making. In their study, fairness and achievement selectively predicted some ethical decisions, while honesty did not predict any ethical choices. These mixed findings are reasonably consistent with the growing literature that attempts to measure individual values and morality and relate them to ethical decisions. To our knowledge, however, no specific study has examined the relationship between moral development or values and the tendencies to use deceptive negotiating tactics.

Contextual Influences on Unethical Conduct

The last set of factors that should have an impact on a negotiator's willingness to act unethically are contextual factors. We briefly examine a number of elements from this group: the negotiator's past experience with using unethical tactics, incentives to use the tactics, the quality of the relationship with the other party, differences in power and status between the two negotiators, the mode of communication between the parties, whether a negotiator is acting as the principal actor or an agent, and the group, organizational, or cultural norms that govern the negotiation process.

Past Experience.   At least one recent study has shown that the simple impact of past experience—particularly failure—can increase the likelihood that a negotiator might attempt to use unethical tactics. Schweitzer et. al. (2002) gave students different kinds of goals (do your best, meet a specific goal, or exceed a specific goal), then asked them to solve puzzles, and manipulated their success or failure at the puzzle task. First, having specific goals clearly influenced reporting of accomplishment; if told to "do your best," parties reported more honestly than if they had a specific goal to meet. Participants who had to meet specific goals were more likely to overstate their productivity than those without, were more likely to overstate their success when their actual performance was closer to the goal, and were more likely to overstate in those situations where they thought they "deserved" the reward based on overall productivity.

Role of Incentives.   A second factor that can influence a negotiator's tendency to use marginally ethical tactics is the role of incentives. Tenbrunsel (1998) demonstrated that greater incentives influenced a negotiator's tendency to misrepresent to the other party, and also enhanced the negotiator's expectation that the other party would misrepresent. However, as we noted in the "justifications" section earlier in this chapter, it is difficult to determine whether the negotiator's heightened sensitivity to misrepresentation was due to an expectation that the other was going to mispresent, or because the negotiator intended to misrepresent himself.

Relationship between the Negotiator and the Other Party.   Two aspects of the negotiator's relationship with the other party affect the negotiator's disposition to use certain tactics: what the relationship has been like in the past and what the parties would like it to be in the future. The negotiators' past relationship will affect current behavior if the parties have been previously competitive or cooperative, are friends or enemies, feel indebted to each other, or hold grudges toward each other. For example, research by Gruder (1971) showed that negotiators were likely to make deceptive arguments, negotiate for a longer period of time, and make fewer concessions when they had previously experienced the other party as exploitative than when the other party had been cooperative. A similar argument can be made for a negotiator's expectations about how the other party will behave in the present or future. If you view the other party with suspicion—as exploitative, competitive, dishonest—you can then justify a relativistic approach to strategy and claim that anticipatory self-defense legitimizes your actions. We see this in the Lewicki and Spencer (1991) study mentioned earlier—expecting the other party to have a competitive motivational orientation legitimized negotiators' use of marginally ethical tactics. We also see this in the Tenbrunsel (1998) study discussed earlier, in the power by which intentions shaped expectations and expectations shaped intentions. Similarly, Schweitzer (1997) demonstrated that students were more likely to lie to strangers than they were to friends, and were particularly more likely to lie to strangers who did not ask any probing questions. However, you can see how this form of rationalization may be easily distorted by fear and suspicion and hence create a self-fulfilling prophecy to justify use of an unethical tactic. All a negotiator needs is to experience some mildly competitive or exploitative bit of behavior from the other party, or even to imagine that it is going to occur. Naturally, this will motivate the other party to seek revenge and act exactly as the negotiator anticipated.

A factor in the relationship that can balance this self-fulfilling dynamic is whether the negotiator expects the relationship to be short term or long term. Another variation in the Lewicki and Spencer (1991) study manipulated whether the negotiator expected to be in a short-term or long-term working relationship with the other party. Respondents who expected to be in a short-term relationship were more likely to see the marginally ethical tactics as appropriate than those expecting a long-term relationship, regardless of their own and the other party's motivations. This was the most powerful finding of the study, and it appears to indicate that when negotiators do not anticipate having to live with the consequences of using marginally ethical tactics, they are far more willing to use them. Anton (1990) reports some anecdotal results that are consistent with this finding.

Relative Power between the Negotiators.   A second situational factor is relative power—how much power one negotiator has relative to the other party. We discussed power earlier in this chapter, in that negotiators use deception as a way to gain temporary information power over the other party. In general, negotiators with relatively more power are more likely to use unethical tactics. For example, in one research study, negotiators with more power bluffed more often and communicated less with their counterpart than those with less power (Crott, Kayser, and Lamm, 1980). This result will seem paradoxical to some people. Why should negotiators with more power, who can presumably get what they want by using their power legitimately, use unethical tactics that increase their power even more? The results seem to support an "intoxication" theory of power, which holds that power corrupts the thinking of the powerful; results confirming the theory have been consistently observed both in laboratory research and in the power dynamics between "haves" and "have nots" in society. A balance of power should lead to more ethical conduct than an imbalance does. (In Chapter 13, we investigate the role of third parties, such as mediators, who often must address power differences between disputants to produce a level playing field.)

Mode of Communication.   Major changes in technology have affected the way negotiators can communicate with each other. With the evolution of e-mail and fax machines, parties have more ways to communicate back and forth than ever before. One question is whether negotiators are more or less likely to use marginally ethical tactics when they are physically removed from each other (using phone, fax, voicemail, or e-mail) than when they are face to face (see Lewicki and Dineen, 2002, for one review of the overall impact of "virtual organization" conditions on negotiation). Research thus far seems to indicate mixed results. Schweitzer, Brodt, and Croson (2002) indicate that negotiators lie more often in face-to-face situations because they want to be able to monitor the other party's reactions, to make sure that the "lie" is having its intended effect. Yet others have argued there is less trust and more suspicion among negotiators when they are *not* face to face (Fortune and Brodt, 2000), since face-to-face situations compel a negotiator to be more honest and cooperative because of the personal and emotional consequences of being caught in a lie in the face-to-face context (Thompson, 1998). Clearly, more work is necessary to refine these ideas.

Acting as an Agent versus Representing Your Own Views.   Acting as an agent for another party often puts you in a different ethical frame of mind than negotiating for yourself. As one author has put it,

> Many negotiators fail to understand the nature of negotiation and so find themselves attempting to reconcile conflicts between the requirements of negotiation and their own sense of personal integrity. An individual who confuses private ethics with business morality does not make an effective negotiator. Those who serve as agents in a negotiation must learn to be objective and to subordinate their own personal goals to the prime purpose of securing the best possible deal for their constituents. (Beckman, 1977, quoted in Lax and Sebenius, 1986, p. 363)

As we point out in Chapter 8, negotiators frequently find themselves representing others' views in negotiation rather than negotiating for their own personal goals and interests. A number of authors have suggested that when people act as an agent for someone else— particularly when the goals for that agent are to get the best possible agreement—they may be more willing to violate personal ethical standards (Bowie and Freeman, 1992). In essence, acting as an agent may release people from their own personal ethical code and allow them to create their own standards of legitimacy—that it is appropriate to do whatever is necessary to maximize the results for the constituent. (See Box 7.3 for a business example.)

Group and Organizational Norms and Pressures.   Many negotiators look to the social norms of the particular situation to decide how to behave. Norms are the informal social rules—the dos and don'ts—that govern social behavior. In negotiation, the rules are defined in two ways: by what people believe is appropriate in negotiation, and by what other people say is appropriate in that situation. As an example of the first case, some negotiators may define negotiation as a game, and thus they feel that gaming rules apply to negotiation. Thus, if negotiating is a game like poker, then it is very appropriate to bluff in order to drive others out of the game. Do other people agree with this analogy? (See Carr, 1968; McDonald, 1963.) What happens when some people believe certain tactics are appropriate but others don't?

Recent research suggests that group and organizational norms and pressures may play a key role in legitimizing inappropriate behavior (although, again, this research has not specifically involved negotiating situations). First, studies have shown that different companies can have distinctly different ethical climates or cultures (Jackall, 1988; Victor and Cullen, 1988). Companies differ in how they value and endorse ethical conduct or appear to condone and tolerate marginally ethical behavior in the service of achieving corporate objectives at any price. Second, whereas the overall company may have a very strong statement of corporate ethics and values, job-related pressures within particular work groups, departments, or divisions may be such that marginally ethical behavior is not only tolerated but even condoned. The actions and practices of the key manager or supervisor in each work group or department probably play a large role in

---

BOX 7.3
Secretaries Learn Ethics on the Job

The following is from an article in *The Wall Street Journal:*

> When Sharon Koehler was taking secretarial classes in high school, no one taught her what to do if her boss broke the law.
>
> But once she began working for a supervisor who, she says, lied, falsified time sheets and tried to trick people into taking drug tests, she quickly learned that loyalty had its limits. After confronting her boss repeatedly, losing lots of sleep, and worrying about whether she was being a good secretary, she finally decided to quit.
>
> "I realized that my values and ethics were totally clashing with this person I was working for," says Ms. Koehler, 36 years old, who now works as an administrative assistant for Zenega AG Products in Des Moines, Iowa. "When you get to the point where it clashes so much, you're not productive."

The article further reported the results of a survey of 2,000 secretaries, which indicated that

- 58 percent have lied about their supervisor's whereabouts.
- 27 percent have shared confidential information about hiring, firing, and layoffs.
- 17 percent have notarized a document without witnessing the signature.
- 12 percent have seen the official minutes of corporate meetings changed.
- 10 percent have removed or destroyed damaging information.

SOURCE: R. Sharpe, "Management: What's a Secretary to Do When the Boss Asks Her to Lie?" *The Wall Street Journal,* February 3, 1998, p. B1.

---

determining what employees believe it is necessary and appropriate to do (see Lewicki and Dineen, 2002, for one study and Murphy, 1992, for a broader review). In fact, it is possible that the more loyalty and commitment people feel toward an organization, the more likely they may be to suspend their own ethical judgment and engage in any and all behavior—even unethical and illegal behavior—to demonstrate that loyalty. Third, norms have to be "salient"—i.e., immediate and relevant to the negotiator—for them to have an impact. In a study of the impact of "ethical climate" on negotiations, Aquino (1998) showed that when specific ethical standards were made salient and relevant to negotiators, they decreased the use of deception by the negotiators and led to more ethical agreements. Fourth, organizations may exert direct pressures on people to breach ethics or even break the law in the service of some corporate or organizational goal. In these circumstances, people have also suspended their best moral judgment—but in the service of obedience, following the rules, and doing what they are told—even if the actions are immoral and unethical.

The pressure to obey authority is very strong, as anyone who has read about Milgram's famous experiments will recall (Milgram, 1974). Such pressure is real in organizations, and many authors are beginning to document how thoroughly it can undermine individual integrity (Brief, 1992; Kelman and Hamilton, 1989). Moreover, at least one group of researchers (Mason and Mudrack, 1997) have shown that the more complex an individual's moral reasoning capability, the more he or she perceives conflict between personal standards and typical organizational demands. In its most extreme forms, organizational pressure leads individuals to commit major crimes against humanity, such as the Holocaust or the infamous My Lai massacre in the Vietnam war. Other authors (e.g., Street, Robertson, and Geiger, 1997) have argued that the pressures of escalating commitment, which can be observed when people are pressured to throw good money after bad or increase their commitment to a failing course of action, may also predispose parties to commit more unethical actions than they otherwise would.

National Culture Norms.   In addition to the pressures of group and organizational norms, national cultures can also create ethical problems and dilemmas because they emphasize different behaviors as acceptable or unacceptable. For example, Volkema (1997) found that for the tactics listed in Table 7.2, Brazilian managers generally felt that questionable negotiating behaviors were more appropriate than American managers did, but also said that they were not significantly more likely to use these behaviors. A follow-up study by Volkema (1999) showed that both cultures were similar in rejecting the use of unethical "indirect" approaches to a negotiation (gathering information through networks and informal contacts), but that Brazilians were more willing to use unethical tactics in their direct relations with an opponent (e.g., bluffing and misrepresentation). Finally, a third study indicated Mexicans saw the same tactics as less appropriate than Americans and were less willing to use them (Volkema, 1998). We will say more about cultural norms in Chapter 11 (also see Box 7.4).

Summary.   Research shows that a number of social forces can encourage negotiators to suspend their own personal and ethical standards and commit acts that are ethically questionable. These forces include

- Acting as an agent for others and responding to their pressures to achieve a very high goal, succeed at any price, or do whatever it takes to accomplish an objective.
- Viewing various forms of business dealings—such as negotiation—as a game (like poker or war) and therefore assuming that the rules of the game are the ones that should be applied.
- Being a member of a group, department, team, or organizational unit that values success and tolerates or even encourages bending or breaking the rules in order to achieve that success.
- Being so loyal to a group or organization that you are willing to do something you would not do as an individual, or convincing yourself that it is permissible to break the rules in order to be rewarded for your loyalty.
- Being willing to follow the direct or implied orders of senior officials in the organization who tell you to get a job done and not worry about how it gets done.

Any of these forces appear to be sufficient, under the right circumstances, to permit individuals to suspend their own good moral judgment in the service of doing what the organization appears to need, want, or request. Combining them can produce an

> **BOX 7.4**
> **Ethical Guidelines for International Business**
>
> People who conduct business in countries other than their own encounter not only differ-
> ent languages but different cultural mores and practices as well. They may find that local
> business practices reflect ethical standards that are dictated by cultural norms that are not
> similar to their own. Such a situation can lead to an ethical dilemma: Which system of
> ethics should guide the interaction? Is it more appropriate to adopt the ethical system of
> the host country, or to remain true to one's own ethical standards? Henry Lane, Joseph
> DiStefano, and Martha Maznevski argue that there are some guidelines for decision mak-
> ers that bridge cultural differences. They offer this list of general advice that can guide
> businesspeople through interactions in a variety of cultural settings:
>
> 1. Identify the stakeholders that have an interest in or will be affected by the decision.
>   This might include the home-country or host-country governments, suppliers, employ-
>   ees, unions, and customers. What are your responsibilities and obligations to each of
>   these stakeholders?
> 2. Ask yourself whether you have the best information possible, and whether it is reliable.
> 3. Do not avoid making ethical decisions that are your responsibility, but also do not
>   accept responsibility for decisions that are not your responsibility.
> 4. Enter into dependent relationships with care. Be certain that you retain enough power
>   to maintain your own standards.
> 5. Do the best for all involved stakeholders, fulfill your obligations, observe laws and
>   contracts, do not use deception, and avoid knowingly doing harm (physical, psycho-
>   logical, economic, or social).
> 6. Remember the "billboard" or "light of day" test: When you drive to work tomorrow
>   morning, would you be happy to see your decision on a billboard at the side of the road?
>   Would your action appear reasonable then?
>
> SOURCE: Adapted from H. W. Lane, J. J. DiStefano, and M. L. Maznevski, *International Manage-
> ment Behavior,* 3rd ed. (Cambridge, MA: Blackwell, 1997).

even more lethal concoction of social pressures that permits people to rationalize their
actions and do whatever is necessary. Such combined pressures often lead to major
breakdowns in legal and ethical behavior.

HOW CAN NEGOTIATORS DEAL WITH THE OTHER PARTY'S USE OF DECEPTION?

A chapter such as this would not be complete without briefly noting some of the
things that you as a negotiator can do when you believe the other party is using deceptive
tactics. We will discuss these in more detail in Chapter 12, when we examine a wide range
of strategies for damage control. If you think the other party is using deceptive tactics (see
Table 7.3), in general you can do the following:

TABLE 7.3   Detecting Deception

Researchers have identified a number of verbal tactics that you can use to determine whether the other party is acting deceptively.

Tactic	Explanation and Examples
Intimidation	Force the other to admit he is using deception by intimidating him into telling the truth. Make a no-nonsense accusation of the other. Criticize the other. Hammer the other with challenging questions. Feign indifference to what he has to say ("I'm not interested in anything you have to say on the matter").
Futility portrayal	Emphasize the futility and impending danger associated with continued deceit: "The truth will come out someday," "Don't dig the hole deeper by trying to cover it up," "If you try to cover it up, it will only be worse in the future," "You are all alone in your deception."
Discomfort and relief	State the maxim "Confession is good for the soul." Help the other reduce the tension and stress associated with being a known deceiver.
Bluffing	Lie to the other to make her believe you have uncovered her deception: "Your sins are about to be uncovered." Indicate that you know what she knows but will not discuss it.
Gentle prods	Encourage the other to keep talking so that he gives you information that may help you separate true facts from deceptions. Ask him to elaborate on the topic being discussed. Ask questions but indicate that you are asking because "other people want to know." Play devil's advocate and ask playful questions. Praise the other so as to give him confidence and support that may lead to information sharing.
Minimization	Play down the significance of any deceptive act. Help the other find excuses for why she was deceptive; minimize the consequences of the action; indicate that others have done worse; shift the blame to someone else.
Contradiction	Get the other to tell his story fully in order to discover more information that will allow you to discover inconsistencies and contradictions in his comments or reports. Point out and ask for explanations about apparent contradictions. Ask the speaker the same question several times and look for inconsistencies in his response. Present contradictions back and ask the speaker to explain. Put pressure on the speaker and get him to slip up or say things he doesn't want to say.
Altered information	Alter information and hopefully trick the other into revealing deception. Exaggerate what you believe is the deception, hoping that the other will jump in to "correct" the statement. Ask the suspected deceiver a question containing incorrect information and hope she corrects you.

TABLE 7.3   *(Concluded)*

Tactic	Explanation and Examples
A chink in the defense	Try to get the other to admit a small or partial lie about some information, and use this to push for admission of a larger lie: "If you lied about this one little thing, how do I know you have not lied about other things?"
Self-disclosure	Reveal a number of things about yourself, including, perhaps, dishonesty on your own part, hoping the other will begin to trust you and reciprocate with disclosures of dishonesty.
Point of deception cues	Point out behaviors you detect in the other that might be an indication he is lying: sweating, nervousness, change of voice, inability to make eye contact, and so on.
Concern	Indicate your true concern for the other's welfare: "You are important to me," "I care deeply about you," "I feel your pain."
Keeping the status quo	Admonish the other to be truthful in order to maintain her good name. "What will people think?" Appeal to her pride and desire to maintain a good reputation.
Direct approach	"Simply tell me the truth." "Let's be honest here." "Surely you have no objection to telling me everything you know."
Silence	Create a "verbal vacuum" that makes the other uncomfortable and gets him to talk and disclose information. When he tells a lie, simply maintain direct eye contact but remain silent.

SOURCE: Adapted from Pamela J. Kalbfleisch, "The Language of Detecting Deceit," *Journal of Language and Social Psychology* 13, no. 4 (1994), pp. 469–96.

Ask Probing Questions.   When the other party is committing acts of omission—that is, not fully disclosing a problem (recall the fourth situation at the beginning of this chapter, about selling the computer with a defective hard drive)—asking a number of probing questions about the other's position, point of view, information, and so on may help you uncover the key information that was omitted. Research by Schweitzer (1997; Schweitzer and Croson, 1998) shows that most buyers fail to ask questions, and that asking questions can reveal a great deal of information, some of which may be intentionally undisclosed by the negotiator. While asking questions may not always expose lies of commission—that is, those in which the actor is intentionally changing information or misrepresenting an issue—excellent and complete questioning may expose some. Police interrogators and prosecuting attorneys have learned to master the art of questioning to discover both lies of omission and commission. Refer back to Chapter 5 for a more extensive examination of asking good questions.

Recognize the Tactic.   In Chapters 3 and 12, we extensively discuss how to respond when the other party is using distributive tactics or dirty tricks. Deceptive tactics certainly fall into the latter category. To summarize, negotiators can do the following things:

- *Ignore the tactic.* If you are aware that the other party is bluffing or lying, simply ignore it.

- *Ask questions.* Researchers Maurice Schweitzer and Rachel Croson (2002) simulated a negotiation over the sale of a new computer. Buyers were either strongly prompted to ask questions of the seller about the condition of the computer, or not prompted to ask questions. Their findings indicate that across the board, asking questions about the condition of the computer reduced the number of deceptive comments made by the seller (lies of commission). However, under some conditions, asking questions also *increased* the seller's use of lies of omission about other aspects of the computer. Thus, while asking questions can help a negotiator determine whether a negotiator is being deceptive, such "cross examination" may actually increase the seller's tendency to be deceptive in areas where questions are not being asked.

- *"Call" the tactic.* Indicate to the other side that you know he is bluffing or lying. Do so tactfully but firmly, and indicate your displeasure. (Recall, though, that spotting lies is not always easy—see Box 7.5.)

- *Respond in kind.* If the other party bluffs, you bluff more. If she misrepresents, you misrepresent. We do not recommend this course of action at all, because it simply escalates the destructive behavior and drags you into the mud with the other party, but if she recognizes that you are lying too, she may also realize that the tactic is unlikely to work.

- *Discuss what you see and offer to help the other party change to more honest behaviors.* This is a variation on calling the tactic but instead tries to assure the other party that telling the truth is, in the long term, more likely to get him what he wants than any form of bluffing or deception will.

CHAPTER SUMMARY

In this chapter, we have discussed the primary factors that negotiators consider when they decide whether particular tactics are deceptive and unethical. We have included this chapter because we believe that the negotiation process raises several critical ethical issues. Much of what has been written on negotiating behavior has been strongly normative about ethics and has prescribed "shoulds" and "should nots." We do not believe that this approach facilitates the understanding of how negotiators actually make decisions about when and where to use specific tactics. To understand this process better, we have approached the study of tactic choice from a decision-making framework, examining the ethical overtones of these choices. We also briefly discussed the ways in which negotiators can respond to another party who may be using deceptive tactics.

We began by considering several negotiation cases, showing how ethical questions can be critical to the selection of particular strategic and tactical options. We then presented four fundamental views of ethics, and showed how each of these approaches was tied to a fundamental approach to ethical reasoning, and how each might be used to make decisions about what is ethically appropriate in negotiations.

We proposed that negotiators who choose to use an unethical tactic usually decide to do so to increase their negotiating power. Power is gained by manipulating the perceived

BOX 7.5
Is There Such a Thing as an "Honest Face"?

Though people in general are not particularly good at spotting lies, some people continue to believe that they can tell by looking into someone's face if that person is inclined to be dishonest or truthful on a regular basis. But how accurate are such assessments?

A study asked participants to view photographs of the same people as children, adolescents, and adults and to rate their attractiveness and honesty based on an assessment of their faces. These results were compared to self-reports of honest behavior provided by the people in the photographs. The results demonstrated that structural qualities of the face, such as attractiveness, "babyfaceness," eye size, and symmetry each individually contributed to perceptions of greater honesty in observers. The self-reports revealed that men who looked more honest early in life actually were more honest as they grew older. On the other hand, women whose behavior was less honest when they were young grew to appear more honest as they aged, even though their behavior did not change significantly. Study participants were able to correctly identify the most honest men in the group as they aged, but their assessment of women was largely inaccurate. The researchers concluded that men's faces accurately reflected their tendency toward honesty, but women's faces were not particularly valid indicators of their truthfulness.

SOURCE: Adapted from L. A. Zebrowitz, L. Voinescu, and M. A. Collins, "Wide-Eyed and Crooked-Faced: Determinants of Perceived and Real Honesty across the Life Span," *Personality and Social Psychology Bulletin* 22 (1996), pp. 1258–69.

base of accurate information in the negotiation, getting better information about the other party's plan, or undermining the other party's ability to achieve his or her objectives. We then presented a simple model of ethical decision making (Figure 7.1). After describing this simple model, we showed how a variety of individual differences and contextual factors may affect the decision to use marginally ethical tactics. We also reported the results of a building stream of research findings that help us understand how negotiators view these tactics, and the individual and situational factors that may predispose their use.

Research on negotiator ethics and on various aspects of this model leads us to the following conclusions:

1. While individual negotiators may disagree as to which negotiating tactics are ethical and which are unethical, the research reported here suggests that there is much more convergence than might have been expected.

2. The decision to use a deceptive tactic can probably best be understood through a decision-making model. It is clear that many individual differences and situational variables are also likely to affect that decision.

3. In deciding to use a deceptive tactic, a negotiator is likely to be more heavily influenced by (*a*) his or her own motivations, (*b*) expectations of what the other negotiator will do, and (*c*) the expected future relationship between the negotiator and the other party.

4. Negotiators who have considered the use of deceptive tactics in the past or who are considering their use in the future should ask themselves the following questions:

   (a) Will they really enhance my power and help me achieve my objective?

   (b) How will the use of these tactics affect the quality of my relationship with the other party in the future?

   (c) How will the use of these tactics affect my reputation as a negotiator?

   Negotiators frequently overlook the fact that, although unethical or expedient tactics may get them what they want in the short run, these same tactics typically lead to diminished effectiveness in the long run.

CHAPTER 8

Social Context:
Relationships and Representatives

We have described the negotiation process as though it occurred between two parties who materialized from nowhere, came together to do a deal, and disappeared. This is clearly not the way actual negotiations unfold. Negotiations occur in a rich and complex social context that has a significant impact on how the parties interact and how the process evolves.

Several social context factors affect negotiations. Major ones include (we draw here on Thompson, Peterson, and Kray, 1995; and Rubin and Brown, 1975):

1. the number of parties and the relationships among those parties;
2. the social knowledge and goals of the parties (what the parties want, what they know about each other, and what their outcome objectives are);
3. the social norms that govern the negotiation (group and cultural norms and practices);
4. the communication processes that the parties use;
5. the informal rules that govern their interaction; and
6. the physical environment and the cultural context in which a negotiation takes place.

In this chapter, we will focus on the first of these context factors—the nature of relationships among and between negotiating parties. Our treatment of relationships will come in four major sections. First, we examine how adding negotiators makes the social environment significantly more complex and dynamic, and thus changes the negotiation. Second, we examine how the parties' past relationship or expectations of a future relationship affect the negotiation process. This discussion considers general assumptions that have been made about the theory and practice of negotiation— assumptions that have not taken into account any relationship between the parties—and provides a critical evaluation of the adequacy of negotiation theory for understanding and managing negotiations within relationships. We present a taxonomy of different kinds of relationships and the negotiations that are likely to occur within them. We also broadly describe research studies that have examined negotiation processes within existing relationships. Third, we look at two major themes—trust and justice—that are particularly critical to effective negotiations within a relationship. In the third and final part of this chapter, we consider contexts in which negotiators are representing the interests of other parties—what we call the agency relationship. We examine the ways that negotiations change when negotiators are representing the interests of others rather than arguing for their own interests. Within this larger context, individuals and groups attempt to exert both direct and indirect pressures on negotiators to advocate their interests. A second dimension of complexity, therefore, is the type of influence strategies that negotiators use, and the different types of influence attempts that occur as the number of parties increases.

Our discussion of other context factors will continue in subsequent chapters. In Chapter 9 we will examine negotiations when there are multiple parties at the table—negotiating either for themselves or on behalf of others. We will discuss the dynamics of coalitions and the ways in which multiparty groups work together to negotiate complex decisions and agreements. In Chapter 11 we consider the important role played by nationality and culture in shaping negotiations, and in Chapter 13 we examine how the availability and use of various third parties can create strong contextual dynamics that will affect the negotiation process.

THE NUMBER OF PARTIES IN A NEGOTIATION

An important aspect to consider in negotiation is how the number of parties affects the dynamics of negotiating. In any given negotiation, there are at least two parties. The following are the basic possible roles for parties in a negotiation:

1. *A negotiating dyad.* The simplest social structure in a negotiation occurs when two isolated individuals negotiate for their own needs and interests. Each member of the dyad is responsible only for stating and defending his or her own positions and needs, and for working with the other party to arrive at an agreement.

2. *Agents and constituencies.* Often a negotiator is not acting for himself but for others. We will call the negotiator in such situations an *agent* and the individuals he is representing a *constituency.* A constituency is one or more parties who have designated someone else (the agent) to represent their positions and interests in a negotiation. Two common examples of an agent and constituent are an attorney and a client, and a salesperson and a boss or company. Constituencies usually do not participate in the actual negotiations (although they may be present); rather, they choose representatives both to advocate their interests and to report accurately on what has transpired during the deliberations. We will consider the dynamics of agent negotiations in more detail later in this chapter.

3. *Additional negotiators.* In some instances there are more than two negotiators. If a family is trying to decide where to spend a summer vacation, each party—Mom, Dad, the two children, and Grandma—has his or her own preferences and priorities. Although each is responsible for stating only his or her own positions and needs, the agreement has to reflect the views of all parties (some parties with low status or power may be forced to go along with the agreement by the others). When there are more than two negotiators, there is a strong possibility that some parties will form alliances, searching for strength in numbers or in the coincidence of their interests. As the number of negotiators increases, the likelihood of finding common ground and thereby satisfying all interests usually decreases. (We will discuss the dynamics of multiparty negotiation in Chapter 9.)

4. *Negotiating teams.* Negotiation can occur between teams of negotiators. A *team* is two or more parties on the same side who are collectively advocating the same positions and interests. The *intra*team dynamics (e.g., whether some members have more power or status than others) will affect the *inter*team negotiation process. We will discuss interteam negotiations to a limited degree later in this chapter and offer a broader treatment of both intrateam and interteam dynamics in Chapter 9.

5. *Unrepresented bystanders and audiences. Bystanders* are those who may have some stake in a negotiation and who care about the substantive issues or the process by which a resolution is reached. Negotiators do not formally represent bystanders, but bystanders frequently follow the negotiation, express public or private views to the negotiators about the potential outcomes or the process, and in some way are affected by what happens. An *audience* is any individual or group of people who are not directly involved in or affected by a negotiation but who have a chance to observe and react to the ongoing events and who may at times offer input, advice, or criticism to the negotiators. Bystanders and constituencies can also serve as audiences. So, too, can members of negotiating teams who are not actively engaged in dialogue with the other party. We will discuss the roles played by audiences and bystanders later in this chapter.

6. *Third parties.* Finally, third parties are bystanders who may be drawn into the negotiation specifically for the purpose of helping to resolve it. Third parties often can reshape a polarized situation into a constructive agreement. Bystanders can be effective as third parties if they have the necessary skills and are seen as neutral. We will examine the key roles played by third parties in Chapter 13.

It is important to understand that although we have attempted to distinguish these different roles, negotiating parties may in fact take on more than one role during the course of a negotiation. We will now explore the structural dynamics of the different roles, first examining the simplest form (two individual negotiators) and then examine how the social structure becomes more complex as additional parties and roles are added.

NEGOTIATING THROUGH OTHERS WITHIN A RELATIONSHIP

Negotiations become more socially complex as the number of participants increases. Social context may play an important role, however, even when there are only two negotiatiors. At this point we will shift the focus and examine the ways in which the negotiation changes when it occurs within an existing relationship.

The Adequacy of Past Theory and Research for Understanding Negotiation within Relationships

Traditionally, researchers studied the negotiation process in two ways. On the one hand, studies of actual negotiations with real negotiators occurred in field situations such as labor relations (Douglas, 1962) and international relations (Ikle, 1964). On the other hand, some researchers brought case studies into the research laboratory. They created simple conflict and negotiating games and simulations, found college students to be willing research participants, and began exploring negotiating problems and situations under controlled laboratory conditions. This latter research tradition has persisted for over 40 years for several reasons. First, this type of research is easier to do than field research; it is far simpler to create a bargaining game and administer questionnaires than to study live negotiators in the middle of a real but complex and often bitter negotiation. It is also difficult to get parties who are in an intense negotiation to allow researchers to do interviews, ask questions, observe, and so on. Second, some research can only be done under controlled laboratory conditions, because one could never manipulate the key variables in an actual negotiation. Thus, if one wanted to study whether making threats increased antagonism in negotiation, one could hardly ask some negotiators in actual negotiations to make threats while others did not, since it would not be genuine behavior if that is not what the parties are predisposed to do. Finally, compared to field situations, the laboratory context allows researchers to collect data more efficiently, institute controls to make sure extraneous factors are eliminated or held constant, and be far more confident about the reliability and validity of the results.

However, there are three serious problems with the laboratory research tradition. The first is that most of our negotiation theory has been drawn from studies using a limited set of bargaining games and classroom simulations. Second, this theory has been extensively used for *prescriptive* purposes; thus, rather than just describe what people do in negotiations (real and simulated), many books (including this one) have used that theory to guide negotiators about what they should do and how they should negotiate. Third—and most problematic—there is a major difference in context between the research laboratory and actual negotiations. In the research laboratory, the subjects (usually college students who don't know one another) are typically brought in, given questionnaires, put in a game or situation, paid, debriefed, and sent home. However, most actual negotiations—business, international, personal, or otherwise—occur between negotiators who have an established relationship. Only recently have researchers begun to examine how our understanding of negotiations must change in order to offer effective prescriptive advice about negotiation situations where the parties have a substantial history and anticipate a long future relationship.

Sheppard and his colleagues (1995; Sheppard and Tuchinsky, 1996a) identified the inadequacy of existing theory to explain negotiation within ongoing relationships. For example, Sheppard and Tuchinsky note the following situations:

> A recently married couple discuss whose parents they will be spending Christmas vacation with. Procter & Gamble and WalMart discuss who will own the inventory in their new relationship. Price Waterhouse discusses a cost overrun with an extremely important audit client. Members of a new task force discuss their new roles only to discover that two wish to serve the same function. Each of these discussions could be modeled quite well as a single issue, distributive negotiation problem. There are two parties: A single, critical dimension and opposing positions. A great portion of each discussion will entail searching for the other's walkaway point and hiding of one's own. But the discussions are also more complicated than the single distributive problem. (pp. 132–33)

The authors note that researchers have usually tried to apply transactional negotiation theory to negotiations in a relationship context. Transactional negotiation theory is based on studies of how people behave in simple marketplace transactions, such as a laboratory-based buyer/seller simulation. In these transactions, the parties have no prior personal relationship or experience with each other and do not expect to have any in the future. There are aspects of relationships, however, that could dramatically change our understanding of negotiation strategy and tactics. As Sheppard and others note:

1. *Negotiating within relationships takes place over time.* In Chapter 4, we noted that one way of turning a distributive negotiation into an integrative one is for the parties to take turns in reaping a benefit or reward. Within a relationship, parties can do this easily. Husband and wife can agree to visit each other's parents on alternate holidays. Negotiators in a laboratory bargaining game cannot agree to do this because their relationship ends when the game is over. Hence, time becomes an important variable in negotiating in relationships; understanding how parties add or trade off issues over time may be critical to managing difficult situations.

2. *Negotiation is often not a way to discuss an issue, but a way to learn more about the other party and increase interdependence.* In a transactional negotiation, the parties seek to get information about each other so they can strike a better deal. People ask questions, listen carefully, test out ideas about the other's position or interests, and then use the resulting information to either maximize individual or joint gain. In a relationship, gathering information about the other's ideas, preferences, and priorities is often the most important activity; this information is usually used to enhance the party's ability to coordinate activities and enhance the ongoing relationship. As a result, "integrative bargaining within a relationship is directly about the people or functions or firms, not about concepts that can be isolated from the parties" (Sheppard and Tuchinsky, 1996a, p.157). Parties may use integrative negotiation processes as a way to learn and understand the other's thinking, work habits, mode of operation, and so on. As we will point out later in this chapter, learning about the other is central to developing trust, which is often the glue that holds relationships together, particularly in difficult circumstances.

3. *Resolution of simple distributive issues has implications for the future.* While time can be an asset, it can also be a curse. The settlement of any one negotiation issue can create undesired or unintended precedents for the future. How Procter & Gamble handles one inventory question may have implications for how similar inventory questions are handled in the future. Alternating visits to their parents in the first two years does not mean the married couple can never change the visitation schedule or that they have to take turns on every issue on which they disagree. But they may have to discuss explicitly when certain precedents apply or do not apply.

Negotiators may not only set precedents, or blueprints for how similar issues should be resolved in the future, but also shift the nature of the future relationship, particularly around power and dependence. The more that the parties learn about each other, the more they may become vulnerable or dependent on each other. Parties may have originally come together because they discovered they could help each other in important ways; in some cases, however, one party can begin to depend too much on the other. For example, if Acme Company is having a difficult time with a challenging manufacturing problem, it may decide to form a strong relationship with one of its very large customers, Battle Corporation, which knows how to solve the problem because of its experience with similar problems in other suppliers. But Battle may insist that Acme sell all of its product to Battle in order to make sure that Battle can benefit from helping Acme with its problem. Acme is now in a dependent relationship; it cannot go back to the market to other customers unless Battle agrees, and its dependence on Battle may lead its costs to rise, its quality to drop, or its competitiveness to decline. Acme will now be highly vulnerable as the demand for its product shifts, as technology changes, or as Battle begins to try to control other strategic issues in Acme's business. This is not an uncommon problem for "big" customer companies, such as one of the Big Three auto makers, or "small" supplier organizations whose entire viability as a business may depend on the whims of that big customer (Sheppard and Tuchinsky, 1996b; Yoshino and Rangan, 1995).

Because distributive negotiations now have implications for the future, negotiators can develop "reputations" based on past behavior. Glick and Croson (2001) created five reputation types (Liar/Manipulator, Tough but Honest, Nice and Reasonable, Cream Puff, and No Reputation) and presented them to students in a negotiation course. For 78 percent of the students, the other's reputation was a significant element in the strategy they used. Reputations also tended to dictate the type of strategy a negotiator used. Against a liar/manipulator, 61 percent of negotiators used distributive tactics and 10 percent used integrative tactics; against tough negotiators, 49 percent used distributive tactics and 35 percent used integrative tactics; against nice negotiators, 30 percent used distributive tactics and 64 percent used integrative tactics; while against cream puff negotiators, 40 percent used distributive tactics and 27 percent used integrative tactics.

4. *Distributive issues within relationship negotiations can be emotionally hot.* If one party feels strongly about the issues or the other acts provocatively, the parties can become angry with each other. Expressing that anger clearly makes negotiating over other issues difficult. The parties may say things they don't mean, hurl blame and accusations at each other, cut off discussions, and even refuse to speak further. At a minimum, the parties may have to cool off or apologize before they can proceed. In extreme cases, the parties can continue feuds for years, carrying emotional baggage from one fight to another that never gets resolved and never permits them to talk about the important substantive issues. Many failed negotiations that show up in the court system—from small-claims cases to major organizational and international disputes—share a common history of bad feeling, failed communication, or a complete breakdown in the ability of the parties to solve their problems.

5. *Negotiating within relationships may never end.* One of the advantages of negotiating in a game or simulation is that there is a defined end. In fact, many participants in laboratory negotiating experiments may develop a specific strategy for

how they are going to play the endgame; often, cooperative strategies are abandoned in favor of getting the other on the last move. In many relationships, however, negotiations are never over. This may have several consequences:

• *Parties may defer negotiations over tough issues in order to start on the right foot.* If the married couple thought their relationship would be over in two years, they would make sure they each got what they wanted while they were married; in addition, they would probably negotiate a very specific agreement about who was to get what when the relationship was over. (Aware of the rising divorce rate in many countries, many couples intending to marry are increasingly turning to complex, legally binding prenuptial agreements.) But if the couple expect the marriage to last forever, they may simply mingle all of their assets and property in the hope that everything will work out in the future. Even if they suspect that they could have a huge fight over property if the marriage soured, they may not wish to raise the issue because talking about it might somehow contaminate the love they have for each other.

• *Attempting to anticipate the future and negotiate everything up front is often impossible.* Two young entrepreneurs who decide to go into business together can't possibly anticipate where their common efforts will take them or what issues they should consider if they decide to separate in five years. At best, all they can do is pledge to communicate with each other and discuss problems as they arise.

• *Issues on which parties truly disagree may never go away.* As we suggested above, some negotiations in relationships are never over. Two roommates who have different standards of cleanliness—one is neat, the other messy—may never settle the question of whose preference is going to govern the living arrangements in their apartment. The messy one will always be disposed to leave things out and around, while the clean one will always be bothered by things left out and around. As long as they live together, the issue may confront them, even though they may go through a range of different possible solutions as they try to accommodate each other.

6. *In many negotiations, the other person is the focal problem.* A well-known prescriptive theory of integrative negotiation teaches that in order to be effective, negotiators must separate the person from the problem (Fisher, Ury, and Patton, 1991). But what happens if the other person is the problem? Return to some of our earlier examples: When one combines emotion-laden issues with people who have major differences in values or preferred lifestyles, there is a recipe for a fight that goes beyond a single-issue negotiation. In the situation of the two roommates, the neatnik's passion for cleanliness may lead her to see the other's messiness not as a simple problem of lifestyle differences, but as intentional and even provocative: "She leaves a mess because she knows how angry I get when this place looks like a dump! She does it just to spite me!" This is no longer a problem of how often to clean, or of whether one cares enough to tolerate the other's idiosyncrasies; this is now a problem of one party seeing the other as spiteful and provocative, causing the problem simply by her very coexistence in the living space. While the parties might

engage in extensive efforts to depersonalize the problem and find lasting solutions, the very fact that one party's existence, preferences, lifestyle, or behavior irritates the other often creates an intractable negotiation problem for which permanent separation or relationship dissolution is the only solution.

7. *In some negotiations, relationship preservation is the negotiation goal, and parties may make concessions on substantive issues to preserve or enhance the relationship.* A potential resolution to the "person-is-the-problem" negotiation is that one or both parties may actually make major concessions on substantive issues simply to preserve the relationship. Parties in traditionally distributive market transactions usually make concessions by starting high or low on an issue and moving toward the middle. Even logrolling concessions can be fairly well understood, because the parties equate their benefits on two separate issues and then trade one off against the other. However, it is difficult to understand how parties trade off the value of the relationship against specific goals on tangible issues. Suppose I have a used car that has a market value of $5,000. However, I decide to sell it to my mother, who needs a car only for occasional trips around town or visits to her grandchildren. How does one set an appropriate target or walkaway price when selling a car to one's mother? This is not a simple market transaction! Can I convince my mother that I should treat her the same way I would treat a buyer off the street? Can I convince *myself* of that? Clearly, the value I place on the past and future relationships between my mother and me will dictate the answer to that question at least as much as (and quite possibly far more than) the market value of the car.

In summary, we have identified several issues that make negotiating in relationships different from and more challenging than conducting either distributive or integrative negotiations between parties who have no past or intended future relationship. It is not always clear how the prescriptive lessons learned from market transactions apply to negotiation within relationships. Both negotiation theory and prescriptions need elaboration and refinement to take into account the importance of ongoing relationships (for example, see Box 8.1). We now turn to defining some of the parameters of relationships that make negotiations within them complex and challenging.

Forms of Relationships

Having identified a number of shortcomings with existing negotiation theory as it may apply to negotiations within relationships, we need to examine the properties of relationships that may affect how negotiations evolve.

Relationships can be described in many ways. The field of social psychology has studied relationships extensively and found several ways to describe them (Holmes and Murray, 1996; Kelley et al., 1983; Reis and Patrick, 1996; Rusbult and Van Lange, 1996). A characteristic of most relationships is that each party has a causal influence on the other party's behavior. How people react to that influence depends on what type of relationship they have (see below). Following Sheppard and Tuchinsky (1996b), we define the word *relationship* as a "*pairing of entities that has meaning to the parties, in*

BOX 8.1
Three Rules for Negotiating a Relationship

International negotiation expert Jeswald Salacuse (1998) suggests three important rules for negotiating a relationship:

- *Don't rush prenegotiation.* Spend ample time getting to know the other party, visiting with him, learning about him, and spending time with him. This process enhances your information gathering and builds a relationship that may include trust, information sharing, and productive discussions. In particular, North American executives have a tendency to rush through things in order to get down to business, which compromises this critical stage for relationship building.

- *Recognize a long-term business deal as a continuing negotiation.* Change and uncertainty are constants in any business deal. The discussions do not end when the contract is signed; the discussions continue as the parties perform according to the contract, and often have to meet to work out problems and renegotiate specific parts of the agreement.

- *Consider mediation or conciliation.* Finally, consider the roles that can usefully be played by third parties. A third party can help monitor the deal, work out disagreements about contract violations, and assure that the agreement does not go sour because the parties cannot resolve differences in interpretation or enforcement.

SOURCE: Adapted from J. Salacuse, "So, What's the Deal Anyway? Contracts and Relationships as Negotiating Goals," *Negotiation Journal* 14, no. 1 (1998), pp. 5–12.

---

which the understood form of present and future interactions influences their behavior today" (p. 354). Two key assumptions accompany this definition: (1) the parties have a history and an expected future with each other that shapes the present interaction, and (2) the link between the parties themselves has meaning (i.e., the relationship contains more than simply what each individual brings to it).

Four Fundamental Relationship Forms.   A clear representation of the types of social relationships is presented by Fiske (1991). Fiske argues for four fundamental forms: communal sharing, authority ranking, equality matching, and market pricing. He defines them as follows:

1. *"Communal sharing* is a relation of unity, community, collective identity, and kindness, typically enacted among close kin" (Fiske, 1991, p. ix). People are bound to one another by feelings of strong group membership; common identity; and feelings of unity, solidarity, and belonging. Collective identity takes precedence over individual identity. The group is the most salient thing; a communal-sharing relationship is based on natural, generous, spontaneous feelings of kindness toward each other, which often derive from a sense of common root, bond, or blood. Such relationships are found in families, clubs, fraternal organizations, and neighborhoods.

2. "*Authority ranking* is a relationship of asymmetric differences, commonly exhibited in a hierarchical ordering of status and precedence, often accompanied by the exercise of command and complementary displays of deference and respect" (Fiske, 1991, p. ix). People follow the principles of organizational hierarchy; higher ranks dominate lower ranks. An authority-ranking relationship is one of inequality, in which high-ranked people control more things or people than others do, and are often thought to have more knowledge or mastery. Control in such relationships is not accomplished by coercion (force) but by legitimate authority, in which those of lower rank submit willingly to those of higher rank (see Chapter 6). Examples include subordinates to bosses, soldiers to their commander, and negotiators to their constituents.

3. "*Equality matching* is a one-to-one correspondence relationship in which people are distinct but equal, as manifested in balanced reciprocity (or tit-for-tat revenge), equal share distributions or identical contributions, in-kind replacement compensation, and turn-taking" (Fiske, 1991, p. ix). People in such relationships see each other as equal and separate, but often interchangeable; each is expected to both contribute equally to others and receive equally from others. Such a process is often best represented as turn taking (where each person does the same function in turn), in-kind reciprocity (where each is expected to give the same and receive the same), or "distributive equality" (where each is expected to receive the same portion or allocation of outcomes). Equality-matching relationships occur within certain teams or groups whose members have to work together to coordinate their actions (recall the example of the roommates and their housekeeping earlier in this chapter).

4. "*Market pricing* is based on an (intermodel) metric of value by which people compare different commodities and calculate exchange and cost/benefit ratios" (Fiske, 1991, p. ix). The values that govern this kind of relationship are determined by a market system. Things are typically measured in some single calibration system, such as utility points or dollars, and exchanges are measured in some ratio of price to goods. In this kind of relationship, people see others as interchangeable; they will deal with anyone who can provide the same goods and services for the same price. In market-pricing relationships, parties can attempt to change the ratio of price to goods in their own favor (maximize their utility) or they can seek what may be defined as a fair price. Examples can be drawn from all kinds of buyer–seller transactions.

The power of Fiske's (1991) typology is that it is a universally applicable grammar of pairs that can be used to understand social dynamics within and across societies around the world. Fiske demonstrates how this typology may be used to understand how people in different societies create and exchange things, make choices, create different social orientations, and make judgments. His definitions are foundational to understanding different social motives that drive relationships, such as power, achievement, equality, and affiliation. Moreover, it is important to understand that *two parties may enact more than one form in their relationship.* As Sheppard and Tuchinsky (1996b) note, a brother and sister may engage in all four relational forms, depending on whether they are discussing the value of a toy one borrowed from the other and then broke, taking turns doing undesirable household chores, running to get a Band-Aid when the other gets hurt, or pulling seniority to claim certain privileges not accorded the other.

Returning to our earlier critique of negotiation research, it is clear that much of the work has been dominated by the assumptions of a market-pricing relationship, a model heavily influenced by the work of economists, game theorists, and social psychologists with an exchange view of interpersonal behavior (Blau, 1964; Kelley, 1966). In the market-pricing paradigm, parties negotiate a price for a commodity, and how parties enact strategy and tactics consistent with this form of exchange is well understood. Far less is known about how negotiations occur within the other three grammars. For example, while considerable negotiation research has occurred in an organizational context (authority ranking), which shows that people with greater authority usually direct those with less authority rather than negotiate (but see Chapter 6), parties with a low level of authority can wield other forms of influence. Similarly, negotiation within a communal-sharing relationship might focus most heavily on discussions of the way in which the group members define and shape their common bond, goals, or identity. Finally, one might expect that negotiations in an equality-matching relationship might consist of discussions about what constitutes equivalence in outcomes, contributions, or resources, particularly when it is impossible to determine objectively true equivalence in treatment for all. Sheppard and Tuchinsky (1996b) suggest that a great deal is known about interpersonal transactions in market-pricing and authority-ranking grammars, but that a better understanding of such transactions in the communal-sharing and equality-matching forms is badly needed.

Dimensions of Relationships.   While Fiske and others have worked to elaborate on the characteristics of different types of relationships within different social contexts (e.g., see Clark and Mills, 1979; Mills and Clark, 1994), other researchers have explored the key features of relationships between parties in a dispute. Greenhalgh (2001; Greenhalgh and Chapman, 1996) defines the word *relationship* as "the meaning assigned by two or more individuals to their *connectedness* or coexistence" (p. 179). These researchers examined features of relationships to which people attend when involved in a dispute. From interview data, Greenhalgh and Chapman derived a list of 14 key components that characterized different kinds of relationships and grouped these components into four key dimensions (see Table 8.1).

Greenhalgh and Chapman's work focuses discussion on the key factors that can affect negotiations in relationships. First, most of the elements can be either unidirectional or symmetrical. For example, A can feel positive affect for B even as B feels no affect for A, or they can feel strongly about each other. Second, the presence of these qualities is likely to affect how the parties negotiate, and, conversely, a negotiation is likely to have impact on these factors. For example, the level of trust between parties is likely to affect whether a particular event has no effect on a negotiation or intensifies it. Similarly, the event may also lead to an overall increase or decrease in trust between the parties. Finally, each relationship is going to differ on the configuration of these qualities, which will then affect how the parties approach negotiation. For example, if we consider only four major dimensions of relationships (level of attraction, level of rapport,

TABLE 8.1   Four Key Dimensions of Relationships

Major Dimension	Key Components
Attraction	Affect: liking the other person Stimulation: experiencing the other as intellectually challenging Commonality: sharing things in common Romantic interest: being physically attracted to the other
Rapport	Trust: reliability, interpersonal integrity, and altruism Disclosure: openness with which the parties deal with each other Empathy: ability to see something from the other party's viewpoint Acceptance: unconditional positive regard for the other Respect: a view of the other as possessing a strong value system and being committed to it
Bonding	Alliance: loyalty as opposed to suspicion, wariness, and so on Exchange: tangible benefits the parties derive from their association with each other Competitive dynamics: degree to which the parties get competitive with each other (competitiveness undermines the relationship)
Breadth	Scope of the relationship: how large the domain of the relationship is (how many different ways the parties know each other and interact) Time-horizon: a focus on relationship as an ongoing entity with a past and a future

SOURCE: Adapted from L. Greenhalgh and D. Chapman, "Relationships between Disputants: Analysis of Their Characteristics and Impact," in Sandra Gleason, ed., *Frontiers in Dispute Resolution and Human Resources* (East Lansing: Michigan State University Press, 1996).

level of bonding, and breadth of relationship), and assume that high versus low levels are possible on each dimension, and also consider whether the other party has the same or a different perspective, we have 32 different combinations of qualities than can affect the way any given negotiation evolves.[1]Admittedly, the major dimensions may not be completely independent (e.g., high positive attraction is also likely to lead to high rapport), but one can easily see how the number of relationship profiles can multiply quickly and become unmanageable.

Negotiations in Communal Relationships

Most negotiation research has been done in the context of the market-pricing or simple exchange relationship. There has been a limited amount of negotiation research in communal-sharing relationships (see Tuchinsky, 1998, for one review). However, studies have shown that, compared to those in other kinds of negotiations, parties who are in a communal-sharing relationship (or who expect to have future interaction):

---

[1]2 levels of attraction × 2 levels of rapport × 2 levels of bonding × 2 levels of breadth × 2 kinds of orientation to the other.

- Are more cooperative and empathetic (Ben-Yoav and Pruitt, 1984b; Greenhalgh and Gilkey, 1993).

- Craft better quality agreements (Sondak, Neale, and Pinkley, 1995).

- Focus their attention more on the other party's outcomes as well as their own (Loewenstein, Thompson, and Bazerman, 1989).

- Focus more attention on the norms that develop about the way that they work together (Macneil, 1980).

- Are more likely to share information with the other and less likely to use coercive tactics (Greenhalgh and Chapman, 1996; Greenhalgh and Kramer, 1990).

- May be more likely to use compromise or problem solving as strategies for resolving conflicts (Dant and Schul, 1992; Ganesan, 1993).

- Are more likely to use indirect communication about conflict issues and develop a unique conflict structure (Tuchinsky, 1998).

It is unclear, however, whether parties in close relationships produce better solutions than other negotiators do. Several studies found that parties who did not have a close relationship produced better integrative solutions (Fry, Firestone, and Williams, 1983; Thompson, Peterson, and Brodt, 1996). It may be that parties in a relationship may not push hard for a preferred solution in order to minimize the conflict level in the relationship, or alternatively may sacrifice their own preferences in order to preserve the relationship (Barry and Oliver, 1996; Tripp, Sondak, and Bies, 1995). Senge (1990) and Argyris and Schon (1996) suggest that this process may be best described as balancing inquiry and advocacy (see Box 8.2).

KEY ELEMENTS IN MANAGING NEGOTIATIONS WITHIN RELATIONSHIPS

Trust and justice are two elements that become more critical and pronounced when they occur within a negotiation. In this section, we discuss how the effects of these elements become intensified in negotiations within relationships.

Trust

Many of the scholars who have written about relationships have identified trust as central to any relationship (Greenhalgh, 2001; Greenhalgh and Chapman, 1996; Tuchinsky, Escalas, Moore, and Sheppard, 1994). McAllister (1995) defined the word *trust* as "an individual's belief in and willingness to act on the words, actions and decisions of another" (p. 25). There are three things that contribute to the level of trust one negotiator may have for another: the individual's *chronic disposition* toward trust (i.e., individual differences in personality that make some people more trusting than others); *situation factors* (e.g., the opportunity for the parties to communicate with each other adequately); and the *history of the relationship* between the parties.

Many researchers have explored trust in negotiation (e.g., Butler, 1991; Kimmel, Pruitt, Magenau, Konar-Goldbaud, and Carnevale, 1980; Lindskold, Bentz, and Walters,

---

BOX 8.2
Balancing Inquiry with Advocacy

Researchers have studied how to minimize interpersonal conflicts in working relationships and how to resolve them effectively when they do arise. They suggest that the key is to balance advocacy skills—what most managers are trained to do—with inquiry skills—the ability to ask questions—in order to promote mutual learning. Guidelines for balancing inquiry and advocacy include the following:

When advocating your own view:
- make your reasoning explicit
- encourage others to explore your view
- encourage others to provide different views
- actively inquire into others' views that differ from your own.

When inquiring into others' views:
- state your assumptions clearly and acknowledge that they are assumptions
- share the "data" on which your assumptions are based;
- don't ask questions if you are not genuinely interested in the others' responses.

When you arrive at an impasse:
- ask what logic or data might change their views;
- ask if there is any way you might jointly design a technique that might provide more information.

When you or others are hesitant to express views or experiment with alternative ideas:
- encourage them (or yourself) to think out loud about what might be making it difficult;
- if mutually desirable, jointly brainstorm ideas about overcoming any barriers.

SOURCE: Adapted from L. A. Hill, "Building Effective One-on-One Work Relationships" (Harvard Business School Note 9-497-028); and P. Senge, *The Fifth Discipline: The Art and Practice of the Learning Organization.*: (New York: Doubleday Currency, 1990).

1986; Schlenkler, Helm, and Tedeschi, 1973; Zand, 1972, 1997). As one might expect, research has generally shown that higher levels of trust make negotiation easier, while lower levels of trust make negotiation more difficult. Similarly, integrative processes tend to increase trust, while more distributive processes are likely to decrease trust. However, a problem with much of the research in this area is that it tends to view trust as a simple, unidimensional construct characteristic of market exchanges (Kimmel et al., 1980; Tedeschi, Heister, and Gahagan, 1969). In contrast, relationships are complex, multifaceted, changing over time, and often grounded in compatibility of personalities, interpersonal styles, and values. Therefore, it would appear likely that more complex models of trust are needed to understand whether trust in a close communal relationship is the same as the trust which occurs in an arm's-length market transaction.

Lewicki and Bunker (1995, 1996) proposed a three-stage developmental model of trust. They suggest that relationships of different depths (closeness) will be characterized by the different types of trust: calculus-based trust, knowledge-based trust, and identification-based trust.

Calculus-Based Trust.   Calculus-based trust is concerned with assuring consistent behavior: It holds that individuals will do what they say because (*a*) they are rewarded for keeping their word and preserving the relationship with others, or (*b*) they fear the consequences of not doing what they say. Trust is sustained to the degree that the punishment for not trusting is clear, possible, and likely to occur. Thus, the threat of punishment is likely to be a more significant motivator than the promise of reward.

This form of trust is most consistent with the market-pricing form of relationships or with the early stages of other types of relationships. In this context, the trustor basically calculates the value of creating and sustaining trust in the relationship relative to the costs of severing it. Compliance with calculus-based trust is often assured both by the rewards of being trusting (and trustworthy) and by the threat that if trust is violated, one's reputation can be hurt because the injured person will tell others about one's lack of trustworthiness and integrity.

Knowledge-Based Trust.   The second form of trust, knowledge-based trust, is grounded in knowing the other sufficiently well so that one can anticipate and predict his or her behavior. Knowledge-based trust relies on information about the other rather than the management of rewards and punishments. It develops over time, largely because the parties develop a history of experience with each other that allows them to predict whether each will act trustworthily or not. Information contributes to the predictability of the other, which contributes to trust. The better one knows the other party, the more accurately one can predict what he or she will do (Kelley and Stahelski, 1970).

Regular communication and *courtship* are key processes in the development of knowledge-based trust (Shapiro, Sheppard, and Cheraskin, 1992). Regular communication places the parties in constant contact with each other so that they can exchange information about wants, preferences, and approaches to problems. Without regular communication, one loses touch with the other, which limits one's ability to predict his or her preferences and reactions. "Courtship" is behavior designed to learn more about the other and to develop the relationship. The other is courted by interviewing him or her, watching the other perform in social situations, and learning how others view him or her. Courtship permits actors to gain enough information to determine whether they can work well together. This kind of trust is not necessarily broken by inconsistent behavior. As long as behavior can be explained adequately or understood based on deeper knowledge, people are willing to accept actions by the other (even if they create costs), talk about breakdowns of trust if they occur, and move on in the relationship. Lewicki and Stevenson (1998) offer the following:

> Consider the example of two friends who agree to meet at a restaurant at 6 P.M. Alan fails to show up until 6:30 and Beth is kept waiting. To the degree that their friendship is based simply on calculus-based trust, Beth will be angry at the high costs she must incur for being "stood up," be upset at Alan's unreliability, and may be angry enough to terminate the relationship.

If they are operating more on knowledge-based trust, however, Beth will tolerate Alan's behavior to the degree that she can muster some adequate explanation for his behavior—"He must have gotten stuck at work," or "He is caught in heavy downtown traffic," or "He is always running behind and that doesn't bother me because I know he will get here eventually."

Identification-Based Trust.   The third type of trust is based on identification with the other's desires and intentions. At this level, trust exists because the parties effectively understand and appreciate each other's wants; this mutual understanding is developed to the point that each can effectively act for the other. Identification-based trust thus permits a party to serve as the other's agent in interpersonal transactions (Deutsch, 1949). The other can be confident that his or her interests will be fully protected, and that no surveillance or monitoring of the actor is necessary. As both knowledge and identification develop, the parties not only know and identify with each other but come to understand what they must do to sustain the other's trust. One comes to learn what really matters to the other, and comes to place the same importance on those behaviors as the other does. This is the type of trust one might expect to see developed in communal-sharing relationships, or market-exchange relationships that transform into communal-sharing ones. Parties affirm strong identification-based trust by developing a *collective identity* (a joint name, title, logo, etc.); *co-locating* (living together in the same building or neighborhood); *creating joint products or goals,* such as a new product line or a new set of objectives; and *committing to commonly shared values,* such that the parties are actually committed to the same objectives and can substitute for each other in external transactions. A suitable metaphor for identification-based trust may be a musical one, such as "harmonizing" or "jamming." Great identification-based trust can be seen in all kinds of teams. When people can anticipate each other's actions and intentions and flawlessly execute a great symphony, a complex surgery, a spectacular touchdown, or an alley-oop pass to the basket with no time left on the clock, we see the product of strong, positive identification-based trust.

Stagewise Development.   Lewicki and Bunker (1995, 1996) proposed that trust develops through these three stages, but will vary depending on the relationship. In a market-based transaction, trust does not proceed beyond the calculus-based stage. In a long-term business relationship, the parties need to develop some knowledge-based

Dilbert © UFS. Reprinted by permission.

TABLE 8.2   Actions to Increase Different Forms of Trust in Negotiations

How to Increase Calculus-Based Trust

1. Create and meet the other party's expectations. Be clear about what you intend to do and then do what you say.
2. Stress the benefits of creating mutual trust. Point out the benefits that can be gained for the other, or both parties, by maintaining such trust.
3. Establish credibility. Make sure your statements are honest and accurate. Tell the truth and keep your word.
4. Keep promises. Make a commitment and then follow through on it.
5. Develop a good reputation. Work to have others believe that you are someone who has a reputation for being trusting and acting trustworthily.

How to Increase Knowledge-Based Trust

1. Have frequent interaction with the other. Meet often. Get to know the other.
2. Let the other learn about you. Tell him or her about yourself. Be transparent.
3. Build familiarity with the other. See him or her in a variety of situations and contexts. Learn each other's thoughts and reactions, likes and dislikes, reasons for doing what you do.
4. Be predictable. Help the other understand how you will respond to certain situations, and then act in that manner. Learn to predict how the other will respond.

How to Increase Identification-Based Trust

1. Develop similar interests. Try to be interested in the same things.
2. Develop similar goals and objectives. Try to develop similar goals, objectives, scenarios for the future.
3. Act and respond similar to the other. Try to do what you know he or she would do in the same situation.
4. Stand for the same principles, values, and so on. Hold similar values and commitments.

---

trust; as they do, they probably also develop some identification-based trust grounded in positive feelings for each other and compatibility of interests and values. In a close personal relationship, the parties are interested in developing both strong knowledge-based trust and high levels of positive attraction to each other. However, based on information or perceived incompatibilities, trust development may slow down or be arrested at any stage. In addition, cheating behavior and other trust violations may drive trust back down to the calculus-based stage. If they are too dramatic and severe, the violations may lead one or both parties to break off the relationship altogether.

Trust Building and Negotiations.   Lewicki and Stevenson (1998) use these concepts to suggest clear action strategies for negotiators who wish to build trust with another party. These strategies are summarized in Table 8.2. Note that if a negotiator is beginning a relationship with another party, or expects that the relationship with the other party will be no more than a market transaction, then the negotiator need only be concerned about developing and maintaining calculus-based trust. However, if the negotiator expects that the relationship could develop into either a long-term market relationship or a communal relationship, then the negotiator should establish calculus-based trust and also work to establish knowledge-based trust by engaging in activities that will encourage information sharing between the parties. However, this process cannot be rushed, nor can it be one-sided. While one party can initiate actions that may move the trust-development process forward, the strongest trust must be mutually developed at a pace acceptable to both parties. Finally, if the parties are negotiating within a relationship in which some trust is already assumed to exist, then each will be making a judgment about the current level of trust and the amount and type of conflict the relationship can handle.

Justice

The second major issue in relationships is the question of what is fair or just. Again, justice has been a major issue in the organizational sciences; individuals in organizations often debate whether their pay is fair, whether they are being fairly treated, or whether the organization might be treating some group of people (e.g., women, minorities, people from other cultures) in an unfair manner.

As research has shown,[2] justice can take several forms:

- *Distributive justice* is about the distribution of outcomes. Parties may be concerned that one party is receiving more than he or she deserves, that outcomes should be distributed equally, or that outcomes should be distributed based on needs (Deutsch, 1985). For example, Benton and Druckman (1974) have shown that outcome fairness is often determined in a distributive negotiation as the point midway between the opening position of the two parties (what is often known as a "split-the-difference" settlement). The presence of such an obvious settlement point appears to increase both concession making and the likelihood of settlement (Joseph and Willis, 1963).

- *Procedural justice* is about the process of determining outcomes. Parties may be concerned that they were not treated fairly during the negotiation, that they were not given a chance to offer their point of view or side of the story, or that they were not treated with respect. For example, people who do not feel that their recent performance appraisals gave them credit for several new workplace innovations are likely to have strong complaints about the procedure (Greenberg, 1986).

- *Interactive justice* is about how parties communicate with each other. Research has shown that people have strong expectations about the process of communication with another party, and when those standards are violated parties feel unfairly treated. Bies and Moag (1986) argue that when the other party practices deception, is not candid and forthcoming, was rude, asks improper questions, makes prejudicial and discriminatory statements, or makes decisions or takes precipitous actions without justifying them, negotiators feel that fairness standards had been violated.

---

[2] See Sheppard, Lewicki, and Minton (1992) for one review of justice issues in organizations, and Albin (1993) for a commentary on the role of fairness in negotiation.

- Finally, *systemic justice* is about how organizations appear to treat groups of individuals. When some groups are discriminated against, disfranchised, or systematically given poorer salaries or working conditions, the parties may be less concerned about specific procedural elements and more concerned that the overall system may be biased or discriminatory in its treatment of certain groups and their concerns.

Given the pervasiveness of concerns about fairness—how parties view the distribution of outcomes, how they view the process of arriving at that decision, or how they treat each other—it is remarkable that more research has not explicitly been done on justice issues in negotiation contexts. Several authors have studied how the actions taken by third parties are particularly subject to concerns about fairness (see Karambayya, Brett, and Lytle, 1992; also see Box 8.3). Justice issues are also raised when individuals negotiate inside their organizations, such as to create a "unique" or specialized set of job duties and responsibilities. These "idiosyncratic deals" have to be managed effectively in order to make sure that they can continue to exist without disrupting others' sense of fairness about equal treatment (see Box 8.4).

Finally, while we have identified these forms of justice (distributive, procedural, interactive, systemic) as separate entities, they are often closely related. For example, many researchers have noted the relationship between procedural and distributive justice (see Brockner and Siegel, 1996, for one review). Thus, parties who feel that a given outcome is unfair are also likely to see that outcome as coming from an unfair procedure, and vice versa. Perceptions of distributive unfairness are likely to contribute to parties' satisfaction with the result of a decision, while perceptions of procedural unfairness are likely to contribute to the parties' dissatisfaction with the result or with the institution that implemented the unfair procedure (see Cropanzano and Folger, 1991).

Summary

In this section, we have examined two core elements common to many negotiations within relationships: trust and justice. Trust issues are central to relationships. While some amount of trust exists in market-transaction negotiations, trust is more critical to communal-sharing relationships in which the parties have some history, an anticipated future, and an attachment to each other. In addition, justice concerns are absolutely central to negotiation in relationships. Negotiations between many parties—husband and wife, business partners, or nations such as those in the Middle East—focus heavily on both fair solutions to distribution problems and fair processes for resolving those disputes.

Finally, although we have reviewed these issues separately, it is clear that they relate very strongly to one another. For example, Brockner and Siegel's (1996) review found that when one party feels the other has acted fairly in the past or will act fairly in the future (give fair outcomes), he or she is much more likely to trust the other. In addition, several theoretical and empirical works have shown that when parties are unfairly treated, they often become angry and retaliate against either the injustice itself or those who are seen as having caused it (Greenberg, 1990; Sheppard, Lewicki, and Minton, 1992; Skarlicki and Folger, 1997). Trust and justice are central to relationship negotiations; we cannot understand negotiation within complex relationships without prominently considering these issues.

BOX 8.3
Fairness in Negotiations

Researcher Cecilia Albin (1993) has examined the role that fairness plays in negotiations. She has noted the following:

1. Fairness in dispute resolution is not a uniquely Western idea. However, cultures differ in the way they determine what is fair.

2. Fairness concerns may be more prominent in some types of disputes, particularly those situations where the benefits and costs of various solutions are not easily distributed among the parties. Thus, negotiations over highly scarce commodities, environmental issues, arms control, family conflicts, or ethics may be rife with fairness issues.

3. Several "structural" factors contribute to judgments about whether a given negotiation is fair or not. These include:
   (*a*) The number and type of parties at the table. For example, ongoing negotiations between Israelis, their Arab neighbors, and the Palestine Liberation Organization have often focused on which parties should be at the table.
   (*b*) The issues to be negotiated, how they appear on the agenda, and whether some issues can be linked to other issues or treated separately. Again, in the Middle East dispute, the linkage of land with peace has been a constant source of tension among the parties.
   (*c*) Rules and codes of conduct for how the negotiations will proceed, how the agenda is constructed, who can communicate, how the role of the media is managed, who is to have voting privileges, and what the time limits are.
   (*d*) The negotiation setting, such as where the negotiation takes place, who has access to information and technical support, and how open the negotiation should be to public scrutiny.

4. Parties will often search for obvious ways to determine what will be a fair outcome. For example, this may be the midpoint in the range defined by the parties' opening offers. When there is no obvious midpoint or settlement point, the parties instead may negotiate the process by which such an outcome can be determined. This may mean negotiating the rules or procedures by which a fair outcome can be selected (e.g., negotiating to decide that a coin flip or a third party will determine the outcome).

5. In integrative negotiations (see Chapter 4), fairness is often one of the most important criteria for deciding on particular settlements or solutions. As the parties discuss interests and invent options, they are often also negotiating joint standards of fairness, and then using these standards to test the viability and acceptability of particular solutions (Fisher, Ury, and Patton, 1991; Lax and Sebenius, 1986).

6. Many negotiations will also require a negotiation about which fairness principles should apply to a particular situation. For example, two boys may agree to paint a neighbor's garage together and to split the money they get paid. One boy winds up doing about two-thirds of the work. The boy who worked harder will probably argue that he should receive two-thirds of the money; the boy who worked less hard may argue that their initial agreement was to split their pay evenly, and that the rule should not be changed. Many negotiations over tough issues (environmental issues, scarce resources, etc.) focus specifically on which outcome-distribution rules should apply in a given situation.

SOURCE: C. Albin, "The Role of Fairness in Negotiation," *Negotiation Journal* 9 (1993), pp. 223–43.

BOX 8.4
The Idiosyncratic Deal: Flexibility versus Fairness

Professor Denise Rousseau of Carnegie Mellon University has long studied the changing nature of employment relationships and "psychological contracts" between employees and employers. In a recent article, she discussed the "idiosyncratic deal"—the unique ways that employers may come to treat certain employees compared to others in the same office or environment. Many idiosyncratic deals are now "negotiated" in the workplace (e.g., educational leaves, flextime, working at home, working on one's own separate project while on the job, doing volunteer work on company time). While idiosyncratic deals were once available only to individuals with long seniority or to jobs with more discretionary job descriptions, Rousseau observes that idiosyncratic deals are much more common today, and not reserved only for a special few. Thus, while idiosyncratic deals are a new source of flexibility and innovation in the workplace, they also raise major concerns about fairness and consistent treatment of classes of employees. Here are some observations about idiosyncratic deals:

1. They are more common when workers:
   - are highly marketable (e.g., have a good BATNA in the job market);
   - are willing to negotiate;
   - have strong market and business knowledge;
   - are located in small or start-up firms;
   - work in more knowledge-oriented firms (specialize in information or services rather than specific products).
2. They are more common in certain countries, such as the United States, the United Kingdom, and New Zealand.
3. Idiosyncratic deals are more likely to work effectively when:
   - there is a high quality relationship between the worker and manager;
   - responsibilities and role requirements are well understood and accepted;
   - performance criteria are clear and well specified;
   - workers trust the performance appraisal process;
   - there is shared understanding of performance criteria among coworkers;
   - coworkers have mutually supportive relations;
   - coworkers trust the manager;
   - when flexibility is limited, legitimate reasons are stated and clear. Such deals are viewed as a source of innovation that can be shared and adopted by others in the firm.

SOURCE: D. Rousseau, "The Idiosyncratic Deal: Flexibility vs. Fairness?" *Organizational Dynamics* 29, 4 (2001), pp. 260–73.

USING REPRESENTATIVES

We now shift our focus to negotiations within another type of relationship: the *agency* relationship. As we noted above, the previous discussion focused on situations where all parties participated in the negotiation, and when the relationship between the negotiators may have been more of a market-pricing and/or communal-sharing one. We shall now consider the roles played by those parties who are not active participants but whose interests are represented by an agent, who will be affected by the outcome achieved by the agent, or who are observing the negotiating process and perhaps offering comments, critiques, or evaluations of the process or outcome. Under such conditions, the chief negotiators will redirect some of their behavior away from the other negotiator and toward these other parties. We will broadly describe the attention paid to the additional parties—regardless of who they are—as *audience effects.*

In this section, we will first examine the different types of audiences that can exist in negotiation and the consequences that audiences have on the agent's behavior. We will then examine the different ways in which agents can manage audiences so as to be more effective in persuading the other party.

Audiences: Team Members, Constituents, Bystanders, and Audiences

There are many different kinds of audiences and audience effects. Initially, we will include all the roles delineated above—negotiating team members, direct constituents, observers or bystanders, and even neutrals (with the sole exception of the focal negotiators themselves)—as audiences because they all tend to serve the function of observers, commentators, and/or stakeholders relative to the focal negotiators' behavior. As we begin to delineate the different roles and functions that audiences play, we will make distinctions among these different roles.

One form of audience is the *additional team members* who are present with the negotiator at the deliberations. Members of a negotiating team may take on one or more important roles: chief spokesperson, expert or resource person on a specific issue, advocate for a particular subgroup with a stake in the outcome, legal or financial counsel, statistician or cost analyst, recorder, or observer. Team members may agree to play a special role in negotiation, but they may also shift into another role as the negotiation evolves. The most frequent role shift is from being the chief negotiator to being a passive observer who is silent while others are speaking. The observer may be taking notes, listening to the discussion, preparing to make comments to be introduced later on, or simply evaluating and judging the actions of those who currently hold the floor. Negotiators also direct their comments toward observers on the other side. So, for example, while a member of one team (chief spokesperson) may appear to be talking directly to a member of the other team (the other chief spokesperson), the purpose of the conversation may be to influence the other team's legal expert (also at the table) on some point. It is important to recognize that team members can play multiple roles because their audience role can do as much to influence and shape a spokesperson's behavior as what the opposing negotiator says or does. Figure 8.1 represents a simple negotiation between two pairs of negotiators—on each side, one may be the primary spokesperson while the other assists, but they may change roles at any time.

FIGURE 8.1   Each Negotiator with a Partner

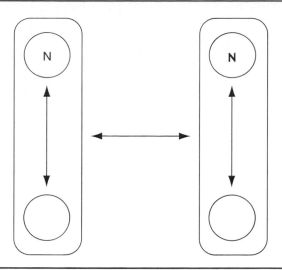

FIGURE 8.2   Negotiator with Constituent versus Other Negotiator

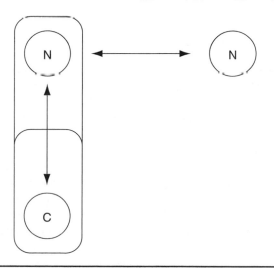

Another type of audience is a direct *constituency*. A constituency is one or more parties whose interests, demands, or priorities are being represented by the focal negotiator at the table. The term *constituency* usually applies to politics; elected officials are usually accountable to the voters who elected them (their constituency). For attorneys or accountants or consultants, their constituents are their clients. The social structure of this negotiation is represented in Figures 8.2, 8.3, and 8.4. In Figure 8.2, the negotiator

FIGURE 8.3   Negotiator with Constituent versus Other Negotiator

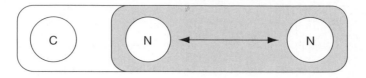

FIGURE 8.4   Negotiator with Several Constituents versus Other Negotiator

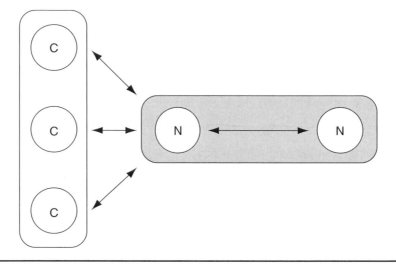

has a constituent who is also a team member; in Figure 8.3, the negotiator represents a constituent who is outside of the negotiating setting; in Figure 8.4, the negotiator represents a group of constituents.

As the figures suggest, negotiators with constituencies are involved in two distinctly different relationships—and often in two separate and distinct negotiations. The first relationship is with the constituency—the negotiator and constituency decide on their collective view of what they want to achieve in the negotiation and the strategy and tactics of how to get it. The constituency then delegates some power and authority to the negotiator to pursue the goals and strategy through negotiation. Constituents expect that the negotiator will accurately and enthusiastically represent their interests in the deliberations, periodically report back as negotiations evolve, and finally report back the outcomes at the end of the process. Constituents therefore expect to profit (or lose) as a direct result of the negotiator's effectiveness, and they often select their agent based on his or her ability to achieve their goals.

The second relationship is with the other party—in this relationship, the negotiator and the other party attempt to reach a viable and effective resolution. Reaching a resolution may require the negotiator to compromise on the goals set by his or her constituency

FIGURE 8.5   Negotiators Representing Constituencies with Input from Audiences

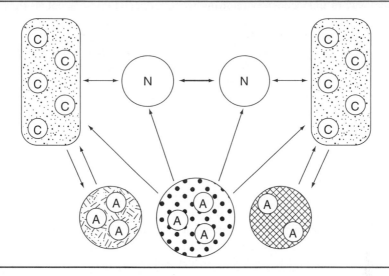

and then to explain and justify those compromises back to the constituent. Because they may be unable to both completely satisfy their constituent and achieve a resolution satisfactory to the other party, representing a constituent creates unique pressures and conflicts for agents. We will have a great deal more to say about these pressures and conflicts later in this chapter.

A third type of audience is composed of external *bystanders* and *observers*. Remember that negotiating team members themselves can act as bystanders and observers. In addition there are often many "pure" bystanders whose interests are not directly represented in the negotiation but who are affected by the negotiation outcome or have a vantage point from which to observe it and some strong need to comment on the process or the emerging outcome. Figure 8.5 represents this most socially complex environment for a negotiation.

A situation that includes bystanders and observers not only offers a context in which many parties are watching and evaluating the negotiation, but also offers many ways for the negotiator to use the audience to bring indirect pressure to bear on the other negotiator. We will examine some of the most common tactics later in this chapter.

Characteristics of Audiences and Bystanders.   We can describe the major characteristics of audiences in several ways (compare Rubin and Brown, 1975). First, audiences vary according to whether they are physically *present at* or *absent from* the negotiation. Some observers (like team members) may be present during negotiations and directly witness the events that occur; others may be physically removed and learn about what happens only through reports and accounts. Whether an audience is present or absent will affect how a negotiator behaves; he or she may say one thing with the audience present and another with the audience absent. In addition, when audiences are absent, negotiators must report what happened in the negotiations; when the audience has no real way of independently knowing what happened, these accounts may not be fully truthful or complete.

Second, audiences can be dependent or nondependent on the negotiators for the outcomes derived from the negotiation process. Audiences who are *outcome-dependent* derive their payoffs as a direct result of the negotiator's behavior and effectiveness. In a labor contract, the amount of salary increase for each union member (constituent as audience member) will be a direct result of the effectiveness of the chief negotiator and the negotiation team. In contrast, a *nondependent* audience will not be directly affected by the results. Although members of the general public may be interested in a contract arrived at by union and management, they will be less directly affected by the settlement.

A third major way in which audiences affect negotiations is by the *degree of their involvement* in the process. Audiences may become *directly* involved in the negotiation process; when they do, the complexity of the interaction increases in a number of ways, depending on who the audience is, what is at stake, how much power the audience has, and what kind of a role the audience chooses to play. In international affairs, the United States has often become involved in some other country's or region's local disputes— the Middle East, Eastern Europe, the former Yugoslavian republics, and emerging African nations. U.S. involvement has occurred in almost every form and variation— from expressing a preference for a particular strategy, process, or outcome, to attempting to facilitate negotiations and work out internal difficulties, to becoming militarily involved and either taking sides or keeping parties separate to help achieve a peaceful resolution. As the principal world superpower following the fall of the Soviet Union, the United States is often a directly involved third party in international affairs.

Audiences also give periodic feedback to the negotiators, evaluating their effectiveness and letting them know how they are doing. Feedback may be verbal, in the form of notes, messages, letters, or personal conversations and advice; or it may be nonverbal, in the form of smiles and nods of affirmation or scowls and frowns of disapproval. Feedback may be directed toward the positions that a negotiator has taken, concessions she has made, agreements she has arrived at, or the manner in which she behaved during the deliberations.

In contrast to this direct involvement, audiences may become *indirectly* involved in the negotiation. Indirect involvement occurs when audiences make their own wishes and desires known (through communication of their ideas) but do not directly try to influence the course of an ongoing negotiation. Again, there are examples in international negotiations as well as labor and political disputes. The United States often makes its views known on how other countries should conduct their affairs but does not directly try to influence those actions. Consumers are often encouraged to boycott a store or product (e.g., grapes, lettuce) to express their sympathy for a labor union and back its demands. Indirect communication also provides a large amount of feedback to the other party, indicating the degree to which the audience approves or disapproves of the agent's words and actions.

Audiences may vary in a number of other ways: identity (who they are and what they stand for); composition (the number and type of different points of view represented); size (which may affect how much power they can have); relationship to the negotiator (emotional ties, amount of informal control they can exercise over the negotiator); and role in the negotiation situation (readiness to try to influence directly the negotiator's behavior, style, or content of communication). In short, as soon as the negotiation setting is expanded to three or more parties, the nature and complexity of their interaction increase. Audiences play several different roles and attempt to shape the progress of negotiation in a variety of different ways. In addition, as the relationship among parties changes from market transaction to some other form, the negotiation issues, strategies, and processes may change as well.

Before we discuss audiences in more detail, we will summarize the most important principles about audiences and the significant ways in which they influence the negotiator's choice of tactics.

Audiences Make Negotiators "Try Harder."   Research has shown that the presence of an audience (a constituency) increases a negotiator's aspirations—that is, the negotiators "try harder" when they know they are being watched. Merely being aware that they are under surveillance can motivate negotiators to act tough (Benton and Druckman, 1974). In one experiment, Carnevale, Pruitt, and Britton (1979) told some subjects in an experimental negotiating situation that they were being watched by their constituents through a one-way window, while others believed they were not being watched. Negotiators who believed they were under surveillance were significantly more likely to conduct their negotiations in a distributive bargaining manner and to use threats, commitment tactics, and put-downs of their opponents to gain advantage (refer to Chapter 3). They were in turn less likely to pursue integrative bargaining strategies, and they obtained lower joint outcomes than negotiators not under surveillance.

Negotiators Seek a Positive Reaction from an Audience.   The presence of an audience motivates a negotiator not only to "try harder," but to seek a positive evaluation from the audience and to avoid a negative evaluation (Gruder and Rosen, 1971). Thus, aspirations are increased because the negotiator is trying to impress the audience to receive a beneficial evaluation. When questioned later about their behavior, negotiators under surveillance said they felt that it was more important to look tough and strong, and as a result they were less likely to make concessions that would facilitate mutual gain. As a result, negotiators under surveillance are likely to be less yielding and will take longer to reach an agreement on their own behalf (Benton and Druckman, 1974).

Pressures from Audiences Can Push Negotiators into "Irrational" Behavior.
In addition to the mere presence of an audience, the presence of a *salient* audience—one valued for its opinions and supportive comments—affects a negotiator even more dramatically. A classic study by Brown (1968) reveals the power of feedback from a salient audience on a negotiator's subsequent behavior. In Brown's experiment, high school students played a competitive negotiation game with someone they thought was another student, but who was in fact an ally of the experimenter playing a preprogrammed strategy. In all cases, the preprogrammed strategy was aggressive and exploitative—thus, the students lost a lot in the early part of the game. The students then received contrived feedback messages from a group of their "peers" (whom they

thought had been observing the first round), telling them either that they looked weak and foolish as a result of the way that they had been exploited in the first game, or that they looked good and strong in the first round because they had played fair. Students then played a second round of the game, during which they were given the choice of using either a retaliatory strategy to get back at the opponent who took advantage of them (a strategy that would also cost them a great deal of money to execute), or a second strategy that did not involve retaliation, thus ignoring the challenge to their self-esteem created by the negative messages from the audience. The experiment, therefore, required the subjects to choose between pursuing a strategy that allowed them to make money but lose face (image and self-respect) in front of the audience or retaliating against the opponent and restoring their image with the important audience, but at great personal cost. As Brown summarized,

> The results were striking: publicly humiliated subjects—those who received the derogatory feedback—were far more likely to retaliate, and with greater severity and self-sacrifice—than subjects who received the more favorable feedback. . . . Of special interest is the fact that when asked why they chose severe retaliation, 75 percent of the subjects who did so reported that they didn't want to look foolish and weak as a result of having been exploited, and that they retaliated in order to reassert their capability and strength. (Rubin and Brown, 1975, p. 45)

In a follow-up study, Brown tested whether knowledge of the costs of retaliation was important in getting subjects to engage in retaliatory behavior. In one variation, the audience knew how much personal cost the subject endured in order to retaliate. In a second variation, the audience did not know the costs. The results of these two variations demonstrated clearly that retaliation was greatest when the audience told the subject that he looked foolish *and* the audience did not know how much it cost the subject to retaliate. Brown's research points to the classic face-saving dilemma for negotiators: to preserve one's image to an audience, often at high costs not known to the audience, or to lose face but conserve resources. The research clearly shows that a bargainer is most aggressive when there is a high need to regain a positive image with an audience who does not know the amount it costs the negotiator to do so.

Brown's study has several important implications for understanding the power of an audience over a negotiator. First, the student subjects in the study did not know the specific identity of anyone in the audience—only that they were from the same high school. The student negotiators never saw the audience, which was only vaguely identified as an important group. Thus, audiences who are viewed only as a somewhat important group to please can nevertheless exert powerful influences over a negotiator's behavior by simply telling the negotiators that they look weak and foolish. A second finding is that some students retaliated against the other party even when there was no audience present. This suggests that the opposing negotiator may act as an audience as well. Negotiators who believe that the opposing negotiator has caused them to look foolish or has evaluated their behavior as weak and ineffective may try to regain a positive evaluation, even from an adversary. Anyone who has ever played a supposedly friendly game of tennis, golf, Ping-Pong, or basketball with some competitive friends will recognize that much of the banter, teasing, and verbal harassment that occur is designed to undermine the opponent's self-confidence or to challenge him or her to play better. All of this is usually done with good-natured humor; yet the banter can quickly turn serious if a comment is made too sharply or taken wrong, and it can both seriously unsettle the opponent and hurt the relationship. One can thus imagine the impact of a message to a negotiator from the other party that he or she was easy to beat. Not only will the bargainer be embarrassed by losing, but the embarrassment will be magnified. Such comments are the fuel for revenge and long-standing, deep-seated animosity.

Brown's research shows how important face-saving is to negotiators whose behavior is highly public, visible, and subject to a great deal of feedback from audiences. For example, in a study of sports agents who represented their clients in salary and contract negotiations, Wheeler (1999) studied the impact of this representation process on agents' perceptions of their reputations. He found that agents who felt that their reputations were at stake as part of the negotiation are more likely to take higher risks, will set higher walkaway points for the negotiation, and will be likely to have higher impasse rates than agents without their reputations at stake. Other examples come to mind from international relations, politics, and labor relations. Decades ago, President Lyndon Johnson characterized the United States' presence in South Vietnam as one of a "pitiful, helpless giant," which soon led to the massive military buildup in Southeast Asia in order to "win" a war that would not humiliate American military capability at home and abroad (but ultimately did). Not only was this effort to "free" South Vietnam ultimately unsuccessful—thus sustaining the actual loss of face that Johnson and others had dreaded—but also the loss was incurred at a phenomenal cost in dollars, military equipment, and human lives whose magnitude was disclosed to the American public only long after the war ended. More recently, strong face-challenging language was used in late 1990 between Iraqi president Saddam Hussein and U.S. president George Bush Sr., leading to Bush's escalation of the war with Iraq following its invasion of Kuwait. A decade later, following the horrific attack on the World Trade Center in New York City, U.S. president George W. Bush Jr. described an "axis of evil" promoting terrorism in the world that must be eliminated, to build support for military actions that the Unied States would take to fight terrorism.

Finally, such tragic twists to face-saving dynamics can also occur when audiences are only indirectly involved. For example, in the mid-1990s, a spokesperson for the state of Ohio's Corrections Department questioned the credibility of a group of prisoners in a prison riot who were holding hostages and threatening their safety. When asked by the press whether the prisoners' threats were real, the spokesperson dismissed the threats, stating that "prisoners threaten to kill hostages all the time." Soon after these comments, the prisoners actually killed a guard—perhaps to prove that their threat was a credible one, and to save face with their own constituents inside and outside the prison.

Audiences Hold the Negotiator Accountable.   Audiences maintain control over negotiators by holding them accountable for their performance and by administering rewards or punishments based on that performance.This accountability will occur under two dominant conditions: when a bargainer's performance is visible to the audience (so that the audience is able to judge how well the bargainer performs) and when the audience is dependent on the bargainer for their outcomes. An audience that is dependent on a negotiator's performance for their outcomes will generally insist that he or she be tough, firm, demanding, and unyielding in the struggle to obtain the best possible outcome for the constituents. Failure to perform in this manner (in the eyes of the audience) may lead to public criticism of the negotiator, with the expectation that this criticism will embarrass him or her into performing in ways that guarantee a larger payoff for the constituency.

Continued characterizations of the negotiator as weak or soft, or as someone who sells out, may lead to unfortunate but predictable outcomes. First, the bargainer may become increasingly inflexible or retaliatory to demonstrate to the constituency that he or she is capable of defending their interests. Second, the bargainer may try to be a more loyal, committed, and dedicated advocate of the constituency's preferred outcomes and priorities, simply as a way to regain their good favor and evaluation. Finally, the negotiator may be forced to resign, judging himself or herself incapable of representing the constituency's best interests. Moreover, the status of the agent does not seem to affect the pressures. High-status members of a group (e.g., senior-level managers or formally designated leaders) do not appear to negotiate more quickly, achieve fewer deadlocks in the negotiating process, or attain better solutions than low-status members (Klimoski and Ash, 1974; Kogan, Lamm, and Trommsdorf, 1972). As a result, the presence of accountability pressures leads to longer, more time-consuming negotiations than when accountability pressures are absent (Benton, 1972; Breaugh and Klimoski, 1977; Haccoun and Klimoski, 1975; Klimoski, 1972).

The effects of accountability to constituents do not have to be all bad, however. Constituents can keep negotiators from making extreme or outrageous commitments that might get them in trouble later. For example, Kirby and Davis (1998) had constituents monitor the investment decisions of managers in a simulated production game. The results of the experiment indicated that those managers were less likely than nonmonitored ones to escalate their commitment to unproductive courses of action, and less likely to pursue risky investment strategies. Thus, accountability can deter individuals from pursuing risky decisions that may have long-term destructive consequences.

Tactical Implications of Social Structure Dynamics: The Negotiator's Dilemma

The presence of an audience—particularly an outcome-dependent audience—creates a paradox for negotiators because of two sets of pressures. One set comes from the constituency, which expects the agent to be tough, firm, unyielding, and supportive of the constituency's demands. The other set comes from the opposing negotiator and from the definition of negotiation itself: that the negotiator should be flexible, conciliatory, and willing to engage in give-and-take. (See again Figure 8.5, which depicts these pressures simultaneously pushing the negotiator from opposite directions.) Cutcher-Gershenfeld and Watkins (1999) have noted that these dynamics create a dilemma of trust. In Chapter 1, we noted a dilemma of trust that most negotiator's face: how much to trust and believe what the other says (Kelley, 1966). To trust and believe everything the other says puts the negotiator under the other's control, but to trust and believe nothing the other says precludes any agreement. A comparable dilemma of trust exists between agents and constituents. Agents enter negotiations with the challenge of representing the interests of their constituents (a "pure" agent), but also bring their own interests as well. There is often a tension between how much they can pursue their own interests versus pursue the interests of their constituents, and the negotiator must decide where s/he will resolve this tension. The dilemma is that the more trust constituents put in a representative, the more autonomy and freedom the representative will feel to "create value" with other negotiators; but the more they are involved in creating value, the more difficult it will be to go back and persuade constituents that the "new" solution truly represents the original interests of the constituents.

The basic dilemma, then, is to determine how a negotiator can satisfy both the constituency's demands for firmness (and a settlement favorable to their interests) and the other party's demand for concessions (and a settlement favorable to the other party or to their mutual gain). The answer is that a negotiator must build relationships with both the constituency and the other party. On the one hand, the relationship with the constituency must be cultivated on the basis of complete support for their demands and willingness to advocate these demands in negotiation. On the other hand, the relationship with the other party must be developed through stressing the similarity and commonality of the parties' collective goals or fate, and the desirability of establishing and maintaining a productive working relationship to find a common goal. However, each of these relationships must be developed privately, outside of the visibility of the other group. Privacy assures that a negotiator can conduct deliberations with the other party without accountability pressures. Maintaining privacy may require a certain degree of duplicity by the negotiator, in that he or she must promise loyalty and dedication to each group, out of view of the others.

Typically, negotiators first meet with the constituency to define their collective interests and objectives. They then meet with opposing negotiators, in private, so that they can candidly state their constituents' expectations but also make necessary concessions without looking weak or foolish to the constituents. Finally, a negotiator returns to the constituents to sell the concessions to them, persuading them that the achieved settlement was the best one possible under the circumstances. Successful management of a constituency therefore requires that negotiators have control over the visibility or invisibility of their negotiating behavior to the constituency and to audiences. A negotiator who does not have such control is going to be on public display all the time. Every statement, argument, concession, and mistake will be in full view of an audience who may pick it apart, critique it, and challenge it as possibly disloyal. Such potential pressure is highly undesirable, and, as we have argued earlier, likely to lead negotiators to appeal to the audience rather than to find an agreement.

Managing these dilemmas is a very important but quite delicate process. In the following sections, we will try to summarize this process by offering two forms of prescriptive advice: first, to negotiators who are faced with constituency management problems and, second, to those constituencies who must manage an agent.

Advice to Negotiators for Managing Their Constituencies and Audiences

1.   Maintain Control over and "Manage" Audience Visibility.   Negotiators can control both the visibility of their behavior and the communication process with constituencies, audiences, and even the other party by employing tactics that make them appear to be highly committed to the bargaining position they support. A few of the most common tactics are described below.

Limit One's Own Concessions by Making Negotiations Visible to the Constituency.
Because negotiators who negotiate in full view of their constituencies are less likely to
make concessions than negotiators who deliberate in private, negotiators can enhance
their own visibility in order to strengthen their position. Negotiators typically go public when they want to remain firm. For example, a negotiator may insist on allowing the
constituency to be present for all negotiations, knowing that most concessions are made
when parties deliberate in private. As a result, observable negotiations are likely to limit
the agent's search for solutions, and hence are likely to increase the frequency of
impasse. They are also likely to see priority placed on issue-by-issue, short-term goals
rather than long-term interests (King and Zeckhauer, 1999; Kurtzberg, Moore, Valley,
and Bazerman, 1999).

Use the Constituency to Show Militancy.   A second way that a constituency can
be used is to make the constituency visible and let them demonstrate that they are more
extreme, radical, committed, and inflexible than the negotiator. Community groups that
want to inspire public officials to enact change often insist that the officials come to an
open meeting, in which community spokespersons confront the officials with their concerns or grievances. Those invited to speak at the meeting are often the most demanding or militant. Militants may also be specifically invited to let the other side know that
concessions will not come easily and that the only way agreement is going to be
reached (or disaster averted) is for the other party to make concessions. In addition to
intimidating the other party, this tactic can have other side benefits. First, a barely-
under-control militant constituency may not only intimidate the other party but also
allow the negotiator to seem like a nice, pleasant, reasonable person in contrast. It is
natural to prefer to deal with nice, pleasant negotiators rather than angry, militant ones.
As a result, a negotiator can look more cool, calm, and rational than the out-of-control
constituency simply through the contrast effect. If the negotiator then says, "Either you
deal with me and my demands or you work with someone else from my constituency
who is far more irrational than me," the negotiator is likely to gain significant ground
with the other party. This is a variation of the classic good cop/bad cop negotiating tactic discussed in Chapter 3.

Use the Constituency to Limit One's Own Authority.   A third way that a negotiator can use a constituency is by showing the other party that the constituency has limited the negotiator's ability to make concessions, particularly unauthorized ones. This
tactic may be used either as a bluff or because of a genuine limit on authority. As a bluff,
the negotiator leads the other party to believe that all concessions must be cleared with
the constituency. As a genuine tactic, the negotiator's constituency has actually defined
limits to what the negotiator can decide on his or her own. In banks, for example, new
loan officers may be able to approve very few loans on their own signature, whereas the
bank's senior loan officer has a wider latitude. Yet although the senior loan officers could
easily approve certain loans on their own authority, they may use the constituency (the
bank's loan committee) both for protection (to make sure that the loan is not granted
foolishly) and also to pressure the borrower into meeting certain terms and conditions.

Negotiators must be careful about revealing how much authority and autonomy
they really have. On the one hand, it might seem that limiting authority would give a
party a distinct advantage. Every minor deviation from the originally stated position

Pepper . . . and Salt

THE WALL STREET JOURNAL

**"OK, let me go pretend to talk to my
manager."**

From *The Wall Street Journal*. Used with permission of Cartoon Features Syndicate.

would have to be approved, a process that is very tedious and time-consuming. If the
other party is in a hurry, he or she may choose to make concessions to avoid the delay.
On the other hand, the tactic may backfire. Not only is it very frustrating for the other
party to wait while every minor change and concession is reviewed and approved, but it
also frustrates the agent, who may feel embarrassed by his or her powerlessness. This
mutual frustration eventually may lead to a complete breakdown in negotiations.
Because negotiation is understood as the process of making concessions toward mutual
agreement, encountering a negotiator who cannot make any concessions on his or her
own violates expectations and creates anger. This may lead the other party to demand
that the constituency send a representative who has the power to negotiate an agreement.

   Use Great Caution in Exceeding One's Authority.   The reverse side of this negotiating dilemma is that negotiators who overextend their authority or exceed the limits
set by their constituency may be unable to persuade the constituency that the achieved
settlement is a good one. This is often a problem in union–management relations, particularly when the union group is militant and has very high aspirations. After a long
and arduous negotiation, a union negotiating team reaches a tentative settlement with
management. But the union rank and file, who may have inflated expectations, reject
the proposed contract offer. This rejection vote is tantamount to a vote of no confidence
in the negotiator. Sometimes negotiators in this position resign; at other times they
return to the table with heightened belligerence to prove their toughness to their constituency, which jeopardizes the possibility of any effective agreement with the other
party. In the extreme, negotiators may be willing to endure extremely high personal
costs—a long strike, personal fines, jail sentences, and negative public opinion—to
restore their image with the constituency.

   For example, in the 1981 strike of the Professional Air Traffic Controllers Organization (PATCO) against the Federal Aviation Authority (FAA), the PATCO leader, Robert
Poli, spent several months negotiating a new package on behalf of his organization. When

the deal was finally presented to the union for ratification, 90 percent of the membership rejected the tentative contract as inadequate. So Poli returned to the FAA and attempted to gain a better package, but the FAA wouldn't budge, and after two weeks of unsuccessful debate, PATCO called a strike. The strike (illegal under the terms of the government's contract with each union member) led the FAA and the administration of President Ronald Reagan to (1) fire all the striking controllers from their jobs; (2) obtain federal injunctions and impose fines of several million dollars per day against the union and its leadership; (3) jail some union members and officials, including Poli; (4) impound the union's strike fund; and (5) ban all striking controllers from any further employment with the U.S. government, either as controllers or in any other federal job. In the early days of this confrontation, 90 percent of the union supported Poli's taking them out on strike and going to jail. Poli was put in the difficult position of either leading the union in its militant demands (and becoming a hero-martyr in going to jail for them) or affirming that the deal he struck with the FAA was a good one and being rejected by his union. As it turned out, the animosity from this dispute lingered for a long time: it was 1993 before President Bill Clinton finally declared that fired air traffic controllers could be rehired.

Increase the Possibility of Concession to the Other Negotiator by Cutting Off Visibility to Audiences. If increased audience visibility increases the likelihood that negotiators will take tougher stands, be less flexible, and make fewer concessions, then a negotiator who wishes to be more flexible and conciliatory would want negotiations to be less visible. There are two approaches to accomplishing this objective:

1. *Establish "privacy" prior to the beginning of negotiations.* In Chapter 2, we mentioned the importance of establishing negotiating ground rules before the actual process begins. One rule that should be considered is that the negotiations will be conducted in private, that no media or public interviews will be granted, and that contact with the other party's constituency (or visibility to audiences) will be strictly controlled. To keep the negotiations private, parties may select a remote location in neutral territory, where their meetings will not be too obvious or visible. When the time comes for announcements about progress or achievements, both parties can make them jointly, coordinating their communications. Needless to say, if the other party wishes the negotiations to be held in a public environment—where communication with constituencies is easy and the constituencies may actually have a direct view—setting the terms and conditions for the visibility of the negotiation will be the first item for deliberations. Given the many ways in which people can communicate these days—telephones, fax machines, closed-circuit video, and electronic mail—finding and maintaining true privacy in a negotiation can be a real challenge, but it can be done.

2. *Screen visibility during negotiations.* If negotiators have not agreed beforehand to a location that is private and secure, there are other options for screening out unwanted observers from sensitive discussions. One of the simplest ways is to have some discussions occur informally, on a strictly unofficial basis. These discussions can occur during coffee breaks, meal breaks, walks around the building, or even in the exercise room or bar of a hotel. Key representatives may agree to

meet for breakfast before the day's formal deliberations begin or for cocktails afterward. During such meetings, parties can speak more candidly off the record, or they can hint about their bottom-line position or their willingness to make certain concessions: "We've been sitting in that room for a long time, and you know, if your side is willing to name a proposal something like the following [insert the specific details here], my people would probably be willing to go along with it."

Heads of state who negotiate major arms and trade agreements are frequently photographed at dinners, receptions, or walks in the garden. Although a large portion of such functions is public and ceremonial, private time is frequently part of them as well. (Blessing's 1988 play, *A Walk in the Woods,* is an interesting re-creation of the way President Jimmy Carter shaped the Camp David accords between Israel and Egypt through a number of informal discussions with Prime Minister Menachem Begin and President Anwar Sadat.) Every formal gathering between heads of state and heads of organizations is also an opportunity for a great deal of informal contact.

In some cases, the meeting may be planned but very secretive. In one industry, for example, labor negotiations occurred every two years. Prior to the beginning of formal talks, the union president and the company president met for dinner in another city half a continent away and broadly discussed the key issues that would be raised in the negotiations. Although the union president could lose his job if the rank and file were to become aware of this meeting, both presidents considered the meeting invaluable to keeping an informal communication channel open between them and permitting them to maintain a personal connection in the midst of the confrontational negotiations that would occur for the next few months.

Other kinds of information can also be privately exchanged in these informal venues. Negotiators can grumble and complain, brag about their constituency and its support, or even let the other party overhear their conversations with their own constituents. All these tactics give the other side information about what is really possible without saying it directly during the formal negotiation.

3. *Be aware of time pressure.* Not unsurprisingly, time pressure in negotiation may also increase competitive behavior, particularly when the negotiator is accountable to a constituency. Research indicates that when negotiators are *not* representing the views of constituents, time pressure tends to make negotiators act less competitive (Mosted and Rutte, 2000). However, when negotiators are acting as agents of others, time pressure results in more competitive dynamics and a higher rate of impasse.

Establish a Reputation for Cooperation.   Finally, agents can establish a strong reputation for being cooperative, both with those they represent and with the other agent. For example, Gilson and Mnookin (1994) have suggested that lawyers can both effectively represent their clients and establish sound relationships with other attorneys:

> Our message is that the relationship between opposing lawyers and their capacity to establish credible reputations for cooperation have profound implications for dispute resolution: If the payoff structure establishes cooperation as the most desirable strategy and supportive institutional structures exist, lawyers may be able to damp conflict, reduce transaction costs and facilitate dispute resolution. (p. 564)

However, concern for reputations can create a problem for agents. Agents who feel that their reputations are at stake in a negotiation may be more likely to take risks, display more contentious behavior, set higher walkaway prices, and have higher impasse rates than agents who do not feel that their reputations are at stake (King and Zeckhauser, 1999; Kurtzberg, Moore, Valley and Bazerman, 1999).

2. Communicate Indirectly with Audiences and Constituents.   Negotiators can often manipulate the observability/accountability dynamics described above by communicating *indirectly*. Indirect communications are efforts by the negotiator to bring the opinions of audiences and constituents to bear on the other party. Although the negotiator may believe that he is well defended against the other party's arguments, he may not be able to defend himself against other people—his constituents, his friends, his superiors, or public opinion—when they appear to side with the other party. Informal communication takes place in several ways:

Communicate through Superiors.   The technique of communicating through superiors is frequently used when negotiators are representatives of two hierarchically structured organizations (e.g., a company and a union, or two companies engaged in a business deal) and when one or both negotiators are dissatisfied with the progress of negotiations or the behavior of the other party. To manage their frustration and dissatisfaction, they may go to their own superiors (who are probably not directly involved) and ask the superiors either to attend a negotiating session or, more commonly, to contact their counterpart in the opposing organization. The situation is represented in Figure 8.6. A salesperson (A) is frustrated in her negotiations with a company over a major sales contract. The buyer (D) wants a major price concession because of the volume of product being purchased. The salesperson finally talks to her boss (B), the vice president of sales, who then approaches the buyer's senior purchasing agent (C). The senior purchasing agent spends several hours describing the details of competitive bids that the company has received from other sellers and explaining why the seller must reduce the price or lose the business. So the salesperson is eventually authorized to sell the product at a considerably discounted price without losing her incentive bonus for completing the sale.

Such indirect processes work under several conditions. First, the tactic's effectiveness depends on a social structure in which the negotiator represents an organization or group that has some formal hierarchy of power—and the other party has a similar accountability structure. Negotiations between representatives of formal private- and public-sector organizations fit this description. Second, the chief negotiator cannot be the person with the most authority, such as the president, chairman, or official leader. The reason chief executives do not negotiate is *not* necessarily that they are too busy doing other things. Rather, conducting negotiations through an agent who is not the senior person allows the organization to limit its concessions by limiting the negotiator's power and authority to make decisions. Senior executives are likely to become involved only when negotiations are extremely delicate, critical, or symbolically significant to the well-being of the organization and its relationships with other organizations. Usually, much of the preliminary groundwork has been laid by subordinates and chief negotiators. In international relations, for example, contacts between nations occur on a number of diplomatic levels; the heads of state may become directly involved in only

FIGURE 8.6   Indirect Communication between Negotiators through Their Bosses

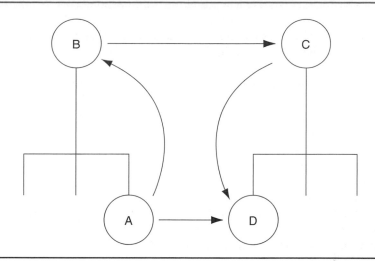

the most delicate, symbolic, or politically important negotiations. Finally, the effectiveness of the tactic depends on indirect communication originating from someone the other party trusts more or is less well-defended against. When the indirect communication comes from superiors, it may be even more effective because the communicator has high status, reputation, and visibility. Thus, in the previous illustration, confronted with a compelling case from the senior purchasing agent of the company (who, although she is still an agent of the company, is defined as a nonnegotiator), the vice president of sales may be more likely to accept and believe the financial information than if the same information were presented during the negotiation.

   Communicate through Intermediaries.   Negotiators communicate through intermediaries when they need to make informal contact with the other party, an opposing negotiator, or a constituency (see Figure 8.7). Here the approach is made through any external contact who can serve as an intermediary or communication conduit. Those selected are usually chosen for some valid reason—past experience in working together, a personal friendship or relationship, or a personal reputation for credibility, trustworthiness, impartiality, and integrity. The tactic is most often used under two major circumstances: when a negotiator wants to feel out the opposing group to attempt to gain inside information, or when deliberations are deadlocked and need to be unfrozen.

   Pruitt (1994, 1995; also see Salacuse, 1999) has proposed a branching-chain model of interorganizational negotiation. This model employs the concept of influence networks (see Chapter 6) and suggests that negotiations between organizations take place between organizational members and interested intermediaries across and within organizational boundaries. At the ends of the chains are major stakeholders, while all other members of the chain are intermediaries of one form or another (diplomats, former and current leaders, friends and allies of each key party), who try to reconcile the needs and values of the different stakeholders. Examining several cases drawn from

FIGURE 8.7   Indirect Communication through an Intermediary

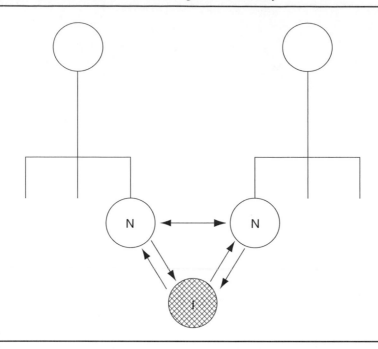

U.S. State Department negotiations, Pruitt offers a number of interesting and testable hypotheses about the ways in which chains can be mobilized to achieve negotiation goals that cannot be achieved by the stakeholders themselves.

Similar to the tactic of communicating through superiors, the effectiveness of informal contact depends on engaging the right individuals: ones who are not subject to the same accountability pressure that binds formal group representatives so they can use informal communication channels that may eventually clear blockages in the formal links.

Communicate Directly to the Other Party's Constituency.   In a third form of indirect communication (see Figure 8.8), one agent seeks to bypass the other party and communicate directly with his or her constituency to persuade those involved to change their position or the instructions they are giving their representative. The agent himself may initiate this tactic, usually when he believes that negotiations are deadlocked, that the other negotiator is not communicating effectively with her constituency, or that the other party is either not representing her constituency's interests clearly or not accurately reporting to her constituency. Thus, the agent attempts to eliminate the intermediary and communicate directly with the other's constituency. In labor–management negotiations, for example, management representatives frequently prefer to speak or write directly to the rank and file rather than go through the union leadership. The intent (and the impact) may be not only to ensure that management's position is clearly heard and understood, but also to subtly undermine the credibility and effectiveness of the

FIGURE 8.8   Indirect Communication through a Constituency

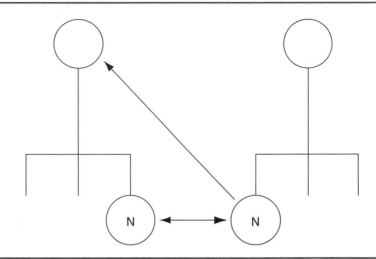

union leadership. In international relations, one country's political message may be broadcast on the other country's news media, or "propaganda" messages may be included with gifts of food, medical supplies, and the like. The tactic, of course, may also be initiated by the other negotiator. In this case, the opponent usually extends the invitation because she believes her credibility or integrity is being questioned and wants the agent to hear the message directly from her constituency.

However, it should be clear that direct communication with the other party's constituency—particularly without the sanction of the other negotiator—is likely to be viewed as an inflammatory tactic. If the other negotiator is not consulted or does not grant permission, the act of going around him or her will usually be interpreted as a hostile act. Negotiators who are undermined by their opponents in this way are likely to become defensive and rigid. The immediate impact on the negotiator's constituency, however, is less clear. They may perceive this tactic as one intended to undermine their leadership's effectiveness and respond by rallying around their leadership more strongly. At other times, particularly when a constituency may already have doubts about the effectiveness of its own representation, direct, open, accurate communication from the other negotiator may undermine confidence in their representative even further.

3. Communicate Directly to Bystanders and Audiences.   Finally, an agent may try to manipulate the opinion of bystanders (other than constituencies) and to mobilize their support, either to build up his or her own position or to undermine the other party's position (see Figure 8.9). Communication through bystanders may occur (1) as an explicit and conscious tactic to exert influence on the other party, but through circuitous channels; (2) as an effort to build alliances and support for one's own position; or (3) as a result of the natural tendency for conflict to proliferate and envelop innocent bystanders. In all cases, agents are public about their own (or their organization's) demands. They will tell

FIGURE 8.9   Negotiating through Constituents, Audiences, and Bystanders

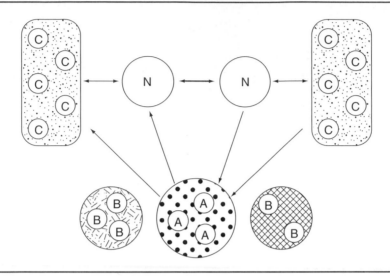

anyone who will listen how fair, legitimate, just, and appropriate their own side's position is, and how unfair, unjust, illegitimate, and inappropriate the other party's position is. The agent's hope is that unaligned parties will openly side with them (hence lending strength and credence to their arguments), and that these parties will communicate their dissatisfaction and displeasure to the other party (thus undermining the strength and credibility of the other party's arguments). (See Box 8.5 on involving constituencies.)

Communication through audiences—particularly the media—is extremely common in major interorganizational negotiations such as intergovernmental, international, or labor–management relations. Most of these deliberations are well known for having a public phase in which the negotiators primarily address their arguments to audiences rather than to one another. In this phase, the media—radio, television, and newspaper— play an integral role by serving as both an audience themselves and a communication vehicle to reach other audiences. Media relations and image management often become ends in themselves; strong negotiators can consciously stage their performance before radio microphones or television cameras in order to win public opinion to their side, which will then put pressure on the other party to concede. Note, too, that communication through the media can also be used to reach one's own constituency. The quickest and most efficient way of letting one's own constituency know the exact elements of one's negotiating posture and personal commitment to this posture is to represent that position in the media—although, admittedly, many agents have learned that the media may not get it right either. This approach is likely to be used when an agent wants to communicate firmness and toughness in a position, and not as likely to be used when the agent wants to communicate concession-making or defeat. For example, in the summer of 1998, the Starr Commission released its report on its investigation of President Bill Clinton and his relationship with Monica Lewinsky. The highly controversial decision

BOX 8.5
The Importance of Involving Constituencies in Solving Community Problems

When a regional government commission proposed to solve its budget problem by selling parklands known as the national capital area's "emerald necklace" [greenbelt], residents in affected neighborhoods feared their open space would fall into the hands of developers. They launched an all-out campaign to block this sale of the "family jewels."

Closed-door negotiations among government officials soon produced a solution that seems to have avoided the residents' worst fears while accomplishing the commission's goals of slashing costs. However, by excluding the public in crafting a solution, these behind-the-scenes arrangements may have so aroused public cynicism about this process that the regional commission would find it even more difficult to rally political support for future planning challenges.

This future failure, disguised as today's success, offers a clear lesson to public-dispute facilitators about the value of involving the public in the design of a consensus-building process.

SOURCE: From a description of a parkland dispute in Ottawa, Canada. Richard Jackman, "Back Room Politics Solve Today's Problem—but Create Tomorrow's?" *Consensus*, April 1996, pp. 1, 12.

to release the detailed and graphic commission report, videotapes, and accompanying materials to the media and the nation was defended by an anti-Clinton political group as an action necessary to convince the public that President Clinton had an affair with Ms. Lewinsky and had lied under oath about it to the commission. In contrast, most political supporters of the president saw these actions, and the subsequent impeachment trial, as an effort to cripple the president or encourage him to resign by shifting public opinion against him.

Communication may also be designed to activate and win over interested audiences who will communicate directly with the other party. In the same example, the release of the documents motivated many political leaders to put pressure on the president to resign, while others were motivated to encourage the president to withstand the media storm of outrage and embarrassment. A comparable example can be found in major addresses given by heads of state in most democratic countries. Once the head of state delivers the speech, various political leaders and all forms of special interest groups who will be affected by the key issues begin to put their spin on the speech and cast it in negative or positive terms.

The effectiveness of communicating through audiences is determined by several factors. First, the success of the tactic depends on the degree to which an audience's outcomes hinge directly on the negotiator's effectiveness and how severe the consequences are likely to be. This degree and severity of effect can vary from outcomes that directly affect the audience in a dramatic way to those that only minimally and indirectly affect the audience. If I live in Canada, a strike by farm workers in the United States may not affect me very strongly, particularly if I can purchase fruit and vegetables grown locally. On the other hand, a strike by school bus drivers in my local area is likely to affect me and my family very strongly. In addition, the farm workers' strike would not affect me if I did not eat many fruits and vegetables; in contrast, I would be greatly affected by the bus driver strike if I had three small children.

The second factor in the effectiveness of communicating through audiences is the degree to which the audience is organized as a coherent unit. An audience may be directly and seriously affected by the results of a particular negotiation but unable to exert leverage on the negotiations because they have no means for determining their collective sentiments or making decisions among themselves. Even a very large group of people is unlikely to have significant impact on the negotiations if their reaction cannot be brought to bear on the negotiators themselves. The many families who may be grossly inconvenienced by a strike of school bus drivers cannot easily organize to provide alternate transportation for all, nor can they bring much pressure on the strikers. Interestingly enough, the media are increasingly providing opportunities for such "disorganized majorities" to have a voice. The last decade has seen a dramatic rise in radio and television talk shows, featuring hosts who stir controversy over politically charged topics and provide both airtime and bait to their listening audiences. Call-in talk shows have been credited with being one of the only vehicles by which average citizens can have a say in governmental and public affairs, and in many cases they have stirred significant public support or opposition for key political issues.

Having stated that audiences cannot have impact without some form of communication leverage, we must note that the reverse is also true: Well-organized audiences can have significant effects on the outcome of negotiations even if their total number is small. The effectiveness of particular political lobbies in state and federal government of all political persuasions and special interest orientations is testimony to the strength of organization. For example, numerous public opinion polls support such government actions as gun control, political campaign financing limits, or environmental protection legislation. Lobbyists succeed according to their ability to identify and contact audience members who support their position, to mobilize these members toward a common purpose, and to bring pressure on all policy makers to engage in a concerted action to forward or block particular initiatives (through massive letter-writing and telephone campaigns, promises of financial contributions to the legislator's campaign, and so on).

Finally, appeals to audiences will be effective to the degree that the negotiator is sophisticated in the use of media relations. To someone who is naive in using the media as an effective but indirect negotiating tool, media relations may involve no more than appearing before a camera or microphone and reading a prepared statement. However, as we implied in Chapters 5 and 6, the content of one's message, particularly on television, often is considerably less important than the visual presentation and the performance. Portraying an image of confidence, control, and steadfast determination is essential. The negotiator needs to be well dressed, well spoken, and in control of the situation. Further, he or she needs to be able to respond to hostile or loaded questions effectively. Finally, an agent may wish to be surrounded by his or her constituency—the rank and file, supporters, close advisers—who will openly demonstrate their solidarity and support. Effective politicians in all industries and contexts have learned how to use the media to get their message across and win the hearts and minds of key audiences to buttress their own positions and agendas.

4. Build Relationships with Audiences, Constituents, and Other Agents.   At the beginning of this chapter, we suggested that negotiators who are intent in building or strengthening a relationship with the other party should negotiate differently than if the negotiation is a simple, one-time market transaction. The same principles are true for how negotiators should manage relations with constituents, audiences, and opposing agents. Rather than undermining the other party's support, negotiators should try to develop personal relationships with the other party. The underlying assumption should be that it is easier (and definitely more pleasant) to work with and persuade a friendly counterpart than an unfriendly one. Individuals who see themselves as similar to each other, who are attracted to each other, or who are likely to experience a common fate are more likely to change their attitudes toward each other (refer back to our discussion of source and receiver factors of leverage in Chapter 6). In addition, building a personal relationship will permit the agent to get the message across to a less defensive, less antagonistic adversary. Thus, the better the relationship between an agent and other agents, the more the final agreement will represent long-term interests rather than short-term gains (Kurtzberg, Moore, Valley, and Bazerman, 1999; McKersie, 1999).

Many of the tactics we described earlier in this chapter can be applied in this setting. Some negotiators meet informally outside the context of negotiations. Shared cocktails, a meal, or even a coffee break are obvious opportunities for promoting friendliness, easy conversation, and cordiality. When parties drop their formal negotiator roles and meet as individual people, they can discover their commonality and develop their liking for each other. The agenda for both sides is usually not to conduct formal deliberations, but to communicate openly and build some trust that will alleviate the tension and conflict inherent in formal negotiations and keep negotiations from ending in deadlock or an angry walkout.

In addition to developing a relationship based on shared personal interests or genuine liking, agents may also stress their common fate—namely, the accountability pressures put on them by their constituencies. If both agents feel strongly pressured by their constituencies, they are likely to stress their common fate as a way to build the relationship. Thus, "You and I are in this together," "We both have our constituencies to deal with," "We want to achieve the best for all of us," and "We want to develop an agreement based

on mutual respect that we can live with successfully in the future" are all statements that typify the opening stages of negotiation. Many experienced negotiators refer to these expressions of common fate as the "harmony-and-light speech." They may believe that the other party is using such expressions merely as a tactical ploy to soften them up before presenting tough demands. Although that allegation may be true, the harmony-and-light speech that opens many formal negotiations does play a critical role. Even if the speech is ritualistic, it communicates that the other party is interested in building a personal relationship. Moreover, the absence of the speech may indicate that the parties are so adamant in their positions or so angry at each other that they cannot bring themselves to make the speech. This may be a clear sign that the negotiations will be tense and are likely to become deadlocked.

A further purpose of informal meetings is to permit each party to get a sense of the other's objectives. In many negotiations, chief negotiators meet before the formal deliberations, much like the corporate and labor leaders we described earlier. The purpose of this meeting is usually twofold: to sense what the other side's major demands will be, and to develop a relationship and an open channel of communication that can be used regardless of how tense the negotiations become. Such meetings are usually held privately because publicizing the event might lead other managers or union members to view the meeting as collusion. However, some negotiators may choose to publicize the event to demonstrate a spirit of cooperation.

Finally, a strong relationship between agents should allow the negotiators to do a better job of coordinating their actions in presenting their settlements back to their constituents. The better the relationship, the better able the agents will be to present their agreement back to constituents in a way that it appears to meet both sides' interests, even if this is not truly the case (Kurtzberg, Moore, Valley, and Bazerman, 1999; McKersie, 1999).

Advice to Constituents in Managing Agents

While most of our prescriptive advice has been to the negotiator in managing one's audience and constituents, we should also spend some time describing how a constituency can effectively manage its agent. Much of this advice can be extracted from our earlier discussion of the impact of audiences on agents—the impact of competing interests, pressures for accountability and face saving, deadlines, and so on. We also draw on Fisher and Davis (1999) and their specific advice to constituencies managing agents, particularly those attempting to achieve an integrative outcome:

1. At the outset, the agent should have no authority to make a binding commitment on any substantive issues.
2. At the outset, the agent should have discretion to design and develop an effective overall negotiation process.
3. The constituent should focus most of his or her communication to the agent on interests, priorities, and alternatives, rather than specific settlement points.
4. The constituent should establish clear expectations about the frequency and quality of reporting back to the constituent.

5. The agent's authority should expand as the agent and constituent gain insight about the other parties through the negotiation.

6. Specific and direct instructions to the agent by constituents (principals) should be put in writing and be available to show to the other side when necessary.

7. The constituent should instruct the agent on exactly what the agent can disclose in negotiation—interests, ranges of acceptable settlement, key facts, the principal's identity (sometimes kept secret in business or real estate deals), and so on.

Section Summary

Sometimes negotiation is a private affair between two parties. At other times, however, there are audiences to a negotiation, and the presence of an audience has both a subtle and a direct impact on negotiations.

Three types of audiences may be encountered. First, when teams of people (rather than individuals) negotiate, the chief negotiators provide much of the actual dialogue. Although these two usually speak directly to one another, they also use their own and opposing team members as an audience. We address these dynamics extensively in the next chapter.

A second type of audience is the constituency the negotiator represents. A husband or wife negotiating for a new house represents a family, division heads on a companywide budget committee negotiate what portion of capital resources their departments will have for the coming year, sales or purchasing people negotiate for their companies, and diplomats negotiate for their countries. The audiences in each case have a stake in the outcome of the negotiation and benefit or suffer according to the skills of their representatives.

The third type of audience is bystanders. Bystanders see or hear about the negotiations and form favorable or unfavorable opinions of the settlement and the parties involved. Bystanders may or may not be indirectly affected by the course and outcome of the negotiations.

Audiences influence negotiators through two different routes. One is that negotiators desire positive evaluations from those who are in a position to observe what they have done. The other is that audiences hold negotiators responsible for the outcomes of negotiations. They can reward negotiators by publicly praising them and punish negotiators by firing them. They can intrude and change the course of negotiations—as when the public requires mandatory arbitration or fact-finding in some disputes. They make their preferences known—for example, by talking to the press—thereby putting pressure on one or both negotiators through the impact of public opinion and support.

Audiences can have both favorable and unfavorable effects on negotiations. Sometimes negotiators try to use an audience to their advantage, as when they try to pressure the other party into taking a more flexible or desirable position; they may also try to prevent an audience from having influence when they think it might be undesirable for their position. Although there are many different ways of influencing an audience, all involve controlling the visibility or communication with that audience. In this section, we suggested four basic strategies to influence audience effects:

1. Limit concessions by making actions visible to one's constituency, thereby putting oneself in a position that the other party will recognize as difficult to change.

2. Increase the possibility of concessions on the part of both sides by cutting off the visibility of negotiations from the audiences.

3. Communicate indirectly with the other negotiator by communicating with his or her audiences.

4. Facilitate building a relationship with the other negotiator by reducing visibility and communication with both parties' audiences.

We also offered several suggestions for constituents that they can use to manage their agents in negotiation. These include processes for managing agent authority, helping the agent understand the constituent's primary interests and alternatives, giving the agent discretion to manage the process, and establishing the process for frequent reporting between agents and constituents.

When negotiations move from a private to a public context, they become more complex and more formal. In setting strategy, a negotiator needs to consider whether negotiations should be held privately or involve audiences in various ways. To ignore this social context is to ignore a potent factor in determining negotiation outcomes.

CHAPTER SUMMARY

In this chapter, we explored the social environment of negotiation. Much of negotiation theory is predicated on the assumption that two negotiating parties are dealing directly with each other, and no other parties are involved. Yet much of the professional negotiation conducted in business, law, government, communities, and international affairs occurs in an environment in which there are several other parties involved. These parties take on various roles—additional negotiators, constituencies, bystanders, audiences, and third parties—and may or may not have a stake in the outcome, care about the process, or wish to make comments and observations about events as they transpire. Depending on the number of additional parties and the roles they play, a negotiation can be quickly transformed from a relatively quiet and calm dialogue to mayhem and confusion. Understanding these dynamics is critical to learning how to manage and control them so one can achieve negotiation objectives.

In addition, we cannot assume that negotiators are involved only in arm's-length market transactions about the exchange of fees for goods and services. Many negotiations take place within highly complex relationships. In this chapter, we have evaluated the status of previous negotiation research—which has focused almost exclusively on market-exchange relationships—and evaluated its status for different types of relationships, particularly communal-sharing and authority-ranking relationships. Within relationships, we see that parties shift their focus considerably, away from a sole focus on price and exchange, to also attend to the future of the relationship, the level of trust between the parties and questions of fairness. We argue that most negotiations occur within these relationship contexts, and future work must attend to their unique complexities.

We turn next in Chapter 9 to other aspects of negotiations involving relationships: coalitions and groups.

Coalitions, Multiple Parties, and Teams

In Chapter 8, we focused on the social context of negotiation and developed two major themes: (1) that negotiation dynamics become more complex when there is an ongoing relationship between the parties, and (2) that negotiation dynamics also become more complex when negotiators represent other parties. We considered negotiators as agents representing the interests of others at the table, and the dynamics between agents and their constituents. In this chapter, we extend the analysis to three situations that involve multiple parties:

1. Multiple (more than two) parties are negotiating with one another, with the parties each striving to achieve their own individual objectives. We will examine how parties ally into *coalitions* to achieve these objectives.

2. Multiple parties are negotiating with one another and attempting to achieve a collective or group consensus. We will discuss this kind of group decision making as a process of *multiparty negotiation*.

3. Multiple individuals are present on each "side" of the negotiation—in other words, the parties to a negotiation are teams rather than individuals. We will discuss this as a process of *interteam negotiation*.

Three major sections of the chapter will address each of these multiparty contexts in turn. The chapter begins, however, with an example illustrating the variations in complexity that occur when multiple parties are involved.

SITUATIONS WITH MORE THAN TWO PARTIES

A negotiation situation becomes more complex when more negotiators are added (see Figure 9.1). For example, let's consider a student who wants to sell a used stereo system. He posts a notice on the bulletin board in the student union, indicating the details about the stereo and a suggested price. Two interested students call. Let us now assume three different variations on this situation:

- In the first case, the two potential buyers are roommates. One roommate has agreed that she will do the talking and try to negotiate the best deal with the seller, while the other one stays silent but comes along for moral support.

- In the second case, the two buyers do not know each other. The seller can sell to the first one who calls, sell to the first one who shows up at his apartment, or ask the two to come at the same time and try to play the two off against each other.

FIGURE 9.1   A Seller and Two Buyers

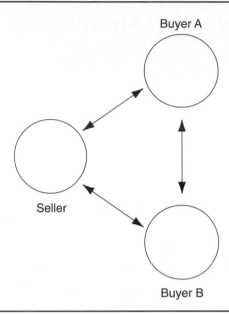

In this case, each buyer's offer on the stereo becomes the seller's alternative (Chapter 3) for the stereo (assuming the alternative offer is an acceptable one), and the seller can, in effect, auction the stereo off to the highest bidder.

- In the third case, the two buyers show up at the door together, exchange greetings, and discover that they live in the same dormitory. They also discover that they were both asked to come at the same time by the seller and figure out that the seller is probably trying to get them to bid against each other. So they agree to make a lowball offer on the stereo and not increase their bids by more than a few dollars. They hope that if they try to hold the price down but offer to pay cash on the spot, they can get the seller to get rid of the stereo now.

We now have three different variations on a three-party negotiation. The first case resembles the typical agency relationship situation we described in Chapter 8. One buyer is representing the other, and we have two negotiations occurring: one between the buyer and the seller, and one between the buyer and her roommate. In the second case, the seller is conducting a sequenced series of one-on-one transactions; he gets one to bid, then goes to the other with the bid and asks her to raise it; thus, he is using each potential buyer as his alternative while he tries to get them to compete in an auction. The seller's success in this case relies heavily on the buyers' unwillingness or inability to communicate with each other. In the third case, the seller is about to be unwittingly compromised by the buyers. Having discovered the seller's intent to get them to compete, the buyers are motivated and able to collude in order for both to hold the price down and to punish the seller for trying to structure the deal as an auction. If the buyers are successful, they may be able to purchase the stereo at a bargain price (although they still may face a nego-tiation between them over who actually gets the stereo or the terms of its use).

In the next section, we explore this third situation—what happens when the par-ties form coalitions or subgroups in order to strengthen their bargaining position through collective action.

COALITIONS IN NEGOTIATION

There has been extensive research on coalitions. Much of this work has been done in laboratory settings with experimental bargaining games or simulations of voting behavior, but some has consisted of applied studies that analyze coalition formation in real-world settings. One particularly appealing context for studying coalitions is complex organizations, where decisions are often made by coalitions of people. For example, a well-known theory of organizational governance and management (see Cyert and March, 1963; March, 1962; Thompson, 1967) refers to the group of people who direct and man-age the organization as the "dominant coalition." This usually includes those with the highest rank, such as president or executive officer, but may also include consultants, sen-ior advisors, attorneys, or others who may not have a major title but have significant influence over the organization's goals and direction.

We begin this section with an overview of what a coalition is and the different forms that coalitions take. We then analyze when and why coalitions form, how coalitions develop, the nature of coalition decision making, and the role of power and leverage in coalitions. The section concludes with some practical advice for building and maintain-ing coalitions.

What Is a Coalition?

There are a number of ways to define a coalition. Pearce, Stevenson, and Porter (1986) suggest that coalitions:

- *Are interacting groups of individuals.* People who may want the same thing but do not specifically interact (the second stereo example) are excluded from this analysis. Coalition members will communicate with each other about pertinent issues. Usually, most people in a coalition are aware of those who belong and those who do not belong.

- *Are deliberately constructed and issue oriented.* In a coalition, the parties are intentionally joining to accomplish some specific purpose that serves their inter-ests. Once interaction concerning these issues ceases to occur, the coalition no longer exists as an active entity.

- *Exist independent of formal structure.* A coalition is not necessarily a formal group, such as a department, team, or task force (whose members may unite because they have been created by design in the organization), although a depart-ment or team could informally also bond together around a common purpose or objective. But the origins of a coalition are informal, based on the interests of the parties rather than created by formal organizational designation.

- *Lack formal structure.* Since coalitions lack formal organizational designation and legitimacy, they also lack any internal hierarchy or formal legitimate authority. Informal leadership and roles may evolve as the coalition persists and grows, however.

- *Focus on a goal(s) external to the coalition.* For the most part, coalitions form to exert influence on a person or body external to the coalition. This may be another individual or group inside their organization (but who is not in the coalition), or an individual or group outside their organization.

- *Require concerted member action.* Finally, a coalition requires the commitment of the members to focus their action on an intended target collectively. The members may act in concert or may focus on refraining from action (e.g., an organized protest of some form), but the objective is to achieve collectively what they cannot accomplish individually.

An essential aspect of a coalition is that its members are trying to achieve outcomes that satisfy the *interests of the coalition, not those of the larger group* within which the coalition is formed (although at times the two may be compatible) (Polzer, Mannix, and Neale, 1998).

Types of Coalitions

Cobb (1986) points out that there are several different types of coalitions:

- A *potential coalition* is an emergent interest group. It has the potential to become a coalition by taking collective action but has not yet done so. Two forms of a potential coalition can also be identified: latent and dormant. *Latent coalitions* are emergent interest groups that have not yet formed into an operating coalition; *dormant coalitions* are interest groups that previously formed but are currently inactive. Potential coalitions can be of interest both to coalition members and to those they oppose; if one can identify what might lead a supportive or opposing coalition to form (or to invigorate a dormant one), one can select courses of action that might be more or less likely to activate that coalition.

- An *operating coalition* is one that is currently operating, active, and in place. Again, two forms are common: established and temporary. *Established coalitions* are relatively stable, active, and ongoing across an indefinite time span. They may continue because they represent a broad range of interests, because the issues are never fully resolved, or because they are in constant opposition to another established coalition that is taking action. For example, in most governmental systems there are established coalitions of liberals, conservatives, and moderates who are engaged in ongoing debates across a range of issues and involving a large cast of actors and operatives. In contrast, a *temporary coalition* operates for a short time and is usually focused on a single issue or problem. These groups form for the express purpose of exerting collective action; when their objectives are met, they disband. Often, however, people in temporary coalitions discover that they have a number of other common interests that are more persistent or long term; thus, temporary coalitions often transform into established ones.

• *Recurring coalitions* are ones that may have started as temporary but then determine that the issue or problem does not remain resolved; hence, the members need to remobilize themselves every time the presenting issue requires collective attention in the future. For example, a citizen's group that successfully opposed the location of a fast-food restaurant in a certain neighborhood may discover that the issue does not completely go away, and that they may need to remobilize when a monster gasoline station applies for a building permit on the same site.

Understanding When and Why Coalitions Form

Coalitions form all the time. In families, parents may be seen as acting in a unified front, creating major obstacles for children who want to influence them about extending curfew times or lightening the load of required household chores. Parents often align with one or more of their children in order to exert pressure on the other parent; "Go tell your mom that it would be great to visit Grandma," says Dad (who doesn't feel like making dinner that night) to the oldest son. Similarly, coalitions form constantly in political organizations (where people are mobilizing their efforts to support or oppose any number of legislative agendas) and in business organizations (where parties get together to support or oppose an action being planned by the organization's formal leadership). In each of these contexts, the fundamental dynamic is the same: parties come together to pool their efforts and resources in pursuit of common or overlapping goals.

Coalition researchers often explore these dynamics through laboratory "games" where individuals possess resources that may have to be pooled in order to realize some desired outcome. The focus is often on how individual actors can form the smallest possible "winning" coalition and the payoffs that each player can obtain from participating in that coalition (Murnighan, 1982). Control over resources is the basis for two critical pieces of the coalition formation process: what each member brings to the coalition, and what each member should receive if the coalition forms.

A Classic Coalition Game.   In order to understand when and why coalitions form, we examine a classic coalition problem: the 4–3–2 game (Murnighan, 1978, 1982). In this game, three players are given an unequal number of votes in order to collect a prize (e.g., a pool of money). Andrea (A) has four votes, Barbara (B) has three votes, and Cecilia (C) has two votes. In order to collect the prize, they must assemble at least five votes; thus, no player can claim the prize without forming a coalition with another player, and each player must use *all* her votes at once. The players can communicate with one another (sometimes by talking, sometimes only by sending written messages); their job is to determine whom they are going to ally with and then how they are going to split the prize. Not surprisingly, the most important factor that determines who aligns with whom is *how* they decide to split the money. Based on a series of research studies, Murnighan (1986, 1991; Murnighan and Brass, 1991) reports the following findings:

• The 3–2 (Barbara–Cecilia) coalition is the most common. This result usually occurs because Andrea (with four votes) argues that she contributes the most to the coalition and hence should receive the largest share of the outcomes. Either because Andrea's demands are seen as excessive (they may be), or because Barbara and Cecilia feel badly treated by Andrea, or because Barbara and Cecilia recognize that they can pool the fewest votes to get the whole pot, Barbara and Cecilia tend to form a coalition most often.

• Once the 3–2 coalition arises, it appears to be stable. That is, on a large number of repeated trials, the Barbara–Cecilia coalition will continue to dominate. Barbara and Cecilia will choose each other to the consistent exclusion of Andrea. The most common distribution of the pool is 50/50 or a small advantage to Barbara (with three votes).

• Occasionally, stable coalitions are broken. This is most likely to occur because Andrea makes a very attractive offer to Barbara or Cecilia that lures one of them away from the Barbara–Cecilia pattern. Interestingly, research results show that if Andrea wants to break the Barbara–Cecilia coalition, she should make Barbara or Cecilia a dramatically good offer (e.g., a 90/10 split). In fact, however, Andrea seldom does this; she may make marginally better offers than she did before, but usually the improvement is so minimal that it does not cause Barbara or Cecilia to defect from their prior agreement.

When Andrea is successful, she is more likely to get Barbara to defect than Cecilia (Murnighan, 1986). Murnighan speculates that this may be due to Barbara's inflated ego—"I'm getting a better deal, probably because I deserve it," she thinks, "and why shouldn't I deserve an even better deal?" (Murnighan, 1991, pp. 131–132). The result may also be due to the increased loyalty of Cecilia to a deal in which she is getting consistently less than the other and has to rationalize continued involvement; hence, she may be less likely to defect.

If a defection occurs, what happens next? The defector (assume Barbara), who probably got a big incentive to defect (e.g., a promise of a large share of the pot), now may insist that she continue to receive the bonus. This is usually seen as greedy by Andrea, even though Andrea encouraged the greediness by offering the hefty bonus to begin with! As a result, Andrea may reject Barbara in future deals because of Barbara's greediness. Moreover, Cecilia is still mad at Barbara for defecting from the stable B–C relationship. Hence, Barbara, who was tempted to defect and took the opportunity, may now be rejected by both sides, who then ally with each other in an Andrea–Cecilia coalition. This coalition may persist for a long time, often until Barbara is able to put a highly tempting offer on the table that will break the Andrea–Cecilia coalition.

A "Real World" Example.   There are a number of real-world parallels to the kind of coalition dynamics found in the 4–3–2 game that we have just described. For example, the first formulation of the European Economic Community (EEC), in 1957, included the charter members Germany, France, Italy, the Netherlands, Belgium, and Luxembourg. Germany, France, and Italy were very large and economically powerful; Belgium and the

Netherlands were weaker than the "big three" but more economically powerful than Luxembourg. In the first EEC treaty, each government had voting power proportional to its economic and physical size (four votes each for Germany, France, and Italy; two votes each for Belgium and Netherlands; and one vote for Luxembourg). Some decisions required unanimous votes, while others required only a majority vote (four out of six countries). These requirements produced a tremendous amount of coalition behavior. When the votes needed to be unanimous, even the smallest countries could exert strong control over the decision, because they could block any deal that came along. In contrast, when the votes only needed to be a majority, smaller countries could ally with larger countries, and it was even possible for all the small countries to be excluded if the big three decided to get together. These dynamics did not fundamentally change until the EEC expanded its membership in 1973. When Denmark, Ireland, and the United Kingdom entered the EEC, the proportional votes held by each party changed, as did the total number of votes necessary to carry a majority and take action (Murnighan, 1991).

The Nature of Coalition Inputs.   In general, people form coalitions to preserve or increase their resources. As Murnighan (1986) notes, there can be several different types of resources: money, information, natural resources, discretion (the ability to make decisions without consulting others), and so on. In the situations we have been discussing—both the 4–3–2 game and the real-world example of the formation of the EEC in the 1950s—the resources involved were potential *votes* that individual parties brought to a decision-making process. Early research on coalitions in laboratory situations tended to define resources as votes (Gamson, 1961), but studies of voting behavior are often difficult to generalize when the votes don't translate into any real power to control anything.

It is important to keep in mind, however, that the resources that serve as *coalition inputs* take many other forms, depending on the specific context involved. In organizations, for example, coalitions realistically form around key resources such as information, money, or control over the future direction of the group or organization. Coalition inputs may also include other kinds of resources: the amount of effort one has exerted, the ability or skill one contributes to the task or problem, or the level of expertise one has obtained. Effort, ability, and skill may be as critical to the coalition as control over specific resources; for example, in the formation of joint ventures in organizations, ability, skill, and expertise are often as critical as money, plant capacity, or raw materials.

For an interesting example involving somewhat unusual inputs into coalition formation, see Box 9.1 on the role of coalitions in string quartets.

The "Tragedy of the Commons."   The coalition games and examples we have discussed to this point involve actors forming coalitions to achieve some desired outcome that meets shared objectives. However, coalitions also form in order to *avoid a poor outcome* that will occur if individuals act alone in a self-interested manner. A classic statement of this type of problem (called a *social dilemma*) is an anecdote developed by Garrett Hardin (1968) known as "The Tragedy of the Commons" drawn from life in 17th-century village life in England. Murnighan (1991, pp. 141–142) relates the story:

BOX 9.1
Coalition Dynamics in String Quartets

Researchers Keith Murnighan and Donald Conlon studied the group dynamics and coalition politics that occur in string quartets (Murnighan and Conlon, 1991). Their analysis was based on interviews with musicians in 80 string quartets in England and Scotland.

In a string quartet, four musicians—two violinists, a viola player, and a cellist—must play together so that their music sounds like it is played by a cohesive unit. But each group, because of the individual talents of its members and their collective work together, develops its own idiosyncratic style; thus, two quartets playing the same piece of music can sound quite different from each other. There is a lot of debate, discussion, and negotiation among the players. Moreover, individual players take on their own reputations:

- The *first violin* is usually the strongest player and the driving force behind the group; he or she usually carries the tune for the group, and much of the best classical music is written explicitly for this role. Therefore, it is not uncommon for the first violinist to develop a big ego.

- The *second violin* always has to follow the first and is usually seen as a weaker player whose only job is to play "second fiddle" and support the first violinist.

- *Viola* players are often seen as the flakiest and most unconventional; it is assumed that many of them began playing the violin early in their career, couldn't make it in the strong competition with other top violinists, and switched to the viola as a less demanding instrument.

- Finally, *cellists* are seen as playing a background role; they often play the bass notes, which set a foundation for the rest of the group.

Compared to the first violinist, the remaining three are often referred to as the "bottom" of the quartet, whose job it is to complement and show off what the first violinist can do. Yet if these roles are weak, the entire group will play poorly and sound bad. Thus (and not surprisingly, as is true of many other groups), the weakest links in the group determine the group's overall strengths. Based on their interviews with quartet members, Murnighan and Conlon determined that coalition dynamics are most common in the bottom and middle of the quartet. The first and second violins often form an alliance because they play the same instrument. In contrast, the researchers observed that the cellist is never excluded from any coalition, even though he or she plays a larger instrument, one that is not held under the chin. Moreover, other differences within the coalition can drive the dynamics (e.g., if one member is female and the others are male, or if three live together in a different part of the city, or if one person's ability and/or commitment to the group creates a significant problem for the other three).

Are string quartets that do a good job managing coalition dynamics somehow "better" than those that don't? At the conclusion of their article, Murnighan and Conlon observe that "for string quartets, especially successful string quartets, the task is so inspiring by itself that diversity and conflict become a secondary and relatively inconsequential interference" (p. 183). Nevertheless, their intriguing analysis of these very specialized groups sheds light on how we negotiate the inherent conflicts and coalitions that lie beneath the surface of groups of all kinds.

SOURCE: Adapted from J. K. Murnighan and D. E. Conlon, "The Dynamics of Intense Work Groups: A Study of British String Quartets," *Administrative Science Quarterly* 36, (1991), pp. 165–86.

Near the center of the town was a common area that everyone in the town could use. Picnics, county fairs, and summer weddings often took place on the commons. Early on, there were no rules about this area. All the townspeople could use the commons in any way they pleased. Unfortunately, a herdsman in one end of the town realized that he could expand his herd without having to buy more land if he grazed his cows on the commons. This way he could make the most of his own farmland and maximize his returns on his now larger herd. Once one herdsman started, the others in the town realized what a beneficial plan this was and they too began to graze their cattle on the commons. Before long, of course, the commons was reduced to a barren field, with no grass, no attraction for anyone, and no social activity. When it rained, the commons was a pool of mud. No one even thought of getting married there anymore. As Hardin put it, "Ruin is the destination toward which all men rush, each pursuing his own best interest in a society that believes in the freedom of the common. Freedom in a common brings ruin to all."

The reader will recognize that the term *social dilemma* applies to a number of major contemporary issues—air and water pollution, use of natural resources, charitable contributions, voting (or not voting) in elections. In each situation, if a large enough number of people reason that their behavior or vote will not make a significant difference, then a major social problem ensues. For instance, a New England lobster fisherman may wish to continue fishing to support a family; if all fishing in the same waters continues unabated, however, there will be little lobster left for future generations. "Commons dilemmas" can be avoided only if a large number of people accept some responsibility for doing their part of not taking advantage of an unlimited good, so that others may also be able to share that resource in the future.

How Coalitions Develop

Through a series of studies, Murnighan and his colleagues (Murnighan, 1986; Murnighan and Brass, 1991) offer a detailed assessment of the coalition formation process. The following steps and activities seem to be the most critical.

Coalitions Start with a Founder.   The founder is the person who initiates the coalition. Typically, founders are those who recognize that they cannot get what they want through existing channels by themselves. Coalition founders usually identify an agenda or course of action that must be accomplished or achieved. In terms of leverage (see Chapter 6), the founder develops some form of action agenda, vision, or commitment, and persuades others to join him or her in pursuing it.

Discussions with others often take the form of a negotiation. In some cases, persuasion efforts alone may be successful—that is, simply by describing the agenda, or by portraying it in glowing and enthusiastic terms, the founder may be able to win the others' support. In other cases, the persuasion effort is not sufficient, and the founder may have to offer tangible rewards or benefits to get others to join the coalition. This is where the negotiation process really takes place. Murnighan and Brass (1991) suggest that early in the coalition-building process, founders may have to offer a disproportionate share of profits or benefits to potential partners. In other words, founders may have to offer an unequal or inequitable share to early prospects. This is done because the prospects may be unwilling to take the risk and make the commitment to join the coalition without some kind of a significant incentive. One apparent paradox of being a founder, therefore, is that early in the coalition-building process the founder may have to give away a lot in order to apparently gain a little. This process does not continue indefinitely, however; as the coalition builds and strengthens, other prospective partners will have more interest in joining on their own, and the founder's power position shifts from weakness (having to give away a lot to gain supporters) to strength (being able to dictate what new members must give in order to join the coalition).

Murnighan and Brass (1991) suggest that there are two key propositions that affect the founder's ability to build a coalition:

- *Successful founders have extensive networks.* In Chapter 6, we discussed the power of having a network and being in a key position within a network. Successful founders usually have a strong network of friends and associates whom they know and whom they can approach when they need support for a particular agenda. As we mentioned in Chapter 8, multiparty negotiations often look like branching chains, and negotiators often work through the chains to eventually make contact with the other party and establish the basis for a more formal meeting or discussion (Pruitt, 1994, 1995).

- *Founders' benefits from early coalitions are likely to be small.* Because others will be skeptical of lending their support to the coalition, a founder needs to give early partners enough to make it worth their while. As we noted above, founders don't immediately get rich from early support; in fact, they may become poorer until several other people join the coalition and it builds some momentum.

Coalitions Build by Adding One Member at a Time.   Coalitions do not come together in a single, defining event; instead, coalitions are built by adding individuals one at a time. The founder or an early ally is instrumental in driving this process. Contacts may be made simply through friends or acquaintances with whom the founder meets on a regular basis. Proximity and convenience influence who is approached, but neither may be enough. This is where another key negotiation principle comes in—*the founder can benefit significantly in coalition building if he or she understands the others' interests.* A founder who knows what others want or need and who can explain how coalition membership may deliver on those needs has powerful tools for attracting new partners. The nature of these wants and needs, and resources one can use to build and leverage them, can be multifaceted and complex. Discussions with others may be tentative, with the founder trying to find out what the others might want instead of making explicit offers; he or she may then get the process started by making such offers, based on one or more of several criteria:

- The other has something important to bring to the coalition that will enhance its strength.
- The other wants less than other people do in order to be a member of the coalition. (The less the other demands, the more desirable he or she may be as a coalition prospect, but a person who demands little may also not be seen as valuable or critical to have on board.)

- The founder can make some form of promise or commitment to the other about future rewards or benefits to be derived. Sometimes these commitments are clear, explicit, or even written; in other situations, they may be vague and oblique. If a founder can get away with making vague and nonspecific promises, he or she clearly maintains more control than if the commitments are clear, specific, and costly.

Coalitions Need to Achieve Critical Mass.   Coalitions continue to grow through pairwise discussions and matching processes. How big they get is determined by a number of factors, but at some point, they reach a "joining threshold"—a level where a minimum number of people have joined—and others begin to join because they recognize that their current friends and associates are already members. Founders and their early supporters make lots of contacts with other people, trying to determine others who might be interested in joining, as well as the "price" of such membership. There is a point at which a coalition, having reached a critical mass (Schelling, 1978), finds that further growth is easier, but at the same time less necessary (Murnighan and Brass, 1991). From that point forward, the coalition may continue to accumulate more members, "especially in particularly politicized, turbulent environments" (Murnighan and Brass, 1991, p. 292).

Weak Ties Can Be Strong.   Earlier, we discussed the strength-is-weakness dynamic in coalitions—that coalition founders will go to those who are the weakest for support, often because the weakest may need to be in the coalition most, and because they will demand the least payoff from joining the coalition. A related action occurs in coalition building, particularly with regard to the founder's network. Founders usually have a large and diverse network of initial contacts and associates whom they can contact for potential membership. Research has shown that those founders who have a large, diverse network of weak ties are often in a better situation to form a coalition than those who have a small, uniform network of strong ties (Granovetter, 1973; Kadushin, 1968).[1] Paradoxically, those who have a few strong ties, with high frequency of interaction and high multiplexity, already have a small coalition that demands a lot of their attention. In organizational settings, veto players (senior managers or those in formal authority positions) are unlikely to be founders because they will not be willing to give much away and will have difficulty selling others on membership. In contrast, veto players are more likely to wait until others approach them with initiatives and "bide their time until offers become attractive enough to accept" (Murnighan and Brass, 1991, p. 293). The founder may use this approach early on, but in a tentative manner, since at some point the founder probably wants to bring the veto player on board. Founders, on the other hand, have extensive networks of weak ties with several other parties, often bring on those who have their own extensive networks (thereby extending the "network reach" of possible members), and use these ties to make contacts and build support.

---

[1]In this context, the strength of ties is determined by the frequency and multiplexity of interaction that founders have with members of their network. Interaction frequency means the number of times that two parties interact. Uniplexity/multiplexity means the number of different ways that the parties interact with each other. If parties only work on a single project together, the relationship is uniplex; if parties work together on different projects, see each other socially, and often eat lunch together, the relationship is multiplex.

Many Successful Coalitions Form Quietly and Disband Quickly.   Coalitions do not have to be permanent, large, or public to be effective. In fact, if they do become permanent and public, their members tend to be seen as the opposition, as naysayers, or as people who are known for challenging the formal leader or established structure. In contrast, successful coalitions are often drawn together quickly around key issues and mobilize simply for the purpose of endorsing or blocking a particular course of action. The coalition seldom meets formally; instead, pairs and subgroups may meet informally (over the lunch table, by e-mail) to exchange ideas, share information and rumors, and perhaps develop a common mind-set about what is going on and how it is happening. When a critical action or decision is forthcoming, they mobilize to work together, then go back to their own individual activities and environments.

Murnighan and Brass (1991) identify several reasons why remaining intact as a coalition after the successful resolution of an issue is risky. First, if a coalition "wins" and is identified, the nonwinners may eventually seek revenge. Revenge can eventually pit coalitions against each other so that each one's sole objective is to keep the other side from succeeding. This is a common dynamic in legislative bodies around the world, as various liberal and conservative groups attempt to block each other's initiatives and agendas. Second, public acknowledgment of the coalition may also lead to turmoil within the coalition that could damage future coalition activity. For example, if the coalition is composed of people who all have strong egos, most will want to take more than their share of the credit for the coalition's success. If the coalition is informal, all can take credit and feel good; if the coalition's activity becomes public, actual contributions may become known and some members will be recognized as actually having contributed very little, which could then lead to in-fighting and threaten the coalition's viability. Finally, some coalition members may want anonymity. The more publicly identified they become with the coalition, the more their future actions may be seen by others as motivated by coalition membership and not by their own interests. They may lose the option to join other coalitions, and they may lose personal effectiveness because they are assumed to be puppets of the coalition's leadership. For this reason, many coalition members do not want to be known as being political or publicly associated with other coalition members, and they definitely want to be able to keep their options open to form other associations as their interests may dictate in the future.

Standards for Coalition Decision Making

Coalition decision rules emphasize the criteria that parties will use to determine who receives what from the results of the coalition's efforts. Decision rules focus on the standards for which members of the coalition will advocate, and how the output or results should be allocated. Decision rules tend to parallel three standards of fairness: equity, equality, and need. Those advocating an *equity standard* argue that anyone who contributed more should receive more, in proportion to the magnitude of the contribution. Those advocating an *equality standard* argue that everyone should receive the same, and those advocating a *need standard* argue that parties should receive more in proportion to some demonstrated need for the resource.

In general, parties tend to argue for the standard that is most likely to serve their individual needs. For example, returning to the 4–3–2 game described above, Andrea, as the player with four votes, will probably argue for the equity standard—that she should receive the larger share of any pool because she contributes more votes. Cecilia, as the player with only two votes, will probably argue for equality, because she stands to make more in an equal split with either Andrea or Barbara than she would from an equitable split. Barbara, as the swing player, might argue for equality if she was trying to form a coalition with Andrea, but might argue for equity when negotiating with Cecilia. If one player had a very strong need—for example, a need for money to repair her car so she could get to her job—that argument might prevail if she could convince the other two of the strength and validity of her need, relative to their needs, to get either an equitable or equal split of the resource pool.

Power and Leverage in Coalitions

Chapter 6 addressed the general nature of power and leverage in negotiations. The dynamics of power and influence are central aspects of the formation and maintenance of coalitions because coalitions tend to arise in situations where multiple actors have competing and partially overlapping interests. Leverage issues in coalitions are discussed from two perspectives: the issue of strength versus weakness in coalitions, and the types of power that underlie coalition formation.

Where Is the Strength in Coalitions?   When the goal is to form the smallest possible winning coalition, those parties who have relatively fewer resources in a coalition may be stronger. This is true because their relatively weaker resource position leads them to ask for less from the winning pool, and hence they are more desirable to have as coalition partners (Murnighan, 1978). Thus, when any winning coalition obtains the same payoff and the structure of the situation indicates that two given actors are interchangeable (either one can contribute the same amount to the dominant coalition), those actors who appear to contribute the fewest resources, have the least power, or exert the least influence will have an advantage. This result is often referred to as the *strength-is-weakness* argument (Murnighan, 1986). As Murnighan notes, "When anyone will do, interchangeability favors those who appear weak. Thus, a supervisor who needs any supportive voice for a new group strategy will almost certainly attempt to convince the weakest, most agreeable group member to concur" (p. 161). Murnighan cautions, however, that although this may lead to adoption of the proposed strategy, the coalition based on weak members may, with its lack of dedicated support, undermine the implementation of that strategy.

In contrast, however, most coalition studies reinforce the opposite—that *strength is strength.* The more resources a party holds or controls, the more likely he or she is to be a critical coalition member. Such a person will be a central figure to pulling the coalition together, dictating its strategy, and influencing the distribution of the resource pool. Note that this centrality directly parallels the type of centrality we discussed in Chapter 6, when we discussed formal and informal power that comes from one's position in a hierarchy and in a network structure. Coalition players with strength often become the center of communication networks that form in the process of both shaping the coalition and deciding on the distribution of the pool (Murnighan and Volrath, 1984).

How Is Power Related to Coalition Formation?   Polzer, Mannix, and Neale (1995, 1998) have identified three key types of power in multiparty negotiations: strategic, normative, and relational. Discussion of these types of power provides a convenient summary of the coalition-formation process:

- *Strategic power* depends on the availability of alternative coalition partners. A negotiator's power comes from the availability of an alternative. If negotiators have good alternatives, then they can walk away from any unacceptable deal and approach others who may be able and willing to discuss a better deal. The more resources a given potential partner brings to a coalition, or the greater variety in resources or types of inputs, the more that partner can add to the coalition, and the more power he or she will have in contributing to the coalition and dictating what the coalition should look like.

- *Normative power* has no strategic function. Instead, normative power derives from what parties consider to be a fair or just distribution of the outcomes and results of a coalition. In essence, the party who proposes the rule or principle of what constitutes a fair distribution of the outcomes has more normative power. One party may argue for an equal distribution, the other for an equitable distribution, and a third for a distribution based on need; the party whose arguments ultimately shape the allocation rule used by the group has the most normative power.

- *Relationship-based power* is shaped by the compatibility of preferences between two or more parties. As we noted in Chapter 8, parties who see each other as having common or compatible interests are more likely to begin and preserve a relationship with each other. The parties' compatibility may be based on shared or complementary interests (mutual gain), common ideology, or simply liking each other and enjoying being together.

Polzer, Mannix, and Neale (1995, 1998) recently examined these three sources of power in a study. Negotiators took the role of one of three divisional vice presidents in a research and development firm, and had to allocate funding from two resource pools. The value of the first resource pool varied depending on which two of the three players were included in the final agreement on the pool; their varying power was based on the size of the division they represented. Thus, strategic power was manipulated by who could coalesce with whom to get the pool. Normative power was manipulated by the degree to which each division, if it received the resources, could use the resources to best contribute to the overall mission of the organization. Finally, relationship power was manipulated through the second pool, in which parties had more or less compatible preferences on negotiation issues. The results indicate that *relationship power from compatibility of interests was the overriding source of power.* As the authors note:

> Players who had compatible interests were able to achieve higher individual outcomes from both portions of the task. This was true even when compatible players did not form exclusive two-way coalitions. These findings indicate that compatible players formed internal coalitions, acting as allies against the incompatible third party—not necessarily to lock the third party out of the final agreement, but to force him or her to accept a reduced share of both resource pools. (Polzer, Mannix, and Neale, 1995, p. 128)

The authors also note that relationship dynamics can significantly affect the process of negotiation, influence the preferences parties have for particular agreements, and therefore significantly affect the formation and stability of coalitions (see Chapter 8). Parties in relationships tend to see themselves as more permanently together in the future; thus, they incorporate a temporal aspect into their relationship and expect that if their interests are not being met now, they certainly will be in the future. As a result, they work together without requiring the certainty of immediate payoff. In addition, they see themselves as having compatible preferences and build a strong concern for ensuring that both are achieving their own outcome goals. Finally, parties in relationships develop trust, in that they are more certain about the other's behavior and intentions and recognize greater opportunities to work together. As a result, relationships clearly become key drivers for sustained, ongoing coalition formation and maintenance.

How to Build Coalitions: Some Practical Advice

We conclude this section with a practical approach to coalitions developed by Peter Block (1987), who proposed a strategy of empowerment and positive politics in organizations. Empowerment, Block states, "comes from acting on our enlightened self-interest. Politics is the pursuit of self-interest, and positive politics is the pursuit of enlightened self-interest" (p. 105). Enlightened self-interest, according to Block, occurs when people

- Pursue activities that have meaning to themselves and to others.
- Are needed.
- Genuinely contribute to the organization and its purpose.
- Act with integrity and tell the truth about what they see happening.
- Treat others well and have a positive impact on them.
- Strive to be as good and productive as they can at what they do.

Parties who pursue enlightened self-interest are likely to use *authentic* tactics with others (in contrast with expedient, unethical power tactics, such as the ones we reviewed in Chapter 7). Block argues that authentic tactics require parties to do the following:

1. *Say no when they mean no.* Rather than hedging a position, refusing to make commitments, sitting on the fence, or being nice to everybody regardless of beliefs, parties need to let others know where they stand.

2. *Share as much information as possible.* Authentic tactics require parties to tell everything they know, so that they can maximize what others know, maximize the common pool of information, and increase the ability of the parties to arrive at a solution that is in their individual and collective interests. As Block notes, this might mean sharing the entire budget rather than only a small part, sharing complete financial data, involving people extensively in proposed changes and giving them this information early in the process, letting people know about possible failures early on so they can plan to avert them or minimize the impact, and letting people know where they stand and how their job performance is rated so they can make informed decisions about their lives and future.

3. *Use language that describes reality.* Instead of using language that obscures, masks, or disguises what is really going on, parties should use language that is straightforward and clear. This is related to the previous point about fully sharing information. Politicians have frequently been criticized for refusing to answer questions clearly or fully, or failing to give complete and accurate accounts of what has happened. Instead of using language that describes reality, politicians skillfully use language that distorts, obscures, misleads, or places the blame elsewhere (see Kurtz, 1998).

4. *Avoid repositioning for the sake of acceptance.* To be complete in their disclosure and use language accurately, parties should not shift their position, endorsement, or support simply to make it more acceptable, palatable, or consistent with what is hot or current. Such repositioning is often viewed as no more than public relations, an effort to polish up old, tired ideas and present them as new ones. For example, companies have often been accused of retreading the same fundamental management programs with new names and slogans, depending on what is hot—corporate culture, quality, productivity, leadership, and so on. Politicians accuse each other of taking old jobs or social welfare programs and giving them new names and buzzwords. The more often this happens—and people recognize it—the more it breeds cynicism about whether real change is desired or can be pursued.

Because Block (1987) is examining empowerment in the context of organizational leadership, he sees the dominant driving force for a coalition as *vision*—getting people collectively to endorse a view of greatness for their unit and organization that others will buy into. However, recall that relationships, common interests, or normative rules can also provide the organizing principle for building a coalition. Political action begins the moment parties try to move from articulating a vision to implementing it; parties begin to talk about their ideas and desires to other people, and test out how those others react. Block suggests that as they engage in these discussions parties can think about other prospective coalition members in one or more roles: bedfellows, fence sitters, adversaries, allies, and opponents (see Figure 9.2). These five types can be considered in terms of whether they are in high or low agreement with the parties' objectives and whether they generate high or low trust (see our discussion of trust in Chapter 8).

Allies.   Allies are parties who are in agreement with a negotiator's goals and vision, and whom the negotiator trusts. Block indicates that the strategy with allies is to treat them as friends, to let them know exactly what is envisioned and planned, and to share vulnerabilities and doubts—because allies can often help a negotiator compensate for the areas where he or she feels weakest. In addition, a negotiator trusts an ally because he or she believes that person will tell the truth and will act in the negotiator's best interests.

Opponents.   Opponents are people with whom a negotiator has conflicting goals and objectives, but who can be trusted to be principled and candid in their opposition. They challenge, ask tough questions, don't accept glib answers, and constantly push the negotiator to be better and stronger at advocating a specific course of action. Negotiators expect that opponents will play by the rules and play to win. As Block points out,

FIGURE 9.2   Trust/Agreement Matrix

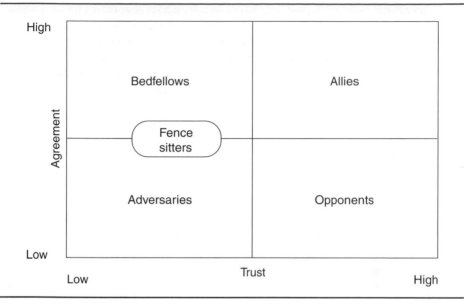

SOURCE: Peter Block, *The Empowered Manager: Positive Political Skills at Work* (San Francisco: Jossey-Bass, 1987). Used with permission of the author.

when people play a game against someone, they want the other person to perform well in order to push them to perform well; when they win, they want to feel that they have played against someone who also tried as hard as possible, and that therefore their victory was deserved.

Bedfellows.   Bedfellows are parties with whom a negotiator has high agreement on the vision or objectives, but low to moderate levels of trust. The low levels of trust arise because either one or both sides don't share information, don't tell the whole truth, play it cagey, and say what they think the other wants to hear rather than the truth. Note that bedfellows can be created either by the other party's actions or by one's own actions; if negotiators are less than open and honest with the other party, or think the other party will be less than open and honest in return, trust levels tend to decrease. As Block notes, "When we have less than complete trust in people, we usually think it is their fault. We talk about the fact that they don't trust us. We have evidence as to what they have done that proves them untrustworthy. Even in the face of this, we need to treat them well" (p. 147).

Fence Sitters.   Fence sitters are parties who will not take a stand one way or the other on a given issue. They fear taking a position because it could lock them in, be politically dangerous, or expose them to risk. They also may truly not know what they want to do. As a result, the negotiator can have little trust in fence sitters because it is not clear where they stand, and they may be actively trying to maintain that ambiguity.

Adversaries.   The last group is adversaries; with an adversary, negotiators are low in agreement and low in trust. Unlike opponents, whom negotiators trust to conduct themselves with dignity, adversaries cannot be trusted. As Block notes, "People become adversaries only when our attempts at negotiating agreement and negotiating trust have failed" (p. 152). Efforts to speak to adversaries usually lead to a failure to agree and a failure to develop trust. Many people become preoccupied with adversaries, often because the failure to negotiate with them reveals weaknesses and defects in their ability to manage relationships. In addition, adversaries often behave in ways parties find unacceptable; therefore, the goal is either to win over the adversary or to destroy the adversary. Unfortunately, as Block notes, it doesn't work this way. The more you focus on trying to convert or pressure other people, the stronger they become, the more they threaten you, and the more you become obsessed with them.

As Block notes, this strategy can be very difficult when your boss is an adversary, because you are working for someone who has a conflicting vision and you don't trust him or her. The lack of trust and lack of common vision undermine your productivity. While you can try to manage your boss (which is likely to come across as manipulation, not management), you are unlikely to be happy and content in this work environment as long as this person is an adversary and you see yourself as highly constrained in your actions because of it. Conversely, if a subordinate is an adversary, you are unlikely to be able to work productively with that individual over the long term, and you would probably be better off if you encouraged that person to find productive employment elsewhere.

Block suggests that it is possible to build a coalition with each of these five types, but that one has to use a different strategy in each case. His prescriptive advice is described in Box 9.2.

Section Summary

In this section, we have addressed the nature of coalitions and explored the processes by which they are formed, maintained, and ultimately disbanded. We suggested that coalition formation occurs when there are more than two negotiating parties, and is most likely when parties need to add the resources or support of others to enhance the likelihood of achieving their own individual outcomes. We discussed when, why, and how coalitions form; addressed how they work (and don't work) once formed; and considered the role of power and leverage in coalition politics. Finally, we offered some advice to those who are building a coalition, particularly regarding how one can think about potential partners, and what should be the agenda in conducting negotiations with those partners.

We conclude this section with a cautionary note about the importance of underlying relationships among the parties to a dispute that may involve the formation of coalitions. As Murnighan (1991) notes, much of the earlier work on coalitions

> ignored one important factor: whether the people who form coalitions together can actually work with each other effectively. . . . Whom you choose as a partner depends on the potential payoffs that can result from that partnership. Those payoffs include the interpersonal benefits you get from your work interactions. . . . More generally, you may maximize your

BOX 9.2
Action Strategies for Building Relationships in Coalitions

Author Peter Block has prescriptive advice for building a coalition with each of the five types of partners he identifies. His major suggestions can be outlined as follows.

With allies:

- Affirm your agreement on the collective vision or objective.
- Reaffirm the quality of the relationship.
- Acknowledge the doubt and vulnerability that you have with respect to achieving your vision and collective goal.
- Ask for advice and support.

With opponents:

- Reaffirm that your relationship is based in trust.
- State your vision or position.
- State in a neutral way what you think their position or vision is.
- Engage in some kind of problem solving.

With bedfellows:

- Reaffirm the agreement.
- Acknowledge the caution that exists.
- Be clear about what you want from bedfellows in terms of their support.
- Ask bedfellows what they want from you.
- Try to reach an agreement on how the two parties are going to work together.

With fence sitters:

- State your position on the project.
- Ask where they stand.
- Apply gentle pressures.
- Encourage them to think about the issue and tell you what it would take to gain their support.

With adversaries:

- State your vision or goals.
- State in a neutral way your understanding of your adversary's position.
- Identify your own contribution to the poor relationship between you and your adversary.
- End the meeting by restating your plan but making no demands.

SOURCE: Peter Block, *The Empowered Manager: Positive Political Skills at Work* (San Francisco: Jossey-Bass, 1987).

monetary outcome in all your negotiations, but if you also sour all your interpersonal relationships, you'll end up rich and lonely. There's more to bargaining (and life) than winning negotiations, especially if you pay the price of alienating the other person. Burn enough personal bridges and the very opportunity to negotiate will disappear. (p. 137)

These issues of relationships between the parties—past, current, and future—clearly have an impact on how the parties select their coalition partners, and whether those partnerships are likely to endure or to shift as economic incentives change.

THE NATURE OF MULTIPARTY NEGOTIATIONS

We now turn to a discussion of negotiation situations where more than two parties are working together to achieve a *collective objective*. This type of negotiation is a *multiparty negotiation.*

To illustrate the nature of multiparty negotiations, we will return to the example of the student selling a stereo system where there was more than one possible buyer. Now assume that there is not one seller, but four roommates who are selling the stereo system. A year ago, each put in $200 to buy the system; they now have different preferences for what they should do. Aaron (A) wants to sell it and simply split up the money because he wants to buy a new bike for himself; Bill (B) wants to sell it and buy a newer but inexpensive stereo system; Chuck (C) wants to sell it and buy a super-high-quality system that will require each of them to chip in a lot more money; and Dan (D) doesn't want to sell it at all and thinks the whole thing is a dumb idea. Each party has his own preferences and priorities, and the roommates must collectively decide what to do as a group if and when the system is sold. They might agree to make a single collective decision about what to do next, or they might agree to align together in subgroups to pool their money, or each might go his separate way. When the parties agree to hold a meeting to discuss the options and make a collective decision, this is a *multiparty negotiation* that involves unique dynamics in a collective decision-making process.

The general model for a multiparty negotiation is represented in Figure 9.3. Each of the parties (there can be three or more) is representing his or her own interests. In a different situation (e.g., they might be representatives of different departments meeting together as a task force), they could be representing the interests of others (see Figure 9.4). Most of the complexities described in this section will increase linearly, if not exponentially, as more parties, constituencies, and audiences are added.

In the remainder of this section, we will note the factors that make multiparty negotiations more difficult to manage than one-on-one negotiations. In the section that follows, we will comment on some of the key stages and phases in multiparty deliberations. For each phase, we will consider a variety of strategies that can be used to manage multiparty negotiations effectively. Our discussion will show that multiparty negotiations are complex and highly susceptible to breakdown, and therefore the process often requires the parties to make a conscious commitment to work toward an effective multiparty agreement.[2]

---

[2]These sections draws heavily on the work of Bazerman, Mannix, and Thompson (1988); Brett (1991); and Kramer (1991), who provided excellent overviews of the problems and challenges of multiparty negotiations.

FIGURE 9.3   A Multiparty Negotiation

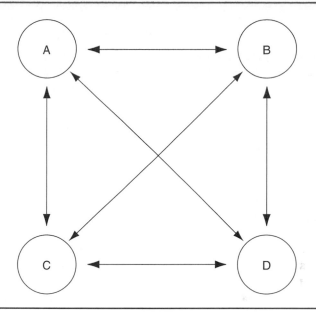

Differences between Two-Party Negotiations and Multiparty Negotiations

There are several important ways in which multiparty negotiations differ from two-party deliberations. In every case, the differences are what make multiparty negotiations more complex, challenging, and difficult to manage.

Number of Parties.   The first difference is the most obvious one: multiparty negotiations have more negotiators at the table. Thus, negotiations simply become bigger. This creates challenges for managing several different perspectives and ensuring that each party has adequate time to speak and be heard. Each party may be acting as a *principal*—that is, representing his or her own interests (Figure 9.3)—or an *agent*—representing the interests of at least one other party (the *constituency*) (Figure 9.4). (Refer back to our discussion of these roles in Chapter 8.) In addition, parties may have different social roles outside the negotiation (e.g., president, vice president, director, board chairman) that may lead to either equal or unequal levels of power and status in the negotiation (see Chapter 6). If the parties are all equals (e.g., all vice presidents), the exchange within the negotiation should be more open than if one party has higher status or power than the others. For instance, if one party is the president and the others are vice presidents, we can expect the president to control and dominate the process more actively.

Informational and Computational Complexity.   A second difference in multiparty negotiations is that more issues, more perspectives on issues, and more total information (facts, figures, viewpoints, arguments, documentary support) are introduced: "One

FIGURE 9.4   A Multiparty Negotiation with Constituents

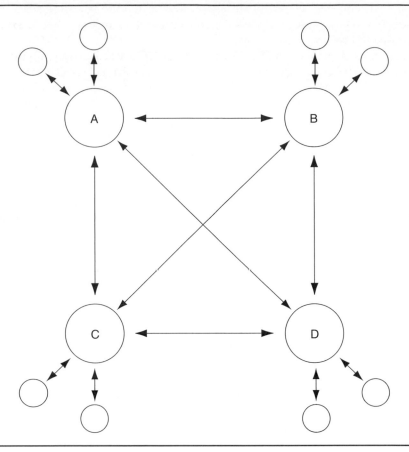

of the most fundamental consequences of increasing the number of parties is that the nego-tiation situation tends to become less lucid, more complex, and therefore, in some respects, more demanding. As size increases, there will be more values, interests, and perceptions to be integrated or accommodated" (Midgaard and Underal, 1977, p. 332, as quoted in Kramer, 1991). Keeping track of all this information, the perspectives of each side, and the parameters into which a solution must fit becomes a major challenge for the negotiators.

Social Complexity.   A third difference is that as the number of parties increases, the social environment changes from a one-on-one dialogue to a small-group discussion. As a result, all the dynamics of small groups begin to affect the way the negotiators behave. First, how the process evolves may depend on the motivational orientation of the parties toward each other. A study by Weingart, Bennett, and Brett (1993) explored the nature of motivational orientation on the behavior of negotiators in a multiparty negotiation. The authors found that parties with a cooperative (versus an individualistic) motivational

orientation were much more likely to achieve a higher quality outcome in their deliberations, and that cooperatively motivated parties were more trusting and engaged in less
argumentation than individualistic ones. This orientation also seemed to affect the way the
parties discussed the issues (see below).

Second, social pressures may develop for the group to act cohesively, yet the members are in conflict with each other and cannot be cohesive unless they can find an
acceptable solution. Members compare themselves to one another, evaluate themselves
against one another, and try to use a variety of influence tactics to persuade one another
toward their point of view (see Chapter 6 for a description of these tactics). Strong pressures for conformity develop as members pressure other members to adopt a common
perspective or definition of the problem or to endorse a particular solution. In addition,
the group can develop dysfunctional group dynamics. For example, if pressures to keep
the group cohesive are strong, the group may attempt to avoid or minimize conflict by
downplaying their differences or not working through them adequately to reach an effective solution. Janis's (1982, 1989) research on policy-making and decision-making
groups has shown that these efforts to minimize and avoid conflict can frequently lead
to disaster. Fiascoes such as the U.S. invasion of the Bay of Pigs in Cuba during the
Kennedy administration or NASA's decision to launch the *Challenger* space shuttle
(Tompkins, 1993) were caused by dynamics in the key decision-making groups that left
group members hesitant to create conflict and express their real reservations about
going ahead with the project (see Box 9.3). This hesitancy led to an illusion of consensus, in which all parties believed that they were the only dissenting member in a fairly
strong emerging agreement about what actions to take. Afraid to express their dissent for
fear of looking weak and foolish (note the face-saving dynamics), group members self-
censored their reservations and concerns, thereby reinforcing the apparent surface consensus and leading to a decision with disastrous consequences.

Procedural Complexity. A fourth way in which multiparty negotiations are
more complex than two-party ones is that the process they have to follow is more complicated. In one-on-one negotiations, the parties simply take turns in either presenting
their issues and perspectives, challenging the other's perspectives, or moving the negotiation along from its early stages to the later ones. When more parties are involved, the
procedural rules become far less clear. Whose turn is it to do what? How do the parties
coordinate where they are in the negotiations (e.g., opening statements, presentation of
viewpoints, moving toward agreement)?

There are several consequences of this procedural complexity. First, negotiations will
take longer (Sebenius, 1983), so more time must be allowed. Second, the greater the number of parties, the more complex and out of control the process can become—particularly
if some parties choose to adopt a strategy of tough positional bargaining and dominate the
process in an effort to railroad through their particular viewpoints (Bazerman, Mannix, and
Thompson, 1988). Third, as a result of the first two elements, negotiators will probably
have to devote explicit discussion time to how they will manage the process to arrive at the
type of solution or agreement they want. Finally, the parties must decide how they want to
approach multiple issues on the table. Weingart, Bennett, and Brett (1993) reported that
parties who discussed multiple issues simultaneously—considered all of the issues at once,

---

BOX 9.3
Space Shuttle *Challenger*

On January 28, 1986, the space shuttle *Challenger* exploded 73 seconds into its flight. All those on the flight were instantly killed, including civilian passengers specially recruited for the trip. Subsequent investigations placed part of the blame for this tragedy on leaders at NASA who failed to create a communication environment that allowed their subordinates to discuss openly potential technical difficulties. If communication had been more open, the *Challenger* might not have been lost.

In his book-length report on the *Challenger* disaster, Philip Tompkins (1993) noted that workers at NASA knew their director did not like to hear bad news. He had a tendency to "kill the messenger," particularly when faced with technical information that might necessitate delays in the launch schedule. Consequently, his subordinates communicated with him in a passive, nondirective style. In the days prior to *Challenger*'s launch, engineers met to discuss potential technical difficulties with the flight based on the colder-than-usual weather. These technical professionals concluded that launching the *Challenger* might be dangerous in cold-weather conditions. However, because meetings at NASA did not generally promote open exchange of ideas and debate, the indirect warnings they issued were ignored. Some professionals testified after the accident that they were intimidated by senior administrators at NASA and did not feel they could bring problems to the table for discussion. Instead, they relied on hints and technical memos to try to get their message across without angering their superiors.

Tompkins wrote that one purpose of his book was "to point out the value of communication, the dangers of defensiveness and unwillingness to face open appraisal" (p. 110). The *Challenger* disaster aptly demonstrates the tragedy that can strike if all members of a work team cannot speak openly in meetings and negotiations.

SOURCE: Adapted from P. K. Tompkins, *Organizational Communication Imperatives: Lessons of the Space Program* (Los Angeles: Roxbury Publishing Company, 1993).

---

and looked for ways to trade one off against another—achieved higher quality agreements and increased the likelihood of achieving agreement compared to groups that approached the issues sequentially (one at a time, in a fixed or negotiated sequence). Groups that approached issues simultaneously also exchanged more information and had greater insight into the preferences and priorities of the other parties at the table.

Strategic Complexity.   Finally, multiparty negotiations are more strategically complex than two-party ones. In one-on-one negotiations, the negotiator need only attend to the behavior of the other negotiator; strategy is therefore driven by the negotiator's objectives, the other party's actions, and the tactics they each use. The strategic and tactical options of two party negotiations were discussed in Chapters 2 and 3.

In a group negotiation, complexity increases significantly. The negotiator must consider the strategies of *all* the other parties at the table and decide whether to deal with each of them separately or as a group. The actual process of dealing with each of them usually evolves into a series of one-on-one negotiations, but conducted within the view of all of the other group members. Viewed in this manner, this series of one-on-one negotiations can have several consequences.

First, these exchanges are subject to the surveillance and audience dynamics described in Chapter 8. In this context, negotiators will be sensitive to being observed and may feel the need to be tough to show their firmness and resolve (both to the other party and to bystanders or audiences). As a result, the social milieu may lead negotiators to adopt distributive strategies and tactics—even if they did not intend to do so—simply to show their toughness and resolve to others. The short-term result is that negotiators in the group may become strongly positional unless specific actions are taken to manage the group beyond this competitive escalation. A related dynamic is that once the parties have become strongly positional, negotiators will have to find satisfactory ways to explain modification of their positions—concession making or movement toward compromises and consensus—to their constituencies without the face-threatening dynamics discussed earlier. Even without constituencies, negotiators will not want to lose face with the other negotiators present. This will be particularly true in the situation shown in Figure 9.4, when negotiators have constituencies.

Second, negotiators who have some way to control the number of parties at the table (or even in the room) may begin to act strategically, using this control to serve their objectives. The tactic used will be determined by the strategic interests to be served by adding other parties. Additional parties may be invited to add support or credence to the negotiator's position, to provide "independent" testimony or support to a point of view, or simply to present a show of force. For example, when communities are in dispute about whether to build a new shopping center or school, change a zoning law, or present a new tax package, it is not uncommon for the agents who will publicly speak to the issue to pack the audience with a large number of supporters who will occasionally show their enthusiasm and support (or opposition) for a position. (Recall the discussion in Chapter 8 of enlisting audience support to pressure an opponent.) Thus, negotiators can strategically add parties to the negotiation, either to enhance their perceived power through sheer numbers or to present some credible threat about the consequences that will occur if the negotiators do not get their way.

Third, negotiators can explicitly engage in coalition building as a way to marshal support. Coalition dynamics were described earlier in this chapter. Parties may explicitly or implicitly agree to support each other's positions in order to add collective weight to their combined view, and then use this coalition to either dominate the negotiation process or shape the desired settlement. Coalitions may be explicitly formed prior to negotiations or during negotiation recesses and breaks, or they may emerge as the discussion proceeds. Two or more parties may begin to realize that they have compatible views and agree to help each other achieve their separate objectives as the group objective is attained.

Members of coalitions can exert their strength in multiparty negotiations in a number of ways: by expressing solidarity with each other, by agreeing to help each other achieve their common or individual objectives, by dominating discussion time, and by agreeing to support each other as particular solutions and negotiated agreements emerge. Murnighan (1986) has suggested that the emergence of consensus in decision-making groups proceeds as a "snowballing coalition." As noted earlier, coalitions are built one party at a time. Thus, in a group discussion, as parties share information and then deliberate possible solutions, a few people will emerge with a common perspective and then tacitly or explicitly agree to support each other's views. Other individuals then negotiate with the emerging coalition to incorporate their own views. Those who may be unwilling to negotiate or modify their views are eventually rejected and left out of the group decision.

The risk for those on the outside of an influential coalition is that they will not be an active participant in the discussions, some of which may occur away in caucuses from the main negotiating table. A study by Kim (1997) demonstrated that negotiators who are excluded from part of a multiparty negotiation receive a lesser share of the outcome than those who are present for the duration. Kim's findings showed that this is particularly damaging to the excluded party when he or she misses the second half of the discussion. The lesson seems to be that simply being present when key discussions occur is important, especially in the later stages as the parties hone in on a final settlement.

Polzer, Mannix, and Neale (1995, 1998) have argued that relationships are the most significant force in shaping which parties will enter coalitions with each other in a multiparty negotiation. When a relationship is in place, parties extensively incorporate the time dimension into their deliberations and side negotiations with each other. Thus, what the parties have done for each other in the past, and/or what they think they can do for each other in the future, has a strong impact on the current discussions. In addition, as we noted in Chapter 8, relationships may lead the parties to have similar preferences, to have strong concern for the others and a desire to help the others achieve their outcomes, and to create and sustain strong trust among group members.

Summary.   There are five ways in which the complexity increases as three or more parties simultaneously engage in negotiation. First, there are simply more parties involved in the negotiation, which increases the number of speakers, increases the demand for discussion time, and increases the number of different roles the parties may play. Second, more parties bring more issues and positions to the table, and thus more perspectives must be presented and discussed. Third, negotiations become socially more complex—social norms emerge that affect member participation, and there may be stronger pressures to conform and suppress disagreement. Fourth, negotiations become procedurally more complex, and the parties may have to negotiate a new process that allows them to coordinate their actions more effectively. Finally, negotiations become more strategically complex, because the parties must monitor the moves and actions of several other parties in determining what each will do next. In addition, the possibility of coalitions increases the likelihood that decisions will not be made by a comprehensive negotiated consensus, but by some subgroup that can dominate the discussion and decision-making processes.

MANAGING MULTIPARTY NEGOTIATIONS

Given the additional complexity that occurs in a multiparty negotiation, what is the most effective way to cope? Touval (1988), who examined many multiparty and treaty negotiations in international diplomacy, outlined three key stages that characterize multilateral negotiations: prenegotiation, actual negotiation, and managing the agreement. In addressing these three stages, we will also identify what a single negotiator can do when:

- The individual is simply one of the parties in a multiparty negotiation and wants to ensure that his or her own issues and interests are clearly incorporated into the final agreement.

- The individual wants to ensure that the group reaches the highest quality and best possible final agreement.

- The individual is responsible for managing a multiparty negotiation process to ensure that many of the strategic and procedural complexities are effectively managed.

The Prenegotiation Stage

This stage is characterized by lots of informal contact among the parties. They tend to work on the following issues:

Participants.   The parties must agree on who is going to be invited to the talks. If the group is already an intact one, this is an easy question. However, many complex international negotiations give a great deal of time to the question of who will be recognized and who can speak for others. Issues about participants can be decided on the basis of the following:

- Who must be included if a deal is to be reached (key coalition members)?

- Who could spoil the deal if they were excluded (veto players)?

- Whose presence is likely to help other parties achieve their objectives (desirable coalition members)?

- Whose presence is likely to keep other parties from achieving their objectives (key coalition blockers)?

- Whose status will be enhanced simply by being at the table? (This was often a key issue in the Palestinian–Israeli talks in the Middle East, and in the Paris Peace Talks to end the Vietnam war, when the Viet Cong were invited to the table as a fully recognized party.)

Coalitions.   We have said much about coalitions in an earlier section of this chapter. It is not uncommon for coalitions to exist before negotiations begin, or for them to organize in anticipation of the meeting of all the parties. Naturally, coalitions will form to either promote or block a particular agenda.

Defining Group Member Roles.   If the group already has a structure, then roles—leaders, mediators, record keepers, and so on—will already have been determined. But if the group has not met before, then parties may begin to jockey for key roles. Some may want to lead, participate actively, and promote a particular agenda; others may wish to stay silent and be invisible; and still others may wish to take a third-party role such as mediator or facilitator (see Chapter 13).

Understanding the Costs and Consequences of No Agreement.   Brett (1991) suggests that negotiators need to understand the costs and consequences that will ensue if the group fails to agree. This suggestion has been given repeatedly for negotiators in one-on-one negotiations. For example, suppose a group of vice presidents in a computer company is trying to decide which models of a new line of personal computers should be built next year and the quantities of each. First, what will happen if the parties fail to agree on what to do? Will someone else (i.e., the president) step in and decide for them? How will the president feel about the group if the members can't agree? Second, are the costs for impasse the same for every negotiator? Usually this is not the case— different agents have different costs associated with no agreement. For example, if the vice presidents cannot agree, the president may mandate the model line and quantities, which may have greater costs for the engineering and manufacturing departments (which would have to change over) than for the marketing and sales departments (which would have to design a new marketing and ad campaign regardless of what was done). The group members with the better impasse alternatives are likely to have more power in the negotiation, because they care less about whether the group reaches a particular solution relative to no agreement. Finally, do group members perceive their agreement and no-agreement options accurately? There is much evidence that negotiators are prone to perceptual biases that lead them to believe that they are better than others (refer back to Chapter 5), their options are better than others' options, they are more likely to achieve their outcomes than others, and they have more control over shaping an outcome than others (Taylor and Brown, 1988; Tyler and Hastie, 1991). In multiparty negotiations, these biases are likely to affect negotiators by inflating their sense of power and ability to win—leading them to believe that the no-agreement alternative is much better than it really is. Reality checking with others is important in keeping these biases under control.

Understanding the Decision Rule.   In addition, each party needs to know how the other members of the group understand the decision rule—that is, how the parties are actually going to decide the final outcome. Is it possible that one member could push his or her entire preferences on the rest of the group, because of either formal status (e.g., president) or persistence in arguing for his or her own views? Could a small group or coalition push their views on everyone else? Will the group vote? If so, will a majority rule? Or is the group aiming for true consensus in the form of a solution that incorporates everyone's views and represents all interests? These are not all the possible decision rules, but they do represent the most common ones. Understanding the decision rule allows individuals to shape the negotiation strategy they will pursue. If the current rule is unsatisfactory—for example, the president will dominate and everyone will acquiesce, but the quality of the agreement may be inferior and create major problems for the company in the future—then it may be desirable (if possible) to challenge the rule early on and convince the group to adopt a decision rule that permits greater opportunities to influence the final outcome and produce a better solution.

Learning the Issues and Constructing an Agenda.   Finally, parties spend a great deal of time familiarizing themselves with the issues, absorbing information, and trying to understand one another's interests. They will also spend time constructing an agenda. An agenda is an effective decision aid for the following reasons:

- It establishes the issues that will be discussed.
- Depending on how the issues are worded, it can also define how each issue is discussed (refer back to our discussion of framing in Chapter 2).
- It can define the order in which issues are discussed.
- It can be used to introduce process issues (decision rules, discussion norms, member roles, discussion dynamics), as well as substantive issues, simply by including them.
- It can assign time limits to various items, thereby indicating the importance of the different issues.

The Formal Negotiation Stage—Managing the Group Process and Outcome

Much of the multiparty negotiation process is a combination of the group discussion, bilateral negotiation, and coalition-building activities described earlier in this chapter. It also incorporates a great deal of what we know about how to structure a group discussion so as to achieve an effective and endorsed result. The following approaches are likely to ensure a high-quality group decision.

Appoint an Appropriate Chair.   Multiparty negotiations will proceed more smoothly when it is clear to everyone involved who is chairing or facilitating the process. Often this role will be played by one of the interested parties, but multiparty negotiations can be greatly facilitated by the presence of a *neutral* chairperson who can implement many of the tactics described below. When feasible, the parties should seriously consider designating a chair who has little stake in the specific outcome but a strong commitment to an open and fair process. In this case, the chairperson functions as a third party who has no stake in any particular outcome but does have a strong interest in ensuring that the group works toward achieving the best possible outcome. As a practical matter, it is frequently the case that the chair will be drawn from within the circle of interested parties. Keep in mind that if a chairperson is also advocating a particular position or preferred outcome, *it will be most difficult for that individual to act or be seen as neutral,* because the solution the person wants to obtain on the issues is likely to compromise (or be perceived to compromise) his or her neutrality or objectivity with respect to facilitating the process. See Box 9.4 for an inventory of constructive approaches to acting as a chair in multiparty negotiations.

Use and Restructure the Agenda.   A critical way to control the flow and direction of negotiation is through an agenda. Either the chair or the parties to the negotiation may introduce and coordinate the agenda. An agenda adds a high degree of structure, organization, and coordination to a discussion. Agendas provide low-power or disadvantaged groups a vehicle for getting their issues heard and addressed, assuming that they can get them on the agenda. However, the manner in which an agenda is built (by collective consensus at the beginning of a meeting versus by one person prior to the

BOX 9.4
Chairing a Multiparty Negotiation

Chairpersons of multiparty negotiations must be sensitive to keeping tight control over the group process while not directly affecting the group's outcome. When a group wants to achieve a consensus or unanimous decision, the responsibility of the chair is to be constantly attentive to the group process. Some pointers for how to chair a multiparty negotiation effectively include:

- *Explicitly describe the role you will take as chair.* Be clear that you are there only to manage process and that the group will determine the outcome.

- *Introduce the agenda or build one based on the group's issues, concerns, and priorities.* Make sure the group has an opportunity to discuss, modify, or challenge the agenda before you begin.

- *Make logistical arrangements that will help the negotiation process.* Does the physical setup of the room offer the best possible configuration for constructive discussion? Arrange for a flip chart, blackboard, or overhead projector to write down issues and interests. Many negotiators find they benefit from common visual access to issues, proposals and other information during the discussion.

- *Introduce necessary ground rules or let the parties suggest them.* How long will the group meet? What is the expected output or final product? Will minutes be taken? Will the group take breaks? Where will negotiations take place? How and when can group members consult with their constituents?

- *Create or review decision standards and rules.* Find standards for what parties believe will be a fair or reasonable settlement. What criteria will be used to assess whether a particular solution is fair, reasonable, and effective? How will the group ultimately decide to adopt an agreement?

- *Assure individual members that they will have an opportunity to make opening statements* or other ways of placing their individual concerns and issues on the table. Be clear that once parties are familiar with the issues, simultaneous discussion of several issues can take place. This will permit trade-offs among issues rather than forcing a compromise on each individual issue.

- *Be an active gatekeeper.* Make sure that people have a chance to speak and that the more vocal people do not dominate so that the less vocal people become silent and drop out. Ask the more vocal people to hold back and explicitly invite the more silent people to make comments and input. Often, as a group moves toward some form of agreement or consensus, some people participate less. Make sure that they have chosen not to participate, rather than simply dropped out because they don't think their views are worthwhile or important.

- *Listen for interests and commonalities.* Encourage people to express interests, mirror them back, and encourage people to identify not only what they want, but also why they want it. Listen for priorities and concerns. Once the issues and interests have been identified, explicitly set aside a time for inventing options. Use brainstorming and other group decision-making techniques to generate options and evaluate them.

BOX 9.4
(Concluded)

- *Introduce external information* (studies, reports, statistics, facts, testimony from experts) that will help illuminate the issues and interests. Ask for hard data to support assertions (but be careful to refrain from engaging in aggressive "cross-examination" that will compromise your neutrality).

- *Summarize frequently,* particularly when conversation becomes stalled, confused, or tense. State where you think the group is, what has been accomplished, and what needs to be done. Paraphrasing and summarizing bring the group back to reality and back on task.

---

meeting) and who builds it will have a great deal of impact on the flow of the negotiation. Unless group members feel comfortable challenging the person who introduces a preemptive agenda, the agenda will go unquestioned and hence the implicit discussion structure and format it suggests will prevail. Negotiators entering a multiparty negotiation for which an (unacceptable) agenda has been created in advance should consider letting other parties know ahead of time that they view the agenda itself as open to discussion or change. In other words, make sure that possible modifications to the agenda are part of the agenda.

Although an agenda may add needed structure to a complex negotiation, a drawback is that it may artificially partition related issues; as a result, issues may be discussed separately rather than coupled or traded off to exploit integrative potential. The parties using an agenda must be sensitive to the implicit structure it imposes, and they must be willing to challenge and reconfigure it if doing so will facilitate the emergence of an integrative, consensus-based agreement.

Ensure a Diversity of Information and Perspectives.   A third way to facilitate the negotiation is to ensure that the group receives a wide variety of different perspectives about the task and different sources of information. Because the nature of the information changes depending on the group's task—for example, designing and implementing a change, finding the best possible solution to a problem, or simply finding a solution that is politically acceptable to several constituencies—it is difficult to prescribe what information is critical and how to ensure that the group is exposed to it. This can simply be a matter of making sure that the voices of all participants are heard (see Box 9.5 for insight on why some group members become silent in a group deliberation). If there is a chair, he or she can ensure that the group receives input from each group member; that various constituencies and stakeholders have an opportunity to provide input (through written comments or opportunities for open testimony before the group); and that relevant reports, documents, or statistical analyses are circulated and discussed.

BOX 9.5
Why Group Members Give Up

Researchers Paul Mulvey, Jack Veiga, and Priscilla Elsass (1996) note that managers are quite cynical about group decision making, and many report that they find group decision making so frustrating and tedious that they often raise the white flag and privately give up in the group rather than continue working to help the group make a good decision. Here are some of the most common reasons why group members engage in self-limiting behavior, quietly giving in rather than continuing to participate in the group discussion:

1. *The presence of a perceived expert.* When they think that someone in the group has a lot of expertise—or, more problematically, when they think that several members have expertise—they will strongly limit their own participation, usually out of fear of looking foolish in front of the expert.

2. *The presence of a compelling argument.* When one or more people make a very strong, persuasive, and convincing argument—and particularly when it is made after a lot of fruitless discussion—other people will self-limit.

3. *Lacking confidence in one's ability to contribute.* If someone is not extremely confident about his or her own views, and doesn't want to take a risk, he or she will self-limit.

4. *An unimportant or meaningless decision.* When people see the decision as having little or no impact on their unit, they will contribute less.

5. *Pressure from others to conform to the group decision.* Strong pressures to align with the team's decision, join a coalition, or fear of retaliation can push people to find their place.

6. *A dysfunctional decision-making climate.* When people see other group members as frustrated, disorganized, or floundering, they may self-limit. Both weak leadership and the early stages of a decision process can lead to this judgment.

The authors proceed to recommend several strategies that team leaders can use—many of which are noted later in this section—to ensure that members do not drop out of the conversation early and create a false consensus.

SOURCE: Adapted from P. W. Mulvey, J. F. Veiga, and P. M. Elsass, "When Team Members Raise a White Flag," *Academy of Management Review* 10, no.1 (1996), pp. 40–49.

Ancona and Caldwell (1988) suggest four group-member roles that may be useful during this information management phase: scouts, ambassadors, coordinators, and guards. *Scouts* patrol the environment and bring in relevant external information—reports, statistics, findings, and others' experience. *Ambassadors* represent a formal link to some important constituency—for example, senior management; they help to acquire the resources the group needs to continue to operate and provide some limited information about the group's activities to constituencies (enough to give the constituency an idea about events and deliberations but not so much as to divulge private or confidential discussions). *Coordinators* provide a formal link between the group members and the constituencies they represent—frequently, negotiators are themselves the coordinators of input from their constituency into the group deliberations. Finally, *guards* are designated to keep some information inside the group and ensure that there are no leaks or premature disclosures of key information or discussions. Clearly, group members can play more than one role and can rotate roles in the course of a multiparty negotiation.

Ensure Consideration of All the Available Information.   One way to ensure that the group discusses all available information is to monitor discussion norms. Discussion norms reflect the way the group engages in sharing and evaluating the information introduced (Brett, 1991).

Although it would be highly desirable to do so, groups seldom consider in advance what discussion norms they are going to follow. In most cases, this failure is probably due to a lack of understanding about how much deliberations can be improved by following norms and rules that will enhance discussion. Several group norms can undermine an effective discussion:

- *Unwillingness to tolerate conflicting points of view and perspectives.* There may be many reasons for this: one or more members dislike conflict, are afraid that conflict will be uncontrollable, or see conflict as destructive to group cohesiveness. But as we noted above, the absence of conflict can also lead to disastrous decisions.

- *No means for defusing an emotionally charged discussion.* Unless there is a way to release it, anger, frustration, or resentment can become mixed in with the substantive issues and hamper the group's efforts. Although a great deal of negotiation literature suggests that parties should simply be calm and rational at all times, doing so is simply not humanly possible. The more the parties care about a particular issue and are invested in it, the more likely it is that emotions will creep in. Vehicles must exist to allow the parties to vent their emotions productively.

- *Coming to a meeting unprepared.* Unfortunately, preparation for a meeting often consists of either no preparation at all or simply preparing one's own position. Attention to the others' positions or to assessing underlying interests and priorities requires thorough preparation.

Several strategies may be used to manage each of these three potentially destructive discussion norms. The parties must generate and exchange ideas in a manner that permits full exploration and allows everyone to have some input, yet avoids some of the destructive conflict and emotions that can occur. Bazerman, Mannix, and Thompson (1988) suggest several group decision-making and brainstorming techniques that are frequently used to achieve this objective:

The Delphi Technique.   A moderator structures an initial questionnaire and sends it out to all parties, asking for input. Parties provide their input and send it back to the moderator. The moderator summarizes the input and sends it back to the parties. Parties then evaluate the report, make further input, and return it to the moderator. Over a number of rounds, through the questions and inquiries shaped by the moderator, the parties can exchange a great deal of information and share different perspectives. The advantages are that the group has little face-to-face interaction, does not get bogged down in personal hostility or inefficient communications, and can go through several iterations. The limitations are that the real priorities and preferences of group members may not be expressed, and the way the problem is defined and shaped early in the process will greatly determine the outcome. The parties may miss opportunities to expand the pie of resources, redefine the problem in an important way, or truly evaluate important trade-offs. Thus, the Delphi technique may tend to generate compromise settlements rather than truly creative, integrative solutions.

Brainstorming.   In brainstorming, the parties are instructed to define a problem and then to generate as many solutions as possible without criticizing any of them. Many of the suggestions may be unrealistic or impractical, but the purpose is to suggest a large number of potential solutions and to be as creative as possible in suggesting them. Brainstorming tends to generate a wider variety of solution options than might normally occur, particularly because it invites everyone to participate rather than just a small, vocal minority. By then inventing criteria to edit and modify the list, the parties can reduce the number of solutions to the two or three that appear most feasible, effective, efficient, or easy to implement.

Nominal Group Technique.   The nominal group technique typically follows brainstorming. Once the brainstormed list of solution options is created, group members can rank, rate, or evaluate the alternatives in terms of the degree to which each alternative solves the problem. The leader collects, posts, and records these ratings so that all group members have an opportunity to formally evaluate the options and to vote on the ones they consider to be most effective.

Review and Manage the Decision Rules.   In addition to monitoring the discussion norms, the parties also need to manage the decision rules—that is, the way the group will decide what to do (Brett, 1991). In decision-making groups, the dominant view is to assume that majority rules and, at some point, take a vote of all members, assuming that any settlement option that receives more than 50 percent of the votes will be the one adopted. Obviously, this is not the only option. Groups can make decisions by dictatorship (one person decides); oligarchy (a dominant minority coalition decides); simple majority (one more person than half the group decides); two-thirds majority; quasi consensus (most of the group agrees, and those who dissent agree not to protest or raise objections); and true unanimity, or consensus (everyone agrees). Determining the group's decision rule before deliberations begin will also significantly affect the group process. For example, if a simple majority will make the decision in a five-person group, then only three people need to agree. Thus, any three people can get together and form a coalition during or even prior to the meeting. In contrast, if the decision rule will be consensus, or unanimity, then the group must meet and work hard enough to ensure that all parties' interests are raised, discussed, and incorporated into the group decision. Whether a coalition-building strategy or a complete sharing of positions and interests and problem solving will be necessary requires significantly different approaches.

Table 9.1 presents a chart that summarizes the three different negotiating strategies and the related tactics, decision rules, goal orientations, and decision aids. Each of the

TABLE 9.1 Tactics, Decision Rules, Goal Orientations, and Decision Aids for Mutual, Coalition, and Individual Gain

Mutual	*Coalition*	*Individual*
Tactics		
1. Share own and elicit others' interests	1. Seek similar others and construct an alternative that meets your interests	1. Open with a high, but not outrageously high, demand
2. Consider many alternatives; be creative; look for ways to use available resources	2. Recruit just enough members to control the group's decision	2. Argue the merits of your alternative; do not reveal your interests
3. Don't just compromise; make trade-offs	3. Encourage interpersonal obligations among coalition members	3. Appear unable or unwilling to concede
4. Encourage positive relations		4. Encourage positive relations
		5. Use threats, time deadlines, and promises, if necessary
Decision Rules		
Consensus	Oligarchy	Dictator
Unanimity	Majority	
Goal Orientation		
Cooperative	Cooperative or individual	Individual
Decision Aids		
Packaging	Packaging	
Search models	Search models	

SOURCE: From J. Brett, "Negotiating Group Decisions," *Negotiation Journal,* July 1991, pp.291–310. Used with permission of Plenum Publishing Corporation.

three strategies—maximizing individual gain, entering into a coalition, or pursuing mutual gain (consensus or unanimity decision rules)—is outlined, along with the tactics, decision rules, goal orientations, and decision aids that accompany each. As the chart reveals, any one set of elements can drive the others—decision rules or goals can drive the approaches, or vice versa. Thus, negotiators would do well to understand the decision rules and goal orientations before selecting a strategy and set of tactics. Similarly, negotiators need to understand the consequences of adopting an approach (strategy and tactics) that may not fit the related decision rules and goal orientations, because mismatches are likely to produce frustration, poor group process, and perhaps suboptimal outcomes.

Strive for a First Agreement.   Finally, if the objective is consensus or the best quality solution, negotiators should not strive to achieve it all at once. Rather, they should strive for a *first agreement* that can be revised, upgraded, and improved. As we have discussed, the additional complexity of multiparty negotiations increases the complexity of the events, the likelihood of communication breakdown, and the likelihood that the parties will negotiate more positionally (either because of the competitive dynamics or the consequences of audience or constituency dynamics). Given these conditions, achieving true consensus among the parties becomes much more difficult, even if a true consensus solution exists. As a result, it is often better to set a more modest objective for these negotiations: to reach a preliminary agreement or a tentative consensus that can then be systematically improved through "renegotiation," using the first agreement as a plateau that can be modified, reshaped, and improved upon in a follow-up negotiation effort.

The drawback, of course, is that many group members may be satisfied with the first solution—either because it already incorporates their views or because the difficulty of achieving it may sap their enthusiasm for exerting any time and energy to improve it. First agreements typically reflect the position of a group's majority or the views of a small number of powerful group members (Brett, 1991; Nemeth, 1986, 1989). These parties may not be open to dissenting views that would otherwise stimulate consideration of a wider set of possible alternative outcomes. As Brett (1991) notes:

> Majority and powerful individuals, however, are often intolerant of dissent. After all, why should they risk losing control over the group decision by providing an opportunity for dissent? A second agreement resolves this dilemma. It preserves the control of the powerful party—if no better agreement is forthcoming, the first agreement will stand. It also protects the interests of both the majority and the minority, letting them reveal information about their weaknesses and hidden agendas without fear that the group will use the information against them. At their best, second agreement deliberations encourage the sharing of minority points of view, the questioning of assumptions, the discussion of decision ramifications, the search for superior alternatives and the testing of consensus. (p. 294)

This resistance to further deliberations by parties who are happy with the first agreement may be overcome by taking a break after the first agreement is reached, encouraging the group to critique and evaluate the first agreement, and explicitly planning to come back with a commitment to try second-agreement negotiations (renegotiations). In addition, if the group has been through a great deal of divisive and unproductive conflict to reach the first agreement, then the renegotiations must specifically attend to changing and managing the conflict process. As Brett (1991) states, effectively attending to this process may also allow a group to achieve a high-quality outcome in their first negotiation effort.

The Agreement Phase

The third and final stage in managing multiparty negotiations is the agreement stage. During the agreement stage, the parties are employing the decision rules and criteria we reviewed above. They are also likely to encounter some last-minute problems and issues, such as deadline pressures, the discovery of new issues that were not previously addressed, the need for more information on certain problems or concerns, and the tendency for some parties to threaten veto power while they lobby to get their specific pet idea or project included in the final group agreement.

Here are some things the chairperson can do to keep the group moving toward a successful completion:

• *Move the group toward selecting one or more of the options.* Use the process rules we discussed earlier, as well as the wide variety of techniques for achieving an integrative agreement presented in Chapter 4. Listen for the emergence of the "snowballing coalition" among key members (see the coalition section earlier in this chapter). Permit and encourage packaging and trade-offs among multiple issues, or modification of the first agreement or tentative agreement reached earlier. If the decision is particularly laden with conflict, pursue a first agreement, with the understanding that the group will take a break and come back to renegotiate the agreement at a later date.

• *Shape a tentative agreement.* Write it down. Work on language. Write the wording on a blackboard, flip chart, or computer screen that can be displayed to the entire group, so that all can see it and edit it freely. Test to make sure all parties understand the agreement and its implications and consequences. Remember that the person who does the writing often has more power than others, because he or she gets to write the agreement in his or her own language and may bias or selectively remember some points and omit others.

• *Discuss whatever follow-up or next steps need to occur.* Make sure that individuals who have a role in this process understand what they need to do. Make assignments to individuals to ensure that key action steps are designed and executed. Schedule a follow-up meeting. Plan for another meeting in the future to evaluate how the agreement is working.

• *Thank the group for their participation, their hard work, and their efforts.* If the discussion has been particularly difficult or required a large time commitment, a small-group celebration and formal thank-you notes or gifts may be in order. Have dinner or a party together to celebrate all of the hard work.

• *If desirable, conduct a postmortem.* Have group members discuss the process and the outcome, and evaluate what they might do better or differently the next time. This will ensure learning for both the group members and the chair.

V S Hixson
VIVIAN SCOTT HIXSON

THE CHRONICLE OF HIGHER EDUCATION

"Okay. The resolution is that since nobody on the committee took notes last week, and nobody can remember what happened, what we did last week probably didn't matter. All in favor say 'Aye.' "

Used by permission of Vivian Scott Hixson.

INTERTEAM NEGOTIATIONS

In this final section of the chapter, we examine negotiations where the parties are working in teams rather than as single individuals. We use the term "interteam negotiation" to describe these situations: two or more co-negotiators sharing interests and priorities who negotiate with two or more co-negotiators on the other side who share their own interests and priorities (Shapiro and Von Glinow, 1999). In Chapter 8 we discussed how additional team members at the negotiation table provide an "audience" that influences the roles individuals assume during the negotiation. Here we address a broader set of questions about negotiation processes when teams are present: Do teams behave differently than individuals? How does the presence of two or more people change the way one party interacts with the other party and advances its own interests? Are teams more likely to act competitively, or are they more inclined to pursue cooperative strategies that would lead to integrative outcomes? Only a small number of research studies have investigated these issues. We can summarize the findings of these studies in four broad conclusions.

Integrative Agreements Are More Likely When Teams Are Involved.   A study by Thompson, Peterson, and Brodt (1996) compared negotiations between teams, negotiations between individuals, and (mixed) negotiations where a team negotiates against an individual. They found that joint profits for the two parties are greater when at least one of the parties is a team. Part of the explanation was that teams exchange more information than solo negotiators, which increases the likelihood that integrative potential can be discovered and exploited. Even when a team negotiates against a solo negotiator, these positive benefits of team negotiation occur. Polzer (1996) showed that the benefit of teams for achieving integrative outcomes may depend on *experience*: when negotiators were novices, the presence of teams reduced the integrativeness of settlements. However, when trained negotiators where involved, the presence of teams led to more integrative outcomes. In general, however, the presence of at least one team seems to trigger behaviors that enhance integrativeness. As Thompson and colleagues (1996, p. 75) state, "team negotiation initiates a process of information exchange that is mutually beneficial for all parties."

Teams Are Sometimes More Competitive Than Individuals, and May Claim More Value.   A substantial research tradition in game theory has shown that groups tend to be highly competitive in their dealings with other groups (e.g., McCallum, Harring, Gilmore, Drenan, Chase, Insko, and Thibaut, 1985). Does this extend to the realm of negotiation? Research efforts to explore this issue have yielded mixed findings. In one study of the effects of negotiating teams on competition, cooperation, and trust, Polzer (1996) found that when teams are present in negotiations, there is more contentiousness and less trust between the parties. Other studies, however, failed to find differences between the competitiveness of negotiating teams versus individuals (O'Connor, 1997; Thompson, Peterson, and Brodt, 1996).

Competitiveness aside, are teams better than individuals at the distributive component of negotiation—claiming the value that the parties have created? Research to date points to an advantage for teams. In one of the key recent studies of team negotiations that we have discussed (Thompson, Peterson, and Brodt, 1996), teams claimed more value than solo negotiators in one experiment, but not in another involving the same negotiation task. Polzer (1996) found that teams did better than the individuals against whom they were negotiating in mixed (team vs. solo) matchups. One partial explanation lies in Polzer's finding that negotiating teams were perceived as having more power than individuals. These studies point to two implications for an individual facing a negotiating team on the other side: First, be attentive to the possibility that the team will be aggressive in pursuing its interests and claiming value, and second, avoid the trap of assuming that the other party has disproportionate power merely because it elected to send a team to negotiate.

Accountability Pressures Are Different for Teams Compared to Individuals. As we discussed in Chapter 8, individual negotiators are more likely to behave in a more competitive manner when they are accountable to constituents than when accountability pressures do not exist. This occurs, at least in part, because negotiators feel a need to show "toughness" when the people on whose behalf they are negotiating can observe their performance. However, a study by O'Connor (1997) reveals that *teams* of negotiators do not respond in the same way to constituent surveillance. In her experiment, accountability increased the competitive behavior of solo negotiators to a significantly greater degree than it did for negotiating teams. O'Connor's findings suggest that the pressures created by accountability are distributed and diffused among the members of a negotiating team, leading individual team members to perceive less responsibility for the outcomes that result from the negotiation.

The Relationship among Team Members Affects Negotiation Process and Outcomes. Peterson and Thompson (1997) examined what happens when teams comprised of friends negotiate against teams of strangers. Not surprisingly, they found that teams of friends were more cohesive as a group, and more focused on maintaining their relationship, than were teams of strangers. For teams of strangers, more cohesiveness was associated with improved negotiating performance. Peterson and Thompson found that the relationship among team members affected how information was used to reach a negotiated outcome. Specifically, when individuals on the team had unique information about the team's interests and preferences, teams of strangers were able to claim more of the joint profit on the table than were teams of friends. The issue of accountability also played a role in Peterson and Thompson's study. When teams of strangers were accountable for their negotiating performance (to a supervisor), they did better (claimed a greater share of joint profit) than did teams of friends who were similarly accountable.

Taken as a whole, these findings indicate that relationships among team members complicate the ways that teams use information and tactics to work toward a negotiated settlement. As a general matter, Peterson and Thompson (1997) found that teams of strangers outperform teams of friends under some conditions, but that teams of friends never outperform teams of strangers. We do not conclude that it is necessarily "bad" for individuals negotiating as a team to be friends or acquaintances, but it does appear that when team members have a pre-existing friendly relationship, they need to be especially vigilant about not allowing those friendships to interfere with the pursuit of optimal outcomes. Teams of strangers, on the other hand, may be able to improve their performance by taking the time to become a more cohesive operating unit before entering the negotiation.

CHAPTER SUMMARY

Most negotiation theory has been developed under the assumption that negotiation is a bilateral process—that there are only two focal negotiators or teams of negotiators opposing each other. Yet many negotiations are multilateral deliberations—more than two negotiators are involved, each with his or her own interests and positions, and the group must arrive at a collective agreement regarding a plan, decision, or course of action. In this chapter, we explored the dynamics of three forms of multiparty negotiations: when the parties form subgroups, or coalitions, as a way to realize their objective; when multiple parties must work together to achieve a collective decision or consensus; and when one or more parties in a negotiation are comprised of a team of people rather than a single individual.

One theme that runs through all forms of multiparty negotiation is the need to manage situations that are significantly more complex than two-party negotiations. We present here a brief set of questions that should be kept in mind by any participant in negotiations involving coalitions, multiple parties, and/or teams:

- What are the consequences of the parties failing to agree due to the increased complexities? What happens if there is no agreement?

- How will the parties involved actually make a decision? That is, what decision rules will be used? Why are these the best possible rules?

- How can the parties use iterations—multiple rounds of discussion—to achieve their objectives? (This may be particularly appropriate when the decision rule is consensus or the best-quality agreement, because consensus may not be achievable in a single iteration.)

- Do we need a designated chair or facilitator? Should it be a neutral outsider, or can one of the parties fill this role? What tactics can a facilitator use to manage group process in order to ensure that the best decision is reached? (These tactics might include ensuring that the group is exposed to a variety of information sources, managing the process to make sure that the group considers and discusses all available information thoroughly, and structuring the group's agenda with care.)

If these issues are raised and thoughtfully considered, the parties involved are considerably more likely to feel better about the process, and to arrive at an effective outcome, than if these factors are left to chance.

CHAPTER 10

Individual Differences

Some people are better negotiators than others. How do the best negotiators behave, think, or feel differently from average negotiators? Researchers have been examining the effects of individual differences on the process and outcome of negotiations for years. An enormous amount of research on this topic has been conducted. Unfortunately, many of the findings in this area are fragmented, contradictory, and difficult to apply in practical settings. Our goal in this chapter is to provide an overview of individual differences and negotiation, and to discuss some new research findings that appear to be particularly promising in this area.

We begin with a review of early research on individual differences. We then examine more recent research on individual differences and negotiation, segmenting our discussion into three major categories: (1) dimensions of *personality* that appear to have an influence on negotiations, (2) the effect of *sex and gender* on negotiation, and (3) the role of native *abilities* in negotiation, including cognitive ability and the relatively new domain of emotional intelligence. The chapter then proceeds with a discussion of the behavioral approach to studying individual differences in negotiations and explores how superior negotiators behave differently from average negotiators. Finally, the chapter concludes with a critique of the research on individual differences in negotiation and some suggestions for future research in this area.

EARLY RESEARCH ON INDIVIDUAL DIFFERENCES AND NEGOTIATION

Research efforts to define the effects of background, demographic, ability, and personality factors in negotiations began in the late 1950s. Jeffrey Rubin and Bert Brown, in their book *The Social Psychology of Bargaining and Negotiation* (1975), reviewed 200 empirical studies of background, demographic, and personality factors that might contribute to differences in bargaining outcomes (detailed reviews of early research were also provided by Hermann and Kogan, 1977, and Terhune, 1970). Studies have examined the impact of differences in age, sex, race, cultural and national heritage, and socioeconomic status on negotiation outcomes. Early research examined personality factors such as risk-taking propensity; perceived locus of control; level of cognitive complexity; tolerance for ambiguity; level of self-concept; nature and strength of social motives (e.g., needs for achievement, power, and/or affiliation); attitudes (e.g., interpersonal trust, cooperativeness, authoritarianism); and normal or abnormal personality structure, to name some of the more prominent variables studied.

The findings from these studies are widely disparate, inconclusive, and sometimes directly contradictory. For example, Rubin and Brown (1975) reviewed more than 100 studies on sex differences and their impact on bargaining behavior: About 30 studies reported no difference between men and women; 20 studies reported that males bargain more cooperatively than females; and a large number of others reported that females bargain more cooperatively than males. Similarly contradictory results can be noted for many other personality variables. Explaining and coping with the reasons for these patterns of contradictory and/or nonsignificant findings became a major challenge in this area of research. We briefly examine three different explanations that account, at least in part, for the contradictory and inconclusive early research findings.

The Effects of Individual Differences Are Too Subtle and Elusive to be Revealed by Contemporary Research Strategies and Methods.   In effect, measuring instruments are too primitive to detect individual differences in negotiation that probably exist. One possible explanation for this, suggested by Hamner (1980), is that the impact of social structure and context variables in negotiation may override the effects of personality variables. Although individual differences may predispose bargainers to particular behavior in the early rounds of negotiation, key structural factors such as the nature of the bargaining problem, the relative power between negotiators, pressures from constituencies, or simply the behavior of the other negotiator may quickly override the effect of any individual differences that existed at the start of bargaining. Moreover, these same structural variables may inhibit opportunities for individual differences to emerge and actually have an effect during negotiations.

The issue of bargaining task may be particularly important. Much of the early research on demographic and personality differences employed a simple, two-choice Prisoner's Dilemma game. The Prisoner's Dilemma is traditionally played by experimental subjects who cannot see each other, do not speak to each other, and whose "negotiating" consists of making simple choices between more cooperative and more competitive decision options. Limited and constrained interaction of this form is hardly comparable to the complex verbal and nonverbal communication processes that occur in face-to-face negotiation. Hence, research scenarios and settings must be rich enough to allow the impact of personality variables to emerge, but not be so dominated by major structural relationships that when personality factors do emerge, they are quickly obscured.

Another possibility is that personality variables may interact with structural variables in complex and perhaps unpredictable ways (Hamner, 1980). Not only do structural variables—relative power, time pressure, accountability, possibilities for joint gain—dominate the prediction of the likely outcomes, but also if personality does have an effect, its impact may be in combination with structural elements. For example, certain types of people may be successful in win-win negotiation situations while other types of people may perform well in win-lose negotiations (Barry and Friedman, 1998, provided evidence to support this proposition, as we will discuss later in this chapter).

Findings Are Inconclusive Because of Flawed or Inconsistent Research Methods.   The variables examined, and the methods by which they were examined, varied considerably from one study to the next in early research on individual differences in negotiation. As a result, contradictory findings can be traced to the use of different research designs, methods, and experimental bargaining problems. An example of a concerted effort to remedy these problems with a comprehensive research design was a study by Hermann and Kogan (1977).

Hermann and Kogan proposed eight personality factors that should influence negotiation outcomes: level of manifest anxiety, authoritarianism, cognitive complexity, tendency to be conciliatory, dogmatism, propensity toward risk taking, level of self-esteem, and predisposition toward suspiciousness. They expected these factors to influence (1) a bargainer's predispositions toward the negotiating situation; (2) the behavior of the negotiator during negotiations, regardless of the conduct of the other party; and (3) the behavior of the negotiator during negotiations, given that the other party's personality dispositions were similar to, or the opposite of, the negotiator's. After administering a battery of personality instruments to Princeton undergraduate males, pairs of these students played several rounds of a Prisoner's Dilemma game. Hermann and Kogan found, however, that only two personality variables–cognitive complexity and self-esteem–predicted a bargainer's predisposed strategy toward the other party, and only two variables—authoritarianism and self-esteem—differentiated how students described their own actual strategy in the game. In all, only 3 out of 32 analyses between personality variables and actual game-playing strategy reached acceptable levels of statistical significance. They did find that certain personality variables emerged as important when bargainers were matched with a partner who scored similarly on the particular trait measure. Hence, the pairing of negotiators with similar styles allowed the interactive effect of personality and behavior to emerge. Overall, although selected results did emerge in Hermann and Kogan's research, many of the predicted results were not significant or conclusive. As in so much of the research that came before, the findings revealed no consistent pattern with regard to the clear effect of any one personality element across all three outcome measures.

One potential problem with research in this area (including the study we have just described) is the issue of *sampling*. The effects of certain personality predispositions may go undiscovered if research is limited to unique, homogeneous populations of research subjects who do not possess that predisposition, or who all possess it to a roughly equivalent extent (Hamner, 1980). Most experimental negotiation studies have been conducted with volunteer college populations, usually students enrolled in psychology or management courses. This particular population may be so homogeneous with respect to age, socioeconomic background, and other demographic or dispositional characteristics that true differences in negotiation style may not be readily identified. In the study by Hermann and Kogan (1977), we do not know the demographic characteristics of Princeton undergraduate males, nor whether this sample of students represents a reasonable approximation of the general population of New Jersey or the United States. We can speculate, however, that concerns about sampling homogeneity apply. Moreover, as we mentioned earlier, the constrained choice options of the Prisoner's Dilemma game may minimize the subtlety and strength that these variables could have and that might emerge in a more complex negotiating scenario. Finally, Hermann and Kogan themselves note that once the gaming interaction had begun, personality elements were considerably less successful at predicting negotiating behavior. This supports the assertion that, in the long run, structural and interactive factors may be likely to dominate initial personality differences.

The Inconclusive Findings Are Due to Flawed Conceptualizations of Individual Difference Factors.   Some early critics argued that researchers were incorrectly defining key personality factors. Perhaps inconsistent results can be explained more productively, the argument went, if personality traits were thought of in terms of broader underlying dimensions that (at that point) had not yet been identified. A significant effort in this regard was by Rubin and Brown (1975). To explain and organize the diverse and often contradictory findings that were revealed by their review, Rubin and Brown proposed a single dimension of personal style—interpersonal orientation (IO).

Individuals may be classified as either high or low in their interpersonal orientation. Someone with a high IO is "responsive to the interpersonal aspects of his relationship with the other. He is both interested in, and reactive to, variations in the other's behavior" (Rubin and Brown, 1975, p. 158). High IOs determine their own behavior in a conflict setting by tuning in to the other's behavior—the other's cooperativeness or competitiveness, relative amount of power, use of power, and adherence to certain bargaining norms such as equity, exchange, and reciprocity.

High IOs use this information in one of two ways, depending on whether they are cooperatively or competitively disposed. *Cooperative* high IOs attend to the other party's behavior for the purpose of maximizing cooperation; they look for behavioral cues that the other can be trusted and, if they find them, will act trustworthily and maximize the exchange and flow of information to enhance a cooperative, mutually satisfactory outcome. In contrast, a *competitive* high IO attends to the behavior of the other person for the purpose of using this information to gain strategic advantage. Competitive high IOs are suspicious of others' motives and intentions (expecting to be exploited), and untrustworthy themselves (either to gain advantage or as a defense against the expected exploitation).

In contrast to either form of high IO, a low IO is characterized by "a nonresponsiveness to the interpersonal aspects of his relationship with the other. His interest is neither in cooperating nor competing with the other, but rather in maximizing his own gain pretty much regardless of how the other fares" (Rubin and Brown, 1975, p. 159). Low IOs determine their behavior in conflict situations on the basis of their own goals and preferred outcomes, and an evaluation of the situation they are in. Low IOs are less concerned with the behavior of the other—either cooperative or competitive—than with the situational variations and complexities that might influence their outcome.

The value of the IO construct is that it provides a unified way to organize and explain some of the discrepant, conflicting findings of earlier research. Rubin and Brown (1975) demonstrated that much of the conflicting research could be successfully explained if IO were considered to be the major element of differentiation between groups. For example, an experiment by Swap and Rubin (1983) compared the effects of sex differences with the effects of IO differences on a preference for equity versus equality in the distribution of outcomes. It has frequently been proposed that, with regard to outcomes, men demonstrate a greater preference for *equity* (parties in the relationship receive outcomes in relation to their inputs), while women demonstrate a greater preference for *equality* (each party receives the same outcomes). In the Swap and Rubin experiment, IO and sex differences were systematically controlled in a resource-distribution task. The results indicate that males and low IOs tended to allocate

BOX 10.1
Taking Conflict Personally—an Individual Difference

Researchers Judith Dallinger and Dale Hample (1995) have determined that individuals differ in the degree to which they take conflict personally—that is, experience strong negative emotional reactions to specific conflict management incidents and episodes. People who take certain conflicts personally are more likely to feel threatened, anxious, damaged, devalued, and/or insulted by a particular conflict event. The researchers argue that taking conflict personally is both a state (a temporary feeling associated with a particular event) and a trait (an enduring predisposition that differs across individuals). Research findings suggest that

- Those who are more likely to take conflict personally are more likely to have nonconfrontational (avoiding or accommodating) styles of managing conflict.
- Those who are more likely to take conflict personally prefer supervisors who have a compromising conflict management style.
- Those who are more likely to take conflict personally are more likely to feel persecuted by, and have a higher stress management reaction to, those supervisors who use a forcing (competing) conflict style, and are much less satisfied with this supervisor.

SOURCE: J. M. Dallinger and B. D. Hample, "Personalizing and Managing Conflict," *International Journal of Conflict Management* 6, no. 3 (1995), pp. 273–89.

rewards according to equity standards, while females and high IOs seemed more concerned with equality of outcomes.

Although research interest in the specific concept of IO did not endure much beyond the early 1980s, it did redirect attention toward more systematic investigations of individual differences having greater direct relevance for the context of negotiation. We discuss this later body of research in the next three sections covering (1) personality, (2) sex and gender, and (3) abilities.

PERSONALITY AND NEGOTIATION

Much of the earlier research on personality effects can be faulted for selecting personality variables more on the basis of convenience than on a strongly reasoned relationship between the variable and the negotiation process. For example, many personality variables seem to have been selected because well-established scales had already been developed for measuring them rather than because they had a clearly logical presumed influence on negotiation. While this rationale may make sense for research reasons—having confidence in the reliability and validity of measurement—the dimensions themselves may have been less important in negotiation settings than other, more meaningful personality distinctions. In this section, we review seven approaches to studying personality and disposition that have shown greater promise as predictors of negotiation behavior (see Box 10.1). These include (*a*) conflict style, (*b*) social value orientation, (*c*) interpersonal trust, (*d*) self-efficacy, (*e*) self-monitoring and locus of control, (*f*) Machiavellianism, and (*g*) the so-called Big Five personality factors.

FIGURE 10.1 Thomas-Kilmann Conflict Styles

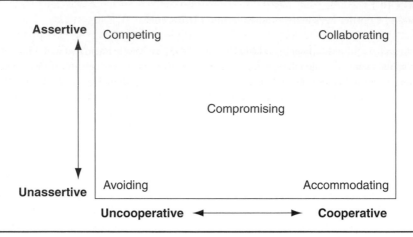

SOURCE: Adapted from K. Thomas and R. H. Kilmann (1974). Thomas Kilmann conflict mode survey. Tuxedo Junction, NY: Xicom. Used with permission.

Conflict Management Style

Dealing with conflict is a central part of the negotiating process. In Chapter 1, we identified five modes of behavior that are commonly used to deal with conflict: contending, problem solving, inaction, yielding, and compromising. We also examined the effect on outcomes that would be created by choosing one style over another; we did not, however, examine the *reasons* that one style is commonly chosen over another. A negotiator may use rational criteria to make this choice, such as selecting the style that is assumed to be most likely to lead to the desired outcomes. It is also possible, however, that people use styles consistently because they have a personality predisposition to do so, and that conscious choice may not be as important. As discussed in Chapter 1, there are two levels of concern underlying the five conflict management styles. One is the degree of concern a party shows for his or her own outcomes, and the other is the degree of concern the party shows for the other's outcomes. Thomas (1976) has proposed that two personality dimensions can represent these two levels of concern: the degree of *assertiveness* that a party maintains for his or her own preferred solutions or outcomes, and the degree of *cooperativeness* a party shows toward working with the other party to achieve their mutual goals. Analogous to the approaches we described in Chapter 1, Thomas's research identified five major conflict management styles (see Figure 10.1):

A *competing* style—high on assertiveness and low on cooperativeness.

An *accommodating* style—low on assertiveness and high on cooperativeness.

An *avoiding* style—low on both assertiveness and cooperativeness.

A *collaborating* style—high on both assertiveness and cooperativeness.

A *compromising* style—moderate on both assertiveness and cooperativeness.

Research by Thomas and his colleagues (Kilmann and Thomas, 1977; Thomas, 1976, 1977) has supported the premise that individual conflict management styles vary according to two factors: the nature of the situation (i.e., that negotiators make rational choices about which strategy to use) and individual tendencies to use certain styles regardless of the situation. In addition, individual differences in conflict management style have been correlated with other dispositions. For example, Thomas (1976) suggests that individuals high in a competing style are lower in risk taking, more internally controlled, higher on needs for power and control, and lower on needs for affiliation. Similarly, individuals strong in collaboration are thought to be more task oriented, creative, and capable of dealing with complexity. Each of these relationships is derived through inference, however, and is not a result of direct research. Similar inferences are drawn between individuals with particular conflict orientations and their actual behavior in conflict situations. If the stakes for winning are high and outcomes are derived through individual effort, then individuals with strong competing modes should dominate the situation; if outcomes are derived from joint efforts, then individuals with a strong collaborative mode should dominate. In contrast, if the stakes are low for an individual, then that individual should be more likely to ignore the conflict (avoiding mode), or allow the other to reap what little resources are available (accommodating mode).

The Thomas–Kilmann model, and subsequent research on the motivational potential of conflict management styles, represents a simple yet coherent model for viewing the effect of personality variables on bargaining and conflict management behavior. Research exploring the two dimensions has generally been supportive (Kabanoff, 1987; Pruitt and Rubin, 1986; Rahim, 1983; Ruble and Thomas, 1976; van de Vliert and Kabanoff, 1988; van de Vliert and Prein, 1989). Although little research has explored the effects of negotiator choice of conflict management styles on actual negotiation behavior (see Butler, 1994), studies where conflict styles were experimentally manipulated have generally supported the model (Ben-Yoav and Pruitt, 1984a, 1984b; Carnevale and Keenan, 1990; O'Connor, 1997; O'Connor and Carnevale, 1997; Pruitt, Carnevale, Ben-Yoav, Nochajski, and Van Slyck, 1983). There is debate about the usefulness of models of conflict styles (see Carnevale and Pruitt, 1992; Thompson, 1990b), but in general, efforts to develop measures of conflict styles, and to explore how these styles are related to conflict behavior, have fared considerably better than did earlier research on the effects of personality variables.

Social Value Orientation

Social value orientations are preferences that people have regarding the kinds of outcomes they prefer in social settings where interdependence with others is required (McLintock and Liebrand, 1988). Some people are said to have a *proself* or *egoistic* orientation, which means they are primarily concerned with personal outcomes and unconcerned with outcomes obtained by the other party; others are said to have a *prosocial* orientation, which means a preference for outcomes that benefit both self and others with whom they are interdependent (De Dreu, Weingart, and Kwon, 2000).

Negotiation is clearly an example of the kind of social interdependence where these social value orientations might be expected to play a role. Research on this issue

"Dickie Wilson attacked my values."

(e.g., De Dreu and Van Lange, 1995; Olekalns and Smith, 1999; Olekalns, Smith, and Kibby, 1996) has shown that proself individuals behave distributively, adopting a style that is relatively tough and contentious, with more emphasis on bargaining over positions than exploring underlying interests that might yield mutual gain. Prosocials, on the other hand, being more concerned with the well-being of others, are more oriented toward problem solving and reciprocal cooperation. As a result, prosocial negotiators achieve more integrative outcomes (higher joint gain) than proself negotiators (De Dreu, Weingart, and Kwon, 2000).

Prosocial versus egoistic motives in negotiation can be rooted either in stable individual differences or in elements of a particular situation (for example, when negotiators are encouraged to act selfishly or cooperatively). However, as De Dreu and his colleagues point out, the effects of these social motives on negotiation appear to be essentially the same regardless of whether they derive from individual differences or situational demands.

Interpersonal Trust

As we discussed in Chapter 1, one of the fundamental dilemmas in negotiation is the degree to which negotiators should trust the other party. Negotiators must gather information and determine how much the other party is likely to be deceptive or deceitful—by misrepresenting true positions, distorting relevant facts, or introducing spurious information and positions. In addition, the trustworthiness of the other party may change over time, depending on whether negotiations are beginning or near the end, and depending on whether the negotiation has proceeded cooperatively or competitively.

Julian Rotter (1967, 1971, 1980) has proposed that interpersonal trust functions as a personality variable with important effects in social relationships. According to Rotter's (1980) research, individuals differ in their level of interpersonal trust—defined as "a generalized expectancy held by an individual that the word, promise, oral, or written statement of another individual or group can be relied upon" (p. 1). Unlike a broad-based belief in the goodness of others and the benign nature of the world, Rotter argues, interpersonal trust is determined by the experiences that individuals have in dealing with others. If individuals have had experiences when they have trusted others, and this trust has been rewarded by reciprocal trust and productive relationships, then generalized interpersonal trust should be high. In contrast, if individuals have had their trust punished by others through exploitation, deception, and dishonesty, then interpersonal trust is likely to be low.

Rotter and his colleagues developed a test for diagnosing an individual's level of interpersonal trust and used the scores to measure levels of interpersonal trustworthiness. The interested reader may find a more detailed description of these and other studies of interpersonal trust in Rotter (1967, 1971, 1980). Individuals who are more trusting are also less likely to lie or cheat. High trusters believe that others will be trustworthy, and that they need to be trustworthy themselves; hence, they are more likely to impose high moral standards on themselves and behave ethically. In contrast, low trusters believe that others cannot be trusted to observe the rules, and therefore feel less pressure themselves to tell the truth. As a result, they believe that lying, cheating, and similar behaviors are necessary defensive reactions.

High trusters were not more gullible than low trusters, a surprising result to some people. It might be assumed that high trusters would be more likely to believe communications from other people without questioning their validity, and therefore would be more likely to be tricked. The studies summarized by Rotter (1980) indicate that the high-trust individual is not more prone to gullibility than the low-trust individual. As Rotter states,

> It seems that high trusters can read the cues as well or as poorly as low trusters. They differ, however, in their willingness to trust the stranger when there are no clear-cut data about previous behavior. The high truster says to himself or herself, "I will trust the person until I have clear evidence that he or she can't be trusted." The low truster says, "I will not trust the person until there is clear evidence that he or she can be trusted." (p. 6)

Both orientations are prone to self-fulfilling prophecies. An individual with high interpersonal trust is likely to approach the other person, in attitude and style, in a way that communicates trust. Should the other be searching for cues about appropriate behavior in this situation, he or she may respond with similarly high levels of trusting behavior. The other's behavior is thus likely to reward and reinforce the initial orientation of the high-trust individual, and lead to a cooperative relationship between the parties. In contrast, a low-trust individual is likely to approach the other, in attitude and style, in a way that communicates suspicion and mistrust of the other's motives and intentions. If the other is searching for cues as to the appropriate behavior, he or she may respond with low self-disclosure, dishonesty, and mistrust of the party. This behavior will thus reward and reinforce the initial low-trust orientation and lead to a less cooperative relationship between the parties.

William Ross and Jessica LaCroix (1996) reviewed the diverse literature on trust and negotiation, concluding that trust may have multiple effects on negotiation. Their review suggests that negotiators who are high in trust may be more cooperative when they negotiate, and that they may also think about negotiations differently than negotiators who are less trusting. Ross and LaCroix hypothesize that trust may influence cognitive processes in negotiation like the illusory correlation bias or cognitive framing (see Chapter 5 for a discussion of communication and cognitive biases), but these hypotheses need to be confirmed by empirical research.

Self-Efficacy and Locus of Control

Perceived self-efficacy is considered to be a critical aspect of mastering complex interpersonal skills, such as those involved in negotiation. Wood and Bandura (1989) define self-efficacy as "people's beliefs in their capabilities to mobilize the motivation, cognitive resources, and courses of action needed to exercise control over events in their lives" (p. 364). In essence, self-efficacy is considered to be a judgment about one's ability to behave effectively in a given situation (Gist, Stevens, and Bavetta, 1991). People with high self-efficacy have been found to obtain higher outcomes in many organizational situations than those with low self-efficacy (Wood and Bandura, 1989). Self-efficacy has been found to influence performance directly, through the setting of higher goals and the adoption of more analytic strategies.

Research by Marilyn Gist, Cynthia Stevens, and Anne Bavetta (1991) suggests that self-efficacy may play an important role in negotiation. Their research used a salary negotiation simulation where participants in an experiment played the role of an employee who was negotiating with his or her manager over the salary of a new job. Gist and her colleagues (1991; also see Stevens, Bavetta, and Gist, 1993; Stevens and Gist, 1997) found that people with higher levels of self-efficacy obtained higher salaries in the simulation. Their research further suggested that self-efficacy leads to higher outcomes in the salary negotiation because people higher in self-efficacy were also more likely to set higher goals before the negotiation (also see Brett, Pinkley, and Jacofsky, 1996). There is also some evidence that one's perceived level of competence at the task of negotiation may increase the likelihood that collaborative problem solving will occur. Alexander, Schul, and McCorkle (1994), in a study of industrial managers participating in a sales negotiation simulation, found that individuals high in *task-specific self-esteem* (one's perceived degree of competence in performing a task) engaged in more cooperative, problem-solving behaviors.

A construct conceptually related to self-efficacy, *locus of control*, has also been investigated by researchers. Rotter (1966) defines locus of control as the extent to which people perceive that they have control over events that occur. Those who attribute the cause of events to external reasons (e.g., luck) have a high *external* locus of control, while those who attribute the cause of events to internal reasons (e.g., ability) have a high *internal* locus of control (Rotter, 1966). In a distributive negotiation task, Ford (1983) found that "internals" had higher resistance points than "externals." In addition, Ford found a tendency for teams composed of internals to be more likely to stalemate during negotiations. In their television advertisement simulation study, Greenhalgh and Neslin (1983) found that externals were more likely to prefer an impasse than a moderately favorable settlement. While neither study found a direct effect of locus of control on negotiation outcomes, a study of distributive negotiations in four-person networks with a sample of female college students by Stolte (1983) suggests that internals may negotiate higher outcomes than externals, especially when they are in noncentral positions in networks. Taken as a whole, the research findings suggest that locus of control may have an influence on negotiator aspirations, preferences, and negotiation outcomes.

Self-Monitoring

Self-monitoring refers to the extent to which people are aware of and responsive to the social cues that come from one's social environment (Snyder, 1974, 1987). High self-monitors are attentive to external, interpersonal information that arises in social settings and are more inclined to treat this information as cues to how one should behave. Low self-monitors are less attentive to external information that may cue behavior and guided more in their behavioral choices by inner, personal feelings. One can think of self-monitoring as the extent to which a person "monitors" the external social environment for cues regarding the role of appropriate behavior of "self."

Jerry Jordan and Michael Roloff (1997) examined the effects of self-monitoring on planning for negotiation. The results of an integrative negotiation simulation demonstrated that high self-monitors were more likely to plan the impressions that they wanted to make on the other negotiator (e.g., to appear friendly), to plan to use logrolling during the negotiation (see Chapter 4), and to consider more strategies while planning. Self-monitoring also had an effect on the outcome of the negotiation, with high self-monitors negotiating outcomes that helped them achieve higher percentages of their goals than low self-monitors.

The Jordan and Roloff (1997) study demonstrates that self-monitoring may be an important individual difference that influences negotiations. Self-monitoring appears to be important during planning, but it may also interact with other situational factors such as the other party's behavior to influence negotiation process and outcomes (see Ohbuchi and Fukushima, 1997). More research is required to understand other ways in which self-monitoring may influence negotiations.

Machiavellianism

Another stream of research that links personality to bargaining behavior is work by Christie, Geis, and their associates on the concept of "Machiavellianism." After extensive study of the writings of Niccolo Machiavelli and similar political philosophers, Christie and Geis (1970) developed an attitude scale based on Machiavelli's classic writings. Those scoring high in Machiavellianism (high Machs) tend to be cynical about others' motives, more likely to behave unaltruistically and unsympathetically toward others, and less willing to change their convictions under social pressure. High Machs are thought to be more likely to tolerate behavior that violates social norms and are more inclined to advocate the use of deception interpersonally.

In numerous research studies, Christie and Geis explored the relationship between a Machiavellian orientation and behavior in various situations. We describe a few of these experiments here because of their applicability to negotiation processes. The interested reader may find a more detailed description of these and other studies of Machiavellianism in Christie and Geis (1970).

- One experiment created opportunities for subjects to dissuade another subject (an experimental confederate) from cheating; expose the confederate to the experimenter; refrain from using unethically obtained information; confess the behavior to the experimenter (either at the first opportunity, or after direct accusation by the experimenter); and lie with varying degrees of plausibility about their own behavior. High Machs initially tried harder to persuade the confederate not to cheat, and initially resisted using the confederate's unethically obtained information in the experimental task. But high Machs were no different from low Machs in the frequency of lying before being directly accused by the experimenter. Once accused, however, high Machs maintained their ability to lie with far greater credibility. They confessed less and were able to maintain more direct, convincing eye contact with the experimenter while lying than were low Machs.

- A second experiment explored the willingness of subjects to engage in manipulative behavior when they were in a high-power position. After the researchers created the legitimacy for subjects to deceive and manipulate other subjects in a test-taking situation, subjects were placed in a role that allowed the manipulative behavior to occur. High Machs attempted significantly more manipulative behaviors than low Machs, in both the total number and variety. They told bigger lies, were more verbally distracting, and were more innovative in the manipulative techniques employed. Finally, high Machs enjoyed their manipulative, high-power role.

- A third experiment described behavior in a game structured to allow players to join coalitions in order to win. Players differed in the amount of power they contributed to the coalition (point values that were assigned to their position); these power differences were either known to all players or known only to one. Compared to other players, high Machs displayed a more opportunistic sense of timing with regard to making or breaking a coalition, and more clearly controlled the initiation of bids and the structure of the coalition negotiations. High Machs initiated more offers, decisively dissolved coalitions when they were not advantageous, and were sought after by others to be in coalitions. As a result, high Machs were usually a member of the winning coalition and seldom lost the game or were shut out of points. Finally, high Machs were less responsive to the personal or ethical concerns of others in the situation. They tended to treat both the game and other players with emotional detachment, rather than becoming personally excited or involved with other people or outcomes.

- An experiment similar to the Prisoner's Dilemma was conducted with high Machs in order both to discover their behavior in this situation and to investigate the effect of real money (as opposed to imaginary points) on behavior. Playing against a variety of preprogrammed strategies, high Machs tended to become more exploitative over time. When real money was introduced into a game that had been previously played for points, high Machs became more cooperative, presumably because this behavior was more rational and would ensure them a positive financial outcome. Thus, high Machs appear to be opportunistic, but only when the outcomes in a situation warrant it.

A few studies since Christie and Geis's experiments have examined the influence of Machiavellianism on negotiation, with mixed findings. In a distributive bargaining task, Greenhalgh and Neslin (1983) reported that high Machs tended to negotiate *lower* outcomes than low Machs. Greenhalgh and Neslin surmised that this counterintuitive finding may have been due to the richness of the negotiation task, which may have reduced or moderated the influence of Machiavellianism (this hypothesis has not been tested empirically). An experiment by Fry (1985), on the other hand, found that high Machs do better than low Machs in distributive negotiation. Interestingly, Fry's findings suggest that the Machiavellianism of *both* negotiating parties may jointly influence negotiations. Fry (1985) found that low Machs change their negotiation style as a function of the Machiavellianism of the other negotiator. When negotiating with a high Mach, low Machs made fewer offers and were less effective negotiators than when negotiating with low Machs. High-Mach negotiators did not change their negotiation style as a function of the other party's Machiavellianism. Lastly, Barry, Fulmer, and Long (2000) included a measure of Machiavellianism in their study of people's attitudes toward the use of ethically marginal negotiation tactics (we discussed ethics more fully in Chapter 7). Barry and colleagues found that high Machs were more likely to approve of the use of deceptive tactics (making false promises; misrepresenting interests) in negotiation.

The "Big Five" Personality Factors

One way of moving the study of personality toward a more unified and coherent position (and away from numerous studies of a multitude of seemingly unrelated traits) is to focus on a very few key personality categories, or "factors," under which most individual traits can be subsumed. This is what personality psychologists had in mind when they developed the Five-Factor Model of personality (e.g., Goldberg, 1993), also known as the "Big Five." The personality factors that comprise the Big Five include (Barrick and Mount, 1991, pp. 3–5):

- *Extraversion*—being sociable, assertive, talkative
- *Agreeableness*—being flexible, cooperative, trusting
- *Conscientiousness*—being responsible, organized, achievement oriented
- *Emotional stability*—being secure, confident, not anxious
- *Openness*—being imaginative, broad-minded, curious

Research by Barry and Friedman (1998) examined how the Big Five personality factors are related to negotiator behavior and outcomes. Their study looked at both distributive and integrative negotiation situations, focusing on the first three of the five factors listed above. With respect to distributive bargaining (a price negotiation simulation), Barry and Friedman found that negotiators higher in extraversion and agreeableness were more likely to do *worse* for themselves. One reason is that these negotiators were more susceptible to the trap of "anchoring," which occurs when one party's extreme offer biases the other party's view of the underlying structure of the situation. For example, imagine that Jack makes an extreme opening offer; to the extent that Jill, after hearing Jack's offer, reframes her view of her own aspirations and probability of success and concedes more than she otherwise would have, she is said to have been "anchored" by Jack's opening. Barry and Friedman argued that anchoring is a greater risk for extraverted and agreeable negotiators because of their greater focus on the maintenance of social relations. Importantly, however, their findings showed that these effects of personality were lessened when negotiators had high aspirations for their own performance. To put it another way, a high degree of motivation to do well overcame the liability of certain personality traits in negotiation.

Barry and Friedman found that these elements of personality did *not* affect how well negotiators did in a separate experiment involving a more complex integrative bargaining simulation. In that situation, personality was less important than the cognitive ability (intelligence) of negotiators (we discuss the role of abilities later in this chapter). Unexpectedly, they found no role for negotiator conscientiousness in either distributive or integrative settings. It is widely assumed, and we agree, that successful negotiators are planful, attentive, organized, and have high aspirations—the very characteristics one might expect from a person high in dispositional conscientiousness. However, we have yet to see research evidence connecting the disposition to be conscientious with negotiation behaviors or outcomes.

Section Summary

In this section, we discussed the role of personality in negotiation in terms of a variety of dispositional traits, including conflict style, social value orientation, interpersonal trust, self-efficacy, locus of control, self-monitoring, and Machiavellianism. Recent convergence by many personality psychologists around the Five-Factor Model has brought into focus the question of whether personality traits are best viewed separately versus in clusters of related traits. The Five-Factor Model is an appealing way to analyze personality because of its parsimonious reduction of the many personality traits that exist into a limited and manageable set of broad categories. Moberg (1998) argues, however, that narrow traits may explain more variance in negotiation behavior than these broad personality factors because the aggregation of traits into factors masks important relationships between specific traits and specific strategies. It seems likely that future research on personality in negotiation will continue to struggle with this tension between the specific and the general.

Personality is also potentially important in negotiation for a reason we have not mentioned to this point: because individuals tend to view the actions of other parties through a lens of personality. A study by Morris, Larrick, and Su (1999) found that although interests and positions determine much of what happens in negotiation, negotiators tend to interpret the behavior of their negotiating counterparts in terms of personality. For example, negotiators who lack sufficient information about the other party's situation may resort to inferences about the other party's agreeableness or cooperativeness as a way to understand what is happening. The result is misperception—negotiators inappropriately explain the actions of others in personality terms even though elements of the situation are actually responsible. Clearly, a full understanding of the role of personality in negotiation requires attention not just to how an individual's personality affects his or her actions, but also to how we use or misuse personality to explain the actions of others with whom we negotiate.

SEX, GENDER, AND NEGOTIATION

We will use the word *sex* to refer to the biological categories of male and female, and the word *gender* to refer to the psychological aspects associated with each category (Deaux, 1985). Most of the empirical research on male/female differences in negotiation has examined sex differences and then posited theoretical aspects of gender to account for any differences found. For instance, a typical experiment may examine how males and females bargain differently in integrative negotiations. If differences are found, they are interpreted in reference to gender (e.g., men and women are socialized differently as children, and this explains an aspect of adult bargaining behavior). We agree with Deaux (1985), that there is more than just a semantic difference between the terms *sex* and *gender*. Rather, investigations of sex differences suggest that investigators implicitly believe that any differences found may be rooted in biological differences, whereas investigators who examine gender lean more heavily toward the social causes of behavior (Deaux, 1985). Few investigators would support pure biological or pure social explanations of behavior; rather, it is a difference in focus or the implicit assumptions underlying the research. One weakness of the research in this area has been the use of sex (i.e., males versus females) rather than gender (male or female sex roles) as the independent variable. We are not aware of studies in the negotiation literature that directly compare individuals by sex roles.

The most empirically researched individual difference factor in negotiation has been the search for sex differences. As a whole, this research has tended to yield contradictory findings; some research suggests that there is little or no difference between male and female negotiators (e.g., Carnevale and Lawler, 1987; Pruitt, Carnevale, Forcey, and Van Slyck, 1986; Putnam and Jones, 1982), while other research documents significant differences between male and female negotiators (e.g., Kimmel, Pruitt, Magenau, Konar-Goldband, and Carnevale, 1980; Neu, Graham, and Gilly, 1988; Pruitt and Syna, 1985; Stuhlmacher and Walters, 1999; Walters, Stuhlmacher, and Meyer, 1998; Watson and Kasten, 1988).

Two recent large-scale meta-analytic reviews[1] of the literature on sex differences in negotiation have concluded that women behave more cooperatively in negotiation than men (Walters, Stuhlmacher, and Meyer, 1998), and that men tend to negotiate better outcomes than women (Stuhlmacher and Walters, 1999). For both of these conclusions, however, the differences, while statistically significant, are small. Indeed, there is no simple answer to the question of how sex and gender influence negotiation, although we have seen worthwhile research progress on this issue. Our discussion here looks first at theoretical critiques of previous research on sex and gender in negotiation, and then reviews recent empirical work that is beginning to yield some interesting findings.

Male and Female Negotiators: Theoretical Perspectives

Recent work in this area has seen the application of feminist theory to negotiation (e.g., Gray, 1994; Kolb and Coolidge, 1991; Kolb and Putnam, 1997; Northrup, 1995; Watson, 1994a). This work clearly delineates that negotiation is a gendered activity (Kolb and Putnam, 1997), whereas the focus of much negotiation theory is on autonomous people who work to achieve instrumental outcomes (Gray, 1994). These theorists identify several key aspects of negotiation that have been undervalued by negotiation theory and research (see Harding, 1986, for a general discussion). For instance, until very recently, the focus on the instrumental value of negotiating has led to the neglect of the value of relationships in negotiation (Bies, Lewicki, and Sheppard, 1995; Gray, 1994; Kolb and Putnam, 1997). Because relationships may influence how negotiations are perceived, framed, and conducted, inattention to relationships by researchers may have undervalued their importance in understanding negotiation dynamics.

Deborah Kolb and Gloria Coolidge (1991) suggest that there are differences in how males and females negotiate, but that research on this topic has been so fundamentally flawed that it has been unable to detect these differences. One of the main problems with research on gender and negotiation has been "its very conception of gender as a stable set of characteristics that describe all women (or men) in negotiation situations" (Kolb and Coolidge, 1991, p. 273). That is, research has tended to treat sex and gender as a factor that may affect many aspects of negotiations for all male and female negotiators. This ignores differences among women and men, and makes the finding of stable differences difficult to detect in research. In addition, it is not clear how gender influences negotiation. Does it influence negotiator preferences? Strategies and tactics? Concessions? Outcomes? Situational factors combine with sex and gender to influence these variables in complex ways, making it difficult for sex and gender to have the generalized influence they are expected to have in much of the research that investigates the effects of sex and gender on negotiations.

---

[1] In a "meta-analytic" literature review, empirical results from many studies on the same subject are combined in order to create a broad statistical estimate of the effect or relationship that the underlying studies investigated. Meta-analysis is a way to capitalize statistically on the fact that the studies being reviewed together provide a much more robust sample than any one of them does individually.

Kolb and Coolidge argue that women and men approach negotiations in at least four fundamentally different ways:

1. *Relational view of others.* Women are very aware of the complete relationship among the parties who are negotiating and are more likely to perceive negotiation as part of the larger context within which it takes place than to focus only on the content of the issues being discussed. As we said in Chapter 4, equally important to the needs and interests that are discussed during the negotiation is learning how the other party perceives the situation. According to Kolb and Coolidge (1991), "Expressions of emotion and feeling and learning how the other experiences the situation are as important, if not more important, than the substance of the discourse" (p. 264). Men tend to be quite task oriented; they want to resolve the matter at hand and not to concentrate on the other party's feelings or perceptions, except to understand them for their pragmatic value during the negotiation. Women are more likely to find value from the relationship itself, regardless of the issues being negotiated.

2. *Embedded view of agency.* Closely related to the importance of relationships is an embedded view of agency. Kolb and Coolidge argue that women tend not to draw strict boundaries between negotiating and other aspects of their relationships with other people but instead see negotiation as a behavior that occurs within relationships without large divisions marking when it begins and ends. In contrast, men tend to demarcate negotiating from other behaviors that occur in the relationship, and to signal the beginning and end of the negotiations behaviorally. They typically begin with a light discussion ("break the ice"), move on to the negotiation phase ("talking turkey"), and conclude with another light discussion ("cement the deal"). Because women are more likely to see negotiations as flowing naturally from the relationship, they may be less likely "to recognize that negotiations are occurring unless they are specifically demarcated from the background against which they occur" (Kolb and Coolidge, 1991, p. 265).

3. *Control through empowerment.* Women and men perceive and use power in different ways. According to Kolb and Coolidge (1991), women are more likely to seek empowerment where there is "interaction among all parties in the relationship to build connection and enhance everyone's power" (p. 265). Men can be characterized as using power to achieve their own goals, or to force the other party to capitulate to their point of view. While women's conceptualization of power may make them more comfortable than men with integrative versus distributive negotiation, the fit is not perfect.

4. *Problem solving through dialogue.* Women and men also tend to use dialogue in different ways, and this first appears in very young children (Sheldon and Johnson, 1994). Women "seek to engage the other in a joint exploration of ideas whereby understanding is progressively clarified through interaction"; they also alternatively listen and contribute, and this results in "the weaving of collective narratives that reflect newly-emerging understanding" (Kolb and Coolidge, 1991, p. 266). Contrast this with men, who use dialogue (*a*) to convince the other party that their position is the only correct one and (*b*) to support various tactics and ploys that are used to win points during the discussion.

Male and Female Negotiators: Recent Empirical Findings

As we noted at the start of our discussion of sex and gender, empirical research on sex differences in negotiation has yielded an inconsistent pattern of results. We mentioned two recent reviews pointing to conclusions that women behave more cooperatively than men, while men reap better outcomes, but cautioned that these effects are small in magnitude. Here we look beyond broad inferences about sex differences; our discussion examines research on how men and women think about negotiation, are treated within negotiation, respond to tactics, and are influenced by stereotypes and other elements of social context.

Men and Women Conceive of Negotiations in Different Ways.   Robin Pinkley (1989, 1990, 1992; Pinkley and Northcraft, 1994) has conducted research that seeks to identify how disputants interpret conflict situations. Her research used a critical incidents methodology where people remembered and described a recent dispute in which they were involved. Pinkley found that disputants use three dimensions to interpret conflicts: relationship versus task, emotional versus intellectual, and compromise versus win. She found that women were more likely to perceive conflict episodes in relationship terms, whereas males were more likely to perceive the task characteristics of conflict episodes. The focus on relationships and task characteristics was also related to better relationship outcomes and task outcomes, respectively (Pinkley, 1989). There were no differences between male and female perceptions of conflict on the other two dimensions. Watson and Kasten (1988) also reported differences in how men and women perceive negotiations. In a simulated negotiation study with managers as participants, Watson and Kasten found that women perceived male behavior as more assertive than men did.

There is evidence to suggest that these male-female variations in perceptions about negotiation translate into differences in behavioral style and strategy when negotiating. Jennifer Halpern and Judi Parks (1996) demonstrated that men and women discuss different things when they negotiate. Halpern and Parks used a low-conflict bargaining simulation to examine how same-sexed pairs of men and women negotiated. They

NON SEQUITUR   **by WILEY**

BOX 10.2
Sex Differences in the Ultimatum Game

Sara Solnick (2001) published the results of a study comparing the behavior of men and women in a common two-person negotiation simulation known as the "ultimatum game." Here's how the game worked in Solnick's experiment: Each pair plays the game for $10 of real money. The first player (the "offerer") proposes a division of the $10 between the two. The second player (the "recipient") independently indicates a division amount that he or she would find minimally acceptable. If the share of the $10 offered by the first player exceeds the minimum acceptable amount stated by the recipient, then the division is accepted, and both players receive their share of the money. If the offer does not exceed the recipient's minimum, then both players receive nothing. The offerer does best for him/herself by proposing a split that only just exceeds the recipient's minimum.

Participants knew the sex of the other person in their pair. Men and women in the role of the offerer did not differ in the size of the divisions that they proposed. However, offers did vary according to the sex of the offer *recipient*. On average, offerers tendered $4.89 to men, but only $4.37 to women. According to Solnick, this may suggest that offerers expected women to demand less payment than men.

Interestingly, however, a comparison of the minimum acceptable amounts stated by recipients shows that women demanded *higher* minimum offers than men. Solnick also found that recipients (of both sexes) stated higher acceptable minimum amounts when paired with female offerers compared to male offerers. Solnick interprets this to mean that people may expect more generosity or fairness from women than from men.

The moral of the story seems to be that negotiators often harbor (and act upon) questionable assumptions that women will demand less and concede more. As Solnick observes, this may help explain findings that women are offered higher prices than men in new car negotiations (Ayers and Siegelman, 1995), and that men receive higher gains than women in salary negotiations (Gerhart and Rynes, 1991). Negotiators—especially women—need to be careful not to allow dubious assumptions to interfere with the successful pursuit of desirable outcomes at the bargaining table.

SOURCE: S. J. Solnick, "Gender Differences in the Ultimatum Game," *Economic Inquiry*, 39 (2001), pp. 189–200.

---

found that men were more likely to discuss positions than women, whereas women were more likely to reveal personal information and feelings than men. In addition, men and women chose different examples to buttress their arguments during the negotiation.

Men and Women Are Treated Differently in Negotiation.   Not only do women and men perceive negotiations in different ways, but there is growing evidence that women in negotiations are often treated worse than men during negotiations (Whittemore, 1996). We will consider research findings from two different domains: negotiating the purchase of a new car, and salary negotiations. (See Box 10.2 for an interesting experimental example.)

Automobile Negotiations.   Ian Ayres and Peter Siegelman (1995; also see Ayres, 1991) conducted an intriguing experiment that documented how men and women are treated during negotiations for a new car. They assigned different pairs of negotiators (black female/white male, black male/white male, white female/white male) to shop for a new car at 153 Chicago-area car dealerships. A white male negotiator participated in all pairs. Each negotiator in the pair separately visited the same car dealership on different days and bargained for a new car (negotiators chose the particular car for each negotiation from a list; no cars were actually purchased). Negotiators received two days of training before visiting their first car dealer. They followed a set script during the negotiations and were similar in terms of age, education, dress, economic class, occupation, and attractiveness. The major dependent variables in the research were estimates of dealer profits from the initial and final offers that negotiators received. Dealer profits were calculated as the difference between published list prices of the cars and the offers received by the negotiators (dealer fixed costs were ignored in the study).

Ayres and Siegelman (1995) found that the offers negotiators received from the car dealers included in the study differed significantly depending on the negotiators' sex and race (see Table 10.1). White males received the most favorable offers, followed in order by white females, black females, and black males. When the bargaining process (number of bids and counterbids) was examined, Ayres found that differences in the opening offers accounted for the majority of the differences in the final offers that the negotiators achieved. Concession rates and the length of the negotiation were not found to differ significantly across the sex and race of the negotiators. Finally, the sex and race of the salesperson had no effect on the results of the Ayres and Siegelman study; that is, women and blacks (versus white men) did not gain any advantage by dealing with a female or black salesperson.

The results of the Ayres and Siegelman (1995) study suggest that people are treated differently when they bargain for new cars—women and blacks may start negotiations at a less favorable position than white males. It is not clear why women and blacks are treated this way—it could be racism, sexism, or opportunistic behavior by the car dealers (dealers may believe that women and blacks are willing to pay more than white males for the same product). Note that there was no evidence that the negotiation

TABLE 10.1   Average Car Dealer Profit (from Ayres & Siegelman, 1995)

	Initial Offer		Final Offer	
Experimenter	*Profit*	*Markup*	*Profit*	*Markup*
White male	$1,019	9.2%	$ 564	5.2%
White female	1,127	10.3	657	6.0
Black male	1,954	17.3	1,665	14.6
Black female	1,337	12.2	975	7.2

Note: Profit figures are estimates that Ayres and Siegelman calculated from published list prices of the new cars.

SOURCE: Adapted from I. Ayres and P. Siegelman, "Race and Gender Discrimination in Bargaining for a New Car," *American Economic Review* 85 (1995), pp. 304–321.

process was different for women and blacks compared to white males; the differences in the final deals obtained were present in the opening offers made to the different negotiators, and these differences carried through to the final offers. Consider what this means to the typical negotiator in the Ayres and Siegelman study. Negotiators received the same average concession from the car dealers during the negotiation, so in a relative sense, they believed that they negotiated good deals. It is only when the results are compared across groups (which typically would not occur, because most people simply don't know a large number of other people who are buying the same car at the same time) that differences based on sex and race become clear. Note, however, that while Ayres and Siegelman controlled for many factors during the study, it is possible that an uncontrolled variable may have accounted for the results.

Salary Negotiations.   Research on salary negotiations by job seekers also documents how men and women may receive different treatment and outcomes during negotiations. In a study of MBA graduates, Gerhart and Rynes (1991) found that males received a higher monetary payoff for bargaining their salary than did females, even though men and women were equally likely to bargain. In order to rule out other possible explanations, Gerhart and Rynes statistically controlled for the effects of industry, college major, GPA, and business experience on the salaries received. However, it is possible that differences other than sex may still account for their results.

Similar Tactics Have Different Effects When Used by Men versus Women.
The results of a study by Dreher, Dougherty, and Whitely (1989) suggest that not only do men and women receive different outcomes during salary negotiations, but that the same negotiation tactic may have opposite effects on salary negotiation outcomes, depending on whether it is used by a male or a female employee (also see Kolb, 1992). Dreher and his colleagues found that the use of exchange tactics had a positive effect on the outcome of salary negotiations of male employees and a negative effect on the outcome of salary negotiations of female employees. That is, women using the same negotiation tactic (exchange) that men used were less successful than men. Exchange tactics include reminding supervisors of previous favors and offering to make sacrifices for outcomes. Dreher and his colleagues suggest that women who use exchange tactics "may violate stereotypic expectations about appropriate female behavior" (1989, p. 547) and are therefore penalized for using this tactic. A possible alternative explanation of the results of this study is that women are less effective in their use of exchange tactics than men; this does not seem very likely, however.

Gender Stereotypes Affect Negotiator Performance.   In a recent and important series of studies, Kray, Thompson, and Galinsky (2001) examined how the performance of male and female negotiators varies depending on the kinds of sex-role stereotypes that are activated in a particular situation. They theorized a link between classic gender stereotypes about how men and women claim resources and perceptions of how men and women will perform in negotiation. Their analysis draws upon a social psychological theory of "stereotype threat" (Steele, 1997). Stereotype threat refers to performance anxiety that afflicts individuals in certain social categories (e.g., race, sex) who fear that their performance will confirm a negative stereotype. Kray and colleagues argued that people who are consciously aware of certain gender stereotypes will act in ways that confirm these stereotypes during negotiation. They predicted and found that when stereotype threat is activated (by telling negotiators that the bargaining task is diagnostic of one's ability as a negotiator), women do worse because of the negative stereotypes that are active, and men do better because of the positive stereotypes in play. In contrast, when negotiators in their studies were told explicitly that the task was *not* diagnostic of ability, there were no differences in the performance of male and female negotiators. Thus, to the extent that men do better in negotiation than women (e.g., Stuhlmacher and Walters, 1999), Kray and her colleagues have shown that the activation of stereotypes about performance—which may or may not have any basis in fact—is part of the reason why.

Tactics May Vary with the Sex of Observers.   The results of two studies indicate that an individual's negotiation behavior may vary depending on the sex of others who are observing the negotiator, although their findings are not consistent with each other. Pruitt, Carnevale, Forcey, and Van Slyck (1986) found that negotiators displayed more contentious behavior when under the surveillance of a male constituent compared to a female constituent. In contrast, Cantrell and Butler (1997), using an integrative negotiation task (the Ugli Orange simulation), found that men placed higher bids for the oranges and were rated as more dominating when observed by women. As we discussed in Chapter 8, surveillance effects are important because negotiators in many situations are observed by constituents or others to whom they are accountable for their actions and outcomes. Additional studies are seemingly needed to sort out the conditions under which sex or sex role effects exist in negotiation situations involving surveillance and accountability.

Section Summary

There is a growing body of evidence that suggests that women and men are treated differently both before and during negotiations. To date, this research has been conducted primarily with distributive negotiations. Taken as a group, however, they suggest that women may be at a disadvantage when they negotiate simply because they are women. The nature of this disadvantage may occur in receiving worse opening offers from the other party than men, receiving worse outcomes in similar negotiations than men, and in being penalized when they use the same negotiation tactic that men use successfully.

Determining the underlying theoretical basis for sex and gender differences in negotiation is the difficult but important work that lays ahead because these effects are open to various alternative explanations. The research we discussed on stereotype threat effects (Kray, Thompson, and Galinsky, 2001) represents one compelling recent approach. Another is found in work by Carol Watson (1994b), who hypothesized that power differences (rather than sex or gender differences alone) are responsible for differences in negotiation behavior by men and women. Watson reviewed 20 years of research from 1975 to 1995 and found eight studies that examined both power and sex of the negotiator. The results of her review showed that power was a better predictor of negotiation outcomes than sex of the negotiators, suggesting that power differences might be able to explain some of the disparate findings in the literature on sex and negotiation. Clearly, more research is needed that goes beyond simple empirical documentation of sex/gender differences to explore the underlying social and psychological mechanisms that account for how men and women experience negotiation differently.

ABILITIES IN NEGOTIATION

Do people who are smarter or more capable in certain cognitive or emotional domains make better negotiators? What does it mean to be "smart"? In this brief section, we examine the relationship between three kinds of abilities and negotiation behavior: (*a*) cognitive ability, which is the traditional conceptualization of intelligence; (*b*) the relatively new concept of emotional intelligence; and (*c*) perspective-taking ability.

Cognitive Ability

Cognitive ability refers to "a very general mental capability that, among other things, involves the ability to reason, plan, solve problems, think abstractly, comprehend complex ideas, learn quickly and learn from experience" (Gottfredson, 1997, p. 13). Cognitive ability, which is synonymous with the general notion of intelligence, has been shown to influence reasoning processes, decision making, information processing capacity, learning, and adaptability to change, particularly in novel or complex situations (e.g., Gottfredson, 1997; Lepine, Colquitt, and Erez, 2000; Ree and Earles, 1991; Schmidt and Hunter, 1998). These aspects of thinking and mental processing are clearly related to much of what goes on the cognitive (as opposed to the emotional) side of negotiation. To the extent that negotiation entails the navigation of complex problem-solving tasks, it is reasonable to expect that individual cognitive ability may predict negotiation processes and outcomes (Fulmer and Barry, 2002).

There has been only limited research attention to the role of cognitive ability in negotiation. A few early studies involving experimental bargaining games, such as the Prisoner's Dilemma, produced mixed and inconclusive findings regarding the role of cognitive ability, leading Rubin and Brown (1975) in their large-scale review of early bargaining research to conclude that intelligence is unrelated to bargaining behavior. However, a different picture emerges from two recent studies examining cognitive ability in more complex integrative negotiation settings. Barry and Friedman (1998) found a strong link between negotiator cognitive ability and the integrativeness of settlements reached by participants in a complex commercial real estate negotiation simulation. Similarly, Kurtzberg (1998) found that cognitive ability predicted the ability of negotiators to reach integrative settlements in a simulation about a syndication contract for a television program. Smarter negotiators, it appears, have an advantage in moving the parties toward recognizing and exploiting joint gain.

What about purely distributive negotiation situations? Do negotiators with high cognitive ability do better? Barry and Friedman (1998) explored this issue using a distributive bargaining task in which a manufacturer and supplier negotiate the price of a component. They found no link between intelligence and performance, but this nonfinding should be regarded with caution because the task in their study was a very basic, single-issue negotiation. The possible role of cognitive ability in distributive bargaining situations of greater complexity remains unexplored.

Emotional Intelligence

In recent years psychologists have proposed that other forms of "intelligence" beyond general cognitive ability may exist as stable abilities capable of predicting behavior. One in particular that has attracted a good deal of attention since the early 1990s is the notion of emotional intelligence. Researchers define emotional intelligence as encompassing a set of discrete but related abilities: (*a*) the ability to perceive and express emotion accurately, (*b*) the ability to access emotion in facilitating thought, (*c*) the ability to comprehend and analyze emotion, and (*d*) the ability to regulate appropriately one's own emotions and those of others (Mayer and Salovey, 1997). A mass-market book published in the mid-1990s (Goleman, 1995) made strong claims about the role of emotional intelligence in a broad range of social domains and attracted widespread attention in the popular press. Although academics criticized those claims as misleading and overstated (Mayer, Salovey, and Caruso, 2000), it is fair to say that the concept of emotional intelligence has resonated with both researchers and the lay public as a way to capture variations in how people analyze and use emotion in social life.

As we discussed in Chapter 5, interest among negotiation researchers in emotional aspects of negotiation has risen in recent years. To the extent that the concept of emotional intelligence captures stable and measurable tendencies involving the perception, comprehension, and regulation of emotion, it may be an important individual difference for the study of negotiation. Fulmer and Barry (2002) made this case in a recent paper. They argued that an emotionally intelligent negotiator's ability to sense subtle emotional cues may give him or her an advantage by providing insight into opportunities for extracting concessions or creating logrolling solutions. They further suggested that negotiators high in emotional intelligence are better able to use emotions to influence the negotiation outcome—part of a process that Thompson, Nadler, and Kim (1999) referred to as "emotional tuning." Despite the intuitive appeal of emotional intelligence as an individual-difference factor in negotiation, empirical research studies of its role have yet to appear in the academic literature.

Perspective-Taking Ability

Negotiators need to perceive, understand, and respond to arguments that the other party makes during negotiations. The ability to take the other person's perspective, especially during preparations for negotiation, should enable negotiators to prepare and respond to the other party's arguments (Neale and Bazerman, 1983). Neale and Northcraft (1991) define perspective-taking ability as "a negotiator's capacity to understand the other party's point of view during a negotiation and thereby to predict the other party's strategies and tactics" (p. 174). Walton and McKersie (1965) suggest that distributive negotiators who better understand the resistance point of the other party will have a strategic advantage during negotiations. Negotiators who understand the other party's perspective will be more likely to form arguments that convince the other party, and should also be more likely to find an agreement that satisfies the other party. Presumably, the ability to perceive the other party's perspective would also be important during integrative negotiations as the negotiator strives to understand the other party's needs and interests and works to craft an agreement that satisfies the interests of both parties.

Neale and Bazerman (1983) investigated the importance of perspective-taking ability in a study of the effect of arbitration on distributive contract negotiations. They found that negotiators with higher perspective-taking ability negotiated contracts of higher value than did negotiators with lower perspective-taking ability. The results of this study suggest that perspective-taking ability may influence the negotiation process by increasing the concession rate of the other negotiator. That is, negotiators who are high in perspective-taking ability appear to be able to increase the concessions that the other party is willing to make. In another study on the effects of perspective-taking ability, Greenhalgh and Neslin (1983) reported that perspective-taking ability was not correlated with settlement preferences or negotiated outcomes in a television advertisement negotiation simulation. Kemp and Smith (1994), however, found that negotiators who were asked about their perspective-taking ability before an integrative negotiation simulation reached higher joint agreements than did negotiators in the control condition. In addition, the mean perspective-taking ability score of the negotiation pairs was strongly correlated with their joint outcomes. Mean perspective-taking ability was not related to information exchange or to identifying the other negotiator's priorities accurately, however.

Perspective-taking ability would appear to be an important individual difference that may influence many aspects of negotiations. Few published studies have investigated the effects of perspective-taking ability on integrative negotiations (see Kemp and Smith, 1994), nor has research clearly explained how perspective-taking ability has an effect on the negotiation process.

THE BEHAVIORAL APPROACH TO DIFFERENCES AMONG NEGOTIATORS

Some research has been conducted to try to identify how superior negotiators behave, rather than to identify their personality characteristics. The implicit assumption underlying this research is that negotiators who can copy or imitate the behavior of successful negotiators will become better negotiators themselves. Three approaches have been used to study the behavior of successful negotiators: (1) comparing superior and average negotiators in actual negotiations, (2) comparing expert and amateur negotiators in simulated negotiations, and (3) comparing experienced and naive negotiators in simulated negotiations. Each of these approaches has strengths and weaknesses; none of them is ideal. However, this research does provide some interesting insights about how superior negotiators behave.

The most comprehensive study comparing superior and average negotiators in actual negotiations was conducted by Neil Rackham (1980), who compared the behavior of labor relations negotiators in 102 actual negotiation sessions. He found important differences between superior and average negotiators during prenegotiation planning, face-to-face negotiations, and postnegotiation review. The results of this study are summarized in Table 10.2. While the results of Rackham's study may not be fully applicable to non-labor-relations negotiations, they provide sensible advice for all negotiators.

TABLE 10.2   Behaviors of Superior Negotiators Identified by Rackham (1980)

During Prenegotiation Planning

Considered more outcome options for the issues being discussed
Spent more time looking for areas of common ground
Thought more about the long-term consequences of different issues
Prepared their goals around ranges rather than fixed points
Did not form their plans into strict sequential order

During Face-to-Face Bargaining

Made fewer immediate counterproposals
Were less likely to describe their offers in glowingly positive terms
Avoided defend-attack cycles
Used behavioral labeling, except when disagreeing
Asked more questions, especially to test understanding
Summarized compactly the progress made in the negotiation
Did not dilute their arguments by including weak reasons when they were trying to persuade
   the other party

During Postnegotiation Review

Reserved time to review what they learned from the negotiation

SOURCE: Adapted from M. Rackam (1980), "The Behavior of Successful Negotiators," Huthwaite Research Group. Reprinted in R. J. Lewicki, D. M. Saunders, and J. W. Minton (eds.), *Negotiation: Readings, Exercises, and Cases,* 3rd ed. (New York: The McGraw-Hill Companies, 1999).

Margaret Neale and Greg Northcraft (1986) compared the performance of expert and amateur negotiators in a simulated negotiation market. This task gives buyers and sellers the opportunity to negotiate with any other seller or buyer in the market, but each buyer/seller pair may make only one deal. There is typically not enough time in market simulations for all possible buyer/seller pairs to make a deal. The expert negotiators in the study were professional negotiators with average formal experience of over 10 years. The amateur negotiators were graduate and undergraduate college students. Neale and Northcraft found that while both experts and amateurs were more likely to reach integrative solutions as the market progressed, experts were more integrative at the beginning of the negotiations than were amateurs. Experts also tended to receive higher average outcomes than amateurs, although this difference was not very strong.

Leigh Thompson (1990a) examined the effects of integrative bargaining experience on judgment accuracy, behavior, and negotiation outcomes in a longitudinal simulation study. In this creatively designed study, Thompson formed two groups of negotiators. In the experienced negotiator group, negotiators bargained with a different person in seven different integrative negotiation simulations; these negotiators increased their experience in integrative negotiation during the study. In the naive negotiator group, negotiators had either no previous experience with integrative negotiation in the simulation or only one experience; these negotiators had only one opportunity to increase their experience in the study. Thompson found that experienced negotiators made more accurate judgments about the other party's priorities as they gained experience, and that the likelihood of negotiating favorable agreements increased with experience, especially when negotiating with a naive negotiator who had no previous experience with the simulation. However, experience with the simulation did not improve the experts' ability to identify issues where both parties had compatible interests.

In summary, research from the behavioral perspective suggests that superior negotiators behave differently from average negotiators in many ways. There is no ideal method for studying expert negotiators. Participant observation may change the process that is being observed, and frequently it is difficult for experimenters to gain access to actual negotiations (see Rackham, 1980). While laboratory simulations give researchers more precision and control, they lack the richness of actual negotiations. The most appropriate approach may be a combination of laboratory studies and field work, be it in the same study or across experiments, as described in the three studies above. Unfortunately, few studies have been conducted that examine the behavior of expert or experienced negotiators. Those studies that have been done need to be replicated and extended, and this would appear to be a particularly fertile ground for further research on individual differences in negotiation.

CLOSING COMMENTS: THE FUTURE OF RESEARCH ON INDIVIDUAL DIFFERENCES IN NEGOTIATION

No single personality type or individual characteristic has been directly and consistently linked to success in negotiation. Yet everyday experience and research suggest that personality and other biographical variables play a role in negotiation processes and outcomes (see Box 10.3). Research in this area has been fragmented, however, and findings are often contradictory and complex. Our review of the research exploring individual differences and negotiation revealed that, in addition to those research ideas discussed throughout the chapter, there are two additional concerns that sorely need to be addressed by future research.

First, the majority of the research examining individual differences and negotiation has concentrated on distributive negotiations. There is much less research on the individual difference factors related to integrative negotiating, and research identifying characteristics that distinguish superior from average integrative negotiators is rare. By limiting the study of the effects of personality and other individual differences to distributive negotiations, researchers have inadvertently constrained the variance of the behaviors measured in their studies. Artificially constraining the variance means that a fair test of the extent to which individual differences have an effect on negotiation processes and outcomes has yet to be conducted (see Johns, 1989). Future researchers need to study a wide range of negotiation situations in addition to the typical distributive negotiation task currently included in studies of the effects of individual differences on negotiation.

The second research concern we have identified relates to how research on individual differences and negotiation has been conducted. Far more attention needs to be given to the design of studies that investigate individual differences and negotiation, especially to the negotiation part of the equation. Researchers in this area have become

BOX 10.3
Personal Styles of U.S. and Japanese Negotiators Clash in Trade Talks

The Wall Street Journal reported that trade talks between the United States and Japan were in serious difficulty at one point several years ago, largely due to the different interpersonal styles of the two negotiators: Charlene Barshefsky, the U.S. trade representative, and Sozaburo Okamatsu, the Japanese negotiator. The stakes were huge. Success in the negotiations would ease long-standing tensions, create billions of dollars in business for Americans, and accelerate a restructuring of the Japanese economy, while failure could raise the price of imports and cripple many Japanese–American alliances. Their styles were described as follows:

> Ms. Barshefsky and Mr. Okamatsu embody the strengths and weaknesses of their countries and illustrate how the two sides are trying to reach an agreement and why they are floundering. Each makes demands that feed into the other's fears, leaving each searching for more senior officials—fixers—who will override the negotiators. In the end, the two heads of state [President Clinton and Prime Minister Morihiro Hosokawa] just might break the impasse.
>
> The negotiators couldn't differ more. He is a 56-year-old Japanese who grew up during the American Occupation and recalls eating powdered eggs distributed by GIs. She's a 43-year-old American baby boomer who quotes John Lennon to explain her negotiating style.
>
> He is a member of Japan's government elite—a Tokyo University graduate, the son of a MITI vice minister—who has spent 34 years diligently climbing the ranks at his ministry. She is the daughter of immigrants who made her mark as a high-priced trade lawyer with blue-chip clients and joined the government only last year. He speaks so softly that he had to utter the threat of "retaliation" twice before any reporters at a news conference noticed. She is as blunt as an exclamation point.
>
> She quickly earned a name in Japan as a brawler, arguing toe-to-toe in Tokyo last June with Mr. Hatakeyama, a MITI man widely reviled by Americans as overbearing . . . Ms. Barshefsky honed her negotiating style at the Washington law firm Steptoe & Johnson, where she was co-head of the international law practice. [While she had some prior international trade experience] . . . , her Japan experience was paltry—and in that respect she shares an all-too-common failing in American government: lack of institutional memory and knowledge of opponents. Before taking the trade negotiator's post, she had never visited Japan and had little recent business experience with the country. Chalmers Johnson, a Japan expert at the University of California, contends that even after eight months of negotiating experience, "Ms. Barshefsky is a lamb going to slaughter."
>
> . . . By contrast, Mr. Okamatsu knows the U.S. well—like most Japanese trade negotiators. One of his first tasks upon joining MITI in 1960 was to try to ease trade frictions by overseeing restrictions on Japanese exports of low-priced silverware. He lived in New York for three years in the mid-1970s and has warm memories of the way he and his family were received . . . But Mr. Okamatsu is under fire, too, for the opposite reason that Ms. Barshefsky is. Even some of his fans say he has the common flaws of a bureaucrat—an overly considerate approach to problems and dogged loyalty to his ministry above all else . . . "Bureaucrats are like cavities," Masao Ogura, the chairman of a major transportation company, wrote in a recent newspaper essay. "The best service to the people is to pull them out completely."
>
> After their tussle in Tokyo, Mr. Okamatsu and Ms. Barshefsky made up. During a negotiating session in Hawaii in September, he sent flowers to her room. She gave him a pewter paperweight with an engraved eagle. He brought—what else?—a camera. Aides snapped photos of the pair on a balcony overlooking the Pacific. Even after, the U.S. negotiating team called the photos "the honeymoon shots." But the next month, they were back at war over the specifics of a trade proposal.

SOURCE: B. Davis and J. M. Schlesinger, "War of Words: U.S. and Japan Send Very Different People to Trade Negotiations," *The Wall Street Journal*, February 9, 1994, pp. A1, A11.

increasingly more sophisticated in identifying and measuring the different individual characteristics that are likely to influence negotiations (Barry and Friedman, 1998; Greenhalgh, Neslin, and Gilkey, 1985). Often lacking in this field of research, however, is attention to the negotiation tasks used. Virtually all of the research in this area uses a measure of personality variables, has subjects negotiate in a simulation, and then compares perceptual, behavioral, or outcome data as a function of personality. The flaw in this approach is that the research designs include only one instance of negotiation from which the dependent measures are collected. Most definitions of personality suggest that *personality is the generalized tendency of people to respond in a similar manner across situations or time* (see Epstein, 1979, 1980).

The appropriate way to study the effects of personality on negotiation is to gather data from many different negotiation situations and to investigate the effects of individual differences on the *average* negotiation outcome (perception, behavior, etc.). This method allows measurement and other errors to cancel each other out across negotiation situations and provides a fair test of the true effects of individual differences. Gathering behavioral data from multiple occurrences has become the standard method of assessing the personality–behavior relationship in other domains of behavioral research. *No study examining the effects of individual differences on negotiation has been conducted in this manner.* Thompson's (1990a) study of experienced and naive negotiators came close, but it did not examine the effects of existing individual differences on negotiation.

While much can be and has been learned from studies of individual differences on negotiation that examine only one negotiation, it is time for researchers to explore this area with a research method that more accurately assesses the effects of individual differences on negotiation. A recent focus by researchers on how personality factors may change their influence based on situational factors, also called the *interactionist approach,* has been a positive trend (e.g., see Cantrell and Butler, 1997; Ohbuchi and Fukushima, 1997). So has the expansion of simulation materials from a reliance on distributive tasks to a variety of integrative materials (e.g., Barry and Friedman, 1998; Halpern and Parks, 1996; Kray, Thompson, and Galinsky, 2001). Though recent research has provided a useful starting point, much remains to be learned about how individual differences influence negotiation preparation, process, and outcomes.

CHAPTER SUMMARY

In this chapter, we reviewed the past and current research on the effects of individual differences on negotiation. This has been a very difficult question to address with controlled, systematic research. A wealth of research has shown that no clear and simple effects exist. In many cases, the research methods have been inadequate to allow personality differences to emerge; in other cases, personality differences were obscured by major structural differences in the bargaining situation (the nature of the bargaining problem, relative power of negotiators, constituency pressures, etc.), or personality and structure have interacted to produce complex effects. Even comprehensive experiments, designed to overcome many of these methodological problems, have yielded inconclusive results.

Nevertheless, efforts to understand the effect of individual differences on negotiation continue. We discussed several approaches to describing personality that may have some promise for characterizing differences among negotiators, including conflict management style, social value orientation, interpersonal trust, self-efficacy, locus of control, self-monitoring, and the five-factor model. Each of these approaches appears to have good *prima facie* reasons for being directly related to individual differences in managing conflictual relationships, and working competitively or collaboratively with others. Future research needs to explore the effect of these approaches in detail, especially paying attention to how they affect both distributive and integrative negotiations.

We also discussed research findings exploring the effects of sex and gender on negotiation. The application of feminist theory to negotiation suggests that negotiation is a gendered activity, whereas research and theory have tended to concentrate on examining instrumental aspects of negotiation and thus have excluded a focus on relationships. Empirical work suggests that women may be treated worse than men when they negotiate, but systematic research is required to verify this finding. Finally, several recent studies have expanded how gender is examined by negotiation researchers.

We examined the role of abilities in negotiation, including cognitive ability, emotional intelligence, and perspective-taking ability. There is some evidence that smarter negotiators from a cognitive perspective are better able to find and exploit integrative potential. Although empirical research on emotional intelligence in negotiation remains scant, there is reason to believe that emotionally intelligent negotiators may have some strategic advantages. Research seems to link perspective-taking ability to the development of integrative outcomes, although the underlying process through which this occurs has not been clearly illuminated.

The behavioral approach to studying individual differences was also examined. Rather than searching for underlying personality dimensions, the behavioral approach concentrates on describing how expert negotiators behave. While there has been relatively little research from this approach, it has the potential to provide unique information about how people can learn to negotiate more effectively.

Many researchers have come to believe that differences in a negotiator's personality play a far less important role in negotiating outcomes than other key elements that we have discussed earlier in this book. It has become popular to believe that if a negotiator has a good understanding of the issues at stake, understands the dynamics of distributive and integrative bargaining, knows the role that is likely to be played by differences in power and constituency pressures, has prepared for negotiation and worked out a plan to use effective persuasion, then it is highly likely that he or she will succeed. It has also been suggested that even if individual differences can explain some of what negotiators think and do, they are still of limited interest because they refer to fixed characteristics that negotiators cannot change (e.g., Bazerman, Curhan, Moore, and Valley, 2000).

We suggest that some researchers may have closed the book prematurely on the effects of individual differences on negotiation, and that individual differences may have an important effect on the process and outcome of negotiations. Although it is true that negotiators cannot "change" their personalities or other stable individual differences, they can learn to compensate for the limitations these characteristics might bring and to capitalize on behavioral tendencies that may follow from the characteristics of other parties. Moreover, constituencies and organizations frequently make choices about who will negotiate on their behalf; in these circumstances, individual differences can play an important role in negotiator selection. Accordingly, we see a future for research in this area. Researchers must be careful, however, to measure differences rigorously and to analyze behavior across diverse negotiation situations, if the influence of individual differences on negotiations is to be assessed appropriately.

CHAPTER 11

Global Negotiation

The number of global negotiations is increasing rapidly. People today travel more frequently and farther, and business is more international in scope and extent than ever before. For many people and organizations, global negotiations have become the norm rather than an exotic activity that occurs only occasionally. Numerous books and articles, from both academic and practitioner perspectives, have been written about the complexities of negotiating across borders, be it with a person from a different country, culture, or region. Although the term *culture* has many possible definitions, we will use it to refer to the shared values and beliefs of a group of people. Culture describes group-level characteristics, which may or may not be accurate descriptors of any given individual within the group (Avruch, 2000). Countries can have more than one culture, and cultures can span national borders. With these caveats in mind, we will use the terms *culture* and *country* loosely in this chapter to refer to negotiation across borders (legal or cultural). As we discussed in Chapters 1 and 8, negotiating is a social process that is embedded in a much larger context. This context increases in complexity when more than one culture is involved, making negotiation a highly complicated process when it occurs across borders (Sebenius, 2002).

So much has been written on this topic that we cannot summarize it all in one chapter (for examples, see Binnendijk, 1987; Brett, 2001; Fisher, Schneider, Borgwardt, and Ganson, 1997; Foster, 1992; Habeeb, 1988; Hendon and Hendon, 1990; Kremenyuk, 1991; Lukov, 1985; Mautner-Markhof, 1989; Weiss, 1996; for earlier work, see Fayerweather and Kapoor, 1976; Hall, 1960; Van Zandt, 1970). Recent additions in this area are studies of negotiations occurring in newly developing economies (e.g., Arino, Abramov, Rykounina, and Vila, 1997; Brouthers and Bamossy, 1997; Pfouts, 1994) and intracultural comparisons of negotiators from several different countries, including Norway and Mexico (Natlandsmyr and Rognes, 1995); China and Canada (Tse, Francis, and Walls, 1994); China and Hong Kong (Leung and Yeung, 1995); the United States and Taiwan (Drake, 1995); and the United States and Mexico (Husted, 1996), among others. Our goal is to highlight and discuss some of the most recent and interesting work that has been written on this topic.

It is important to recognize that this book has been written from a North American perspective, and that this cultural filter has influenced how we think about negotiation, what we consider to be important aspects of negotiation, and our advice about how to become a better negotiator. This chapter also reflects our own cultural filter, both in our choices about what we discuss, and because we use Americans as the base from which to make comparisons to other cultures. That is not to say that all Americans share the same culture. In fact, there is evidence that people from countries as similar as the United

States and Canada negotiate differently (see Adler and Graham, 1987; Adler, Graham, and Schwarz, 1987). Within the United States and Canada, there are systematic regional and cultural differences (e.g., among English and French Canadians, and among Hispanics, African Americans, Southerners, New Yorkers, and other groups in many areas of the United States). At some level, however, Americans do share (more or less) a common culture that is different from that of other countries. While recognizing the differences within the United States, we will use some common aspects of American culture in our discussion of international and intercultural negotiation.

This chapter is organized in the following manner. First we discuss the American negotiating style, from both non-American and American perspectives. Next we present the results of a program of research that has demonstrated that negotiators in different countries use different negotiation processes to reach similar negotiation outcomes. Then we will discuss some of the factors that make negotiations across borders difficult, including both the environmental context (macropolitical factors) and the immediate context (microstrategic factors). We then turn to a discussion of perhaps the most critical issue of cross-border negotiation: the effect of culture, be it national, regional, or organizational. We discuss how culture can be conceptualized in cross-border negotiations, how academics and practitioners use the concept of culture, and the influence of culture on negotiations. The chapter concludes with a discussion of some culturally responsive strategies available to the global negotiator. Boxes throughout the chapter present examples of factors to think about when negotiating with people from other cultures (see Acuff, 1993; Hendon and Hendon, 1990; and Kennedy, 1985, among others, for further examples).

THE AMERICAN NEGOTIATING STYLE

Several authors have written about the American negotiation style (see Druckman, 1996; Koh, 1996; Le Poole, 1989; McDonald, 1996). Labeling any culture's traits is risky business, however, because labels are at best a guide to an average person from the country or culture in question, and there is a great deal of variation around that average. Labels tend to constrain our thinking and expectations such that we may perceive more consistency in the other person than actually exists, and labels may lock us into perceiving the other party's behavior in a historically dated manner. For instance, it is likely that negotiators from countries undergoing economic restructuring will become increasingly influenced by the new organizational cultures that develop rather than the old national culture, perhaps making national-level trait descriptions less useful as time passes (see Derong and Faure, 1995). With this caution in mind, cultural or national trait labels can provide us with at least a good starting point for knowing how to negotiate across borders.

We'll start by looking at how some non-Americans describe the American style, and conclude this section with an American's own view of the American negotiating style. Tommy Koh (1996), the former ambassador from Singapore to the United States, had the opportunity to observe American negotiators in the international political arena for several years. Koh notes the following strengths of the American negotiators: (1) good preparation; (2) clear and plain speaking; (3) a focus on pragmatism over doctrine;

(4) strong ability to recognize the other party's perspective, and to recognize that nego-tiations do not have to be win-lose; (5) good understanding of the concession–making process that is fundamental to negotiation; and (6) candid and straightforward commu-nication. In contrast, he lists the following as major weaknesses of American political negotiators: (1) serious intergovernmental agency conflicts that cause problems in reaching consensus within the American team; (2) the separation of political power between the presidency and Congress, which complicates the negotiation process; (3) the influence of interest groups on negotiations; (4) media interference, which makes it more difficult to negotiate sensitive parts of an agreement discreetly; (5) negotiator impatience; and (6) cultural insensitivity. Koh says that the strengths of American polit-ical negotiators outweigh their weaknesses, but he also cautions to focus on the indi-vidual characteristics of each negotiator and not to be guided by trait labels alone.

A much more biting view of the American negotiating style is offered by Samfrits Le Poole (1989) in his article "Negotiating with Clint Eastwood in Brussels." Le Poole writes that American business negotiators have an "arrogant ignorance" that handicaps them when negotiating globally. Le Poole, a European, argues that Europeans are much more adept at cross-border negotiations because the geography of Europe provides them with the opportunity to understand an international perspective from a very early age. For Le Poole, American business negotiators are always in a hurry, do not under-stand the role of small talk in building relationships, and are too quick to concede in negotiations. Le Poole argues that these characteristics weaken the American negotiator dealing with a European. For instance, knowing the Americans' love for efficiency and their tendency to give large concessions, many European negotiators will deliberately delay the negotiation process and reap the benefits of more concessions. Le Poole's central argument is that all negotiators need to understand the ways in which their own culture influences how they negotiate across borders.

McDonald (1996) offers an American perspective on the American negotiating style. From his 40 years of experience as a U.S. diplomat and international negotiator, McDon-ald's balanced view of the American negotiating style dovetails nicely with the perspec-tives of Koh (1996) and Le Poole (1989). For McDonald, the weaknesses of American negotiators include (1) impatience, (2) arrogance, (3) poor listening skills, (4) insularity, (5) legalism, and (6) naïveté. On the other hand, McDonald perceives the following strengths of American negotiators: (1) friendliness, (2) fairness and honesty, (3) flexibil-ity, (4) innovativeness, (5) pragmatism, (6) preparedness, and (7) cooperativeness.

NOT EVERYONE NEGOTIATES LIKE AMERICANS!

Graham and his colleagues (see Graham, 1993, for a review) have conducted a series of experiments comparing negotiators from the United States and several other countries. These studies each used the same research materials—a version of the buyer/seller negotiation simulation developed by Kelley (1966), in which negotiators have to decide on the prices of three products (televisions, typewriters, air conditioners). The participants in the studies were business people who were attending either man-agement seminars or graduate business courses. Participants in the studies negotiated with people from their own countries (thus, these were intracultural, not cross-cultural, negotiations). The major dependent measures in these studies were (1) the individual profit level made by the two negotiators in the simulation and (2) the level of satisfaction that the negotiators had with the negotiation outcomes.

The results of this research have been quite consistent across studies. Graham and his colleagues found no differences in the profit levels obtained by negotiators in the simulation from the United States and the other countries studied, which included Japan (Graham, 1983, 1984); China (Adler, Brahm, and Graham, 1992); Canada (Adler and Graham, 1987; Adler, Graham, and Schwarz, 1987); Brazil (Graham, 1983); and Mexico (Adler, Graham, and Schwartz, 1987). Taken as a whole, these results suggest that negotiators from different countries were equally effective in obtaining negotiation outcomes when they negotiate with other people from their own country.

Graham and Adler did find, however, that there were significant differences in the negotiation *process* in the countries that they studied (also see Graham, Evenko, and Rajan, 1992). In other words, although negotiators from different countries obtained the same average outcomes, the ways in which they negotiated to obtain those outcomes were quite different. For instance, Graham (1983) concludes that "in American negotiations, higher profits are achieved by making opponents feel *un*comfortable, while in Japanese negotiations, higher profits are associated with making opponents feel comfortable" (p. 63). In addition, Graham (1983) reports that Brazilian negotiators who used powerful and deceptive strategies were more likely to receive higher outcomes; these strategies were not related to the outcomes attained by the American negotiators. Further, Adler, Graham, and Schwartz (1987) report that representational strategies (gathering information) were negatively related to profits attained by Mexican and French-Canadian negotiators, whereas these strategies were unrelated to the profits that American negotiators received. Finally, although Adler, Brahm, and Graham (1992) found that Chinese and American negotiators used similar negotiation strategies when they negotiated, their communication patterns were quite different—the Chinese asked more questions, said no less frequently, and interrupted each other more frequently than did American negotiators.

Adler and Graham (1989) also compared intracultural and cross-cultural negotiation outcomes and processes. They found that Japanese and English-Canadian negotiators received lower profit levels when they negotiated cross-culturally than when they negotiated intraculturally; American and French-Canadian negotiators negotiated the same average outcomes in cross-cultural and intracultural negotiations. These results support Adler and Graham's hypothesis that cross-cultural negotiations will result in poorer outcomes compared to intracultural negotiations, at least some of the time. In addition, Adler and Graham found some differences in the cross-cultural negotiation process. For instance, French-Canadian negotiators used more cooperative strategies in cross-cultural negotiations than in intracultural negotiations, and American negotiators reported higher levels of satisfaction with their cross-cultural negotiations (versus intracultural negotiations).

A study by Natlandsmyr and Rognes (1995) generally supports and extends Graham's research. Natlandsmyr and Rognes examined the negotiation process and outcome of Mexican and Norwegian negotiators who participated in a negotiation simulation similar to the one used by Graham and his colleagues in their research. Natlandsmyr and Rognes found that when negotiating intraculturally, Norwegian negotiators reached higher joint outcomes than Mexican negotiators. During intercultural negotiations, however, the Mexican–Norwegian dyads reached agreements closer to the intracultural Mexican dyads than to the intracultural Norwegian dyads. Natlandsmyr and Rognes report that the progression of offers that Mexican and Norwegian negotiators made was different, and they suggest that culture may have a significant effect on the negotiation process.

In summary, research suggests that negotiators from different cultures (countries) use different negotiation strategies and communication patterns when negotiating intraculturally than when negotiating cross-culturally. However, it is important to note that there were few differences in the negotiation outcomes attained by the negotiators across these studies (see Natlandsmyr and Rognes, 1995). This suggests that there are many different ways to negotiate agreements that are, on average, worth the same value, and that negotiators should employ the process that fits the culture they are in. Further, the culture of the negotiator appears to be an important predictor of both the negotiation process that will occur and how the chosen negotiation strategies will influence negotiation outcomes. In addition, this research suggests that cross-cultural negotiations may yield poorer outcomes than intracultural negotiations, at least on some occasions.

WHAT MAKES CROSS-BORDER NEGOTIATIONS DIFFERENT?

Phatak and Habib (1996) suggest that two overall contexts have an influence on cross-border negotiations: the environmental context and the immediate context (see Figure 11.1). The *environmental context* includes "forces in the environment that are beyond the control of either party" that influence the negotiation (Phatak and Habib, 1996, p. 30). The *immediate context* "includes factors over which the negotiators have influence and some measure of control" (Phatak and Habib, 1996, p. 30). In order to understand the complexity of cross-border negotiations, one must understand how the factors in both the environmental and the immediate contexts can influence negotiation processes and outcomes.

Environmental Context

In an important article about the environmental context, Salacuse (1988) suggested six factors that make global negotiations more challenging than domestic negotiations: political and legal pluralism, international economics, foreign governments and bureaucracies, instability, ideology, and culture. Phatak and Habib (1996) have suggested an additional factor: external stakeholders. These factors can act to limit or constrain organizations that operate in the international arena, and it is important that negotiators who bargain across borders understand and appreciate their effects.

Political and Legal Pluralism.   When organizations make business deals that cross a national border, they come into contact with the legal and political system of another country. There may be implications for the taxes that an organization pays, the labor codes or standards that it must meet, and the different codes of contract law and standards of enforcement (e.g., case law versus common law versus no functioning

FIGURE 11.1   The Contexts of International Negotiations

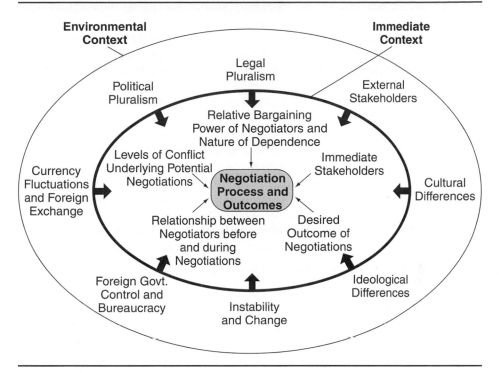

SOURCE: Adapted from A.V. Phatak and M.H. Habib, "The Dynamics of International Business Negotiations," *Business Horizons* 39 (1996), pp. 30–38; and from J.W. Salacuse, "Making Deals in Strange Places: A Beginner's Guide to International Business Negotiations," *Negotiation Journal* 4 (1988), pp. 5–13.

legal system). In addition, political considerations may enhance or detract from the conduct of business negotiations in various countries at different times. For instance, the open business environment in the former Soviet republics in the 1990s is quite different than the closed environment of the 1960s.

International Economics.   The value of international currencies naturally fluctuates, and this factor must be considered when making deals across borders. In which currency will the deal be made? According to Salacuse (1988), the risk is typically greater for the party who must pay in the other country's currency. The less stable the currency, the greater the risk for both parties. In addition, any change in the value of a currency (upward or downward) can significantly affect the value of the deal for both parties, changing a mutually valuable deal into a windfall profit for one and a large loss for the other. Many countries also control the currency flowing across their borders. Frequently, purchases within these countries may be made only with hard currencies that are brought into the country by foreign parties, and domestic organizations are unable to purchase foreign products or negotiate outcomes that require payment in foreign currencies.

Foreign Governments and Bureaucracies.   Countries differ in the extent to which the government regulates industries and organizations. Organizations in the United States are relatively free from government intervention, although some industries are more heavily regulated than others (e.g., power generation, defense) and some states have tougher environmental regulations than others. Generally, however, business negotiations in the United States occur without government approval, and the parties to a negotiation decide whether or not to engage in a deal based on business reasons alone. In contrast, the governments of many developing and (former) communist countries closely supervise imports and joint ventures (see Brouthers and Bamossy, 1997; Derong and Faure, 1995; Pfouts, 1994); frequently, an agency of the government has a monopoly in dealing with foreign organizations (Salacuse, 1988). In addition, political considerations, such as the effect of the negotiations on the government treasury and the general economy of the country, may influence the negotiations more heavily than what Western business people would consider to be legitimate business reasons.

Instability.   Although the world continues to change rapidly, business people negotiating domestically in the United States are accustomed to a degree of stability that is not present in many areas of the world. Instability may take many forms, including a lack of resources that Americans commonly expect during business negotiations (paper, electricity, computers); shortages of other goods and services (food, reliable transportation, potable water); and political instability (coups, sudden shifts in government policy, major currency revaluations). The challenge for international negotiators is to predict changes accurately and with enough lead time to adjust for their consequences if they occur. Salacuse suggests that negotiators faced with unstable circumstances should include clauses in their contracts that allow for easy cancellation or neutral arbitration, and consider purchasing insurance policies to guarantee contract provisions. This advice presumes that contracts will be honored and that specific contract clauses will be culturally acceptable to the other party.

Ideology.   Negotiators within the United States generally share a common ideology of the benefits of individualism and capitalism. According to Salacuse (1988), Americans believe strongly in individual rights, the superiority of private investment, and the importance of making a profit in business. Negotiators from other countries do not always share this ideology. For example, negotiators from some countries (e.g., China, France) may instead stress group rights as more important than individual rights and public investment as a better allocation of resources than private investment; they may also have different prescriptions for earning and sharing profit. Ideological clashes increase the communication challenges in cross-border negotiations in the broadest sense because the parties may disagree at the most fundamental levels about what is being negotiated.

Culture.   As we suggested earlier, people from different cultures appear to negotiate differently (e.g., Graham and Mintu-Wimsat, 1997). In addition to behaving differently, people from different cultures may also interpret the fundamental processes of negotiations differently (such as what factors are negotiable and the purpose of the negotiations). According to Salacuse (1988), people in some cultures approach negotiations deductively (they move from the general to the specific) whereas people from other cultures are more inductive (they settle on a series of specific issues that become the area of general agreement) (see Xing, 1995). In some cultures, the parties negotiate the substantive issues while considering the relationship between the parties to be more or less incidental. In other cultures, the relationship between the parties is the main focus of the negotiation, and the substantive issues of the deal itself are more or less incidental (see Tinsley, 1997). There is also evidence that preference for conflict resolution models varies across cultures (Tinsley, 1997, 1998).

One does not have to leave the United States to see the influence of culture on negotiations. Contrast the negotiation described in Box 11.1 with a stereotypical Wall Street negotiation. Clearly there is a large challenge negotiating across borders when the fundamental beliefs about what negotiation is and how it occurs are different. We will spend the latter part of this chapter exploring various aspects of this issue in more detail.

External Stakeholders.   Phatak and Habib defined external stakeholders as "the various people and organizations that have an interest or stake in the outcome of the negotiations" (1996, p. 34). These stakeholders include business associations, labor unions, embassies, and industry associations. For example, labor unions often oppose negotiations with foreign companies because they are afraid that domestic jobs will be lost. International negotiators can receive a great deal of promotion and guidance from their government via the trade section of their embassy, and from other business people via their chamber of commerce in the country in which they are negotiating.

Immediate Context

Throughout this book we have discussed many of the immediate context factors in reference to domestic negotiations. In this section, we will discuss the concepts in the Phatak and Habib (1996) model from a cross-border perspective; more detailed discussion of the theories and models underlying this model can be found elsewhere in this book.

Relative Bargaining Power.   One factor in cross-border negotiations that has received considerable research attention is the relative bargaining power of the two parties in the negotiation. Joint ventures have been the subject of a great deal of research on cross-border negotiations, and relative power has frequently been operationalized as the amount of equity (financial and other investment) that each side is willing to invest in the new venture (see Yan and Gray, 1994, for a review). The presumption is that the party that invests more equity has more power in the negotiation and therefore will have more influence on the negotiation process and outcome. Research by Yan and Gray (1994) questions this perspective, however, and suggests that relative power is not simply a function of equity, but appears to be due to management control, which was found to be heavily influenced by negotiating. In addition, several factors seem to be able to influence relative power, including special access to markets (e.g., in current or former communist countries); distribution systems (e.g., in Asia, where creating a new distribution system is so expensive that it may be a barrier to entering markets); or managing government relations (e.g., where the language and culture are quite different).

BOX 11.1
Cross-Cultural Negotiations within the United States

I had a client in West Virginia who bought from me for several years. He had a family business that he'd started in a small town with his grandfather, and it had now grown to be the major employer in the town. We had developed quite a close relationship. Every few months, I would make a trip up from North Carolina to see him, knowing after a while that he would need to place an order with me as long as I spaced our visits out every few months. When we got together, at first we would talk about everything but business, catching up with each other. I would ask him about his life, the business, his family, the town, etc., and he would ask me about my work and the company and life in the big city in North Carolina where I lived and worked. Once we'd caught up with each other, we would get down to some business, and this was often after lunch. Each and every time, it would take a few hours of this and that, but I'd always leave with an order, and it was always a pleasant break, at least for me, from my usual hectic pace.

One day I phoned in preparation for my next trip, to see if he would be in, to arrange a convenient day, and he told me that he'd like me to meet a friend of his next time I was up there to visit him. His friend, he said, was interested in some of the things my company was selling, and he thought I should meet him. Of course I was delighted, and we arranged a convenient day for the three of us to meet.

When I arrived at my client's office, his friend, Carl, was already there. We were very casually introduced, and my client began explaining Carl's work, and how he thought what my company sold could be useful to him. Carl then took over and spoke a little about what he did, and I thought for a moment that we were going to go straight into business talk. However, in just a few moments, the conversation between the three of us quickly turned back to discussions of life in town, North Carolina, our respective families, and personal interests. It turned out that Carl liked to hunt, and he and my client began regaling me with stories of their hunting adventures. I'd hunted a little, and shared my stories with them. One thing led to another, and soon we were talking about vacations, the economy, baseball—you name it.

Occasionally, we would make a brief journey back to the business at hand, but it always seemed to be in conjunction with the small talk, like how the tools we manufactured were or were not as precise as the mechanisms on the guns we used for hunting, things like that. I realized that quite a lot of information about our mutual work, my company, their needs, and their work was being exchanged in all this, even though business was never directly addressed. I remember the first few meetings my client and I had had with each other many years ago—how we learned about each other this way then, too. I was struck with how quaint it felt now, how different it was from the way I usually had to sell, and yet how much I enjoyed working like this!

Well, our discussions went on this way through the rest of the morning, weaving some business back and forth through the larger context of informal chit-chat about each other and our lives. Just before lunch, my client leaned back and began what seemed to be a kind of informal summary of who I was and what I did, and how what I did seemed to him to be just the thing that Carl and his company could use. Carl agreed, and my client asked him, almost on my behalf, how much he wanted to order, and Carl thought for a moment and gave me the biggest order I ever got from West Virginia. "Now that that's

---

BOX 11.1
(Concluded)

done," my client said, "how about some lunch?" We all went to the same place we always go to when I'm in West Virginia, talking about life and things and some business. By midafternoon I said I had to be heading home. We all agreed to stay in touch. We've been in touch ever since, and now I've got two clients to visit whenever I'm in West Virginia.

SOURCE: D. A. Foster, *Bargaining across Borders: How to Negotiate Business Successfully Anywhere in the World* (New York: McGraw-Hill, 1992), pp. 108–109. Reproduced with the permission of the McGraw-Hill companies.

Levels of Conflict.   The level of conflict and type of interdependence between the parties to a cross-border negotiation will also influence the negotiation process and outcome. High-conflict situations, or conflicts that are ethnically, identity, or geographically based, will be more difficult to resolve (see Isajiw, 2000; Ross, 2000; Stein, 1999; Zartman, 1997). Ongoing conflicts in Northern Ireland, the Middle East, East Timor, and Sudan are but a few examples. There is historical evidence, however, that civil wars concluded through a comprehensive, institutionalized agreement that prohibits the use of coercive power and promotes the fair distributions of resources and political power lead to more stable settlements (Hartzell, 1999). Also important is the extent to which negotiators frame the negotiation differently or conceptualize what the negotiation concerns (see Chapters 2 and 5 for extended discussions of framing), and this appears to vary across cultures (Abu-Nimer, 1996), as do the ways in which negotiators respond to conflict (Ohbuchi and Takahashi, 1994; Tinsley, 1998; see Weldon and Jehn, 1995, for a review). For example, Fisher, Ury, and Patton (1991) discuss how conflicts in the Middle East were difficult to deal with for several years because the different parties had such different ways of conceptualizing what the dispute was about (e.g., security, sovereignty, historical rights).

Relationship between Negotiators.   Phatak and Habib (1996) suggest that the relationship the principal negotiating parties develop before the actual negotiations will also have an important impact on the negotiation process and outcome. Negotiations are part of the larger relationship between two parties. The history of relations between the parties will influence the current negotiation (e.g., how the parties frame the negotiation), just as the current negotiation will become part of any future negotiations between the parties. (See Chapter 8 for a detailed discussion of this point.)

Desired Outcomes.   Tangible and intangible factors will play a large role in determining the outcomes of cross-border negotiations. In the political arena, countries often use international negotiations to achieve both domestic and international political goals. For instance, one of the main goals of the North Vietnamese during the Paris Peace Talks to end the war in Vietnam was to be recognized formally by the other parties to the negotiation. Similarly, in recent ethnic conflicts around the world, numerous parties have threatened that unless they are recognized at the formal negotiation table they will disrupt the successful resolution of the conflict (e.g., Northern Ireland). Ongoing tension can exist between one party's short-term objectives for the current negotiations and their influence on the parties' long-term relations. In trade negotiations between the United States and Japan, both sides often settle for less than their desired short-term outcomes because of the importance of the long-term relationship (see Phatak and Habib, 1996).

Immediate Stakeholders.   The immediate stakeholders in the negotiation include the negotiators themselves as well as the people they directly represent, such as their managers, employers, or boards of directors (Phatak and Habib, 1996). Stakeholders can influence negotiators in many ways (see Chapter 8). The skills, abilities, and international experience of the negotiators themselves clearly can have a large impact on the process and outcome of cross-border negotiations. In addition, the personal motivations of the principal negotiators and the other immediate stakeholders can have a large influence on the negotiation process and outcomes. People may be motivated by several intangible factors in the negotiation, including how the process or outcome will make them look in the eyes of both the other party and their own superiors, as well as other intangible factors like their personal career advancement (Phatak and Habib, 1996).

In summary, Phatak and Habib's (1996) model provides a good overview of how several factors in the environmental and immediate contexts can have a large influence on cross-border negotiations. The next section of this chapter provides examples of how these factors can interact to determine the processes and outcomes of negotiations.

HOW DO WE EXPLAIN GLOBAL NEGOTIATION OUTCOMES?

As we have seen in the discussion of the Phatak and Habib (1996) model, global negotiations can be much more complicated than domestic negotiations. At times it may be tempting to attribute the outcomes of negotiations to a single variable, such as cultural differences or the relative power of a country (the size of the national economy, for instance). This would be a serious mistake, however. Recent studies of negotiations in very different contexts suggest that simple, one-variable arguments cannot explain conflicting global negotiation outcomes (see Mayer, 1992).

Schoppa (1993) examined the results of five different discussions between Japan and the United States under the 1989 Structural Impediments Initiative, which focused on changing trade relations between the two countries. These negotiations were between the same countries during the same time period, so one would expect that similar explanations should be found for the outcome of each negotiation. For instance, if the United States were more powerful than Japan, or if the Japanese were better listeners than the Americans, then this should more or less equally influence the outcomes of all five negotiations. Schoppa found that the results of the five negotiations (whose subjects were public investment, distribution systems, land policy, exclusionary business practices, and Keiretsu groups) were quite different, and that no single variable could explain them. Schoppa also found that different negotiation strategies had different levels of effectiveness across the different issues. For instance, a strategy of expanding the number of participants involved in the negotiation process seemed to produce concessions in the public investment and distribution system negotiations, but had no effect in the exclusionary business practices and Keiretsu negotiations.

Derong and Faure's (1995) study of the negotiation process between Chinese companies and the various levels of government in China is also enlightening. The study examined a series of negotiations between a high-technology company in Beijing and six government regulatory bureaus. Much has been written about the Chinese negotiation style (e.g., the need for harmony, the meaning of time, etc.; see Pye, 1992), and we would expect intra-Chinese negotiations to be more or less similar. What Derong and Faure found, however, was that a wide variety of different strategies and tactics were used in the negotiations, depending on the goals of the negotiators and the situation. While the national culture appeared to determine the overall negotiation process, the role of the organization and the organizational culture also appeared important. With respect to time, for instance, Derong and Faure found that "the [government] bureaus act according to the usual temporality of bureaucracies which requires a huge amount of time to attain any result. On the other hand, the company works on the unspoken assumption that time is a limited resource whose use has a cost in managerial terms" (p. 49). The interplay between organizational culture and national culture, and how this changes as countries reform their economic systems, will make it even less likely that researchers can use simplistic explanations of global negotiations.

In summary, models such as Phatak and Habib's (1996) are very good devices for guiding our thinking about global negotiations. It is always important to remember, however, that negotiation processes and outcomes are influenced by many factors, and that the influence of these factors can change in magnitude over time (see Yan and Gray, 1994). The challenge for every global negotiator is to understand the simultaneous, multiple influences of several factors on the negotiation process and outcome, and to update this understanding regularly as circumstances change. This also means that planning for global negotiations is especially important, as is the need to adjust plans as new information is obtained through monitoring the environmental and immediate contexts.

CONCEPTUALIZING CULTURE AND NEGOTIATION

The most frequently studied construct in research examining global negotiation is culture (for reviews see Brett, 2001; Gelfand and Dyer, 2000). While many international negotiation experts consider culture the critical factor in negotiations across borders, there are in fact many different meanings of the concept of culture (see Avruch, 2000). Robert Janosik (1987) has identified four ways that culture has been conceptualized in international negotiation: as learned behavior, as shared values, as dialectic, and in context. While there are similarities and differences among the four ways, each approach does stress the importance of understanding how culture affects negotiation.

Culture as Learned Behavior

The first approach to understanding the effects of culture concentrates on documenting the systematic negotiation behavior of people in different cultures. Rather than focusing on why members of a given culture behave in certain ways, this pragmatic, nuts-and-bolts approach concentrates on creating a catalogue of behaviors that the foreign negotiator should expect when entering a host culture (Janosik, 1987). Many of the books and articles in the popular press use the concept of culture as learned behavior in negotiations across borders, yielding lists of dos and don'ts to obey when negotiating with people from various cultures. For instance, Solomon (1987) suggests that global negotiators should recognize that Chinese negotiators will begin negotiations with a search for broad principles and building a relationship. This will be followed by a long period of assessment in which the boundaries of the relationship will be explored; a decision about whether or not to strike an agreement will eventually be made, and this agreement will form the foundation for further concessions and modifications. More recent research consistent with this perspective has examined the effects of culture on displaying emotion during negotiation (George, Jones, and Gonzalez, 1998) and face-saving behavior (Ogawa, 1999; Ting-Toomey and Kurogi, 1998).

Culture as Shared Values

The second approach concentrates on understanding the central values and norms of a culture and then building a model for how these norms and values influence negotiations within that culture (see Faure, 1999; Sebenius, 2002). Cross-cultural comparisons are made by finding the important norms and values that distinguish one culture from another, and then understanding how these differences will influence negotiation across borders. For instance, Sebenius (2002) argues that culture has an important effect on both decision making during negotiation as well as the negotiation process itself, including who participates in the negotiation, who makes decisions during the negotiation, and the informal factors that help or hinder negotiations.

While the culture-as-learned-behavior approach concentrates exclusively on behavior, the culture-as-shared-values approach recognizes that thought precedes behavior and seeks to understand how culture influences thought processes in general (Janosik, 1987). For example, a central value in the United States is individualism. Americans are expected to make individual decisions, defend their points of view, and take strong stands on issues that are important to them. Contrast this with a central value of the Chinese—collectivism (see Faure, 1999, for systematic analysis of the effects of culture on the Chinese negotiation style). Chinese negotiators are expected to make group decisions, defend the group above the individual, and take strong stands on issues important to the group. When American and Chinese people negotiate, differences in the individualism/collectivism cultural value may be expected to influence negotiations in many ways. For instance, (1) the Chinese will likely take more time when negotiating because they have to gain the consensus of their group before they strike a deal; (2) the use of multiple lines of authority by the Chinese will lead to mixed signals about the true needs of the group, and no single individual may understand all of the requirements; and (3) because power is shared by many different people and offices, it may be difficult for foreigners to identify their appropriate counterpart in the Chinese bureaucracy (Pye, 1992).

Culture as Dialectic

The third approach to using culture to understand global negotiation identified by Janosik (1987) recognizes that, among their different values, all cultures contain dimensions or tensions that are called *dialectics*. These tensions are nicely illustrated in parables from the Judeo-Christian tradition. Consider the following examples: "too many cooks spoil the broth" and "two heads are better than one." These parables offer conflicting guidance for those considering whether to work on a task alone or in a group. This reflects a dialectic, or tension, within the Judeo-Christian tradition regarding the values of independence and teamwork. Neither complete independence nor complete teamwork works all of the time; each has advantages and disadvantages that vary as a function of the circumstances (e.g., the type of decision to be made or task to be addressed). According to Janosik (1987), the culture-as-dialectic approach has advantages over the culture-as-shared-values approach because it can explain variations within cultures (i.e., not every person in the same culture shares the same values to the same extent). While this may yield accurate academic understanding of the effects of culture on international negotiations, it does not appear to offer clear guidelines for practitioners faced with negotiations across borders.

Culture in Context

Proponents of the fourth approach to using culture to understand negotiations across borders recognize that no human behavior is determined by a single cause. Rather, all behavior may be understood at many different levels simultaneously, and a social behavior as complex as negotiation is determined by many different factors, one of which is culture. Other factors that may be important determinants of negotiation behavior include personality, social context, and environmental factors. In other words, proponents of the culture-in-context approach recognize that negotiation behavior is multiply determined, and using culture as the sole explanation of behavior is oversimplifying a complex social process. Many academic models of negotiation recognize the multiple determinants of negotiation behavior and are excellent guides for research and understanding negotiation. As the models become more complex, however, they may become less useful for practitioners of negotiations across borders because they are just too complicated to put into practice (Janosik, 1987).

HOFSTEDE'S DIMENSIONS OF CULTURE

As discussed above, the term *culture* has taken on many different meanings. Hofstede's research (1980a, 1980b, 1989, 1991) defines culture as the shared values and beliefs held by members of a group, and is considered the most comprehensive and extensive program of research on cultural dimensions in international business. Hofstede examined data on values that had been gathered from over 100,000 IBM employees from around the world; to date, over 53 cultures and countries have been included in his study. Statistical analysis of this data suggests that four dimensions could be used to describe the important differences among the cultures in the study.[1] Table 11.1 lists the countries included in Hofstede's study and their ranking on the four dimensions described below.

Individualism/Collectivism

The individualism/collectivism dimension describes the extent to which the society is organized around individuals or the group. Individualistic societies encourage their young to be independent and to look after themselves. Collectivistic societies integrate individuals into cohesive groups that take responsibility for the welfare of each individual. Individualistic countries include the United States, Great Britain, and Australia, while collectivistic countries include Indonesia, Pakistan, and Costa Rica. Hofstede suggests that the focus on relationships in collectivist societies plays a critical role in negotiations—negotiations with the same party can continue for years, and changing a negotiator changes the relationship, which may take a long time to rebuild. Contrast this with individualistic societies, in which negotiators are considered interchangeable and competency, rather than relationship, is an important consideration when choosing a negotiator. The implication is that negotiators from collectivist cultures will strongly depend on cultivating and sustaining a long-term relationship, whereas negotiators from individualistic cultures may be more likely to swap negotiators, using whatever short-term criteria seem appropriate. In addition, Smith, Dugan, Peterson, and Leung (1998) found that within collectivistic countries disagreements are resolved based on rules, whereas in individualistic countries conflicts tend to be resolved through personal experience and training.

The individualism/collectivism dimension of culture has received considerable attention from negotiation researchers, and it appears to influence a broad range of negotiation processes, outcomes, and preferences for conflict resolution procedures.

Negotiation Processes.   Cai (1998) demonstrated how individualism/collectivism influenced negotiation planning: negotiators from a more collectivist culture (Taiwan) spent more time planning for long-term goals, while negotiators from a more individualistic culture (U.S.) spent more time planning for short-term goals. Gelfand and Christakopoulou (1999) found that negotiators from a relatively individualistic culture (U.S.) were more susceptible to fixed-pie errors (see Chapter 5) than were negotiators from a more collectivist culture (Greece). In addition, examination of the negotiation process revealed that negotiators from the more individualistic culture made more extreme offers during the negotiation than did negotiators from the more collectivist culture (Gelfand and Christakopoulou, 1999). Individualism-collectivism also appears

---

[1]Subsequent research by Hofstede and Bond (1988) suggested that a fifth dimension, labeled Confucian Dynamism, be added. Confucian Dynamism contains three elements: work ethic, time, and commitment to traditional Confucian values. The dimension has received little attention in the negotiation literature (cf., Chan, 1998).

TABLE 11.1   Ranking of Countries/Cultures on Cultural Dimensions
Reported by Hofstede (1991)

Country	Individualism	Rank Order On: Power Distance	Masculinity	Uncertainty Avoidance
Arab countries	26/27	7	23	27
Argentina	22/23	35/36	20/21	10/15
Australia	2	41	16	37
Austria	18	53	2	24/25
Belgium	8	20	22	5/6
Brazil	26/27	14	27	21/22
Canada	4/5	39	24	41/42
Chile	38	24/25	46	10/15
Colombia	49	17	11/12	20
Costa Rica	46	42/44	48/49	10/15
Denmark	9	51	50	51
East Africa	33/35	21/23	39	36
Ecuador	52	8/9	13/14	28
Finland	17	46	47	31/32
France	10/11	15/16	35/36	10/15
Germany F.R.	15	42/44	9/10	29
Great Britain	3	42/44	9/10	47/48
Greece	30	27/28	18/19	1
Guatemala	53	2/3	43	3
Hong Kong	37	15/16	18/19	49/50
India	21	10/11	20/21	45
Indonesia	47/48	8/9	30/31	41/42
Iran	24	29/30	35/36	31/32
Ircland (Rep.)	12	49	7/8	47/48
Israel	19	52	29	19
Italy	7	34	4/5	23
Jamaica	25	37	7/8	52
Japan	22/23	33	1	7
Malaysia	36	1	25/26	46
Mexico	32	5/6	6	18
Netherlands	4/5	40	51	35
New Zealand	6	50	17	39/40
Norway	13	47/48	52	38
Pakistan	47/48	32	25/26	24/25
Panama	51	2/3	34	10/15
Peru	45	21/23	37/38	9
Philippines	31	4	11/12	44
Portugal	33/35	24/25	45	2
Salvador	42	18/19	40	5/6
Singapore	39/41	13	28	53
South Africa	16	35/36	13/14	39/40

TABLE 11.1   *(Concluded)*

		Rank Order On:		
Country	*Individualism*	*Power Distance*	*Masculinity*	*Uncertainty Avoidance*
South Korea	43	27/28	41	16/17
Spain	20	31	37/38	10/15
Sweden	10/11	47/48	53	49/50
Switzerland	14	45	4/5	33
Taiwan	44	29/30	32/33	26
Thailand	39/41	21/23	44	30
Turkey	28	18/19	32/33	16/17
Uruguay	29	26	42	4
U.S.	1	38	15	43
Venezuela	50	5/6	3	21/22
West Africa	39/41	10/11	30/31	34
Yugoslavia	33/35	12	48/49	8

SOURCE: Based on G. Hofstede, *Culture and Organizations: Software of the Mind* (London, England: McGraw-Hill, 1991). Reproduced with permission of the McGraw-Hill Companies.

to influence the effects of negotiator accountability on the negotiation process. Gelfand and Realo (1999) found that "high accountability enhanced competition for representatives with low levels of collectivism, yet enhanced cooperation for those with high levels of collectivism" (p. 730).

Negotiation Outcomes.   Researchers have also found that the effects of individualism/collectivism may also influence negotiation outcomes. Lituchy (1997) reported that negotiators from a more collectivist culture (Japan) reached more integrative solutions than negotiators from a more individualist culture (U.S.) or negotiation dyads where both cultures were present (Japan, U.S.). Arunachalam et al. (1998) found that negotiators from a more collectivistic culture (Hong Kong) reached higher joint outcomes on an integrative negotiation task than did negotiators from a more individualistic culture (U.S.). Brett and Okumura (1998) did not find a direct effect of individualism/collectivism on negotiation outcomes but, rather, found that same-culture negotiators (Japan-Japan or U.S.-U.S. dyads) reported higher joint gains than intercultural dyads (Japan-U.S.). Brett and Okumura suggest that lack of information sharing in intercultural dyads may have caused lower integrative outcomes in these groups. More research on the effects of individualism/collectivism on negotiation outcomes needs to be conducted in order to understand better the extent of its influence on negotiation.

Conflict Resolution Styles.   Kim and Kitani (1998) demonstrated how individualism/collectivism influenced preference for conflict resolution styles in romantic relationships as partners from a more collectivist culture (Asian Americans) preferred obliging, avoiding, and integrating conflict management styles, while partners from a more individualistic culture (Caucasian Americans) preferred a dominating conflict management style. Similarly, Pearson and Stephan (1998) found that negotiators from a more collectivist culture (Brazil) preferred accommodation, collaboration, and withdrawal compared to negotiators from a more individualist culture (U.S.), who had a stronger preference for competition. A study by Mintur-Wimsatt and Gassenheimer (2000) provided further evidence of the effects of individualism/collectivism on conflict resolution styles as they found that exporters from the Philippines (a "high context" culture that is more collectivist) preferred less confrontational problem solving than did exporters from the United States (a "low context" culture that is more individualistic). Gire (1997) found that while negotiators from both a more individualistic culture (Canada) and more collectivist culture (Nigeria) preferred negotiation to arbitration as a conflict management procedure, negotiators from the more collectivist culture had a stronger preference for negotiation than did negotiators from the more individualistic culture, who much preferred arbitration compared to negotiators from the more collectivist culture. In addition, Arunachalam, Wall, and Chan (1998) found that mediation had a stronger effect on negotiation outcomes with negotiators from a more individualistic culture (U.S.) than those with negotiators from a more collectivist culture (Hong Kong).

In summary, the individualism/collectivism dimension of culture appears to influence a broad range of negotiation processes, outcomes, and preferences for conflict resolution procedures. More systematic research is required to further explicate the extent of these effects, however, as well as to identify what specific aspects of differences in individualism/collectivism account for these findings.

Power Distance

The power distance dimension describes "the extent to which the less powerful members of organizations and institutions (like the family) accept and expect that power is distributed unequally" (Hofstede, 1989, p. 195). According to Hofstede, cultures with greater power distance will be more likely to have decision making concentrated at the top, and all of the important decisions will have to be finalized by the leader. Cultures with low power distance are more likely to spread the decision making throughout the organization, and while leaders are respected, it is also possible to question their decisions. Countries that are high in power distance include Malaysia, Guatemala, and Panama, while countries that are low in power distance include Norway, Sweden, and Great Britain. The consequences for international negotiations are that negotiators from comparatively high power distance cultures may need to seek approval from their supervisors more frequently, and for more issues, leading to a slower negotiation process. In addition, Smith Dugan, Peterson, and Leung (1998) found that "out group" disagreements were less likely to occur in high power distance cultures than lower power distance cultures.

Masculinity/Femininity

Hofstede found that cultures differed in the extent to which they held values that were traditionally perceived as masculine or feminine. Masculine cultures were characterized by "assertiveness, the acquisition of money and things, and *not* caring for others, the quality of life, or people" (Hofstede, 1980a, p. 46). Feminine cultures were characterized by concern for relationships, nurturing, and quality of life. Countries that are higher in masculinity include Japan, Austria, and Venezuela, while countries that are higher in femininity include Costa Rica, Chile, and Finland. According to Hofstede (1989), this dimension influences negotiation by increasing the competitiveness when negotiators from masculine cultures meet; negotiators from feminine cultures are more likely to have empathy for the other party and to seek compromise.

Uncertainty Avoidance

Uncertainty avoidance, the fourth dimension identified by Hofstede, "indicates to what extent a culture programs its members to feel either uncomfortable or comfortable in unstructured situations" (1989, p. 196). Unstructured situations are characterized by rapid change and novelty, whereas structured situations are stable and secure. Countries that are higher in uncertainty avoidance include Greece, Portugal, and Guatemala, while countries that are lower in uncertainty avoidance include Sweden, Hong Kong, and Ireland. Negotiators from uncertainty avoidance cultures are less comfortable with ambiguous situations and are more likely to seek stable rules and procedures when they negotiate. Negotiators from cultures more comfortable with unstructured situations are likely to adapt to quickly changing situations and will be less uncomfortable when the rules of the negotiation are ambiguous or shifting.

Section Summary

Hofstede's dimensions have received a great deal of attention in cross-cultural research and international business. Although the model is not without its critics (see, e.g., Kale and Barnes, 1992; Triandis, 1982), it has become a dominating force in cross-cultural research in international business. Other than work on individualism-collectivism, however, little systematic research exploring the effects of Hofstede's dimensions on negotiation has been conducted (see Kozan, 1997; Tse, Francis, and Walls, 1994), and the extent to which these dimensions influence cross-cultural and intracultural negotiations needs to be further explored (see Foster, 1992). In addition, there is evidence of considerable variation within more individualistic or more collectivist cultures. For instance, Miyahara, Kim, Shin, and Yoon (1998) studied preferences for conflict resolution styles in Japan and Korea, which are both collectivist cultures. Miyahara et al. found significant differences between Japanese and Koreans, with Koreans reporting more concern about avoiding impositions and avoiding dislike during conflict resolution, while Japanese reported more concern about obtaining clarity than the Koreans. For these reasons, interpretations of the effects of Hofstede's dimensions on negotiations should be considered tentative.

HOW DO CULTURAL DIFFERENCES INFLUENCE NEGOTIATIONS?

Given that cultural differences exist, can be measured, and operate on different levels, the issue becomes how they influence negotiations. Drawing upon work by Weiss and Stripp (1985), Foster (1992), and others, we suggest that culture can influence negotiations across borders in at least eight different ways:

1. *Definition of negotiation.* The fundamental definition of negotiation, what is negotiable, and what occurs when we negotiate can differ greatly across cultures (see Ohanyan, 1999; Yook and Albert, 1998). For instance, "Americans tend to view negotiating as a competitive process of offers and counteroffers, while the Japanese tend to view the negotiation as an opportunity for information-sharing" (Foster, 1992, p. 272).

2. *Selection of negotiators.* The criteria used to select who will participate in the negotiations vary across cultures. These criteria can include knowledge of the subject matter being negotiated, seniority, family connections, gender, age, experience, and status. Different cultures weigh these criteria differently, leading to varying expectations about what is appropriate in different types of negotiations.

3. *Protocol.* Cultures differ in the degree to which protocol, or the formality of the relations between the two negotiating parties, is important. American culture is among the least formal cultures in the world. A generally familiar communication style is quite common; first names are used, for example, while titles are ignored. Contrast this with the situation in other cultures. Many European countries (e.g., France, Germany, England) are very formal, and not using the proper title when addressing someone (e.g., Mr., Dr., Professor, Lord) is considered insulting (see Braganti and Devine, 1992). The formal calling cards or business cards used in many countries in the Pacific Rim (e.g., China, Japan) are essential for introductions there. Negotiators who forget to bring business cards or who write messages on them are frequently breaching protocol and insulting their counterpart (Foster, 1992). Even the ways that business cards are presented, hands are shaken, or dress codes are observed are subject to interpretation by negotiators and can be the foundation of attributions about a person's background and personality.

4. *Communication.* Cultures influence how people communicate, both verbally and nonverbally. There are also differences in body language across cultures; a behavior that may be highly insulting in one culture may be completely innocuous in another (Axtell, 1990, 1991, 1993). To avoid offending the other party in negotiations across borders, the international negotiator needs to observe cultural rules of communication carefully. For example, placing feet on a desk in the United States signals power or relaxation; in Thailand, it is considered very insulting (see Boxes 11.2 and 11.3 for more examples). Clearly, there is a lot of information about how to communicate that an international negotiator must remember in order not to insult, anger, or embarrass the other party during negotiations. Culture-specific books and articles can provide considerable advice to international negotiators about how to communicate in various cultures; seeking such advice is an essential aspect of planning for global negotiations (Binnendijk, 1987; Graham and Sano, 1989; Pye, 1992; Tung, 1991).

5. *Time.* Cultures largely determine what time means and how it affects negotiations (see Mayfield, Mayfield, Martin, and Herbig, 1997). In the United States, people tend to respect time by appearing for meetings at an appointed hour, being sensitive to not wasting the time of other people, and generally holding that "faster" is better than "slower" because it symbolizes high productivity. Other cultures have quite different views about time. In more traditional societies, especially

---

BOX 11.2
Example of Communication Rules for Global Negotiators

Never touch a Malay on the top of the head, for that is where the soul resides. Never show the sole of your shoe to an Arab, for it is dirty and represents the bottom of the body, and never use your left hand in Muslim culture, for it is reserved for physical hygiene. Touch the side of your nose in Italy and it is a sign of distrust. Always look directly and intently into your French associate's eye when making an important point. Direct eye contact in Southeast Asia, however, should be avoided until the relationship is firmly established. If your Japanese associate has just sucked air in deeply through his teeth, that's a sign you've got real problems. Your Mexican associate will want to embrace you at the end of a long and successful negotiation; so will your Central and Eastern European associates, who may give you a bear hug *and* kiss you three times on alternating cheeks. Americans often stand farther apart than their Latin and Arab associates but closer than their Asian associates. In the United States people shake hands forcefully and enduringly; in Europe a handshake is usually quick and to the point; in Asia, it is often rather limp. Laughter and giggling in the West Indies indicates humor; in Asia, it more often indicates embarrassment and humility. Additionally, the public expression of deep emotion is considered ill-mannered in most countries of the Pacific Rim; there is an extreme separation between one's personal and public selves. The withholding of emotion in Latin America, however, is often cause for mistrust.

SOURCE: D. A. Foster, *Bargaining across Borders: How to Negotiate Business Successfully Anywhere in the World* (New York: McGraw-Hill, 1992), p. 281. Reproduced with the permission of the McGraw-Hill Companies.

---

in hot climates, the pace is slower than in the United States. This tends to reduce the focus on time, at least in the short term. Americans are perceived by other cultures as enslaved by their clocks, because time is watched carefully and guarded as a valuable resource. In some cultures, such as China and Latin America, time per se is not important. The focus of negotiations is on the task, regardless of the amount of time that it takes. The opportunity for misunderstandings because of different perceptions of time is great during cross-cultural negotiations. Americans may be perceived as always being in a hurry and as flitting from one task to another, while Chinese or Latin American negotiators may appear to the Americans to be doing nothing and wasting time.

6. *Risk propensity.* Cultures vary in the extent to which they are willing to take risks. Some cultures tend to produce bureaucratic, conservative decision makers who want a great deal of information before making decisions. Other cultures produce negotiators who are more entrepreneurial and who are willing to act and take risks when they have incomplete information (e.g., "nothing ventured, nothing gained"). According to Foster (1992), Americans fall on the risk-taking end of the continuum, as do some Asian cultures (e.g., the "Dragons"), and some European cultures are quite conservative (e.g., Greece). The orientation of a culture toward risk will have a large effect on what is negotiated and the content of the negotiated

---

BOX 11.3
Cross-Cultural Miscommunication

Though many multinational organizations have extensive experience in overseas markets, some problems persist. Language and cultural differences make it difficult to translate slogans and ideas effectively in new environments. For example:

- In Taiwan, the Pepsi slogan "Come alive with the Pepsi Generation" translated into "Pepsi will bring your ancestors back from the dead."

- In Chinese, Kentucky Fried Chicken's "Finger-lickin' good" became "Eat your fingers off."

- Salem cigarette's slogan, "Salem—Feeling Free" became "When smoking Salem, you feel so refreshed that your mind seems to be free and empty" in Japan.

- When Chevrolet introduced the Nova in South America, they were apparently unaware that in Spanish "*No va*" means "It won't go."

- When Parker Pen marketed a ballpoint in Mexico, the slogan was supposed to inform customers that the pen "won't leak in your pocket and embarrass you." However, the company used the word *embarazar* for *embarrass*. Mexican consumers read the advertisement as "It won't leak in your pocket and make you pregnant."

- In Italy, a campaign for Schweppes tonic water translated the name as "Schweppes Toilet Water."

SOURCE: Anonymous

---

outcome. Negotiators in risk-oriented cultures will be more willing to move early on a deal and will generally take more chances. Those in risk-avoiding cultures are more likely to seek further information and take a wait-and-see stance.

7. *Groups versus individuals.* Cultures differ according to whether they emphasize the individual or the group. The United States is very much an individual-oriented culture, where being independent and assertive is valued and praised. Group-oriented cultures, in contrast, favor the superiority of the group and see individual needs as second to the group's needs. Group-oriented cultures value fitting in and reward loyal team players; those who dare to be different are socially ostracized—a large price to pay in a group-oriented society. This cultural difference can have a variety of effects on negotiation. Americans are more likely to have one individual who is responsible for the final decision, whereas group-oriented cultures like the Chinese are more likely to have a group responsible for the decision. Decision making in group-oriented cultures involves consensus and may take considerably more time than American negotiators are used to. In addition, because so many people can be involved in the negotiations in group-oriented cultures, and because their participation may be sequential rather than simultaneous, American negotiators may be faced with a series of discussions over the same issues and materials with many different people. In a negotiation in China, one of the authors of

this book met with more than six different people on successive days, going over the same ground with different negotiators and interpreters, until the negotiation was concluded.

8. *Nature of agreements.* Culture also has an important effect both on concluding agreements and on what form the negotiated agreement takes. In the United States, agreements are typically based on logic (e.g., the low-cost producer gets the deal), are often formalized, and are enforced through the legal system if such standards are not honored. In other cultures, however, obtaining the deal may be based on who you are (e.g., your family or political connections) rather than on what you can do. In addition, agreements do not mean the same thing in all cultures. Foster (1992) notes that the Chinese frequently use memorandums of agreement to formalize a relationship and to signal the start of negotiations (mutual favors and compromise). Frequently, however, Americans will interpret the same memorandum of agreement as the completion of the negotiations that is enforceable in a court of law. Again, cultural differences in how to close an agreement and what exactly that agreement means can lead to confusion and misunderstandings when we negotiate across borders.

In summary, a great deal has been written about the importance of culture in cross-border negotiations. While academics and practitioners may use the word *culture* to mean different things, they agree that it is a critical aspect of international negotiation that can have a broad influence on many aspects of the process and outcome of negotiations across borders.

CULTURALLY RESPONSIVE NEGOTIATION STRATEGIES

Although a great deal has been written about international negotiation and the extra challenges that occur when negotiating across borders, cultures, or nationalities, far less attention has been paid to what the individual negotiator should specifically *do* when faced with negotiating with someone from another culture. The advice by many theorists in this area, either explicitly or implicitly, has been, "When in Rome, act as the Romans do" (see Francis, 1991, and Weiss, 1994, for reviews of the over simplicity of this advice). In other words, negotiators are advised to be aware of the effects of cultural differences on negotiation and to take them into account when they negotiate. Much of the material discussed in this chapter reflects this tendency. Many theorists appear to assume implicitly that the best way to manage cross-border negotiations is to be sensitive to the cultural norms of the person with whom you are negotiating and to modify your strategy to be consistent with behaviors that occur in that culture. Contrast this with the less culturally sensitive view, "Business is business everywhere in the world," which suggests that the other party can adapt to your style of negotiating, that style is unimportant, or, more arrogantly, that your style should dictate what other people do. Although it is important to avoid cultural gaffes when negotiating, it is not clear that the best approach is to modify your strategy to match the other person's approach.

Several factors indicate that cross-border negotiators should not make large modifications to their approach:

1. Negotiators may not be able to modify their approach *effectively*. It takes years to understand another culture deeply, and you may not have the time necessary to gain this understanding before beginning negotiations. Although a little understanding of another culture is clearly better than total ignorance, it may not be enough to let you make effective adjustments to your negotiation strategy. Attempting to match the strategies and tactics used by negotiators in another culture is a daunting task that requires fluency in their language as only one of many preconditions. Even simple words may be translated in several different ways with different nuances, making the challenge of communicating across languages a daunting task (see Adachi, 1998).

2. Even if negotiators can modify their approach effectively, it does not mean that this will translate automatically into a better negotiation outcome for their side. It is quite possible that those on the other side will modify their approach too. The results in this situation can be disaster, with each side trying to act like the other "should" be acting, and both sides not really understanding what the other party is doing. Consider the following example contrasting typical American and Japanese negotiation styles (also see Box 11.4). Americans are more likely to start negotiations with an extreme offer in order to leave room for concessions. Japanese are more likely to start negotiations with gathering information in order to understand whom they are dealing with and what the relationship will be. Assume that both parties understand their own and the other party's cultural tendencies (this is a large assumption that frequently is not met). Now assume that each party, acting out of respect for the other, decides to "act like the Romans do" and to adopt the approach of the other party. The possibilities for confusion are endless. When the Americans gather information about the Japanese, are they truly interested or are they playing a role? It will be clear that they are not acting like Americans, but the strategy that they are using may not be readily identified. How will the Americans interpret the Japanese behavior? The Americans have prepared well for their negotiations and understand that the Japanese do not present extreme positions early in negotiations. When the Japanese *do* present an extreme position early in negotiations (in order to adapt to the American negotiation style), how should the Americans interpret this behavior? The Americans likely will think, "That must be what they really want, because they don't open with extreme offers." Adopting the other party's approach does not guarantee success, and in fact may lead to more confusion than acting like yourself (where at least your behavior is understood within your own cultural context).

3. Research suggests that negotiators may naturally negotiate differently when they are with people from their own culture than when they are with people from other cultures (Adler and Graham, 1989; Natlandsmyr and Rognes, 1995). The implications of this research are that a deep understanding of how people in other cultures negotiate, such as Costa Ricans negotiating with each other, may not help an American negotiating with a Costa Rican (see Drake, 1995; Weldon and Jehn, 1995).

BOX 11.4
A Simple "Hai" Won't Do

When a TV announcer here reported Bill Clinton's comment to Boris Yeltsin that when the Japanese say yes they often mean no, he gave the news with an expression of mild disbelief.

Having spent my life between East and West, I can sympathize with those who find the Japanese yes unfathomable. However, the fact that it sometimes fails to correspond precisely with the Occidental yes does not necessarily signal intended deception. This was probably why the announcer looked bewildered, and it marks a cultural gap that can have serious repercussions.

I once knew an American who worked in Tokyo. He was a very nice man, but he suffered a nervous breakdown and went back to the United States tearing his hair and exclaiming, "All Japanese businessmen are liars." I hope this is not true. If it were, all Japanese businessmen would be driving each other mad, which does not seem to be the case. Nevertheless, since tragedies often arise from misunderstandings, an attempt at some explanation might not be amiss.

A Japanese yes in its primary context simply means the other person has heard you and is contemplating a reply. This is because it would be rude to keep someone waiting for an answer without supplying him with an immediate response.

For example: A feudal warlord marries his sister to another warlord. (I am back to TV.) Then he decides to destroy his newly acquired brother-in-law and besieges the castle. Being human, though, the attacking warlord worries about his sister and sends a spy to look around. The spy returns and the lord inquires eagerly, "Well, is she safe?" The spy bows and answers, *"Hai,"* which means yes. We sigh with relief, thinking, "Ah, the fair lady is still alive!" But then the spy continues, "To my regret she has fallen on her sword together with her husband."

Hai is also an expression of our willingness to comply with your intent even if your request is worded in the negative. This can cause complications. When I was at school, our English teacher, a British nun, would say, "Now children, you won't forget to do your homework, will you?" And we would all dutifully chorus, "Yes, mother," much to her consternation.

A variation of hai may mean, "I understand your wish and would like to make you happy but unfortunately . . ." Japanese being a language of implication, the latter part of this estimable thought is often left unsaid.

Is there, then, a Japanese yes that corresponds to the Western one? I think so, particularly when it is accompanied by phrases such as *"sodesu"* (it is so) and *"soshimasu"* (I will do so).

A word of caution against the statement "I will think about it." Though in Tokyo this can mean a willingness to give one's proposal serious thought, in Osaka, another business center, it means a definite no. This attitude probably stems from the belief that a straightforward no would sound too brusque.

When talking to a Japanese person, it is perhaps best to remember that although he may be speaking English, he is reasoning in Japanese. And if he says, "I will think about it," you should inquire as to which district of Japan he hails from before going on with your negotiations.

4. Research by Francis (1991) suggests that moderate adaptation may be more effective than "acting as the Romans do." In a simulation study of Americans' responses to negotiators from other countries, Francis found that negotiators from a familiar culture (Japan) who made moderate adaptations to American ways were perceived more positively than negotiators who made no changes or those who made large adaptations. Although these findings did not replicate for negotiators from a less familiar culture (Korea), more research needs to be conducted to understand why. At the very least, the results of this study suggest that large adaptations by international negotiators will not always be effective.

Stephen Weiss (1994) has advanced our understanding of the options that people have when negotiating with someone from another culture. Weiss observes that a negotiator may be able to choose among up to eight different culturally responsive strategies. These strategies may be used individually or sequentially, and the strategies can be switched as the negotiation progresses. According to Weiss, when choosing a strategy, negotiators should be aware of their own and the other party's culture in general, understand the specific factors in the current relationship, and predict or try to influence the other party's approach. Weiss's culturally responsive strategies may be arranged into three groups, based on the level of familiarity (low, moderate, high) that a negotiator has with the other party's culture. Within each group there are some strategies that the negotiator may use individually (unilateral strategies) and others that involve the participation of the other party (joint strategies).

Low Familiarity

Employ Agents or Advisers (Unilateral Strategy).   One approach for negotiators who have very low familiarity with the other party's culture is to hire an agent or adviser who is familiar with the cultures of both parties. This relationship may range from having the other party conduct the negotiations under your supervision (agent) to receiving regular or occasional advice during the negotiations (adviser). Although agents or advisers may create other problems (such as tensions between that person and you), they may be quite useful for negotiators who have little awareness of the other party's culture and little time to become aware.

Bring in a Mediator (Joint Strategy).   Many types of mediators may be used in cross-cultural negotiations, ranging from someone who conducts introductions and then withdraws to someone who is present throughout the negotiation and takes responsibility for orchestrating the negotiation process (see Kolb, 1983a). Interpreters will often play this role, providing both parties with more information than the mere translation of words during negotiations. Mediators may encourage one side or the other to adopt one culture's approaches or a third cultural approach (the mediator's home culture).

Induce the Other Party to Use Your Approach (Joint Strategy).   The third option is to persuade the other party to use your approach. There are many ways to do this, ranging from making a polite request to asserting rudely that your way is best. More subtly, you can continue to respond to the other party's requests in your own language because you "cannot express yourself well enough" in the other's language. Although this strategy has many advantages for the negotiator with low familiarity, there are also some disadvantages. For instance, the other party may become irritated at or insulted by having to make the extra effort to deal with you on your own cultural terms. In addition, the other party may also have a strategic advantage because he or she may now attempt more extreme tactics and, if you object, excuse their use on the basis of his or her "cultural ignorance" (after all, you can't expect the other party to understand everything about how you conduct business).

Moderate Familiarity

Adapt to the Other Party's Approach (Unilateral Strategy).   This strategy involves making conscious changes to your approach so that it is more appealing to the other party. Rather than trying to act like the other party, negotiators using this strategy maintain a firm grasp on their own approach but make modifications to help relations with the other person. These modifications may include acting in a less extreme manner, eliminating some behaviors, and including some of the other party's behaviors. The challenge in using this strategy is to know which behaviors to modify, eliminate, or adopt. In addition, it is not clear that the other party will interpret your modifications in the way that you have intended.

Coordinate Adjustment (Joint Strategy).   This strategy involves both parties making mutual adjustments to find a common process for negotiation. Although this can be done implicitly, it is more likely to occur explicitly ("How would you like to proceed?"), and it can be thought of as a special instance of negotiating the process of negotiation. This strategy requires a moderate amount of knowledge about the other party's culture and at least some facility with his or her language (comprehension, if not the ability to speak). Coordinate adjustment occurs on a daily basis in Montreal, the most bilingual city in North America (85 percent of Montrealers understand both English and French). It is standard practice for businesspeople in Montreal to negotiate the process of negotiation before the substantive discussion begins. The outcomes of this discussion are variations on the theme of whether the negotiations will occur in English or French, with a typical outcome being that either party may speak either language. Negotiations often occur in both languages, and frequently the person with the best second-language skills will switch languages to facilitate the discussion. Another outcome that occasionally occurs has both parties speaking in their second language (i.e., the French speaker will negotiate in English while the English speaker will negotiate in French) to demonstrate respect for the other party. Another type of coordinate adjustment occurs when the two negotiating parties adopt aspects of a third culture to facilitate their negotiations. For instance, during a recent trip to Latin America, one of the authors of this book conducted discussions in French with a Latin American colleague who spoke Spanish and French, but not English. On a subsequent trip to China, negotiations were conducted in French, English, and Chinese since each of the six participants spoke two of the three languages.

High Familiarity

Embrace the Other Party's Approach (Unilateral Strategy). This strategy involves adopting completely the approach of the other party. To be used successfully, the negotiator needs to be completely bilingual and bicultural. In essence, the negotiator using this strategy doesn't act like a Roman, he or she *is* a Roman. This strategy is costly (in preparation time and expense) and places the negotiator using it under considerable stress (it is difficult to switch back and forth rapidly between cultures). However, there is much to gain by using this strategy because the other party can be approached and understood completely on his or her own terms.

Improvise an Approach (Joint Strategy). This strategy involves crafting an approach that is specifically tailored to the negotiation situation, other party, and circumstances. To use this approach, both parties to the negotiation need to have high familiarity with the other party's culture and a strong understanding of the individual characteristics of the other party. The negotiation that emerges with this approach can be crafted with aspects from both cultures adopted when they will be useful. This approach is the most flexible of the eight strategies, which is both its strength and weakness. Flexibility is a strength because it allows the approach to be crafted to the circumstances at hand, but it is a weakness because there are few general prescriptive statements that can be made about how to use this strategy.

Effect Symphony (Joint Strategy). This strategy works to "transcend exclusive use of either home culture" (Weiss, 1994, p. 58) and instead allows the negotiation parties to create a new approach that may include aspects of either home culture or adopt practices from a third culture. Professional diplomats use such an approach when the customs, norms, and language that they use transcend national borders and form their own culture (diplomacy). Use of this strategy is complex and involves a great deal of time and effort. It works best when the parties are familiar with each other, familiar with both home cultures, and have a common structure (like that of professional diplomats) for the negotiation. Risks of using this strategy include costs due to confusion, lost time, and the overall effort required to make it work.

CHAPTER SUMMARY

This chapter examined various aspects of a growing field of negotiation that explores the complexities of negotiating across borders. We began the chapter with a discussion of the American negotiating style, from both American and non-American perspectives. While there is a great deal of consistency in perceptions of the American negotiating style (e.g., Americans are straightforward, impatient), it is important to remember that there is also a lot of variability within cultures (i.e., not every American negotiates in the same way).

Next, we examined the results of a research program by John Graham and his colleagues (Graham, 1993) that compared American negotiators with negotiators from several countries. Graham and his colleagues found that regardless of where negotiators were from, they negotiated the same level of outcomes on a standard negotiation task. The process of negotiation differed across countries, however, suggesting that there is more than one way to attain the same negotiation outcome. Finally, this research program also suggested that negotiators seem to use different strategies when negotiating with people domestically and internationally (see Natlandsmyr and Rognes, 1995).

We then examined some of the factors that make cross-border negotiations different. Phatak and Habib (1996) suggest that both the environmental and the immediate context have important effects on global negotiations. We then discussed Salacuse's (1988) description of the environmental factors that influence global negotiations: (1) political and legal pluralism, (2) international economics, (3) foreign governments and bureaucracies, (4) instability, (5) ideology, and (6) culture. We added one more environmental factor—external stakeholders—from Phatak and Habib (1996). Phatak and Habib's five immediate context factors were discussed next: (1) relative bargaining power, (2) levels of conflict, (3) relationship between negotiators, (4) desired outcomes, and (5) immediate stakeholders. Each of these environmental and immediate context factors acts to make cross-border negotiations more difficult, and effective international negotiators need to understand how to manage them. We concluded this section of the chapter with a discussion of how to make sense of global negotiation outcomes in light of the multiple factors that can simultaneously influence them.

Next, we turned to a discussion of Robert Janosik's (1987) work on the conceptualization of culture. Janosik suggests that culture is used in at least four different ways by researchers and practitioners in global negotiations: (1) culture as learned behavior, (2) culture as shared values, (3) culture as dialectics, and (4) culture in context. Each of these approaches to understanding culture has strengths and weaknesses, and occasionally there are communication breakdowns between researchers and practitioners when they use the same word (*culture*) in such different ways. We then turned to a discussion of Hofstede's work on culture, the factor that has been most frequently used to explain differences in negotiations across borders. Hofstede's research (1980a, 1980b, 1989, 1991) defines culture as the shared values and beliefs held by a group of people, and is the most comprehensive study of cultural dimensions in international business. He concluded that four dimensions could summarize cultural differences: (1) individualism/collectivism, (2) power distance, (3) masculinity/femininity, and (4) uncertainty avoidance.

Next, we examined how cultural differences can influence negotiations. Foster (1992), adapting work by Weiss and Stripp (1985), suggests that culture can influence global negotiations in several ways, including (1) the definition of negotiation, (2) the selection of negotiators, (3) protocol, (4) communication, (5) time, (6) risk propensity, (7) groups versus individuals, and (8) the nature of agreements.

The chapter concluded with a discussion of how to manage cultural differences when negotiating across borders. Weiss presents eight different culturally responsive strategies that negotiators can use with a negotiator from a different culture. Some of these strategies may be used individually, whereas others are used jointly with the other negotiator. Weiss indicates that one critical aspect of choosing the correct strategy for a given negotiation is the degree of familiarity (low, moderate, or high) that a negotiator has with the other culture. However, even those with high familiarity with another culture are faced with a daunting task if they want to modify their strategy completely when they deal with the other culture.

CHAPTER 12

Managing Difficult Negotiations: Individual Approaches

INTRODUCTION

Michele is having a terrible dispute with her neighbor in the condo next door. The neighbor, who recently moved in to the apartment, brought a large German Shepherd dog with her that barks ALL the time. Michele is a writer who likes to work at home in the morning, but the dog is so distracting that she cannot get anything done. Michele has talked to the neighbor, who has apologized for the problem but has done nothing to keep the dog quiet. Michele is considering filing a nuisance complaint with the police and taking the neighbor to court.

Donna and her coworker Max are at it again. They both work as website administrators for a major marketing firm. Max just can't seem to get to work on time, and Donna always has to cover for him on the website problems that crop up during the night before. Max always stays later than Donna, but there is much less work in the late afternoon than first thing in the morning. She and Max have talked about it; he promises to get to work earlier, and for a few days he is fine, but then he slips back into his old pattern. Donna doesn't want to report him to the boss, but she doesn't see any other alternative.

Simon, a manufacturer's representative for a machine tool company, finds that a client's recent expansion has resulted in Simon having to follow the client into another sales representative's territory. Simon is sure that the problem can be worked out to everyone's satisfaction and advantage, but so far the other rep seems to want it all—in fact, he seems to act like it's some sort of contest.

In this chapter, we address situations where negotiations become especially difficult, often to the point of impasse, stalemate, or breakdown. As we have noted several times, negotiation is a conflict management process, and all conflict situations have the potential for becoming derailed. The parties become angry or entrenched in their positions. Perceptions become distorted, and judgments are biased. The parties cease to communicate effectively and instead accuse and blame each other. One party maintains a conflict management style that is not compatible with the other. Issues are viewed in such a way that the parties do not believe that there is any possible compatibility between them, or they cannot find a middle ground where agreement is possible. In short, destructive conflict processes override the negotiation, and the parties cannot proceed.

When negotiations become difficult to resolve, problems may be traced to one or more of the following causal elements:

- Characteristics of the way parties perceive themselves or other negotiators (the parties involved directly and indirectly—their styles, preferences, and behaviors).
- Characteristics of the *issues* of their communication (i.e., the substance of the negotiation, or how the parties view the substance).
- Characteristics in the *process* used to negotiate or manage conflict (the play of the game, or the actual conduct of negotiation).
- Characteristics of the context of their negotiation (the negotiation setting—temporal, relational, and/or cultural).

As the title suggests, the current chapter deals with managing difficult negotiations and remedies that negotiators can use on their own, without outside assistance. The chapter is organized into three major sections. In the first section, we discuss the nature of negotiations that are "difficult to resolve." We examine the causes of stalemate, impasse, or breakdown, and explore characteristics of difficult negotiations, including characteristics of the parties, the types of issues involved, and the process in play. In the second section, we will discuss the specific actions that the parties can take *jointly* to try to move the conflict back to a level where successful negotiation and conflict resolution can ensue. Finally, in the third section, we will discuss *mismatched* situations where one party wants to negotiate to an integrative resolution, and the other party is being "difficult"—and hence, what the integrative party can do to draw the other into a more constructive process. In Chapter 13 we will address those difficult situations in which third parties (i.e., parties other than the disputants themselves) work to facilitate resolution, either by their own initiative or because they are invited in by the negotiators.

THE NATURE OF "DIFFICULT TO RESOLVE" NEGOTIATIONS AND WHY THEY OCCUR

It is not uncommon for negotiations, especially distributive ones, to become contentious to the point of breakdown. In extreme cases, conflict escalates and interpersonal enmity increases. What are the characteristics of these "difficult to resolve" negotiations, and what actions are most effective in making them easier to resolve? Not unsurprisingly, any number of things can go wrong. Before examining these things in some detail, we define the notion of "impasse" as a way to understand difficult negotiations, and examine what causes negotiations to become intractable (and hence reach impasse).

The Nature of Impasse

We describe "difficult to resolve" negotiations broadly as being at *impasse*. Impasse is a condition or state of the conflict in which there is no apparent quick or easy resolution. When impasse exists, the parties are unable to create mutually advantageous deals that satisfy their aspirations and expectations (Ross and Stillinger, 1991).

- *Impasse is not necessarily bad or destructive (although it can be).* There can be numerous reasons why negotiations are at impasse, and there can be very good reasons why parties choose to stay at impasse until a viable resolution can be recognized (Mayer, 2000).

- *Impasse does not have to be permanent.* By suggesting that impasse is a "state" of the negotiation, this means that it is not resolvable given the current situation in the content, context, process, or people. Thus, if the content, context, process, or people are altered in some way—either intentionally or simply by the passage of time and change of circumstances—negotiators can move "out of impasse" and into resolution. Conditions of impasse that persist over a long period of time may lead us to define that negotiation as *intractable*. Putnam and Wondolleck (2003) have determined that intractable conflicts (conflicts that are *long-standing* and *elude resolution*) vary along several different dimensions:

  1. *Divisiveness*—the degree to which the conflict divides people, such that they are "backed into a corner" and can't escape without losing face.

  2. *Intensity*—the level of participant involvement, emotionality, and commitment in a conflict.

  3. *Pervasiveness*—the degree to which the conflict invades the social and private lives of people.

  4. *Complexity*—the number and complexity of issues, the number of parties involved, the levels of social systems involved in the conflict, and the degree to which it is impossible to resolve one issue without resolving several others simultaneously.

- *Impasse can be tactical or genuine.* Tactical impasse occurs when parties deliberately refuse to proceed with negotiation as a way to gain leverage or put pressure on the other party to make concessions—in other words, "intentionally using impasse as a means for advancing their goals" (Mayer, 2000, p. 169). According to Ross and Stillinger (1991) this sort of intransigence occurs when "one or both parties in a conflict . . . [believes] that a willingness to forgo immediate gains in trade (and thereby deprive its adversary of similar gains) will win for itself even more favorable terms in future negotiations" (p. 391). Genuine impasse, in contrast, occurs "when the parties feel unable to move forward without sacrificing something important to them. . . . usually, disputants experience this kind of impasse as beyond their control, and they feel they have no acceptable choice but to remain there" (Mayer, 2000, p. 171). Thus, as Mayer notes, impasses that start out as tactical may become genuine.

- *Impasse perceptions versus reality.* The difference between tactical and genuine impasse may be perceived rather than real—but if it is perceived, that may be "real enough" for the parties to believe they are at impasse. Thus, perceived intransigence is created by the expectation that the other party will experience deterioration in his or her negotiation position, making compromise and concessions more likely in the future. Intransigence can be defined more specifically as a party's unwillingness to move to any fallback position through concession or compromise. Such toughness in bargaining may lead to short-term gain if agreement ensues, but toughness that calls forth toughness in response may well lead to no agreement whatsoever, making such a tactic a "powerful but dangerous card for a negotiator to play in multilateral negotiations" (Brams and Doherty, 1993, p. 706).

What Makes a Negotiation Intractable?

Because negotiations change with time and change in the issues, parties, and context in which they occur, a negotiation becomes more "tractable" when it becomes easier to resolve, and "intractable" when it is more difficult to resolve. Putnam and Wondolleck (2003) have concluded that the following characteristics make a negotiation more *intractable*:

- The parties themselves are unorganized, loosely connected, and lacking structure.
- The social system from which the parties come is ill defined, dispute resolution procedures are chaotic and uncertain, and there is an absence of clear governing authority.
- There are fundamental value differences on the key issues.
- The conflict repeatedly escalates: the parties grow in size, the number of issues on the table expands, and the costs of resolution increase. Parties are polarized against each other, and conflict repeatedly spirals.

In contrast, the following characteristics make a negotiation more *tractable*:

- The parties themselves are well organized; group members are clear, the parties have clearly defined roles and agree on a common mission.
- The social system from which the parties come is clearly structured, there are clear procedures and rules for resolving disputes, and clear, legitimate authority exits.
- There is general consensus on underlying values, but a disagreement on how resources are to be allocated.
- The conflict frequently de-escalates: the negotiation remains contained and focused, the parties are strongly committed to finding a mutually acceptable resolution, and cycles of high conflict are frequently broken up by long cycles of relative peace and calm.

In the remainder of this section, we will discuss the four dimensions—aspects of the *parties,* aspects of the *issues,* aspects of the conflict *process,* and aspects of the *context* of the negotiation—that cause negotiations to be difficult to resolve. We will not extensively explore the dimensions of the social system, since in the short term, parties in dispute can do little about the "social system" in which their conflict may be embedded.

Characteristics of the Parties

How One Defines One's Self.   Many impasses originate because of the way parties define themselves. Issues of identity are central to many difficult-to-resolve negotiations. "Identity" is about the way that individuals answer the question "Who am I?" (Hoare, 1994, p. 25). Individuals may answer this question in a variety of ways, depending on the social groups to which they belong, and how they understand themselves to be (Gray, 2003; Hogg, Terry, and White, 1995; Smyth, 1994). Rothman (1997) indicates that conflict is likely to occur when people's identities are threatened, because such threats challenge people's fundamental sense of who they are. Examples from world and domestic affairs abound. Calls for ethnic self-determination or a national homeland, calls for the correction of perceived institutionalized discrimination against aggrieved minorities, and appeals for the universal extension of human or political rights are all often major causal elements in intractable negotiations. Moreover, as we noted in Chapter 2, parties often "frame" a negotiation around an identity issue when they believe that one outcome of the conflict could be to either strengthen or weaken their sense of identity (Gray, 2003).

Comparing One's Self to Others.   If issues of identity focus on the question "Who am I," issues of characterization reflect the way that individuals define "Who are they?" (Gray, 2003). The development of one's social identity is often inextricably tied to the process of comparing one's self to others. When we define ourselves by virtue of the groups to which we belong, we also begin to define others as members of groups to which we do not belong, or as strongly dissimilar. Moreover, parties in conflict tend to fall into a psychological trap called "the fundamental attribution error" (Ross, 1997)—tending to blame others for their fate when things go wrong, but taking personal credit for their successes; conversely, they tend to see others' successes as due to luck, but failures as due to others' defects and deficiencies.

Babcock, Wang, and Loewenstein (1996) examined the effect of this social comparison process as it occurs in negotiation impasses, with two principal findings. First, negotiators chose comparison groups to reflect a supportive, self-serving bias for their own positions (they compared themselves to others whose positions make their own demands seem fair and reasonable). Second, negotiation breakdowns or impasses (in this case, the occurrence of a work stoppage) were positively correlated with perceived differences between the negotiators' chosen comparison groups. In short, the greater the perceived differences between the comparison groups, the greater the likelihood of a breakdown. While the first finding could be based on an intentional, strategic choice, the second finding is consistent with our earlier comments regarding extreme positions, perceptual differences, and resultant impasses.

Perceptions of Power.   The decision to bargain tough may arise from a negotiator's belief that he or she can effectively exercise coercive power (see Chapter 6) to levy costs on the other party or to make that party accept a settlement that is not in his or her best interest. The effectiveness of such a tactic, in the short run and without regard to its effect on the long-term negotiation relationship, clearly depends on the other party's belief that the negotiator has such power and will use it (Brams and Doherty, 1993; de Dreu, 1995). Negotiators in such confrontations are likely to develop a tendency to see each other as extreme, biased, and decidedly uncooperative. If the other party is perceived to be politically or philosophically the opposite, and if good manners lead one or both of you to avoid mutual disclosure of your views on volatile subjects, the level of negotiation difficulty is likely to rise. Keltner and Robinson (1993) found such negotiations to be marked by excessive length, few agreements overall, and, in retrospect, little perceived cooperation.

Smyth (1994) examined two aspects of the role of power on impasses: whether the parties believe that their power was subject to change, and whether there were agreed-on social institutions for dealing with power changes between parties. The resulting matrix indicates how parties will react to power relationships (see Figure 12.1). Smyth suggests that the most intractable situations occur in the lower left quadrant, in which there is a change in the power balance but no existing, mutually acceptable social institutions to govern or manage the change. Intractability is seen to result from the strengths of and interaction among four variables:

- The saliency (perceived importance and relevance) of a group's social identity.
- The attractiveness to each party of the substance of the deal.
- The attractiveness to the low-power party of gaining more power.
- The saliency (perceived importance and relevance) of the institutions governing changes in issues of autonomy and control.

According to Smyth, successful negotiation in these situations depends on the prior resolution of social identity issues among the disputing parties. Impasses often result from the perceived need to negotiate simultaneously about the change in power and the applicable, appropriate institutions for maintaining that power shift. When social identification is strong (as it is, for example, among the Serbs in the former Yugoslav republics, or the Israelis and Palestinians in the Middle East), the consequential in-group/out-group

FIGURE 12.1   Conflicts, Power Relationships, and Institutions

	Power Relationship Altered	**Power Relationship Does Not Change**
Agreed-Upon Institutions	**II** Democratic elections Mergers	**I** Market transactions Civil suits
No Agreed-Upon Institution	**VI** Revolutions Secessions Devising new international agreements	**III** Football riots Spontaneous civil disturbances

SOURCE: L. F. Smyth, "Intractable Conflicts and the Role of Identity," *Negotiation Journal* 10 (1994), p. 312. Used with permission of Plenum Publishing Corporation.

bias often leads one or both parties to demonize the other, and to discount the validity and acceptability of the other's bargaining position. This often results in an unwillingness to deal with the other party at all (see Spector, 1998). It is in the nature of intergroup negotiations that some adjustment of each party's own identity, or the rigor with which it is defended, must be made in order for negotiations to proceed productively (Ring and Van de Ven, 1994). In short, there has to be some give on both sides (particularly the high-power side), and a willingness to at least consider that the other party may have a legitimate interest and a valid perspective.

Getting Mad, Getting Even.   Impasse may also result from an expression of fear and anger (Adler, Rosen, and Silverstein, 1998) or from a commitment to seek revenge on the offending party, trading "harm for harm" (Kim and Smith, 1993). The escalation of conflict through revenge seems to be driven by one or more of three things: an interest in retribution to correct injustice, the necessity to stand up and express one's self-worth, and the wish to deter future occurrences of undesirable behaviors (Kim and Smith, 1993). These emotions and motivations, in turn, exacerbate the tendency for conflict to escalate and for negotiations to break down fully and fatally. Pruitt, Parker, and Mikolic (1997) propose that escalation often occurs in response to persistent annoyance of one party by another, while Jones and Remland (1993) suggest that escalation might also be explained by "nonverbal status displays" (p. 119). Such displays, meant to express power, dominance, or relative status in face-to-face conflicts for clearly strategic purposes, are of two general types: those made to degrade the other party's physical presence, and those intended to degrade the other party's intellectual presence. Again, the intractable disputes seen in the news each day reflect these dynamics. (We will discuss these tactics in greater detail later in this chapter.)

Conflict Management Style.   Finally, impasses may also result from too little engagement in the negotiation, rather than too much. Mayer (2000) observed that parties often prefer to avoid conflict in a number of creative ways:

- Aggressive avoidance ("Don't start with me or you will regret it")—intimidate others to keep them away.
- Passive avoidance ("I refuse to dance")—try to ignore the other.
- Passive aggressive avoidance ("If you are angry at me, that's *your* problem")—put the blame on the other party and walk away.
- Avoidance by claiming hopelessness ("What's the use . . .").
- Avoidance through surrogates ("Let's you and her fight")—deflect the conflict to a "surrogate" to take the other on.
- Avoidance through denial ("If I close my eyes, it will all go away")—make believe it isn't there.
- Avoidance through premature problem solving ("There is no conflict—I fixed everything").
- Avoidance by folding ("OK, we'll do it your way; now can we talk about something else?").

Note that these eight different approaches can be used singly or combined together. The function is to NOT engage in the conflict in a productive way, which may in and of itself perpetuate the impasse until the other party, or the circumstances, change in some way (Mayer, 2000). (See also our discussion of avoidance as a strategy in Chapter 1, and as a personal style preference in Chapter 10.)

Characteristics of the Negotiation Context

The second reason that negotiation can become intractable concerns characteristics of the context: the negotiation setting, temporal issues, relational issues, and cultural issues (see Chapter 11 for a discussion of the influence of culture on negotiation). Very little research and theory has been written about how the negotiation context leads negotiators to impasses. Experienced negotiators understand, however, that changing the negotiation context—the physical location in which it occurs—can be an important tactic for getting negotiations back on track. For instance, changing locations from one hotel or city to another can be used as a symbol for a new start to negotiations and a signal that the previous approach was "left at the old location." Alternatively, changing from a more formal space—such as a formal conference or Board room—to an informal space   such as a living room, lounge or restaurant—can make people more comfortable and change the interpersonal dynamics. Even more importantly, replacing an aggressive member of the negotiating team with a quieter member, either temporarily or permanently, can signal the other party that one is also willing to change the substance of the negotiation. Finally, timing is critical in a negotiation (see Chapter 3). Compromises that are presented too early may be rejected outright, but if they can be repackaged and presented later "for exploration," they may be able to break an impasse. (See Box 12.1 for an illustration of the importance of physical location, timing, and compatibility on "energy flow" or "chi" in negotiation.)

Agreement on the Rules and Procedures.   Another way that parties can manage the context is to obtain mutual agreement about the rules that will govern the negotiation. (We discussed this as a core element of planning in Chapter 2.) Escalated conflict tends to exceed its original bounds; as parties become more upset, they may be more likely to resort to any and all tactics to defeat the other. Efforts at effective conflict de-escalation and control may require that the parties rededicate themselves to basic ground rules for how they will manage the impasse. Establishing ground rules might include the following steps (see also Dukes, Piscolish, and Stephens, 2000):

- Determining a site for a meeting (changing the site or finding a neutral location).
- Setting a formal agenda as to what may or may not be discussed, and agreeing to abide by that agenda.
- Determining who may attend the meetings. (Changing key negotiators or representatives may be a signal of the intention to change the negotiation approach.)
- Setting time limits for the individual meeting and for the overall negotiation session. (As we have pointed out, progress in negotiation is often paced according to the time available; therefore, setting limits is likely to allow for more progress than not setting them.)

BOX 12. 1
Negotiate with Feng Shui

Most of the prescriptive writing on negotiation, including much of what is in this volume, focuses on achieving a better understanding of the issues and the other party. Few negotiators understand how important the context of the negotiation can be, or ways to control and manage that context to achieve better results.

Jose Armilla is an experienced U.S. government advisor and international negotiator. In a recent book, Armilla writes about the ancient Chinese traditions of focusing on factors other than the issues and the parties in order to achieve effective results. This tradition gives significant emphasis to three factors that many Western negotiators ignore— location (*ti tian*), compatibility between parties (*hsiang rong*), and timing (*chun shi*)—that tap into the "hidden energies" of one's surroundings and bring them to bear in the negotiation. This hidden energy is called *chi;* chi can be contained both within individuals and in the environment around them. The process of tapping into the hidden energies is called *feng shui*, or ". . . the ancient Chinese art of balancing the chi energy in the environment with the flow of a person's chi in order to increase his or her effectiveness in human affairs" (Armilla, 2001, pp. 9–10).

Armilla offers a number of important and useful tips for connecting with chi flow (getting in touch with stress, monitoring energy flow, exercise, and consumption of liquids), concentrating the chi (through meditation, movement exercises, and focusing energy), and using the chi to assist you in a number of different types of negotiations. For example, in purchasing a house, Armilla advises negotiators to attend to features of the house that affect their own chi level, as well as features of a house which are likely to create "good vibes," such as:

- Attending to how the entrance to the house is configured
- Attending to the foyer of the house, and the location of the stairs relative to the central entrance
- Location of the stove and arrangement of the kitchen to offer the cook security and command of the kitchen area
- Location and configuration of bedrooms

Other interesting suggestions are offered for "bargain hunting" at bazaars and yard sales, buying a car, or many other negotiators.

Finally, Armilla offers assessments of a number of successful and failed negotiations that could be explained by positive or negative chi. Perhaps the best known success is the meeting between American President Ronald Reagan and Soviet General Secretary Mikhail Gorbachev in Geneva, Switzerland, 1985. The timing of the event was selected based on predictions by Reagan's astrologer(!) with an eye to "enhancing Gorbachev's receptivity to Reagan's message as well as a safe trip to Geneva" (p. 165). But even more important, Armilla argues that both men were feng shui compatible, and Geneva was the right place because of its good feng shui. This positive chi was enhanced further by the arrangement of furniture in the meeting, dining and sleeping rooms, selection of specific locations for specific topic discussions, timing of the various meetings, and the food served at meals!

SOURCE: J. Armilla, *Negotiate with Feng Shui* (St. Paul, MN: Llewellyn Publications, 2001).

- Setting procedural rules, such as who may speak, how long they may speak, how issues will be approached, what facts may be introduced, how records of the meeting will be kept, how agreements will be affirmed, and what clerical or support services are required.

- Following specific "dos and don'ts" for behavior (e.g., don't attack others).

Finally—and perhaps this may be a radical step for some negotiators—the parties may agree to set aside a short period during negotiations to critique how they are doing. This mechanism effectively designates a selected time for the parties to evaluate their own progress. It provides time to reevaluate ground rules, change procedural mechanisms, or perhaps even change negotiators. Voice systems—internal systems for receiving comments and feedback from constituents or organization members—are also effective ways to monitor process and find out how things are progressing (see Box 12.2). This process orientation may provide the opportunity for the parties to self-correct the procedural mechanisms that will allow them to make greater progress on their substantive disagreements (Walton, 1987).

In summary, contextual factors can play an important role in breaking an impasse, especially through their symbolic value. More research and theory addressing how and when such interventions will be successful need to be conducted, however.

Characteristics of the Issues

At least three aspects of the issues under discussion can contribute to a "difficult to resolve" negotiation:

- *Value differences.* Many negotiations that are difficult to resolve can be traced to fundamental value differences between the parties. Value differences can vary from very minor differences in preference to major differences in ideology, lifestyle, or what is considered to be most sacred and critical. The critical question is how individuals or groups with distinct differences in values choose to deal with these differences—by attempting to force their views on the other versus by supporting efforts to accommodate and respect the other. Many of the most intractable conflicts that societies grapple with—religious, political, economic, legal, and environmental—are rooted in core value differences. Recent research on the nature of ideologically based negotiations (Wade-Benzoni, Hoffman, Thompson, Moore, Gillespie, and Bazerman, 2002) has helped to create new insights on why these disputes are difficult to negotiate.

- *High stakes distributional bargaining.* "Difficult to resolve" negotiations may also result from distributive bargaining in which there is no apparent overlap in the parties' bargaining range. As we noted in Chapters 3 and 6, parties may have inflated their negotiating positions to the point that there is no apparent zone of possible agreement, the costs of settling are seen as higher than the costs of protracting the dispute, the parties have locked themselves into public postures from which they are unwilling to back down, and the parties are inclined to use power to force the other side to back down. Many of these impasses will be very responsive to the tactics we describe later in this chapter.

BOX 12.2
New Ways to Get Feedback

Like most large organizations, Pillsbury had a problem. Though they recognized the value of employee feedback on company policies, few employees were willing to provide their insight for fear of retaliation or punishment.

So the company installed a private hotline for employee input. Calls are transcribed so that even the caller's gender is not revealed. The transcripts are then sent to top management on a regular basis. Management was stunned to find how much genuinely useful information had been bottled up because employees feared ridicule or recrimination. Callers identified problems from inaccurate clocks to poor product placement in retail outlets. One caller even suggested a successful new product line for the company. Even management decisions are second-guessed: A plant manager in Tennessee was being chastised by his superiors for closing the plant during a snowstorm, until dozens of appreciative employees phoned headquarters to voice their approval.

Certainly face-to-face communication is a more effective mechanism for feedback. But until large organizations learn to establish more open relationships with their rank-and-file employees, programs like the one at Pillsbury can provide valuable information to upper management.

SOURCE: Thomas Petzinger, "Two Executives Cook Up Ways to Make Pillsbury Listen," *The Wall Street Journal,* September 27, 1996, p. B1.

• *Risk to human health and safety.* Finally, a number of negotiations—particularly those in the area of health and the environment—become intractable because the threat to human survival is so clear and apparent, and often because the issues themselves are rooted in complex science which is difficult for the layperson to understand, much less believe and/or blindly trust. Environmental cleanup, nuclear power, disposal of toxic waste, pollution control, and related issues create intense debate and deeply felt argument. Burgess and Burgess (1995) note that negotiating parties often compete in "bidding wars" of one-upsmanship over who has the greatest concern for public health and safety.

Characteristics of the Conflict Resolution Processes

Finally, negotiations are "difficult to resolve" to the extent that the process of conflict resolution is characterized by the following dynamics:

1. The atmosphere is charged with anger, frustration, and resentment. Mistrust and hostility are directed at the opposing negotiator.
2. Channels of communication, previously used to exchange information and supporting arguments for each party's position, are now closed or constrained. Each party uses communication channels to criticize and blame the other, while simultaneously attempting to limit the same type of communication from the other party.

3. The original issues at stake have become blurred and ill defined, and perhaps new issues have been added. Negotiators have become identified with positions on issues, and the conflict has become personalized. Even if a negotiator could make a concession, he or she would not make it due to a strong dislike for the other party.

4. The parties tend to perceive great differences in their respective positions. Conflict heightens the magnitude of these differences and minimizes areas of perceived commonality and agreement. The parties see themselves as further apart than they may actually be, and they do not recognize areas where they may be in agreement.

5. As anger and tension increase, the parties become more locked in to their initial negotiating positions. Rather than searching for ways to make concessions and move toward agreement, the parties become firmer in stating their initial demands, and they resort to threats, lies, and distortions to force the other party to comply with those demands. The other usually meets these threats with counterthreats and retaliation.

6. If there is more than one person on a side, those on the same side tend to view each other favorably. They see the best qualities in the people on their side and minimize whatever differences exist, yet they also demand conformity from their team members and will accept a militant, autocratic form of leadership. If there is dissension in the group, it is hidden from the other party; group members always attempt to present a united front to the other side (Adler, Rosen, and Silverstein, 1998; Blake and Mouton, 1961a, 1961b, 1961c; Corwin, 1969; Harvey, 1953; Keltner and Robinson, 1993).

Faulty Group Process. Beyond the dynamics just described, impasse can also occur within a group when members are interested in conveying a strong appearance of cooperation and agreement. An inflexible preference for maintaining an appearance of collaboration at any cost may lead parties to be excessively civil with each other, leading them to self-censor potentially critical or discomforting comments and inquiries, and/or ignore thorny, controversial issues (e.g., Janis, 1982; Janis and Mann, 1977). The result is excessive cohesion within the group, with parties avoiding difficult points in order not to endanger (in their minds) valuable, desirable relationships among group members.

Remedies. In bargaining situations where parties want to work together, the prescriptive remedy is reducing the predictable pressures that fuel a breakdown of group process, while enhancing intellectual or constructive conflict necessary to work through the impasse. Researchers (e.g., Janis, 1982) suggest that groups can engage in a variety of practices to ensure a better exchange of ideas: using outside experts and devil's advocates, assigning some group members to the role of critical evaluator, breaking into subgroups, holding second-chance meetings where previous decisions can be easily reconsidered, and ensuring that the leader does not overly control the discussion. Turner and Pratkanis (1994) suggested ways that groups can stimulate intellectual conflict, and hence facilitate the critical exchange and evaluation of ideas, assumptions, and plans:

- Ensure that the group conducts a thorough, balanced, comprehensive discussion of the issues (see the discussion of group decision making in Chapter 9).

- Establish procedures for protecting minority viewpoints and opinions, such as ensuring that all ideas are pooled and considered without attaching them to the particular individuals who initiated them.

- Use directed discussion aids, such as a logical, clear procedure for discussing the issues, considering the advantages and disadvantages of every possible action alternative, and requiring groups to come up with more than one solution or action strategy so that multiple strategies are seriously proposed and considered (see also Maier, 1952; Maier and Hoffman, 1960).

Section Summary

In this section, we have reviewed four factors that can make negotiations and conflict "difficult to resolve": characteristics of the parties and their views of each other, characteristics of the issues in dispute, characteristics of the conflict management process, and characteristics of the negotiation context. In the next section, we turn our attention to actions that the parties can take to try to overcome these difficulties on their own initiative.

STRATEGIES FOR RESOLVING IMPASSE: JOINT APPROACHES

Mayer (2000) suggests that dispute resolution involves three major components:

1. Cognitive resolution. The purpose of cognitive resolution is to change how the parties view the situation. For parties to achieve cognitive resolution, ". . . they must *perceive* that the key issues have been resolved, think that they have reached closure on the situation, and view the conflict as part of their past as opposed to their future . . ." (p. 98). Cognitive resolution is often difficult to achieve because people tenaciously hang on to beliefs and perceptions in spite of new data to the contrary. New information and reframing are often key to this process.

2. Emotional resolution involves the way the parties feel about the impasse and the other party, and the amount of emotional energy they put into the negotiation. When parties have emotionally resolved an impasse, they no longer experience negative feelings, relations with the other are less intense, and they have reached some kind of "emotional closure" on the conflict events. Emotional resolution often involves trust rebuilding, forgiveness, and apology.

3. Behavioral resolution processes address exactly what people will do in the future, and what agreements they make about how that future will be realized. Behavioral resolution agreements usually specify ways that the parties can discontinue the problematic conflict dynamics, and mechanisms for instituting those new behaviors which prompt resolution.

In this section, we will describe five major conflict-reduction strategies that can be used to resolve impasses. For the most part, and since we wish to prescribe strategies for changed behavior, all of these processes are aimed at behavioral resolution. However, it will be clear that these behaviors are also aimed at cognitive and emotional resolution as well. The strategies are:

1. Reducing tension and synchronizing the de-escalation of hostility.
2. Improving the accuracy of communication, particularly improving each party's understanding of the other's perspective.

3. Controlling the number and size of issues in the discussion.

4. Establishing a common ground on which the parties can find a basis for agreement.

5. Enhancing the desirability of the options and alternatives that each party presents to the other.

Before describing each of these approaches in detail, it is important to note that there is nothing firm or rigid about the number of different techniques for resolving impasses. Research on the nature of conflict and its resolution has suggested a wide array of different dispute resolution techniques that can be assembled and applied in several different ways (e.g., Deutsch, 1973; Deutsch and Coleman, 2000; Pruitt and Rubin, 1986; Susskind, McKearnan, and Thomas-Larmer, 1999; Walton, 1987). We suggest that the most productive procedure for resolving a highly polarized impasse is to approach it using the steps for conflict management in roughly the order presented. The first step should be some effort at reducing tension, followed by efforts to improve the accuracy of communication and to control the proliferation of issues. Finally, the parties should engage in techniques for establishing common ground and enhancing the attractiveness of each other's preferred alternatives. This procedure is by no means firm and inflexible; many impasses have been successfully resolved by invoking the steps in a different order (see, for example, Box 12.3). However, the order in which we present these procedures is the one most frequently used by third parties in resolving impasses, and hence we believe it will also be the most effective if employed by the negotiators themselves. If the conflict cannot be effectively controlled, third-party intervention may become necessary (see Chapter 13).

BOX 12.3
Save That Sale!

Thomas Keiser (1988), in his *Harvard Business Review* article entitled "Negotiating with a Customer You Can't Afford to Lose," addresses the question of what you do "when your customer turns into Attila the Hun." He proposes eight strategies for handling such situations:

1. Prepare by knowing your walkaway point and by building the number of variables you can work with during the negotiation.

2. When under attack, listen.

3. Keep track of the issues requiring discussion.

4. Assert your company's needs.

5. Commit to a solution only if it's certain to work for both sides.

6. Save the hardest issues for last.

7. Start high and concede slowly.

8. Don't be trapped by emotional blackmail.

SOURCE: Adapted from T. Keiser, "Negotiating with a Customer You Can't Afford to Lose," *Harvard Business Review* 66, no. 6 (1988), pp. 30–37.

Reducing Tension and Synchronizing De-escalation

Unproductive deliberations can easily become highly emotional. Parties are frustrated, angry, and upset. They are strongly committed to their viewpoints and have argued strenuously for their preferred alternatives, seeing themselves as firm, principled, or deserving. The other side, behaving the same way, is seen as stubborn, bull-headed, inflexible, and unreasonable. The longer the parties debate, the more likely it is that emotions will overrule reason—name-calling and verbal assaults replace logic and reason. When the negotiation becomes personalized, turning into a win-lose feud between individuals, all hope of productivity is lost. Several approaches for controlling conflict are specifically directed at defusing volatile emotions.

Separating the Parties.   The most common approach to de-escalating conflict is to break off face-to-face relations. Declare a recess, call a caucus, or agree to adjourn and come back later when there has been a chance to unwind and reflect. The parties should acknowledge explicitly that the purpose of the caucus is to allow tempers to cool so the dialogue will become less emotional. Each party should also agree to return with a renewed effort to make deliberations more productive—either by simply regaining composure or by attempting a new or different way to address the issue that created the anger.

The parties may be separated for a few minutes or hours to several days or weeks. Variations in the time period are related to the level of hostility, as well as to unique situational circumstances. Parties may use the time to check with their constituencies, gather new information, and reassess their position and commitments.

Tension Release.   Tension is a natural by-product of negotiations. Consequently, negotiators should be aware that it is bound to increase, and they should know how to act to address or diminish it. Some negotiators who are sensitive to increases in tension know how to make a witty remark or crack a joke that causes laughter and releases tension. Others know that it is sometimes appropriate to let the other party ventilate pent-up anger and frustration without having to respond in kind. Skilled negotiators also know that allowing the other party such a catharsis will clear the air and may permit negotiations to return to a calmer pace.

Acknowledging the Other's Feelings: Active Listening.   When one party states her views and the other openly disagrees, the first negotiator often hears the disagreement as more than just disagreement. She may hear a challenge, a put-down, an assertion that her statement is wrong or not acceptable, an accusation of lying or distorting of the facts, or another form of personal attack. Whether or not this is the message that was intended is beside the point; the negotiator has to deal with the way it was received. Understandably, such misinterpretations escalate conflict.

There is a difference between accurately hearing what the other party has said and agreeing with it. One can let the other party know that both the content and the emotional strength of his or her message have been heard and understood, but that does not mean that one agrees with or accepts it. This technique is called *active listening* (Rogers, 1961), and it is frequently used in interviews and therapy settings as a way of encouraging a person to speak more freely (see Chapter 5). Rather than challenging and confronting the other negotiator's statements by bolstering one's own statements and position, it is possible to respond with statements that probe for confirmation and elaboration. Comments may include: "You see the facts this way," "You feel very strongly about this point," and "I can see that if you saw things this way, you would feel threatened and upset by what I have said." Again, these statements do not indicate that a negotiator agrees with the other party; rather, they communicate that the other has been accurately heard and understood.

Synchronized De-escalation.   Charles Osgood (1962), writing about the cold war and disarmament, suggested a unilateral strategy for conflict de-escalation called "graduated and reciprocated initiatives in tension reduction" (GRIT). The party who desires to de-escalate a conflict initiates the action. He or she decides on some small concession that each side could make to signal both sides' good faith and desire to de-escalate. The concession should be large enough to be read as an unambiguous signal of a desire to change the relationship, but not so large that if only one side followed through it would be weak or vulnerable. The party should then make a public announcement stating:

1. Exactly what the concession is.
2. That the concession is part of a deliberate strategic policy to reduce tension.
3. That the other side is explicitly invited to reciprocate in some specified form.
4. That the concession will be executed on some stated time schedule.
5. That each party commits to execute the concession without knowing whether the other will reciprocate.

The party who initiated the de-escalation then executes the concession. The specific concession should be something that is obvious, unambiguous, and subject to easy verification. Making it public and symbolic also helps. If the opposing party does not respond, then the initiator goes through with the action and repeats the sequence, selecting a simple, low-risk concession in an effort to attract the other into synchronized de-escalation. If the other does respond, then the initiator proposes a second action, slightly riskier than the first, and once again initiates the sequence. As the synchronized de-escalation takes hold, the parties can both propose larger and riskier concessions that will bring them back into a productive negotiating relationship.

In a more recent variation of this approach to de-escalation, a negotiator invites the other party to make a small, initial concession, providing a short list of such offers from which the other might choose. Such a proposal would be accompanied by a promise to respond in kind, choosing an answering concession from a list to be provided by the other party (Ross and Stillinger, 1991).

Improving the Accuracy of Communication

The second step in conflict reduction is to ensure that both parties accurately understand the other's position. (For a broader treatment of communication processes in negotiation, see Chapter 5.) When conflict becomes heated, communication efforts concentrate on managing emotions and directing the next assault at the other. Effective

---

BOX 12.4
Language Strategies to Facilitate Communication

Linguist Deborah Tannen argues that Americans live in an argument culture, where the language we use in talking about issues reflects a preference for adversarial relationships. The words we choose to describe our interactions shape our perceptions of the experience. Consequently, when we refer to the "opponent" in a "debate," we shape our communication as adversarial and are more likely to escalate the conflict.

   Tannen proposed the following naming alternatives to help defuse the argument culture:

Instead of This . . .	*Say This . . .*
Battle of the sexes	Relations between women and men
Critique	Comment
Fight	Discussion
Both sides	All sides
Debate	Discuss
The other side	Another side
Having an argument	Making an argument
The opposite sex	The other sex
War on drugs	Solving the drug problem
Litigation	Mediation
Provocative	Thought-provoking
Most controversial	Most important
Polarize	Unify
Attack-dog journalism	Watchdog journalism
Automatic opposition	Genuine opposition
Focus on differences	Search for common ground
Win the argument	Understand another point of view
The opposition party	The other party
Prosecutorial reporting	Investigative reporting
The argument culture	The dialogue culture

SOURCE: From Deborah Tannen, "How to Turn Debate into Dialogue," *USA Weekend*, February 27–March 3, 1998, pp. 4–5.

---

listening decreases. Each party thinks that they know what the other side is going to say and does not care to listen anymore. During impasses listening becomes so diminished that the parties are frequently unaware that their positions may have much in common. Rapoport (1964) labeled this the "blindness of involvement" because it inhibits the development of trust and the problem-solving process. Several approaches can be used to rectify this situation (see also Box 12.4).

   Role Reversal.   Although it is often easy to see the logic, rationale, and potential common ground on both sides of a conflict when one is an outsider, recognizing them when one is personally involved in a conflict is another matter. Role reversal can help negotiators to put themselves in the other party's shoes and look at the issue from

BOX 12.5
What Did You Say?

When you are on the receiving end of offensive comments in a negotiation setting, your first response may be to offend back, or to stalk off in anger and displeasure. For important negotiations, though, this creates the risk of denying you (as well as the other parties) any mutual gains from the exchange, as well as diverting your attention from the issues that brought you to the table in the first place. Andrea Schneider (1994) suggests that your basic options when faced with offensive comments involve first trying to understand why the offense occurred and then deciding what to do about it. To understand the behavior, she suggests four steps:

- Check your assumptions.
- Check the data on which your assumptions are based.
- Seek and evaluate other data, even (or especially) if those data tend to disconfirm your assumptions.
- Evaluate and adjust your assumptions, as appropriate.

Once your assumptions seem correct and appropriate, then decide whether to handle the behavior by

- Ignoring it (just act like it never occurred).
- Confronting it (i.e., counterattack: "That's racist," or "How juvenile").
- Deflecting it (i.e., acknowledge it and move on—a sense of humor often helps here).
- Engaging it (talk with the other party about his or her purpose in being offensive, and about your reaction to the offense).

SOURCE: Adapted from A. K. Schneider, "Effective Responses to Offensive Comments," *Negotiation Journal* 10 (1994), pp. 107–15.

his or her perspective. For instance, a manager can take the position of an employee, a salesperson that of a customer, a purchasing agent that of a supplier. Negotiators can play out scenarios in their imagination, ask a friend or colleague to assume the other role and act out a dialogue, or, more effectively, include role reversal as part of a unilateral strategy-preparation process. Although role reversal will not identify exactly how the other party thinks and feels about the issues, the process can provide useful and surprising insights (for example, see Box 12.5 on dealing with offensive comments).

During negotiations, one side often tries to encourage the other to reverse roles. He may plead, "Look at this from my perspective. What you're saying (or doing) puts me in this position, and thus how could you expect . . . ?" A variation on this occurs when one party tells the other, "If I were in your shoes, I would . . . ?" If role reversal gives the negotiator an accurate understanding of the other's position and shows that a previous view was incorrect, it gives a chance to correct specific misperceptions. This corrected understanding gives the negotiator a broader, more integrated view of the options. Role reversal also gives the negotiator an opportunity to explore how some planned action may affect the relationship. Hence, a member of management taking labor's role may discover that some of management's arguments or tactics may have an ineffective or undesirable effect, which may lead management to drop the tactics before they cause problems (Johnson and Dustin, 1970).

One purpose of role reversal is to highlight areas of commonality and overlap between positions; however, this cannot be achieved unless such compatibilities actually exist and at least one party moves toward them by proposing compromises. When no actual compatibility exists, role reversal may simply sharpen the differences between actual positions. Although some negotiators find that a lack of compatibility inhibits the search for common ground, others prefer to be aware of it so they can find other means to break the impasse. In order to negotiate integratively, both parties need accurate knowledge of the other's goals. If the parties' goals are actually incompatible, integrative negotiation is impossible, and the sooner that is discovered, the better. As we showed in Chapter 3, the existence of a negative settlement range also has severe consequences for the distributive bargaining process. Thus, role reversal can be a powerful tool for uncovering the true goals of both parties and determining how the negotiation should proceed.

Imaging.   Imaging, like role reversal, is a method for gaining insight into the other party's perspective. In the imaging process, parties in conflict are asked to engage in the following activities separately:

1. Describe how they see themselves.
2. Describe how the other party appears to them.
3. State how they think the other party would describe them.
4. State how they think the other party sees themselves.

The parties then exchange this information, in order. The two sets of statements frequently reveal dissimilarities and inconsistencies. Imaging usually produces animated discussion as the parties clarify and substantiate what they have said or heard. A common result is that the parties recognize that many apparent differences and areas of conflict are not real, and thus they begin to understand those that are real. Alderfer (1977) gives an example of imaging in negotiations between top executives who met to work out an organizational structure for a new firm that resulted from a merger of two organizations. Executives from both sides were deeply concerned that they would be outmaneuvered by the other and would "lose" as a result of the merger. A consultant suggested having an imaging meeting prior to actual negotiations. This meeting sharply altered the perceptions of both parties, and successful integrative negotiations became possible.

When parties complete role reversal or imaging processes, they have usually accomplished several things. First, they have clarified and corrected misconceptions and misinterpretations. In addition, they have brought to the surface both parties' interests, goals, and priorities, as well as limitations, which can then be used in the problem-solving process. One side often gains an understanding of the other side's true needs. Finally, and perhaps even more important, the process sets a positive tone for the negotiation. Parties find that they can make their needs and concerns heard and not be interrupted. This reduces defensiveness and encourages people to listen. Most people begin the negotiation process with a rather clear idea of what they need from the other party; in this phase, they learn more about what the other needs from them. Joint problem solving moves from being an unattainable ideal to an achievable process.

Controlling Issues

A third major difficulty that inhibits parties from reaching agreement is that as conflict intensifies, the size and number of the issues expand. As the impasse escalates, it snowballs; bits and pieces of other issues accumulate into a large, unmanageable mass. Although small conflicts can be managed satisfactorily one at a time, large conflicts become unwieldy and less amenable to easy resolution. The problem for negotiators in escalated impasses, therefore, is to develop strategies to contain issue proliferation and reduce the negotiation to manageable proportions.

Fractionate the Negotiation.   "Fractionating" is a method of issue control that involves dividing a large conflict into smaller parts (Fisher, 1964). According to Fisher, fractionating can involve several actions: reducing the number of parties on each side; controlling the number of substantive issues involved; stating issues in concrete terms rather than as principles; restricting the precedents involved, both procedural and substantive; searching for ways to narrow the big issues; and depersonalizing issues, separating them from the parties advocating them. We will examine each of these approaches in more detail below.

1. Reduce the Number of Parties on Each Side.   When there is an impasse, both parties seek to build alliances for strength or to bring their constituencies into the negotiation; either they increase the number of parties at the negotiation or they bring more clout to the table. Additional parties, such as lawyers, experts, or parties with formal authority, are often brought into negotiations for the information or the leverage they can provide. Because the sheer number of parties at the table can considerably increase the complexity of the negotiation (more parties equal more perspectives on the issues, more time needed to hear each side, more opportunities for disagreement, etc.), negotiation ground rules should provide ways to limit how many people can be added. One way to control an impasse that has escalated is to reduce the number of actors. Having fewer actors present, or even limiting the discussion to two individuals, will increase the chances of reaching a settlement.

2. Control the Number of Substantive Issues Involved.   A second way to fractionate a conflict is to keep the number of issues small enough to manage. When conflict builds to impasse, the size and number of issues proliferate. Some negotiations escalate to the point where there are too many issues to manage constructively. At the same time, limiting negotiations to a very few issues also raises problems. Single-issue negotiations are frequently harder to manage because they quickly lead to win-lose polarization over the issue. In such circumstances, it is often desirable to expand the number of issues so both sides can see themselves as having gained something and can achieve an integrative solution. The number of issues can be expanded by defining the issue broadly enough so that resolution can benefit both sides or by coupling the issue with another issue so that each party can receive a preferred settlement on at least one issue. (We discussed defining the bargaining mix, bundling and packaging issues, and inventing options in Chapters 2, 3, and 4.)

3. State Issues in Concrete Terms Rather Than as Principles.   Negotiation issues become difficult to control when events or issues are treated as matters of principle. Small conflicts can rapidly become intractable disputes when their resolution is not treated as an isolated event but instead must be consistent with a broader policy or principle. Negotiators may view any deviation from policy as a threat to that policy. Because it is far more difficult to change broad policy than to make a concession on a single issue, negotiations can immediately become problematic. For example, an employee needs to take her child to the doctor during her work hours and requests an excused absence from the company. The company does not have a policy that permits employees to take time off for this reason, and the employee's supervisor tells her she has to take sick leave or vacation time instead. "It's a matter of principle," the manager asserts. Resorting to arguments of principle and policy is often a strategic defense by high-power parties against any change from the status quo; however, the longer the discussion remains at the level of policy or principle, the less likely it is that the dispute can be successfully resolved.

There are, of course, times when a single event is properly seen as indicative of a new principle or policy. When this is the case, negotiations should be arranged specifically to address the policy or principle. Many times, people are reluctant to address principles because they know negotiations over principles are difficult and lengthy. However, attempting to negotiate a concrete issue when the negotiation really should address the broader principle may result only in frustration and a sense of futility. If this occurs, it is wise to face the underlying issue and raise it directly. There are at least two strategies that can be used to do so:

- Question whether the issue needs to be addressed at the principle or policy level. Inquire about the link between the specific issue and the broader policy or principle. If none exists, and one party wants to look at the matter from a policy or principle level, suggest that the immediate concrete issue be handled and discussed separately from the underlying principle or policy. If need be, the parties can agree that the concrete issue can be settled in this instance, with no expectation as to how the policy will later be established.

- Point out that exceptions can be made to all policies, and that principles and policies can be maintained even if deviations are agreed to under special circumstances. The parties may be willing to agree that this specific case might be one of those times.

4. Restrict the Precedents Involved, Both Procedural and Substantive.   Another type of issue magnification occurs when the parties treat concessions on a single issue as violations of some substantive or procedural precedent. When a substantive precedent is at stake, one party will imply that to concede on this issue at this time will render him or her vulnerable to conceding on the same issue, or a similar issue, in the future. To return to our previous example, the manager is likely to argue that if she grants the employee an excused absence in this case, when no policy exists, then she will be obligated to grant every other employee the same request. Belief in the power of precedent is strong. The high-power party, who supports the precedent, believes that if she gives in to this one request, there will be no end to the number and types of requests she may get in the future. In contrast, procedural precedents are at stake when parties agree to follow a process they haven't followed before. In the same employment example, the manager may not want to give the employee the excused absence because the employee did not submit any proof that she was, in fact, taking a child to the doctor. So they agree that the employee will return with some evidence that the doctor's visit was made.

Issues of precedent are usually as thorny to control as issues of principle. Once again, a negotiator trying to move a conflict toward de-escalation and resolution should try to prevent single issues from being translated into major questions of precedent. Focusing the dialogue on the key issue and persisting in arguments that concessions on this issue at this time do not necessarily dictate any precedents—substantive or procedural—for the future is a way to undermine the power of precedent.

5. Search for Ways to Fractionate the Big Issues.   Fisher (1964) calls these "salami tactics": ways to slice a large issue into smaller pieces. Issues that can be expressed in quantitative measurable units are easy to slice. For example, compensation demands can be cut up into pennies-per-hour increments, or lease rates can be reduced to dollars per square foot. When working to fractionate issues of principle or precedent, parties may use the time horizon (when the principle goes into effect or how long it will last) as a way to fractionate the issue, or vary the number of ways that the principle may be applied. For example, a company may devise a family emergency leave that allows employees the opportunity to be away from the company for a period of no longer than three hours, and no more than once a month, for illness in the employee's immediate family.

6. Depersonalize Issues: Separate Them from the Parties Advocating Them. Positional bargaining tends to create conflict over the issues and enhance tension in the relationship between negotiators. People become identified with positions on issues, and vice versa. Effective negotiation requires separating the issues from the parties, not only by working to establish a productive relationship between the parties (leaving only the issue conflict at stake), but also by trying to resolve the issues in a fair and impartial way independent of the parties who hold the conflicting views. Fisher, Ury, and Patton (1991) elaborate on this point, suggesting that effective integrative negotiation is tough on the negotiating problem but soft on the people.

Establishing Common Ground

As we noted earlier, parties in escalated conflict tend to magnify perceived differences and to minimize perceived similarities (Pruitt and Rubin, 1986). The parties tend to see themselves as further apart and having less in common than may actually be the case. Therefore, a fourth major action that parties can take to de-escalate conflict is to establish common ground and focus on common objectives. Several approaches are possible: establishing common (superordinate) goals (see also Box 12.6), aligning against common enemies, agreeing to follow a common procedure, establishing a common framework for approaching the negotiation problem, including managing time

---

BOX 12.6
Trying to Please Everyone: The Use of a Common Goal

Disputes over the use of water are common among environmentalists, water recreation enthusiasts, and industry. Early in 1996, the Deerfield River Hydroelectric Project in Vermont was simply another battle site in this long-standing, multiparty war. More recently, however, creative negotiation has transformed the heated discussions over the Deerfield project into cooperative ventures that have benefited most of the parties involved.

Each of the stakeholders in this dispute brought different priorities to the negotiation table. The rafting and canoeing companies wanted the power company to agree to a regular schedule of water release into the Deerfield River so they could coordinate recreation activities with their clients. Fishing enthusiasts felt that the flow into the river should be continuous and steady so that regular cycles of fish breeding and migration would be undisturbed. Local environmental groups wanted the power company to set aside land for conservation to offset damage that might be caused by the water release. Finally, local towns worried that the use of land for conservation would reduce their property tax revenue. Ultimately, it was a lose-lose situation for the power company: there was no activity they could envision that would satisfy all constituents.

The typical strategy for the power company would have been to divide and conquer, asking that the federal government or court agree to the proposed release schedule as originally presented simply because the other parties could not agree. But they noted the potential for long, costly court battles and appeals, coupled with the risk that the final settlement may not be to their liking, and opted instead to renew negotiation efforts.

Ultimately, the company agreed to spend $7 million to protect both fish and land, while agreeing to coordinate release of whitewater with local recreation companies. Local towns are thrilled with the increase in sales tax revenue that accompanies an increase in recreation activity. More important, the lines of communication in Vermont remain open. The stakeholders in this dispute realized that they shared a common goal: protection of the Deerfield River.

SOURCE: N. Ulman, "Unlikely Allies: Pact for River's Use Unites Conservationists and a Power Company," *The Wall Street Journal,* May 20, 1996, pp. A6 and A9.

---

and deadlines. As we discussed in Chapter 2, these approaches might also be viewed as efforts to reframe the conflict away from a focus on differences and toward a focus on common areas. Once this reframing has occurred, it becomes possible to use fewer distributive negotiation approaches, and to move from a purely distributive approach to one that accommodates a mix of distributive and integrative strategies.

Superordinate Goals.   Superordinate goals are common goals; both parties desire them, and both parties must cooperate to achieve them. In a corporation, for example, people perform different jobs (e.g., marketing, manufacturing, distribution) that have different objectives, yet they must work together (e.g., to get the product to the customer) or the corporation will not survive. A local city council may disagree with community members about the ways to spend limited funds for community development; however, the two sides may be able to agree if it is possible for them to write a joint grant proposal that will provide enough money to meet all objectives. Two entrepreneurs may be in a heated conflict over how to resolve a design problem in a new product, but if they share the common objective of resolving the problem in time to present their case to a group of venture capitalists who could fund the design, they may improve their chances of finding a solution.

To have significant impact on negotiations, superordinate goals must be jointly desired by both parties and must not be seen as benefiting one more than the other. Johnson and Lewicki (1969) demonstrated that superordinate goals that were closely related to the issues of the conflict and that were introduced by one party in the dispute often became caught up in the conflict dynamics and lost their effectiveness. Random events (under neither party's control) or events created by neutral third parties are frequently better superordinate goals than those that are sought out and planned by the parties involved. For example, disasters such as floods, storms, blackouts, fires, and the like—witness the impact of the World Trade Center attack of September 11, 2001— bring people and communities together with a common purpose of survival; the same impact can be seen in negotiations.

Common Enemies.   A common enemy is a negative form of superordinate goal. The parties find new motivation to resolve their differences to avoid intervention by a third party, or to pool resources to defeat a common enemy. Political leaders of all persuasions often invoke outside enemies (the other political party) to bring their own constituencies together. Managers who are in conflict learn that if they don't resolve their differences themselves, someone else (their boss) will make the decision for them. Labor and management may behave more collaboratively when threatened with binding arbitration, declining market share, foreign competition, or government intervention.

Common Expectations.   We noted earlier in this chapter that parties can manage the social context by creating common ground rules to govern their conflict. However, ground rules are often badly introduced and mismanaged, such that efforts to use and monitor them become part of the conflict rather than a process for effectively managing it. For example, ground rules are often introduced in a directive manner; they are formal, limiting, and prohibitive, trying to prevent people from doing (the wrong) things rather than encouraging people to do (the right) things; they are not consistently applied, deviations are handled arbitrarily, and there is no agreed-upon procedure for revisiting and revising the ground rules. As a result, Dukes, Piscolish, and Stephens (2000) suggest that the more effective process is to move from ground rules to "higher ground," a process that is more about creating common and shared expectations. The process of creating common or shared expectations—a process for how the parties will move forward—is called "creating a group covenant" (Dukes, Piscolish, and Stephens, 2000).

A group covenant is a process for addressing differences, managing expectations, establishing ground rules, and so on for moving a group to "higher ground." There are six key elements to this process:

1. Establish the need for creating shared expectations.
2. Educate and inspire people to create a new covenant that all will agree to follow.

3. Begin by envisioning desired outcomes for the future, and then develop common ground rules that will enable the group to reach that future.

4. Promote full participation by giving everyone a voice in the process.

5. Be accountable by honoring the agreements contained in the new covenant.

6. Evaluate, modify, revise, and recommit to these new principles as necessary. (Dukes et al., 2000, p. 83)

Each of these steps needs to be enacted to create a new covenant to work in a way that will facilitate agreement rather than sidetrack it.

Manage Time Constraints and Deadlines.   Time, while a source of power and leverage in many negotiations (see Chapter 6), can also be an impediment to integrative bargaining. Gersick (1988, 1989) suggests that time and timing are critical aspects of effective group process. Not only should parties try to agree to a time schedule for moving discussions along, but they also should realize that under the time pressure of an approaching deadline, any substantive issues that remain unresolved may surface, changing one or both parties to a more competitive, less collaborative frame of mind. The remedies for this problem are fairly straightforward:

- Conduct thorough and open problem diagnosis and issue identification steps so as to identify both parties' motives.

- To the extent possible, address and identify the clearly distributive issues, and do so early enough that they will not linger and derail the collaborative process when a deadline approaches.

- Be generous in estimating the time necessary to accomplish the negotiation, making allowances for extra time to manage difficult or linked issues.

- Recognize tentative deadlines for what they are, reserving the right (if not the obligation) of benchmarking progress against the time allotted, and be willing to let both sides sleep on tentative settlements before closing on them.

- Be willing to entertain the possibility of extending the deadline set early in the negotiation. If the deadline is not movable, pay additional attention to timing, pacing, and benchmarking.

Reframe the Parties' View of Each Other.   In Chapter 2, we discussed the power of frames in shaping the way the parties view each other, the issues, and the conflict management process. For example, Lewicki, Gray, and Elliott (2003) offer many detailed examples of the ways that frames shape (or misshape) the ways that parties view "difficult to resolve" environmental disputes and the processes available for their resolution. In an examination of several of the approaches by which disputes can be "reframed," Lewicki et al. suggest that parties must be able to gain perspective on the dispute. This perspective-taking requires standing back from the negotiation, observing it, and reflecting on it in a way that allows parties to recognize that there is more than one way to view the other party, the issues, and the process of resolving it (see Schön and Rein, 1994). Many of the processes we describe in this chapter presume that the parties are able to engage in this perspective-taking on their own. However, if they are unable to, the suggestions we offer here will be difficult for the parties to employ. A major characteristic of "difficult to resolve" disputes, therefore, may be the inability of parties to engage in the perspective taking that appears to be essential to the reframing process. Once again, this is often a key role for third parties, which we will discuss in Chapter 13.

Build an Integrative Framework.   Though often time-consuming, diligent application of the integrative process (as described in Chapter 4) can produce lasting resolutions to thorny, complex problems. In the terms of the dual concerns model (Chapter 1), both parties are committed to pursue both their own interests *and* the other's; each party wants to ensure a substantive win-win agreement as well as to strengthen the future relationship. How do parties build an integrative framework to maximize their ability to achieve a mutually acceptable agreement?

Integrative frameworks are ways of redefining issues to create a common perspective from which initial positions appear more compatible. Eiseman (1978) refers to this process as creating an integrative conceptual framework, and Fisher, Ury, and Patton (1991) explain that successful negotiators focus on interests, not positions. By defining negotiated issues in terms of positions—my position on this issue is X—parties tend to simplify complex phenomena by defining a single point and then refusing to move from it. To create movement, parties must establish ways of redefining the conflict so that they can explore compatible interests. Recall the classic example from Chapter 4 (adapted from Follett, 1940): Two men are quarreling in a library about whether a window should be open or shut. They bicker back and forth about how much to leave it open. Enter the librarian. She asks one why he wants the window open, and he responds that he wants some fresh air. She asks the other why he wants it closed, and he responds that he wants to avoid a draft. So she goes into the next room and opens a window, meeting the needs of both parties.

There are four approaches to reorienting a "difficult" negotiation toward a more integrative process: building trust, training the parties, seeking semantic resolutions, and generating creative alternatives

i) Build Trust.   Strong, constructive bargaining relationships are typically marked by conditions of high trust (characterized by hope, faith, confidence, assurance, and initiative) and low distrust (characterized by the absence of fear, skepticism, and cynicism), and are accompanied by low vigilance and low monitoring behaviors between the parties (Lewicki, McAllister, and Bies, 1998; Lewicki and Stevenson, 1998). Healthy interdependence, characterized by strong trust and either low distrust or the effective management of any distrust that exists, will likely support the pursuit of mutually beneficial opportunities. The collaborative ideal of high trust/low distrust refers to each party's expectation that the other will cooperate, will be predictable, and will be committed to solving the problem (Ross and LaCroix, 1996). Such attitudes and behaviors are critically important to moving parties to create value in negotiations, and to move beyond impasses. The trust produced by successful collaboration—based on enhanced knowledge of, or even identification with, the other party and his or her needs—reinforces itself through multiple iterations of bargaining situations (e.g., Lewicki and Stevenson, 1998; Shapiro, Sheppard, and Cheraskin, 1992). (Refer back to our discussion of trust in Chapter 8.)

ii) Train the Parties in Integrative Negotiation and Interactive Problem Solving.
Several recent studies have demonstrated the impact of training parties to use integrative and problem-solving processes. While these approaches are technically "third party" approaches, in that the training and facilitation is done by third parties who are not active participants in the dispute, we will briefly describe the work here. Kelman (1996) shows how negotiation can be employed as a process of interactive problem solving, with the goal of transforming the relationship between the parties, through developing an agreement that addresses the fundamental needs and fears of both parties on a basis of reciprocity. He then discusses four components of negotiation—identification and analysis of the problem, joint shaping of ideas for a solution, influencing the other side, and creating a supportive political environment—and shows how interactive problem solving leads to specific prescriptions for each component. Subsequent work by Cross and Rosenthal (1999) showed that training in interactive problem solving (compared to distributive and integrative bargaining models) led Jewish and Arab students to be less pessimistic about their ethnic conflict and showed positive change in attitudes toward members of the other group. Coleman and Lim (2001) specified a broader framework for measuring and calibrating the impact of such training on a variety of conflict reduction initiatives.

iii) Search for Semantic Resolutions.   Negotiations where the parties are negotiating over specific words and ideas—contract language, setting policy, or establishing memoranda of agreement—can lead to an impasse over key words, phrases, and expressions. Sometimes these discussions can be reduced to irrelevant linguistic hairsplitting, yet to the parties involved the wording is significant in both meaning and intent. Discovering how parties attach different meanings to some words, or exploring language that can accommodate both sides, is another alternative for achieving an integrative framework. More specific treatment of the integrative solution-building process can be found in Chapter 4.

iv) Generate Creative Alternatives.   For many negotiators, the prescriptive advice to create value (see Chapter 4) is easy to say but hard to accomplish. Perhaps part of the difficulty lies in the tendency to see all or most negotiations in competitive win-lose terms; this perception leads to the unconscious assumption that winning the substantive contest is all that matters. Even when collaboration may be the appropriate strategy, it may be very difficult to convince oneself and the other party to engage in the creative processes necessary to secure a collaborative outcome. One needs to generate creative alternatives, where creativity refers to "the process by which novel outcomes are developed that are viewed as acceptable, and satisfying to a given audience" (Spector, 1995, p. 86). The long-standing interest in creative thinking (e.g., De Bono, 1990; Sternberg, 1988; Von Oech, 1992; Whiting, 1958) is testimony to the depth and breadth of this problem.

Spector (1995) has written about applying creative decision-making approaches to negotiation, especially in difficult or intractable cases. Going beyond basic creativity heuristics such as brainstorming, role-playing, and role reversal, Spector proposes that the metaphorical process of analogical reasoning (the illustrative use of analogies) provides considerable power to reframe intractable conflict. Analogical reasoning is defined as the inferential process by which a resemblance, similarity, or correspondence, perceived between two or more things in some respect, suggests that they will probably agree in other ways as well. When using analogies, the problem is restated in terms of something very familiar. By comparison and through different lenses, new ideas and options may be generated. (Spector, 1995, p. 87)

This might be a particularly fruitful remedy for impasse problems, since "the way a dispute is framed can constrain the options for resolution" (p. 82). Several kinds of analogies may prove useful:

- *Direct analogies,* in which the problem is placed or examined in a totally different field of information (e.g., "This conflict is like a can of worms").

- *Fantasy analogies,* in which the problem is restated in terms of a party's fantasized or wished-for state (e.g., "I wish I could sweep this thing away like a pile of dust").

- *Personal analogies,* in which a party puts herself in the problem situation, attempting to identify with it or empathize with those in the situation ("You must feel like a large picture in a small frame").

- *Symbolic analogies,* in which a different, often graphic image is conjured up to focus attention and provide a starting point for more open discussion ("This conflict reminds me of trying to land an airplane whose landing gear won't go down"). (p. 88)

The desired outcome—fresh ideas and new perspectives—becomes possible when parties use the analogy to develop a new or amended cognitive orientation to the problem.

Enhancing the Desirability of Options to the Other Party

Another method that parties can use to increase the likelihood of agreement is to make their desires and preferences appear more palatable to the other. We have noted that as conflict escalates, the parties may lock into a rigid position on an issue. Moreover, as this position is interpreted and reinterpreted over time, negotiators try to remain consistent with the original position—that is, to establish a clear-cut policy that applies in all circumstances. Because these policies are designed to apply to a variety of circumstances, they become broader rather than more specific. If the other party does not readily comply with a negotiator's position or policy, the negotiator's tendency is to escalate demands or increase the magnitude threats for noncompliance. These actions make impasse more likely.

Roger Fisher (1969) suggests that most influence situations can be characterized by a demand (what you want) and offers and threats (the consequences of meeting or not meeting the demand). The who, what, when, and why of this influence process are depicted in Table 12.1. Fisher suggests that in most negotiation situations, the parties tend to emphasize the demand and the threat, and he claims this emphasis is greatly misplaced and self-destructive. Rather, negotiators should direct their efforts to the following question: How can we get the other party to make a choice that is best for us, given that our interests diverge? This approach is largely a matter of focusing on the other's interests rather than one's own. Like role reversal, it requires negotiators to

TABLE 12.1   Fisher's "Demand" Dynamics

	Decision (The Decision You Desire)	Offer (The Consequences of Making the Decision)	Threat (The Consequences of Not Making the Decision)
Who?	Who is to make the decision?	Who benefits if the decision is made?	Who gets hurt if the decision is not made?
What?	Exactly what decision is desired?	If the decision is made, what benefits/costs can be expected?	If the decision is not made, what risks/ potential benefits can be expected?
When?	By what time does the decision have to be made?	What, if ever, will be the benefit of making the decision occur?	How soon will the consequences of not making the decision be felt?
Why?	What makes this a right, proper, and lawful decision?	What makes these consequences fair and legitimate?	What makes these consequences fair and legitimate?

Every feature of an influence problem can be located somewhere on this schematic map. The nature of a given problem can be discovered through estimating how the presumed adversary would answer the above questions.

SOURCE: R. Fisher, *International Conflict for Beginners* (New York: Harper & Row, 1969), p. 48. Used with permission.

focus less on their own position, and more on clearly understanding and addressing the other party's needs. Moreover, once those needs are understood, effort should be invested in but in moving toward the other party, not in getting the other party to come to you. This can be done in most cases by making offers rather than demands and threats. Fisher suggests several alternative strategies:

Give the Other Party a "Yesable" Proposal.   Rather than emphasizing one's own position and letting the other party suggest alternatives that can be approved or overruled, a negotiator should direct effort to understanding the other side's needs and devising a proposal that will meet those needs. Fisher terms this a "yesable" proposal, one to which the only answer can be "Yes, it is acceptable." To succeed, however, this approach requires negotiators to consider what the other party wants or would agree with, rather than exclusively considering their own goals and needs.

Ask for a Different Decision.   Rather than making demands more general, to fit with their policy, negotiators should endeavor to make demands more specific. Negotiators must determine what specific elements of their demands are most palatable or offensive to the other party, then use this information to refine the demand. "Ask for a different decision," asserts Fisher. Reformulate, repackage, reorganize, or rephrase. Fractionate, split, divide, or make more specific. Making demands more specific is not making them more rigid; rather, specific demands can be reformulated to meet the other's needs. Fisher, Ury, and Patton (1991) recommend that successful negotiators be skilled at inventing options for mutual gain (see Chapter 4). Inventing and refining ways in which both parties can succeed, and providing a variety of these options to the other party, greatly enhance the likelihood that both parties can select a desirable option.

Sweeten the Offer Rather Than Intensifying the Threat.   Negotiators can also make options more palatable by enhancing the attractiveness of accepting them. Again, this is a matter of placing the emphasis on the positive rather than the negative. In the language of traditional carrot-and-stick tactics for motivating workers, the approach should make the carrot more attractive rather than making the stick larger. Promises and offers can be made more attractive in several ways: maximizing the attractive qualities and minimizing the negative ones, showing how the offer meets the other party's needs, reducing the disadvantages of accepting the offer, making offers more credible (i.e., you will do what you promise to do), or setting deadlines on offers so they expire if not accepted quickly. Many would argue that these are common sales tricks akin to rebates, discount coupons, "two-for-the-price-of-one" offers, "today only" sales, and "extra added attraction" elements. They are! Negotiators can and should use the same techniques that salespeople use to move their products. Some of these techniques were described more fully in Chapter 6 under the topic of leverage.

Use Legitimacy or Objective Criteria to Evaluate Solutions.   Finally, negotiators may insist that alternative solutions be evaluated by objective criteria that meet the tests of fairness and legitimacy. Negotiators on all sides should be able to demonstrate that their demands are based on sound facts, calculations, and information, and that preferred solutions are consistent with those facts and information. This procedure will frequently require disclosing and sharing those facts, rather than disguising and distorting them. "Here's how we arrived at our proposal. Here are the facts we used, the cost data we used in our estimates, the calculations we made. You can verify these by the following procedures." The more this data is open to public verification and demonstrated to be within the bounds of fairness and legitimacy, the more convincing it will be that the position is independent of the negotiator who advocates it, and the more persuasive the position will be in achieving a settlement.

Section Summary

In this section, we reviewed five major strategies that negotiators can use to get derailed negotiations back on track and return to a more productive flow of events: reducing tension, improving communication, controlling issues, finding common ground, and making options more attractive for joint resolution. Taken together, these strategies create a large portfolio of alternatives that negotiators can pursue to manage derailed discussions, enhance deteriorating communications, and find ways to invent acceptable solution alternatives. These various techniques are ways that parties can work together to overcome intractability and improve the odds that successful resolution can occur. In some negotiations, however, the two parties may not place the same value on overcoming conflict or stalemate, or bring the same working theories of negotiation to the table. These mismatches between negotiator approaches are the focus of the next section.

MISMATCHED MODELS: INTENTIONAL AND OTHERWISE

We turn now to situations where parties have chosen *different* models to guide their negotiation, either because they have diagnosed the negotiation differently or because they possess different levels of negotiation sophistication. We believe that collaborative negotiation is less used and less familiar to many negotiators than it should be, and that broader applications of integrative negotiating (where appropriate) would produce better agreements. We will direct our discussion and advice, then, to parties who wish to be collaborative but find they must deal with parties who are reluctant to do so—who wish, intend, or try to be distributive.

Negotiators always run the risk of encountering parties who, for any number of reasons, are difficult negotiators. That difficulty may be *intentional* (i.e., the result of a clear strategic, behavioral, or philosophical choice by the other party). It may also be due to *inadequate skill* on the other party's part, including faulty skill in diagnosing negotiation opportunities—the other just doesn't see any value or potential for a collaborative approach, or doesn't know how to craft and pursue such an approach at all. In this section, we address methods negotiators can use when dealing with an intentionally difficult party. We then proceed to explain the skills and behaviors needed to defend against such parties and/or to convert them to use a more productive negotiation process. Quite simply, what the collaborative party is trying to do is to change the game, that is, to convince the other party to move from distributive to integrative negotiations. At least four challenges exist:

- What to do when the other side uses hard distributive tactics.
- What to do if the other side is more powerful.
- What to do if the other side is just generally difficult to deal with.
- The special problem of ultimatums.

We will now discuss the tactical responses to each of these situations.

Responding to the Other Side's Hard Distributive Tactics

By *hard tactics* we mean the distributive tactics that the other party applies in a negotiation to put pressure on negotiators to do something that is not in their best interest to do. The temptation to use hard tactics is inherent in the distributive model: get information, but don't give it; convince the other party of the value of staying in the deal, or the cost of leaving it; and so on. Distributive tactics were presented in Chapter 3, where we also discussed strategies for responding to or dealing with these tactics. To summarize briefly, as a pressured party you can respond to these tactics in any of these ways:

1. *Ignore them.* A tactic ignored is, essentially, a tactic defeated; even if it is recognized later, it has no power to bring undue pressure to bear. Unfortunately, some bargainers are slow learners; if you ignore them, they may simply not get the message that you want something different to happen.

2. *Call them on it.* Negotiators should let the other party know they are aware of what they are trying to do when they use hard tactics by identifying the tactic and raising it

to the level of open discussion. This should be done tactfully, but firmly. Negotiators may indicate their distress or displeasure with the tactic and explain why it is problematic. Sometimes, the embarrassment value of such an observation is sufficient to make negotiators disavow the tactic and abandon its future use, or even convert their behavior to more win-win negotiating.

3. *Respond in kind.* The possibility of responding to a hard tactic with a hard tactic was discussed in Chapter 3. Recall, however, that responding in kind is likely to escalate the conflict, and it is not consistent with the principles we are proposing here.

4. *Offer to change to more productive methods.* Negotiators may announce that they have noted the other party's behavior and suggest a better way to negotiate. Fisher, Ury, and Patton (1991), in advising well-intentioned bargainers not to let themselves be victimized, suggest a comprehensive strategy: "Recognize the tactic, raise the issue explicitly, and question the tactic's legitimacy and desirability—negotiate over it" (p. 130). The logic of this advice lies in the assumption that once the trickster understands that (1) their behavior is understood and (2) continuing this behavior will entail certain costs (including the possibility that you will walk away from the negotiation), he or she will respond to a suggestion for a more integrative exchange.

Responding When the Other Side Has More Power

Relative power can be a good predictor of how a conflict will evolve. Other things being equal, when power is unequal, victory typically goes to the more powerful party. Power imbalances in negotiation can represent clear dangers to the satisfaction of personal needs and to the collaborative process. First, high-power parties tend to pay little heed to the needs of low-power parties, who either don't get their needs met or use disruptive, attention-getting tactics that make collaboration very difficult (Donohue and Kolt, 1992). Second, low-power parties are not usually in a position to trigger and advance an integrative process. Integrative negotiation requires a tolerance of change and flexibility, which often requires negotiators to give up some control over outcomes; low-power parties "have less to give, and thus less flexibility to offer the other party" (Donohue and Kolt, p. 107).

When dealing with a party with more power, negotiators have at least four alternatives. They can

1. Protect themselves.
2. Cultivate their best alternative (BATNA).
3. Formulate a "trip wire alert system."
4. Correct the power imbalance.

Negotiators can *protect themselves* by keeping in mind that they have real interests, that negotiation may be the preferred approach of achieving those interests, and that excessive accommodation to the high-power party will not serve them well over the long term. A note of caution, though: Knowing the resistance point may provide a clear measure of minimum acceptability (lowest price, maximum monthly payment, etc.), but too strict an adherence to it may deprive negotiators of creativity and flexibility, which are critical components to the design of an integrative arrangement. It may also limit the ability to use information that emerges during the exchange (Fisher, Ury, and Patton, 1991).

Alternatively, negotiators should *cultivate their BATNA,* which represents the best they can accomplish without the negotiation. Many negotiators bargain without a clear definition of their BATNA; we pointed out in Chapters 3 and 4 that the lack of such a critical reference point gives negotiators less power and limits what they can achieve in the current negotiation (Fisher, Ury, and Patton, 1991). Even after negotiations have started, one can continue to seek to improve one's BATNA. For example, a job seeker who is discussing an offer with a particular employer may continue to cultivate alternatives by pursuing other opportunities. Keep in mind also that "cultivating a BATNA" has important perceptual elements: Does the other party perceive that BATNA is worthwhile and it is likely to be accepted if sufficiently favorable terms are not accepted? Negotiators can also help the other party to see that their BATNA is not really as good as they think it is. A low-power negotiator's hand is strengthened to the extent that alternatives improve, but it may not be enough simply to *have* an improved alternative; the other party must accurately perceive its existence and its strength in relation to their own alternative.

A clear, strong BATNA may also be reinforced by additional safety measures. Low-power negotiators are also advised to *formulate a trip wire alert system,* which serves as an early warning signal when bargaining enters the safety zone close to the walkaway option or the BATNA (Fisher, Ury, and Patton, 1991). The trip wire tells the negotiator to exercise special caution and pay increased attention to the negotiation in progress. Given that negotiations often become intense and engrossing at such points, it might be appropriate to assign a co-negotiator to attend to the trip wire and to notify the involved negotiator at the critical time.

The foregoing options involve dealing with an extant power imbalance. A final option for dealing with more powerful parties is to *correct the imbalance.* Three approaches to this are possible: low-power parties taking power, high-power parties giving power, and third parties managing the transfer and balance of power. The first approach, power-taking, is typically not feasible in negotiations; as we already mentioned, using disruptive or attention-getting actions to try to take power typically contributes to a distributive exchange, generating in-kind responses from the high-power party. However, as we pointed out in Chapter 6, power in negotiation is multifaceted, and power may be gained on dimensions different from those currently held by the high-power party. The third approach—using a third party to manage power transfer—*is* feasible and is commonly used (see Chapter 13 for a discussion of mediators and other third parties).

The middle, remaining approach is for the high-power party to give power to the other party. Such actions include sharing resources; sharing control over certain processes or outcomes (e.g., agendas or decisions); focusing on common interests rather than solely on the high-powered party's interests; or educating the low-power party about what power he or she does have and how to use it more effectively (Donohue and Kolt, 1992). The immediate question is why high-power parties would ever choose to give power away. The answer is complex, but there are good reasons. First, sharing power may facilitate a better integrative process. Second, even if one party does have power over the other, the best the high-power party can hope for is compliance rather than enthusiastic cooperation. Finally, no power imbalance exists forever, and when the low-power party does gain a power base or a BATNA, he or she is likely to either sever the relationship or look for some form of revenge.

The Special Problem of Handling Ultimatums

One particularly troublesome hard tactic used by distributive negotiators is the use of ultimatums. An ultimatum is an attempt "to induce compliance or force concessions from a presumably recalcitrant opponent" (Kramer, Shah, and Woerner, 1995, p. 285). Ultimatums typically have three components: (1) a demand; (2) an attempt to create a sense of urgency, such that compliance is required; and (3) a threat of punishment if compliance does not occur (George, 1993). For example, one particular type of ultimatum is the "exploding offer," in which one party presents the other with a classic no-win, "use-it-or-lose-it" dilemma. An exploding offer has a specific time limit or deadline attached to it, forcing the other party to decide on a less-than-attractive offer or run the risk of going without anything (Robinson, 1995). Such offers have several other components, including:

- A clear asymmetry of power between the parties.
- A pressure-inducing test of faith for the respondent.
- A restricted set of options.
- A lack of consideration and respect for the offerer by the respondent.
- An apparent lack of good faith on the offerer's part. (Robinson, 1995, pp. 278–79)

The strategic logic of this type of ultimatum often involves an attempt to force a negotiator into a premature agreement, thereby bringing an early end to a negotiation process that might eventually produce a more equitable outcome. It might also have the effect of limiting the negotiator's ability to comparison-shop among multiple competing offers.

While one analysis of ultimatums might suggest that such a take-it-or-leave-it tactic should be successful, given that something (anything) must be preferable to nothing (a failed negotiation), empirical studies have not found this to be so (Guth, Schmittberger, and Schwarze, 1982; Guth and Tietz, 1990). Conflicts involving ultimatums often fall prey to escalation problems, as noted elsewhere in this chapter, through severe "action–reaction" spirals. Reactions to the making of ultimatums seem to go beyond the violation of simple fairness concerns, in that they

> are motivated by asymmetric moral imperatives. Most offerers define the situation as the opportunity for . . . gain; they tend to be blatantly strategic. Many respondents, on the other hand, owing to their relatively powerless situation, define the situation morally . . . This asymmetry can lead to disagreement and unhappiness for both parties—for the offerer, following a rejection, or for the respondent, in accepting an offer that he or she feels is unfair. (Murnighan and Pillutla, 1995, p. 265)

The pervasive unhappiness resulting from the use of such ultimatums can taint future dealings between the parties, sometimes permanently.

Robinson (1995) has developed one possible response to ultimatums, which he calls the "farpoint gambit" (after the name of a maneuver on a *Star Trek* episode). The success of the response hangs on the ability to say "Yes, but . . ." to an ultimatum. (Robinson cautions—and we agree—that this approach is a last resort; other remedies should be exhausted first.) When first presented with an ultimatum, negotiators should probably try a reasonable approach: be forthright in addressing the ultimatum; make sensible, reasonable counteroffers; or attempt to engage the offerer in joint problem solving. If that fails, Robinson suggests "an exploding offer can be defused by *embracing* it" (p. 282)—that is, agree to the ultimatum provisionally, subject to some qualifying event or condition. Robinson advises that the farpoint gambit be used only when all three of the following conditions exist:

1. When the initiator is perceived as behaving unethically and ignores appeals to reason.
2. When the respondent is truly interested in the basic offer but needs more time to consider it.
3. When there are issues central to the deal that genuinely need clarification.

Responding When the Other Side Is Being Difficult

When the other side presents a clearly problematic pattern of difficult behavior, two possibilities exist: On the one hand, it is possible that the negotiator does not know any other way to negotiate, but might be responsive to suggestions for changing his or her behavior. On the other hand, there is the possibility that the person is a difficult person whose behaviors are consistent both within and outside of the negotiation context. However, in most cases it is not likely that enough is known about the other to make the distinction. In the following section, we will review several approaches for dealing with difficult negotiators. The first, proposed by Ury (1991), suggests a broad-based approach that may be used with any difficult other party, including one using hard distributive tactics. The second, based on the work of Bramson (1981), suggests different strategies for dealing with negotiators who have particularly difficult styles.

Ury's Breakthrough Approach.   William Ury (1991) suggests a five-stage "breakthrough approach," which sees obstacles set by the other party as challenges that can be addressed through specific strategies. Ury's plan involves creating a favorable negotiation environment by regaining your "mental balance" and controlling one's own behavior, helping the other party achieve similar balance and control, changing the game from a distributive one to an integrative one, overcoming the other party's skepticism by jointly crafting a mutually satisfactory agreement, and achieving closure through firm, even-handed use of negotiating power. Ury suggests that his approach operates on the principle of acting counterintuitively. This requires negotiators to do the opposite of what they might naturally do in difficult situations. When the other party stonewalls or attacks, people often feel like responding in kind. When they insist on their position, negotiators want to reject it and assert their own. When others exert pressure, negotiators are inclined to retaliate with direct counterpressure. But in trying to break down the other party's resistance, these counterpressure responses only increase it. In contrast,

TABLE 12.2   Ury's Strategies for Managing Difficult Negotiations

Steps	Barriers to Cooperation	Challenges	Strategies
Step 1	Your natural reaction to opponent's cooperative behavior	Don't react	Go to the balcony
Step 2	Other's negative emotions	Disarm them	Step to the side
Step 3	Other's positional behavior	Change the game	Don't reject, reframe
Step 4	Other's skepticism about benefits of agreement	Make it easy for them to say yes	Build them a golden bridge
Step 5	Other's perceived power	Make it hard to say no	Bring them to their senses, not their knees

SOURCE: Adapted from "Strategy Table," from *Getting Past No* by William Ury. Copyright © 1991 by William Ury. Used by permission of Bantam Books, a division of Random House, Inc.

The essence of the breakthrough strategy is indirect action. You try to *go around* his resistance. Rather than pounding in a new idea from the outside, you encourage him to reach from within. Rather than telling him what to do, you let him figure it out. Rather than trying to break down his resistance, you make it easier for him to break through it himself. In short, breakthrough negotiation is the art of letting the other person have it your way. (Ury, 1991, p. 9)

Ury proposes a five-step process for this counterintuitive pattern of responding (the titles of the steps are adapted from Ury's strategies for managing difficult negotiations; see Table 12.2).

Step 1: Don't React—Go to the Balcony.   A natural reaction to aggressive tactics is to strike back, give in, or break off negotiations. None of these behaviors serve the negotiator's legitimate interests, let alone move the process in an integrative direction. The resulting challenge to this obstacle is to not react, thereby avoiding the destructive effect reacting naturally would have on the process. Instead, Ury recommends, negotiators should "go to the balcony"—that is, psychologically remove themselves from the interaction so that they become an observer to their own interaction with the other party. The advantages of this are that it

- Provides some distance from the conflict, and from one's own emotions.
- Creates breathing space, allowing negotiators to cool off so their eventual response can be more reasoned.
- Creates an opportunity for negotiators to see the situation in context and to remind themselves why they are there in the first place.

Step 2: Disarm Them—Step to Their Side.   As noted above, negativeness and attack in negotiation tend to breed more of the same; tensions heighten, and damaging exchanges tend to escalate. Confrontation and impending impasse typically elicit negative emotions for both sides. The negotiator's challenge is to act counterintuitively—to deflect or sidestep the other party's negativeness, disarming him or her through positive, constructive communication. The strategy of stepping to the other side conveys the compelling image of "coming around" the table to listen to and acknowledge the other party's legitimate points, needs, and concerns. This strategy of disarmament includes:

- Active listening.
- Acknowledging the other's points, without necessarily conceding their truth or accuracy.
- Agreeing, wherever one can, to recognize points of understanding that might provide the foundation for subsequent agreement.
- Acknowledging the other party personally, as a mark of recognition of and respect for his or her authority, sensitivities, and competencies.
- Expressing one's own views clearly and considerately.

Step 3: Change the Game—Don't Reject, Reframe.   Framing the problem is an important step in preparing for any negotiation (see Chapter 2). Given the obstacle of the other party's positional behavior, the challenge at this stage is to change the negotiation by proactively reframing his or her tactics. A reframing strategy includes the following active behaviors:

- Asking open-ended, problem-solving questions.
- Reframing the other party's tactics (for example, if presented with a stone wall, ignore it, test it, or reinterpret it as just wishful thinking; if attacked, ignore it, deflect it from you to the problem, or recast it in less confrontational terms that highlight common goals and interests).
- Negotiating, directly and openly, the rules of the negotiation process.

Step 4: Make It Easy to Say Yes—Build Them a Golden Bridge.   This is the persuasive stage of the process, wherein the challenge and opportunity for negotiators is to make it easy for the other party to say yes to an offer (see, e.g., Fisher, 1969). According to Ury (1991, p. 89), the four most common objections from the other party are these:

- It's not my idea (i.e., "not invented here").
- It doesn't address one of my basic interests.
- It might cause me to lose face or look bad to some important constituency.
- It requires too big of an adjustment for me (i.e., "too much, too fast").

The proposed strategy is to close this gap by building a golden bridge, to entice the other party to cross over to agreement by:

- Involving him or her in the actual design of an agreement that addresses both the interests and aversions of all parties.
- As much as possible, satisfying his or her unmet needs without jeopardizing the basic fabric of the agreement.
- Recognizing and being empathetic to the range of personal and organizational demands and expectations that he or she faces.

- Helping him or her to save face and deal with constituencies by providing justifications for the agreement—changed conditions, third-party advice or expertise, or some objective standard of fairness.

- "Going slow to go fast" (Ury, p. 105), walking him or her through complex agreements step by step and not demanding closure until everyone is ready.

Step 5: Make It Hard to Say No—Bring Them to Their Senses, Not Their Knees. Throughout the first four stages, the other party may maintain an abiding belief in the value of his superior power or wits. Having made it easy for the other party to say yes, negotiators must now address the challenge of making it hard for them to say no. Confronting power plays with power plays will most likely return the negotiation to the competitive dynamics the parties have worked to change; a better strategy is to bring the other negotiators to their senses without bringing them to their knees. The components of this strategy are to:

- Tend to one's own BATNA, strengthening it and making sure the other party knows what it is.

- Help the other party think about the consequences of no agreement.

- If necessary, actually use one's own BATNA, being careful to anticipate and defuse the other's reaction to what may be perceived as a punitive move.

- Keep sharpening the other's choice—refer back to the attractive terms that got the other party to cross the bridge and help them maintain their focus on the advantages of completing the deal.

- Fashion a lasting agreement, thinking through and planning for implementation.

Responding to Difficult People. Sometimes problems in negotiation can be traced to difficulties in the other's behavioral style. The subject of how to deal with difficult people in the workplace has received increasing attention in recent years from several authors (e.g., Bernstein and Rosen, 1989; Bramson, 1981, 1992; Solomon, 1990). These authors make several important points. First, everyone can exhibit difficult behaviors or be difficult to deal with at times; some people, however, are *invariably* difficult, and their behavior conforms to predictable and identifiable patterns. Second, what is difficult behavior to one person may not be difficult for another. Labeling an action "difficult" may say as much about the receiver as it does about the sender. Person A may have a great deal of difficulty contending with a very aggressive negotiator, whereas Person B has no difficulty with that person. Third, difficult people do what they do because it works for them. Their behavior gives them control, feels comfortable, and lets them get their way. By giving in to it, negotiators reinforce the behavior, providing the difficult person ample reasons to continue behaving in ways that were useful in the past. Difficult people also may continue their difficult ways because they honestly are not aware of the long-term costs to people and organizations that must contend with them. Finally, it is possible to cope with invariably difficult people—contending with their behavior on equal behavioral terms—as opposed to giving in to them, accepting their behavior, or getting them to change their values, beliefs, or attitudes. In short,

BOX 12.7
Why, You No Good, Uncooperative, Double-Dealing, . . . Etc.

Emotionality is frequently an aspect of difficult, high-stakes negotiation. All the same, emotion run wild can be detrimental to the process, distorting perceptions and diverting attention from the real issues. Adler, Rosen, and Silverstein (1998) looked at the problem and effects of fear and anger in negotiations, and suggest some tactics for managing such emotions.

Regarding your *own* emotions, you can

- Determine which situations tend to trigger inappropriate anger.
- Decide, when angry, whether or not to display your anger.
- Use behavioral techniques (e.g., taking a break, counting to 10) to reduce your anger.
- Express your anger and disappointment effectively (e.g., openly and in a nonaccusatory fashion).
- Avoid the negotiator's bias ("I'm fair and reasonable, you're not . . .").
- Try to promote trust.

Regarding the *other party's* emotions, you can

- Defuse emotional buildups by direct confrontation ("You seem angry; are you?").
- Assess the real significance of emotional displays (Is it an act? A distributive dirty trick?).
- Address the other's anger directly, perhaps apologizing for a comment or pointing out the effects of a bad situation.
- Respond to the other's anger strategically (call a break, use silence to "wit him out," make a modest concession, etc.).
- Help the other party save face (especially when losing face contributed to his anger).
- Consider calling in a mediator when you anticipate anger rising.

SOURCE: R. S. Adler, B. Rosen, and E. M. Silverstein, "Emotions in Negotiation: How to Manage Fear and Anger," *Negotiation Journal* 14, No. 2 (1998), pp. 161–79.

negotiators must effectively counterbalance the potential power these behaviors give to those who use them. Box 12.7 offers a general framework for coping with a difficult other. Relating to difficult people in negotiation or other highly charged, results-oriented exchanges is a critically important skill. We encourage anyone wishing to go beyond the basics presented here to refer to Bramson (1981), Solomon (1990), and (Ury (1991) to build their skills and insights.

CHAPTER SUMMARY

Through any number of different avenues—breakdowns in communication, escalation of anger and mistrust, polarization of positions and refusal to compromise, the issuance of ultimatums, or even the avoidance of conflict—negotiations often hit an impasse. Productive dialogue stops. The parties may continue talking, but the communication is usually characterized by trying to sell or force one's own position, talking about the other's unreasonable position and uncooperative behavior, or both. When these breakdowns occur, the parties may simply agree to recess, cool off, and come back tomorrow. More commonly, however, the parties break off negotiation and walk away angry and upset. Although they may privately wish there was some way to get back together, they usually don't know how to arrange a reconciliation.

This chapter explored the various reasons that conflicts become "difficult to resolve" and more likely to reach impasse. We discussed the fundamental nature of "difficult to resolve" conflicts and proposed four groups of reasons why they were difficult: characteristics of the negotiation parties, characteristics of the issues under discussion, characteristics of the conflict resolution process being pursued by the parties, and characteristics of the context of the negotiation. We then suggested five major strategies that the parties could use to attempt to resolve a dispute on their own:

- Reduce tension by separating themselves from one another through cooling-off periods, releasing tension, talking about emotions and feelings, or attempting to synchronize de-escalation of the conflict.

- Improve the accuracy of communication by role reversal or mirroring the other's statements.

- Keep the number of issues under control so that issues are managed effectively, new issues are not carelessly added, and large issues are divided into smaller ones.

- Search for common ground through exploring superordinate goals, common enemies, creating common ground rules and effective time management, developing common expectations through a "covenant," and reframing.

- Enhancing the desirability of the options and alternatives for both parties by providing "yesable" proposals, asking for different decisions, sweetening offers, and using objective criteria to evaluate solutions.

Finally, in the third section of this chapter, we explored what negotiators can do when they are already in an integrative mode, and the other party is being competitive or "difficult." We reviewed several major works which provide clear and important advice to parties who want to convert the other party by curtailing their use of power, curtailing their use of hard distributive and unethical tactics, responding to their ultimatums, or simply dealing with their counterproductive behavior.

The tools that we discussed are broad in function and in application, and they represent self-help for negotiators in dealing with stalled or problematic exchanges. None of these methods and remedies is a panacea, and each should be chosen and applied with sensitivity to the needs and limitations of the situations and of the negotiators involved. Their successful application may require a significant amount of individual skill at interpersonal communication. A truly confrontational breakdown, especially one that involves agreements of great impact or importance, sometimes justifies the introduction of individuals or agencies who themselves are not party to the dispute. That is the subject of Chapter 13.

CHAPTER 13

Managing Difficult Negotiations:
Third-Party Approaches

In Chapter 12 we reviewed a number of techniques that negotiators themselves can use to break deadlocks, reduce tension and hostility, and return negotiations to a productive pace. However, frequently the parties cannot implement these techniques effectively by themselves. When negotiators have tried all options and are not making progress, when mistrust and suspicion are high, or when the parties cannot take actions toward defusing conflict without those actions being misinterpreted and mistrusted by others, third-party involvement may become necessary. In this chapter we will describe the typical roles that third parties play and the ways in which those roles can contribute to conflict resolution. We will also discuss the institutionalization of third-party processes through the establishment and maintenance of alternative dispute resolution (ADR) systems within organizations.

ADDING THIRD PARTIES TO THE TWO-PARTY NEGOTIATION PROCESS

Third parties work to manage conflict in several different situations, using a variety of styles and techniques. Often, third parties need do no more than implement some of the dispute resolution techniques reviewed in Chapter 12, such as aiding in the reduction of tension, controlling the number of issues, enhancing communication, establishing a common ground, or highlighting certain decision options to make them more attractive to the parties. As we will discuss, certain third-party styles use more of these techniques than others. (For a broad treatment of these and related issues, see Lewicki, Weiss, and Lewin, 1992; Singer, 1990, 1994; Ury, 2000; Mayer, 2000.)

The negotiation process we have described in most of this book presumes that there are two or more parties working face-to-face, without the direct involvement of others. The parties' personal involvement can create a deep understanding of the issues and a commitment to resolve their differences in a constructive manner. As long as this direct form of negotiation remains productive, it is best to allow it to proceed without the involvement of other parties. As we have described, however, negotiations are often tense and difficult, and can lead to frustration and anger. Negotiation over critical issues may also reach an impasse, leaving the parties unable to move the process beyond a particular sticking point. At these points (when passions are high, when the parties are deadlocked on the issues, or both) third-party intervention may be a productive way (if not the only way) to get the negotiations back on track. Our premise is that third-party intervention should be avoided as long as negotiations have a chance of proceeding unaided—that is, as long as progress is occurring or is likely to occur within reasonable limits of time and other resources. However, if intervention becomes advisable, it should be done in a timely and thoughtful manner.

The negotiators themselves may seek third-party intervention, or it may be imposed from the outside by choice, custom, law, or regulation. Outside imposition of intervention by a third party (addressed later in this chapter in the section on informal third-party styles) may bring in the perspective of someone who is not part of the dispute per se, but is nonetheless interested in its resolution. The third party may be a manager or a friend or a peer of the negotiators. As a rule of thumb, interventions that are not sanctioned by the parties—or reinforced by a third party's expertise, friendship, or authority—are unwelcome and ineffective (see Arnold and O'Connor, 1999). Uninvited third parties may find themselves bearing the brunt of hostility from one or even both parties in a negotiation, regardless of the third party's intentions or motivations. For example, law enforcement officers who attempt to intervene in domestic disputes, if only to separate the parties and cool down the situation, often find that the battling parties unite in turning on the officers as unwelcome outsiders. Many law enforcement agencies, in fact, caution officers to respond to domestic dispute calls in pairs in order to separate the disputants and to protect the officers' safety.

Benefits and Liabilities of Third-Party Intervention

Benefits.   At a minimum, third parties can provide (or even enforce) the stability, civility, and forward momentum the negotiators need in order to address the problems that remain to be solved—especially those problems that are central to the negotiation and that have stalled or derailed discussions. Further, third-party interventions can provide a number of other general benefits:

- Creating breathing space or a cooling-off period.
- Reestablishing or enhancing communications.
- Refocusing on the substantive issues.
- Remedying or repairing strained relationships.
- Establishing or recommitting to time limits and deadlines.
- Salvaging sunk costs.
- Increasing levels of negotiator satisfaction with, and commitment to, the conflict resolution process and its outcomes.

Even if the relationship between the parties is so damaged that future exchanges would be highly problematic, third parties may enable the parties to reduce hostility levels, manage their emotions, and achieve some closure on the key issues (Jones and Bodtker, 2001). Organizations may adopt and support ADR systems and conflict management skills training. Such commitments are likely to result in a constructive, collaborative work environment, leading to greater individual and organizational effectiveness (Costantino and Merchant, 1996).

TABLE 13.1   Conditions Where Third-Party Intervention May Help

- Intense emotions that appear to be preventing a settlement.
- Poor communication, beyond the ability of the negotiators to fix it (see Chapter 5).
- Misperceptions or stereotypes that hinder productive exchanges.
- Repeated negative behaviors (anger, name-calling, blaming others, etc.), creating barriers between the parties.
- Serious disagreement over the importance, collection, or evaluation of data.
- Disagreement as to the number or type of issues under dispute.
- Actual or perceived incompatible interests that the parties are unable to reconcile.
- Unnecessary (but perceived-as-necessary) value differences that divide the parties.
- Absence of a clear, agreed-on negotiation procedure or protocol, or not using established procedures (such as caucuses or cooling-off periods) to their best advantage.
- Severe difficulties in getting negotiations started, or in bargaining through an impasse.

SOURCE: Adapted from C. Moore, *The Mediation Process: Practical Strategies for Resolving Conflict,* 2nd ed. (San Francisco: Jossey-Bass, 1996), pp. 13–14. Also see Arnold and Carnevale (1997).

Limitations and Liabilities.   Third-party interventions may also have certain liabilities and limitations. At a minimum, the involvement of third parties signals a failure of the negotiation process, even if only temporarily. Intervention by a third party may signal that the parties have failed to grow, to build relationships, or to become adept in managing their own interdependencies. This is especially true when parties turn to arbitration (see our later discussion), which requires the parties to give up control over determining their outcomes. Arbitration hearings can be viewed as the result of the negotiators' agreement to disagree, and a willingness to surrender control over the outcome of their dispute. In contrast, the dominant purpose of other types of third-party interventions (especially mediation and process consultation, also discussed later) is to enhance the parties' dispute resolution skills. Their goal is to allow the parties to maintain control of the outcomes, while regulating the process of their interaction. Thus, each type of third-party intervention has its own particular advantages and disadvantages.

When Is Third-Party Involvement Appropriate?

Serious negotiators must make a realistic effort to resolve their own disputes. In labor–management negotiations, for example, failure to bargain in good faith has been codified as an unfair labor practice under current U.S. labor law [N.L.R.A., Sections 8(a)(5) and 8(b)(3)]. In general, though, negotiators initiate third-party interventions when they believe they can no longer manage the dispute on their own. When one negotiator requests intervention, that process must be acceptable to all the disputing parties. If only one party recognizes a need for third-party intervention, he or she must usually persuade the other party to agree. However, as we said earlier, someone with power or authority over the negotiators may also impose interventions, particularly when a failure to resolve the dispute threatens to lead to significant costs for the affected organization or individuals. A list of conditions under which negotiators might seek third-party involvement is presented in Table 13.1.

Which Type of Intervention Is Appropriate?

There are several different ways to describe the variety of third-party styles available to negotiators. Moore (1996) suggests that approaches to conflict management and resolution can be placed on a single continuum (see Figure 13.1), in which the styles are in increasing order according to the amount of coercion used on the negotiating parties to get them to accept and endorse the third-party settlement. Thus, under conditions of very low coercion, the parties don't even engage in the issue themselves, choosing to avoid the issue or to discuss it informally. At the other extreme, third parties with the force of law or legitimate authority impose settlements, or the parties go outside the bounds of the legal and regulatory system by using violent or nonviolent pressure tactics directly on the other.

Thibaut and Walker (1975) presented an important framework suggesting that negotiators may surrender control over neither, either, or both the dispute process (the *how*) and the dispute outcome (the *what*) (see Figure 13.2). Surrender of neither process nor outcome control by the bargainers constitutes negotiation (lower right cell), as addressed in the other chapters of this book; surrender of both outcome and process controls constitutes a complete withdrawal of the negotiators from the process (upper left cell), indicating their willingness to have the dispute taken over by an otherwise uninvolved person who will manage the dispute and determine its outcome in whatever manner he or she sees fit. Of the remaining two mixed situations (arbitration and mediation, both discussed in detail later in this chapter), mediation is the most common form of third-party involvement that is largely procedural in nature. Mediation (and other similar forms of process-only control, such as facilitation or process consultation), then, is less intrusive in that negotiators surrender control only over the process while maintaining control over outcomes. Mediation can be highly effective in many disputes (Carnevale and Pruitt, 1992; Moore, 1996), while helping to preserve an important benefit of unassisted negotiation: The parties retain control over shaping the actual outcome or solution, which enhances their willingness to implement it. Our corollary to the rule "No third-party involvement unless necessary," then, is "If involvement is necessary, use a minimally intrusive intervention" (one toward the left side of the chart in Figure 13.1), such as mediation.

Procedure-only third-party interventions support the needs of negotiators who desire guidance or procedural assistance but wish to maintain control over the choice and implementation of the ultimate outcome. Frustrated negotiators may feel they just want an end to the dispute, but completely abdicating control to a third party could have a number of detrimental effects (see the discussion of arbitration later in this chapter). In addition, negotiators may not know how to screen potential third parties to determine what they will do, or the negotiators may be at the mercy of whatever help is most conveniently available. Failure to use third-party intervention when appropriate is just as wasteful and damaging to the ultimate negotiation process as using the wrong intervention method (e.g., arbitration rather than mediation, when negotiator commitment to outcomes is critical for a lasting resolution), or even using the right method at the wrong time (e.g., before negotiators have exhausted the unassisted methods we outlined in Chapter 12, or after expressed anger and personal attacks have soured one or both parties on the entire process—see also Conlon and Fasolo, 1990).

FIGURE 13.1 Continuum of Conflict Management and Resolution Approaches

	Decisions Made by Negotiators			*Decisions Made by Private Third Parties*		*Decisions Made by Legal (Authoritative) Third Parties*		*Extralegal Decisions*	
Conflict avoidance	Discussion and problem solving	Informal negotiation	Mediation	Administrative decision	Arbitration	Judicial decision	Legislative decision	Nonviolent direct action	Violence

——— Increased coercion and more likelihood of win-lose decisions ———→

SOURCE: Adapted from C. Moore, *The Mediation Process: Practical Strategies for Resolving Conflict,* 2nd ed. (San Francisco: Jossey-Bass, 1996), p. 7, Table 1.1.

FIGURE 13.2 Categories of Third-Party Intervention

Level of Negotiator Control over Outcome

		Low	High
Level of Negotiator Control over Procedure	**Low**	Autocracy	Mediation
	High	Arbitration	Negotiation

SOURCE: Adapted from B.H. Sheppard, "Third Party Conflict Intervention: A Procedural Framework," in B.M. Staw and L.L. Cummings, eds., *Research in Organizational Behavior*, vol. 6 (Greenwich, CT: JAI Publishing, 1984), pp.141–90; and from J. Thibaut and L. Walker, *Procedural Justice: A Psychological Analysis* (Hillsdale, NJ: Lawrence Erlbaum Associates, 1975).

The same issues of propriety and timeliness apply to uninvited interventions, as when a manager chooses to intervene in a dispute between two subordinates. The third party has the advantage of being potentially more objective than the disputants about the choices of whether to intervene, and what style to use. In addition, naive third parties may lack objectivity (i.e., impartiality), in that they have a personal feeling or value position about what is right for this situation, as opposed to having a specific or direct interest in helping to resolve the dispute solely by working "to reconcile the competing interests of the two parties" (Moore, 1986, p. 17). Finally, research by Conlon and Ross (1993) suggests that partisan third parties—who lack impartiality, due to a prior relationship with one or both parties, or who have a clear bias to settle the dispute more in favor of one side than the other—could have a significant negative effect on disputant satisfaction regarding the third-party intervention. However, the third party must keep in mind the likely effect of the intervention on the negotiators—specifically on their willingness and ability to address and manage disputes more effectively in the future.

Third-party interventions, particularly arbitration, may have strong negative consequences, such as decreasing the ability of the parties to negotiate effectively and increasing dependency on the third party (see Beckhard, 1978). The rules for third parties to use are rules of moderation: (1) to borrow the medical dictum, "First, do no harm," and (2) intervene only when necessary and control only as much as necessary to enable the parties to find resolution. In other words, don't let the intervention make the situation worse, do use surgery when needed, and don't use surgery when simple first aid would be sufficient. This advice assumes an overriding value in the negotiators' continued (or improved) ability to interact constructively; it also assumes that resolution of the specific dispute is not critically urgent. To the extent that the negotiators will have little or no interaction in the future or that timeliness is critical, relatively more controlling interventions (the middle of Figure 13.1) may be acceptable or necessary. Quite often, however, neither of these conditions applies; we discuss choice processes in these less drastic situations in more detail later in this chapter.

TYPES OF THIRD-PARTY INTERVENTION

In the following sections, we discuss several different forms of third-party intervention. Before we proceed, we wish to note that third-party intervention may be formal or informal. *Formal* interventions are intentionally designed and generally follow a set of rules or standards; they are used by judges, labor arbitrators, divorce mediators, referees, and group facilitators (e.g., psychologists or organization development practitioners). *Informal* interventions are incidental to the negotiation; a manager or a concerned friend, for example, may become involved in someone else's dispute. While it is important to know whether the third party is following a clear, public, specified set of procedures or "making it up on his own," the proliferation of hybrid forms of dispute resolution, both formal and informal, has blurred this traditional separation.

FORMAL INTERVENTION METHODS

In this section, we describe three important types of more formal third-party interventions: arbitration, mediation, and process consultation. We will review the objectives, style, and procedural impact of each approach and describe how each affects negotiation outcomes. (By describing these three approaches, we do not mean to suggest that there are only three. Numerous authors [e.g., Diehl, Druckman, and Wall, 1998; Ury, 2000;] have suggested numerous other formal roles.) As with many of the other areas of research that we have reviewed, the literature on third-party intervention in dispute resolution is large and growing rapidly (see Devinatz and Budd, 1997). Interested readers should refer to references used in this chapter to explore the research and practice in greater detail. In the next section of this chapter, we will address informal intervention techniques.

Arbitration

Arbitration involves low or nonexistent levels of negotiator control over outcomes, but it retains high levels of negotiator control over process (see again Figure 13.2). Even though arbitration represents a loss of outcome control by the negotiating parties, it is probably the most common and well-known form of third-party dispute resolution. The process is fairly clear-cut: Parties in dispute, after having reached a deadlock or a time deadline without successful resolution of their differences, present their positions to a neutral third party. The third party listens to both sides and then decides the outcome of the dispute (Elkouri and Elkouri, 1985; Prasow and Peters, 1983). Arbitration is used widely in disputes between different businesses (Corley, Black, and Reed, 1977) and between managers and their union-organized workers (e.g., Elkouri and Elkouri, 1985), and has clearly become an accepted international process for resolving commercial disputes globally (Beechey, 2000; Swacker, Redden and Wenger, 2000).

There are several different forms of arbitration. First, arbitrators may hear and rule on a single issue under dispute, or on multiple issues in a total settlement package (Feigenbaum, 1975). Second, arbitration may be voluntary or binding. Under *voluntary arbitration,* the parties may submit their arguments to an arbitrator, but they are not required to comply with the arbitrator's decision. In contrast, *binding arbitration* requires the parties to comply with the decision, either by law or by precedent within that sphere of arbitral practice. In arbitrating labor–management contract disagreements, the arbitrator's ruling typically amends an existing agreement and becomes part of the agreement for the remaining life of the contract. A third variation concerns the arbitrator's discretion. At one extreme, arbitrators are free to craft (and impose) any resolution they deem appropriate; at the other, their choice is severely constrained, as in "final-offer" arbitration, in which the arbitrator must approve, without amendment, one of the positions presented by the two disputing parties. In labor–management settings, management will frequently attempt to control this situation by requiring the arbitrator to neither add to nor detract from the labor contract being interpreted; that is, management will try to curtail the arbitrator's discretion to change the contract or to rule outside of a strict interpretation of it. The pros and cons of these variations will become evident as we examine arbitration in more detail. (See Box 13.1 for a twist on arbitration.)

Formal arbitration is most commonly used as a dispute resolution mechanism in labor relations or in claims about violations of legal contracts. For example, in most states, "lemon laws"—legal protection given to consumers if they buy a product that does not work and cannot be effectively fixed, such as a car or major appliance—specify that most claims will be resolved through arbitration. Arbitration is being used in a number of new areas—for example see Box 13.2 on the use of arbitration to resolve problems on the Internet. New contracts, typically in the public sector, that cannot be achieved through negotiation are frequently submitted for consideration to an arbitrator. When a new contract is submitted to arbitration this process is called "interest arbitration." A highly visible form of interest arbitration is the awarding of salaries and compensation packages to professional athletes. On the other hand, "grievance arbitration" refers to decisions about the interpretation of existing contracts. For instance, a union may grieve management's decision to discipline an employee if they felt that management did not follow the negotiated discipline policy (e.g., did management act

---

BOX 13.1
Arbitration with a Twist

The Council of Better Business Bureaus, Inc., offers arbitration of consumer complaints on vehicles manufactured by participating corporations. Under the council's Auto-Line program, local Better Business Bureaus offer arbitration by trained volunteers, with a twist: The arbitrator's decision is binding on the manufacturer, but not on the consumer-complainant, who is free to pursue other remedies (primarily through litigation) if he or she finds the arbitration decision unacceptable.

BOX 13.2
Arbitrating the Internet

In 2000, five law professors formed one of the first organizations to arbitrate disputes over ownership of Internet domain names (domain names, such as yahoo.com, serve as addresses on the Internet for World Wide Web and e-mail accounts). Disputes are commonly over ownership of a specific address, or whether the choice of an address infringes on a company's name or trademark.

The law professors arbitrate the disputes entirely on line. Operating as Disputes.org, they have the authority to stop the use of a domain name, or transfer the name to its rightful owner.

"This new arbitration body will make a useful contribution to the world of the Internet," said Prof. Ethan Katsch, a professor of undergraduate legal studies at the University of Massachusetts at Amherst and one of the organization's founders. "Resolving domain-name disputes on-line will be quicker and far less expensive than going to court."

SOURCE: W. R. Leibowitz, "Law Professors Create Group to Arbitrate Disputes over Domain Names," *Chronicle of Higher Education,* January 28, 2000, p. A45.

---

in a fair and consistent manner?). While interest and grievance arbitration have many similarities, the fundamental difference between them concerns the types of decisions that they process.

Arbitration has come under increasing scrutiny and criticism as a dispute resolution mechanism, even in the labor relations area (e.g., Brett and Goldberg, 1983; Kanowitz, 1985). Arbitration initially appears to have two distinct advantages as a resolution procedure: It imposes a clear-cut resolution to the problem in dispute, and it helps the parties avoid the costs of prolonged, unresolved disputes. However, as noted by Kochan (1980) and others (see Devinatz and Budd, 1997), arbitration appears to have several negative consequences as well, which we describe below.

The Chilling Effect.   If the parties in negotiation anticipate that their own failure to agree will lead to binding arbitration, they may lose their incentive to work seriously for a negotiated settlement. This chilling effect occurs as "the parties avoid making compromises they might be otherwise willing to make, because they fear that the fact finder or arbitrator will split the difference between their stated positions" (Kochan, 1980, p. 291). If negotiators anticipate that the arbitrator will split the difference, then it is in their best interest to maintain an extreme, hard-line position because difference splitting is likely to result in the hard-liner's favor. Some early research supported this claim (Grigsby and Bigoness, 1982; Long and Feuille, 1974; Starke and Notz, 1981) and suggested that final-offer arbitration (discussed above) is a better alternative. In final-offer arbitration, the arbitrator must choose either one party's position or the other's— nothing in between, no splitting the difference. Given this constraint, it is believed that bargainers will be more motivated to settle, or to close the gap that will be arbitrated as much as possible, in order to increase the likelihood that the arbitrator will choose your final offer. If both parties act this way it also minimizes the loss that will occur if the arbitrator picks the other party's position as the basis for the arbitration award. However, recent work has shown that "splitting the difference" may not be common practice in professional business arbitration. Keer and Naimark (2001) examined a sample of arbitration cases and found that two-thirds of arbitrators ruled either 100 percent for the claimants or 0 percent for the claimants, while only one-third of the cases involved some form of "splitting." A related study cited by these authors showed that 72 percent of a large sample of commercial arbitration awards gave below 20 percent or above 80 percent of the award to the claimant. Taken together, these findings suggest that the tendency for the arbitrator to "split the difference" may be far less common than assumed.

The Narcotic Effect.   When arbitration is anticipated as a result of the failure of parties to agree, negotiators may also lose interest in the process of negotiating. Because bargaining takes time and effort, especially in complex situations, and there is no guarantee that agreement will be reached, negotiators may take the easy way out and accept the guarantee of an imposed settlement under arbitration. Negotiator passivity, loss of initiative, and dependence on the third party are common results of recurring dispute arbitration. These results are even more likely when negotiators are accountable to constituencies, because then negotiators can take tough, unyielding stands on issues and blame compromise settlements on the arbitrator rather than on their own concessions.

The Half-Life Effect.   Parents are often aware that as the demand for arbitration from siblings increases, both the sheer number of decisions required and the likelihood that those decisions will not please one or both sides increase as well. This is known as the *half-life effect*. For example, as one of the authors worked at home one Sunday afternoon, he was frequently subject to his children's demands to arbitrate disputes over sharing a video game. After a series of decisions involving both his own children and half of the surrounding neighborhood, he was informed by one of his children that his decisions were generally viewed as outrageous, unfair, and without appropriate compassion, and that his services were no longer desired. As the frequency of arbitration increases, disenchantment with the adequacy and fairness of the process develops (Anderson and Kochan, 1977), and the parties may resort to other means to resolve their disputes.

The Biasing Effect.   Arbitrators must be careful that their decisions do not systematically favor one side or the other and that they maintain an image of fairness and impartiality (see Conlon and Ross, 1993). Even if each decision, taken separately, appears to be a fair settlement of the current conflict, perceived patterns of partiality toward one side may jeopardize the arbitrator's acceptability in future disputes. Parties to potential labor arbitration frequently review different arbitrators' published decisions in an effort to secure one who is likely to favor their own side (i.e., labor or management) or to avoid one who tends to make awards more consistently supportive of the other side.

The Decision-Acceptance Effect.   Finally, arbitrated disputes may engender less commitment to the settlement than alternative forms of dispute resolution. Research on the dynamics of group decision making (e.g., Vroom, 1973) has demonstrated that commitment to a given solution and willingness to implement it are significantly greater when group members participate in developing that solution than when it is imposed by a single member. Lasting dispute resolution requires timely and effective implementation, and "one of the most powerful drivers of effective implementation is the commitment to [a] decision that derives from *prior participation in making it*" (Leavitt and Bahrami, 1988, p. 173; emphasis added). For this reason, arbitration is likely to lead to situations in which disputants are less than fully committed to following through, especially if they feel dissatisfied with the arbitrator's decision.

Mediation

In contrast to arbitration, mediation has developed increasing support (Bush, 1996; Kochan, 1980; Kochan and Jick, 1978) and it has been studied with increasing frequency (for literature reviews see Carnevale and Pruitt, 1992; Lewicki, Weiss, and Lewin, 1992; and Wall and Lynn, 1993). Brett, Barsness, and Goldberg (1996) found that mediation, when compared to arbitration, was less costly, less time-consuming, and produced greater disputant satisfaction. Although the ultimate objective of mediation is the same as arbitration—to resolve the dispute—the major difference is that mediation seeks to achieve the objective by having the parties themselves develop and endorse the agreement. In fact, mediation has been called a form of "assisted negotiation" (Susskind and Cruikshank, 1987, p. 136), "an extension and elaboration of the negotiation process" (Moore, 1996, p. 8), and "has always been an informal accompanist of negotiation" (Wall and Blum, 1991, p. 284). Mediation can help reduce or remove barriers to dispute settlement, adding value to the negotiation process because it tends to produce or enhance much of what parties desire and value in negotiation itself (Bush, 1996). These sentiments have received empirical support from both field and laboratory studies (Esser and Marriott, 1995a). Finally, mediators may be used to help to resolve the root causes of an ongoing conflict rather than simply resolving a presenting dispute (Brown, 1999); it is almost impossible for arbitration to accomplish this goal.

It is important to note that formal or contractual mediation is based on established and accepted rules and procedures. Later in this chapter, when examining informal interventions, we will discuss emergent mediation, which is less well defined (Pruitt and Carnevale, 1993). Mediators have no formal power over outcomes, and they cannot resolve the dispute on their own or impose a solution. Instead, their effectiveness comes from their ability to meet with the parties individually, secure an understanding of the issues in dispute, identify areas of potential compromise in the positions of each side, and encourage the parties to make concessions toward agreement.

As with arbitration, mediation's roots are in the field of labor relations, sometimes as a preliminary step to arbitration in grievance and contractual negotiations. Mediation has also been described, though, as "the second oldest profession," having been around as long as conflict itself (Kolb, 1983a), and has become a very popular alternative to the courts—particularly when the parties desire low-cost solutions that they can largely shape themselves (see Lovenheim, 1989). (See Box 13.3.) Singer (1994) has noted the many different contexts in which mediation and ADR (see the section later in this chapter) have been used: malpractice suits, tort cases, liability claims, pretrial diversions of

---

BOX 13.3
Not Just for Baseball Anymore

More employers are realizing the benefits of settling disputes out of court by using arbitrators or mediators. Employers generally view arbitration and mediation as quicker, cheaper, and more confidential than a lawsuit.

"Most disputes center around claims of race, sex, or age discrimination," said Sara Cole, Associate Professor of Law at Ohio State University. And employers are tending to favor arbitration or mediation over a jury trial, because a jury is more likely to sympathize with an employee than an arbitrator or mediator, because jury members can identify with an employee who has been discriminated against. And employers can force their employees to use arbitration or mediation, by having employees sign an agreement to use alternative dispute resolution (ADR) rather than go to court. Thus, by using these methods, employers can maintain more control, while at the same time have a process that tends to be faster, cheaper, and seen by both sides as most fair.

SOURCE: E. Swartzlander, "Not Just for Baseball Anymore," *Business First,* December 29, 2000, pp. B1–B2.

---

alcohol and drug cases to treatment centers rather than criminal proceedings, business disputes, consumer complaints, and community and government disputes, to name a few. Mediation has become an extremely popular alternative in divorce proceedings because the parties must be willing to abide by the terms of the settlement and therefore have the most influence in shaping its terms (Donohue, 1991; Kressel, 1985). Mediation has also become a more common form of resolution for civil and community disputes (Duffy, Grosch, and Olczak, 1991; Kessler, 1978). Community mediation centers, staffed by trained volunteers, have opened across the United States (Duffy, Grosch, and Olczak, 1991; Lovenheim, 1989; Singer, 1994). Mediation is also used increasingly to avoid costly litigation in business settings (Coulson, 1987) and to resolve business–government disputes, particularly in the area of environmental regulation (Drayton, 1981; Reich, 1981; Susskind and Cruikshank, 1987). Finally, mediation is being suggested more frequently as a mechanism for the resolution of international disputes. Rubin (1981) documented Henry Kissinger's success as an extremely skilled international mediator, and Jandt and Pedersen (1996) show how mediation is used around the world to resolve both local and cross-border disputes.

When to Use Mediation. Several elements of the mediation process are integral to its success. The first is timing: The mediation effort needs to occur when the parties are open to receiving help. Because mediation is frequently a voluntary process—the parties usually are not forced to enter into mediation—it cannot be effective if the parties choose not to cooperate. If they believe that they have more to gain by holding out or protracting the dispute, then mediation cannot work. Many parties in a dispute don't seek mediation because they don't really understand the process. They may also get caught up in the momentum of conflict, becoming involved in a "metadispute" (that is, a dispute about the dispute), or they may fear a loss of leverage or advantage at the hands of a third party (McEwen and Milburn, 1993). Mediators who identify that the parties are not ready for their intervention frequently say, "Call me when you're ready," and leave until the parties have achieved a greater willingness to participate in the process. Formal mediation in some settings (e.g., divorce, international hostilities, or certain types of organized labor strikes) may be imposed if doing so might prevent a situation from escalating or deteriorating beyond any hope of reclamation. This is usually a judgment call by an experienced mediator who is empowered by some external agency or authority to intervene (Bercovitch, 1989; Donohue, 1991). Research suggests that when parties are pressured or required to enter mediation, they generally come away finding it to be a fair and satisfactory process (Brett, Barsness, and Goldberg, 1996; McEwen and Milburn, 1993).

Second, the mediator must be acceptable to all the parties to the dispute. The mediator is traditionally viewed as a neutral individual whom the parties recognize as impartial, experienced, and potentially helpful. Some would argue, however, that a completely "neutral" mediator is virtually impossible to find because any active intervention by a mediator may influence the process and outcome of a negotiation in a way that unintentionally favors one of the parties (see Gibson, Thompson, and Bazerman, 1996). In addition to unknown mediators, a friend, peer, or supervisor may intervene to act as a mediator, and this person is not likely to be completely neutral. Mediators may be certified by an organization of third parties, such as the Federal Mediation and Conciliation Service of the U.S. Department of Labor, or a local mediation service or dispute settlement center, adding to their credibility. In addition, a variety of qualities such as integrity, impartiality, and experience in comparable disputes may be required for a potential mediator to be viewed as acceptable by both sides. At times, however, the most appropriate (or only) mediator available is not without bias, to some degree. Although mediator bias has usually been thought to be incompatible with mediation effectiveness (Young, 1972), recent research has produced a more complex view of this issue (e.g., Carnevale and Conlon, 1990; Conlon and Ross, 1993; Kaufman and Duncan, 1992; Smith, 1985; Touval and Zartman, 1985; van de Vliert, 1992). Carnevale and Conlon (1990) suggest that mediator bias has two forms: that of general alignment or affiliation with parties prior to mediation, and that of greater support for one side than the other during mediation. However, disputants may overlook bias of the first sort if they are convinced that the mediator in question shows no bias of the second sort and mediates evenhandedly. This tends to be supported by recent research (e.g., Conlon and Ross, 1993; Wall and Stark, 1996).

Mediator Models, Choices, and Behaviors.   The idea of a neutral individual sitting down to mediate a dispute between two parties seems simple enough, but a more complete description of the process would have to identify and address a large number of facets (see Table 13.2). A complete framework for understanding mediation would have to take into consideration a very large number of factors (see Wall and Lynn, 1993), and a complete understanding of the role and impact of these factors is considerably beyond the scope of this book.

Mediators may choose any of a variety of levels and approaches to accomplish what they feel needs to be done (see Herrman, Hollett, Gale, and Foster, 2001, for an extensive

TABLE 13.2   Facets of the Mediation Framework

Mediation determinants: previous agreement, job requirement, perception that mediation is useful or is preferable to dispute, expected benefits to negotiator or negotiator's constituents

Technique determinants: formal rules, ethical specifications, source of conflict, difficulty of reaching agreement, mediator's reading of the conflict (i.e., importance of parties' reaching their goals, obtainable outcomes for parties), characteristics of dispute, culture, mediator's training, mediator's structural role, mediator's ideology, sex of mediator, time pressures

Parties' outcomes: settlement/agreement, prevention of future disputes, improvement of current relationship, compromise from positions, fair agreements, compliance to agreement, parties' satisfaction

Outcome determinants: level of conflict, parties' motivation to reach agreement, commitment to mediation process, parties' relationship, availability of resources, type of issue, relative power of parties, discord within parties' constituencies, admission of fault, speed of mediator's entry, mediator's characteristics, parties' aspirations, factors altering conflict level

Mediator's net outcomes: benefits from mediating (and any settlement), costs from mediating (and any settlement), benefits from each technique, costs from each technique

Mediation process: mediation stages or steps, speed of mediation, frequency of use

---

SOURCE: Adapted from J.A. Wall and A. Lynn, "Mediation: A Current Review," *Journal of Conflict Resolution* 37 (1993), pp.160–94.

list of mediator skills and knowledge areas; also see Barrett, 1999). Esser and Marriott (1995b) tested three types of mediation: content mediation (helping the parties manage trade-offs); issue identification (enabling the parties to prioritize the issues); and positive framing of the issues (focusing on desired, positively stated outcomes). While content mediation proved to be the most effective type in the study, all three approaches were found to be more satisfying to disputants than no mediation at all. As Rubin (1980) noted, mediators primarily "facilitate concession-making without loss of face by the parties, and thereby promote more rapid and effective conflict resolution than would otherwise occur" (p. 380).

A somewhat more organized way to think about the mediation process is to understand the key stages or phases of a mediation. Recall that in Chapter 5 we reviewed phase models of negotiation. Stage models of mediation are no different, and a number of such models have been proposed, most often as important tools for training mediators (see Folberg and Taylor, 1984; Kochan, 1980; Kressel, 1972; Lovenheim 1989; Moore, 1996; Wall, 1981). Figure 13.3 represents a model from a book by mediation expert Christopher Moore (1996). As we noted when we discussed stages of negotiation, stages in the mediation process can be roughly grouped into four categories: premediation preparation (Stages 1–5); beginning stages of the actual mediation (Stages 6 and 7); middle stages of the mediation (Stages 8, 9, and 10); and ending stages of the mediation (Stages 11 and 12). In the premediation stages, the mediator is attempting to get to know the parties, helping them to understand the process that will be followed, and gaining their confidence. The mediator is most concerned with understanding the nature of the dispute and with securing acceptance by the parties. Mediator strategies

FIGURE 13.3   Twelve Stages of Mediator Moves

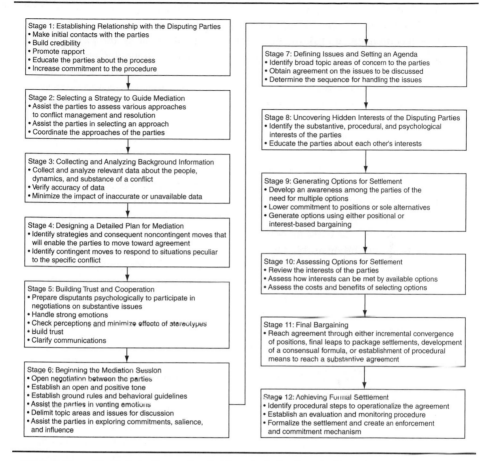

Stage 1: Establishing Relationship with the Disputing Parties
- Make initial contacts with the parties
- Build credibility
- Promote rapport
- Educate the parties about the process
- Increase commitment to the procedure

Stage 2: Selecting a Strategy to Guide Mediation
- Assist the parties to assess various approaches to conflict management and resolution
- Assist the parties in selecting an approach
- Coordinate the approaches of the parties

Stage 3: Collecting and Analyzing Background Information
- Collect and analyze relevant data about the people, dynamics, and substance of a conflict
- Verify accuracy of data
- Minimize the impact of inaccurate or unavailable data

Stage 4: Designing a Detailed Plan for Mediation
- Identify strategies and consequent noncontingent moves that will enable the parties to move toward agreement
- Identify contingent moves to respond to situations peculiar to the specific conflict

Stage 5: Building Trust and Cooperation
- Prepare disputants psychologically to participate in negotiations on substantive issues
- Handle strong emotions
- Check perceptions and minimize effects of stereotypes
- Build trust
- Clarify communications

Stage 6: Beginning the Mediation Session
- Open negotiation between the parties
- Establish an open and positive tone
- Establish ground rules and behavioral guidelines
- Assist the parties in venting emotions
- Delimit topic areas and issues for discussion
- Assist the parties in exploring commitments, salience, and influence

Stage 7: Defining Issues and Setting an Agenda
- Identify broad topic areas of concern to the parties
- Obtain agreement on the issues to be discussed
- Determine the sequence for handling the issues

Stage 8: Uncovering Hidden Interests of the Disputing Parties
- Identify the substantive, procedural, and psychological interests of the parties
- Educate the parties about each other's interests

Stage 9: Generating Options for Settlement
- Develop an awareness among the parties of the need for multiple options
- Lower commitment to positions or sole alternatives
- Generate options using either positional or interest-based bargaining

Stage 10: Assessing Options for Settlement
- Review the interests of the parties
- Assess how interests can be met by available options
- Assess the costs and benefits of selecting options

Stage 11: Final Bargaining
- Reach agreement through either incremental convergence of positions, final leaps to package settlements, development of a consensual formula, or establishment of procedural means to reach a substantive agreement

Stage 12: Achieving Formal Settlement
- Identify procedural steps to operationalize the agreement
- Establish an evaluation and monitoring procedure
- Formalize the settlement and create an enforcement and commitment mechanism

SOURCE: C. Moore, *The Mediation Process: Practical Strategies for Resolving Conflict,* 2nd ed. (San Francisco, CA: Jossey-Bass, 1996), pp. 66–67.

may include separating the parties, questioning them about the issues, and actively listening to each side. The mediator must be able to separate rhetoric from true interest in order to identify each side's priorities. Once this has been accomplished, the mediator may then begin managing the exchange of proposals and counterproposals, testing each side for areas where concessions may be possible.

As mediation progresses, mediators often become increasingly active and aggressive. They may bring the parties together for face-to-face deliberations, or they may continue to keep them separate. They may press one or both sides to make concessions that the mediator judges to be essential. At this stage, mediators use many of the tactics we described in Chapter 12—in essence, doing them for the disputants. They may invent proposals and solutions they think will be acceptable, testing them with each side or even announcing them publicly. Mediators may also use decision support systems to organize the needs and positions of the disputing parties (Mumpower and Rohrbaugh, 1996). The mediator will try to get the parties to agree in private before announcing anything to the public, so that the parties may consult with their constituencies if necessary. If the mediation effort has been successful, the mediator will ultimately bring the parties together to endorse a final agreement or to publicly announce their settlement. Cobb (1993) suggests that effective mediators empower bargainers by balancing power, controlling the process, and being neutral—and that their ability to repackage otherwise thorny exchanges into less confrontational verbiage helps create "descriptions of responsibility without blame" (p. 256).

The influence of "mediator style" has been studied extensively (e.g., Bowling and Hoffman, 2000). In the field of divorce and child custody mediation, Kressel and his associates identified two distinct mediator orientations: a settlement orientation (marked by strict neutrality and a narrow focus on arriving at a specific resolution) and a problem-solving orientation (marked by attempts to deal with underlying problems, and possibly departures from strict neutrality). Participants found the problem-solving orientation to be a more structured, active approach to resolving conflict, and one leading to more frequent and desirable outcomes. It also seemed to produce more positive attitudes toward mediation (Kressel, Frontera, Forlenza, Butler, and Fish, 1994). As mediators involve the parties in more joint problem solving, disputant hostility, especially with regard to intangible issues such as fairness, face-saving, and pride seems to decrease (Zubek, Pruitt, Pierce, McGillicuddy, and Syna, 1992).

Kolb's (1983a) study of mediator styles identified two main types of mediators: "deal makers," whose style was marked by a high degree of issue management, issue packaging, and coordination of exchanges between the parties; and "orchestrators," whose style was less issue-specific but more oriented toward sequencing conversations between the parties. Recent research that has tested and extended Kolb's model suggests that the two mediator styles vary as a function of the degree of third-party control exercised over (1) the process, (2) the outcome, or (3) the motivation of the parties to continue deliberations. Field studies revealed four types of approaches: parties who controlled all three, controlled only outcome and motivation, controlled only process and outcome, and—interestingly enough—controlled none of these (Baker and Ross, 1992). More recent research on mediator style reveals, in fact, that styles vary tremendously in terms of the degree of process and outcome control, with all types and variations depending on the individual and the context in which he or she is mediating (Kolb et al., 1994). What does seem to be emerging, however, is a strong case in favor of mediator flexibility. Botes and Mitchell (1995) suggest that flexibility is a prerequisite for effective mediators, just as it is for negotiators (see the dual concerns model in Chapter 1). In this case, mediator flexibility is defined as decreased constraints, increased freedom of action, increased autonomy, and increased ability to entertain imaginative ideas.

Recognizing that mediators deal with a variety of situations and may choose their behaviors based on what they feel a given situation warrants, Carnevale (1986) developed a "strategic choice model" of mediator behavior. Carnevale proposes that the mixture of high or low levels of two variables—concern for the disputing parties' aspirations and perception of parties' common ground (i.e., areas of agreement)—will produce four basic mediation strategies: problem solving, compensation, pressure, or inaction (see

FIGURE 13.4   Carnevale's Strategic Choice Model of Mediator Behavior

Mediator's Perception of "Common Ground"

	Low	**High**
High	Compensation	Problem solving
Low	Pressure	Inaction

Mediator's Concern for Parties' Aspirations

SOURCE: Adapted from P. J. D. Carnevale, "Strategic Choice in Negotiation," *Negotiation Journal* 2 (1986), pp. 41–56.

Figure 13.4). *Problem solving* (high concern for parties' aspirations, high perception of common ground) takes the form of assisting the parties to engage in integrative exchange, as they would in win-win negotiation in the mediator's absence (see Chapter 4). *Compensation* (high concern for aspirations, low perception of common ground) involves mediator application of rewards and inducements to entice the parties into making concessions and agreements. *Pressure* (low concern for aspirations, low perception of common ground) involves trying to force the parties to reduce their levels of aspiration in the absence of perceived potential for an integrative (win-win) resolution. Finally, *inaction* (low concern for aspirations, high perception of common ground) involves standing back from the dispute, leaving the parties to work things out on their own. Subsequent research has provided support and additional evidence for the model (e.g., Carnevale and Conlon, 1988; Chaudhry and Ross, 1989; Harris and Carnevale, 1990). Some debate exists as to whether Carnevale's (1986) model is complete, however, because it does not take into account power imbalances between parties or the mediator's aspirations (Carnevale, 1992; van de Vliert, 1992). Possible effects of mediator aspirations and preferences on the negotiators' subsequent perceptions and behaviors raise interesting questions about the nature of mediator bias. The results of one study suggest that it comes down to a matter of degree, with mediator alignment (i.e., "unequal rapport, partiality, or bias") falling short of overt support for a particular party or position (Wittmer, Carnevale, and Walker, 1991, p. 595). In this study, disputants were found to distrust even favorable recommendations from mediators whom they saw as biased, while perceived favorable bias was sufficient to offset unfavorable recommendations.

Mediator-applied pressure, mentioned earlier, seems to interact with the type of situation being mediated. Parties who are in disputes marked by high intensity (e.g., major conflicts involving many issues and disagreement over major priorities) and high levels of interparty hostility tend to respond well to forceful, proactive mediation behaviors. In contrast, disputants in low-hostility situations tend to respond better to a less active, more facilitative mediator approach (Donohue, 1989; Hiltrop, 1989; Lim and Carnevale, 1990). When high hostility was accompanied by high levels of problem-solving behavior by the negotiators, mediators assisted best by posing problems, challenging negotiators to solve them, and suggesting new ideas and soliciting negotiator responses to them (Zubek, Pruitt, Pierce, McGillicuddy, and Syna, 1992). These last findings also suggest that mediators may get in the way when negotiators are capable of solving their own problems; although a mediator's forceful intervention and a proactive style may be appropriate when hostility is high, these same qualities may be counterproductive when hostility is low, or even when high hostility is accompanied by high negotiator problem-solving skill (see Hiltrop and Rubin, 1982). In such situations, process consultation (which we discuss later) may be a better intervention choice.

When Is Mediation Effective?   Carnevale and Pruitt (1992) report that "mediation is effective in general—agreements are usually reached, participants are ordinarily satisfied, and compliance is high" (p. 562). They also suggest that mediation effectiveness can be viewed from a variety of perspectives, including the mediator-parties relationship, the relationship between the parties, the issues, and the parties (see Table 13.3). Kressel and Pruitt (1989) report that mediation was effective in about 60 percent of the cases studied, ranging from 20 to 80 percent across a variety of settings; greatest effectiveness occurred in situations marked by only moderate levels of conflict (see Glasl, 1982; Hiltrop and Rubin, 1982). By *moderate conflict,* we mean situations in which tension is apparent and tempers are beginning to fray, but in which negotiations have not deteriorated to the point of physical violence or other irrevocably damaging threats and actions. Disputes beyond the moderate stage are often characterized by drastic actions and reactions, through which the parties harm the relationship beyond repair. Other research suggests that mediation is more effective when negotiators experience a "hurting stalemate" (Touval and Zartman, 1985). Several other studies have shown that mediation is effective only in certain kinds of disputes (see Carnevale and Pruitt, 1992). Kochan and Jick (1978), for example, in their review of mediation in the public sector, report that mediation was most successful in conflicts that involved a breakdown in negotiations due to bargainers' inexperience or over commitment to their positions. In contrast, mediation was less effective when one or both of the negotiating parties had internal conflict, for example, when major differences exist between the demands of a union's rank and file and their chief negotiator's belief about what was attainable at the negotiating table. Mediation was also less effective as a strategy when the parties differed on important economic issues or had major differences in their expectations for a settlement.

In negotiating terms, if the resistance points of the two sides don't overlap (see Chapter 3), then mediators may have to exert greater direct and indirect pressure on the negotiators to create a "positive bargaining zone," or an overlap of resistance points (Stevens, 1963). Direct pressure occurs if the mediator uses tactics to encourage the parties to soften their positions; indirect pressure typically comes through wearing the parties down over time and increasing the cost of holding out. Some mediators achieve results by being aggressive (Johnson, 1993) and applying pressure on the negotiators to settle or to consider options (Kolb, 1983a, 1983b). It appears that mediation is not always effective in

TABLE 13.3   Aspects of Effective Mediation

Mediator-parties relationship
  Improve acceptance of mediation by the parties.
  Increase parties' trust in the mediator.

Relationship between the parties
  Control communication between the parties.
  Have separate meetings with the parties to influence them.

The issues
  Uncovering the underlying interests and concerns.
  Setting agendas.
  Packaging, sequencing, and prioritizing agenda items.
  Interpreting and shaping proposals.
  Making suggestions for possible settlements.

The parties
  Helping parties save face when making concessions.
  Helping parties resolve internal disagreements.
  Helping parties deal with constituents.
  Applying positive incentives for agreement or concession making.

SOURCE: Adapted from P. J. D. Carnevale and Dean G. Pruitt, "Negotiation and Mediation," *Annual Review of Psychology* 43 (1992), pp. 531–42.

highly intense conflicts (Rubin, 1980), such as those in which many issues are at stake or the parties disagree on major priorities. Again, under such conditions, mediation tactics may be insufficient to move the parties toward mutual agreement.

Zubek, Pruitt, Pierce, McGillicuddy, and Syna (1992) examined the process and outcome of 73 hearings at two community dispute resolution centers. They found that some mediator behaviors were perceived as positively related to mediation success, some as negatively related, and others as unrelated to mediation success. For instance, mediator behaviors positively related to successful mediation included demonstrating empathy, structuring discussions, (creating and controlling the agenda), helping the parties establish priorities, and maintaining calm, friendly, but firm control over the mediation process. On the other hand, mediator behaviors negatively related to mediation success included displaying expertise, criticizing, and asking embarrassing questions. Finally, mediator behaviors unrelated to mediation success included providing reassurance, order keeping, and mediator experience.

Gibson, Thompson, and Bazerman (1996) took a different approach to examining mediator effectiveness by analyzing common cognitive errors made by mediators. The results of their analysis led them to generate "symmetric prescriptive advice" for mediators, including to:

Push for agreement only when a positive bargaining zone exists (see Chapter 3).

Search for "fully efficient" agreements (i.e., "there exists no other outcome or set of outcomes that at least one party prefers and toward which the other party would at least be indifferent," p. 74).

Help the parties think through the issue(s) of fairness.

Avoid reaching an agreement for "agreement's sake" (the agreement-is-good bias).

Avoid accepting the first agreement discovered (the first acceptable agreement may not be the best agreement).

Avoid the 50-50 split if it doesn't treat both parties equally.

Trading Off the Advantages and Disadvantages of Arbitration versus Mediation

It should be clear from this review that both mediation and arbitration have their advantages and disadvantages. The disadvantages of arbitration include:

- Negative consequences for negotiators when they anticipate a third-party intervention (e.g., chilling and narcotic effects).
- Removal of outcome control from negotiators.
- Possible lack of commitment to implementing the imposed outcome.

The disadvantages of mediation include:

- Lack of impetus or initiative to adhere to any particular settlement or to settle at all.
- Possible perpetuation of the dispute, perhaps indefinitely.
- Possible escalation of the dispute into more damaging, more costly forms.

Several researchers have proposed that combining mediation and arbitration into a two-stage dispute resolution model may minimize the disadvantages of each (Grigsby, 1981; Grigsby and Bigoness, 1982; Starke and Notz, 1981). Starke and Notz proposed that mediation, as a preliminary step to arbitration, should have a complementary and facilitating effect, but only when the arbitration is of the final-offer format. In conventional arbitration, the parties expect a compromise ruling by the arbitrator; because mediation also promises a compromise, the parties may choose to wait for the arbitration ruling rather than make concessions during mediation, when a conventional arbitration rule is used. In contrast, under the expectation of final-offer arbitration, mediation provides the parties with an incentive to evaluate the reasonableness of their current positions. As a result, they may be more willing to modify their positions prior to expected arbitration to improve their chances that the arbitrator will rule in favor of their side. Efforts to test these assertions have been mixed. In a laboratory study of arbitration and negotiation, Grigsby and Bigoness (1982, also see Grigsby, 1981) found that anticipated mediation reduced the chilling effect in negotiators expecting final-offer-by-issue arbitration, but negotiators expecting conventional arbitration, final-offer-by-package arbitration, or no arbitration were more subject to the chilling effect when they were anticipating mediation as an intervening step. Other studies have suggested that final-offer arbitration resulted in resolution of a larger number of issues than conventional arbitration and encouraged higher value concessions by the negotiators (Neale and Bazerman, 1983).

Ross and Conlon (2000) have summarized much of this work and acknowledged that there is still a great deal to be done. They argued that current research can help us suggest conditions under which mediation might be preferred to precede arbitration, and the conditions under which arbitration might be preferred to precede mediation. They propose that mediation followed by arbitration (referred to as "med-arb") might be preferred because:

1. Disputants would prefer the procedure, because they will have more influence over the process early in the dispute resolution effort.
2. The process might move faster, because mediation might resolve the case before it has to go through a longer, more formal arbitration process.
3. The cost of the settlement process might be lower (for the same reason).
4. The disputants might be more likely to see the process as fairer, because they had more voice and more process control in the mediation phase before the issue went to arbitration.
5. There might be greater compliance with mediation-arbitration decisions, again because of the feelings of satisfaction and fairness generated by participation in the earlier mediation process.

In contrast, they propose that arbitration followed by mediation ("arb-med") might be preferred for these reasons:

1. Disputants will have lowered expectations for settlement and be more reasonable in their expectations for the outcome, because the arbitrator's decision is likely to be more "reasonable" than the parties' initial expectations.
2. Disputants will engage in more cooperative behavior, because their expectations will be lower (see previous point) and they will more anxious to please the arbitrator.
3. Because they are likely to be more cooperative, disputants will reveal more confidential information in arb-med.
4. Disputants will be more responsive to suggestions for settlement presented by a mediator, because they fear complete loss if the arbitration decision is revealed.
5. Disputants will also agree to specific mediator settlement proposals more frequently, for the same reason.
6. There will be more voluntary settlements in the mediation phase under arb-med, in order to avoid the uncertainty of an arbitration judgment.
7. Mediated settlements will be of higher quality, because of the greater sharing of information in this particular sequence.

Note that these propositions build upon the work of Sheppard (1984) (Figure 13.2) mentioned earlier. Moreover, as we will note later in this chapter (e.g., Elangovan, 1995a, Figure 13.6), situational factors will also help to dictate when one combined approach may be favored over the other.

Process Consultation

A third formal approach to the resolution of disputes is *process consultation* (Walton, 1987), which has been defined as "a set of activities on the part of the consultant that helps the client to perceive, understand, and act upon the process events which occur in the client's environment" (Schein, 1987, p. 34). As used here, the objective of process consultation is to defuse the emotional aspect of conflict and improve communication between the parties, leaving them with renewed or enhanced abilities to manage future disputes.

The difference between mediation and process consultation is that mediators are at least somewhat concerned with addressing the issues in the dispute (i.e., the deal-making style described earlier, per Kolb, 1983a), whereas process consultants focus only on improving communication and conflict management procedures (similar to Kolb's orchestration style). Process consultants assume that teaching the parties how to manage conflict more productively and effectively will lead them to produce better outcomes. The purpose of the third party's intervention is to create the foundation for productive dialogue over substantive issues and to teach the parties how to prevent conflicts from escalating destructively in the future.

Process Consultation Behaviors.   Process consultants usually employ a variety of tactics. Their first step is often to separate the parties and interview them individually to determine each side's view of the other side, position, and a history of the relationship and its conflicts. The consultant uses this information gathered in the diagnostic phase to structure a series of dialogues or confrontations between the parties (Walton, 1987). These meetings are designed specifically to address the causes of past conflicts and each side's perceptions of the other. Meetings are held on neutral turf, and who should attend and what issues should be discussed are planned ahead of time. The purpose of the third party is to encourage the negotiators to confront their differences and the reasons for them. The process consultant is the referee, timekeeper, and gatekeeper of the process, working to keep the parties on track while also ensuring that the conflict does not escalate. Finally, the third party directs all sides toward some type of problem solving and integration, assuming that by confronting and airing their differences the parties can create a format for working on their substantive differences in the future and can pursue this agenda without a recurrence of unproductive escalation. The process consultant works to change the climate for conflict management, promote constructive dialogue around differences of opinion, and create the capacity for other people to act as their own third parties.

This description of successful process consultation suggests that process consultants should possess many of the same attributes that we have ascribed to other third parties. First, they should be perceived as experts in the technique, knowledgeable about conflict and its dynamics, able to be emotionally supportive while confronting the parties, and able to diagnose the dispute. Second, they should be perceived as clearly neutral, without bias toward one side or the other. Third, they should be authoritative—that is, able to establish power over the process that the conflicting parties are pursuing, thereby intervening in and controlling it. Although they do not attempt to impose a particular solution or outcome, process consultants must be able to shape the manner in which the parties interact, separating them or bringing them together, and to control the agenda that they follow when interaction occurs. Without such control, the parties will resort to their earlier pattern of destructive hostility.

The primary focus of process consultation is to teach the parties how to resolve substantive differences themselves, not to resolve their differences for them. Thus, process consultation goes the farthest in putting the issues under dispute back in the hands of the disputing parties. To make process consultation work, however, the parties must be able to manage their own potentially destructive conflict processes in order to be able to work through these substantive differences—something that is frequently very hard for them to do.

Process consultation has been used most commonly to improve long-standing relationships that the parties want to continue. Marital and family therapy are forms of process consultation, as are organizational development and team building among work groups. Process consultation has also been tried in labor–management relationships and in international conflict among ethnic, political, and cultural groups such as Protestants and Catholics in Northern Ireland, or Palestinians and Israelis in the Middle East (Kelman, 1996). Many of the early efforts at process consultation in these environments were less than completely successful (Benjamin and Levi, 1979; Boehringer, Zeruolis, Bayley, and Boehringer, 1974; Brown, 1977; Cohen, Kelman, Miller, and Smith, 1977; Hill, 1982; Lewicki and Alderfer, 1973). However, these research studies have contributed to a better understanding of process consultation in the following ways:

1. Process consultation is less likely to work as an intervention technique when the parties are deeply locked in a dispute over one or more major unresolved issues. Because process consultation seeks to change the nature of the working relationship between the parties, it may only work before the parties are in open conflict, or between major outbreaks of hostility (Walton, 1987).

2. Process consultation may be an ineffective technique when dealing with short-term relationships. There is probably little need to teach parties to resolve disputes effectively when they will not be working together in the future.

3. Process consultation may be ineffective when the substantive issues in the dispute are distributive, or zero-sum. The objectives of process consultation are to improve both the relationship and the skills for integrative bargaining. If the nature of the dispute or constituency pressures on the bargainers do not encourage and support the integrative process, then process consultation is not likely to be effective. Divisive issues or constituency pressures to maintain a hard-line stance will constantly undermine efforts at process consultation.

4. Process consultation may be ineffective when the level of conflict is so high that the parties are more intent on revenge or retribution than on reconciliation. (See our discussion of forceful mediation intervention in the previous section.) In effect, process consultation may work only when sustained conflict has worn the parties out, making them want resolution more than continued warfare, or when the parties sincerely want to coexist but do not have the skills to do so. If the parties do not have sufficient incentive to work together, efforts at process consultation will be undermined. One side will exploit trust, cooperation, and honesty, and the dispute will quickly escalate.

In contrast, a great deal has been learned in the last decade about when process consultation is likely to be successful, and how it can work most effectively. A number of leading practitioners have detailed procedures for using facilitation to structure dialogue between parties, move them toward problem solving, and transform their relationship. Kelman (1996) conducted a large number of interactive problem-solving workshops between Israelis and Palestinians, and describes how the process not only improves the relationship between the parties but also improves the basis for larger negotiations between the two groups. Mitchell and Banks (1996) provide a useful roadmap for how the workshop model can be used, and offer a number of specific exercises and activities that can be used to bring strongly adversarial groups together. Finally, Bunker and Alban (1997) reviewed a variety of large group interventions, in which the objective is to bring together many diverse groups, stakeholders, or constituencies in order to coordinate and facilitate systemwide planning and change. Bunker and Alban show how facilitation and process consultant techniques can be applied to organizational development in order to enhance the ability of large groups and systems to coordinate change efforts in a single planning initiative.

INFORMAL INTERVENTION METHODS

In this chapter we have reviewed several major approaches used by third parties to resolve disputes. These approaches—arbitration, mediation, and process consultation—represent formal approaches to the resolution of disputes, and they are the three most commonly described in the research on third-party behavior. However, other third-party approaches are possible, most of them used informally by managers, parents, counselors, and others who become involved in other people's disputes. Sheppard (1984) proposed a generic classification of third-party intervention procedures. Rather than prescribing how managers should intervene in conflicts, Sheppard's model describes how they actually do intervene. The model was developed from an earlier model proposed by Thibaut and Walker (1975) to describe the psychological aspects of procedural justice systems (e.g., courts or tribunals). Thibaut and Walker conceived of dispute resolution as involving two stages: a procedural or process stage, in which evidence and arguments are gathered and presented, and an outcome or decision stage, in which the evidence is evaluated to determine which party the weight of evidence favors. They then distinguished among major conflict intervention styles based on the amount of process control, decision control, or both used by the third party. These two approaches to control may be thought of as independent dimensions of conflict intervention, and a third party may exert varying amounts of each in handling a dispute. For our current purposes, we shall simply refer to situations where a third party exerts high or low amounts of process or decision control and represent the possibilities in matrix form (refer back to Figure 13.2). Sheppard (1983) asked practicing managers to describe the last time they intervened in a dispute between their subordinates and then coded their responses according to the amount of process and decision control the third party used. He concluded that managers use one of three dominant styles when they intervene in a subordinate conflict (see Figure 13.5):

1. *Inquisitorial intervention.* This was the most common style. A manager who uses inquisitorial intervention exerts high control over both the process and the decision. She tells both sides to present their cases, asks lots of questions to probe

FIGURE 13.5   Managerial Third-Party Intervention Styles

Degree of Managerial Outcome Control

	High	**Low**
High	Inquisitorial Intervention	Mediational Intervention
Low	Adversarial Intervention	Providing Impetus

(Row labels under "Degree of Managerial Process Control")

SOURCE: Adapted from B. H. Sheppard, "Managers as Inquisitors: Some Lessons from the Law," in M. Bazerman and R. J. Lewicki, eds. *Negotiating in Organizations* (Beverly Hills, CA: Sage Publications, 1983).

into each side's position, and frequently controls who is allowed to speak and what they say. She then invents a solution that she thinks will meet both parties' needs and usually enforces that solution on both parties. Inquisitorial intervention is a judicial style of handling conflicts that is found most commonly in European courtrooms.

2. *Adversarial intervention.* Managers who use adversarial intervention exert high control over the decision, but not the process. The manager does not control the process in that he does not ask questions, try to get the whole story, or control the destructive aspects of the conflict between the parties. Instead, he passively listens to what each side chooses to tell him and then makes a decision (tells the parties how to solve the conflict) based exclusively on the presentations. This style is most similar to the style used by most American courtroom judges.

3. *Providing impetus.* Managers who provide impetus typically do not exert control over the decision, and they exert only a small amount of control over the process. The manager typically tries to make a quick diagnosis of what the conflict is about and then tells the parties that if they don't find a solution, she will impose one on them. In short, the manager first asks, "What's going on here?" When she finds out what's going on, she says, "You'd better solve this problem, or else I'll solve it for you, and neither of you will like the solution!"

Which Approach Is More Effective?

Sheppard's research indicates that managers spontaneously tend to act like an inquisitorial judge or an arbitrator, or to provide a common enemy by threatening to settle the dispute for the parties in an undesirable way if they can't settle it themselves. Note that the remaining cell in Figure 13.5, which we have labeled "mediational intervention," is the mediation style we have described above, but not a style commonly observed among managers. Although subsequent research on how managers act has shown that managers claim to prefer mediation as a third-party style (Lewicki and Sheppard, 1985), it is not clear that managers actually use mediation unless they are specifically trained in the process. When handling a conflict, managers seem to assume that because the parties cannot seem to resolve the dispute on their own, the manager must primarily deal with the outcome of their conflict (see Sheppard, Blumenfeld-Jones, Minton, and Hyder, 1994). Therefore, managers may be very uncomfortable using a mediation strategy that, by Sheppard's definition, requires them to control the process of conflict but leaves the solution in the hands of the disputants. Managers often think they mediate, but when observed in actual situations they seem to exert far more control over the outcome than would be recommended by the formal mediation process we have described thus far.

Sheppard's work has generated a growing body of research on informal managerial dispute intervention. Elangovan (1995a; 1998) has expanded and enhanced Sheppard's work in a variety of ways. More specifically, Elangovan has developed a prescriptive model to guide managers in choosing intervention strategies (see Figure 13.6). Elangovan's model is premised on a similar model of managerial decision making developed by Vroom and Yetton (1973). The model attempts to provide a decision tree in which potential third parties need to ask a series of diagnostic questions about the dispute (see the questions at the top of Figure 13.6). Based on whether the dispute is judged to be high or low on each of these questions, the potential third party arrives at an end point on the decision tree that prescribes a particular style. These styles—described as means-control, ends-control, full control, part control, and low control—are similar to the styles described in Figures 13.2 and 13.5, except that Elangovan explicitly chooses not to use the more common terms *mediation* and *arbitration* to describe these styles (see Table 13.4 for his description of the styles). Rather, Elangovan prefers to describe the degrees of outcome and process control, which provides more precision about what the third party should do, while avoiding value-laden terms like *arbitration* or *mediation,* which may be confusing because of their numerous variations and forms. Extending his thinking to the global environment, Elangovan (1995b) has also done preliminary work on the role that culture plays in third-party intervention processes. His studies show that preferences for third-party intervention vary as a function of cultural differences, as one might predict from Hofstede's categories of cross-cultural differences (see Chapter 11).

In other work on the key factors that motivate a third party to assume a particular style, Pinkley and her colleagues (Pinkley, Brittain, Neale, and Northcraft, 1995) found evidence that judgments along five key dimensions could account for a manager's choice of intervention. Those five dimensions were:

1. The amount of attention the manager gives to the parties' statements of the issues in dispute rather than trying to deal with underlying problems.
2. The degree of voluntary (versus mandated) acceptance of the solution proposed by the third party.
3. Third-party versus disputant control over shaping the outcomes.
4. The third party's personal approach to, or avoidance of, conflict (see Chapter 10).
5. Whether the dispute is to be handled publicly or privately.

FIGURE 13.6   A Prescriptive Model for Managerial Dispute Intervention

DI   How important is this dispute to the effective functioning of the organization?
TP   How important is it to resolve the dispute as quickly as possible?
ND   Does the dispute concern the interpretation of existing rules, procedures, and
      arrangements or the changing of existing rules, procedures, and arrangements?
NR   What is the expected frequency of future work-related interactions between the
      disputants?
CP   If you were to impose a settlement on your subordinates (disputants), what is the
      probability that they would be committed to it?
DO   What is the orientation of the disputants? That is, if you were to let your subordinates
      (disputants) settle the dispute, what is the probability that they would come to an
      organizationally compatible settlement?

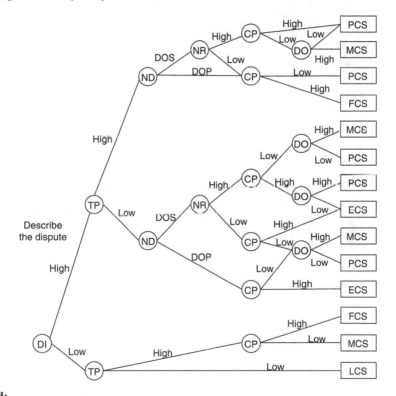

Legend:

MCS = Means-control strategy
ECS = Ends-control strategy
LCS = Low control strategy
FCS = Full control strategy
PCS = Part control strategy

SOURCE: Reprinted with permission of Academy of Management, P. O. Box 3020, Briarcliff Manor, NY 10510-8020. From A. R. Elangovan, "Managerial Third-Party Dispute Intervention: A Prescriptive Model of Strategy Selection," *Academy of Management Review* 20, no. 4 (1995), p. 820. Reproduced by permission of the publisher via Copyright Clearance Center.

TABLE 13.4   Managerial Dispute Intervention Strategies

MCS   Means-control strategy: Manager intervenes in the dispute by influencing the process of resolution (i.e., facilitates interaction, assists in communication, explains one disputant's views to another, clarifies issues, lays down rules for dealing with the dispute, maintains order during talks) but does not attempt to dictate or impose a resolution (though he or she might suggest solutions); the final decision is left to the disputants; high on process control but low on outcome control (e.g., mediation, conciliation).

ECS   Ends-control strategy: Manager intervenes in the dispute by influencing the outcome (i.e., takes full control of the final resolution, decides what the final decision will be, imposes the resolution on the disputants) but does not attempt to influence the process; the disputants have control over what information is presented and how it is presented; high on outcome control but low on process control (e.g., arbitration, adjudication, adversarial intervention).

LCS   Low control strategy: Manager does not intervene actively in resolving the dispute; he or she either urges the parties to settle the dispute on their own or merely stays away from the dispute; low on both process and outcome control (e.g., encouraging or telling the parties to negotiate or settle the dispute by themselves, providing impetus).

FCS   Full control strategy: Manager intervenes in the dispute by influencing the process and outcome (i.e., decides what information is to be presented and how it should be presented and also decides on the final resolution); he or she asks the disputants specific questions about the dispute to obtain information and imposes a resolution; manager has full control of the resolution of the dispute; high on both process and outcome control (e.g., inquisitorial intervention, autocratic intervention).

PCS   Part control strategy: Manager intervenes in the dispute by sharing control over the process and outcome with the disputants (i.e., manager and disputants jointly agree on the process of resolution as well as strive for a consensus on the settlement decision); he or she works with the disputants to help them arrive at a solution by facilitating interaction, assisting in communication, discussing the issues, and so on. In addition, he or she takes an active role in evaluating options, recommending solutions, persuading the disputants to accept solutions, pushing for a settlement; moderate on managerial process and outcome control (e.g., group problem solving, mediation/arbitration).

SOURCE: Reprinted with permission of Academy of Management, P. O. Box 3020, Briarcliff Manor, NY 10510-8020. From A. R. Elangovan, "Managerial Third-Party Dispute Intervention: A Prescriptive Model of Strategy Selection," *Academy of Management Review* 20, no. 4 (1995), p. 807. Reproduced by permission of the publisher via Copyright Clearance Center.

It is clear that managers and others in authority usually have the right to intervene in dispute. Not only are they likely to be interested in workplace disputes and their resolutions, but they usually have the power to involve themselves. Conlon, Carnevale, and Murnighan (1994) found that managers-as-third-parties did choose to impose outcomes about two-thirds of the time in the sample studied, and even more often when they perceived the disputants as being uncooperative. This is consistent with other empirical findings related to managerial dispute intervention (e.g., Sheppard, Blumenfeld-Jones, Minton, and Hyder, 1994). Watkins and Winters (1997) have extended this model to illustrate some of the dilemmas associated with each intervention style.

There is reasonably strong evidence that the net benefit would be positive if mediation were used more often as an informal third-party intervention style than it is currently used. Karambayya and Brett (1989), studying classroom simulations, found that managers do assume a number of roles, depending on how they diagnose the situation. They found general support for Sheppard's (1983, 1984) research and reported that mediation in particular led to fairer outcomes than did other forms of dispute resolution, and was perceived to be a fairer process by disputants, lending support to Brett and Rognes's (1986) advice that managers should act as mediators when acting as third parties. More recent research by Karambayya, Brett, and Lytle (1992), again using classroom subjects, found that managers were most likely to intervene in autocratic or mediational manners, but that relative authority and experience had distinct effects. Experience aside, third parties in authority over the disputants were more likely to be autocratic than those who were not in authority, and peer interveners were no more likely to be mediator-like. Autocratic interventions tended to produce one-sided outcomes and impasses, whereas mediational interventions tended to produce compromises. It is likely that managers' failure to use mediation more extensively is due to beliefs about the managerial role, in that managers have a tendency to frame conflicts as hands-on opportunities and this may cause them to decide not to mediate (Sheppard Blumenfeld-Jones, Minton, and Hyder, 1994). Interveners with greater managerial experience, though, were significantly less likely to be autocratic than those with less experience, and third parties with both authority and more experience tended to exhibit the most mediational behavior in the study group.

Finally, research by Conlon and Fasolo (1990) suggests that, although mediational interventions may be preferable to autocratic ones, timing may be critical. More specifically, the speed of intervention (i.e., earlier versus later in the dispute) was found to affect disputants' perceptions of procedural fairness. Quick interventions tended to produce disputant feelings of lack of control and loss of voice—that is, the negotiators felt they had lost their ability to have a say and present their case to their satisfaction. Disputants also expressed lower satisfaction with third-party interventions that they felt were inappropriate due to violations of due process; in other words, negotiators were not satisfied when they felt that they were denied access to normal procedural steps and safeguards.

The most extensive treatment of the role that third parties can play in informal dispute resolution and conflict management can be found in William Ury's (2000) recent book *The Third Side*. Ury describes 10 roles that third parties can play to help others resolve their disputes (see Table 13.5, right column). In addition, Ury suggests that third parties can influence conflict at three general stages: (1) prevent conflicts, where interventions inhibit latent conflict from emerging; (2) resolve conflict, where conflicts that have emerged are managed; and (3) contain conflict, where ongoing conflicts that have been a challenge to resolve are contained. Each of these stages and potential third-party roles will be discussed in more detail below.

Conflict may escalate at the "prevent" stage for three reasons: (1) frustrated needs; (2) poor skills; and (3) weak relationships (see Table 13.5). Humans have several fundamental needs (e.g., security, love, recognition) and frequently the blocking of these needs can lead to conflict. The role of the Provider is to enable others to fulfill their needs. For instance, a good manager should ensure that her staff receives positive recognition for

TABLE 13.5   Ten Roles Third Parties Play

Why Conflict Escalates	*Ways to Transform Conflict*
Prevent	
Frustrated needs	The Provider
Poor skills	The Teacher
Weak relationships	The Bridge-Builder
Resolve	
Conflicting interests	The Mediator
Disputed rights	The Arbiter
Unequal power	The Equalizer
Injured relationships	The Healer
Contain	
No attention	The Witness
No limitation	The Referee
No protection	The Peacekeeper

SOURCE: From William Ury, *The Third Side* (New York: Penguin, 2000), p. 190.

their work with regular merit increments or promotions in order that the staff do not become disgruntled and create conflicts at work. Conflicts can also results from poor conflict management skills and intolerance of differences of opinion. The role of the Teacher is to educate people in the skills of managing differences and conflict. Weak relationships are another source of conflict that third parties may help to prevent escalating. The role of the Bridge-Builder is to find ways to bring parties together to improve relationships in order to prevent conflict from escalating. For instance, a manager may assign members of two office factions to the same project teams in order to create ties across the office.

Conflict may escalate at the "resolve" stage for four reasons: (1) conflicting interests; (2) disputed rights; (3) unequal power; and (4) injured relationships (see Table 13.5). The role of the Mediator is to help parties reconcile their differences of opinion by opening channels of communication between parties and helping them search for their own solution. The role of the Arbiter is to choose from opposing positions when disputing parties are unable to decide for themselves. For instance, a manager may choose which of two marketing plans the organization will adopt when her subordinates are divided on which to support. The role of the Equalizer is to ensure that the voices of weaker parties are heard when resolving conflicts. For instance, the influence of quiet members of a project team may be minimized unless the Equalizer takes action to ensure that they are heard. The role of the Healer is to ensure that the emotional aftermath of a conflict is managed so that it does not become the source of a future conflict. For instance, after an angry dispute between two co-workers has been settled, the Healer may still need to listen to both parties and help them deal with residual hurt feelings that could lead to further conflict.

Conflict may escalate at the "contain" stage for three reasons: (1) lack of attention; (2) lack of limitation; and (3) lack of protection. The role of the Witness is to contain escalating conflict by watching and remembering the events that occur in his or her presence. The mere presence of a neutral witness can act to contain conflict because people are often less willing to escalate a conflict when witnesses are present. The role of the Referee is to place limits on the extent to which behaviors are tolerated. For instance, the Referee may endorse harsh, pointed words but not sanction physical violence in an argument. The role of the Peacekeeper is to intervene in a dispute to prevent violence, or to stop it once it occurs. The United Nations plays this role between warring states, but it is also a role that individuals may play between hostile individuals.

Taken as a whole, Ury's model is a very creative way of looking at third-party interventions, formal or informal, in any kind of conflict. This is not a stage model in the sense that third parties should act in a prescribed order when dealing with conflict. Rather, Ury notes that different disputes will require different interventions, and that third parties will find themselves using different interventions in different sequences depending on the challenges that they face. Ury does offer one clear piece of advice that is appropriate for all third parties, however: "Contain if necessary, resolve if possible, best of all prevent" (2000, p. 113).

Although research findings suggest that negotiators should increase their use of mediation as an informal third-party intervention, further research is necessary. More attention needs to be focused on determining how managers can better identify mediational opportunities, how they can learn to mediate more effectively, and whether the managerial findings of recent research are true for third parties in other conflict situations (e.g., among peers or friends).

DISPUTE RESOLUTION SYSTEMS: WHEN THE ORGANIZATION IS THE THIRD PARTY

From an organizational standpoint, conflict seems inevitable, and perhaps a certain type and level of conflict is healthy and advisable. It has been our position throughout this book that conflict resolution is best left to the disputants. This chapter addresses a variety of situations, though, that sometimes call for a departure from that standard—such as when disputants are incapable of self-resolution or when the consequences of ongoing, unresolved conflict become damaging. So it is with organizations. Conflict costs for organizations include the following:

- Wasted time and money, emotional damage, drained energy, and lost opportunities (see Box 13.4).
- Potentially low levels of disputant satisfaction.
- Potential damage to necessary relationships.
- The likelihood of conflict spreading and/or recurring. (Brett, Goldberg, and, Ury 1990)

The glow of a resolved dispute is not likely to last forever because "resolving a dispute will not alter the underlying conflict of interests that generated the dispute. As long

---

BOX 13.4
Peers Decide Co-worker's Fate

A waitress in a Red Lobster restaurant was accused of stealing a guest comment card from the comment card box at the restaurant where she worked. The comment card complained that the prime rib was "rare" and their waitress had been "uncooperative." Ms. Hatton, a 19-year veteran of the restaurant, said she intended to show the comment card to her boss, not to steal it. But because the boss discovered the card missing when the customers verbally complained as well, she fired Ms. Hatton. In Ms. Hatton's words, being fired felt like "a knife going through me."

Normally, workers who feel that they have been unjustly treated will take legal action and sue the restaurant. But Red Lobster is one of a growing number of employers who permit fired or disciplined workers to appeal to a peer review panel of co-workers, who can hear testimony, overturn management decisions, and even award damages. So a general manager, an assistant manager, a server, a hostess, and a bartender, all of whom worked for other Red Lobster restaurants, met to decide Ms. Hatton's fate. And Ms. Hatton enthusiastically chose the peer review procedure, because she said it was a lot cheaper and she felt better being judged by people who knew how things work in a small restaurant. The panel interviewed the general manager, Ms. Hatton, and the hostess, reconstructing the events that occurred and what the parties had said and done that day. After an hour and a half of deliberation, they unanimously restored Ms. Hatton's job. They said she had done all she could in trying to placate the unhappy customers, and that the unofficial policy against reading the contents of a comment card box had not been enforced at the restaurant. But because the policy had been violated, they decided to punish Ms. Hatton by not granting her the three weeks of lost wages she also sought. The waitress was happy with the decision, the restaurant counsel said that the panel had made the right choice, and the restaurant manager was cooperative and helpful when Ms. Hatton returned to her job.

Darden Industries, the company that owns the Red Lobster chain, adopted peer reviews in 1994. In four years, the company estimates that it had saved $1 million in legal fees set aside for handling employee disputes. They said about 100 cases per year went to peer review. The program has also been credited with reducing racial tension between workers and customers.

SOURCE: Adapted from Margaret A. Jacobs, "Red Lobster Tale: Peers Decide Fired Waitress's Fate," *The Wall Street Journal*, January 20, 1998, pp. B1, B6.

---

as the relationship endures, future disputes will arise" (Brett et al., 1990, p 164). Beginning in the 1980s, many large organizations experimented with alternative dispute resolution (ADR) systems, but the results have been mixed. These systems incorporate many of the third-party approaches we have described in this chapter, as well as other hybrid variations and forms. For example, Costantino and Merchant (1996) suggest six broad categories of ADR options (see Figure 13.7):

1. *Preventive ADR systems* are those that companies put in to prevent disputes. For example, companies can build clauses into contracts so that any dispute automatically goes to ADR; the company can also specify a number of ways for parties to meet and problem-solve if disputes occur.

FIGURE 13.7   Dynamics of ADR Techniques

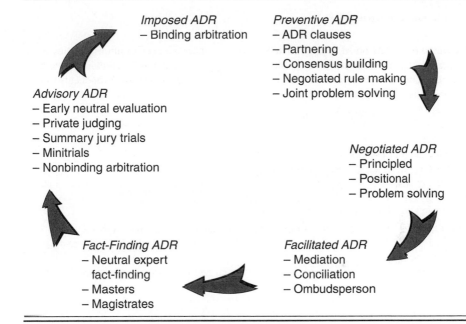

Imposed ADR
– Binding arbitration

Preventive ADR
– ADR clauses
– Partnering
– Consensus building
– Negotiated rule making
– Joint problem solving

Advisory ADR
– Early neutral evaluation
– Private judging
– Summary jury trials
– Minitrials
– Nonbinding arbitration

Negotiated ADR
– Principled
– Positional
– Problem solving

Fact-Finding ADR
– Neutral expert
  fact-finding
– Masters
– Magistrates

Facilitated ADR
– Mediation
– Conciliation
– Ombudsperson

SOURCE: From C. A. Costantino and C. S. Merchant, *Designing Conflict Management Systems* (San Francisco: Jossey-Bass, 1996), p. 38.

2. *Negotiated ADR systems* are mechanisms that allow the parties to resolve their own disputes without the help of any third party, using the negotiation processes we discussed earlier in this book.

3. *Facilitated ADR systems* provide a third-party neutral (an ombudsperson) who assists the parties in negotiating a resolution. We have described mediation and process consultation, and will discuss ombudspersons in the next few paragraphs.

4. *Fact-Finding ADR systems* use the technical expertise of third parties to determine the facts in a specific situation and how the facts should be interpreted. The parties usually agree in advance about whether they are going to abide by the information or conclusion provided by the fact-finder.

5. *Advisory ADR systems* use the expertise of a third party to determine what the resolution would likely be if the dispute went to arbitration, court, and so on. In this approach, each party can get a realistic idea of how strong the other's case is, and what the arbitrator or judge might do, without having to pay the full cost of that process or actually live with the outcome.

6. *Imposed ADR systems* are those in which the third party makes a binding decision that the parties must live with. Binding arbitration is the most common form of imposed ADR.

According to Carver and Vondra (1994), there is both good and bad news about ADR. The good news is that many companies have learned to use ADR effectively, and

---

BOX 13.5
If Only There Were a Better Way . . .

Interested in starting an ADR program in your organization? Cathy Costantino, writing in the periodical *Government Executive,* shared her experience in doing just that in her work with the Federal Deposit Insurance Corporation (FDIC). She advises that proponents follow 10 steps in establishing ADR programs:

1. Identify the stakeholders in the process.
2. Assess the current system.
3. Clarify your goals.
4. Obtain buy-in from management and disputants.
5. Select the types of ADR to use and the types of cases to use them on.
6. Train and educate both operators and users.
7. Maximize the incentives to use the system, and minimize the constraints.
8. Launch a pilot program.
9. Measure the pilot program's results.
10. Make modifications and implement thoroughly.

SOURCE: Adapted from C. A. Costantino, "How to Set Up an ADR Program," *Government Executive,* 26 (1994), pp. 44–47.

---

that they are reaping the benefits of the process: an immense savings of time and money, and relationships that are not destroyed and may in fact be improved by the process (for example see Bourdeaux, O'Leary, and Thorburgh, 2001). What makes ADR effective, these authors note, is the commitment of the company to make it work as an alternative to litigation with employees, customers, suppliers, regulators, and so on (see Box 13.5). The bad news is that many systems that start out as well-intended efforts to handle employee conflict are poorly designed and poorly operated, often mutating "into a private judicial system that looks and costs like the litigation it's supposed to prevent" (p. 120). Carver and Vondra identify the following factors that can undermine ADR in some companies:

- Some people believe that winning is the only thing that matters, rather than settling of disputes (or, conversely, some people use ADR only when they believe that they cannot win in court).
- Some people (particularly attorneys) see ADR as an alternative to litigation, rather than the preferred alternative.
- Some people see ADR as nothing more than litigation in disguise.

Several authors have suggested some of the key factors that should drive the design of an effective dispute resolution system (e.g., Brett, Goldberg, and Ury, 1990; Costantino and Merchant, 1996; Lynch, 2001; Sheppard, Lewicki, and Minton, 1992; Ury, Brett, and Goldberg, 1988). One is to make sure that the parties understand what their choices are before they begin using a particular procedure, to ensure that any procedure chosen is well understood by disputants, and that low-cost options are tried first. Second, it appears that users need to be involved in the design of alternate dispute resolution systems in order for them to be effective (Carter, 1999). A third is to appoint, train, and support individuals (e.g., ombudsmen) to advise and assist disputants in dispute resolution (Gadlin, 2000; Stieber, 2000). An ombudsman is typically charged with being "a confidential and informed information resource, communications channel, complaint-handler, and a person who helps an organization work for change" (Rowe, 1995, p. 103). Ombudsmen traditionally are generators of options, working in strict confidentiality to assist disputants by serving as "mediators, counselors, and third-party interveners" (Rowe, p. 105). Finally, McEwen (1999) suggests that the way to improve alternative dispute resolution systems is through systematic research and suggests several directions that this research should take.

Should the organization decide to take a more expansive approach, Brett and her colleagues (1990) suggest following several key principles in designing and operating such a system:

1. Consult before disputing, and give feedback after (that is, attempt to air issues and decisions that are potential conflict creators, and make sure that the lessons learned in handling the dispute are recorded and reported).

2. Keep the focus on interests, not positions or personalities (per Fisher, Ury, and Patton, 1991).

3. Build in "loop-backs" to disputants (that is, make sure the disputing process is informed by the lessons learned through system operations).

4. Develop and use cost-efficient mechanisms for protection of rights and for restoring power imbalances.

5. Arrange and pursue remedies in a cost-efficient manner, by using and exhausting low-cost remedies before trying higher-cost approaches.

6. Provide disputants with the necessary skills, resources, and motivation to use the system easily and constructively.

7. Work with all concerned parties to make the system design viable and valuable.

It is likely that a well-designed dispute resolution system will offer users a variety of alternatives. When deciding which alternatives to try, Sander and Goldberg (1994) suggest asking two simple questions:

- Will the procedures satisfy the user's objectives (timeliness, thoroughness, etc.)?
- Will the procedures and the system overcome likely barriers or impediments to settlement?

CHAPTER SUMMARY

If negotiators are unable to engage in remedial dispute resolution activities when necessary, third-party intervention may help. In this chapter, we reviewed three formal styles of third-party intervention: arbitration, mediation, and process consultation. Each of these styles has its strengths and weaknesses as an intervention and dispute resolution approach. The styles differ in the degree to which the disputants surrender control to the third party over the negotiation process and/or the outcome. Arbitration typically involves a structured process in which disputing parties have relatively free rein to present their stories, while the arbitrators decide the outcome, often imposing a resolution on the disputants. Mediators exert a great deal of control over how the parties interact, both physically and when communicating; although mediators may point the parties toward possible resolutions through suggestions and guidance, they typically do not choose the resolution for the disputants. Finally, process consultants are less involved in the disputed issues than arbitrators or mediators, but they are heavily involved in helping to establish or enhance communication and dispute resolution skills that the parties can then apply to the immediate dispute and future communication.

Other third-party roles and styles, including informal versions of the three formal approaches we addressed, are increasingly being studied systematically to determine their application and impact. Continuing interest in organizational support for alternative dispute resolution procedures promises great dividends for organizations willing to invest the necessary resources in system design and operations. A great deal remains to be done to determine the mastery and propriety of particular informal third-party styles and techniques for various types of conflict and to achieve a better understanding of how third parties—individually and organizationally—can effectively assist in resolving disputes.

Finally, we briefly reviewed some of the emerging work on alternative dispute resolution (ADR). The description of ADR encompasses a variety of techniques that employers put in place to handle workplace disputes and avoid litigation with employees and with others outside the organization. ADR can include not only mediation and arbitration but also a number of hybrid methods that allow employees to have their concerns heard by neutral third parties. The purpose of ADR is to find resolution processes that minimize lawsuits, court cases, and so on, and that allow organizations to handle employee conflicts efficiently and effectively.

Bibliography

Aaronson, K. (1989). *Selling on the fast track.* New York: Putnam.

Abu-Nimer, M. (1996). Conflict resolution approaches: Western and Middle Eastern lessons and possibilities. *American Journal of Economics and Sociology, 55,* 35–52.

Acuff, F. L. (1993). *How to negotiate anything with anyone anywhere around the world.* New York: AMACOM.

Adachi, Y. (1998). The effects of semantic difference on cross-cultural business negotiation: A Japanese and American case study. *The Journal of Language for International Business, 9,* 43–52.

Adler, N. J., Brahm, R., & Graham, J. L. (1992). Strategy implementation: A comparison of face-to-face negotiations in the People's Republic of China and the United States. *Strategic Management Journal, 13,* 449–466.

Adler, N. J., & Graham, J. L. (1987). Business negotiations: Canadians are not just like Americans. *Canadian Journal of Administrative Sciences, 4,* 211–238.

Adler, N. J., & Graham, J. L. (1989). Cross-cultural interaction: The international comparison fallacy? *Journal of International Business Studies, 20,* 515–537.

Adler, N. J., Graham, J. L., & Schwarz, T. (1987). Business negotiations in Canada, Mexico, and the United States. *Journal of Business Research, 15,* 411–429.

Adler, R., Rosen, B., & Silverstein, E. (1996). Thrust and parry: The art of tough negotiating. *Training and Development, 50,* 42–48.

Adler, R. S., Rosen, B., & Silverstein, E. M. (1998). Emotions in negotiation: How to manage fear and anger. *Negotiation Journal, 14,* 161–179.

Albin, C. (1993). The role of fairness in negotiation. *Negotiation Journal, 9,* 223–243.

Alderfer, C. P. (1977). Group and intergroup relations. In J. R. Hackman & J. L. Suttle (Eds.), *Improving life at work. Behavioral science approaches to organizational change* (pp. 227–296). Santa Monica, CA: Goodyear.

Alexander, J. F., Schul, P. L., & Babakus, E. (1991). Analyzing interpersonal communications in industrial marketing negotiations. *Journal of the Academy of Marketing Science, 19,* 129–139.

Alexander, J. F., Schul, P. L., & McCorkle, D. E. (1994). An assessment of selected relationships in a model of the industrial marketing negotiation process. *Journal of Personal Selling & Sales Management, 14*(3), 25–41.

Allred, K. G. (1998). Anger-driven retaliation: Toward an understanding of impassioned conflict in organizations. In R. Bies, R. J. Lewicki, & B. H. Sheppard (Eds.), *Research on negotiation in organizations* (Vol. 7), in press.

Allred, K. G., Mallozzi, J. S., Matsui, F., & Raia, C. P. (1997). The influence of anger and compassion on negotiation performance. *Organizational Behavior and Human Decision Processes, 70,* 175–187.

Ancona, D., & Caldwell, D. F. (1988). Beyond task and maintenance: External roles in groups. *Group and Organizational Studies, 13,* 468–491.

Anderson, J. C., & Kochan, T. (1977). Impasse procedures in the Canadian Federal Service. *Industrial and Labor Relations Review, 30,* 283–301.

Anton, R. J. (1990). Drawing the line: An exploratory test of ethical behavior in negotiations. *The International Journal of Conflict Management, 1,* 265–280.

Antonioni, D. (1994). The effects of feedback accountability on upward appraisal ratings. *Personnel Psychology, 47,* 249–256.

Aquino, K. (1998). The effects of ethical climate and the availability of alternatives on the use of deception during negotiations. *International Journal of Conflict Management, 9*(3), 195–217.

Argyris, C., & Schön, D. (1996). *Organizational learning II: Theory, method, and practice.* Reading, MA: Addison-Wesley Longman.

Arino, A., Abramov, M., Rykounina, I., & Vila, J. (1997). Partner selection and trust building in west European–Russian joint ventures. *International Studies of Management and Organization, 27,* 19–37.

Armilla, J. (2001). *Negotiate with Feng Shui.* St. Paul, MN: Llewellyn Publications.

Arnold, J., & Carnevale, P. (1997). Preferences for dispute resolution procedures as a function of intentionality, consequences, expected future interaction, and power. *Journal of Applied Psychology, 27,* 371–398.

Arnold, J. A., & O'Connor, K. M. (1999). Ombudspersons or peers? The effect of third-party expertise and recommendations on negotiation. *Journal of Applied Psychology, 84,* 776–785.

Arunachalam, V., & Dilla, W. N. (1995). Judgment accuracy and outcomes in negotiation: A causal modeling analysis of decision-aiding effects. *Organizational Behavior and Human Decision Processes, 61,* 289–304.

Arunachalam, V., Wall, J. A., Jr., & Chan, C. (1998). Hong Kong versus U.S. negotiations: Effects of culture, alternatives, outcome scales, and mediation. *Journal of Applied Social Psychology, 28,* 1219–1244.

Asherman, I. G., & Asherman, S. V. (1990). *The negotiation sourcebook.* Amherst, MA: Human Resource Development Press.

Athos, A. G., & Gabarro, J. J. (1978). *Interpersonal behavior: Communication and understanding in relationships.* Englewood Cliffs, NJ: Prentice Hall.

Austin, R. A. (1989). *Power listening: An empirical investigation of the effects of listening instruction on the listening skills of white collar business executives.* Unpublished master's thesis, University of Maryland, College Park, MD.

Avruch, K. (2000). Culture and negotiation pedagogy. *Negotiation Journal, 16,* 339–346.

Axtell, R. E. (1990). *Do's and taboos of hosting international visitors.* New York: John Wiley and Sons.

Axtell, R. E. (1991). *Gestures: The do's and taboos of body language around the world.* New York: John Wiley and Sons.

Axtell, R. E. (1993). *Do's and taboos around the world* (3rd ed.). New York: John Wiley and Sons.

Ayres, I. (1991). Fair driving: Gender and race discrimination in retail car negotiations. *Harvard Law Review, 104,* 817–872.

Ayres, I., & Siegelman, P. (1995). Race and gender discrimination in bargaining for a new car. *American Economic Review, 85,* 304–321.

Babcock, L., & Loewenstein, G. (1997). Explaining bargaining impasse: The role of self-serving biases. *Journal of Economic Perspectives 11*(1) 109–126.

Babcock, L., Wang, X., & Loewenstein, G. (1996). Choosing the wrong pond: Social comparisons in negotiations that reflect a self-serving bias. *The Quarterly Journal of Economics, 111,* 1–19.

Baker, C., & Ross, W. (1992). Mediation control techniques: A test of Kolb's "orchestrators" vs. "deal-makers" model. *The International Journal of Conflict Management, 3,* 319–341.

Bales, R. F. (1950). *Interaction process analysis: A method for the study of small groups.* Cambridge, MA: Addison-Wesley.

Ball, S. B., Bazerman, M. H., & Carroll, J. S. (1991). An evaluation of learning in the bilateral winner's curse. *Organizational Behavior and Human Decision Processes, 48,* 1–22.

Bar-Hillel, M. (1980). The base-rate fallacy in probability judgments. *Acta Psychologica, 44,* 211–213.

Baranowski, T. A., & Summers, D. A. (1972). Perceptions of response alternatives in a prisoner's dilemma game. *Journal of Personality and Social Psychology, 21,* 35–40.

Barnard, C. (1938). *The functions of the executive.* Cambridge, MA: Harvard University Press.

Baron, R. A. (1990). Environmentally induced positive affect: Its impact on self efficacy and task performance, negotiation and conflict. *Journal of Applied Social Psychology, 20,* 368–384.

Barrett, J. T. (1999). In search of the Rosetta Stone of the mediation profession. *Negotiation Journal, 15,* 219–227.

Barrick, M. R., & Mount, M. K. (1991). The Big Five personality dimensions and job performance: A meta-analysis. *Personnel Psychology, 44,* 1–26.

Barry, B. (1999). The tactical use of emotion in negotiation. In R. Bies, R. J. Lewicki, & B. H. Sheppard (Eds.), *Research on negotiation in organizations* (Vol. 7, pp. 93–121), Stamford, CT: JAI Press.

Barry, B. (2001). Influence tactics in organizations from a social expectancy perspective. In A. Y. Lee-Chai & J. A. Bargh (Eds.), *The use and abuse of power,* Psychology Press, 2001.

Barry, B., & Friedman, R. (1998). Bargainer characteristics in distributive and integrative negotiation. *Journal of Personality and Social Psychology, 74,* 345–359.

Barry, B., & Fulmer, I. S. (2001, June). How influence in organizations is affected by computer-mediated communication: A theoretical framework. Paper presented at the annual meeting of the International Association for Conflict Management, Cergy, France.

Barry, B., Fulmer, I. S., Long, A. (2000). Ethically marginal bargaining tactics: Sanction, efficacy, and performance. Presented at the annual meeting of the Academy of Management, Toronto.

Barry, B., Fulmer, I. S., & Van Kleef, G. A. (2002). I laughed, I cried, I settled: The role of emotion in negotiation. In M. Gelfand and J. Brett (Eds.), *Culture and negotiation: Integrative approaches to theory and research,* in press.

Barry, B., & Oliver, R. L. (1996). Affect in dyadic negotiation: A model and propositions. *Organizational Behavior and Human Decision Processes, 67,* 127–143.

Bateson, B. (1972). *Steps to an ecology of mind.* New York: Ballantine Books.

Batson, C. D., & Thompson, E. R. (2001). Why don't moral people act morally? Motivational considerations. *Current Directions in Psychological Science, 10*(2), 54–57.

Bazerman, M. (1998). *Judgment in managerial decision making* (4th ed.). New York: John Wiley and Sons.

Bazerman, M. H., & Carroll, J. S. (1987). Negotiator cognition. In B. Staw & L. L. Cummings. *Research in organizational behavior* (Vol. 9, pp. 247–288), Greenwich, CT: JAI Press.

Bazerman, M. H., Curhan, J. R., Moore, D. A., & Valley, K. L. (2000). Negotiation. *Annual Review of Psychology, 51,* 279–314.

Bazerman, M. H., Magliozzi, T., & Neale, M. A. (1985). Integrative bargaining in a competitive market. *Organizational Behavior and Human Decision Processes, 35,* 294–313.

Bazerman, M. H., Mannix, E. A., & Thompson, L. L. (1988). Groups as mixed motive negotiations. In E. J. Lawler & B. Markovsky (Eds.), *Advances in group processes* (Vol. 5, pp. 195–216). Greenwich, CT: JAI Press.

Bazerman, M. H., Moore, D. A., & Gillespie, J. J. (1999). The human mind as a barrier to wiser environmental agreements. *The American Behavioral Scientist, 42,* 1277–1300.

Bazerman, M. H., & Neale, M. A. (1983). Heuristics in negotiation: Limitations to effective dispute resolution. In M. Bazerman & R. J. Lewicki. *Negotiating in organizations.* Beverly Hills, CA: Sage.

Bazerman, M. H., & Neale, M. A. (1992). *Negotiating rationally.* New York: Free Press.

Bazerman, M. H., Neale, M. A., Valley, L., Zajac, E. J., & Min Kim, J. (1992). The effect of agents and mediators on negotiation outcomes. *Organizational Behavior and Human Decision* Processes, *53,* 55–73.

Bazerman, M. H., & Samuelson, W. F. (1983). I won the auction but don't want the prize. *Journal of Conflict Resolution, 27,* 618–634.

Beckhard, R. (1978, July–September). The dependency dilemma. *Consultants' Communique, 6,* 1–3.

Beckman, N. (1977). *Negotiations.* Lexington, MA: Lexington Books.

Beebe, S. A. (1980). Effects of eye contact, posture, and vocal inflection upon credibility and comprehension. *Australian SCAN: Journal of Human Communication, 7–8,* 57–70.

Beechey, J. (2000). International commercial arbitration. *Dispute Resolution Journal, 55,* No. 3, pp. 32–34.

Beisecker, T., Walker, G., & Bart, J. (1989). Knowledge versus ignorance in bargaining strategies: The impact of knowledge about other's information level. *The Social Science Journal, 26,* 161–172.

Bem, D. (1972). Self-perception theory. In L. Berkowitz (Ed.), *Advances in experimental social psychology* (Vol. 6, pp. 1–62). New York: Academic Press.

Benjamin, A. J., & Levi, A. M. (1979). Process minefields in intergroup conflict resolution: The Sdot Yam workshop. *Journal of Applied Behavioral Science, 15,* 507–519.

Bentham, J. (1789). *An introduction to the principles of morals and legislation.* Oxford: Oxford Press.

Benton, A. A. (1972). Accountability and negotiations between representatives. *Proceedings, 80th Annual Convention, American Psychological Association,* Hawaii, 227–228.

Benton, A. A., & Druckman, D. (1974). Constituent's bargaining orientation and intergroup negotiations. *Journal of Applied Social Psychology, 4,* 141–150.

Ben-Yoav, O., & Pruitt, D. G. (1984a). Accountability to constituents: A two-edged sword. *Organizational Behavior and Human Performance, 34,* 283–295.

Ben-Yoav, O., & Pruitt, D. G. (1984b). Resistance to yielding and the expectation of cooperative future interaction in negotiation. *Journal of Experimental Social Psychology, 34,* 323–335.

Bercovitch, J. (1989). Mediation in international disputes. In K. Kressel & D. Pruitt (Eds.), *Mediation research* (pp. 284–299). San Francisco: Jossey-Bass.

Berkowitz, L. (1989). The frustration-aggression hypothesis: An examination and reformulation. *Psychological Bulletin, 106,* 59–73.

Berlo, D. K., Lemert, J., & Mertz, R. (1966). *Dimensions for evaluating the acceptability of message sources.* East Lansing, MI: Michigan State University.

Bernstein, J., & Rosen, S. (1989). *Dinosaur brains: Dealing with all those impossible people at work.* New York: John Wiley and Sons.

Bettinghaus, E. P. (1966). *Message preparation: The nature of proof.* Indianapolis: Bobbs-Merrill.

Bettinghaus, E. P. (1980). *Persuasive communication* (2nd ed.). New York: Holt, Rinehart & Winston.

Bies, R. J., Lewicki, R. J., & Sheppard, B. H. (1995). Preface. In R. J. Bies, R. J. Lewicki, & B. H. Sheppard (Eds.), *Research on negotiation in organizations* (Vol. 5, p. ix). Greenwich, CT: JAI Press.

Bies, R., & Moag, J. (1986). Interactional justice: Communication criteria of fairness. In R. J. Lewicki, B. H. Sheppard, and M. H. Bazerman (Eds.), *Research on negotiation in organizations* (Vol. 1, pp. 43–55). Greenwich, CT: JAI Press.

Bies, R., & Shapiro, D. (1987). Interactional fairness judgments: The influence of causal accounts. *Social Justice Research, 1,* 199–218.

Bies, R., & Tripp, T. (1998). Revenge in organizations: The good, the bad and the ugly. In R. W. Griffin, A. O'Leary-Kelly, & J. Collins (Eds.), *Dysfunctional behavior in organizations, Volume 1: Violent behavior in organizations* (pp. 49–68). Greenwich, CT: JAI Press.

Binnendijk, H. (1987). *National negotiating styles*. Washington, DC: Foreign Service Institute, Department of State.

Blake, R. R., & Mouton, J. S. (1961a). *Group dynamics: Key to decision making*. Houston, TX: Gulf Publications.

Blake, R. R., & Mouton, J. S. (1961b). Comprehension of own and outgroup positions under intergroup competition. *Journal of Conflict Resolution, 5,* 304–310.

Blake, R. R., & Mouton, J. S. (1961c). Loyalty of representatives to ingroup positions during intergroup competition. *Sociometry, 24,* 177–183.

Blau, P. (1964). *Exchange and power in social life*. New York: John Wiley and Sons.

Bless, H., Bohner, G., Schwarz, N., & Strack, F. (1988). Happy and mindless: Moods and the processing of persuasive communication. Unpublished manuscript, Mannheim, GR.

Blessing, L. (1988). *A walk in the woods*. New York: New American Library, Dutton.

Block, P. (1987). *The empowered manager: Positive political skills at work*. San Francisco: Jossey-Bass.

Blumenstein, R. (1997, December 30). Haggling in cyberspace transforms car sales. *The Wall Street Journal,* pp. B1, B6.

Boatright, J. R. (1993). *Ethics and the conduct of business*. Englewood Cliffs, NJ: Prentice Hall.

Boehringer, G. H., Zeruolis, V., Bayley, J., & Boehringer, K. (1974). Stirling: The destructive application of group techniques to a conflict. *Journal of Conflict Resolution, 18,* 257–275.

Bok, S. (1978). *Lying. Moral choice in public and private life,* New York: Pantheon.

Bone, D. (1988). *The business of listening*. Los Altos, CA: Crisp Publications.

Bonoma, T., Horai, J., Lindskold, S., Gahagan, J. P., & Tedeschi, J. T. (1969). Compliance to contingent threats. *Proceedings of the 77th Annual Convention of the American Psychological Association, 4,* 395–396.

Boster, F. J., & Mongeau, P. (1984). Fear-arousing persuasive messages. In R. N. Bostrom (Ed.), *Communication Yearbook* (Vol. 8, pp. 330–375). Beverly Hills, CA: Sage.

Bostrom, R. N. (1990). *Listening behavior: Measurement and application*. New York: Guilford.

Botes, J., & Mitchell, C. (1995). Constraints on third-party flexibility. *Annals of the American Academy of Political and Social Science, 542,* 168–184.

Bottom, W. P. (1998). Negotiator risk: Sources of uncertainty and the impact of reference points on negotiated agreements. *Organizational Behavior And Human Decision Processes, 76,* 89–112.

Bottom, W. P., & Paese, P. W. (1999). Judgment accuracy and the asymmetric cost of errors in distributive bargaining. *Group Decision & Negotiation, 8,* 349–364.

Bottom, W. P., & Studt, A. (1993). Framing effects and the distributive aspect of integrative bargaining. *Organizational Behavior and Human Decision Processes, 56,* 459–474.

Bourdeaux, C., O'Leary, R., & Thorburgh, R. (2001). Control, communication, and power: A study of the use of alternative dispute resolution of enforcement actions at the U. S. Environmental Protection Agency. *Negotiation Journal, 17,* 175–191.

Bowers, J. W. (1964). Some correlates of language intensity. *Quarterly Journal of Speech, 50,* 415–420.

Bowers, J. W., & Osborn, M. M. (1966). Attitudinal effects of selected types of concluding metaphors in persuasive speeches. *Speech Monographs, 33,* 147–155.

Bowie, N. (1993). Does it pay to bluff in business? In T. L. Beauchamp & N. E. Bowie (Eds.), *Ethical theory and business* (pp. 449–454). Englewood Cliffs, NJ: Prentice Hall.

Bowie, N., & Freeman, R. E. (1992). *Ethics and agency theory*. New York: Oxford University Press.

Bowling, D., & Hoffman, D. (2001). Bringing peace into the room: The personal qualities of the mediator and their impact on the mediation. *Negotiation Journal, 16,* 5–28.

Braganti, N. L., & Devine, E. (1992). *European customs and manners: How to make friends and do business in Europe* (rev. ed.). New York: Meadowbrook Press.

Braginsky, D. D. (1970). Machiavellianism and manipulative interpersonal behavior in children. *Journal of Experimental Social Psychology, 6,* 77–99.

Brams, S. J., & Doherty, A. E. (1993). Intransigence in negotiations: The dynamics of disagreement. *Journal of Conflict Resolution, 37,* 692–708.

Bramson, R. (1981). *Coping with difficult people*. New York: Anchor Books.

Bramson, R. (1992). *Coping with difficult bosses*. New York: Carol Publishing Group.

Brass, D. J. (1984). Being in the right place: A structural analysis of individual influence in an organization. *Administrative Science Quarterly, 29,* 518–539.

Breaugh, J. A., & Klimoski, R. J. (1977). Choice of group spokesman in bargaining member or outsider. *Organizational Behavior and Human Performance, 19,* 325–336.

Brehm, J. W. (1976). Responses to loss of freedom: A theory of psychological reactance. In J. W. Thibaut, J. T. Spence, & R. C. Carson (Eds.), *Contemporary topics in social psychology* (pp. 53–78). Morristown, NJ: General Learning Press.

Brett, J. (1991). Negotiating group decisions. *Negotiation Journal, 7,* 291–310.

Brett, J., Barsness, Z., & Goldberg, S. (1996). The effectiveness of mediation: An independent analysis of cases handled by four major service providers. *Negotiation Journal, 12,* 259–269.

Brett, J., Goldberg, S., & Ury, W. (1990). Designing systems for resolving disputes in organizations. *American Psychologist, 45,* 162–170.

Brett, J. F., Pinkley, R. L., & Jacofsky, E. F. (1996). Alternatives to having BATNA in dyadic negotiation: The influence of goals, self-efficacy, and alternatives on negotiated outcomes. *International Journal of Conflict Management, 7,* 121–138.

Brett, J. M. (2001). *Negotiating globally.* San Francisco: Jossey-Bass.

Brett, J. M., & Goldberg, S. B. (1983). Grievance mediation in the coal industry: A field experiment. *Industrial and Labor Relations Review, 37,* 3–17.

Brett, J. M., & Okumura, T. (1998). Inter- and intracultural negotiation: U. S. and Japanese negotiators. *Academy of Management Journal, 41,* 495–510.

Brett, J. M., & Rognes, J. (1986). Intergroup relations in organizations: A negotiations perspective. In P. Goodman (Ed.), *Designing effective work groups* (pp. 202–236). San Francisco: Jossey-Bass.

Brett, J. M., Shapiro, D. L., & Lytle, A. L. (1998). Breaking the bonds of reciprocity in negotiation. *Academy of Management Journal, 41,* 410–424.

Brief, A. (1992). *Sanctioned corruption in the corporate world.* Unpublished manuscript.

Brock, T. C. (1963). Effects of prior dishonesty on post-decision dissonance. *Journal of Abnormal and Social Psychology, 66,* 325–331.

Brockner, J. (1992). The escalation of commitment to a failing course of action: Toward theoretical progress. *Academy of Management Review, 17,* 39–61.

Brockner, J., & Siegel, P. (1996). Understanding the interaction between procedural and distributive justice: The role of trust. In R. Kramer & T. Tyler (Eds.), *Trust in organizations* (pp. 390–413). Thousand Oaks, CA: Sage.

Brodt, S. E. (1994). "Inside information" and negotiator decision behavior. *Organizational Behavior and Human Decision Processes, 58,* 172–202.

Brooks, E., & Odiorne, G. S. (1984). *Managing by negotiations,* New York: Van Nostrand.

Brouthers, K. D., & Bamossy, G. J. (1997). The role of key stakeholders in international joint venture negotiations: Case studies from Eastern Europe. *Journal of International Business Studies, 28,* 285–308.

Brown, B. L. (1999). Contextual mediation. *Meditation Quarterly, 16,* 349–356.

Brown, B. R. (1968). The effects of need to maintain face on interpersonal bargaining. *Journal of Experimental Social Psychology, 4,* 107–122.

Brown, L. D. (1977). Can "haves" and "have-nots" cooperate? Two efforts to bridge a social gap. *Journal of Applied Behavioral Science, 13,* 211–224.

Brown, L. D. (1983). *Managing conflict at organizational interfaces.* Reading, MA: Addison-Wesley.

Bruner, J. S., & Tagiuri, R. (1954). The perception of people. In G. Lindzey (Ed.), *The handbook of social psychology* (Vol. 2, pp. 634–654). Reading, MA: Addison-Wesley.

Buber, M. (1958). *I and thou.* New York: Charles Scribners & Sons.

Buber, M. (1963). *Pointing the way.* New York: Harper & Row.

Buechler, S. M. (2000). *Social movements in advanced capitalism.* New York, Oxford University Press.

Bunker, B. B., & Alban, Billie T. (1997). *Large group interventions: Engaging the whole system for rapid change.* San Francisco: Jossey-Bass.

Burgess, G., & Burgess, H. (1995). Constructive confrontation: A transformative approach to intractable conflicts. *Mediation Quarterly, 13,* 305–322.

Burgoon, J. K., Coker, D. A., & Coker, R. A. (1986). Communication of gaze behavior: A test of two contrasting explanations. *Human Communication Research, 12,* 495–524.

Burgoon, M., & King, L. B. (1974). The mediation of resistance to persuasion strategies by language variables and active-passive participation. *Human Communication Research, 1,* 30–41.

Burgoon, M., & Stewart, D. (1975). Empirical investigations of language: The effects of sex of source, receiver, and language intensity on attitude change. *Human Communication Research, 1,* 244–248.

Burnstein, D. (1995). *Negotiator pro.* Beacon Expert Systems, 35 Gardner Road, Brookline, MA.

Burton, J. (1984). *Global conflict.* Center for International Development, University of Maryland, College Park, MD.

Bush, R. B. (1996). "What do we need a mediator for?": Mediation's "value-added" for negotiators. *American Psychologist, 45,* 162–170.

Butler, J. K. (1991). Toward understanding and measuring conditions of trust: Evolution of a conditions of trust inventory. *Journal of Management, 17,* 643–663.

Butler, J. K., Jr. (1994). Conflict styles and outcomes in negotiation with fully-integrative potential. *International Journal of Conflict Management, 5,* 309–325.

Butler, J. K. Jr. (1996). Two integrative win-win negotiating strategies. *Simulation and Gaming, 27,* 387–392.

Butler, J. K. Jr. (1999). Trust expectations, information sharing, climate of trust, and negotiation effectiveness and efficiency. *Group and Organization Management, 24,* 217–238.

Cacioppo, J. T., & Petty, R. E. (1985). Central and peripheral routes to persuasion: The role of message repetition. In L. F. Alwitt & A. A. Mitchell (Eds.), *Psychological processes and advertising effects: Theory, research, and application* (pp. 91–111). Hillsdale, NJ: Lawrence Erlbaum.

Cai, D. A. (1998). Culture, plans, and the pursuit of negotiation goals. *Journal of Asian Pacific Communication, 8,* 103–123.

Calero, H. H., & Oskam, B. (1983). *Negotiate the deal you want.* New York: Dodd, Mead & Company.

Camerer, C. F., & Loewenstein, G. (1993). Information, fairness, and efficiency in bargaining. In *Psychological perspectives on justice. Theory and applications* (pp. 155–179). Cambridge: Cambridge University Press.

Cantrell, R. S., & Butler, J. K., Jr. (1997). Male negotiators: Chivalry or machismo or both? *Psychological Reports, 80,* 1315–1323.

Carlisle, J. A., & Parker, R. C. (1989). *Beyond negotiation: Redeeming customer-supplier relations.* Chicester, G. B. : John Wiley.

Carnevale, A., Gainer, L., Meltzer, A., & Holland, S. (1988). Workplace basics: The skills that employers want. *Training and Development Journal, 42,* 283–290.

Carnevale, P. J., & Isen, A. M. (1986). The influence of positive affect and visual access on the discovery of integrative solutions in bilateral negotiation. *Organizational Behavior and Human Decision Processes, 37,* 1–13.

Carnevale, P. J. D. (1986). Strategic choice in negotiation. *Negotiation Journal, 2,* 41–56.

Carnevale, P. J. D. (1992). The usefulness of mediation theory. *Negotiation Journal, 8,* 387–390.

Carnevale, P. J. D., & Conlon, D. E. (1988). Time pressure and strategic choice in mediation. *Organizational Behavior and Human Decision Processes, 42,* 111–133.

Carnevale, P. J. D., & Conlon, D. E. (1990, June). *Effects of two forms of bias in mediation of disputes.* Paper presented at the third International Conference of the International Association of Conflict Management, Vancouver, B. C., Canada.

Carnevale, P. J. D., & Keenan, P. A. (1990). *Decision frame and social goals in integrative bargaining: The likelihood of agreement versus the quality.* Paper presented at the annual meeting of the International Association of Conflict Management, Vancouver, B. C., Canada.

Carnevale, P. J. D., & Lawler, E. J. (1987). Time pressure and the development of integrative agreements in bilateral negotiations. *Journal of Conflict Resolution, 30,* 636–659.

Carnevale, P. J. D., & Pruitt, D. G. (1992). Negotiation and mediation. In M. Rosenberg & L. Porter (Eds.), *Annual Review of Psychology* (Vol. 43, pp. 531–582). Palo Alto, CA: Annual Reviews, Inc.

Carnevale, P. J. D., Pruitt, D. G., & Britton, S. D. (1979). Looking tough: The negotiator under constituent surveillance. *Personality and Social Psychology Bulletin, 5,* 118–121.

Carnevale, P. J. D., Pruitt, D. G., & Seilheimer, S. D. (1981). Looking and competing: Accountability and visual access in integrative bargaining. *Journal of Personality and Social Psychology, 40,* 111–120.

Carr, A. Z. (1968, January–February). Is business bluffing ethical? *Harvard Business Review, 46,* 143–153.

Carroll, J., Bazerman, M., & Maury, R. (1988). Negotiator cognitions: A descriptive approach to negotiators' understanding of their opponents. *Organizational Behavior and Human Decision Processes, 41,* 352–370.

Carroll, J., Delquie, P., Halpern, J., & Bazerman, M. (1990). *Improving negotiators' cognitive processes.* Working paper, Massachusetts Institute of Technology, Cambridge, MA.

Carter, S. (1999). The importance of party buy-in in designing organizational conflict management systems. *Mediation Quarterly, 17,* 61–66.

Carver, C. S., & Scheir, M. E. (1990). Origins and foundations of positive and negative affect: A control process view. *Psychological Review, 97,* 19–35.

Carver, T., & Vondra, A. (1994 May/June). Alternative dispute resolution: Why it doesn't work and why it does. *Harvard Business Review, 72,* 120–130.

Cellich, C. (1997). Closing your business negotiations. *International Trade Forum, 1,* 14–17.

Chaiken, S. (1986). Physical appearance and social influence. In C. P. Herman, M. P. Zanna, & E. T. Higgins (Eds.), *Physical appearance, stigma, and social behavior: The Ontario symposium* (Vol. 3, pp. 143–177). Hillsdale, NJ: Lawrence Erlbaum.

Chaiken, S. (1987). The heuristic model of persuasion. In M. Zanna, J. Olson, & C. Herman (Eds.), *Social influence: The Ontario symposium* (Vol. 5, pp. 3–39). Hillsdale, NJ: Lawrence Erlbaum.

Chan, C. W. (1998). Transfer pricing negotiation outcomes and the impact of negotiator mixed-motives and culture: empirical evidence from the U. S. and Australia. *Management Accounting Research, 9,* 139–161.

Charan, R. (1991). How networks reshape organizations—for results. *Harvard Business Review, 69*(5), Sept./Oct., pp. 104–115.

Chatman, J., Putnam, L., & Sondak, H. (1991). Integrating communication and negotiation research. In M. Bazerman, R. Lewicki, & B. Sheppard (Eds.), *Research on negotiation in organizations* (Vol. 3, pp. 139–164). Greenwich, CT: JAI Press.

Chaudrhy, S. S., & Ross, W. R. (1989). Relevance trees and mediation. *Negotiation Journal, 5,* 63–73.

Chen, C. C., Chen, X., & Meindl, J. R. (1998). How can cooperation be fostered? The cultural effects of individualism-collectivism. *Academy of Management Review, 23,* 285–304.

Chertkoff, J. M., & Conley, M. (1967). Opening offer and frequency of concessions as bargaining strategies. *Journal of Personality and Social Psychology, 7,* 181–185.

Christie, R., & Geis, F. L. (Eds.). (1970). *Studies in Machiavellianism.* New York: Academic Press.

Cialdini, R. B. (2001). *Influence: Science and practice* (4th ed.). Boston: Allyn and Bacon.

Clark, M. S., & Mills, J. (1979). Interpersonal attraction in exchange and communal relationships. *Journal of Personality and Social Psychology, 37*(1), 12–24.

Clark, R. A. (1984). *Persuasive messages.* New York: Harper & Row.

Cobb, A. (1986). Coalition identification in organizational research. In R. J. Lewicki, B. H. Sheppard, & M. H. Bazerman (Eds.), *Research on negotiation in organizations* (Vol. 1, pp. 139–154). Greenwich, CT: JAI Press.

Cobb, S. (1993). Empowerment and mediation: A narrative perspective. *Negotiation Journal, 9,* 245–259.

Cohen, A. R., & Bradford, D. L. (1989). Influence without authority: The use of alliances, reciprocity, and exchange to accomplish work. *Organizational Dynamics, 17*(3), 5–17.

Cohen, H. (1980). *You can negotiate anything.* Secaucus, NJ: Lyle Stuart.

Cohen, S. P., Kelman, H. C., Miller, F. D., & Smith, B. L. (1977). Evolving intergroup techniques for conflict resolution: An Israeli–Palestinian pilot workshop. *Journal of Social Issues, 33,* 165–189.

Coleman, P., & Lim, Y. Y. J. (2001). A systematic approach to evaluating the effects of collaborative negotiation training on individuals and groups. *Negotiation Journal,* October, 364–392.

Conger, J. A. (1998). The necessary art of persuasion. *Harvard Business Review, 76*(3), 84–95.

Conlon, D., Carnevale, P. J. D., & Murnighan, K. (1994). Intravention: Third-party intervention with clout. *Organizational Behavior and Human Decision Processes, 57,* 387–410.

Conlon, D. E., & Fasolo, P. M. (1990). Influence of speed of third-party intervention and outcome on negotiator and constituent fairness judgments. *Academy of Management Journal, 33,* 833–846.

Conlon, D. E., & Ross, W. H. (1993). The effects of partisan third parties on negotiator behavior and outcome perceptions. *Journal of Applied Psychology, 78,* 280–290.

Cooper, W. (1981). Ubiquitous halo. *Psychological Bulletin, 90,* 218–244.

Corley, R. N., Black, R. L., & Reed, O. L. (1977). *The legal environment of business* (4th ed.). New York: McGraw-Hill.

Corwin, R. G. (1969). Patterns of organizational conflict. *Administrative Science Quarterly, 14,* 504–520.

Coser, L. (1956). *The functions of social conflict.* New York: Free Press.

Costantino, C. A. (1994). How to set up an ADR program. *Government Executive, 26,* 44.

Costantino, C. A., & Merchant, C. S. (1996). *Designing conflict management systems.* San Francisco: Jossey-Bass.

Coulson, R. (1987). *Business mediation: What you need to know.* New York: American Arbitration Association.

Cronkhite, G., & Liska, J. (1976). A critique of factor analytic approaches to the study of credibility. *Communication Monographs, 32,* 91–107.

Cronkhite, G., & Liska, J. (1980). The judgment of communicant acceptability. In M. E. Roloff & G. R. Miller (Eds.), *Persuasion: New directions in theory and research* (pp. 101–139). Beverly Hills, CA: Sage.

Cropanzano, R., & Folger, R. (1991). Procedural justice and worker motivation. In R. M. Steers & L. W. Porter (Eds.), *Motivation and work behavior* (2nd ed.) (pp. 131–143). New York: McGraw-Hill.

Croson, R. T. A. (1999). Look at me when you say that: An electronic negotiation simulation. *Simulation & Gaming, 30,* 23–37.

Cross, S., & Rosenthal, R. (1999). Three models of conflict resolution: Effects on intergroup experiences and attitudes. *Journal of Social Issues, 55*(3), 561–580.

Crott, H., Kayser, E., & Lamm, H. (1980). The effects of information exchange and communication in an asymmetrical negotiation situation. *European Journal of Social Psychology, 10,* 149–163.

Crumbaugh, C. M., & Evans, G. W. (1967). Presentation format, other persons' strategies and cooperative behavior in the prisoner's dilemma. *Psychological Reports, 20,* 895–902.

Cutcher-Gershenfeld, J., & Watkins, M. (1999). Toward a theory of representation in negotiation. In R. H. Mnookin and L. E. Susskind, *Negotiating on behalf of others* (pp. 23–51). Thousand Oaks. CA: Sage Books.

Cyert, R., & March, J. (1963). *A behavioral theory of the firm.* Englewood Cliffs, NJ: Prentice Hall.

Dahl, R. A. (1957). The concept of power. *Behavioral Science, 2,* 201–215.

Dallinger, J. M., & Hample, D. (1995). Personalizing and managing conflict. *The International Journal of Conflict Management, 6,* 273–289.

Daly, J. (1991). The effects of anger on negotiations over mergers and acquisitions. *Negotiation Journal, 7,* 31–39.

Dant, R. P., & Schul, P. L. (1992). Conflict resolution processes in contractual channels of distribution. *Journal of Marketing, 56,* 38–54.

Davidson, M. N., & Greenhalgh, L. (1999). The role of emotion in negotiation: The impact of anger and race. In R. Bies, R. J Lewicki, & B. H. Sheppard, *Research on negotiation in organizations* (Vol. 7, pp. 3–26). Stamford, CT: JAI Press.

Dawson, R. (1997). Ethical differences between men and women in the sales profession. *Journal of Business Ethics, 16,* 1143–1152.

Deaux, K. (1985). Sex and gender. *Annual Review of Psychology, 36,* 49–81.

De Bono, E. (1990). *Lateral thinking: Creativity step-by-step* (Reissue ed.). New York: Harper Collins.

de Dreu, C. K. W. (1995). Coercive power and concession making in bilateral negotiation. *Journal of Conflict Resolution, 39,* 646–670.

de Dreu, C. K. W., Carnevale, P. J. D., Emans, B. J. M., & van de Vliert, E. (1994). Effects of gain-loss frames in negotiation: Loss aversion, mismatching, and frame adoption. *Organizational Behavior and Human Decision Processes, 60,* 90–107.

de Dreu, C. K. W., Giebels, E., & van de Vliert, E. (1998). Social motives and trust in integrative negotiation: The disruptive effects of punitive capability. *Journal of Applied Psychology, 83,* 408–422.

de Dreu, C. K. W., Koole, S. L., & Steinel, W. (2000). Unfixing the fixed pie: A motivated information processing approach to integrative negotiation. *Journal of Personality and Social Psychology, 79,* 975–987.

de Dreu, C. K. W., Nauta, A., & van de Vliert, E. (1995). Self-serving evaluations of conflict behavior and escalation of the dispute. *Journal of Applied Social Psychology, 25,* 2049–2066.

de Dreu, C. K. W., & van Lange, P. A. M. (1995). The impact of social value orientation on negotiator cognition and behavior. *Personality and Social Psychology Bulletin, 21,* 1178–1188.

de Dreu, C. K. W., Weingart, L. R., & Kwon, S. (2000). Influence of social motives on integrative negotiation: A meta-analytic review and test of two theories. *Journal of Personality and Social Psychology, 78,* 889–905.

Deep, S., & Sussman, L. (1993). *What to ask when you don't know what to say: 555 powerful questions to use for getting your way at work.* Englewood Cliffs, NJ: Prentice Hall.

Delbecq, A. L., & Van de Ven, A. H. (1971). A group process model for problem identification and program planning. *Journal of Applied Behavioral Science, 7,* 466–492.

Demick, B. (1998). Saddam, United States play high stakes chicken. Night Ridder Newspapers: Tribue Media Service.

Derong, C., & Faure, G. O. (1995). When Chinese companies negotiate with their government. *Organization Studies, 16,* 27–54.

Deutsch, M. (1949). A theory of cooperation and competition. *Human Relations, 2,* 129–151.

Deutsch, M. (1958). Trust and suspicion. *Journal of Conflict Resolution, 2,* 265–279.

Deutsch, M. (1962). Cooperation and trust: Some theoretical notes. In M. R. Jones (Ed.), *Nebraska symposium on motivation* (pp. 275–318). Lincoln, NE: University of Nebraska Press.

Deutsch, M. (1973). *The resolution of conflict.* New Haven, CT: Yale University Press.

Deutsch, M. (1985). *Distributive justice: A social-psychological perspective.* New Haven: Yale University Press.

Deutsch, M., & Coleman, P. (2000). *The handbook of conflict resolution.* San Francisco: Jossey-Bass.

Devinatz, V. G., & Budd, J. W. (1997). Third-party dispute resolution. Interest disputes. In D. Lewin, D. J. R. Mitchell, & M. A. Zaida (eds.), *The human resource management handbook* (Vol. 1, pp. 95–135). Greenwich, CT: JAI Press.

Diehl, P. F., Druckman, D., & Wall, J. (1998). International peacekeeping and conflict resolution: A taxonomic analysis with implications. *Journal of Conflict Resolution, 42*(1), pp. 33–55.

Diekmann, K. A., Tenbrunsel, A. E., Shah, P. P., Schroth, H. A., & Bazerman, M. H. (1996). The descriptive and prescriptive use of previous purchase price in negotiations. *Organizational Behavior and Human Decision Processes, 66,* 179–191.

Donaldson, T., & Werhane, P. (1993). *Ethical issues in business: A philosophical approach* (4th ed.). Englewood Cliffs, NJ: Prentice Hall.

Donohue, W. A. (1981). Analyzing negotiation tactics: Development of a negotiation interact system. *Human Communication Research, 7,* 273–287.

Donohue, W. A. (1989). Communicative competence in mediators. In K. Kressel & D. Pruitt (Eds.), *Mediation research.* (pp. 322–343). San Francisco: Jossey-Bass.

Donohue, W. A. (1991). *Communication, marital dispute and divorce mediation.* Hillsdale, NJ: Lawrence Erlbaum.

Donohue, W. A., & Kolt, R. (1992). *Managing interpersonal conflict.* Newbury Park, CA: Sage.

Donohue, W. A., & Roberto, A. J. (1996). An empirical examination of three models of integrative and distributive bargaining. *The International Journal of Conflict Management, 7,* 209–299.

Douglas, A. (1962). *Industrial peacemaking.* New York: Columbia University Press.

Drake, L. E. (1995). Negotiation styles in intercultural communication. *The International Journal of Conflict Management, 6,* 72–90.

Drayton, W. (1981, July–August). Getting smarter about regulation. *Harvard Business Review, 59,* 38–52.

Dreher, G. F., Dougherty, T. W., & Whitely, W. (1989). Influence tactics and salary attainment: A gender specific analysis. *Sex Roles, 20,* 535–550.

Drolet, A. L., & Morris, M. W. (2000). Rapport in conflict resolution: Accounting for how face-to-face contact fosters mutual cooperation in mixed-motive conflicts. *Journal of Experimental Social Psychology, 36,* 26–50.

Drory, A., & Ritov, I. (1997). Effect of work experience and opponent's power on conflict management style. *The International Journal of Conflict Management, 8,* 148–161.

Druckman, D. (1996). Is there a U.S. negotiating style? *International Negotiation, 1,* 327–334.

Druckman, D., & Broome, B. (1991). Value difference and conflict resolution: Familiarity or liking? *Journal of Conflict Resolution, 35*(4), 571–593.

Dudley, B. S., Johnson, D. W., & Johnson, R. T. (1996). Conflict-resolution training and middle school students' integrative negotiation behavior. *Journal of Applied Social Psychology, 26,* 2038–2052.

Duffy, K., Grosch, J., & Olczak, P. (1991). *Community mediation: A handbook for practitioners and researchers.* New York: Guilford.

Dukes, E. F., Piscolish, M. A., & Stephens, J. B. (2000). *Reaching for higher ground in conflict resolution.* San Francisco: Jossey-Bass.

Eagly, A. H., & Chaiken, S. (1975). An attribution analysis of the effect of communicator characteristics on opinion change: The case of communicator attractiveness. *Journal of Personality and Social Psychology, 32,* 136–144.

Eiseman, J. W. (1978). Reconciling incompatible positions. *Journal of Applied Behavioral Science, 14,* 133–150.

Elangovan, A. R. (1995a). Managerial third-party dispute intervention: A prescriptive model of strategy selection. *Academy of Management Review, 20,* 800–830.

Elangovan, A. R. (1995b). Managerial conflict intervention in organizations: Traversing the cultural mosaic. *The International Journal of Conflict Management, 6,* 124–146.

Elangovan, A. R. (1998). Managerial interventions in organizational disputes: Testing a prescriptive model of strategy selection. *The International Journal of Conflict Management, 9,* 301–335.

Elkouri, F., & Elkouri, E. (1985). *How arbitration works* (4th ed.). Washington, DC: BNA, Inc.

Elliott, M., Gray, B., & Lewicki, R. J. (2003). Lessons learned about the framing and reframing of intractable environmental conflicts. In Lewicki, R. J., B. Gray, & M. Elliott, *Making Sense of Intractable Environmental Disputes.* Washington, DC: Island Press.

Emerson, R. M. (1962). Power-dependence relations. *American Sociological Review, 27,* 31–44.

Epstein, Y. (1979). The stability of behavior: I. On predicting most of the people much of the time. *Journal of Personality and Social Psychology, 37,* 1097–1126.

Epstein, Y. (1980). The stability of behavior: II. Implications for psychological research. *American Psychologist, 35,* 790–806.

Esser, J., & Marriott, R. (1995a). Mediation tactics: A comparison of field and laboratory research. *Journal of Applied Social Psychology, 25,* 1530–1546.

Esser, J., & Marriott, R. (1995b). A comparison of the effectiveness of substantive and contextual mediation tactics. *Journal of Applied Social Psychology, 25,* 1340–1359.

Exline, R., Thibaut J., Hickey, C., & Gumpert, P. (1970). Visual interaction in relation to Machiavellianism and an unethical act. In R. Christie & F. Geis (Eds.), *Studies in Machiavellianism* (pp. 53–75). New York: Academic Press.

Eyuboglu, N., & Buja, A. (1993). Dynamics of channel negotiations: Contention and reciprocity. *Psychology & Marketing, 10,* 47–65.

Faure, G. O. (1999). The cultural dimension of negotiation: The Chinese case. *Group Decision and Negotiation, 8,* 187–215.

Fayerweather, J., & Kapoor, A. (1976). *Strategy and negotiation for the international cooperation.* Cambridge, MA: Ballinger.

Feigenbaum, C. (1975). Final-offer arbitration: Better theory than practice. *Industrial Relations, 14,* 311–317.

Feingold, P. C., & Knapp, M. L. (1977). Anti-drug abuse commercials. *Journal of Communication, 27,* 20–28.

Felstiner, W. L. F., Abel, R. L., & Sarat, A. (1980–81). The emergence and transformation of disputes: Naming, blaming, and claiming. *Law and Society Review, 15,* 631–654.

Fern, E. F., Monroe, K. B., & Avila, R. A. (1986). Effectiveness of multiple request strategies: A synthesis of research results. *Journal of Marketing Research, 23,* 144–152.

Festinger, L. A., & Maccoby, N. (1964). On resistance to persuasive communication. *Journal of Abnormal and Social Psychology, 68,* 359–366.

Filley, A. C. (1975). *Interpersonal conflict resolution.* Glenview, IL: Scott Foresman.

Fishbein, M., & Azjen, I. (1975). *Belief, attitude, intention, behavior.* Reading, MA: Addison-Wesley.

Fisher, R. (1964). Fractionating conflict. In R. Fisher (Ed.), *International conflict and behavioral science: The Craigville papers.* New York: Basic Books.

Fisher, R. (1969). *International conflict for beginners.* New York: Harper & Row.

Fisher, R. (1997). *Interactive conflict resolution.* Syracuse, NY: Syracuse University Press.

Fisher, R. & Davis. W. (1999). Authority of an agent: When less is better. In R. H. Mnookin and L. E. Susskind, *Negotiating on behalf of others.* Thousand Oaks, CA: Sage Publications, pp. 59–80.

Fisher, R., & Ertel, D. (1995). *Getting ready to negotiate: The getting to yes workbook.* New York: Penguin.

Fisher, R., Schneider, A. K., Borgwardt, E., & Ganson, B. (1997). *Coping with international conflict.* Upper Saddle River, NJ: Prentice Hall.

Fisher, R., Ury, W., & Patton, B. (1991). *Getting to yes: Negotiating agreement without giving in* (2nd ed.). New York: Penguin.

Fiske, A. P. (1991). *Structures of social life.* New York: The Free Press.

Fiske, S. T., & Taylor, S. W. E. (1991). *Social cognition.* Reading, MA: Addison-Wesley.

Folberg, J., & Taylor, A. (1984). *Mediation: A comprehensive guide to resolving conflicts without litigation.* San Francisco: Jossey-Bass.

Folger, J. P., Poole, M. S., & Stutman, R. K. (1993). *Working through conflict: Strategies for relationships, groups and organizations* (2nd ed.). New York: Harper Collins.

Follett, M. P. (1940). *Dynamic administration: The collected papers of Mary Parker Follett.* H. C. Metcalf & L. Urwick (Eds.). New York: Harper & Brothers.

Follett, M. P. (1942). Constructive conflict. In H. C. Metcalf & L. Urwick (Eds.), *Dynamic administration: The collected papers of Mary Parker Follett* (pp. 30–49). New York: Harper & Brothers.

Ford, D. L., Jr. (1983). Effects of personal control beliefs: An explanatory analysis of bargaining outcomes in intergroup negotiation. *Group and Organization Studies, 8,* 113–125.

Foreman, P., & Murnighan, J. K. (1996). Learning to avoid the winner's curse. *Organizational Behavior and Human Decision Processes, 67,* 170–180.

Forgas, J. P. (1992). Affect in social judgments and decisions: A multiprocess model. *Advances in Experimental Social Psychology, 25,* 227–275.

Fortune, A., & Brodt, S. E. (2000). Face-to-face or virtually, for the second time around: the influence of task, past experience and media on trust and deception in negotiation. Paper presented at the Academy of Management Meetings, Toronto, Canada.

Foster, D. A. (1992). *Bargaining across borders: How to negotiate business successfully anywhere in the world.* New York: McGraw-Hill.

Francis, J. N. P. (1991). When in Rome? The effects of cultural adaptation on intercultural business negotiations. *Journal of International Business Studies, 22,* 403–428.

Freedman, J. L., & Fraser, S. C. (1966). Compliance without pressure: The foot in the door technique. *Journal of Personality and Social Psychology, 4,* 195–202.

French, J. R. P., & Raven, B. (1959). The bases of social power. In D. Cartwright (Ed.), *Studies in social power.* Ann Arbor, MI: Institute for Social Research.

Freund, J. C. (1993). *Smart Negotiating: How to make good deals in the real world.* New York: Simon & Shuster, 1993.

Freund, J. C. (1994). Being a smart negotiator. *Board and Directors, 2*(18), Winter, 33–36.

Froman, L. A., & Cohen, M. D. (1970). Compromise and logrolling: Comparing the efficiency of two bargaining processes. *Behavioral Sciences, 15,* 180–183.

Fry, W. R. (1985). The effect of dyad Machiavellianism and visual access on integrative bargaining outcomes. *Personality and Social Psychology Bulletin, 11,* 51–62.

Fry, W. R., Firestone, I. J., & Williams, D. (1979, April). Bargaining process in mixed-singles dyads: Loving and losing. Paper presented at the Eastern Psychological Association meetings, Philadelphia, PA.

Fry, W. R., Firestone, I. J., & Williams, D. L. (1983). Negotiation process and outcome of stranger dyads and dating couples: Do lovers lose? *Basic and Applied Social Psychology, 4,* 1–16.

Fuller, R. G. C., & Sheehy-Skeffington, A. (1974). Effects of group laughter on responses to humorous materials: A replication and extension. *Psychological Reports, 35,* 531–534.

Fulmer, I. S., & Barry, B. (2002). *The "smart" negotiator: Cognitive ability and emotional intelligence in negotiation.* Presented at the annual meeting of the International Association of Conflict Management, Park City, Utah.

Gadlin, H. (2000). The ombudsman: What's in a name? *Negotiation Journal, 16,* 37–48.

Gahagan, J. P., Long, H., & Horai, J. (1969). Race of experimenter and reactions to black preadolescents. *Proceedings of the 77th Annual Meeting of the American Psychological Association, 4,* 397–398.

Gamson, W. A. (1961). A theory of coalition formation. *American Sociological Review, 26,* 565–573.

Ganesan, S. (1993). Negotiation strategies and the nature of channel relationships. *Journal of Marketing Research, 30,* 183–203.

Garcia, S. M., Darley, J. M., & Robinson, R. J. (2001). Morally questionable tactics: Negotiations between district attorneys and public defenders. *Personality and Social Psychology Bulletin, 27*(6), 731–743.

Geis, F. L., & Moon, T. H. (1981). Machiavellianism and deception. *Journal of Personality and Social Psychology, 41,* 766–775.

Gelfand, M. J., & Christakopoulou, S. (1999). Culture and negotiator cognition: Judgment accuracy and negotiation processes in individualistic and collectivistic cultures. *Organizational Behavior and Human Decision Processes, 79,* 248–269.

Gelfand, M. J., & Dyer, N. (2000). A cultural perspective on negotiation: Progress, pitfalls, and prospects. *Applied Psychology: An International Review, 49,* 62–99.

Gelfand, M. J., & Realo, A. (1999). Individualism-collectivism and accountability in intergroup negotiations. *Journal of Applied Psychology, 84,* 721–736.

George, A. L. (1993). *Bridging the gap: Coercive diplomacy as an alternative to war.* Washington, DC: U.S. Institute of Peace Press.

George, J. M., Jones, G. R., & Gonzalez, J. A. (1998). The role of affect in cross-cultural negotiations. *Journal of International Business Studies, 29,* 749–772.

Gerhart, B., & Rynes, S. (1991). Determinants and consequences of salary negotiations by male and female MBA graduates. *Journal of Applied Psychology, 76,* 256–262.

Gersick, C. J. G. (1988). Time and transition in work teams: Toward a new model of group development. *Academy of Management Journal, 31,* 9–41.

Gersick, C. J. G. (1989). Making time: Predictable transitions in task groups. *Academy of Management Journal, 32,* 274–309.

Geyelin, M. (1997). Mississippi becomes first state to settle suit against big tobacco companies. *Wall Street Journal,* July 7, p. B1.

Ghosh, D. (1996). Nonstrategic delay in bargaining: An experimental investigation. *Organizational Behavior and Human Decision Processes, 67,* 312–325.

Gibb, J. (1961). Defensive communication. *Journal of Communication, 3,* 141–148.

Gibbons, P., Bradac, J. J., & Busch, J. D. (1992). The role of language in negotiations: Threats and promises. In L. Putnam & M. Roloff (Eds.), *Communication and negotiation* (pp. 156–175). Newbury Park, CA: Sage.

Gibson, K., Thompson, L., & Bazerman, M. (1996). Shortcomings of neutrality in mediation: Solutions based on rationality. *Negotiation Journal, 12,* 69–80.

Gillespie, J. J., & Bazerman, M. H. (1998, April). Pre-settlement settlement (PreSS): A simple technique for initiating complex negotiations. *Negotiation Journal, 14,* 149–159.

Gillespie, J. J., & Bazerman, M. H. (1997). Parasitic integration: Win-win agreements containing losers. *Negotiation Journal, 13,* 271–282.

Gilson, R. J., & Mnookin, R. H. Disputing through agents: Cooperation and conflict between lawyers in litigation. *Columbia Law Review, 94*(2), 509–566.

Gilligan, C. (1982). *In a different voice*. Cambridge, MA: Harvard University Press.

Girard, J. (1989). *How to close every sale*. New York: Warner Books.

Gire, J. T. (1997). The varying effect of individualism-collectivism on preference for methods of conflict resolution. *Canadian Journal of Behavioural Science, 29*, 38–43.

Gist, M. E., Stevens, C. K., & Bavetta, A. G. (1991). Effects of self-efficacy and post-training intervention on the acquisition and maintenance of complex interpersonal skills. *Personnel Psychology, 44,* 837–861.

Glasl, F. (1982). The process of conflict escalation and roles of third parties. In G. B. J. Bomers & R. B. Peterson (Eds.), *Conflict management and industrial relations* (pp. 119–141). Boston: Kluwer.

Glick, S., & Croson, R. (2001). Reputations in negotiation. In S. Hock & H., Kunreuther (Eds.), *Wharton on decision making*. New York: John Wiley & Sons, Ch. 10, pp. 177–186.

Glover, S. H., Bumpus, M. A., Logan, J. E., & Ciesla, J. R. (1997). Re-examining the influence of individual values on ethical decision making. *Journal of Business Ethics, 16,* 1319–1329.

Goering, E. M. (1997). Integration versus distribution in contract negotiations: An interaction analysis of strategy use. *Journal of Business Communications, 34,* 383–400.

Goffman, E. (1969). *Strategic interaction*. Philadelphia, PA: University of Philadelphia Press.

Goffman, E. (1974). *Frame analysis*. New York: Harper & Row.

Goldberg, L. R. (1993). The structure of phenotypic personality traits. *American Psychologist, 48,* 26–34.

Goleman, D. (1995). *Emotional intelligence*. New York: Bantam Books.

Goodstadt, B. E., & Hjelle, L. A. (1973). Power to the powerless: Locus of control and the use of power. *Journal of Personality and Social Psychology, 27,* 191–196.

Gordon, T. (1977). *Leader effectiveness training*. New York: Wyden Books.

Gottfredson, L. (1997). Mainstream science on intelligence: An editorial with 52 signatories, history and bibliography. *Intelligence, 24,* 13–23.

Gouldner, A. W. (1960). The norm of reciprocity: A preliminary statement. *American Sociological Review, 25,* 161–178.

Graham, J. L. (1983). Brazilian, Japanese, and American business negotiations. *Journal of International Business Studies, 14,* 47–61.

Graham, J. L. (1984). A comparison of Japanese and American business negotiations. *International Journal of Research in Marketing, 1,* 50–68.

Graham, J. L. (1993). The Japanese negotiation style: Characteristics of a distinct approach. *Negotiation Journal, 9,* 123–140.

Graham, J. L., Evenko, L. L., & Rajan, M. N. (1992). An empirical comparison of Soviet and American business negotiations. *Journal of International Business Studies, 23,* 387–418.

Graham, J. L., & Mintu-Wimsat, A. (1997). Culture's influence on business negotiations in four countries. *Group Decision and Negotiation, 6,* 483–502.

Graham, J. L., & Sano, Y. (1989). *Smart bargaining*. New York: Harper Business.

Granovetter, M. (1973). The strength of weak ties. *American Journal of Sociology, 78,* 1360–1380.

Gray, B. (1991). *The framing of disputes: Partners, processes and outcomes in different contexts*. Paper presented at the annual conference of the International Association of Conflict Management, Den Dolder, The Netherlands.

Gray, B. (1994). The gender-based foundation of negotiation theory. In B. H. Sheppard, R. J. Lewicki, & R. Bies (Eds.), *Research in negotiation in organizations* (Vol. 4, pp. 3–36). Greenwich, CT: JAI Press.

Gray, B. (1997). Framing and reframing of intractable environmental disputes. In *Research on negotiation in organizations*. R. J. Lewicki, R. Bies & B. Sheppard (Eds). 6: 163–188.

Gray, B. (2003). Framing of environmental disputes. In Lewicki, R. J., B. Gray & M. Elliott, *Making Sense of Intractable Environmental Disputes*. Washington, DC: Island Press.

Gray, B., & Donnellon, A. (1989). *An interactive theory of reframing in negotiation*. Unpublished manuscript.

Gray, B., Younglove-Webb, B., & Purdy, J. M. (1997). *Frame repertoires, conflict styles and negotiation outcomes*. Paper read at the International Association of Conflict Management, Bonn, Germany.

Green, R. M. (1993). *The ethical manager*. New York: Macmillan.

Greenberg, B. S., & Miller, G. R. (1966). The effects of low-credible sources on message acceptance. *Speech Monographs, 33,* 135–136.

Greenberg, J. (1986). Organizational performance appraisal procedures: What makes them fair? In R. J. Lewicki, B. H. Sheppard, & M. H. Bazerman (Eds.), *Research on negotiation in organizations* (Vol. 1, pp. 25–42). Greenwich, CT: JAI Press.

Greenberg, J. (1990). Organizational justice: Yesterday, today, tomorrow. *Journal of Management, 16,* 299–432.

Greenhalgh, L. (1986). Managing conflict. *Sloan Management Review, 27,* 45–51.

Greenhalgh, L. (2001). *Managing strategic relationships.* New York: Free Press.

Greenhalgh, L., & Chapman, D. (1996). Relationships between disputants: Analysis of their characteristics and impact. In S. Gleason (Ed.), *Frontiers in dispute resolution and human resources* (pp. 203–228). East Lansing, MI: Michigan State University Press.

Greenhalgh, L., & Chapman, D. (1998). Negotiator relationships, construct measurement, and demonstration of their impact on the process and outcomes of negotiation. *Group Decision and Negotiation, 7,* 465–489.

Greenhalgh, L., & Gilkey, R. W. (1993). The effect of relationship orientation on negotiators cognitions and tactics. *Group Decision and Negotiation, 2,* 167–186.

Greenhalgh, L., & Kramer, R. M. (1990). Strategic choice in conflicts: The importance of relationships. In K. Zald (Ed.), *Organizations and nation states: New perspectives on conflict and cooperation* (pp. 181–220). San Francisco: Jossey-Bass.

Greenhalgh, L., & Neslin, S. A. (1983). Determining outcomes of negotiations. In M. H. Bazerman & R. J. Lewicki (Eds.), *Negotiating in organizations* (pp. 114–134). Beverly Hills, CA: Sage.

Greenhalgh, L., Neslin, S. A., & Gilkey, R. W. (1985). The effects of negotiator preferences, situational power, and negotiator personality on outcomes of business negotiations. *Academy of Management Journal, 28,* 9–33.

Grigsby, D. W. (1981, November). *The effects of an intermediate mediation step on bargaining behavior under various forms of compulsory arbitration.* Paper presented to the Annual Meeting of the American Institute for Decision Sciences, Boston, MA.

Grigsby, D. W., & Bigoness, W. J. (1982). Effects of mediation and alternative forms of arbitration on bargaining behavior: A laboratory study. *Journal of Applied Psychology, 67,* 549–554.

Gruder, C. L. (1971). Relationships with opponent and partner in bargaining. *Journal of Conflict Resolution, 15,* 403–416.

Gruder, C. L., & Duslak, R. J. (1973). Elicitation of cooperation by retaliatory and nonretaliatory strategies in a mixed motive game. *Journal of Conflict Resolution, 17,* 162–174.

Gruder, C. L., & Rosen, N. (1971). Effects of intragroup relations on intergroup bargaining. *International Journal of Group Tension, 1,* 301–317.

Gulliver, P. (1979). *Disputes and negotiations: A cross-cultural perspective.* New York: Academic Press.

Guth, W., Schmittberger, R., & Schwarze, B. (1982). An experimental analysis of ultimatum bargaining. *Journal of Economic Behavior and Organization, 3,* 367–388.

Guth, W., & Tietz, R. (1990). Ultimatum bargaining behavior: A survey and comparison of experimental results. *Journal of Economic Psychology, 11,* 417–449.

Habeeb, W. M. (1988). *Power and tactics in international negotiation.* Baltimore, MD: Johns Hopkins University Press.

Haccoun, R. R., & Klimoski, R. J. (1975). Negotiator status and source: A study of negotiation behavior. *Organizational Behavior and Human Performance, 14,* 342–359.

Hall, E. T. (1960, May–June). The silent language of overseas business. *Harvard Business Review, 38,* 87–96.

Hall, J. (1969). *Conflict management survey: A survey of one's characteristic reaction to and handling conflict between himself and others.* Conroe, TX: Teleometrics International.

Halpern, J. J., & Parks, J. M. (1996). *Vive la difference:* Differences between males and females in process and outcomes in a low-conflict negotiation. *International Journal of Conflict Management, 7,* 45–70.

Hamilton, J. B., & Strutton, D. (1994). Two practical guidelines for resolving truth telling problems in business transactions. *Journal of Business Ethics, 13,* 899–912.

Hammond, J. S., Keeney, R. L., & Raiffa, H. (1998). The hidden traps in decision making. *Harvard Business Review, 76*(5), 47–58.

Hamner, W. C. (1980). The influence of structural, individual, and strategic differences. In D. L. Harnett & L. L. Cummings (Eds.), *Bargaining behavior* (pp. 21–80). Houston, TX: Dame Publications.

Hardin, R. G. (1968). The tragedy of the commons. *Science, 162,* 1243–1248.

Harding, S. (1986). *The science question in feminism.* Ithaca, NY: Cornell University Press.

Harinck, F., De Dreu, C. K. W., & Van Vienen, A. E. M. (2000). The impact of conflict issues on fixed-pie perceptions, problem solving, and integrative outcomes in negotiation. *Organizational Behavior and Human Decision Processes, 81,* 329–358.

Harris, K. L., & Carnevale, P. J. D. (1990). Chilling and hastening: The influence of third-party power and interests on negotiation. *Organizational Behavior and Human Decision Processes, 47,* 138–160.

Hartzell, C. A. (1999). Explaining the stability of negotiated settlements to intrastate wars. *Journal of Conflict Resolution, 43,* 3–22.

Harvey, O. J. (1953). An experimental approach to the study status relations in informal groups. *Sociometry, 18,* 357–367.

Hassett, J. (1981, June). Is it right? An inquiry into everyday ethics. *Psychology Today,* 49–53.

Hassett, J. (1981, November). But that would be wrong . . . *Psychology Today,* 34–53.

Hassett, J. (1982, August). *Correlates of moral values and behavior.* Paper presented at the annual meeting of the Academy of Management, New York.

Hegarty, W., & Sims, H. P. (1978). Some determinants of unethical decision behavior: An experiment. *Journal of Applied Psychology, 63,* 451–457.

Hegtved, K. A., & Killian, C. (1999). Fairness and emotions: Reactions to the process and outcomes of negotiations. *Social Forces, 78,* 269–303.

Heider, F. (1958). *The psychology of interpersonal relations.* New York: John Wiley and Sons.

Heller, J. R. (1967). The effects of racial prejudice, feedback, strategy, and race on cooperative–competitive behavior. *Dissertation Abstracts International, 27,* 2507–2508b.

Henderson, B. (1973). *The nonlogical strategy.* Boston, MA: Boston Consulting Group.

Hendon, D. W., & Hendon, R. A. (1990). *World-class negotiating: Dealmaking in the global marketplace.* New York: John Wiley and Sons.

Henkoff, R. (1997, December 8). Are you (more than) ready for a pay raise? *Fortune,* pp. 233–238.

Hermann, M. G., & Kogan, N. (1977). Effects of negotiators' personalities on negotiating behavior. In D. Druckman (Ed.), *Negotiations: Social-psychological perspectives* (pp. 247–274). Beverly Hills, CA: Sage.

Herrman, M. S., Hollett, N., Gale, J., & Foster, M. (2001). Defining mediator knowledge and skills. *Negotiation Journal, 17,* 139–154.

Higgins, E. T. (1987). Self discrepancy theory: A theory relating self and affect. *Psychological Review, 94,* 319–340.

Hill, B. J. (1982). An analysis of conflict resolution techniques: From problem-solving workshops to theory. *Journal of Conflict Resolution, 26,* 109–138.

Hiltrop, J. (1989). Factors associated with successful labor mediation. In K. Kressel & D. Pruitt (Eds.), *Mediation research* (pp. 241–262). San Francisco: Jossey-Bass.

Hiltrop, J. M., & Rubin, J. Z. (1982). Effects of intervention mode and conflict of interest on dispute resolution. *Journal of Personality and Social Psychology, 42,* 665–672.

Hilty, J. A., & Carnevale, P. J. (1993). Black-hat/white-hat strategy in bilateral negotiation. *Organizational Behavior and Human Decision Processes, 55,* 444–469.

Hinton, B. L., Hamner, W. C., & Pohlan, N. F. (1974). Influence and award of magnitude, opening bid and concession rate on profit earned in a managerial negotiating game. *Behavioral Science, 19,* 197–203.

Hirokawa, R. Y. (1981). Improving intra-organizational communication: A lesson from Japanese management. *Communication Quarterly, 30,* 35–40.

Hitt, W. (1990). *Ethics and leadership: Putting theory into practice.* Columbus, OH: Battelle Press.

Hoare, C. H. (1994). Psychological identity development in United States society: Its role in fostering exclusion of other cultures. In E. P. Salett & D. R. Koslow, (Eds.) *Race, ethnicity and self: Identity in multicultural perspective.* Washington, DC. National Multicultural Institute, 24–41.

Hochberg, A. M., & Kressel, K. (1996). Determinations of successul and unsuccessful divorce negotiations. *Journal of Divorce & Remarriage, 25,* 1–21.

Hocker, J. L., & Wilmot, W. W. (1985). *Interpersonal conflict* (2nd ed.). Dubuque, IA: Wm. C. Brown.

Hofstede, G. (1980a). Motivation, leadership, and organization: Do American theories apply abroad? *Organizational Dynamics, 9,* 42–63.

Hofstede, G. (1980b). *Culture's consequences: International differences in work related values.* Beverly Hills, CA: Sage.

Hofstede, G. (1989). Cultural predictors of national negotiation styles. In. F. Mautner-Markhof (Ed.), *Processes of international negotiations* (pp. 193–201). Boulder, CO: Westview Press.

Hofstede, G. (1991). *Culture and organizations: Software of the mind.* London, UK: McGraw-Hill.

Hofstede, G., & Bond, M. H. (1988). Confucius and economic growth: New trends in culture's consequences. *Organizational Dynamics, 16,* 4–21.

Hogg, M. A., Terry, D. J., & White, K. M. (1995). A tale of two theories: A critical comparison of identity theory with social identity theory. *Social Psychology Quarterly, 58,* 255–269.

Hollingshead, A. B., & Carnevale, P. J. (1990, August). *Positive affect and decision frame in integrative bargaining: A reversal of the frame effect.* Paper presented at the 50th Annual Meeting of the Academy of Management, San Francisco.

Holmes, M. (1992). Phase structures in negotiation. In L. Putnam & M. Roloff (Eds.), *Communication and negotiation* (pp. 83–105). Newbury Park, CA: Sage.

Holmes, J. G., & Murray, S. I. (1996). Conflict in close relationships. In E. T. Higgins & A. W. Kruglanski (Eds.), *Social psychology: Handbook of basic principles* (pp. 579–621). New York: Guilford.

Holmes, M., & Poole, M. S. (1991). Longitudinal analysis of interaction. In S. Duck & B. Montgomery (Eds.), *Studying interpersonal interaction* (pp. 286–302). New York: Guilford.

Homans, G. C. (1961). *Social behavior: Its elementary forms.* New York: Harcourt, Brace & World Co.

Hornstein, H. (1965). Effects of different magnitudes of threat upon interpersonal bargaining. *Journal of Experimental Social Psychology, 1,* 282–293.

Hovland, C. I., & Mandell, W. (1952). An experimental comparison of conclusion drawing by the communicator and by the audience. *Journal of Abnormal and Social Psychology, 47,* 581–588.

Husted, B. W. (1996). Mexican small business negotiations with U. S. companies: Challenges and opportunities. *International Small Business Journal, 14,* 45–54.

Ikle, F. C. (1964). *How nations negotiate.* New York: Harper & Row.

Isajiw, W. W. (2000). Approaches to ethnic conflict resolution: paradigms and principles. *International Journal of Intercultural Relations, 24,* 105–124.

Isen, A. M., & Baron, R. A. (1991). Positive affect as a factor in organizational behavior. In B. M. Staw & L. L. Cummings (Eds.), *Research in organizational behavior* (Vol. 13, pp. 1–53). Greenwich, CT: JAI Press.

Ivey, A. E., & Simek-Downing, L. (1980). *Counseling and psychotherapy.* Englewood Cliffs, NJ: Prentice Hall.

Jackall, R. (1988). *Moral mazes.* New York: Oxford University Press.

Jackson, S., & Allen, M. (1987). *Meta-analysis of the effectiveness of one-sided and two-sided argumentation.* Paper presented at the annual meeting of the International Communication Association, Montreal, Quebec.

Jacobs, A. T. (1951). *Some significant factors influencing the range of indeterminateness in collective bargaining negotiations.* Unpublished doctoral dissertation, University of Michigan, Ann Arbor, MI.

Jandt, F., & Pedersen, P. B. (Eds.). (1996). *Constructive conflict management: Asia-Pacific cases.* Thousand Oaks, CA: Sage.

Janis, I. (1982). *Groupthink: Psychological studies of policy decisions and fiascoes.* Boston, MA: Houghton Mifflin.

Janis, I. (1989). *Crucial decisions: Leadership in policymaking and crisis management.* New York: Free Press.

Janis, I., & Mann, L. (1977). *Decision making.* New York: Free Press.

Janosik, R. J. (1987). Rethinking the culture-negotiation link. *Negotiation Journal, 3,* 385–395.

Jensen, L. (1995). Issue flexibility in negotiating internal war. *The Annals of the American Academy of Political and Social Science, 542,* 116–130.

Johns, G. (1989). Substantive and methodological constraints on behavior and attitudes in organizational research. *Organizational Behavior and Human Decision Processes, 49,* 80–104.

Johnson, B. T., & Eagly, A. H. (1989). Effects of involvement on persuasion: A meta-analysis. *Psychological Bulletin, 106,* 290–314.

Johnson, B. T., & Eagly, A. H. (1990). Involvement and persuasion: Types, traditions, and the evidence. *Psychological Bulletin, 107,* 375–384.

Johnson, D. W. (1971). Role reversal: A summary and review of the research. *International Journal of Group Tensions, 1,* 318–334.

Johnson, D. W., & Dustin, R. (1970). The initiation of cooperation through role reversal. *Journal of Social Psychology, 82,* 193–203.

Johnson, D. W., & Lewicki, R. J. (1969). The initiation of superordinate goals. *Journal of Applied Behavioral Science, 5,* 9–24.

Johnson, R. (1993). *Negotiation basics: Concepts, skills, and exercises.* Newbury Park, CA: Sage.

Johnston, R. W. (1982, March–April). Negotiation strategies: Different strokes for different folks. *Personnel, 59,* 36–45.

Jones, E. E. (1964). *Ingratiation.* New York: Appleton-Century-Crofts.

Jones, E. E., & Nisbett, R. E. (1976). The actor and the observer: Divergent perceptions of causality. In J. W. Thibaut, J. T. Spence, & R. C. Carson (Eds.), *Contemporary topics in social psychology* (pp. 37–52). Morristown, NJ: General Learning Press.

Jones, S. B., & Burgoon, M. (1975). Empirical investigations of language intensity: 2. The effects of irrelevant fear and language intensity on attitude change. *Human Communication Research, 1,* 248–251.

Jones, T. S., & Bodtker, A. (2001). Mediating with heart in mind: Addressing emotion in mediation practice. *Negotiation Journal, 17,* 217–244.

Jones, T. S., & Remland, M. S. (1993). Nonverbal communication and conflict escalation: An attribution-based model. *The International Journal of Conflict Management, 4,* 119–137.

Jordan, J. M., & Roloff, M. E. (1997). Planning skills and negotiator goal accomplishment. *Communication Research, 24,* 31–63.

Joseph, M. L., & Willis, R. H. (1963). An experimental analog to two-party bargaining. *Behavioral Science, 8,* 1117–1127.

Kabanoff, B. (1987). Predictive validity of the MODE conflict instrument. *Journal of Applied Psychology, 72,* 160–163.

Kadushin, C. (1968). Power, influence and social circles: A new methodology for studying opinion makers. *American Sociological Review, 33,* 685–699.

Kahneman, D., Knetsch, J. L., & Thaler, R. H. (1990). Experimental tests of the endowment effect and the Coase Theorem. *Journal of Political Economy, 98,* 1325–1348.

Kahneman, D., & Tversky, A. (1979). Prospect theory: An analysis of decisions under risk. *Econometrica, 47,* 263–291.

Kale, S. H., & Barnes, J. W. (1992). Understanding the domain of cross-national buyer-seller interactions. *Journal of International Business Studies, 23,* 101–132.

Kanowitz, L. (1985). *Alternative dispute resolution.* St. Paul, MN: West.

Kant, I. (1963). *Lectures on ethics.* New York: Harper & Row.

Kant, I. (1964). *Groundwork of the metaphysic of morals.* New York: Harper & Row.

Kanter, R. (1979). Power failures in management circles. *Harvard Business Review, 57,* pp. 65–75.

Kaplan, Robert. (1984, Spring). Trade routes: The manager's network of relationships. *Organizational Dynamics, 12,* 37–52.

Karambayya, R., & Brett, J. M. (1989). Managers handling disputes: Third-party roles and perceptions of fairness. *Academy of Management Journal, 32,* 263–291.

Karambayya, R., Brett, J. M., & Lytle, A. (1992). Effects of formal authority and experience on third-party roles, outcomes, and perceptions of fairness. *Academy of Management Journal, 35,* 426–438.

Karrass, C. (1974). *Give and take.* New York: Thomas Y. Crowell.

Karrass, C. (1999). *Purchasing,* May 6, p. 28.

Karrass, G. (1985). *Negotiate to close: How to make more successful deals.* New York: Simon & Schuster.

Kaufman, S., & Duncan, G. (1992). A formal framework for mediator mechanisms and motivations. *Journal of Conflict Resolution, 36,* 688–707.

Keer, S., & Naimark, R. W. (2001). Arbitrators do not "split the baby": Empirical evidence from international business arbitration. *Journal of International Arbitration, 18*(5): 573–578.

Keiser, T. (1988). Negotiating with a customer you can't afford to lose. *Harvard Business Review, 66*(6), pp. 30–37.

Kelman, H. C. (1996). Negotiation as interactive problem solving. *International Negotiation, 1,* 99–123.

Kellerman, J. L., Lewis, J., & Laird, J. D. (1989). Looking and loving: The effects of mutual gaze on feelings of romantic love. *Journal of Research in Personality, 23,* 145–161.

Kelley, H. H. (1966). A classroom study of the dilemmas in interpersonal negotiation. In K. Archibald (Ed.), *Strategic interaction and conflict: Original papers and discussion* (pp. 49–73). Berkeley, CA: Institute of International Studies.

Kelley, H. H., Berscheid, E., Christensen, A., Harvey, J., Houston, T. L., Levinger, G., McClintock, E., Peplau, A., & Peterson, D. R. (1983). Analyzing close relationships. In H. H. Kelley et al. (Eds.), *Close relationships* (pp. 20–67). San Francisco: Freeman.

Kelley, H. H., & Schenitzki, D. P. (1972). Bargaining. In C. G. McClintock (Ed.), *Experimental social psychology* (pp. 298–337). New York: Holt, Rinehart & Winston.

Kelley, H. H., & Stahelski, A. J. (1970). Social interaction basis of cooperators' and competitors' beliefs about others. *Journal of Personality and Social Psychology, 16,* 66–91.

Kelley, H. H., & Thibaut, J. (1969). Group problem solving. In G. Lindzey & E. Aronson (Eds.), *Handbook of social psychology* (2nd ed.), (Vol. 4, pp. 1–101). Reading, MA: Addison-Wesley.

Kelman, H. C. (1996). Negotiation as interactive problem solving. *International Negotiation, 1,* 99–123.

Kelman, H. C., & Hamilton, V. L. (1989). *Crimes of obedience.* New Haven, CT: Yale University Press.

Keltner, D., & Robinson, R. J. (1993). Imagined ideological differences in conflict escalation and resolution. *The International Journal of Conflict Management, 4,* 249–262.

Kemp, K. E., & Smith, W. P. (1994). Information exchange, toughness, and integrative bargaining: The roles of explicit cues and perspective-taking. *International Journal of Conflict Management, 5,* 5–21.

Kennedy, G. (1985). *Doing business abroad.* New York: Simon & Schuster.

Kessler, S. (1978). *Creative conflict resolution: Mediation.* Atlanta, GA: NIPT.

Kilmann, R. H., & Thomas, K. W. (1977). Developing a forced-choice measure of conflict-handling behavior: The MODE instrument. *Educational and Psychological Measurement, 37,* 309–325.

Kim, M. S., & Kitani, K. (1998). Conflict management styles of Asian- and Causcasion-Americans in romantic relationships in Hawaii. *Journal of Asian Pacific Communication, 8,* 51–68.

Kim, P. H. (1997). Strategic timing in group negotiations: The implications of forced entry and forced exit for negotiators with unequal power. *Organizational Behavior and Human Decision Processes, 71,* 263–286.

Kim, S. H., & Smith, R. H. (1993). Revenge and conflict escalation. *Negotiation Journal, 9,* 37–43.

Kimmel, M. J., Pruitt, D. G., Magenau, J. M., Konar-Goldband, E., & Carnevale, P. J. D. (1980). Effects of trust aspiration and gender on negotiation tactics. *Journal of Personality and Social Psychology, 38,* 9–23.

King, D. C., & Zeckhauer, R. (1999). Legislators as negotiators. In R. H. Mnookin and L. E. Susskind, *Negotiating on behalf of others.* Thousand Oaks, CA: Sage Publications, pp. 203–225.

Kinsman, M. (1992, November 30). Résumé lies seem to be on increase. *Upper Arlington (Ohio) This Week,* p. 26.

Kipnis, D. (1976). *The powerholders.* Chicago: University of Chicago Press.

Kirby, S. L., & Davis, M. A. (1998). A study of escalating commitment in principal-agent relationships: Effects of monitoring and personal responsibility. *Journal of Applied Psychology, 83,* 2, 206–217.

Kleinke, C. L. (1986). Gaze and eye contact: A research review. *Psychological Bulletin, 100,* 78–100.

Kleinke, C. L., & Pohlan, P. D. (1971). Effective and emotional responses as a function of other person's gaze and cooperativeness in two person games. *Journal of Personality and Social Psychology, 17,* 308–313.

Klimoski, R. J. (1972). The effects of intragroup forces on intergroup conflict resolution. *Organizational Behavior and Human Performance, 8,* 363–383.

Klimoski, R. J., & Ash, R. A. (1974). Accountability and negotiator behavior. *Organizational Behavior and Human Performance, 11,* 409–425.

Kochan, T. A. (1980). *Collective bargaining and industrial relations.* Homewood, IL: Richard D. Irwin.

Kochan, T. A., & Jick, T. (1978). The public sector mediation process: A theory and empirical examination. *Journal of Conflict Resolution, 22,* 209–240.

Koehn, D. (1997). Business and game playing: The false analogy. *Journal of Business Ethics, 16,* 1447–1452.

Kogan, N., Lamm, H., & Trommsdorf, G. (1972). Negotiation constraints in the risk taking domain: Effects of being observed by partners of higher or lower status. *Journal of Personality and Social Psychology, 23,* 143–156.

Koh, T. T. B. (1996). American strengths and weaknesses. *Negotiation Journal, 12,* 313–317.

Kohlberg, L. (1969). Stage and sequence: The cognitive development approach to socialization. In D. Goslin (Ed.), *Handbook of socialization theory and research* (pp. 347–380). Chicago: Rand McNally.

Kolb, D. (1983a). *The mediators.* Cambridge, MA: MIT Press.

Kolb, D. (1983b). Strategy and the tactics of mediation. *Human Relations, 36*(3), 247–268.

Kolb, D. (1985). *The mediators.* Cambridge, MA: MIT Press.

Kolb, D. (1992, August). *Is it her voice or her place that makes a difference? A consideration of gender issues in negotiation.* Paper presented at the annual meeting of the Academy of Management, Las Vegas, Nevada.

Kolb, D. (1995). The love for three oranges, or: What did we miss about Ms. Follett in the Library? *Negotiation Journal, 11,* 339–348.

Kolb, D., & Coolidge, G. G. (1991). Her place at the table: A consideration of gender issues in negotiation. In J. Z. Rubin and J. W. Breslin (Eds.), *Negotiation theory and practice* (pp. 261–277). Cambridge, MA: Harvard Program on Negotiation.

Kolb, D. M., & Associates. (1994). *When talk works: Profiles of mediators.* San Francisco: Jossey-Bass.

Kolb, D. M., & Putnam, L. L. (1997). Through the looking glass: Negotiation theory refracted through the lens of gender. In S. Gleason (Ed.), *Frontiers in dispute resolution in labor relations and human resources* (pp. 231–257). East Lansing, MI: Michigan State University Press.

Kolb, D. M., & Williams, J. (2001). Breakthrough bargaining. *Harvard Business Review, 79*(2), 89–97.

Komorita, S. S., & Brenner, A. R. (1968). Bargaining and concessions under bilateral monopoly. *Journal of Personality and Social Psychology, 9,* 15–20.

Komorita, S. S., & Mechling, J. (1967). Betrayal and reconciliation in a two person game. *Journal of Personality and Social Psychology, 6,* 349–353.

Kotter, J. (1977, July–August). Power, dependence and effective management. *Harvard Business Review, 55,* 125–136.

Kotter, J. (1979). *Power in management.* New York: AMACOM.

Kozan, M. K. (1997). Culture and conflict management: A theoretical framework. *International Journal of Conflict Management, 8*(4), 338–360.

Krackhardt, D., & Hanson, J. R. (1993, July–August). Informal networks: The company behind the chart. *Harvard Business Review, 71,* 104–111.

Kramer, R. M. (1991). The more the merrier? Social psychological aspects of multiparty negotiations in organizations. In M. Bazerman, R. Lewicki, & B. H. Sheppard, *Research on negotiation in organizations* (Vol. 3, pp. 307–332). Greenwich, CT: JAI Press.

Kramer, R. M., Newton, E., & Pommerenke, P. L. (1993). Self-enhancement biases and negotiator judgment: Effects of self-esteem and mood. *Organizational Behavior and Human Decision Processes, 56,* 110–133.

Kramer, R. M., Pommerenke, P., & Newton, B. (1993). The social context of negotiation: Effects of trust, aspiration and gender on negotiation tactics. *Journal of Personality and Social Psychology, 38*(1), 9–22.

Kramer, R. M., Shah, P. P., & Woerner, S. L. (1995). Why ultimatums fail: Social identity and moralistic aggression in coercive bargaining. In R. M. Kramer & D. M. Messick (Eds.), *Negotiation as social process* (pp. 285–308). Thousand Oaks, CA: Sage.

Kray, L. J., Thompson, L., & Galinsky, A. (2001). Battle of the sexes: Gender stereotype confirmation and reactance in negotiation. *Journal of Personality and Social Psychology, 80,* 942–958.

Kremenyuk, V. A. (Ed.). (1991). *International negotiation: Analysis, approaches, issues.* San Francisco: Jossey-Bass.

Kressel, K. (1972). *Labor mediation: An exploratory survey.* Albany, NY: Association of Labor Mediation Agencies.

Kressel, K. (1985). *The process of divorce.* New York: Basic Books.

Kressel, K., Frontera, E., Forlenza, S., Butler, F., & Fish, L. (1994). The settlement-orientation vs. the problem-solving style in custody mediation. *Journal of Social Issues, 50,* 67–84.

Kressel, K., & Pruitt, D. (Eds.). (1989). *Mediation research.* San Francisco: Jossey-Bass.

Kristensen, H., & Garling, T. (1997). The effects of anchor points and reference points on negotiation process and outcome. *Organizational Behavior and Human Decision Processes, 71,* 85–94.

Kumar, R. (1997). The role of affect in negotiations: An integrative overview. *Journal of Applied Behavioral Science, 3*(1), 84–100.

Kurtz, H. (1998). *Spin cycle.* New York: Free Press.

Kurtzberg, T., Moore, D., Valley, K., & Bazerman, M. H. (1999). Agents in negotiations: Toward testable propositions. In R. H. Mnookin and L. E. Susskind, *Negotiating on behalf of others.* Thousand Oaks, CA: Sage Publications, pp. 283–298.

Kurtzberg, T. R. (1998). Creative thinking, cognitive aptitude, and integrative joint gain: A study of negotiator creativity. *Creativity Research Journal, 11,* 283–293.

Landon, E. L., Jr. (1997). For the most fitting deal, tailor negotiating strategy to each borrower. *Commercial Lending Review, 12,* 5–14.

Large, M. D. (1999). The effectiveness of gifts as unilateral initiatives in bargaining. *Sociological Perspectives, 42,* 525–542.

Larrick, R. P., & Boles, T. L. (1995). Avoiding regret in decisions with feedback: A negotiation example. *Organizational Behavior and Human Decision Processes, 63,* 87–97.

Laubach, C. (1997). Negotiating a gain-gain agreement. *Healthcare Executive,* January–February, p. 14.

Lax, D., & Sebenius, J. (1986). *The manager as negotiator: Bargaining for cooperation and competitive gain.* New York: Free Press.

Lazarus, R. S. (1991). *Emotion and adaptation.* New York: Oxford University Press.

Leavitt, H. J., & Bahrami, H. (1988). *Managerial psychology: Managing behavior in organizations* (5th ed.). Chicago, IL: University of Chicago Press.

Lefcourt, H. M. (1982). *Locus of control: Current trends in theory and research* (2nd ed.). Hillsdale, NJ: Lawrence Erlbaum.

Lepine, J. A., Colquitt, J. A., & Erez, A. (2000). Adaptability to changing task contexts: Effects of general cognitive ability, conscientiousness, and openness to experience. *Personnel Psychology, 53,* 563–593.

Le Poole, S. (1989). Negotiating with Clint Eastwood in Brussels. *Management Review, 78,* 58–60.

Leung, T., & Yeung, L. L. (1995). Negotiation in the People's Republic of China: Results of a survey of small businesses in Hong Kong. *Journal of Small Business Management, 33,* 70–77.

Leventhal, H. (1970). Findings and theory in the study of fear communications. In L. Berkowitz (Ed.), *Advances in experimental social psychology* (Vol. 5, pp. 120–186). New York: Academic Press.

Levinson, J. C., Smith, M. S. A., & Wilson, O. R. (1999). *Guerilla negotiating.* New York: John Wiley.

Lewicki, R. J. (1983). Lying and deception: A behavioral model. In M. H. Bazerman & R. J. Lewicki (Eds.), *Negotiating in organizations* (pp. 68–90). Beverly Hills, CA: Sage.

Lewicki, R. J. (1992). Negotiating strategically. In A. Cohen (Ed.), *The portable MBA in management* (pp. 147–189). New York: John Wiley and Sons.

Lewicki, R. J., & Alderfer, C. P. (1973). The tensions between research and intervention in intergroup conflict. *Journal of Applied Behavioral Science, 9,* 424–468.

Lewicki, R. J., & Bunker, B. B. (1995). Trust in relationships: A model of trust development and decline. In B. B. Bunker & J. Z. Rubin (Eds.), *Conflict, cooperation and justice* (pp. 133–174). San Francisco: Jossey-Bass.

Lewicki, R. J., & Bunker, B. B. (1996). A model of trust development and decline. In R. Kramer & T. Tyler (Eds.), *Trust in organizations* (pp. 114–139). Newbury Park, CA: Sage.

Lewicki, R. J., & Dineen, B. R. (2003). Negotiating in virtual organizations. In Heneman, R. & Greenberger, D. *Human resource management in virtual organizations,* New York: John Wiley and Sons.

Lewicki, R. J., Gray, B., & Elliott, M. (2003). *Making sense of intractable environmental disputes.* Washington, DC: Island Press.

Lewicki, R. J., & Hiam, A. (1999). *The fast forward MBA in negotiation and dealmaking.* New York: John Wiley and Sons.

Lewicki, R. J., Hiam, A., & Olander, K. (1996). *Think before you speak: The complete guide to strategic negotiation.* New York: John Wiley and Sons.

Lewicki, R. J., McAllister, D., & Bies, R. H. (1998). Trust and distrust: New relationships and realities. *Academy of Management Review. 23*(3), 438–458.

Lewicki, R. J., & Robinson, R. (1998). A factor-analytic study of negotiator ethics. *Journal of Business Ethics, 18,* 211–228.

Lewicki, R. J., & Sheppard, B. H. (1985). Choosing how to intervene: Factors affecting the use of process and outcome control in third party dispute resolution. *Journal of Occupational Behavior, 6,* 49–64.

Lewicki, R. J., & Spencer, G. (1990, June). *Lies and dirty tricks.* Paper presented at the meeting of the International Association for Conflict Management, Vancouver, B. C., Canada.

Lewicki, R. J., & Spencer, G. (1991, August). *Ethical relativism and negotiating tactics: Factors affecting their perceived ethicality.* Paper presented at the meeting of the Academy of Management, Miami, FL.

Lewicki, R. J., & Stark, N. (1995). What's ethically appropriate in negotiations: An empirical examination of bargaining tactics. *Social Justice Research, 9,* 69–95.

Lewicki, R. J., & Stevenson, M. (1998). Trust development in negotiation: Proposed actions and a research agenda. *Journal of Business and Professional Ethics, 16*(1–3), 99–132.

Lewicki, R. J., Weiss, S., & Lewin, D. (1992). Models of conflict, negotiation and third-party intervention: A review and synthesis. *Journal of Organizational Behavior, 13,* 209–252.

Lewis, M. (1990). *Liar's poker.* New York: Penguin Books.

Lewis, M. H., & Reinsch, N. L. (1988). Listening in organizational environments. *Journal of Business Communication, 25,* 49–67.

Liebert, R. M., Smith, W. P., & Hill, J. H. (1968). The effects of information and magnitude of initial offer on interpersonal negotiation. *Journal of Experimental Social Psychology, 4,* 431–441.

Liebschutz, M. (1997). Negotiating the best deal requires a poker strategy. *The Wall Street Journal,* June 8, p. B1.

Lim, R. G. (1997). Overconfidence in negotiation revisited. *The International Journal of Conflict Management, 8,* 52–70.

Lim, R. G., & Carnevale, P. J. D. (1990). Contingencies in the mediation of disputes. *Journal of Personality & Social Psychology, 58,* 259 272.

Lim, R. G., & Murnighan, J. K. (1994). Phases, deadlines, and the bargaining process. *Organizational Behavior and Human Decision Processes, 58,* 153–171.

Lindskold, S., Bentz, B., & Walters, P. D. (1986). Trust development, the GRIT proposal and the effects of conciliatory acts on conflict and cooperation. *Psychological Bulletin, 85,* 772–793.

Lipin, S. (1996). In many merger deals, ego and pride play big roles in which way talks go. *The Wall Street Journal,* August 22, C1, C6.

Lituchy, T. R. (1997). Negotiations between Japanese and Americans: The effects of collectivism on integrative outcomes. *Canadian Journal of Administrative Sciences, 14,* 386–395.

Loewenstein, G. F., Thompson, L., & Bazerman, M. H. (1989). Social utility and decision making in interpersonal contexts. *Journal of Personality and Social Psychology, 57*(3), 426–441.

Long, G., & Feuille, P. (1974). Final offer arbitration: Sudden death in Eugene. *Industrial and Labor Relations Review, 27,* 186–203.

Lovenheim, P. (1989). *Mediate, don't litigate: How to resolve disputes quickly, privately, and inexpensively without going to court.* New York: McGraw-Hill.

Lowe, T. (1986, January). Eight ways to ruin a performance appraisal. *Personnel Journal, 65,* 60–62.

Luce, R. D., & Raiffa, H. (1957). *Games and decisions: Introduction and critical survey.* New York: John Wiley and Sons.

Lukov, V. (1985). International negotiations of the 1980s: Features, problems and prospects. *Negotiation Journal, 1,* 139–148.

Lumsden, G., & Lumsden, D. (1996). *Communicating with credibility and confidence.* San Francisco: Wadsworth.

Lynch, J. E. (2001). Beyond ADR: A systems approach to conflict management. *Negotiation Journal, 17,* 207–216.

Lytle, A. L., Brett, J. M., & Shapiro, D. L. (1999). The strategic use of interests, rights, and power to resolve disputes. *Negotiation Journal, 15*(1), 31–51.

Macneil, I. R. (1980). *The new social contract.* New Haven, CT: Yale University Press.

Maier, N. R. F. (1952). *Principles of human relations.* New York: John Wiley and Sons.

Maier, N. R. F., & Hoffman, L. R. (1960). Quality of first and second solution in group problem solving. *Journal of Applied Psychology, 44,* 278–283.

Maier, R. A., & Lavrakas, P. J. (1976). Lying behavior and the evaluation of lies. *Perceptual and Motor Skills, 42,* 575–581.

Mannix, E. A., Tinsley, C. H., & Bazerman, M. (1995). Negotiating over time: Impediments to integrative solutions. *Organizational Behavior and Human Decision Processes, 62,* 241–251.

March, J. (1962). The business firm as a political coalition. *The Journal of Politics, 24,* 662–678.

Marcus, A. D. (1996, September 30). In Mideast politics, controlling the past is a key to the present. *The Wall Street Journal,* pp. A1, A13.

Martin, J. (1996). How to negotiate with really tough guys. *Fortune,* May 27, pp. 173–174.

Mason, E. S., & Mudrack, P. E. (1997). Do complex moral reasoners experience greater ethical work conflict? *Journal of Business Ethics, 16,* 1311–1318.

Mautner-Markhof, F. (Ed.). (1989). *Processes of international negotiations.* Boulder, CO: Westview Press.

Mayer, B. (2000). *The dynamics of conflict resolution.* San Francisco: Jossey-Bass.

Mayer, J. D., & Salovey, P. (1997). What is emotional intelligence? In P. Salovey & D. J. Sluyter (Eds.), *Emotional development and emotional intelligence: Educational implications* (pp. 3–31). New York: BasicBooks.

Mayer, J. D., Salovey, P., & Caruso, D. (2000). *Emotional intelligence.* In R. Sternberg (Ed.), *Handbook of intelligence* (pp. 396–420). Cambridge: Cambridge University Press.

Mayer, F. W. (1992). Managing domestic differences in international negotiations: The strategic use of internal side-payments. *International Organization, 46,* 793–818.

Mayfield, M., Mayfield, J., Martin, D., & Herbig, P. (1997). Time perspectives of the cross-cultural negotiations process. *American Business Review, 15,* 78–85.

McAllister, D. J. (1995). Affect- and cognition-based trust as foundations for interpersonal cooperation in organizations. *Academy of Management Journal, 38,* 24–59.

McCallum, D. M., Harring, K., Gilmore, R., Drenan, S., Chase, J. P., Insko, C., & Thibaut, J. (1985). Competition and cooperation between groups and between individuals. *Journal of Experimental Social Psychology, 21,* 301–320.

McClintock, C. G., & Liebrand, W. B. (1988). Role of interdependence structure, individual value orientation, and another's strategy in social decision making: A transformation analysis. *Journal of Personality and Social Psychology, 55,* 396–409.

McCornack, S. A., & Levine, T. R. (1990). When lies are uncovered: Emotional and relational outcomes of discovered deception. *Communication Monographs, 57,* 119–138.

McCroskey, J. C., Jensen, T., & Valencia, C. (1973, November). *Measurement of the credibility of mass media sources.* Paper presented at the Western Speech Communication Association, Albuquerque, NM.

McDonald, J. (1963). *Strategy in poker, business & war.* New York: William Norton.

McDonald, J. W. (1996). An American's view of a U. S. negotiating style. *International Negotiation, 1,* 323–326.

McEwen, C., & Milburn, T. (1993). Explaining a paradox of mediation. *Negotiation Journal, 9*(1), 23–36.

McEwen, C. A. (1999). Toward a program-based ADR research agenda. *Negotiation Journal, 15,* 325–338.

McGraw, D. (1997, October 20). Will he own the road? *U. S. News & World Report,* pp. 45–54.

McGuire, W. J. (1964). Inducing resistance to persuasion: Some contemporary approaches. In L. Berkowitz (Ed.), *Advances in experimental social psychology* (Vol. 1, pp. 191–229). New York: Academic Press.

McGuire, W. J. (1973). Persuasion, resistance and attitude change. In I. S. Poole, F. W. Frey, W. Schramm, N. Maccoby, & E. B. Parker (Eds.), *Handbook of communication* (pp. 216–252). Skokie, IL: Rand McNally.

McKersie, R. (1999). Agency in the context of labor relations. In R. H. Mnookin and L. E. Susskind, *Negotiating on behalf of others.* Thousand Oaks, CA: Sage Publications, pp. 181–195.

Michelini, R. L. (1971). Effects of prior interaction, contact, strategy, and expectation of meeting on gain behavior and sentiment. *Journal of Conflict Resolution, 15,* 97–103.

Michener, H. A., Vaske, J. J., Schleiffer, S. L., Plazewski, J. G., & Chapman, L. J. (1975). Factors affecting concession rate and threat usage in bilateral conflict. *Sociometry, 38,* 62–80.

Michener, S. K., & Suchner, R. W. (1971). The tactical use of social power. In J. T. Tedeschi (Ed.), *The social influence process* (pp. 235–286). Chicago: AVC.

Midgaard, K., & Underal, A. (1977). Multiparty conferences. In D. Druckman (Ed.), *Negotiations: Social psychological perspectives* (pp. 329–345). Beverly Hills, CA: Sage.

Milgram, S. (1974). *Obedience to authority: An experimental view.* New York: Harper & Row.

Mill, J. S. (1962). *Utilitarianism, on liberty, essay on Bentham.* New York: New American Library.

Miller, D. T., & Ross, M. (1975). Self-serving bias in the attribution of causality: Fact or fiction? *Psychological Bulletin, 82,* 213–225.

Miller, D. T., & Vidmar, N. (1981). The social psychology of punishment reactions. In M. J. Lerner (Ed.), *The justice motive in social behavior* (pp. 145–172). New York: Plenum Press.

Miller, S. K., & Burgoon, M. (1979). The relationship between violations of expectations and the induction of the resistance to persuasion. *Human Communication Research, 5,* 301–313.

Mills, H., & Clark, M. S. (1994). Communal and exchange relationships: Controversies and research. In R. Erber & R. Gilmour (Eds.), *Theoretical frameworks for personal relationships* (pp. 29–42). Hillsdale, NJ: Lawrence Erlbaum.

Mintu-Wimsatt, A., & Gassenheimer, J. B. (2000). The moderating effects of cultural context in buyer-seller negotiation. *The Journal of Personal Selling and Sales Management, 1,* 1–9.

Mintzberg, H. (1973). *The nature of managerial work.* New York: Harper & Row.

Mintzberg, H., & Quinn, J. B. (1991). *The strategy process: Concepts, contexts, cases* (2nd ed.). Englewood Cliffs, NJ: Prentice Hall.

Missner, M. (1980). *Ethics of the business system.* Sherman Oaks, CA: Alfred Publishing Company.

Mitchell, C. P., and Banks, M. (1996). *Handbook of conflict resolution: The analytical problem solving approach.* London: Pinter.

Miyahara, A., Kim, M. S., Shin, H. C., & Yoon, K. (1998). Conflict resolution styles among "collectivist" cultures: A comparison between Japanese and Koreans. *International Journal of Intercultural Relations, 22,* 505–525.

Mnookin, R. H. (1993). Why negotiations fail: An exploration of barriers to the resolution of conflict. *The Ohio State Journal on Dispute Resolution, 8,* 235–249.

Moberg, P. J. (1998). Predicting conflict strategy with personality traits: Incremental validity and the five factor model. *International Journal of Conflict Management, 9,* 258–285.

Moore, C. (1996). *The mediation process: Practical strategies for resolving conflict* (2nd ed.). San Francisco: Jossey-Bass.

Moore, D. A., Kurtzberg, T. R., Thompson, L. L., & Morris, M. W. (1999). Long and short routes to success in electronically mediated negotiations: Group affiliations and good vibrations. *Organizational Behavior and Human Decision Processes, 77,* 22–43.

Morley, I., & Stephenson, G. (1977) *The social psychology of bargaining.* London: Allen and Unwin.

Morris, M. W., Larrick, R. P., & Su, S. K. (1999). Misperceiving negotiation counterparts: When situationally determined bargaining behaviors are attributed to personality traits. *Journal of Personality and Social Psychology, 77,* 52–67.

Mosted, I., & Rutte, C. R. (2000). Effects of time pressure and accountability to constituents on negotiation. *The International Journal of Conflict Management, 22*(3), 227–247.

Mulvey, P. W., Veiga, J. F., & Elsass, P. M. (1996). When team members raise a white flag. *Academy of Management Executive, 10*(1), 40–49.

Mumpower, J. L., & Rohrbaugh, J. (1996). Negotiation and design: Supporting resource allocation decisions through analytical mediation. *Group Decision and Negotiation, 5,* 385–409.

Murnighan, J. K. (1978). Models of coalition behavior: Game theoretic, social psychological and political perspectives. *Psychological Bulletin, 85,* 1130–1153.

Murnighan, J. K. (1982). Game theory and the structure of decision-making groups. In R. Guzzo (Ed.), *Improving group decision in organizations.* New York: Academic Press.

Murnighan, J. K. (1986). Organizational coalitions: Structural contingencies and the formation process. In R. J. Lewicki, B. H. Sheppard, & M. H. Bazerman (Eds.), *Research on negotiation in organizations* (Vol. 1, pp. 155–173). Greenwich, CT: JAI Press.

Murnighan, J. K. (1991). *The dynamics of bargaining games.* Englewood Cliffs, NJ: Prentice Hall.

Murnighan, J. K., & Brass, D. J. (1991). Intraorganizational coalitions. In M. H. Bazerman, R. J. Lewicki, & B. H. Sheppard (Eds.), *Research on negotiation in organizations: The handbook of negotiation research* (Vol. 3, pp. 283–306). Greenwich, CT: JAI Press.

Murnighan, J. K., & Conlon, D. E. (1991). The dynamics of intense work groups: A study of british string quartets. *Administrative Science Quarterly, 36,* 165–186.

Murnighan, J. K., & Pillutla, M. M. (1995). Fairness versus self-interest: Asymmetric model imperatives in ultimatum bargaining. In R. M. Kramer & D. M. Messick (Eds.), *Negotiation as a social process* (pp. 240–267). Thousand Oaks, CA: Sage.

Murnighan, J. K., & Volrath, D. A. (1984). Hierarchies, coalitions and organizations. In S. B. Bacharach & E. J. Lawler (eds.), *Research in the sociology of organizations.* (Vol. 3, pp. 157–187). Greenwich, CT: JAI Press.

Murphy, K. (1992). *Honesty in the workplace.* Pacific Grove, CA: Brooks-Cole.

Nash, J. F. (1950). The bargaining problem. *Econometrica, 18,* 155–162.

Nash, L. L. (1990). *Good intentions aside: A manager's guide to resolving ethical problems.* Boston, MA: Harvard Business School Press.

Natlandsmyr, J. H., & Rognes, J. (1995). Culture, behavior, and negotiation outcomes: A comparative and cross-cultural study of Mexican and Norwegian negotiators. *The International Journal of Conflict Management, 6,* 5–29.

Neale, M. A. (1984). The effect of negotiation and arbitration cost salience on bargainer behavior: The role of arbitrator and constituency in negotiator judgment. *Organizational Behavior and Human Performance, 34,* 97–111.

Neale, M., & Bazerman, M. H. (1983). The role of perspective-taking ability in negotiating under different forms of arbitration. *Industrial and Labor Relations Review, 36,* 378–388.

Neale, M., & Bazerman, M. H. (1985). The effects of framing and negotiator overconfidence on bargaining behaviors and outcomes. *Academy of Management Journal, 28,* 34–49.

Neale, M., & Bazerman, M. H. (1991). *Cognition and rationality in negotiation.* New York: Free Press.

Neale, M., & Bazerman, M. H. (1992a). Negotiating rationally: The power and impact of the negotiator's frame. *Academy of Management Executive, 6*(3), 42–51.

Neale, M., Huber, V., & Northcraft, G. (1987). The framing of negotiations: Contextual vs. task frames. *Organizational Behavior and Human Decision Processes, 39,* 228–241.

Neale, M. A., & Bazerman, M. H. (1992b). Negotiator cognition and rationality: A behavioral decision theory perspective. *Organizational Behavior and Human Decision Processes, 51,* 157–175.

Neale, M. A., & Northcraft, G. B. (1986). Experts, amateurs, and refrigerators: Comparing expert and amateur negotiators in a novel task. *Organizational Behavior and Human Decision Processes, 38,* 305–317.

Neale, M. A., & Northcraft, G. B. (1991). Behavioral negotiation theory: A framework for conceptualizing dyadic bargaining. In L. Cummings & B. Staw (Eds.), *Research in organizational behavior* (Vol. 13, pp. 147–190). Greenwich, CT: JAI Press.

Nemeth, C. J. (1986). Differential contributions to majority and minority influence. *Psychological Review, 93,* 23–32.

Nemeth, C. J. (1989). *The stimulating properties of dissent.* Paper presented at the first annual Conference on Group Process and Productivity, Texas A & M University, College Station, TX.

Neslin, S. A., & Greenhalgh, L. (1983). Nash's theory of cooperative games as a predictor of the outcomes of buyer-seller negotiations: An experiment in media purchasing. *Journal of Marketing Research, 20,* 368–379.

Neu, J., Graham, J. L., & Gilly, M. C. (1988). The influence of gender on behaviors and outcomes in a retail buyer-seller negotiation simulation. *Journal of Retailing, 64,* 427–451.

Nierenberg, G. (1976). *The complete negotiator.* New York: Nierenberg & Zeif Publishers.

Nierenberg, G., & Calero, H. (1971). *How to read a person like a book.* New York: Simon & Schuster.

Northcraft, G. B., & Neale, M. A. (1987). Experts, amateurs, and real estate: An anchoring and adjustment perspective on property pricing decisions. *Organizational Behavior and Human Decision Processes, 39,* 228–241.

Northrup, H. R. (1964). *Boulwarism.* Ann Arbor, MI: Bureau of Industrial Relations, University of Michigan.

Northrup, T. A. (1995). *The uneasy partnership between conflict theory and feminist theory.* Syracuse University, unpublished paper.

O'Connor, K. M. (1997). Motives and cognitions in negotiation: A theoretical integration and an empirical test. *International Journal of Conflict Management, 8,* 114–131.

O'Connor, K. M. (1997). Groups and solos in context: The effects of accountability on team negotiation. *Organizational Behavior and Human Decision Processes, 72,* 384–407.

O'Connor, K. M., & Arnold, J. A. (2001). Distributive spirals: Negotiation impasses and the moderating role of disputant self-efficacy. *Organizational Behavior and Human Decision Processes, 84,* 148–176.

O'Connor, K. M., & Carnevale, P. J. (1997). A nasty but effective negotiation strategy: Misrepresentation of a common-value issue. *Personality and Social Psychology Bulletin, 23,* 504–515.

Ogawa, N. (1999). The concept of facework: Its function in the Hawaii model of mediation. *Mediation Quarterly, 17,* 5–20.

Ohanyan, A. (1999). Negotiation culture in a post-Soviet context: An interdisciplinary perspective. *Mediation Quarterly, 17,* 83–104.

Ohbuchi, K., & Fukushima, O. (1997). Personality and interpersonal conflict: Aggressiveness, self-monitoring, and situational variables. *International Journal of Conflict Management, 8,* 99–113.

Ohbuchi, K., & Takahashi, Y. (1994). Cultural styles of conflict management in Japanese and Americans: Passivity, covertness, and effectiveness of strategies. *Journal of Applied Social Psychology, 24,* 1345–1366.

O'Keefe, D. J. (1990). *Persuasion: Theory and research.* Newbury Park, CA: Sage.

Olekalns, M., & Smith, P. L. (1999). Social value orientations and strategy choices in competitive negotiations. *Personality and Social Psychology Bulletin, 25,* 657–668.

Olekalns, M., Smith, P. L., & Kibby, R. (1996). Social value orientations, negotiator strategies and outcomes. *European Journal of Social Psychology, 26,* 299–313.

Olekalns, M., Smith, P. L., & Walsh, T. (1996). The process of negotiating: Strategy and timing as predictors of outcomes. *Organizational Behavior and Human Decision Processes, 68,* 68–77.

Oliver, R. L., Balakrishnan, P. V., & Barry, B. (1994). Outcome satisfaction in negotiation: A test of expectancy disconfirmation. *Organizational Behavior and Human Decision Processes, 60,* 252–275.

Osgood, C. E. (1962). *An alternative to war or surrender.* Urbana, IL: University of Illinois Press.

Oskamp, S. (1970). Effects of programmed initial strategies in a prisoner's dilemma game. *Psychometrics, 19,* 195–196.

Ostermeier, T. H. (1967). Effects of type and frequency of reference upon perceived source credibility and attitude change. *Speech Monographs, 34,* 137–144.

Parrott, W. (1994). Beyond hedonism: Motives for inhibiting good moods and for maintaining bad moods. In D. M. Wegner & J. W. Pennebaker (Eds.), *Handbook of mental control* (pp. 278–305). Englewood Cliffs, NJ: Prentice Hall.

Parrott, W. G. (2001). Emotions in social psychology: Volume overview. In W. G. Parrott (Ed.), *Emotions in social psychology* (pp. 1–19). Philadelphia: Psychology Press.

Patterson, J., & Kim, P. (1991). *The day America told the truth.* New York: Prentice Hall.

Pearce, J. L., Stevenson, W. B., & Porter, L. W. (1986). Coalitions in the organizational context. In R. J. Lewicki, B. H. Sheppard, & M. H. Bazerman (Eds.), *Research on negotiation in organizations* (Vol. 1, pp. 97–115). Greenwich, CT: JAI Press.

Pearson, V. S., & Stephan, W. G. (1998). Preferences for styles of negotiation: A comparison of Brazil and the U. S. *International Journal of Intercultural Relations, 22,* 67–83.

Peterson, E., & Thompson, L. (1997). Negotiation teamwork: The impact of information distribution and accountability on performance depends on the relationship among team members. *Organizational Behavior and Human Decision Processes, 72,* 364–383.

Petty, R. E., & Brock, T. C. (1981). Thought disruption and persuasion: Assessing the validity of attitude change experiments. In R. E. Petty, T. M. Ostrom, & T. C. Brock (Eds.), *Cognitive responses in persuasion* (pp. 55–79). Hillsdale, NJ: Lawrence Erlbaum.

Petty, R. E., & Cacioppo, J. T. (1986a). *Communication and persuasion: Central and peripheral routes to attitude change.* New York: Springer Verlag.

Petty, R. E., & Cacioppo, J. T. (1986b). The elaboration likelihood model of persuasion. In L. Berkowitz (Ed.), *Advances in experimental social psychology* (Vol. 19, pp. 123–205). New York: Academic Press.

Petty, R. E., & Cacioppo, J. T. (1990). Involvement and persuasion. Tradition versus integration. *Psychological Bulletin, 107,* 367–374.

Petty, R. E., Cacioppo, J. T., Strathman, A., & Priester, J. R. (1994). To think or not to think: Exploring two routes to persuasion. In S. Shavitt & T. Brock (Eds.), *Persuasion: Psychological insights and perspectives.* Needham Heights, MA: Allyn & Bacon.

Petty, R. E., Cacioppo, J. T., Strathman, A. J., & Priester, J. R. To think or not to think: Exploring two routes to persuasion. In T. Brock & S. Shavitt (Eds.), *Psychology of persuasion.* San Francisco, CA: Freeman, in press.

Petty, R. E., Wells, G., & Brock, T. (1976). Distraction can enhance or reduce yielding to propaganda: Thought disruption versus effort justification. *Journal of Personality and Social Psychology, 34,* 874–884.

Pfeffer, J. (1992). *Managing with power.* Boston, MA: Harvard Business School Press.

Pfeffer, J., & Salancik, G. R. (1974). Organizational decision making as a political process: The case of a university budget. *Administrative Science Quarterly, 19,* 135–151.

Pfouts, R. W. (1994). Buying a pig when both buyer and seller are in a poke. *AEJ, 22,* 80–85.

Phatak, A. V., & Habib, M. H. (1996). The dynamics of international business negotiations. *Business Horizons, 39,* 30–38.

Pilisuk, N., & Skolnick, P. (1978). Inducing trust: A test of the Osgood proposal. *Journal of Personality and Social Psychology, 8,* 121–133.

Pillutla, M. M., & Murnighan, J. K. (1996). Unfairness, anger and spite: Emotional rejections of ultimatum offers. *Organizational Behavior and Human Decision Processes, 68,* 208–224.

Pinkley, R. L. (1989). *Dimensions of conflict frame: Disputant interpretations of conflict.* Unpublished dissertation, University of North Carolina at Chapel Hill, NC.

Pinkley, R. L. (1990). Dimensions of conflict frame: Disputant interpretations of conflict. *Journal of Applied Psychology, 75,* 117–126.

Pinkley, R. L. (1992). Dimensions of conflict frame: Relation to disputant perceptions and expectations. *The International Journal of Conflict Management, 3,* 95–113.

Pinkley, R. L. (1995). Impact of knowledge regarding alternatives to settlement in dyadic negotiations: Whose knowledge counts? *Journal of Applied Psychology, 80,* 403–417.

Pinkley, R. L., Brittain, J., Neale, M., & Northcraft, G. (1995). Managerial third-party dispute intervention: An inductive analysis of intervenor strategy selection. *Journal of Applied Psychology, 80,* 386–402.

Pinkley, R. L., Griffith, T. L., & Northcraft, G. B. (1995). "Fixed pie" a la mode: Information availability, information processing, and the negotiation of suboptimal agreements. *Organizational Behavior and Human Decision Processes, 62,* 101–112.

Pinkley, R. L., Neale, M. A., & Bennett, R. J. (1994). The impact of alternatives to settlement in dyadic negotiation. *Organizational Behavior and Human Decision Processes, 57,* 97–116.

Pinkley, R., & Northcraft, G. B. (1994). Cognitive interpretations of conflict: Implications for dispute processes and outcomes. *Academy of Management Journal, 37,* 193–205.

Polzer, J. T. (1996). Intergroup negotiations: The effects of negotiating teams. *Journal of Conflict Resolution, 40,* 678–698.

Polzer, J. T., Mannix, E. A., & Neale, M. A. (1995). Multiparty negotiations in a social context. In R. Kramer & D. Messick (Eds.), *Negotiation as a social process* (pp. 123–142). Thousand Oaks, CA: Sage.

Polzer, J. T., Mannix, E. A., & Neale, M. A. (1998). Interest alignment and coalitions in multiparty negotiation. *Academy of Management Journal, 41*(1), 42–54.

Poole, M., & Doelger, J. (1986). Developmental processes in group decision-making. In R. Hirokawa & M. Poole (Eds.), *Communication in group decision-making* (pp. 35–62). Beverly Hills, CA: Sage.

Post, F. R., & Bennett, R. J. (1994). Use of collaborative collective bargaining processes in labor negotiations. *The International Journal of Conflict Management, 5*(1), pp. 34–61.

Prasow, P., & Peters, E. (1983). *Arbitration and collective bargaining: Conflict resolution in labor relations* (2nd ed.). New York: McGraw-Hill.

Provis, C. (1996). Interests vs. positions: A critique of the distinction. *Negotiation Journal, 12,* 305–323.

Pruitt, D. G. (1981). *Negotiation behavior.* New York: Academic Press.

Pruitt, D. G. (1983). Strategic choice in negotiation. *American Behavioral Scientist, 27,* 167–194.

Pruitt, D. G. (1994). Negotiation between organizations: A branching chain model. *Negotiation Journal, 10,* 217–230.

Pruitt, D. G. (1995). Networks and collective scripts: Paying attention to structure in bargaining theory. In R. Kramer & D. Messick (Eds.), *Negotiation as a social process* (pp. 37–47). Thousand Oaks, CA: Sage.

Pruitt, D. G., & Carnevale, P. J. D. (1993). *Negotiation in social conflict.* Pacific Grove, CA: Brooks-Cole.

Pruitt, D. G., Carnevale, P. J. D., Ben-Yoav, O., Nochajski, T. H., & Van Slyck, M. (1983). Incentives for cooperation in integrative bargaining. In L. Tietz (Ed.), *Aspiration levels in bargaining and economic decision making* (pp. 22–34). Berlin: Springer.

Pruitt, D. G., Carnevale, P. J. D., Forcey, B., & Van Slyck, M. (1986). Gender effects in negotiation: Constituent surveillance and contentious behavior. *Journal of Experimental Social Psychology, 22,* 264–275.

Pruitt, D. G., & Lewis, S. A. (1975). Development of integrative solutions in bilateral negotiation. *Journal of Personality and Social Psychology, 31,* 621–633.

Pruitt, D. G., Parker, J. C., & Mikolic, J. M. (1997). Escalation as a reaction to persistent annoyance. *The International Journal of Conflict Management, 8,* 252–270.

Pruitt, D. G., & Rubin, J. Z. (1986). *Social conflict: Escalation, stalemate and settlement.* New York: Random House.

Pruitt, D. G., & Syna, H. (1985). Mismatching the opponent's offers in negotiation. *Journal of Experimental Social Psychology, 21,* 103–113.

Putnam, L. L. (1994). Productive conflict: Negotiation as implicit coordination. *The International Journal of Conflict Management, 5,* 284–298.

Putnam, L. L., & Geist, P. (1985). Argument in bargaining: An analysis of the reasoning process. *Southern Speech Communication Journal, 50,* 225–245.

Putnam, L. L., & Holmer, M. (1992). Framing, reframing, and issue development. In L. Putnam & M. Roloff (Eds.), *Communication and negotiation* (pp. 128–155). Newbury Park, CA: Sage.

Putnam, L. L., & Jones, T. S. (1982). Reciprocity in negotiations: An analysis of bargaining interaction. *Communication Monographs, 49,* 171–191.

Putnam, L. L., & Poole, M. (1987). Conflict and negotiation. In F. Jablin, L. Putnam, K. Roberts, & L. Porter (Eds.), *Handbook of organizational communication: An interdisciplinary perspective* (pp. 549–599). Newbury Park, CA: Sage.

Putnam, L. L., & Wilson, S. R. (1989). Argumentation and bargaining strategies as discriminators of integrative outcomes. In M. A. Rahim (Ed.), *Managing conflict: An interdisciplinary approach* (pp. 121–131). New York: Praeger.

Putnam, L., Wilson, S., & Turner, D. (1990). The evolution of policy arguments in teachers' negotiations. *Argumentation, 4,* 129–152.

Putnam, L. & Wondolleck, J. (2003). Intractability: Definitions, dimensions and distinctions. In Lewicki, R. J., B. Gray & M. Elliott, *Making sense of intractable environmental disputes.* Washington, D. C.: Island Press.

Pye, L. W. (1992). *Chinese negotiating style.* New York: Quorum Books.

Quinn, J. B. (1991). Strategies for change. In H. Mintzberg & J. B. Quinn (Eds.), *The strategy process: Concepts, contexts, cases* (2nd ed., pp. 4–12). Englewood Cliffs, NJ: Prentice Hall.

Rachels, J. (1986). *The elements of moral philosophy.* New York: McGraw-Hill.

Rackham, N. (1980). The behavior of successful negotiators. Huthwaite Research Group. Reprinted in R. J. Lewicki, D. M. Saunders, & J. W. Minton (Eds.), *Negotiation: Readings, exercises and cases* (1999, 3rd ed.). Chicago, IL: Irwin/McGraw-Hill.

Rackham, N. (1980). *The behavior of successful negotiators.* London: Huthwaite Research Group Limited.

Rahim, M. A. (1983). A measure of styles of handling interpersonal conflict. *Academy of Management Journal, 26,* 368–376.

Rahim, M. A. (1990). *Rahim Organizational Conflict Inventory: Professional Manual.* Palo Alto, CA: Consulting Psychologists Press.

Rahim, M. A. (1992). *Managing conflict in organizations* (2nd ed.). Westport, CT: Praeger.

Raider, E. B., Coleman, S., & Gerson, J. (2000). Teaching conflict resolution skills in a workshop. In Deutsch, M. & Coleman, P. *Handbook of conflict resolution.* San Francisco: Jossey-Bass.

Raiffa, H. (1982). *The art and science of negotiation.* Cambridge, MA: Belknap Press of Harvard University Press.

Rapoport, A. (1964). *Strategy and conscience.* New York: Harper & Row.

Rapoport, A., Erev, I., & Zwick, R. (1995). An experimental study of buyer-seller negotiation with one-sided incomplete information and time discounting. *Management Science, 41,* 377–394.

Raven, B. H., & Rubin, J. Z. (1973). *Social psychology: People in groups.* New York: John Wiley and Sons.

Reardon, K. K. (1981). *Persuasion theory and context.* Beverly Hills, CA: Sage.

Ree, M. J., & Earles, J. A. (1991). Predicting training success: Not much more than g. *Personnel Psychology, 44,* 321–332.

Reich, R. B. (1981, May–June). Regulation by confrontation or negotiation. *Harvard Business Review, 59,* 82–93.

Reis, H. T., & Patrick, B. C. (1996). Attachment and intimacy: Component processes. In E. T. Higgins & A. W. Kruglanski (Eds.), *Social psychology: Handbook of basic principles* (pp. 523–563). New York: Guilford.

Richardson, R. C. (1977). *Collective bargaining by objectives.* Englewood Cliffs, NJ: Prentice Hall.

Ring, P. S., & Van de Ven, A. H. (1994). Developmental processes of cooperative interorganizational relationships. *Academy of Management Review, 19,* 90–118.

Ritov, I. (1996). Anchoring in simulated competitive market negotiation. *Organizational Behavior and Human Decision Processes, 67,* 16–25.

Robinson, R. J. (1995). Defusing the exploding offer: The fairpoint gambit. *Negotiation Journal, 11,* 389–404.

Robinson, R., Lewicki, R. J., & Donahue, E. (2000). Extending and testing a five factor model of ethical and unethical bargaining tactics: The SINS scale. *Journal of Organizational Behavior, 21,* 649–664.

Rogers, C. R. (1957). *Active listening.* Chicago, IL: University of Chicago Press.

Rogers, C. R. (1961). *On becoming a person: A therapist's view of psychotherapy.* Boston, MA: Houghton Mifflin.

Rogers, C. R., & Roethlisberger, F. J. (1991). Barriers and gateways to communication. *Harvard Business Review, 69,* 105–111.

Rosnow, R. L., & Robinson, E. J. (1967). *Experiments in persuasion.* New York: Academic Press.

Ross, L. (1997). The intuitive psychologist and his shortcomings: Distortions in the attribution process. In L. Berkowitz (Ed.), *Advances in Experimental Social Psychology.* Vol 10. Orlando, Fl: Academic Press, 173–220.

Ross, L., Green, D., & House, P. (1977). The false consensus phenomenon: An attributional bias in self-perception and social-perception processes. *Journal of Experimental Social Psychology, 13,* 279–301.

Ross, L., & Stillinger, C. (1991). Barriers to conflict resolution. *Negotiation Journal, 7,* 389–404.

Ross, M. H. (2000). "Good-enough" isn't so bad: Thinking about success and failure in ethnic conflict management. *Peace and Conflict: Journal of Peace Psychology, 6,* 21–27.

Ross, W., & Conlon, D. E. (2000). Hybrid forms of third-party dispute resolution: The theoretical implications of combining mediation and arbitration. *Academy of Management Review,* Vol. 25, No. 2, 416–427.

Ross, W., & LaCroix, J. (1996). Multiple meanings of trust in negotiation theory and research: A literature review and integrative model. *International Journal of Conflict Management, 7,* 314–360.

Roth, A., & Malouf, M. (1979). Game-theoretic models and the role of information in bargaining. *Psychological Review, 86,* 574–594.

Roth, A. E., Murnighan, J. K., & Schoumaker, F. (1988). The deadline effect in bargaining: Some empirical evidence. *American Economic Review, 78,* 806–823.

Roth, J., & Sheppard, B. H. (1995). Opening the black box of framing research: The relationship between frames, communication, and outcomes. *Academy of Management Proceedings.*

Rothman, J. (1997). *Resolving identity-based conflict in nations, organizations and communities.* San Francisco, CA: Jossey-Bass.

Rotter, J. B. (1966). Generalized expectancies for internal versus external control of reinforcement. *Psychological Monographs, 80*(1).

Rotter, J. B. (1967). A new scale for the measurement of interpersonal trust. *Journal of Personality, 35,* 651–665.

Rotter, J. B. (1971). Generalized expectancies for interpersonal trust. *American Psychologist, 26,* 443–452.

Rotter, J. B. (1980). Interpersonal trust, trustworthiness, and gullibility. *American Psychologist, 35,* 1–7.

Rousseau, J. J. (1947). *The social contract.* New York: Hafner Publishing Commune.

Rowe, M. (1995). Options, functions, and skills: What an organizational ombudsman might want to know. *Negotiation Journal, 11,* 103–114.

Rubin, J., Pruitt, D., & Kim, S. H. (1994). *Social conflict: Escalation, stalemate and settlement* (2nd Edition). New York: McGraw-Hill.

Rubin, J. Z. (1980). Experimental research on third party intervention in conflict: Toward some generalizations. *Psychological Bulletin, 87,* 379–391.

Rubin, J. Z. (Ed.). (1981). *Dynamics of third party intervention: Kissinger in the Middle East.* New York: Praeger.

Rubin, J. Z., & Brown, B. R. (1975). *The social psychology of bargaining and negotiation.* New York: Academic Press.

Ruble, T. L., & Thomas, K. W. (1976). Support for a two-dimensional model of conflict behavior. *Organizational Behavior and Human Performance, 16,* 143–155.

Rusbult, C., & Van Lange, P. A. M. (1996). Interdependence processes. In E. T. Higgins & A. W. Kruglanski (Eds.), *Social psychology: Handbook of basic principles* (pp. 564–596). New York: Guilford.

Rusk, T., with Miller, D. P. (1993). *The power of ethical persuasion.* New York: Penguin.

Russo, J. E., & Schoemaker, P. J. H. (1989). *Decision traps: The ten barriers to brilliant decision making and how to overcome them.* New York: Simon & Schuster.

Salacuse, J. (1998). So, what's the deal anyway? Contracts and relationships as negotiating goals. *Negotiation Journal, 14*(1), pp. 5–12.

Salacuse, J. (1999). Law and power in agency negotiations. In R. H. Mnookin and L. E. Susskind, *Negotiating on behalf of others* (pp 157–175). Thousand Oaks, CA: Sage Books.

Salacuse, J. (2001?). Renegotiating existing agreements: How to deal with "life struggling against form." *Negotiation Journal, 17*(4), 311–332.

Salacuse, J. W. (1988). Making deals in strange places: A beginner's guide to international business negotiations. *Negotiation Journal, 4,* 5–13.

Salacuse, J. W. (1995). The art of advising negotiators. *Negotiation Journal, 11,* 391–401.

Salancik, G. R., & Pfeffer, J. (1977). Who gets power and how they hold on to it: A strategic-contingency model of power. *Organizational Dynamics, 5,* 3–21.

Sander, F., & Goldberg, S. (1994). Fitting the forum to the fuss: A user-friendly guide to selecting an ADR procedure. *Negotiation Journal, 10,* 49–68.

Savage, G. T., Blair, J. D., & Sorenson, R. L. (1989). Consider both relationships and substance when negotiating strategically. *Academy of Management Executive, 3*(1), 37–48.

Schapiro, N. (1993). *Negotiating for your life.* New York: Henry Holt.

Schatzski, M. (1981). *Negotiation: The art of getting what you want.* New York: Signet Books.

Schein, E. (1987). *Process consultation Volume II: Lessons for managers and consultants.* Reading, MA: Addison-Wesley.

Schell, G. R. (1991). When is it legal to lie in negotiation? *Sloan Management Review,* pp. 93–101.

Schelling, T. C. (1960). *The strategy of conflict.* Cambridge, MA: Harvard University Press.

Schelling, T. C. (1978). *Micromotives and macrobehavior.* New York: Norton.

Schlenker, B. R., Helm, B., & Tedeschi, J. T. (1973). The effects of personality and situational variables on behavioral trust. *Journal of Personality and Social Psychology, 25*(3), 419–427.

Schlenker, B. R., & Riess, M. (1979). Self-presentation of attitudes following commitment to proattitudinal behavior. *Journal of Human Communication Research, 5,* 325–334.

Schmidt, F. L., & Hunter, J. E. (1998). The validity and utility of selection methods in personnel psychology: Practical and theoretical implications of 85 years of research findings. *Psychological Bulletin, 124,* 262–274.

Schneider, A. K. (1994). Effective responses to offensive comments. *Negotiation Journal, 10,* 107–115.

Schön, D. A., & M. Rein (1994). *Frame reflection: Toward the resolution of intractable policy controversies.* New York: Basic Books.

Schoppa, L. J. (1993). Two-level games and bargaining outcomes: Why gaiatsu succeeds in Japan in some cases but not in others. *International Organization, 47,* 353–386.

Schreisheim, C., & Hinkin, T. R. (1990). Influence strategies used by subordinates: A theoretical and empirical analysis and refinement of the Kipnis, Schmidt, and Wilkinson subscales. *Journal of Applied Psychology, 75,* 246–257.

Schurr, P. H. (1987). Effects of gain and loss decision frames on risky purchase negotiations. *Journal of Applied Psychology, 72,* 351–358.

Schweitzer, M. E. (1997). *Omission, friendship and fraud: Lies about material facts in negotiation.* Unpublished manuscript.

Schweitzer, M., Brodt, S., & Croson, R. (working paper). *Visual access and context-dependent lies: The use of deception in videoconference and telephone mediated negotiations.* Wharton School OPIM Working Paper #99–07–02.

Schweitzer, M. E., & Croson, R. (2001). Curtailing deception: The impact of direct questions on lies and omissions. *International Journal of Conflict Management, 10*(3), 225–248.

Schweitzer, M. E., L. Ordonez, & B. Douma, (2002). The dark side of goal setting: The role of goals in motivating unethical behavior. Unpublished manuscript.

Sebenius, J. K. (1983). Negotiation arithmetic: Adding and subtracting issues and parties. *International Organization, 37,* 1–34.

Sebenius, J. K. (1992). Negotiation analysis: A characterization and review. *Management Science, 38,* 18–38.

Sebenius, J. K. (2002). The hidden challenge of cross-border negotiations. *Harvard Business Review, 80,* 76–85.

Selekman, B. M., Fuller, S. H., Kennedy, T., & Baitsel, J. M. (1964). *Problems in labor relations.* New York: McGraw-Hill.

Selekman, B. M., Selekman, S. K., & Fuller, S. H. (1958). *Problems in labor relations.* New York: McGraw-Hill.

Seligman, C., Bush, M., & Kirsch, K. (1976). Relationship between compliance in the foot in the door paradigm and size of first request. *Journal of Personality and Social Psychology, 33,* 517–520.

Sen, A. K. (1970). *Collective choice and individual values.* San Francisco: Holden-Day.

Sermat V. (1967). The effects of an initial cooperative or competitive treatment on a subject's response to conditional operation. *Behavioral Science, 12,* 301–313.

Sermat, V., & Gregovich, R. P. (1966). The effect of experimental manipulation on cooperative behavior in a checkers game. *Psychometric Science, 1,* 435–436.

Shannon, E., & Weaver, W. (1948). *The mathematical theory of communication.* Urbana, IL: University of Illinois Press.

Shapiro, D. L. (1991). The effects of explanations on negative reactions to deceit. *Administrative Science Quarterly, 36,* 614–630.

Shapiro, D. L., & Bies, R. J. (1994). Threats, bluffs and disclaimers in negotiation. *Organizational Behavior and Human Decision Processes, 60,* 14–35.

Shapiro, D. L., Sheppard, B. H., & Cheraskin, L. (1992). Business on a handshake. *Negotiation Journal, 8,* 365–377.

Shapiro, D. L., & Von Glinow, M. A. (1999). Negotiation in multicultural teams: New world, old theories? In R. Bies, R. J. Lewicki, & B. H. Sheppard (Eds.), *Research on negotiation in organizations* (Vol. 7, pp. 231–262). Stamford, CT: JAI Press.

Shea, G. F. (1983). *Creative negotiating.* Boston, MA: CBI Publishing Co.

Sheldon, A., & Johnson, D. (1994). Preschool negotiators: Linguistic differences in how girls and boys regulate the expression of dissent in same-sex groups. In B. H. Sheppard, R. J. Lewicki, & R. Bies (Eds.), *Research on negotiation in organizations* (Vol. 4, pp. 37–67). Greenwich, CT: JAI Press.

Shell, R. (1999). *Bargaining for advantage.* New York: Viking Books.

Sheppard, B. H. (1983). Managers as inquisitors: Some lessons from the law. In M. H. Bazerman & R. J. Lewicki (Eds.), *Negotiating in organizations* (pp. 193–213). Beverly Hills, CA: Sage.

Sheppard, B. H. (1984). Third-party conflict intervention: A procedural framework. In B. M. Staw & L. L. Cummings (Eds.), *Research in organizational behavior* (Vol. 6, pp. 141–190). Greenwich, CT: JAI Press.

Sheppard, B. H. (1995). Negotiating in long term mutually interdependent relationships among relative equals. In R. J. Bies, R. J. Lewicki, & B. H. Sheppard (Eds.), *Research on negotiation in organizations* (Vol. 5, pp. 3–44). Greenwich, CT: JAI Press.

Sheppard, B. H., Blumenfeld-Jones, K., Minton, J. W., & Hyder, E. (1994). Informal conflict intervention: Advice and dissent. *Employee Rights and Responsibilities Journal, 7,* 53–72.

Sheppard, B. H., Lewicki, R. J., & Minton, J. W. (1992). *Organizational justice: The search for fairness in the workplace.* New York: Lexington Books.

Sheppard, B. H., & Tuchinsky, M. (1996a). Micro-OB and the network organization. In R. Kramer & T. Tyler (Eds.), *Trust in organizations* (pp. 140–165). Thousand Oaks, CA: Sage.

Sheppard, B. H., & Tuchinsky, M. (1996b). Interfirm relations: A grammar of pairs. In B. M. Staw & L. L. Cummings (Eds.), *Research on organizational behavior* (Vol. 18, pp. 331–373). Greenwich, CT: JAI Press.

Sherif, M., Harvey, L., White, B., Hood, W., & Sherif, C. (1988). *The Robbers' Cave experiment: Intergroup conflict and cooperation.* Middletown, CT: Wesleyan University Press. (Original work published 1961.)

Short, J., Williams, E., & Christie, B. (1976). *The social psychology of telecommunications.* London: John Wiley.

Siegel, S. R., & Fouraker, L. E. (1960). *Bargaining and group decision making: Experiments in bilateral monopoly.* New York: McGraw-Hill.

Simons, T. (1993). Speech patterns and the concept of utility in cognitive maps: The case of integrative bargaining. *Academy of Management Journal, 36,* 139–156.

Singer, L. R. (1990). *Settling disputes: Conflict resolution in business, families, and the legal system.* Boulder, CO: Westview Press.

Singer, L. R. (1994). *Settling disputes: Conflict resolution in business, families, and the legal system* (2nd ed.). Boulder, CO: Westview Press.

Sitkin, S. B., & Bies, R. J. (1993). Social accounts in conflict situations: Using explanations to manage conflict. *Human Relations, 46,* 349–370.

Skarlicki, D. P., & Folger, R. (1997). Retaliation in the workplace: The roles of distributive, procedural and interactive justice. *Journal of Applied Psychology, 82*(3), 434–443.

Skinner, B. F. (1953). *Science and human behavior.* New York: Macmillan.

Slutsky, J., & Slutsky, M. (1998). Learning others' goals is important to successful negotiations. *The Columbus (Ohio) Dispatch,* February 23, p. 9.

Smith, P. B., Dugan, S., Peterson, M. F., & Leung, K. (1998). Individualism/collectivism and the handling of disagreement: A 23 country study. *International Journal of Intercultural Relations, 22,* 351–367.

Smith, W. P. (1985). Effectiveness of the biased mediator. *Negotiation Journal, 1,* 363–372.

Smyth, L. F. (1994). Intractable conflicts and the role of identity. *Negotiation Journal, 10,* 311–321.

Snyder, M. (1974). Self-monitoring of expressive behavior. *Journal of Personality and Social Psychology, 30,* 526–537.

Snyder, M. (1987). *Public appearances/private realities.* New York: Freeman.

Solnick, S. J. (2001). Gender differences in the ultimatum game. *Economic Inquiry, 39,* 189–200.

Solomon, L. (1960). The influence of some types of power relationships and game strategies upon the development of interpersonal trust. *Journal of Abnormal and Social Psychology, 61,* 223–230.

Solomon, M. (1990). *Working with difficult people.* Englewood Cliffs, NJ: Prentice Hall.

Solomon, R. H. (1987). China: Friendship and obligation in Chinese negotiating style. In H. Binnendijk (Ed.), *National negotiating styles* (pp. 1–16). Washington, DC: Foreign Service Institute.

Sondak, H., Neale, M. A., & Pinkley, R. (1995). The negotiated allocation of benefits and burdens: The impact of outcome valence, contribution and relationship. *Organizational Behavior and Human Decision Processes, 64*(3), 249–260.

Spector, B. I. (1995). Creativity heuristics for impasse resolution: Reframing intractable negotiations. *Annals of the American Academy of Political and Social Science, 542,* 81–99.

Spector, B. I. (1998). Deciding to negotiate with villains. *Negotiation Journal, 14,* 43–59.

Spitzberg, B. H., & Cupach, W. R. (1984). *Interpersonal communication competence.* Beverly Hills, CA: Sage.

Sproull, L., & Kiesler, S. (1986). Reducing social context cues: Electronic mail in organizational communication. *Management Science, 32,* 1492–1512.

Stacks, D. W., & Burgoon, J. K. (1981). The role of non-verbal behaviors as distractors in resistance to persuasion in interpersonal contexts. *Central States Speech Journal, 32,* 61–80.

Starke, F. A., & Notz, W. W. (1981). Pre- and postintervention effects of conventional vs. final-offer arbitration. *Academy of Management Journal, 24,* 832–850.

Staw, B. M. (1981). The escalation of commitment to a course of action. *Academy of Management Review, 6,* 577–587.

Steele, C. M. (1997). A threat in the air: How stereotypes shape intellectual identity and performance. *American Psychologist, 52,* 613–629.

Steers, R. M. (1984). *Introduction to organizational behavior,* 2nd ed. Glenview, IL: Scott Foresman.

Stein, J. (1996). The art of real estate negotiations. *Real Estate Review, 25,* 48–53.

Stein, J. G. (1999). Problem solving as metaphor: Negotiation and identity conflict. *Peace and Conflict: Journal of Peace Psychology, 5,* 225–235.

Steinberg, L. (1998). *Winning with integrity.* New York: Random House.

Stieber, C. (2000). 57 varieties: Has the ombudsman concept become diluted? *Negotiation Journal, 16,* 49–57.

Sternberg, R. (Ed.). (1988). *The nature of creativity.* New York: Cambridge University Press.

Stevens, C. M. (1963). *Strategy and collective bargaining negotiations.* New York: McGraw-Hill.

Stevens, C. K., Bavetta, A. G., & Gist, M. E. (1993). Gender differences in the acquisition of salary negotiation skills: The role of goals, self-efficacy, and perceived control. *Journal of Applied Psychology, 78,* 723–735.

Stevens, C. K., & Gist, M. E. (1997). Effects of self-efficacy and goal-orientation training on negotiation skill maintenance: What are the mechanisms? *Personnel Psychology, 50,* 959–978.

Stewart, J. B. (1992). *Den of thieves.* New York: Touchstone Books.

Stillenger, C., Epelbaum, M., Keltner, D., & Ross, L. (1990). *The "reactive devaluation" barrier to conflict resolution.* Working paper, Stanford University, Palo Alto, CA.

Stolte, J. F. (1983). Self-efficacy: Sources and consequences in negotiation networks. *Journal of Social Psychology, 119,* 69–75.

Street, M. D., Robertson, C., & Geiger, S. W. (1997). Ethical decision making: The effects of escalating commitment. *Journal of Business Ethics, 16,* 1153–1161.

Stuhlmacher, A. F., Gillespie, T. L., & Champagne, M. V. (1998). The impact of time pressure in negotiation: A meta-analysis. *The International Journal of Conflict Management, 9*(2), 97–116.

Stuhlmacher, A. F., & Walters, A. E. (1999). Gender differences in negotiation outcomes: A meta-analysis. *Personnel Psychology, 52,* 653–677.

Susskind, L., & Cruikshank, J. (1987). *Breaking the impasse: Consensual approaches to resolving public disputes.* New York: Basic Books.

Susskind, L., McKearnan, S., & Thomas-Larmer, J. (1999). *The consensus building handbook.* Thousand Oaks: Sage Publications.

Sutton, S. R. (1982). Fear-arousing communications: A critical examination of theory and research. In J. R. Eiser (Ed.), *Social psychology and behavioral medicine* (pp. 303–337). New York: John Wiley and Sons.

Swacker, F. W., Redden, K. R., & Wenger, L. B. (2000). The World Trade Organization and dispute resolution. *Dispute Resolution Journal, 55*(3), pp. 35–39.

Swap, W. L., & Rubin, J. Z. (1983). Measurement of interpersonal orientation. *Journal of Personality and Social Psychology, 44,* 208–219.

Swenson, R. A., Nash, D. L., & Roos, D. C. (1984). Source credibility and perceived expertness of testimony in a simulated child-custody case. *Professional Psychology, 15,* 891–898.

Swinth, R. L. (1967). Review of *A behavioral theory of labor negotiations. Contemporary Psychology, 12,* 183–184.

Tannen, D. (1990). *You just don't understand: Women and men in conversation.* New York: Ballantine Books.

Tannenbaum, D., & Norris, E. (1966). Effects of combining congruity principle strategies for the reduction of persuasion. *Journal of Personality and Social Psychology, 3,* 233–238.

Taylor, S. E., & Brown, J. D. (1988). Illusion and well-being: A social-psychological perspective on mental health. *Psychological Bulletin, 103,* 193–210.

Tedeschi, J. T., Heister, D. S., & Gahagan, J. P. (1969). Trust and the prisoner's dilemma game. *Journal of Social Psychology, 79,* 43–50.

Tedeschi, J. T., Schlenker, B. R., & Bonoma, T. V. (1973). *Conflict, power and games: The experimental study of interpersonal relations.* Chicago: AVC.

Teger, A. (1980). *Too much invested to quit.* New York: Pergamon Press.

Tenbrunsel, A. E. (1998). Misrepresentation and expectations of misrepresentation in an ethical dilemma: The role of incentives and temptation. *Academy of Management Journal, 4*(3), 330–339.

Tenbrunsel, A. E. (1999). Trust as an obstacle in environmental-economic disputes. *American Behavioral Scientist, 42,* 1350–1367.

Terhune, K. W. (1970). The effects of personality in cooperation and conflict. In P. Swingle (Ed.), *The structure of conflict* (pp. 193–234). New York: Academic Press.

Thibaut, J., & Walker, L. (1975). *Procedural justice: A psychological analysis.* Hillsdale, NJ: Lawrence Erlbaum.

Thomas, K. W. (1976). Conflict and conflict management. In M. D. Dunnette (Ed.), *Handbook of industrial & organizational psychology* (pp. 889–935). Chicago: Rand McNally.

Thomas, K. W. (1977). Toward multidimensional values in teaching: The example of conflict behavior. *Academy of Management Review, 2,* 484–490.

Thomas, K. W. (1992). Conflict and negotiation processes in organizations. In M. D. Dunnette and L. H. Hough, *Handbook of industrial & organizational psychology* (2nd ed., Vol. 3, pp. 651–718). Palo Alto, CA: Consulting Psychologists Press.

Thomas, K. W., & Kilmann, R. H. (1974). *Thomas-Kilmann conflict mode survey.* Tuxedo, NY: Xicom.

Thompson, J. D. (1967). *Organizations in action.* New York: McGraw-Hill.

Thompson, L. (1990a). An examination of naïve and experienced negotiators. *Journal of Personality and Social Psychology, 59,* 82–90.

Thompson, L. (1990b). Negotiation behavior and outcomes: Empirical evidence and theoretical issues. *Psychological Bulletin, 108,* 515–532.

Thompson, L. (1991). Information exchange in negotiation. *Journal of Experimental Social Psychology, 27,* 161–179.

Thompson, L. (1995). They saw a negotiation: Partnership and involvement. *Journal of Personality and Social Psychology, 68,* 839–853.

Thompson, L. (1998). *The mind and heart of the negotiator*. Upper Saddle River, NJ: Prentice Hall.

Thompson, L., & Hastie, R. (1990a). Social perception in negotiation. *Organizational Behavior and Human Decision Processes, 47,* 98–123.

Thompson, L., & Hastie, R. (1990b). Judgment tasks and biases in negotiation. In B. H. Sheppard, M. H. Bazerman, & R. J. Lewicki (Eds.), *Research on negotiation in organizations* (Vol. 2, pp. 31–54). Greenwich, CT: JAI Press.

Thompson, L., & Hrebec, D. (1996). Lose-lose agreements in interdependent decision making. *Psychological Bulletin, 120,* 396–409.

Thompson, L., & Loewenstein, G. (1992). Egocentric interpretations of fairness and interpersonal conflict. *Organizational Behavior and Human Decision Processes, 51,* 176–197.

Thompson, L., Peterson, E., & Brodt, S. E. (1996). Team negotiations: An examination of integrative and distributive bargaining. *Journal of Personality and Social Psychology, 70,* 66–78.

Thompson, L., Peterson, E., & Kray, L. (1995). Social context in negotiation: An information processing perspective. In R. Kramer & D. Messick (Eds.), *Negotiation as a social process* (pp. 5–36). Beverly Hills, CA: Sage.

Thompson, L., Valley, K. L., & Kramer, R. M. (1995). The bittersweet feeling of success: An examination of social perception in negotiation. *Journal of Experimental Social Psychology, 31,* 467–492.

Thompson, L. L., Nadler, J., & Kim, P. H. (1999). Some like it hot: The case for the emotional negotiator. In L. L. Thompson, J. M. Levine, & D. M. Messick (Eds.), *Shared cognition in organizations: The management of knowledge* (pp. 139–161). Mahwah, NJ: Erlbaum.

Ting-Toomey, S., & Kurogi, A. (1998). Facework competence in intercultural conflict: An updated face-negotiation theory. *International Journal of Intercultural Relations, 22,* 187–225.

Tinsley, C. H. (1998). Models of conflict resolution in Japanese, German, and American cultures. *Journal of Applied Psychology, 83,* 316–323.

Tinsley, C. H. (1996, June). Understanding conflict in other cultural contexts: The Chinese example. Paper presented at the International Association of Conflict Management, Ithaca, New York.

Tinsley, C. H. (1997). Understanding conflict in a Chinese cultural context. In R. J. Bies, R. J. Lewicki, & B. H. Sheppard (Eds.), *Research on negotiation in organizations* (Vol. 6: 209–225). Greenwich, CT: JAI Press.

Tinsley, C. H. (2001). How negotiators get to yes: Predicting the constellation of strategies used across cultures to negotiate conflict. *Journal of Applied Psychology, 86,* 583–593.

Tjosvold, D. (1988). *Getting things done in organizations*. Lexington, MA: Lexington Books.

Tompkins, P. K. (1993). *Organizational communication imperatives: Lessons of the space program*. Los Angeles: Roxbury Publishing Company.

Touval, S. (1988). Multilateral negotiation: An analytical approach. *Negotiation Journal, 5*(2), 159–173.

Touval, S., & Zartman, I. (1985). *International mediation in theory and practice*. Boulder, CO: Westview Press.

Trenholm, S. (1989). *Persuasion and social influence*. Englewood Cliffs, NJ: Prentice Hall.

Trevino, L. K. (1986). Ethical decision making in organizations: A person-situation interactionist model. *Academy of Management Review, 11,* 601–617.

Trevino, L. K., & Youngblood, S. (1990). Bad apples in bad barrels: A causal analysis of ethical decision-making behavior. *Journal of Applied Psychology, 75,* 378–385.

Triandis, H. C. (1982). Review of *Culture's consequences: International differences in work values. Human Organization, 41,* 86–90.

Tripp, T. M., Sondak, H., & Bies, R. J. (1995). Justice as rationality: A relational perspective on fairness in negotiations. In R. J. Lewicki, B. H. Sheppard, & R. Bies (Ed.), *Research on negotiation in organizations* (Vol. 5, pp. 45–64). Greenwich, CT: JAI Press.

Tse, D. K., Francis, J., & Walls, J. (1994). Cultural differences in conducting intra- and inter-cultural negotiations: A Sino-Canadian comparison. *Journal of International Business Studies, 25,* 537–555.

Tuchinsky, M. (1998). *Negotiation approaches in close relationships*. Duke University. Unpublished doctoral dissertation.

Tuchinsky, M. B., Edson Escalas, J., Moore, M. B., & Sheppard, B. H. (1994). Beyond name, rank and function: Construals of relationships in business. In D. P. Moore, *Proceedings of the Academy of Management,* 79–83.

Tung, R. L. (1991). Handshakes across the sea: Cross-cultural negotiating for business success. *Organizational Dynamics, 19,* Winter. 30–40.

Turner, M. E., & Pratkanis, A. R. (1994). Social identity maintenance prescriptions for preventing groupthink: Reducing identity protection and enhancing intellectual conflict. *International Journal of Conflict Management, 5,* 254–270.

Tutzauer, F. (1991). Bargaining outcome, bargaining process, and the role of communication. *Progress in Communication Science, 10,* 257–300.

Tutzauer, F. (1992). The communication of offers in dyadic bargaining. In L. Putnam & M. Roloff (Eds.), *Communication and negotiation* (pp. 67–82). Newbury Park, CA: Sage.

Tversky, A., & Kahneman, D. (1981). The framing of decisions and the psychology of choice. *Science, 211,* 453–458.

Tye, L. (1998). They're not in it for the long haul. *The Columbus (Ohio) Dispatch.* April 19, p. 10E.

Tyler, T., & Hastie, R. (1991). The social consequences of cognitive illusions. In M. H. Bazerman, R. J. Lewicki, and B. H. Sheppard (Eds.), *Research on negotiation in organizations* (Vol. 3, pp. 69–98). Greenwich, CT: JAI Press.

Tzu, Sun (1983). *The art of war.* New York: Dellacorte Press.

Ury, W. (1991). *Getting past no: Negotiating with difficult people.* New York: Bantam Books.

Ury, W. (2000). *The third side.* New York: Penguin.

Ury, W. L., Brett, J. M., & Goldberg, S. B. (1988). *Getting disputes resolved.* San Francisco: Jossey-Bass.

Ury, W. L., Brett, J. M., & Goldberg, S. B. (1993). *Getting disputes resolved.* (2nd ed.). San Francisco: Jossey-Bass.

Valley, K. L., Moag, J., & Bazerman, M. H. (1998). A matter of trust: Effects of communication on the efficiency and distribution of outcomes. *Journal of Economic Behavior and Organization, 34,* 211–238.

van de Vliert, E. (1985). Escalative intervention in small group conflicts. *Journal of Applied Behavioral Science, 21,* 19–36.

van de Vliert, E. (1992). Questions about the strategic choice model of mediation. *The International Journal of Conflict Management, 8,* 379–386.

van de Vliert, E., & Kabanoff, B. (1988). *Toward theory-based measures of conflict management.* Paper presented at the annual meeting of the Academy of Management, Anaheim, CA.

van de Vliert, E., & Prein, H. C. M. (1989). The difference in the meaning of forcing in the conflict management of actors and observers. In M. Rahim (Ed.), *Managing conflict: An interdisciplinary approach* (pp. 51–63). New York: Praeger.

Van Zandt, H. F. (1970 November–December). How to negotiate in Japan. *Harvard Business Review, 48*(6), 45–56.

Veitch, R., & Griffith, W. (1976). Good news–bad news: Affective and interpersonal affects. *Journal of Applied Social Psychology, 6,* 69–75.

Victor, B., & Cullen, J. (1988). The organizational bases of ethical work climates. *Administrative Science Quarterly, 33,* 1010–1025.

Vitz, P. C., & Kite, W. A. R. (1970). Factors affecting conflict and negotiation within an alliance. *Journal of Experimental Social Psychology, 5,* 233–247.

Volkema, R. (1997). Perceptual differences in appropriateness and likelihood of use of negotiation behaviors: A cross-cultural analysis. *The International Executive, 39*(3), 335–350.

Volkema, R. (1998). A comparison of perceptions of ethical negotiation behavior in Mexico and the United States. *The International Journal of Conflict Management, 9*(3), pp. 218–233.

Volkema, R. (1999). Ethicality in negotiations: An analysis of perceptual similarities and differences between Brazil and the United States. *Journal of Business Research, 45,* 49–67.

Volkema, R. (2001). *Predicting unethical negotiating behavior: An empirical examination of the incidents in negotiation questionnaire.* Paper Presented at the Annual Meeting of the Academy of Management, Washington, DC. August.

von Neumann, J., & Morgenstern, O. (1944). *Theory of games and economic behavior.* Princeton, NJ: Princeton University Press.

Von Oech, R. (1990). *A whack on the side of the head: How you can be more creative* (rev. ed.). New York: Warner Books.

Vroom, V. H. (1973). A new look at managerial decision making. *Organizational Dynamics, 4,* 66–80.

Vroom, V. H., & Yetton, P. (1973). *Leadership and decision making.* Pittsburgh, PA: University of Pittsburgh Press.

Wade-Benzoni, K., Hoffman, A., Thompson, L., Moore, D., Gillespie, J., & Bazerman, M. (2002). Barriers to resolution in ideologically based negotiations: The role of values and institutions. *Academy of Management* Review, *27*(1), 41–57.

Walcott, C., & Hoppmann, P. (1975). Interaction analysis and bargaining behavior. *Experimental Study of Politics, 4,* 1–19.

Walcott, C., Hopmann, P. T., & King, T. D. (1977). The role of debate in negotiation. In D. Druckman (Ed.), *Negotiations: Social psychological perspectives* (pp. 193–211). Beverly Hills, CA: Sage.

Wall, J. A. (1977). Intergroup bargaining: Effects of opposing constituent's stance opposing representative's bargaining, and representative's locus of control. *Journal of Conflict Resolution, 21,* 459–474.

Wall, J. A. (1981). Mediation: An analysis, review and proposed research. *Journal of Conflict Resolution, 25,* 157–180.

Wall, J. A., & Blum, M. (1991). Negotiations. *Journal of Management, 17,* 273–303.

Wall, J. A., & Lynn, A. (1993). Mediation: A current review. *Journal of Conflict Resolution, 37,* 160–194.

Wall, J., & Stark, J. (1996). Techniques and sequences in mediation strategies: A proposed model for research. *Negotiation Journal, 12,* 231–239.

Walters, A. E., Stuhlmacher, A. F., & Meyer, L. L. (1998). Gender and negotiator competitiveness: A meta-analysis. *Organizational Behavior and Human Decision Processes, 76,* 1–29.

Walton, R. (1987). *Managing conflict: Interpersonal dialogue and third-party roles* (2nd ed.). Reading, MA: Addison-Wesley.

Walton, R. E., & McKersie, R. B. (1965). *A behavioral theory of labor negotiations: An analysis of a social interaction system.* New York: McGraw-Hill.

Watkins, M., & Winters, L. (1997). Intervenors with interests and power. *Negotiation Journal, 13,* 119–142.

Watson, C. (1994a). Gender differences in negotiating outcomes: Fact or artifact? In A. Taylor & J. Beinstein-Miller (Eds.), *Conflict and gender* (pp. 191–210). Cresskill, NJ: Hampton Press.

Watson, C. (1994b). Gender versus power as a predictor of negotiation behavior and outcomes. *Negotiation Journal, 10,* 117–127.

Watson, C., & Kasten, B. (1988). *Separate strengths? How men and women negotiate.* Newark, NJ: Center for Negotiation and Conflict Resolution, Rutgers University.

Watson, C., & Hoffman, L. R. (1996). Managers as negotiators: A test of power versus gender as predictors of feelings, behavior, and outcomes. *Leadership Quarterly, 7,* 63–85.

Weick, K., & Bougon, M. (1986). Organizations as cognitive maps: Charting ways to success and failure. In H. Sims, D. Gioia, and Associates (Eds.), *The thinking organization: Dynamics of organizational social cognition* (pp. 102–133). San Francisco, CA: Jossey-Bass.

Weingart, L. R., Bennett, R. J., & Brett, J. M. (1993). The impact of consideration of issues and motivational orientation group negotiation process and outcome. *Journal of Applied Psychology, 78*(3), 504–517.

Weingart, L. R., Hyder, E. B., & Prietula, M. J. (1996). Knowledge matters: The effect of tactical descriptions on negotiation behavior and outcome. *Journal of Personality and Social Psychology, 70,* 1205–1217.

Weingart, L. R., Prietula, M. J., Heider, E. B., & Genovese, C. R. (1999). Knowledge and the sequential processes of negotiation: A Markov Chain analysis of response-in-kind. *Journal of Experimental Social Psychology, 35,* 366–393.

Weingart, L. R., Thompson, L. L., Bazerman, M. H., & Carroll, J. S. (1990). Tactical behaviors and negotiation outcomes. *The International Journal of Conflict Management, 1,* 7–31.

Weiss, S. E. (1994). Negotiating with "Romans": A range of culturally-responsive strategies. *Sloan Management Review, 35*(1), 51–61; (2), 1–16.

Weiss, S. E. (1996). International negotiations: Bricks, mortar, and prospects. In B. J. Punnett & O. Shenkar (Eds.), *Handbook for international management research* (pp. 209–265). Cambridge, MA: Blackwell.

Weiss, S. E. (1997). Explaining outcomes of negotiation: Toward a grounded model for negotiations between organizations. In R. J. Lewicki, R. J. Bies, & B. H. Sheppard (Eds.), *Research on negotiation in organizations* (Vol. 6, pp. 247–333). Greenwich, CT: JAI Press.

Weiss, S. E., & Stripp, W. (1985). *Negotiating with foreign business persons: An introduction for Americans with propositions on six cultures.* New York: New York University Graduate School of Business Administration, Working Paper 85–6.

Weitzman, E. B., & Weitzman, P. F. (2000). Problem solving and decision making in conflict resolution. In Deutsch, M. & Coleman, P. *Handbook of conflict resolution.* San Francisco: Jossey-Bass.

Weldon, E., & John, K. A. (1995). Examining cross-cultural differences in conflict management behavior: A strategy for future research. *The International Journal of Conflict Management, 6,* 387–403.

Werth, L. F., & Flannery, J. (1986). A phenomenological approach to human deception. In R. W. Mitchell & N. S. Thompson (Eds.), *Deception: Perspectives on human and nonhuman deceit* (pp. 293–311). Albany, NY: State University of New York Press.

Wheeler, M. (1999). First, let's kill all the agents! In R. H. Mnookin and L. E. Susskind, *Negotiating on behalf of others.* (pp. 235–262). Thousand Oaks, CA: Sage Publications.

Whiting, C. S. (1958). *Creative thinking.* New York: Reinhold.

Whittemore, M. (1996). Hard-ball negotiation. *Success, 43,* 14.

Whyte, G., & Sebenius, J. K. (1997). The effect of multiple anchors on anchoring in individual and group judgment. *Organizational Behavior and Human Decision Processes, 69,* 75–85.

Wilson, S. R., & Putnam, L. L. (1990). Interaction goals in negotiation. In J. Anderson (Ed.), *Communication yearbook* (Vol. 13, pp. 374–406.) Newbury Park, CA: Sage.

Wittmer, J., Carnevale, P., & Walker, M. (1991). General alignment and overt support in biased mediation. *Journal of Conflict Resolution, 35,* 594–610.

Wolff, F. I., Marsnik, N. C., Tacey, W. S., & Nichols, R. G. (1983). *Perceptive listening.* New York: Holt, Rinehart & Winston.

Wolvin, A. D., & Coakley, C. G. (1988). *Listening* (3rd ed.). Dubuque, IA: Wm. C. Brown.

Wolvin, A. D., & Coakley, C. G. (1991). A survey of the status of listening training in some Fortune 500 corporations. *Communication Education, 40,* 152–164.

Wood, R., & Bandura, A. (1989). Social cognitive theory of organizational management. *Academy of Management Review, 14,* 361–384.

Xing, F. (1995). The Chinese cultural system: Implications for cross-cultural management. *SAM Advanced Management Journal, 60,* 14–20.

Yan, A., & Gray, B. (1994). Bargaining power, management control, and performance in United States-China joint ventures: A comparative case study. *Academy of Management Journal, 37,* 1478–1517.

Yankelovich, D. (1982, August). Lying well is the best revenge. *Psychology Today, 71,* 5–6, 71.

Yook, E. L., & Albert, R. D. (1998). Perceptions of the appropriateness of negotiation in educational settings: A cross-cultural comparison among Koreans and Americans. *Communication Education, 47,* 18–29.

Yoshino, M. Y., & Rangan, U. S. (1995). *Strategic alliances.* Boston: Harvard University Press.

Young, O. (1972). Intermediaries: Additional thoughts on third parties. *Journal of Conflict Resolution, 16,* 51–65.

Yukl, G. (1974). Effects of the opponent's initial offer, concession magnitude, and concession frequency on bargaining behavior. *Journal of Personality & Social Psychology, 30,* 323–335.

Yukl, G., & Tracey, J. A. B. (1992). Consequences of influence tactics used with subordinates, peers and the boss. *Journal of Applied Psychology, 77,* 525–535.

Zand, D. (1972). Trust and managerial problem solving. *Administrative Science Quarterly, 17,* 229–239.

Zand, D. (1997). *The leadership triad: Knowledge, trust and power.* New York: Oxford University Press.

Zartman, I. W. (1977). Negotiation as a joint decision making process. In I. Zartman (Ed.), *The negotiation process: Theories and applications* (pp. 67–86). Beverly Hills, CA: Sage.

Zartman, I. W. (1997). Conflict and order: Justice in negotiation. *International Political Science Review, 18,* 121–138.

Zartman, I. W., & Berman, M. (1982). *The practical negotiator.* New Haven: Yale University Press.

Zebrowitz, L. A., Voinescu, L., & Collins, M. A. (1996). "Wide-eyed" and "crooked-faced": Determinants of perceived and real honesty across the life span. *Personality & Social Psychology Bulletin, 22,* 1258–1269.

Zimbardo, P. G., Ebbesen, E. B., & Maslach, C. (1977). *Influencing attitudes and changing behavior.* Reading, MA: Addison-Wesley.

Zubek, J., Pruitt, D., Pierce, R., McGillicuddy, N., & Syna, H. (1992). Disputant and mediator behaviors affecting short-term success in mediation. *Journal of Conflict Resolution, 36,* 546–572.

Name Index

Subject Index

Index

Index